BEYOND SMART

LAWYERING WITH EMOTIONAL INTELLIGENCE

Ronda Muir

Cover design by Cory Ottenwess/ABA Design

Library of Congress Cataloging-in-Publication Data

Names: Muir, Ronda, author.
Title: Beyond Smart : lawyering with emotional intelligence / Ronda Muir.
Description: [Chicago] : American Bar Association, [2017] | Includes bibliographical references and index.
Identifiers: LCCN 2017018064 | ISBN 9781634259163 | ISBN 1634259165
Subjects: LCSH: Practice of law—Psychological aspects. | Lawyers—Psychological aspects. | Emotional intelligence. | Cognitive psychology.
Classification: LCC K120 .M83 2017 | DDC 340/.19—dc23
LC record available at https://lccn.loc.gov/2017018064

Printed in the United States of America.

21 20 19 18 17 5 4 3 2 1

ISBN: 978-1-63425-916-3
e-ISBN: 978-1-63425-917-0

Discounts are available for books ordered in bulk. Special consideration is given to state bars, CLE programs, and other bar-related organizations. Inquire at Book Publishing, ABA Publishing, American Bar Association, 321 N. Clark Street, Chicago, Illinois 60654-7598.

www.shopABA.org

Contents

Preface

You must have heard of "emotional intelligence." It refers to our ability to recognize, understand, and regulate emotions, both our own and those of others. The concept ricocheted around the world starting in the mid-1990s after Daniel Goleman published a book contending emotional intelligence (or EI) is more important than IQ.

Goleman's claim was quite startling. At the time, the psychological research community had long held the opinion that IQ was the best indicator of success. Our institutions of higher learning used notions of cognitive intelligence to admit, evaluate, and graduate the "best" students. There was, of course, the troubling statistic that in the "real world" people with average IQs outperformed those with the highest IQs 70 percent of the time.[1] But no one really knew why.

Many industries have, over the last twenty-plus years, gone on to embrace emotional intelligence as the attribute that can both predict and achieve superior individual and organizational performance. Emotional intelligence is also key to better physical and mental health, resulting in lower organizational costs from attrition, healthcare, and professional liability. Businesses like Google, Aetna, and Johnson & Johnson have built programs for their entire workforce around enhancing emotional intelligence. Doctors, to whom we lawyers like to compare ourselves, are including EI in medical school admissions and physician training because it promotes both good medical care and physician health.

Probably no other profession relies so heavily on cognitive intelligence as law. Law schools rely on LSATs to find the most logical applicants and then rigorously use the Socratic method in classrooms to ferret out any nonrational tendencies that remain. Law firms and law departments hire the top law school graduates and then enforce cultures of strict rationality. Emotion is what we in the law business have been intent on eliminating. So emotional intelligence may seem like an oxymoron to us. What do lawyers need it for?

While some lawyers flourish in their work, troubling data on law people have been accumulating for years. Lawyers suffer outsized levels of emotional distress—six times the level of depression, for example—as any other professional group, outdoing even those oft-maligned dentists. The extremely high rates of suicide and substance abuse (both still underreported), divorce, and health issues among lawyers testify to a degree of personal dysfunction that is astonishing. As testament to this dysfunction, lawyers have left the practice of law in droves, and those who stay are often deeply dissatisfied. A distressed, unhappy lawyer may well be on the front line advising our clients on critical issues. It should be no surprise that reports of client dissatisfaction have soared in recent years, and that malpractice liability is an increasing concern.

As a legal workplace consultant, I often get a distress call from firms, corporate law departments, or individual lawyers who are facing what seem to them like insurmountable problems. Clients are irate, partners are contemptuous, and associates are resentful. Underperformance threatens their organizations and their personal positions. Client and/or attorney defections may be dangerously reducing revenue and damaging reputations. Dissension among individual lawyers, factions, or practice groups can be severely hampering productivity and conflicts may develop into open war, even threatening a firm's continued existence.

The tool of choice for lawyers dealing with these emotionally charged issues in the workplace is usually avoidance, so these feelings have often been purposely unattended to even as they amp up in intensity. My clients are then taken off-guard by how powerful these unwanted, unruly emotions become and are at a loss as to how to react to them.

With emotions running high, clients call on me to get rid of them. Most often, I am told that compensation is the likely culprit. In my experience, that is rarely the case. But whatever is at issue rides on emotional tides that have become so turbulent as to engulf individuals, groups, departments, and firms.

Few research studies on emotions and EI have focused on how they relate to law students, lawyers, or legal practices: of over one million books and scholarly articles on emotional intelligence outstanding in 2017, only a handful relate to law. So it is challenging for lawyers and their advisors to assess how this relatively new, rapidly expanding science applies to the unique circumstance of practicing law.

Some notable attempts have been made over the years to highlight the role of emotions in law. In 2002, consultant Dr. Larry Richard, a psychologist and lawyer, published an article entitled "Herding Cats: The Lawyer Personality Revealed," in which he demonstrated that certain psychological attributes, including low emotional intelligence, occur among lawyers more often than among members of other professions.[2] In 2004, Susan Swaim Daicoff, then a Professor of Law at the Florida Coastal School of Law, published *Lawyer, Know Yourself: A Psychological Analysis of Personality Strengths and Weaknesses*, which comprehensively reviewed more than forty years' worth of empirical studies on lawyers and law students, and was one of the earliest efforts to parse how typical lawyer personalities, including attitudes toward emotions, impact our practices.[3] But little has been done in the industry to follow up on their findings.

I have repeatedly seen how helping lawyers develop emotional intelligence skills produces a more functional and productive law practice. Instead of being surprised and dismayed by powerful emotions hijacking their work, emotionally intelligent lawyers are better able to assess the emotional landscape in a timely manner and make use of emotion to improve their workplaces: individual lawyers become better negotiators, litigators, and judges; practices enjoy more effective leadership and teamwork; personal dynamics with clients and colleagues improve; and increased productivity and client satisfaction raise the bottom line for everyone.

But I have also seen how unintuitive recognizing, understanding, and employing emotions are to many of us. And how daunting the body of research on emotional intelligence can be when it comes to learning how best to use those concepts in the field of law.

While emotional intelligence would have been an advantage to legal practices in times past, it has become critical to survival in the 21st century. Competing providers that have arisen with globalization and technological advances have narrowed the expertise that lawyers provide, which a faltering demand is making clear. One of the few strategies that will make a difference is offering emotionally intelligent professional services—services that promote smart, healthy practitioners who can gain and keep clients.

The good news is that we can raise our emotional intelligence by learning or improving critical skills. And that starts simply with awareness of the importance of emotion in our work. After that awareness has been realized, there are steps to take as an individual lawyer, a practice group, a department, and a firm to fully reap the many benefits of emotional intelligence.

This book is the first comprehensive overview of the burgeoning field of emotional intelligence as it relates to the practice of law. I have made it my business to review the extensive research and widespread uses of emotional intelligence by other industries in order to piece together what that means to us in our daily lives in the law.

First, Chapter 1 reviews what emotional intelligence is: its origins, the industries that find it compelling, its demographics, and its physiology. Then Chapter 2 outlines where we lawyers stand both statistically and reputation-wise when it comes to EI, the traditions behind law's skepticism, a lawyer who made EI history, and in which of the four critical components of emotional intelligence we fall short.

Chapter 3 articulates four advantages that being emotionally intelligent brings to our personal success in practicing law:

1. *Emotionally Intelligent Lawyers Are Smarter*
2. *Emotionally Intelligent Lawyers Are Stronger Practitioners: Negotiators, Case Managers, Litigators, and Judges*

3. *Emotionally Intelligent Lawyers Make More Money*
4. *Emotionally Intelligent Lawyers Are Healthier and Happier*

The advantages of aggregating high EI individuals culminate in Chapter 4, "Four Ways Emotional Intelligence Builds More Successful Law Firms and Law Departments." Then Chapter 5, "Four Steps to Achieving an Emotionally Intelligent Workplace," details how to raise your organization's EI.

In Chapter 6 ("What's My Emotional Intelligence?"), you can find out your own personal emotional intelligence level and then leverage that up with the advice in Chapter 7, which includes development tactics for each of the EI components.

Law schools, too, have a role in increasing lawyers' emotional intelligence, as discussed in Chapter 8. Finally, the urgency of developing more emotionally intelligent practices in the 21st century is summarized in Chapter 9, "Now Is the Time to Lawyer with Emotional Intelligence."

My hope is that you will use this resource and its practical tools to make your practice, and your life, more successful and satisfying.

Preface Endnotes

1. "People with average IQs outperform those with the highest IQs 70 per cent of the time." Travis Bradberry, "Habits of highly emotionally intelligent people," *PS News*, June 15, 2016, http://www.psnews.com.au/vic/508/personal_development/habits-of-highly-emotionally-intelligent-people.
2. Larry Richard, "Herding Cats: The Lawyer Personality Revealed," *Altman Weil Report to Legal Management*, 29(2002): 1–12.
3. Susan Swaim Daicoff, *Lawyer, Know Yourself: A Psychological Analysis of Personality Strengths and Weaknesses* (Washington, DC: American Psychological Association, 2004).

Acknowledgments

My thanks to the American Bar Association and its Section of Dispute Resolution for seeing the timeliness and value of publishing a book promoting how emotional intelligence can make 21st-century lawyers "beyond smart." Editor Rick Paszkiet and Peer Review Committee Chair Daniel Bowling were invaluable advisors during the early stages of putting this material together and editor Kimberly Rosenfield finished it up and got it out to the public with aplomb.

I appreciate the many hours put in seriatim by my fellow Swarthmore College alumni who diligently helped make this book accurate and look good—Felix Richardo, Jane Abell, and Genevieve McGahey. My thanks to Christy Cassisa, J.D., founder of The Institute of Mindful Works; marketing consultant Susan Zangler; Robin Rolfe, founder of Robin Rolfe Resources; and Michael Mills, co-founder and chief strategy officer of Neota Logic, for their insightful suggestions. My heartfelt thanks to my many clients and lawyer colleagues who have each contributed in their own way to this book.

I am most grateful to my ever-patient family and friends, who teach me every day the importance of emotions.

Acknowledgments

About the Author

Ronda Muir, Founder and Principal of Law People Management, LLC, is a leading authority on solutions to people management challenges unique to the legal industry. She draws from years of practicing law in New York and Europe, both as outside counsel and in-house counsel, coupled with advanced study in behavioral science. Ronda has advised corporate law departments and law firms of all sizes across the country on increasing profitability by aligning structure, leadership, compensation, professional development, and culture to enhance client service. She is a frequent speaker, an award-winning author, and publishes http://www.LawPeopleBlog.com.

Chapter One

What Is Emotional Intelligence? Understanding Emotional Intelligence and Its Benefits

Even if we aren't familiar with the precise definition of emotional intelligence or the array of research with respect to it, many of us would guess from our own experience that "emotional intelligence" sounds valuable: we know there are people who excel at "getting along well" with others, whether at the office or socially. These are people who are attuned to what's going on personally with those around them, who don't inflame others, and who, when confronted with trying circumstances, manage to calm the waters and even turn the situation around. They are masters of saying and doing the right thing at the right time to resolve conflicts, improve morale, encourage acceptance of change, and inspire and motivate those around them.

The benefits of "getting along well" that intuitively seem valuable long appeared too difficult, if not impossible, to systematically analyze in a scholarly way. What behaviors or attitudes are the critical ones? Being nice? Being flexible? Being accommodating? How do we assess that stuff? And what are the tangible results, if any, that these attributes produce? How do we measure the practical effect of someone who "gets along well" on the individual and the organization that individual is a part of?

In the world of law, people with these kinds of personal skills may be named as mentors, hiring partners, or client relationship partners. Or they may simply be known within their workplace as conducting themselves appropriately, listening attentively, or giving sound interpersonal advice. But often lawyers with these traits are viewed as being too soft, too sentimental, or too emotional—not as tough or smart as lawyers should be.

So what is this "getting along well" quality, and what is it good for? The following sections of this chapter explore where the concept of emotional intelligence comes from and what it means.

The Origins of Emotional Intelligence Theory

So there is a reason that emotional Captain Kirk was first in command and purely logical Mr. Spock was second . . .

You could say it all started with a lawyer. The idea of emotional intelligence first burst onto the scientific scene in the early 1990s. Daniel Goleman,[1] equipped with a Harvard degree in psychology, was a *New York Times* science reporter who started reporting on two psychology professors, John D. (Jack) Mayer at SUNY Purchase and Peter Salovey at Yale University, who had coined a new concept they called "emotional intelligence" (EI, sometimes referred to as "emotional quotient" or EQ) and introduced a system for measuring it.[2]

Mayer and Salovey had been spurred to investigate the subject by what they considered to be inexplicably unintelligent behavior in someone who undoubtedly had a high IQ—Democratic senator and presidential candidate Gary Hart. A graduate of both Yale Divinity School and Yale Law School, Hart had seen his promising political career go up in flames after he responded to accusations of an extramarital affair by challenging the press in April 1987 to "follow me around" and see if they found anything untoward in his personal life. The press took him up on the challenge and found plenty.[3]

The groundbreaking conclusion of Mayer and Salovey's research was that we perform at our best when we engage both our intellect and our emotions: emotions can enhance intellectual functioning and provide important information to inform decisions and behavior better suited to our goals. In short, emotions offer an *intelligence* that we ignore at our peril.[4]

Goleman's articles on EI in the *New York Times* generated a huge interest in the topic nationally. In 1995 he published his book *Emotional Intelligence: Why It Can Matter More Than IQ,* which remained on the *New York Times* Best Sellers list for over eighteen months, was translated into forty languages, and has sold more than five million copies around the world.

Over the last thirty years this new psychological field of emotional intelligence has been extensively studied. Virtually all theorists have come to agree that four critical components of emotional intelligence are (1) emotional perception, (2) emotional empathy, (3) emotional understanding, and (4) emotional regulation. That is, the emotionally intelligent have an accurate awareness of emotions in themselves and others, can tap into how those emotions feel, and are able to understand and manage emotions so as to produce the desired results.

We now have a wealth of research that provides tools to measure emotional intelligence, that illustrates what emotional intelligence looks like day to day, that explains how and why emotional intelligence impacts not only a person's bottom-line performance, but also their personal well-being and the organizations they are part of, and that identifies specific steps that can raise our emotional intelligence.

The Business Community Embraces Emotional Intelligence

Emotional intelligence was a topic that immediately resonated with the business community. In 1998, when *Harvard Business Review* first published an article on the concept, it attracted a higher percentage of readers than any other article published in that periodical in the prior forty years.[5] The then chief executive officer (CEO) of Johnson & Johnson, Ralph S. Larsen, was so enthusiastic about the idea that he had copies sent out to the company's four hundred top executives worldwide. After a review of more than 1,400 of its employees in thirty-seven countries found that the highest-performing managers were indeed those with the highest EI, Johnson & Johnson soon became one of the corporate leaders in raising emotional intelligence in their workplaces through extensive company-wide educational and development programs.[6]

The benefits of emotional intelligence have been well documented over the last two decades. Compelling evidence from industries worldwide demonstrates that having emotional intelligence helps people work smarter, produce more, have more satisfying careers, stay longer in their jobs, and enjoy greater overall physical and mental health, all of which builds more successful organizations and drives increased profits.

A number of industries have been attuned to the importance of emotional intelligence as vital to their success, including:

Healthcare
Accounting
Technology
Marketing
Primary and Secondary Education
Graduate Business Schools

Healthcare

Every major emotional intelligence conference I've attended has included representatives of one or more distinguished medical schools. The healthcare profession recognizes the critical importance of emotional intelligence to the practice of medicine, and particularly to the patient–physician relationship.[7] As one study concluded, "Medicine is an emotionally demanding practice and medical education is an emotional process and yet it has been customary to regard emotional experience as collateral to . . . competence. Views, however, are changing . . . the fact that doctors' EI affects their patients' and their own health outcomes makes it too important a construct to ignore."[8]

Emotionally intelligent doctors make, by many measures, better doctors.[9] Healthcare workers' emotional intelligence translates into greater patient safety, better clinical results, and better patient and physician health.[10] High EI physicians also have better communication skills, higher patient satisfaction, and more effective stress management skills, resulting in fewer patient complaints to regulatory authorities, fewer medical errors, and fewer malpractice cases.[11] As an example, the judgments of doctors with higher EI don't deteriorate as much when they are sleep deprived.[12] High EI dentists, nurses, and hospital administrators also stand out among their peers.[13]

Emotional intelligence is not just a theoretical component of improved healthcare—a broad-based and advanced implementation effort is incorporating EI testing and instruction into medical school education, as well as into healthcare practices in various settings.[14]

Some advocate for testing all medical school applicants for emotional intelligence, and 80 percent of doctors polled agree.[15] A group of incoming University of South Florida (USF) medical students are being admitted each year into the SELECT program based on an evaluation of their emotional intelligence, with the expectation that they "will become more engaged, compassionate physicians who will connect deeply with their patients and their patients' families; feel more comfortable with and be more effective as team leaders and team members; and have the relationship building skills and systems perspectives to more effectively lead change in healthcare organizations."[16] Both the NYU Langone Hospital for Joint Diseases and the Rush University Medical Center are starting to use EI measures to select residents, while other hospitals offer on-the-job mentoring for residents by mentors selected for their emotional intelligence.[17]

Medical schools around the world still using traditional admissions criteria are adding EI training to their curriculum.[18] USF

Medical School intends to eventually incorporate its EI training from the SELECT program into the curriculum for all medical students.[19] Eight out of the seventeen Canadian medical schools have piloted a Student Leadership Curriculum that teaches components of EI, and a version of that curriculum is being taught to undergraduate medical students at the University of Toronto as well.[20] In the United Kingdom, all medical schools formally teach students to display appropriate emotional reactions to patients and assess their ability to do so in clinical examinations.[21] Those medical schools here in the United States and abroad that don't offer classes dedicated to EI often offer classes in listening, building trust, and using empathy to enhance communication, all of which involve the development of EI skills.[22]

What is not questioned in the healthcare community is whether emotional intelligence is relevant to providing better healthcare from higher performing healthcare workers.

Accounting

Accounting industry leaders, such as the American Institute of Certified Public Accountants and the Institute of Management Accountants, have been advocating for recognition of the role of emotional intelligence in accounting for over fifteen years.[23] Researchers have found that possessing emotional intelligence "allows accountants to excel in strategic decision making, teamwork, leadership, and client relations."[24] And it is being recognized as an essential attribute for accounting firm partners.[25] Yet accounting students score significantly lower in EI than do students in other undergraduate majors, in spite of significantly higher grade point averages.[26]

To raise low EI, large accounting firms are investing in EI training, as well as experimenting with using EI tests during the hiring process and in balancing teams.[27] Deloitte's consulting arm recommends to its clients EI-based interviews and assessments in evaluating applicants and follows its own advice by focusing almost exclusively on candidates' soft skills.[28] PwC provides its leaders with emotional intelligence coaching and regularly conducts staff EI training programs.[29] KPMG considers emotional intelligence one of the key skills of internal auditors, and for its high-performing senior managers runs an annual event that assesses and builds EI skills.[30] The KPMG Business Institute offers advanced coursework in emotional intelligence both inside and outside the firm.[31]

This focus on emotional intelligence in talent selection and development is largely foreign to law firms, which have traditionally been a good five to ten years behind accounting firms in adopting sophisticated human resources processes.[32]

Technology

Since the debut of sinister HAL 9000 in *2001: A Space Odyssey*, we've been fascinated by the possibility that technology might recognize and react to our emotions. In the 21st century, the advance of just such emotion-based technology and its rapidly expanding use in business is astonishing.

The first "emotionally intelligent" robot, named "Pepper," released in 2015, sold out within a minute, according to its Japanese creator, SoftBank Robotics Corp. Pepper stands four feet tall, weighs sixty-one pounds, and uses sophisticated emotion recognition software: he can read your emotions as well as further develop his own through learning. The reviewers rave that he "may just decompress your next domestic row with a witty remark or well-timed turn of phrase," and he is already being used in the marketplace to sell coffee machines.[33]

Pepper reflects advances in the field of "affective computing," which strives to "restore a proper balance between emotion and cognition" by making technology more emotionally intelligent.[34] One undertaking, Eyeris, showcases "deep learning-based emotion recognition software that reads facial micro-expressions in real-time."[35] Dr. Rosalind Picard, director of the Affective Computing Research Group at MIT, and her team teach robots how to read "very subtle and very fleeting expressions," such as "doubtfulness," which can be useful to those who have difficulties reading those cues, including sufferers of autism and posttraumatic stress disorder (PTSD).[36] A University of Amsterdam and University of Illinois team has even deciphered the enigmatic smile of Leonardo da Vinci's *Mona Lisa,* concluding that she was mostly happy: specifically, 83 percent happy, 9 percent disgusted, 6 percent fearful, and 2 percent angry.[37]

Applications of this emotion-reading technology are flourishing. Matilda is a robot barely a foot tall whose primary job is interviewing candidates for sales positions by reading their emotions.[38] SimSensei virtual agents developed at the University of Southern California Institute for Creative Technologies have such high levels of artificial emotional intelligence that they can engage convincingly in back-and-forth interactions with humans. The SimSensei star is Ellie, a virtual therapist that has performed better than her human counterparts, partly because of being perceived as nonjudgmental.[39] The enormity of this accomplishment cannot be overstated in the context of delivering professional services.

This technology is being used to promote EI in humans, as well. Facebook has worked with the Yale Center for Emotional Intelligence on a large-scale project designed to prevent and decrease online bullying, a form of emotional aggression that indicates a lack of emotional empathy.[40] The Cogito Corporation software injects machine-driven emotional intelligence cues into healthcare call center interactions with patients to help keep stress levels down on both sides. "Cogito's algorithms parse each nanosecond of a caller's and patient's speech and simultaneously flash recommendations to the customer service worker," such as "you're speaking too much" or "pause between phrases." The founder of Cogito, who studied at the MIT Human Dynamics Lab, says that this "ability to provide an instant window into customer perception is helping drive dramatic improvements in customer satisfaction and employee engagement."[41]

More applications of the artificial ability to read and understand emotions are coming. Research envisions programs to analyze and respond to a user's moods, such as those of soldiers during training and combat to improve their functioning, of drivers whose confusion or fatigue can be identified and alerted through onboard computers,[42] and of callers whose distressed voices can be directed past voicemail to the intended recipient or emergency responders.[43]

Marketing

> *While emotional intelligence and behavioral sales/marketing techniques are a relatively new phenomenon, they are really less of a trend and more of a paradigm shift.*[44]
>
> —Brent Emler, Director of sales and marketing at Velma.com, a mortgage industry software provider

We buy because of emotion, and no business uses emotion and emotion-based technology more than marketing. Brain imagery shows that consumers primarily use emotions (personal feelings and experiences) rather than cognitive information (brand attributes, features, and facts) when evaluating products. The emotional response to an ad, for example, has far greater influence on a consumer's reported intent to buy a product than does the ad's content—by a factor of three-to-one for television commercials and two-to-one for print ads.[45] Appealing to an emotional connection is more effective as a marketing approach than even the pitches of hot celebrities. And the greater the emotional connection, the more loyalty from the customer. In short, EI "helps you sell bigger deals, in less time, at full margin."[46]

It is the emotional intelligence at every level of a business's outreach that establishes trust and loyalty.[47] As an example, in 2013 Johnson & Johnson had come off a few challenging years—over 280 million packages of over-the-counter medications and two popular artificial hip replacement models were recalled; 10,000 lawsuits related to those artificial hip devices had been filed; and a jury awarded a plaintiff $8.3 million in damages. So the company launched its first corporate branding campaign in more than ten years, unabashedly focusing on emotion to instill a sense of trust in the company again.[48]

Research on emotion is driving the design and implementation of advertising campaigns. Affectiva, an MIT Media Lab spin-off, develops emotion-sensing algorithms for Fortune Global 100 companies by mining the world's largest emotion database: 12 billion emotion data points from 2.9 million face videos submitted by volunteers in seventy-five countries.[49] It has used that information to produce 75 percent accuracy in predicting whether sales of products will rise, fall, or stay the same after a campaign is aired, all based on the audience's specific emotional reactions to the ads.[50] Adoreboard, named the Best Technology Start-up of 2014 by the Silicon Valley Global Leadership Forum, scours thousands of online news, social media, and blogs for twenty-four emotions to advise companies before content goes out on what the emotional reaction is likely to be, how to increase click-through rates, and likely sales.[51]

In social media, headlines and content that quickly connect with the targeted audience have rocketed some sites, like *Upworthy,* to astounding numbers of viewers, a result "strongly linked with emotional intelligence."[52] Even websites are being designed for emotional intelligence: "more and more corporately branded websites will be engineered and developed with the goal of becoming emotionally intelligent . . . not only will they be capable of augmenting and reflecting a user's emotional triggers in line with a proprietary brand, but they will also be capable of tuning themselves to an individual's emotional preferences."[53]

The up-close relationship with consumers that portable devices allow presents an even more personalized marketing arena where companies can appeal to users' emotions in real time. Apple was recently granted a patent registration for a product that analyzes facial expressions, heartbeats, and vocal patterns, a technology that some claim is equal to or better than most humans in reading emotions, which, when coupled with other data such as location and content, allows advertisers to display ads on the device that is targeted to the consumer's mood in the moment.[54] Similarly, Microsoft has applied for a patent that would enable a Kinect for Xbox 360 or some future gaming system to track the emotions of people in their living rooms, so that, by combining location, gender, age, and other metrics with specific moods, advertisers would be able to provide more targeted ads.[55]

Primary and Secondary Education

Higher emotional intelligence in educational settings makes for better schools—more effective administrators and teachers and higher-performing students. Those high-achieving middle schools denominated by the US government as "the Middle Schools to Watch" were found to have principals with high levels of emotional intelligence.[56] With greater EI skills, teachers report more effectiveness and job satisfaction.[57] Classroom exercises in EI yield profoundly improved student behavior, grades, and attendance, and reduce their drug involvement and criminal activity.[58] Even small improvements in interpersonal skills in childhood have been found to greatly increase adult success.[59]

The Yale Center for Emotional Intelligence, one of the few academic initiatives formulating interventions for raising EI, designs Social and Emotional Learning (SEL) programs that teach five key principles about emotions using the acronym RULER (recognition, understanding, labeling, expression, and regulation) and has reported many of the most significant school-based improvements.[60]

Yale's SEL principles are being disseminated through the marketplace. A new line of preschool toys and books called *The Moodsters* features five little detectives who learn how to come to their friends' rescue whenever they have a feelings emergency.[61] An SEL-based game, *If You Can,* created by the game-maker who designed the 1988 game *Madden NFL,* is touted as an "emotional IQ game" for primary schoolers. Each episode is keyed to challenges in twenty areas that involve emotions, such as emotional awareness, resilience, gratitude, sensitivity, empathy, listening, humor, leadership, and collaboration.[62] The movie *Inside Out* drew on SEL principles to teach a young (and even older) audience EI skills by showing what eleven-year-old Riley learns from her experience with her emotions—Joy, Sadness, Fear, Disgust, and Anger—after having to move to another city.[63]

Other countries are experimenting with raising emotional intelligence in their educational systems. Britain's Department for Education has adopted its Social and Emotional Aspects of Learning curriculum based on its findings about "how children's emotional and social competence and wellbeing could most effectively be developed" and how to promote teachers' social competence and emotional well-being.[64] School systems as far away as Singapore and Argentina are teaching EI competencies.[65] In 2017, Yale announced the founding of the Yale China Fund for Emotional Intelligence at the Yale Center Beijing, funded by two Chinese alumni, to assist Chinese educators in incorporating principles of emotional intelligence into programs for children three to six years old.

Graduate Business Schools

"Soft skills" are being prioritized by corporate employers over technical knowledge. An in-depth investigation to better understand employer expectations for MBA graduates determined that the traditional focus of MBA programs—"knowledge of fundamental business concepts"—was ranked only twelfth out of fifteen dimensions identified as important by business executives, and that "the most significant shortcoming of the current [MBA] curriculum . . . was in the courses that aided the development of interpersonal skills."[66] As one study concluded, a typical MBA curriculum does not provide opportunities for students to develop "emotional competencies."[67]

Even a highly technical company like BASF Corp., which used to look for expertise in functional areas like engineering and chemistry, trains managers who interview MBA candidates to assess soft qualities, because it found that "job candidates with proficiency in softer skills ended up leading better, no matter their functional background."[68]

Business schools' awareness of the corporate world's embrace of emotional intelligence is driving a trend to further EI research and to test and train MBA students for emotional intelligence, not only to help their graduates succeed in the job market but also to raise the schools' rankings based on postgraduation placements.[69]

In 2013, the Yale School of Management instituted as part of their admissions process a version of the Mayer-Salovey-Caruso Emotional Intelligence Test (MSCEIT) on a volunteer basis and anticipates using that data to eventually revise its admissions criteria.[70] In 2015 the dean of the Wharton School of the University of Pennsylvania declared that "Emotional intelligence is crucial to business success" and announced the establishment of the Katz Fund for Research on Leadership and Emotional Intelligence to "enhance[e] the creation and dissemination of knowledge on emotional intelligence in the workplace."[71]

And the list goes on.[72] Harvard's MBA program has a required course called FIELD Foundations for students that incorporates EI assessments "to deepen their emotional intelligence and develop a growing awareness of their own leadership styles."[73] Columbia Business School's Program on Social Intelligence includes activities throughout the course of their MBA studies that develop EI and social intelligence skills.[74] Dartmouth's Tuck School of Business recommendation form asks for reflections on an applicant's EI skills, and the school is expecting to select an EI test for admissions purposes. Notre Dame's Mendoza School of Business requires applicants to complete a Personal Characteristics Inventory considered in admissions decisions. The entire 2008 class of Chicago Templeton School of Business is being tested and followed over forty years to see how technical and personal skills, including emotional intelligence attributes like empathy, relate to their business success, the results of which will inform future curriculum.[75]

In response to business schools' increased focus on these personal abilities, applicants can now take a personal style assessment as part of the application-prep packages offered by the admissions consulting firm Veritas Prep.[76] The Graduate Management Admission Council (GMAT) in collaboration with Hogan Assessment Systems also created a test called "Reflect" to measure "soft skills," intended for both business school applicants and admissions committees, which in 2013 was named a Human Resource Executive Magazine Top Product Winner.[77]

THE BUSINESS COMMUNITY EMBRACES EMOTIONAL INTELLIGENCE

- Healthcare
- Accounting
- Technology
- Marketing
- Primary and Secondary Education
- Graduate Business Schools

The Demographics of Emotional Intelligence

The occurrence of emotional intelligence doesn't vary significantly among various demographic groups, but there are some interesting differences. Where do you fall within the groups of geography, age, trends affecting our society at large, race, socioeconomic class, and gender?

Emotional Intelligence and Geography

For a number of years, little research addressed possible variations in EI across cultures or geography, but now the concept of emotional intelligence has traveled widely—it is being taught in schools in Malta, Tasmania, and Lebanon,[78] and is being featured at conferences in South Africa, Saint Petersburg, Buenos Aires, and Nepal.[79] Studies conducted around the world have all come to the same conclusion[80]: the higher your EI, the more likely you are to succeed, and your emotional intelligence is unlikely to differ because of your geography, whether you are from the Netherlands, New Guinea, Thailand, Pakistan, the Ukraine, or any other country.[81]

Even the Chinese recognize the importance of emotional intelligence, which was once thought to clash with their values. While touring a job fair in Tianjin in May 2013, China's President Xi Jiping asked a local official: "Intelligence quotient and emotional quotient—which is more important?" When the official answered "both," Xi responded that emotional intelligence is most important. *Study Times,* a publication of the Central Party School of the Communist Party of China, shortly thereafter published a 3,000-word article entitled "Emotional Quotient and its three major components."[82]

Emotional Intelligence and Age

Unlike IQ, which peaks at age seventeen and remains essentially constant throughout adulthood, there is evidence that average EI rises at least slightly[83] and also steadily from our late teens into our sixties, after which it starts to decrease a little.[84]

A survey reviewing the four generations currently in the workplace—Traditionalists, born 1922 to 1945; Baby Boomers, 1946 to 1964; Gen X, 1965 to 1979; and Gen Y or Millennials, 1980 to 2000—found that the average emotional regulation score went up with each decade and also with each generation, with the biggest jump occurring from Gen Xers to Boomers, apparently due to greater experience.[85] Gaining more experience also appears to teach us to recognize our emotions better.[86]

According to a University of California–Berkeley professor, people age sixty and older are better able to see the positive side of a stressful situation and are more likely to empathize with others, using coping mechanisms that draw heavily on life experience to "positively reappraise" a situation, while younger participants are more likely to cope by adopting an objective, unemotional attitude, which is a less successful strategy.[87]

Emotional Intelligence and Society at Large

There is also the question whether over time our collective emotional intelligence changes. The general population's IQ has been increasing over the last few generations[88]—denominated the "Flynn Effect"[89]—in large measure because of improved environmental factors, "such as better nutrition, increased and better schooling, and exposure to technology."[90]

Although a small amount of evidence confirms a corresponding mass improvement in EI,[91] most of the scant historical data we have show a decline in society-wide EI: a psychologist who assessed thousands of children in the mid-1970s, and a different group again in the late 1980s found that over that period his samples of children, on average, "had become more anxious and depressed, more impulsive and mean, more demanding and disobedient, more hot-tempered and aggressive—and . . . the rate of decline was the same for all, privileged and impoverished alike."[92]

One factor that may be limiting emotional intelligence is the rise of social media and other technology as a preferred mode of interacting, robbing us of the face-to-face social learning that builds and exercises our EI. After preteens are deprived of their screens for only a few days, for example, forcing more interpersonal social interaction, they register significantly higher emotional perception abilities.[93]

Another trend that may be lowering the general population's EI is the increasing use, especially by young people, of prescribed antidepressants and other psychiatric drugs, as well as illegal drugs like opioids and heroin, that dull or hide emotional sensations, making them "emotionally illiterate,"[94] as one researcher contends. Medications are oftentimes appropriate or necessary, of course, but both legal and illegal drugs can inhibit the ability to experience at least part of our emotions, and can therefore deprive us of the opportunity to learn from them.

Emotional Intelligence and Race

Emotional intelligence seems to be race blind. For example, when the Air Force used EI assessments to select US Air Force recruiters, not only did it save nearly $3 million annually from improved recruiting and retention, but it also found no significant differences in EI among ethnic or racial groups.[95] Similarly, several EI assessments—the Bar-On EQ-i, EQ-i 2.0, and MSCEIT—all show no statistically significant differences in the average EI of African Americans, Hispanic/Latinos, Caucasians, and Asians in North America.[96]

Emotional Intelligence and Class

There is little to no research on whether average EI differs by socioeconomic class. Research does show that, whatever our class, we are likely to be most like those we spend the most social time with in terms of relationship skills.[97]

Education seems to make a person more self-aware, a component of EI, and more education evidently makes people appear more emotionally intelligent, even if they aren't.[98] Since high EI predicts higher academic success, better career performance, and also higher compensation, those results would be expected to propel people with higher EI into higher socioeconomic classes. On the other hand, there is some evidence that those with higher socioeconomic standing are less accurate in reading emotions and less empathic than those in lower socioeconomic classes, perhaps because they are less dependent on those around them.[99]

Emotional Intelligence and Gender

In November 2013, Lady Ashton, then the European Union's High Representative of the European Union for Foreign Affairs and Security Policy, brokered a deal with Iran on nuclear proliferation to effusive praise from Herman van Rompuy, then President of the European Council, and John Kerry, the US Secretary of State. The accomplishment was "hailed as one of the great diplomatic triumphs of the new century," and "the diplomatic breakthrough of the decade, [involving] a problem and a dispute so intractable it could have led to a devastating war engulfing the entire Middle East and beyond."[100]

To what does Lady Ashton owe this herculean accomplishment?—to "what is described in Brussels as her 'emotional intelligence' in steering and mediating the highly complex talks."[101] Oh, and one person slyly suggested, her gender was evidence of that higher EI.

So is it? Is one gender more likely than the other to have higher emotional intelligence?

While there are marked gender differences in brain function,[102] the research to date as to which gender has higher EI is decidedly mixed, on average giving a slight nod to women. Some studies show women scoring slightly to significantly higher than men in overall EI,[103] while others show little or no difference between the sexes.[104] Then again, some studies find gender differences only on certain EI subscales, slightly favoring women in most cases and most often in empathy, and men in others, primarily in emotional regulation.[105] One study found that while women and men generally rate their own performance comparably, women tend to underrate themselves compared to others' ratings of them, whereas men tend to overrate themselves.[106]

Some gender differences in emotional intelligence appear depending on where on the organizational chart the person stands. The Hay Group found that with respect to more than 17,000 individuals worldwide, it was at the middle executive level that women exhibit significantly higher EI than their male counterparts.[107]

Men and women do not differ in *how much* emotion they experience: both go through over a hundred emotions in any given day and both experience both pleasant and uncomfortable emotions.[108] Differences between the genders arise in *which emotions* they experience, their *reactions to their emotional experiences,* how they *express their emotions,* and how others *view those expressions.*

Women report greater levels of sadness and other negative emotions than men, but comparable levels of anger. Men apparently suffer a more profound physiological reaction—that is, higher blood pressure, higher pulse, and more perspiration—than women during and after highly emotional states, and remember fewer details of it afterwards.[109] Probably because of these impacts, men try to move out of strong emotions more quickly, "switch[ing] to other brain areas that try to solve the problem that's creating the emotional disturbance."[110] Women tend to remain longer in negative emotions than men, but then recover more easily and remember more details of the experience.[111]

These divergent tendencies may account for the traditional complaint by women that men are less empathic (as women remain in their negative emotions), and the one by men that women are too emotional (as men try to extricate themselves from those emotions).[112] It may also account for preferences in male-dominated workplaces to "tone down" the emotions that they find so debilitating.

Expression of emotions also differs by gender. Women express their anger verbally, which may make them appear "more emotional," whereas men tend to express their anger behaviorally, by acting out in an aggressive way—slamming a door or throwing something—or turning to alcohol or drugs.[113] Women also cry in the workplace more often than men—41 percent of women compared to 9 percent of men had cried during the prior year, according to one study.[114] Evidently a good number of lawyers (whether men or women) are also shedding tears—one in three lawyers report crying on the job,[115] though perhaps behind closed doors. Criers thought crying made no difference in their career success; male managers agreed they were fine with female employees crying, while female managers, interestingly, were much less tolerant.[116]

What's particularly important is that these gender differences in expression of emotions impact *how we judge* the competence of those we work with. Women who express sadness or other negative emotions are judged to be less competent regardless of their actual competence. Women who express anger are also consistently seen as less competent than both angry men and unemotional women. And a woman expressing anger is perceived as an angrier person with less control than a man expressing the same level of anger.[117]

Why do we make such different evaluations depending on which gender is expressing the emotions? Women's emotions are typically attributed to an internal, abiding part of their nature, while men's emotions are attributed to an immediate external provocation.[118] So an expression of emotions by a woman is considered evidence of her being generally overemotional and out of control, while a man's emotional displays are assumed to be an understandable reaction to a single provocation. The take-away apparently is that expressing anger is considered gender appropriate for men but not for women.[119]

Perhaps because of the significance of these judgments to their careers, women as a rule are more aware of and pay more attention to their and others' emotions, compared to men. "Women show more complex conceptualizations of emotion, with a greater understanding of what emotions they or others would feel in different contexts and why." They are also more likely to "see their emotions as providing useful information that is important to analyze."[120]

One of the most striking differences between the genders is that men are much more likely to suppress their emotions.[121] In trying to engage in a "logical, non-emotional approach to problems . . . men more frequently 'stonewall'" the emotion in an interaction "by inhibiting their facial action and minimizing their listening and eye contact."[122] These reactions reduce the ability to be empathic. High emotional suppression rates may be due to the importance men place on portraying an image of maintaining control, something emotional women are seen as not having,[123] and may also be an attempt to ward off disability during strong emotional events, even though suppression has its own negative fallout, like reducing cognitive functioning and accurate recall.[124]

So the results to date on the differences in emotional intelligence between the sexes might be simplified by saying that women are slightly more likely to be emotionally intelligent, and specifically to be more empathic—to "feel your pain"—while men may be somewhat more likely to manage emotions well. The women's higher empathy fosters stronger relationships, while the men's emotional management skills keep matters moving forward.[125] These differences are not likely to be the differences between any two individuals, but reflect an overall bell curve for each gender.

These gender differences, especially those based on self-reports, are colored by the demonstrated impact that socialized expectations, conscious or unconscious, have on both women and men.[126] Particularly in males, social influences may be responsible for delays in the development or the suppression of EI, who "when they become adults . . . shut down their emotional intelligence," perhaps fearful of looking too "sentimental." The hope is that "now that we live in a culture that is beginning to value emotional awareness and intimate relationships, with luck, that trend will diminish."[127]

THE DEMOGRAPHICS OF EMOTIONAL INTELLIGENCE	
Geography:	There are no significant differences in emotional intelligence geographically.
Age:	Emotional intelligence appears to rise somewhat with age.
Society:	Emotional intelligence appears to be declining in society as a whole, perhaps in part because of less personal interaction and the increased use of drugs that detach us from our emotions.
Race:	There are no significant differences in emotional intelligence by race.
Class:	Higher education and performance may indicate upper classes have higher emotional intelligence but also possibly lower empathy because of less dependence on others.
Gender:	Women and men are roughly similar in emotional intelligence, with some small differences in components of EI: women generally appear to be more attentive to emotions and more empathic. Men's and women's emotional experiences and their degree of impairment differ in some ways, and similar emotional expressions are viewed differently by others, depending on gender.

The Physiology of Emotional Intelligence

> *For the most part, we cannot dictate what emotions we are going to feel, when we're going to feel them, nor how strongly we feel them. They come unbidden from the amygdala and other subcortical areas. Our choice point comes once we feel a certain way. What do we do then? How do we express it?*[128]
>
> —Daniel Goleman, author and emotional intelligence expert

Our emotional intelligence reflects how the neural circuitry in our brain was hardwired at birth and then has subsequently developed over years of emotional experiences. Here's a simplified guide (Figure 1-1) to the role different parts of our brains play in our emotional intelligence.

The amygdala, a small area situated toward the base of our brain and developed early in man's evolution, formulates and stores emotional memories and manages our fight-or-flight response, which prompts the production of adrenaline and cortisol, the stress hormones.

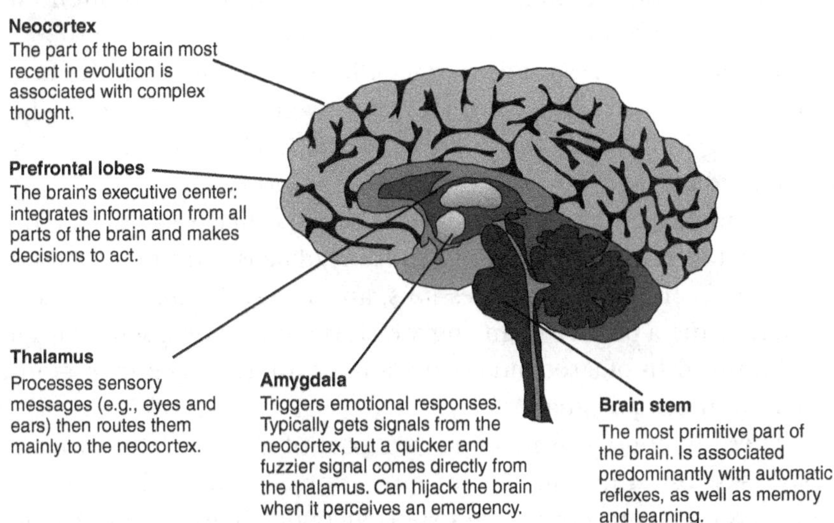

Figure 1-1: The human brain.
Source: Enio Velazco, "Just in Time Coaching," June 14, 2005, Slide 20, http://www.slideshare.net/evelazco/just-in-time-coaching-emotional-intelligence.

The prefrontal cortex (part of our neocortex) is at the front of our brain and developed later in human evolution. It is where our cognition and working memory reside, where we analyze physical and visual data, and also where we process our emotions, reflect on them, and manage them. Its two lobes have been correlated with different types of feelings—the left lobe with more positive feelings and the right lobe with more negative feelings. The ratio of positive/negative feelings gives each person a distinct emotional profile or set-point.[129]

The thalamus acts like an air traffic controller directing outside data in an orderly fashion to the prefrontal cortex for processing. The prefrontal cortex cognitively "thinks" about the data it receives to make sense of it. If it decides, "Aha, this means I should get excited," a signal is then sent to the amygdala, where peptides and hormones are released that produce feelings and action.

But during any sixteen-hour day when we get hundreds of sensations, many are not processed in so orderly a manner.[130] The air-traffic controller thalamus can react quickly to new data by immediately copying the amygdala or bypassing the prefrontal cortex altogether and sending the data directly to the amygdala. Bodily sensations coming up through the brainstem also often hit the amygdala before they make it to the thalamus.

The amygdala responds to data 100 times faster than the prefrontal cortex can think, so even if the prefrontal cortex is in the processing loop, *we usually feel before we think.* The amygdala makes an immediate and often unconscious emotional response to any real or perceived threat even if we're at the office and not in danger of being eaten. For example, the amygdala is activated when we see spiders, frightening expressions, and faces of a different race. Even flashing a picture of an angry or foreign face on a screen for a few hundredths of a second creates an instant, usually unconscious reaction in our amygdala.[131]

These unconscious reactions are part of our "gut" or intuitive responses, often literally felt in our stomachs, which have developed over years of emotional experience and help form our conscious evaluations.[132]

Although fast, the amygdala is also often sloppy and may not read incoming impulses accurately or may generate habitual emotional responses to possibly misperceived signals while the prefrontal cortex is not yet active.

The amygdala's fight-or-flight hormones can also temporarily inhibit the analytical activity in the prefrontal cortex—sometimes referred to as an "amygdala hijack."[133] The hormones driving the hijacking dissipate in three to six seconds, but even during the hijacking, we can still quickly engage the prefrontal cortex consciously.

More importantly, research into brain plasticity has found that, through the process of neurogenesis, which produces new brain cells every day, and by affirmatively practicing preferred response patterns, we can actually change our brains physiologically, as we would a muscle, so as to reformulate both our automatic and deliberate responses,[134] and often within only a matter of weeks.[135]

The role of emotional intelligence is to build the ability of the neocortex to recognize our and others' emotional states, to understand what data those emotional cues are providing, and to consciously use that information to manage the emotional aspects of our responses and relationships so as to achieve the results we desire.[136]

The Proof Is in the Pudding

Companies across the United States know the practical value of emotional intelligence, whether or not they've read the studies or understand how it occurs demographically or physiologically. In a CareerBuilder survey[137] of more than 2,600 hiring managers and human resource professionals nationwide,

- 71 percent value emotional intelligence in an employee more than IQ,
- 75 percent would promote a high EI worker over a high IQ candidate,
- 59 percent would not hire someone who has a high IQ but low EI, and

- 34 percent are placing even greater emphasis on EI when hiring and promoting postrecession.

What specifically is it about these high EI workers that hiring managers value so much? According to the employers surveyed, high EI employees

- are more likely to stay calm under pressure,
- know how to resolve conflict effectively,
- are empathetic to their team members and react accordingly,
- lead by example, and
- make more thoughtful business decisions.

What behaviors do these managers look for that indicate high EI? They look for employees who

- admit to and learn from mistakes,
- keep emotions in check,
- have thoughtful discussions on tough issues,
- listen as much or more than they talk,
- take criticism well, and
- show grace under pressure.

WHAT IS EMOTIONAL INTELLIGENCE?

- In the 1990s, psychology researchers at Yale and the University of New Hampshire explored why some "smart" people did not function as high as one would expect from their cognitive ability.
- They defined a new concept called "emotional intelligence," and concluded that those with high emotional intelligence have an accurate awareness of emotions in themselves and others, can tap into how those emotions feel, and are able to understand and manage emotions so as to produce the desired results. They also developed one of the first assessments for measuring emotional intelligence.
- Daniel Goleman popularized their research in his best-selling book, *Emotional Intelligence: Why It Can Matter More Than IQ.*

(Continued)

- The business community, including the healthcare, accounting, technology, marketing, and education industries, quickly recognized the value of the attribute and embraced testing and training to increase emotional intelligence.
- Research shows that emotional intelligence occurs fairly uniformly throughout populations.
- The physiology of emotional intelligence resides in the neural system that sends both external and internal (including "gut") signals to the amygdala (the emotional brain) and the prefrontal cortex (the rational brain) for processing.
- The proof of the value of emotional intelligence in a business setting is that professionals in charge of hiring across the country prefer high emotional intelligence to high IQ for a number of reasons.

Chapter Endnotes

1. Goleman had studied with one of the researchers concerned with how poorly traditional tests of cognitive intelligence predict future success: David C. McClelland, "Testing for Competence Rather Than 'Intelligence,'" *American Psychologist* 28 (1973): 1–14. John D. Mayer and Peter Salovey, "Emotional Intelligence," *Imagination, Cognition, and Personality* 9 (1989): 185–211.
2. There is no clear answer to who first coined the terms. Many agree that Mayer and Salovey first used "emotional intelligence" in 1989. Ibid. Some cite Wayne L. Payne's 1985 doctoral thesis, "A Study of Emotion: Developing Emotional Intelligence: Self Integration; Relating to Fear, Pain and Desire," accessible in full here: http://eqi.org/payne.htm. Reuven Bar-On reportedly used the term in an unpublished draft of his dissertation, of which apparently no copy remains. The term may have appeared in a 1964 paper: Beldoch, M. "Sensitivity to Expression of Emotional Meaning in Three Modes of Communication," in J. R. Davitz et al., *The Communication of Emotional Meaning*, McGraw-Hill (1964), pp. 31–42. A 1966 paper by B. Leuner was entitled "Emotional Intelligence and Emancipation," *Praxis der Kinderpsychologie und Kinderpsychiatrie*, 15: 193–203. In 1983, Howard Gardner's *Frames of Mind: The Theory of Multiple Intelligences* contended IQ fails to fully explain cognitive ability, and suggested multiple intelligences, including interpersonal intelligence (the capacity to understand the intentions, motivations and desires of other people) and intrapersonal intelligence (the capacity to understand oneself, to appreciate one's feelings, fears and motivations) (New York: Basic Books, 1983). Keith Beasley used the abbreviation "EQ" in "The Emotional Quotient," published in *The British Mensa Magazine* in May, 1987.

3. E.J. Dionne Jr., "Gary Hart the Elusive Front-Runner," *New York Times,* May 3, 1987.
4. Mayer and Salovey, "What Is Emotional Intelligence: Implications for Educators," in *Emotional Development and Emotional Intelligence: Educational Implications,* ed. Salovey and D. Sluter (New York: Basic Books, 1997), 5; Mayer and Salovey, "Emotional Intelligence," *Imagination, Cognition, and Personality,* 189.
5. Goleman et al., *Harvard Business Review on What Makes a Leader* (Boston: Harvard Business School Publishing Corporation, 2001).
6. Kathleen Cavallo and Dottie Brienza, "Emotional Competence and Leadership Excellence at Johnson & Johnson: The Emotional Intelligence in Organizations," *Consortium for Research on Emotional Intelligence in Organizations,* 2001, http://www.eiconsortium.org/reports/jj_ei_study.html.
7. Anemona Hartocollis, "In Medical School Shift, Meeting Patients on Day 1," *New York Times,* September 2, 2010; Peggy Wagner, "Does High EI (Emotional Intelligence) Make Better Doctors," *Virtual Mentor* 8 (2006): 477.
8. Natalie J. Lewis et al., "Emotional Intelligence in Medical Education: Measuring the Unmeasurable?" *Advances in Health Sciences Education* 10 (2005): 339–55.
9. Lewis et al., "Emotional Intelligence in Medical Education," 339–55.
10. Jodi Halpern, "What Is Clinical Empathy?" *Journal of General Internal Medicine* 18 (2003): 670–74. See also: Bernie Wong and Neha John-Henderson, "Does Your Manager Feel Your Pain?" *Greater Good,* May 13, 2013, http://greatergood.berkeley.edu/article/research_digest/does_your_manager_feel_your_pain; David B. Resnik and Gregg E. Dinse, "Do U.S Research Institutions Meet or Exceed Federal Mandates for Instruction in Responsible Conduct of Research?" *Academic Medicine* 87 (9): 1237–42. Doctors who are more emotionally attuned to their patients are less likely to experience burnout. Maura Anfossi and Gianmauro Numico, "Empathy in the Doctor-Patient Relationship," *Journal of Clinical Oncology* 22 (2004): 2258–59.
11. Wagner et al., "Physicians' Emotional Intelligence and Patient Satisfaction," *Family Medicine Journal* 34 (2002): 750–54. See also Deborah L. Kasman, Kelly Fryer-Edwards, and Clarence H. Braddock III, "Educating for Professionalism: Trainees' Emotional Experiences on IM and Pediatrics Inpatient Wards," *Academic Medicine* 78 (2003): 730–41; Terry D. Stratton et al., "Emotional Intelligence and Clinical Skills: Preliminary Results from a Comprehensive Clinical Performance Examination," *Academic Medicine* 80 (2005): S34–S37. Robyn Tamblyn et al., "Physician Scores on a National Clinical Skills Examination as Predictors of Complaints to Medical Regulatory Authorities," *Journal of the American Medical Association* 98 (2007): 992–1001; Hardeep Singh et al., "Medical Errors Involving Trainees: A Study of Closed Malpractice Claims from Five Insurers," *Archives of Internal Medicine* 167 (2007): 2030–36.
12. Shaheen E. Lakhan, "Building Emotional Intelligence," *Canadian Family Physician* 55 (2009): 351–52.
13. High EI dentists produce higher patient satisfaction. Shahram Azimi et al., "Emotional Intelligence of Dental Students and Patient Satisfaction," *European Journal of Dental Education* 14 (2010): 129–32. Clinical nurses with higher emotional intelligence perform better, stay in their jobs longer, and have longer

careers. Estelle Codier et al., "Emotional Intelligence, Performance, and Retention in Clinical Staff Nurses," *Nursing Administration Quarterly* 33 (2009): 310. EI is a core competency for healthcare administrators as well. Brenda Freshman and Louis Rubino, "Emotional Intelligence: A Core Competency for Healthcare Administrators," *The Healthcare Manager* 20 (2002); Michelle T. Renaud et al., "Preparing Emotionally Intelligent Doctor of Nursing Practice Leaders," *Journal of Nursing Education* 51 (2012): 454–60.

14. M. Gemma Cherry et al., "Emotional Intelligence in Medical Education: A Critical Review," *Medical Education Journal* 48 (2014): 468–78.
15. Carol Elam and Terry D. Stratton, "Should Medical Schools Applicants Be Tested for Emotional Intelligence?" *American Medical Association Journal of Ethics* 8 (2006): 473–76; Robert M. Carrothers, Stanford W. Gregory, Jr., and Timothy J. Gallagher, "Measuring Emotional Intelligence of Medical School Applicants," *Academic Medicine* 75 (2000): 456–63. Clinical exam exercises are being developed for applicants to demonstrate their EI skills. Kevin W. Eva et al., "The Ability of the Multiple Mini-Interview to Predict Preclerkship Performance in Medical School," *Academic Medicine* 79 (2004): S40–S42. American Medical Association Ethics Poll, July 2006, cited in Wagner, "Does High EI (Emotional Intelligence) Make Better Doctors?" *Virtual Mentor,* 477–79.
16. "MD Select Program Overview," *USF Health,* 2016, http://health.usf.edu/medicine/mdprogram/select/.
17. Jess White, "Social Skills Are Important for Your Doctors," *Healthcare Business & Technology,* November 3, 2014, http://www.healthcarebusinesstech.com/social-skills-doctors/; Mona M. Signer, "NRMP Update," presented at the annual meeting of the Association of Program Directors in Internal Medicine National Meeting, Phoenix, AZ, October 12, 2012. Wagner, "Does High EI (Emotional Intelligence) Make Better Doctors?" *Virtual Mentor,* 478; Hui-Ching Weng et al., "Doctors' Emotional Intelligence and the Patient-Doctor Relationship," *Medical Education* 42 (2008): 703–11; Lewis et al., "Emotional Intelligence in Medical Education," *Advances in Health Sciences Education,* 339–55.
18. "Pharmacy Students Learn about Emotional Intelligence," *Lebanese American University News & Events,* July 3, 2013, http://www.lau.edu.lb/news-events/news/archive/pharmacy_students_learn_about/; "Workshop: Emotional Intelligence, Psychological Agility and Resilience for Health Professionals (VIC)," *Occupational Therapy Australia,* November 15, 2015, https://www.otaus.com.au/professionaldevelopment/event/emotional-intelligence-nov-2015; Lewis et al., "Emotional Intelligence in Medical Education," *Advances in Health Sciences Education,* 339–55.
19. Daisy Grewal and Heather A. Davidson, "Emotional Intelligence and Graduate Medical Education," *Journal of the American Medical Association* 10 (2008): 1200–1202.
20. Jimmy Bejjani, "Emotional Intelligence: Use in Medical Education and Practice," *McGill Journal of Medicine: MJM* 12 (2009): 5; "Physician Leadership Institute," *Canadian Medical Association,* 2016, https://www.cma.ca/En/Pages/physician-leadership-institute.aspx; "CanMEDS: Better standards, better physicians, better care," *Royal College of Physicians and Surgeons of Canada,* 2016, http://

www.royalcollege.ca/rcsite/canmeds/canmeds-framework-e; "MD Program Competencies," University of Toronto, 2016, http://www.md.utoronto.ca/program/competencies/manager.htm.

21. Cherry et al., "Emotional Intelligence in Medical Education," *Medical Education Journal*, 468–78.
22. Shen H. Comrey, "Predicting Medical Students' Academic Performances by Their Cognitive Abilities and Personality Characteristics," *Academic Medicine* 72 (9): 781–86; Filip Lievens et al., "Personality Scale Validities Increase Throughout Medical School," *Journal of Applied Psychology* 94 (2009): 1514–35; Richard F. Brown and Carma L. Bylund, "Communication Skills Training: Describing a New Conceptual Model," *Academic Medicine* 83 (2008): 37–44.
23. Pat Griffith, "The Emotionally Intelligent Accountant: An Oxymoron?" *Pat Griffith Executive Development Blog*, March 15, 2011, citing the American Institute of Certified Public Accountants 2000, 1996; Ken McPhail, "An Emotional Response to the State of Accounting Education: Developing Accounting Students' Emotional Intelligence," *Critical Perspectives on Accounting* 15 (2004): 646; Jeffrey Pawlow, "Emotional Intelligence Is Critical to Personal and Firm Success," *The Growth Partnership*, January 6, 2010, http://www.thegrowthpartnership.com/news/tgp_blog/emotional_intelligence_is_critical_to_personal_and_firm_success.
24. Lyn Daff, Paul de Lange, and Beverley Jackling, "A Comparison of Generic Skills and Emotional Intelligence in Accounting Education," *Issues in Accounting Education* 27 (2012): 627–45.
25. Cindy Blanthorne, Sak Bhamornsiri, and Robert E. Guinn, "Are Technical Skills Still Important?" *CPA Journal* 75 (2005): 64–65.
26. Darlene Bay and Kim McKeage, "Emotional Intelligence in Undergraduate Accounting Students: Preliminary Assessment," *Accounting Education: An International Journal* 15 (2006): 451; Connie Esmond-Kiger, Mary L. Tucker, and Christine A. Yost, "Emotional Intelligence: From the Classroom to the Workplace," *Management Accounting Quarterly* 7 (2006): 35–41.
27. While serving as KPMG's national director of Women's Initiatives and other Workplace Solutions, Sandra Bushby had over 1,500 U.S. partners take personal style assessments to assemble teams with varied talents, including EI. As an unexpected bonus, KPMG also achieved more culturally, gender, and racially diverse teams. Susan Bushby, "Presented at an ARK Group conference in 2009 on Women in Professional Service Firms," 2009; Gail Lynn Cook et al., "Emotional Intelligence: The Role of Accounting Education and Work Experience," *Issues in Accounting Education* 26 (2011): 268.
28. John Henry and Peter MacLean, "Courting the Candidate-Customer: The Unlikely Attraction," *Deloitte University Press*, July 24, 2013; Melissa Korn and Joe Light, "On the Lesson Plan: Feelings," *The Wall Street Journal*, June 7, 2011.
29. Stephen P. Robbins et al., *Management: The Essentials* (Frenchs Forest, Australia: 2014), 260.
30. "A Focus on Change," *Forbes Insights: Audit 2020*, 2015, 7, https://assets.kpmg.com/content/dam/kpmg/pdf/2015/08/us-audit-2020-report.pdf; "KPMG Case Study," *Speak First Directory*, March 23, 2011, 30.

31. "Emotional Intelligence," *KPMG Business Institute,* 2016, http://kpmg-businessinstitute.cz/en/skoleni/manazerske-a-obchodni-dovednosti/emocni-inteligence.
32. "The general consensus is that the 'Big Four' professional services firms are between five-to-10 years ahead of 'BigLaw' in their operational sophistication and integration." Ernst & Young legal services head Trevor Faure writing in *The Lawyer Management: A Guide to Change,* quoted in Matt Byrne, "Lawyers Years behind Accountants on Process and BD, *The Lawyer* Research Reveals," *The Lawyer,* June 24, 2014. Richard agrees. Larry Richard, "Hiring Emotionally Intelligent Associates," *Bench & Bar of Minnesota,* October, 1999.
33. Aaron Krumins, "It's Happening: 'Pepper' Robot Gains Emotional Intelligence," *ExtremeTech,* June 22, 2015, http://www.extremetech.com/extreme/208666-its-happening-pepper-robot-gains-emotional-intelligence. See also Angad Singh, "'Emotional' Robot Sells Out in a Minute," *CNN,* June 23, 2015, http://www.cnn.com/2015/06/22/tech/pepper-robot-sold-out/.
34. "Affective Computing" n.d., http://affect.media.mit.edu/.
35. Sophie Curtis, "Welcome to a New Era of Machine Emotional Intelligence," *Rework Blog,* March 23, 2015, https://www.re-work.co/blog/deep-learning-eyeris https://www.re-work.co/blog/deep-learning-eyeris-modar-alaoui; "Eyeris," 2016, http://www.emovu.com.
36. "The computer that reads 'subtle' emotions," *BBC News,* May 30, 2012, http://news.bbc.co.uk/today/hi/today/newsid_9724000/9724921.stm. See also "Rosalind W. Picard," n.d, http://web.media.mit.edu/~picard/index.php.
37. "Mona Lisa 'happy', computer finds," *BBC News,* December 15, 2005, http://news.bbc.co.uk/2/hi/entertainment/4530650.stm.
38. "Robots Muscle in on the Job Interview," *Financial Times,* November 17, 2016. Designed by the Research Centre for Computers, Communication and Social Innovation at Australia's La Trobe University, she asks seventy-six questions over twenty-five minutes.
39. Geraldine Cremin, "Robots Are Learning to Fake Empathy," *Motherboard,* April 6, 2016, http://motherboard.vice.com/read/robots-are-learning-to-fake-empathy. On a smaller plane, Google has a new feature of Google+ called +Emotion, which emotionally tags photos by analyzing the emotions expressed. Emotion recognition technology will also be deployed by future versions of Siri, Google Now, Amazon Echo, and other virtual assistants who will "empathize" by reflecting your emotions in their voices. Mike Elgan, "Why 'Emotion' Is the New Killer App," *Datamation,* April 10, 2013, http://www.datamation.com/applications/why-emotion-is-the-new-killer-app-2.html.
40. "Bullying Prevention Hub," *Facebook.com,* 2016, https://www.prod.facebook.com/safety/bullying/. Kimberly Van der Elst, Na'ahmon Razon, and Janelle Caponigro, "Do Bullies Feel Your Pain?" *Greater Good: The Science of a Meaningful Life,* February 3, 2011, http://greatergood.berkeley.edu/article/research_digest/do_bullies_feel_your_pain. Mark Zuckerberg believes that, "What [members] really want is the ability to express empathy," so Facebook is introducing a "dislike" button for users to respond to sad news. Biz Carson, "Finally: You'll soon be able to 'dislike' things on Facebook, says Mark Zuckerberg," *Business Insider,* September 15, 2015, *Business Insider,* http://

www.businessinsider.com/mark-zuckerberg-facebook-is-working-on-a-disk-like-button-2015-9?utm_content=bufferfddbc&utm_medium=social&utm_source=twitter.com&utm_campaign=ASteinman+Twitter.

41. "Cogito Secures $15M in Series B Funding to Bring Emotional Intelligence to Customer Experience," *Business Wire,* November 18, 2016, http://www.businesswire.com/news/home/20161118005048/en/Cogito-Secures-15M-Series-Funding-Bring-Emotional.
42. "Honda's latest concept car unveiled . . . [in January 2016] has Honda's Automated Network Assistant (HANA), built with SoftBank, on board . . . Through HANA, the car becomes aware of a driver's emotions and moods, and can support driving choices as well as suggest media." Darrell Etherington, "Honda's NeuV Is a Mini Electric Concept Car with Emotional Intelligence," *TechCrunch,* January 5, 2017, https://techcrunch.com/2017/01/05/hondas-neuv-is-a-mini-electric-concept-car-with-emotional-intelligence/.
43. "'Mind Reading' Computer Research at Bangor University," *BBC News,* January 25, 2011, http://www.bbc.co.uk/news/uk-wales-north-west-wales-12250845; Elgan, "Why 'Emotion' Is the New Killer App," *Datamation.com.*
44. Brent Emler, "Emotional Intelligence and Mortgage Advertising." *National Mortgage Professional Magazine,* June 10, 2015, http://nationalmortgageprofessional.com/news/54428/emotional-intelligence-and-mortgage-advertising.
45. Peter Noel Murray, "How Emotions Influence What We Buy," *Psychology Today,* February 26, 2013.
46. 81 Media International, "Colleen Stanley on Emotional Intelligence for Sales Success," YouTube video, 8:35, posted [November 7, 2012], https://www.youtube.com/watch?v=SqDucFtkUnY. See also Journal of Consumer Research, Inc., "Product Promotion: When Do Emotional Appeals Trump Celebrity Spokespeople?" *ScienceDaily,* March 3, 2013, http://www.sciencedaily.com/releases/2013/03/130305130734.htm.
47. Emler, "Emotional Intelligence and Mortgage Advertising," *National Mortgage Professional Magazine.* The emotional connection is "particularly essential in terms of working with Millennials."
48. Tanzina Vega, "Trying to Burnish Its Image, J.&J. Turns to Emotions," *New York Times,* April 24, 2013.
49. NPR Staff, "Will Our Screens Soon Be Able to Read Our Emotions?" *NPR,* September 11, 2015, http://www.npr.org/2015/09/11/439190272/will-our-screens-soon-be-able-to-read-our-emotions.
50. Chuck Longanecker, "Give Your Website Soul With Emotionally Intelligent Interactions," *Smashing Magazine,* March 28, 2012, http://uxdesign.smashingmagazine.com/2012/03/28/give-your-website-soul-with-emotionally-intelligent-interactions/; Ian Cocoran, "The Art of Digital Branding: The Emotionally Intelligent Website," *Graphics.com,* 2011, http://www.graphics.com/modules.php?name=Sections&op=viewarticle&artid=1010.
51. Bronwen Morgan, "Emotional Intelligence," *Impact Magazine,* August 19, 2015.
52. Drake Baer, "The Link Between Viral Content and Emotional Intelligence: Want to Get 30 Million Page Views in a Month? Then You Need to Understand the Murky Forces That Compel Us to Click," *Fast Company,* January 29, 2014.
53. Cocoran, "The Art of Digital Branding," *Graphics.com.*

54. "Apple Granted 55 Patents Today Covering Wearable Displays, Inductive Charging, Face Recognition & More," *Patently Apple,* October 25, 2016, http://www.patentlyapple.com/patently-apple/2016/10/apple-granted-55-patents-today-covering-wearable-displays-inductive-charging-face-recognition-more.html. ThirdSight is developing software for purposes of market research that analyzes via cell phones facial expressions, eye movements, hand and body gestures, and tone of voice when users view the product. Sharif Sakr, "Market Research and the Primitive Mind of the Consumer," *BBC News,* March 6, 2011, http://www.bbc.co.uk/news/business-12581446.
55. Wook Jin Chung, Pritesh Patwa, and Martin Miroslavov Markov, "US Patent Application: 20120143693—Targeting Advertisements Based on Emotion," June 7, 2012. The MIT Affective Computing lab is considering replacing Nielsen ratings by recording real-time audience emotion during programming that shows exactly what responses are and when. Adam Higginbotham, "Welcome to Rosalind Picard's Touchy-Feely World of Empathic Tech," *Wired,* November 27, 2012.
56. Michele Reynolds, *An Investigation of the Emotional Intelligence Competencies of National Middle Schools to Watch Principals,* (PhD diss., Eastern Kentucky University, 2011), 97–98. The EI of these principals did not show correlations with gender, geographic location, socioeconomic standing, or the degree of minority enrollment in the school.
57. Susan E. Rivers et al., "Improving the Social and Emotional Climate of Classrooms: A Clustered Randomized Controlled Trial Testing the RULER Approach," *Prevention Science* 14 (2013): 77–87; Marc A. Brackett et al., "Emotion Regulation Ability, Job Satisfaction, and Burnout among British Secondary School Teachers," *Psychology in the Schools* 47 (2010): 406–17.
58. Brackett and Rivers, "Transforming Students' Lives with Social and Emotional Learning," in *International Handbook of Emotions in Education,* ed. Reinhard Pekrun and Lisa Linnenbrink-Garcia (New York: Routledge, 2014), 366–86. See also "Evidence," *RULER,* 2016, http://ei.yale.edu/ruler/.
59. Damon E. Jones, Mark Greenberg, and Max Crowley, "Early Social-Emotional Functioning and Public Health: The Relationship Between Kindergarten Social Competence and Future Wellness," *American Journal of Public Health* 105 (2015): 2283–90.
60. "Yale Center for Emotional Intelligence," *Yale Center for Emotional Intelligence,* 2013, http://ei.yale.edu/. RULER participants show improved attention, higher academic performance, better leadership skills, improved social skills, less substance abuse and negative social behavior, and decreased anxiety and depression. School climates improve, with less bullying. Faculty benefit through better relationships with students and administration, lower anxiety, lower stress and burnout, and higher job satisfaction.
61. "Meet the Moodsters: A Groundbreaking Line of Toys and Books Designed to Teach Emotional Intelligence to Preschoolers Now Available," *PR Newswire,* September 9, 2015, http://www.prnewswire.com/news-releases/meet-the-moodsters-a-groundbreaking-line-of-toys-and-books-designed-to-teach-emotional-intelligence-to-preschoolers-now-available-300139699.html. See also "The Moodsters," *TheMoodsters.com,* http://themoodsters.com/.

62. Wade Roush, "From Madden NFL to Emotional Intelligence: Trip Hawkins' Journey," *Xconomy*, January 27, 2014, http://www.xconomy.com/san-francisco/2014/01/27/from-madden-nfl-to-emotional-intelligence/?utm_source=rss&utm_medium=rss&utm_campaign=from-madden-nfl-to-emotional-intelligence.
63. Mary Ryerse, "12 Ways to Use Inside Out to Teach Emotional Intelligence," *The Gottman Institute Blog*, August 17, 2015, https://www.gottman.com/blog/12-ways-to-use-inside-out-to-teach-emotional-intelligence/. "Joy, the predominant emotion/character, scrambles to provide Riley with enough happy memories to bolster resiliency, while keeping . . . sadness at bay. While Joy and Sadness wrestle at the helm of Riley's brain, Joy comes to recognize that . . . sometimes sadness leads to wisdom and self-preservation." Linda Esposito, "Inside Out—A Major Emotional IQ Picture," *Psychology Today*, June 26, 2015.
64. Instituted in 2005, this program "focuses on five social and emotional aspects of learning: self-awareness, managing feelings, motivation, empathy and social skills . . . The materials help children develop skills such as understanding another's point of view, working in a group, sticking at things when they get difficult, resolving conflict and managing worries." "Social and Emotional Aspects of Learning (SEAL): Improving Behaviour, Improving Learning," *National Archives*, May 2005, http://webarchive.nationalarchives.gov.uk/20110809101133/nsonline.org.uk/node/87009. See also Katherine Weare and Gay Gray, *What Works in Developing Children's Emotional and Social Competence and Wellbeing?* (Nottingham: DfES Publications, 2003), 74.
65. Tani Ruiz, "Social and Emotional Learning in Schools: Essentials for Holistic Development," *UNICEF.org*, n.d. http://www.unicef.org/eapro/media_7792.html; "Argentina Schools Add 'Emotional Education' to Curriculum," *Gulf Times*, June 2, 2013, http://www.gulf-times.com/us-latin percent20america/182/details/354898/argentina-schools-add-%E2%80%98emotional-education%E2%80%99-to-curriculum.
66. Fredricka F. Joyner and Derek T. Y. Mann, "Developing Emotional Intelligence in MBA Students: A Case Study of One Program's Success," *American Journal of Business Education (AJBE)* 4 (2011): 61.
67. Ibid. 61, 60.
68. Korn and Light, "On the Lesson Plan: Feelings," *The Wall Street Journal*.
69. Max Niesen, "Now You Might Have to Show Emotional IQ to Get into Business School," *Business Insider*, May 2, 2013, http://www.businessinsider.com/mbas-and-emotional-intelligence-2013-5.
70. Vivian Giang, "Your Boss Probably Wouldn't Pass Yale's Emotional Intelligence Assessment," *Business Insider*, May 10, 2013, http://www.businessinsider.com/yales-emotional-intelligence-assessment-2013-5.
71. "The Wharton School of the University of Pennsylvania Announces Gift to Establish the Katz Fund for Research on Leadership and Emotional Intelligence," *Wharton Magazine*, July 7, 2015, http://whartonmagazine.com/press-releases/launch-of-new-wharton-leadership-research/.
72. The Stern School of Business at NYU claims the Stern Advantage arises from recognizing the contribution of both EI and IQ to success in business. "The Stern Advantage," *NYU Stern*, http://www.stern.nyu.edu/programs-admissions/

full-time-mba/the-stern-advantage/iq-eq. Wake Forest University's Masters in Management program emphasizes the importance of EI throughout the curriculum. "Your Ten-Month Path to Success," *Wake Forest University School of Business,* https://business.wfu.edu/ma-management/curriculum/. Arizona State's W. P. Carey School of Business asks entrants to self-assess their strengths and weaknesses, including their EI, and uses additional assessments and feedback to plan development during the first year. "Leadership Development," W.P Carey School of Business, https://wpcarey.asu.edu/mba-programs/full-time/leadership. The Hough Business School at the University of Florida requires all MBA students to take a leadership course that includes instruction in EI. "Career Accelerator Program," University of Florida, http://floridamba.ufl.edu/full-time/careerAccelerator.asp.

73. "Required Curriculum," Harvard Business School, http://www.hbs.edu/mba/academic-experience/curriculum/Pages/required-curriculum.aspx.
74. "Leadership Lab," Columbia Business School, http://www8.gsb.columbia.edu/psi/.
75. Max Nisen, "Now You Might Have to Show Emotional IQ to Get into Business School," *Business Insider,* May 2, 2013, http://www.businessinsider.com/mbas-and-emotional-intelligence-2013-5; Korn, "Business Schools Know How You Think, but How Do You Feel?" *The Wall Street Journal,* May 1, 2013; Ernesto Reuben, Paola Sapienza, and Luigi Zingales, "A Description of the Templeton-Chicago MBAs Longitudinal Study," January 2008, http://www.ereuben.net/research/TCMLS.pdf. All first-year MBAs participate in the Leadership Effectiveness and Development program (LEAD) "where students practice and perfect key communication skills such as negotiation, team-building, and giving feedback."
76. "MBA Admissions Consulting Services," *Veritas Prep,* https://www.veritasprep.com/business-school/school-packages/.
77. Korn, "B-Schools Know How You Think, but How Do You Feel?" *The Wall Street Journal.* See also GMAC, "Reflect™ by GMAC," http://www.gmac.com/reflect/why-it-matters.aspx. GMAC noted that more than forty schools had joined a pilot program of the test. As of 2016, GMAC is no longer selling the product; however, there is still interest among business school applicants and test prep companies alike in incorporating personality assessments into business school admissions. Elana Goodwin, "Where to Go to Business School Based on Your Personality Type," *Business School Insider,* June 10, 2016, http://www.kaptest.com/blog/business-school-insider/2016/06/10/where-to-go-to-business-school/.
78. Claudette Portelli, "Personal Growth and Emotional Intelligence," *Times of Malta,* April 5, 2012. Emily Baker, "Rural Tasmania Says Emotional Intelligence Key," *The Examiner,* March 22, 2016, http://www.examiner.com.au/story/3805743/emotional-intelligence-key/. Pharmacists at the Lebanese American University are also being taught EI. "Pharmacy Students Learn about Emotional Intelligence," *Lebanese American University,* July 3, 2013, http://www.lau.edu.lb/news-events/news/archive/pharmacy_students_learn_about/.
79. The Second Annual African Emotional Intelligence Conference was held in Cape Town, South Africa, in March 2014. "Emotional Intelligence African

Summit & Education Forum," *SBS Conferences,* March 1–5, 2014, http://www.sbs.co.za/eq2014/. The author's article "Emotional Intelligence for Lawyers" was featured in the 2014 Saint Petersburg International Legal Forum organized by the Ministry of Justice of Russia ("St. Petersburg International Legal Forum," *SPBLegalForum,* 2017, http://www.spblegalforum.ru); the Fifth Annual International Congress on Emotional Intelligence was held in September 2015 in Buenos Aires, Argentina ("5th International Congress on Emotional Intelligence," *ICPA,* September 15–17, 2015, http://icpa.ca/events/5th-international-congress-on-emotional-intelligence/); and World Without Anger's Sixth International Conference on Emotional Intelligence was held in July 2016 in Nepal. "World Without Anger," *WWA,* 2016, http://worldwithoutanger.org/eiconference.php.

80. Steven J. Stein and Howard E. Book, *The EQ Edge: Emotional Intelligence and Your Success,* 3rd ed. Toronto, Canada: Multi-Health Systems, Inc., 2011, 5; "New Study of Leaders Reveals Emerging Global Talent Crisis, Emotional Intelligence Seen as Solution," *PR Newswire,* April 17, 2012, http://www.prnewswire.com/news-releases/new-study-of-leaders-reveals-emerging-global-talent-crisis-emotional-intelligence-seen-as-solution-147740315.html.
81. Cavallo and Brienza, *Emotional Competence and Leadership Excellence at Johnson & Johnson;* Rosete and Ciarrochi, "Emotional Intelligence and Its Relationship to Workplace Performance Outcomes of Leadership Effectiveness," *Leadership and Organization Development,* 26 (2005): 388–99. For example, in a study of 515 senior executives in Latin America, Germany, and Japan, those who were primarily strong in EI were more likely to succeed than those who were strongest in either relevant experience or IQ, regardless of their ethnic origins or the country of their workplace. Executives high in EI accounted for 74 percent of the successes and only 24 percent of the failures, results that were almost identical in all three cultures. Cherniss, *The Business Case for Emotional Intelligence* (New Brunswick, NJ: Consortium for Research on Emotional Intelligence in Organizations, 1999).
82. Amy Li, "Xi Jinping's 'Emotional Intelligence' Comments Spark Debate," *South China Morning Post,* May 21, 2013, http://www.scmp.com/news/china/article/1242750/xi-jinpings-emotional-intelligence-comments-spark-debate.
83. Fariselli, Ghini, and Freedman, "Age and Emotional Intelligence," *SixSeconds.* Young children are often perceived as emotionally astute, but older adults rate themselves and are rated by others somewhat higher in EI than young adults.
84. Stein and Book, *The EQ Edge,* 17–19.
85. Travis Bradberry and Jean Greaves, *Emotional Intelligence 2.0* (San Diego: TalentSmart, 2009), 237–40.
86. Among undergraduate business students in the United Kingdom and Malaysia, "the older the student, the more they were able to deal with emotions like self-esteem, stress management, commitment ethic, empathy, comfort, assertion and aggression." "Predicting Academic Strength Emotionally," *Science Daily,* July 5, 2011, http://www.sciencedaily.com/releases/2011/06/110628173051.htm.
87. "'Increasingly, it appears that the meaning of late life centers on social relationships and caring for and being cared for by others,' UC Berkeley psychologist Robert Levenson said in a statement. 'Evolution seems to

have tuned our nervous systems in ways that are optimal for these kinds of interpersonal and compassionate activities as we age.'" Yasmin Anwar, "Emotional Intelligence Peaks as We Enter our 60s, Research Suggests," *Berkeley Research,* December 16, 2010, http://vcresearch.berkeley.edu/news/emotional-intelligence-peaks-we-enter-our-60s-research-suggests.

88. Robert J. Sternberg, Elena Grigorenko, and Donald A Bundy, "The Predictive Value of IQ," *Merrill-Palmer Quarterly* 47 (2001): 16.
89. David Brooks, "The Heart Grows Smarter." *New York Times,* November 4, 2012.
90. Ulric Neisser ed., *The Rising Curve: Long-term Gains in IQ and Related Measures* (Washington, DC: American Psychological Association, 1998).
91. From 2003 to 2007, the percentage of people with high EQ that one vendor tested edged up single digits during each of those years, although in 2008 the percentage dropped, which the vendor speculates was because of the fierce emotions that could not easily be dealt with during the recession that year. Bradberry and Greaves, *Emotional Intelligence 2.0,* 230.
92. Goleman mentions a study of engineers that also found decreasing levels of EI over time. Goleman, "The Decline of the Nice-Guy Quotient." *New York Times,* September 10, 1995.
93. Yalda T. Uhlsa, et al., "Five Days at Outdoor Education Camp without Screens Improves Preteen Skills with Nonverbal Emotion Cues," *Computers in Human Behavior* 39 (2014): 387–92.
94. Katherine Sharpe, "The Medication Generation," *The Wall Street Journal,* June 29, 2012.
95. Cherniss, "Emotional Intelligence."
96. Stein and Book, *The EQ Edge,* 6–7.
97. Aimee Groth, "You're the Average of the Five People You Spend the Most Time with," *Business Insider,* July 24, 2012, http://www.businessinsider.com/jim-rohn-youre-the-average-of-the-five-people-you-spend-the-most-time-with-2012-7.
98. Steven B. Wolff, *Emotional Competence Inventory (ECI) Technical Manual,* 2nd ed. (St. Petersburg, FL: Hay Acquisition Company, Inc.), 2005.
99. A group of seven studies found that upper-class individuals tend to behave more unethically than lower-class individuals—they are more likely to break the law while driving, take valued goods from others, lie in a negotiation, cheat to increase their chances of winning a prize, and endorse unethical behavior at work, in part because they had more favorable attitudes toward greed. Michael W. Kraus, Cote, and Dacher Keltner, "Social Class Contextualism and Emphatic Accuracy," *Psychological Science* 21 (2010): 1716–23. "At least since Plato.., one line of thought in political philosophy views elites as possessing superior capacities for moral reasoning that uniquely qualify them for positions of leadership and governmental power. However, an opposing view associated with critical social theorists like Karl Marx . . . argues that the class hierarchy is a morally corrupting force, undermining the legitimacy of economic elites and justifying class conflict and revolution. But despite this long-standing debate, little research has investigated how the moral reasoning of individuals from different social classes might systematically diverge." In these studies, upper-class participants were more likely than lower-class ones to choose the "utilitarian

option" in a strongly moral dilemma, i.e., "more likely to take resources from one person to benefit several others" due to "their lower empathy for the person whose resources were taken." Artificially inducing empathy reduced the tendency. Côté, Paul K. Piff, and Robb Willer, "For Whom Do the Ends Justify the Means? Social Class and Utilitarian Moral Judgment," *Journal of Personality and Social Psychology.*

100. "Emotional Intelligence: A Clincher in Lady Ashton's Diplomatic Triumph," *The Guardian*, November 24, 2013.
101. Ian Traynor, "Iran Nuclear Talks: Lady Ashton's Geneva Triumph Takes Center Stage," *The Guardian*, November 24, 2013, http://www.theguardian.com/politics/2013/nov/24/iran-nuclear-talks-lady-ashton-geneva-triumph.
102. While the genders score comparably in IQ, men have nearly 6.5 times the amount of gray matter in their brains, the site of information processing, whereas women have nearly ten times the amount of white matter, which networks the processing centers. So men may excel at tasks requiring more localized processing, such as mathematics, while women may excel at integrating and assimilating information, which aids language skills. Bjorn Carey, "Men and Women Really Do Think Differently," *Livescience*, January 20, 2005, http://www.livescience.com/3808-men-women-differently.html.
103. In an early administration of the MSCEIT, "women performed about a 0.5 standard deviation higher than men." Mayer, Salovey, and Caruso, "Emotional Intelligence Meets Traditional Standards for an Intelligence," *Intelligence* 27 (1999): 293. A 2003 study found, "a significant . . . difference . . . in the emotional intelligence scores of male and female managers. The mean total emotional intelligence score of females was 109.56 and that of males was 98.31." "Relationship between Emotional Intelligence and Transformational Leadership Style: A Gender Comparison," *Journal of Business and Psychology*, 397. A later study again found, "overall female EI . . . was significantly higher than overall male EI." Bracket, Mayer, and Rebecca M. Warner, "Emotional Intelligence and Its Relation to Everyday Behavior," *Personality and Individual Differences* 36 (2004): 1393.
104. Goleman, "An EI-based Theory of Performance," in Goleman and Cherniss eds., *The Emotionally Intelligent Workplace: How to Select for, Measure, and Improve Emotional Intelligence in Individuals, Groups, and Organizations* (San Francisco: Jossey-Bass, 2000).
105. One MSCEIT study showed women outperforming men to a small extent in total EI score and also in all four branch subscores. Brackett and Mayer, "Convergent, Discriminant, and Incremental Validity of Competing Measures of Emotional Intelligence," *Personality and Social Psychology Bulletin* 29 (2003). In one instance, the largest difference was in the critical branch of Managing Emotions, but gender accounted for only 5 percent of the variance. Mayer, Salovey, and Caruso, *Meyer-Salovey-Caruso Emotional Intelligence Test User's Manual* (New York: Multi-Health Systems, 2002). Among high school and college students, more significant differences were found, with women scoring significantly higher both in overall EI and in subscores. Brackett et al. "Emotional Intelligence and Its Relation to Everyday Behavior," *Personality and Individual Differences* 36 (2004): 1387. Curiously, despite the small advantage

in EI that women demonstrate on the MSCEIT, their higher scores may not necessarily produce more emotionally intelligent behavior, perhaps because increases over a competency threshold don't significantly impact behavior. Rivers et al., "Improving the Social and Emotional Climate of Classrooms: A Clustered Randomized Controlled Trial Testing the RULER Approach," *Prevention Science.* Another possible explanation is that "emotional abilities may manifest differently for men and women and the MSCEIT is biased towards accurately capturing male behavior." Brackett et al., "Emotional Intelligence and Its Relation to Everyday Behavior," *Personality and Individual Differences.* The trait EI model has shown no significant gender differences in total EI, although "females scored higher than males on the 'social skills' factor." K.V. Petrides and Adrian Furnham, "Gender Differences in Measured and Self-Estimated Trait Emotional Intelligence," *Sex Roles* 42 (2000): 449. Researchers in Lebanon observed significant gender differences "in EI sub-competency scores with males scoring higher on self-regulation and self-motivation, and females scoring higher on self-awareness, empathy and social skills." D. Jamali et al., "Emotional Intelligence and Management Development Implications: Insights from the Lebanese Context," *Journal of Management Development* 27 (2008): 356. In 7,700 administrations of the EQ-i, women scored higher than men in the "interpersonal" category overall and in each of its subcategories: Empathy, Interpersonal Relationships, and Social Responsibility. Men did not demonstrate strength in any of the five major EI categories but rather scored higher than women in a variety of subcategories: Actualization, Assertiveness, Stress Tolerance, Impulse Control, and Adaptability. Bar-On, "Emotional and Social Intelligence," in *The Handbook of Emotional Intelligence.* On the EQ-i 2.0, there were "small to medium gender effects . . . for some subscales. The largest difference was on Empathy, with women scoring higher than men with a moderate effect size." "Smaller differences were found with women scoring higher than men on the Interpersonal Composite, Emotional Expression, and Emotional Self-Awareness. Men scored higher than women with small effect sizes on Stress Tolerance, Problem Solving, and Independence." "EQ-i 2.0 FAQ," *MHS,* 2013, http://ei.mhs.com/EQi20FAQ.aspx. The Hay Group analyzed 10,000 of Goleman's ECIs taken between March 1999 and May 2001 and found "gender differences . . . on both self and others ratings on the ECI," with women rating themselves higher, and being rated higher by both men and women, than men." Wolff, *Emotional Competence Inventory.* With respect to specific ECI competencies, an early study found females were rated higher than males were by peers on some measures (Emotional Self-Awareness, Conscientiousness, Developing Others, Service Orientation, and Communication) and by supervisors on Adaptability and Service Orientation, but not by their direct reports. Cavallo and Brienza, *Emotional Competence and Leadership Excellence at Johnson & Johnson,* 5.

106. Scott N. Taylor and Jacqueline N. Hood, "It May Not Be What You Think: Gender Differences in Predicting Emotional and Social Competence," *Human Relations* 64 (2011): 627–52.
107. "Women Poised to Effectively Lead in Matrix Work Environments, Hay Group Research Finds," *Hay Group.*

108. Robin W. Simon and Leda E. Nath, "Gender and Emotion in the United States: Do Men and Women Differ in Self-Reports of Feelings and Expressive Behavior?" *American Journal of Sociology* 109 (2004): 1137–76.
109. S. Whittle et al., "Sex Differences in the Neural Correlates of Emotion: Evidence from Neuroimaging," *Biological Psychology* 87 (2011): 319–33.
110. Goleman, "Are Women More Emotionally Intelligent Than Men?" *Psychology Today*.
111. S. Nolen-Hoeksema, "Emotion Regulation and Psychopathology: The Role of Gender," *Annual Review of Clinical Psychology* 8 (2012): 170.
112. Goleman, "Are Women More Emotionally Intelligent Than Men?" *Psychology Today*. This phenomenon is the basis of such popular books as Deborah Tannen's *You Just Don't Understand: Women and Men in Conversation*, in which women are portrayed as wanting emotional company while men want to solve the problem.
113. Simon and Nath, "Gender and Emotion in the United States," *American Journal of Sociology*. This difference is attributed to differences in the social status of men and women, with women usually at a lower status and therefore experiencing more taxing, powerless circumstances, and also to differences in the cultural expectations of appropriate gender behavior—good girls don't act aggressively.
114. Rosman, "Read It and Weep, Crybabies," *The Wall Street Journal*. Women are physically wired to shed tears more than men because of higher levels of the hormone prolactin and smaller tear ducts. The incidence of males tearing up goes up as their testosterone levels decrease with age. A study of thirty-seven countries determined that women in developed Western economies not only cry much more than men, but also cry much more than women in societies where women have fewer rights. Cultural inhibitions that arose in the late nineteenth century "when factory workers—mostly men—were discouraged from indulging in emotion lest it interfere with their productivity" likely discourage men from crying.
115. Hazel Thompson, "Is It OK for Men to Cry at Work?" *Forbes*, June 12, 2012; Laura Manning, "Lawyers Can't Handle Tuesdays, Survey Reveals," *The Lawyer*, January 24, 2011, http://www.thelawyer.com/1006739.article.
116. Anne Kreamer, *It's Always Personal: Navigating Emotion in the New Workplace* (New York: Random House, 2011). See an interview with Kreamer here: http://www.youtube.com/watch?v=q_ha3pL_Rtk. Facebook CEO's Sheryl Sandberg in her 2013 book *Lean In: Women, Work and the Will to Lead* says it's okay to cry at work, that emotions are hardwired as survival mechanisms, and the lines between professional and personal conduct are increasingly becoming blurred.
117. Victoria L. Brescoll and Eric Luis Uhlmann, "Can an Angry Woman Get Ahead?: Status Conferral, Gender, and Expression of Emotion in the Workplace," *Harvard Kennedy School*, 2008, http://gap.hks.harvard.edu/can-angry-woman-get-ahead-status-conferral-gender-and-expression-emotion-workplace.
118. Nolen-Hoeksema, "Emotion Regulation and Psychopathology: The Role of Gender," *Annual Review of Clinical Psychology*, 165.

119. L.F Barrett and E. Bliss-Moreau, "Affect as a Psychological Primitive," *Advances in Experimental Social Psychology*, 41 (2009): 650. This attribution reflects at least in part the belief throughout our society that gender differences (not just emotions) are primarily biological in origin, rather than "determined by both biological and social factors." Leslie R. Brody, "Gender and Emotion: Beyond Stereotypes," *Journal of Social Issues* 53 (1997): 370.
120. Nolen-Hoeksema, "Emotion Regulation and Psychopathology: The Role of Gender," *Annual Review of Clinical Psychology*, 169, 170.
121. Ibid.
122. Leslie R. Brody, "Gender and Emotion: Beyond Stereotypes," *Journal of Social Issues* 53 (2): 369–93, 371.
123. Some research has questioned "[t]he widespread belief that men's modus operandi when it comes to emotion regulation is denial and suppression," suggesting men may be using an automatic, unconscious method of regulating their emotions that simply looks like suppression when compared to the "more conscious, linguistically based emotion regulation of women." Nolen-Hoeksema, "Emotion Regulation and Psychopathology: The Role of Gender," *Annual Review of Clinical Psychology*, 171.
124. Simon and Nath, "Gender and Emotion in the United States," *American Journal of Sociology*. In a study in which participants were asked to watch a negative-emotion-eliciting film, "those randomly assigned to hide their feelings during the film showed poorer memory for its auditory and visual details," a deficit that "was pronounced enough to be evident to suppression participants themselves, who reported less confidence in their memory than participants who simply watched the film." Jane M. Richards and James A. Gross, "Emotion Regulation and Memory: The Cognitive Costs of Keeping One's Cool," *Journal of Personality and Social Psychology* 79 (3): 414.
125. "Empathy fosters rapport and chemistry. People who excel in emotional empathy make good counselors, teachers, and group leaders because of this ability to sense in the moment how others are reacting . . . If the other person is upset, or the emotions are disturbing, women's brains tend to stay with those feelings. But men's brains do something else: they sense the feelings for a moment, then tune out of the emotions and switch to other brain areas that try to solve the problem that's creating the disturbance." Goleman, "Are Women More Emotionally Intelligent Than Men?" *Psychology Today*.
126. Simon and Nath, "Gender and Emotion in the United States," *Journal of Personality and Social Psychology*. "[W]omen may be socialized to pay more attention to emotions, or they may be better biologically prepared to perform at such tasks." Salovey, Brackett, Mayer eds., *Emotional Intelligence*, 152.
127. Brooks, "The Heart Grows Smarter," *New York Times*. Some differences between the genders may be disappearing as improvements in testing, awareness, and achievement occur over time. In one study, improvements in emotion management by men between 2003 and 2008 eliminated an originally starkly lower performance compared to women. Bradberry and Greaves, *Emotional Intelligence 2.0*, 232–33.
128. Goleman, *Emotional Intelligence: Why It Can Matter More Than IQ* (New York: Bantam Books, 2005).

129. R.J Davidson and W. Irwin, "The Functional Neuroanatomy of Emotion and Affective Style," *Trends in Cognitive Style* 3 (1), 11–21.
130. Daniel Goleman, *The Brain and Emotional Intelligence: New Insights* (Florence, MA: More Than Sound, 2011).
131. Paul J. Whalen et al., "Masked Presentations of Emotional Facial Expressions Modulate Amygdala Activity Without Explicit Knowledge," *Journal of Neuroscience* 18 (1): 411–18; Elizabeth Phelps et al., "Performance on Indirect Measures of Race Evaluation Predicts Amygdala Activation," *Journal of Cognitive Neuroscience* 12 (5): 729–38.
132. Carlin Flora, "Gut Almighty," *Psychology Today,* May 1, 2007. See also Bruce Kasanoff, "Intuition Is the Highest Form of Intelligence," *Forbes,* February 21, 2017.
133. Goleman first introduced the term "amygdala hijacking" in his 2005 book, *Emotional Intelligence: Why It Can Matter More Than IQ.* See also Ralph Richard Banks and Richard Thompson Ford, "(How) Does Unconscious Bias Matter?" *Emory Law Journal* 1053 (2009).
134. Rick Hanson, *Buddha's Brain* (Oakland, CA: New Harbinger Publications, Inc., 2009).
135. Richard Davidson and Sharon Begley, *The Emotional Life of Your Brain* (New York: Penguin Group, 2013).
136. Roderick Gilkey, Ricardo Caceda, and Clinton Kilts, "When Emotional Reasoning Trumps IQ," *Harvard Business Review* 88 (12): 20–21; Goleman and Richard Boyatzis, "Social Intelligence and the Biology of Leadership," *Harvard Business Review* 86 (9): 74–81; Joo Kim et al., "The Effects of Serotonin Transporter Promoter and Monoamine Oxidase A Gene Polymorphisms on Trait Emotional Intelligence," *Neuropsychobiology* 64 (4): 224–30; Benjamin Kreifelts et al., "Association of Trait Emotional Intelligence and Individual fMRI-Activation Patterns During the Perception of Social Signals from Voice and Face," *Human Brain Mapping* 31 (7): 979–91.
137. "Seventy-One Percent of Employers Say They Value Emotional Intelligence over IQ, According to CareerBuilder Survey," *CareerBuilder.com,* August 18, 2011, http://www.careerbuilder.com/share/aboutus/pressreleasesdetail.aspx?id=pr652&sd=8/18/2011&ed=08/18/2011.

Chapter Two

Are Lawyers Emotionally Intelligent?

To help understand the emotional intelligence (EI) of lawyers as a group, this chapter looks over the available evidence from EI assessment and other data, sees how "non-lawyers" evaluate our relationship skills, and reviews the general attitude of law with regard to emotions. Finally, we can learn a lot from a famous groundbreaking case study of cognition and emotions that involved a lawyer.

Emotional Intelligence Assessment and Other Data on Lawyers
The View from the Bleachers
Law's Skeptical View of Emotions
The Lawyer Who Had No Emotions

Then, in *Where Do We Lawyers Fall Short?*, we review the data on where lawyers stand in each of the four critical components of EI.

Emotional Intelligence Assessment and Other Data on Lawyers

Emotional intelligence, that's an oxymoron, right?

—Author's unnamed lawyer client

Not all EI assessments keep track of scores by profession, and even those that do often do not have a large number of lawyers to report on, so there is no definitive answer to how lawyers score as a group. What we do have are the scores of several hundred lawyers on at least a few of the EI assessments to compare to the general population's scores.

With those caveats, how are we doing?

We lawyers score below the national average in overall emotional intelligence. While lawyers score well *above* the national average of 100 in IQ—an average of 115 to 130—their average scores in emotional intelligence are consistently reported, at least anecdotally, to be in the 80 to 95 range, significantly *below* the national EI average of 100.[1]

My experience attests to the reliability of these average numbers. In the law firms and law departments where I have done testing, the average EI scores nearly always fall within that range, with only a few exceptions scoring lower or higher.

We lawyers apparently score lower than do doctors, whose mean EI score on a number of different assessments is 100, or the national average.[2] Yet in the healthcare field, there is a drumbeat to further improve EI for better patient and provider results.

Lawyers are used to acing their academic work and passing their IQ, SAT, LSAT, and other exams with higher than average scores. So a low score on an EI assessment can be quite a blow. Not unexpectedly, the typical reaction from a lawyer contemplating a low score is to question the validity of the assessment, and even the concept altogether.

Yet there is substantial and widespread evidence of how poorly lawyers manage their emotions (with instances of mismanaged romantic feelings particularly abundant)—a prime indication of low EI: lawyers at all levels and types of practice have been charged with emotion-generated crimes[3]; motions to suspend and sanction lawyers because of unmanaged emotions are legion[4]; and then there is the flood of instances of incivility that can make lawyers look emotionally unhinged.[5]

Not all unruly emotions are so publicly apparent or even privately obvious, however. Missteps in emotional management that are not publicized—caused by outsized fear, unbridled pride, misdirected passion, unmanaged jealousy, or intense desire for revenge, for example—can still exact a high cost personally and to workplaces and families. Further, management decisions to merge with or acquire a firm, recruitment committee decisions about whether to hire a lateral "star" and on what terms, and day-to-day decisions by individual lawyers as to how to interact with colleagues and respond to clients all risk being undermined by emotions that we don't recognize or manage.

These types of missteps, which can be major, certainly plague other professions as well and are not solely because of low EI. But lawyers could well avoid behaviors that increasingly risk derailing their careers, jeopardizing their companies or firms, as well as damaging their personal relationships, if they employed greater emotional intelligence.

The View from the Bleachers

Lawyers' low EI means that those who aren't lawyers whom we deal with every day—our staff, witnesses, business and financial types, community leaders, and most importantly clients of all stripes—are likely to have higher overall emotional intelligence than we do. That's right. We lawyers, accustomed to thinking of ourselves as smarter and higher performing than most of those around us, are in fact likely to have lower EI than the office manager, executive, or litigant we are working with.

Our interactions with "non-lawyers" have earned us a reputation that reflects others' opinions of our interpersonal skills. As Daicoff noted, "By the end of the twentieth century . . . lawyers were not particularly well-liked in society."[6] Matters haven't gotten any better in the 21st century.[7]

The (very) old perception of lawyers as trusted advisors has given way to appellations of "snake," "shark," "bottom-feeder," and "bloodsucker."[8] Inappropriate and objectionable behavior repeatedly reinforces the image of our being society's outliers[9] and has lowered the public's trust in lawyers individually, in our justice system generally,[10] and even in judges[11] and the Supreme Court.[12]

A Gallup Poll regularly asks respondents to rate the honesty and ethical standards of people in different fields. Nurses, doctors, and police officers are routinely rated as highly trustworthy by over 50 percent of those polled. Lawyers are usually found settled at the bottom, alongside members of Congress, business executives, and stockbrokers, with a recent poll showing only 15 percent of respondents rating lawyers as highly trustworthy.[13] In the Pew Research Center's latest poll asking which professions "contribute to society," lawyers ranked last.[14]

Portrayals of lawyers in film and TV are another indication of how low our EI skills are in the eyes of the public. Long gone is Perry Mason, reassuring the wronged and skillfully bringing evildoers to justice. The TV series about a lawyer entitled "The Shark" pretty much says it all from an image standpoint, only one-upped by the arrival of a lawyer drama entitled "Damages" starring Glenn Close, who will always be remembered as depicting one of the most frightening personas in cinematic history—the man-eating, marriage-dashing, family-unfriendly *Fatal Attraction* psychopath, now dispensing legal advice.

Even our clients, some of whom are lawyers themselves, are bad-mouthing lawyers and our emotional skills. The BTI Consulting Group compiles an annual list of the "most arrogant" lawyers, built on the responses of corporate counsel at hundreds of Fortune 1,000 companies, a list that includes some firms with high standing in the industry.[15] Arrogance is a type of emotional aggression, characterized by a pattern of behavior that "demeans others in an attempt to prove competence and superiority,"[16] a strategy that is obviously not working to lawyers' advantage.

Perhaps most discouraging is the finding of an American Bar Association (ABA) poll that the most negative perceptions of lawyers and the legal profession are held by those people who have the most regular dealings with lawyers. In fact, the survey showed a "disturbing pattern that the more a person knows about the legal profession and the more he or she is in direct personal contact with lawyers, the lower an individual's opinion of them."[17] As a result, the legal lexicon now includes concepts like "legal abuse syndrome" and "secondary victimization" resulting from litigants' interaction with the legal system.[18]

This lack of appreciation of lawyers by our clients and the general public may well stem at least in part from how differently we and they view the world in terms of emotions. As one commentator points out, lawyers' typically unemotional approach makes them seem, "odd, rigid, and even amoral to a public who uses both thinking and feeling."[19]

Law's Skeptical View of Emotions

> *(M)en decide far more problems by hate, or love, or lust, or rage, or sorrow, or joy, or hope, or fear, or illusion, or some other inward emotion, than by reality, or authority, or any legal standard, or judicial precedent, or statute.*[20]
>
> —Cicero

> *It is perhaps the quintessential error of the modern Western world view to suppose that thought can occur without feeling.*[21]
>
> —Mary E. Clark, author and political activist

The historical legal view has been that the judicial system should be elevated above emotions, which were thought to poison objective analysis and undermine the predictable and uniform application of the law.[22] That may be one of the reasons law practice is so "aggressively rational, linear, and goal oriented," making lawyers unaware of the "wishes, fear, beliefs and defenses that motivate our actions."[23]

This view of emotions reflects the position that dominated during early centuries of debate on the subject by our greatest thinkers. During the 1st century BCE, Cicero recognized emotions as important in making decisions, but Stoic philosophers such as Seneca and Cato the Younger contended that emotion undermined rational thought. Then in the 4th century BCE, Plato described emotion and reason as two horses pulling us in opposite directions, and Publilius Syrus cautioned, "Rule your feelings, lest your feelings rule you."[24]

Conflicting attitudes have continued to prevail in recent history. During the late 18th and early 19th centuries, the Romantic Movement promoted the notion that emotions could provide valuable insight unavailable through rational thought alone, but into the early part of the 20th century emotions were still considered by some philosophers and even psychologists to be purely negative: "acute disturbances" or "disorganized response[s], largely visceral, resulting from the lack of an effective adjustment."[25] One prominent psychologist predicted that the concept of "emotion" was an "unneeded term" that would soon pass out of scientific consideration altogether.[26] Nonetheless, a number of different theories began to coalesce during the 20th century around the importance of emotions and the recognition of some sort of interpersonal intelligence involving the awareness and management of emotions.[27]

Given these long-standing debates through the centuries, it is no wonder that there has been uncertainty as to how best, or even whether, to consider emotions in delivering justice. Historically, the law has erred on the side of denying the importance of emotions.[28]

In administering justice in civil cases, we lawyers deal with the "reasonable man" unburdened by outsized emotions. In tort cases, the law tiptoes around identifying and quantifying mental functioning. Personal injury victims are entitled to recover reasonable medical expenses for even minor physical injuries, but significant barriers usually bar recovery for psychological or emotional harm. Even lawsuits for emotional distress often require a showing of some sort of bodily injury. Similarly, determining "pain and suffering" damages for anything beyond physical injury often involves either a complex analysis that is not necessarily consistent with principals of neuroscience or, on the other hand, a simple formula that avoids assessments or calculations of actual emotional damage.[29] Even when emotional damages are found, in many cases they are limited by caps.

Criminal cases are also challenged by the introduction of internal brain function or emotion. "Insanity" and "diminished capacity," for example, are complicated concepts that theoretically free a person from some or all legal responsibility for his or her actions, but definitions vary from state to state and are often independent of, or even at odds with, relevant modern psychological theory. In fact, mental health practitioners are usually restrained from making a judgment on the issue of whether a defendant is or is not insane. Attributes of "crimes of passion" are also often not analyzed consistent with current psychological research.[30]

The inability of our conventional justice system to adequately assess the complex interplay between brain function, emotion management, and criminality is highlighted by the creation of special veterans' courts to adjudicate the wave of criminal cases involving posttraumatic stress disorder suffered by many of our troops.[31] These troubled veterans, although criminals according to our traditional justice system, are increasingly being treated with a different perspective aimed "at helping them regain the sense of discipline and camaraderie they had in uniform, and steering them onto a more positive course in life." In other words, the specialized courts hope to help them achieve emotional equilibrium.[32]

Dr. Russell Swerdlow, a neurologist who testifies as an expert witness, maintains that physiological conditions that impact emotional management and therefore decision making should be highly relevant to criminal responsibility where criminal intent is key, and some courts have been entertaining that notion. The number of US criminal cases since 2004 in which defense lawyers introduced neuroscientific evidence, including evidence that relates to emotions, has dramatically increased, with currently 20 percent resulting in favorable outcomes for the accused, such as a reduction of charges or sentences, although none have been exonerated based on such evidence.[33] Similarly, in the United Kingdom, the annual average of cases using neuroscientific evidence has nearly doubled from the years 2005–2009 to 2009–2012.[34]

Certainly, in a comeuppance to the rationalist tradition of legal thought, research clearly shows that, not unsurprisingly, the juries themselves who are applying these rationalist principles often are more influenced by their emotions than by the clear rationale of the law.[35]

Law schools and other graduate schools are starting to explore how neuroscience and law interface. The University of Wisconsin in Madison has launched a dual degree program in neuroscience and law, and neuroscientist David Eagleman heads Baylor College of Medicine's Initiative on Neuroscience and the Law. The MacArthur Foundation Research Network on Law and Neuroscience, headquartered at Vanderbilt University in Nashville, Tennessee, and led by Owen Jones, professor of law and biology, has engaged academics across the country in exploring the roles of brain function and emotions on legally responsible behavior.

Not only are emotions traditionally excluded from courtroom considerations, but individual lawyers are also supposed to be emotionless, an attitude reinforced in the education of law students. Most lawyers were taught in law school that, "how they feel about the cases they read is irrelevant; what matters is the soundness of their logic . . . Resistance to the human dimension of the lawyer's work is built into most law training."[36]

So would we in fact be better off if we lawyers had no emotions?

LAW'S SKEPTICAL VIEW OF EMOTIONS

- The current default position that law is "above" emotions follows centuries of changing attitudes about the relative roles of emotion and reason.
- Civil and criminal law reflect law's resistance to considering and quantifying brain function, emotions, and emotional damage.
- The introduction of neuroscience principles in legal cases and the increasing collaboration between schools of neuroscience and law hold out the possibility of legal proceedings that are more integrated with the principles of behavioral sciences, including those relating to emotions.
- Juries defy the "all reason" rule in law by often deciding cases for emotional reasons.
- Individual lawyers are still expected to personally adhere to the "no emotion" standard of the law in their practices.

The Lawyer Who Had No Emotions

> *The Law seems to offer an either-or choice: You can be objective (and be a good lawyer) or you can be emotional.*[37]
>
> —Jill Breslau, trained psychiatrist and lawyer, and Susan Swaim Daicoff, law professor and author of *Lawyer, Know Yourself*

> *Just as there is a stream of thought, there is a parallel stream of feeling. The notion that there is 'pure thought,' rationality devoid of feeling, is a fiction, an illusion based on inattention to the subtle moods that follow us through the day.*[38]
>
> —Daniel Goleman, author and emotional intelligence expert

In Ridley Scott's 1982 dystopian film *Blade Runner*, set in Los Angeles in 2019, Rick Deckard (Harrison Ford) is charged with exterminating "replicants"—bioengineered organic robots that are visually indistinguishable from humans but designed not to have advanced emotions.[39] To distinguish replicants from humans, Deckard subjects them to a test to expose their inadequate capacity to feel. One female replicant, Rachael, suspects the blade runner himself of low emotional capacity. "Did you ever take that test yourself?" she asks Deckard.

The film makes for good science fiction, but some would argue that lawyers should be "designed" not to have emotions.

Let's take a look at a lawyer who in fact had no emotions to see how that worked for him.

Antonio Damásio is a world-renowned neuroscientist who has conducted groundbreaking work in the area of emotions and their role in decision making. In his 1994 book *Descartes' Error: Emotion, Reason and the Human Brain,* regarded as one of the most influential books of the past two decades,[40] Damásio reports that, in the 1970s, he was asked to consult on the case of a commercial lawyer from New York in the prime of his career named "Elliot" who had undergone brain surgery to remove a tumor the size of an orange from his frontal lobe.[41] The lawyer's doctors had informed him that he had a good prognosis for retaining full brain function after the surgery, with the possible exception that there might be disruption in his access to his emotions.

After the surgery, numerous assessments found that the patient had the identical spectrum of cognitive intelligence that he had had before the operation—his IQ, attention, memory, and language were all fully intact. He was not eligible for disability and could go back to work.

But Elliot soon lost his job. And his wife. And his house. And he started living in his brother's spare bedroom.

Consultations with the man then in a desperate situation led Damásio to understand that severing some of the connections between his thinking brain (the prefrontal cortex) and his emotional brain (the amygdala) had resulted, as predicted, in a loss of access to his emotions. Elliot couldn't feel. But it was also almost impossible for him to make good decisions—his cognitive abilities allowed him to analyze and weigh various factors, but without strong "gut" reactions, he was unable to determine the best course of action. The first indication of this crucial deficit came when Damásio tried to set up follow-up appointments with his patient. While the man could reason the pros and cons of each potential appointment, because he could not "feel" a preference, he was locked into a pathological indecisiveness.

For all practical purposes, without his emotions Elliot had become cognitively paralyzed and effectively stupid. Damasio said, "The tragedy of this otherwise healthy and intelligent man was that he was neither stupid nor ignorant, and yet he acted often as if he were . . . [because] the machinery for his decision making was so flawed."[42]

Since this lawyer was "all thought and no feeling," Damásio considered Descartes' centuries-old declaration of "I think, therefore I am" to be in error: thinking alone is woefully insufficient in accounting for what makes us human.[43]

The lesson from Elliot's tragedy and from years of ensuing research has a direct impact on lawyers' lives and work today: lawyers are not at their best when they stop feeling, when they wall off their emotions. In fact, we now know how to use emotional cues and regulate emotions so as to produce legal practices that are smarter, more productive, more profitable, and more satisfying.

ARE LAWYERS EMOTIONALLY INTELLIGENT?

- Based on limited data, lawyers on average score lower than the general public in overall emotional intelligence.
- Low emotional intelligence may well fuel the increasing incidences of lawyer misconduct recounted in criminal, civil, and disciplinary proceedings, as well as complaints of widespread incivility.
- Emotional intelligence that is lower than that of the general public may be the source of the public's impressions of lawyers as being untrustworthy, clients' impressions of their arrogance, and the media's negative portrayals of lawyers.
- The ABA has found that the more a person interacts with lawyers, the lower his or her opinion is of lawyers, who also figure in concepts like "legal abuse syndrome" and "secondary victimization" suffered by those who go through the legal process.
- Law's historical bias toward being "above" emotions is reflected in our proceedings and remedies, despite juries often deciding cases for emotional reasons.
- Individual lawyers are expected to personally adhere to the "no emotion" standard, even though the groundbreaking case of a lawyer who lost access to his emotions showed him catastrophically impaired professionally and personally.

Where Do We Lawyers Fall Short? The Four Components of Emotional Intelligence

What makes lawyers as a group low in emotional intelligence? The following four components of EI are recognized by most theorists as the most significant building blocks of emotional intelligence, and various data reveal in which areas lawyers fall short.

1. *Emotional Perception*
2. *Emotional Empathy*
3. *Emotional Understanding*
4. *Emotional Regulation*

Emotional perception is our ability to recognize different feelings. When we are upset, do we know the name of the specific emotion we are feeling? When looking at someone's face, do we recognize the difference between joy and contentment, or surprise and contempt? Emotional empathy is our ability to tap into what someone else is going through emotionally. How does it feel to lose a loved one? To win unexpected praise?

Understanding emotions is our ability to identify the causes and consequences of different feelings. What behavior will make our colleagues curious rather than angry? Do we know what has led an associate to become so apprehensive? Regulating emotions is our ability to effectively change what we and others feel. If we have a bad day but need to give an inspiring speech, can we psych ourselves up and motivate our audience anyway?

These interconnected components can be thought of as a pyramid where each additional attribute is built on and supported by the prior one(s): emotional perception is a key precedent to being empathic, both of which are significant in building emotional understanding, and all three in turn give us the information and ability to manage our emotions and relationships well.[44]

1. Emotional Perception

> *Research shows that if you name it, you can tame it. If you can't name [your] feelings, it's very hard to know what to do with them.*[45]
>
> —Marc Brackett, Director of the Yale Center for Emotional Intelligence

All EI theories start with emotional perception, or what is sometimes called emotional awareness or clarity—that is, the accurate recognition of both our own emotions and those of others. Without this critical skill of emotional awareness, we end up chasing our own tails—we don't realize what emotions are driving us, we don't "see" the emotional impact of our actions on others, and we don't "get" the emotional feedback that they are telegraphing, so we risk repeating the same maladaptive behaviors again and again.

By first accurately assessing our emotional states and those of others, we can see the relationship between emotions and behavior and then use that understanding to produce better outcomes. This ever-expanding knowledge gives the aware a huge advantage over those who are blindly driven into mystifying behaviors by unknown and uncontrollable feelings that produce even more mystifying responses.

However, emotional perception does not come easily to most of us.[46] For example, what are the differences between jealousy and envy? Or shame and guilt? In how they feel? In how others look when they experience them? Yet identifying an emotion as one instead of another can take us down divergent paths.

The data from EI assessments tell us that lawyers are especially vulnerable to deficits in this important area of emotional perception—on average it is our lowest EI subscore, and it is a significant deficit.[47] One legal journal gave its readers an assessment in hopes of identifying "what is it specifically about attorneys that might explain their ill repute when it comes to creating and maintaining quality relationships with people?" The results showed that, compared with a worldwide database containing scores of more than half a million people, "As a group, lawyers had trouble recognizing other peoples' emotions and therefore responding appropriately."[48]

Because of their emotion-avoidant cultures, lawyers may also lack an extensive emotional vocabulary to help pinpoint what they are feeling, unlike expert wine lovers who can draw on a broad viniculture vocabulary to distinguish among hundreds of wines based on nuances in color, taste, and "legs."

The bottom line is that we are more likely than non-lawyers to get blindsided by emotions we can't see—caught off guard by a disgruntled client, an overwhelmed associate, an angry partner, or even by our own powerful reactions.[49]

Emotional perception can be divided into the following:

Emotional Self-Awareness
Awareness of Others' Emotions

Emotional Self-Awareness

Individuals who are emotionally self-aware know what they are feeling at any given time—irritable, sad, resentful, proud, or any number of other emotions or combinations of emotions.

It is estimated we experience over 100 emotions every day.[50] Researchers recognize five to eight primary emotions that can morph or combine into many variations,[51] for example, sadness can range in intensity from dissatisfaction to distress to sorrow, with variations in between. Our negative feelings outnumber positive ones, and the emotions of anger, joy, and sadness are the ones that we most easily recognize.[52]

A strong body of research shows that the ability to differentiate what we're feeling helps us in many ways: to regulate emotions, to promote greater well-being, to improve our relationships, to adapt to changes in social environments, to build supportive social networks, and to recover more quickly from distress.[53] The emotionally self-aware have a better memory, are more effective leaders, and have better judgment.[54] Not surprisingly, then, 83 percent of people high in self-awareness are top performers, while only 2 percent of bottom performers are high in self-awareness.[55] And the universality of the importance of self-awareness has been confirmed in research conducted in ninety-four countries.[56]

Yet a test of over 500,000 globally found that "only 36% . . . [were] able to accurately identify their emotions as they happen," leaving an astonishing two-thirds of us who are typically not aware of the emotions we are experiencing at any given time.[57] At the extreme, a rare disability in labeling and expressing what we and others feel is called alexithymia, and may be caused by brain damage.[58] But most often we just tend to be vague in talking to ourselves and others about emotions. A lawyer may say to herself, "I yelled because I was really stressed out," which doesn't really identify the emotion and gives her little concrete information to work with. Being able to recognize that she was feeling resentful or betrayed or overwhelmed provides more information and starts her on the path to both understanding and regulating her emotions.[59]

A highly successful patent lawyer came to me to help her improve relations with her colleagues. Although she had been soundly criticized by firm management, she felt she was demanding but reasonable when supervising associates and interacting with her partners: she simply applied to her colleagues the same exacting standards she applied to herself. One of her difficulties was in identifying what her feelings were when she was correcting a colleague: was it righteous anger at sloppy mistakes, irritation at lost efficiency, indignation at not having her instructions followed, or shame that her reputation was being sullied? By keeping notes about when these situations occurred, studying the circumstances and her reactions, and being more explicit and open to feedback in an emotionally neutral way, she was able to answer those questions, which led to improved interactions.

Awareness of Others' Emotions

"Othello's Error" refers to the tragic mistake Othello made in reading his wife's emotional cues, as recounted in Shakespeare's *The Tragedy of Othello, the Moor of Venice.*[60] Othello incorrectly attributed his beloved Desdemona's sobbing to be longing for her lover, while in truth she was heartbroken that Othello was accusing her of having had an affair of which she was innocent. Othello killed her for what he mistook as infidelity.

Psychologists at Harvard concluded decades ago that those best at identifying others' emotions are more successful in their work and their social lives.[61] To perceive others' emotional states, we largely use the same neural circuitry that makes us self-aware, so those who are emotionally self-aware are more likely to correctly assess the emotions of others.[62] Therefore, lawyers' low scores in emotional perception likely reflect both low self-awareness and low awareness of others' emotions.

Decoding the emotions in others has long been of academic interest. In 1872, Darwin published *The Expression of the Emotions in Man and Animals,* a study of facial expressions that he contended corresponded to the same emotions being expressed across countries, mental abilities, and even species. He theorized that the ability to read these expressions—accurately distinguishing between a friend and a predator, for example—is a critical survival skill.[63]

Starting in the 1950s, Dr. Paul Ekman's groundbreaking research cataloged the specific emotional content of hundreds of facial expressions.[64] The TV show *Lie to Me,* in which the protagonist solved crimes by detecting how people truly feel rather than what they try to project, is based on Ekman's findings.[65] Ekman believes that most of us can be trained to determine the emotional content of someone's face in one-hundredth of a second, essentially without conscious processing.[66]

Accurately recognizing others' emotions involves accessing several data sources besides facial expressions. The verbal expressions of others—"I am angry, disappointed," etc.—are often the most direct indicators of people's emotions, but nonverbal behavior, body language, verbal tone, the situational context, cultural norms, and vocabulary are also important, and sometimes can lead us to a different conclusion about others' emotions than what is said or facially registered.[67]

2. Emotional Empathy

Do you feel like we do?[68]

—Peter Frampton, rock legend

Empathy is widely recognized as a critical component of emotional intelligence. EI assessments often do not produce subscores on empathy, and fewer track lawyers' scores on empathy, so we have little data as to whether lawyers are more or less empathic than the general population. In his early work, however, consultant Dr. Larry Richard found that successful rainmakers and managing partners exhibited higher levels of empathy than most other lawyers he had tested.[69]

Theorists distinguish between two types of empathy: cognitive and emotional. Cognitive empathy refers to the ability to shift perspectives so as to intellectually understand what other people are experiencing emotionally: "Her anger must make her unable to focus on the details of this project."[70] Emotional empathy refers to our personal emotional experience that is triggered by others' emotions: "Her anger makes me relive the clenched stomach and headache that I experience when I'm angry and that make it hard for me to focus on the details of a project."[71]

Physiologically, neuroscientists theorize that humans are wired to be automatically emotionally empathic through "mirror neurons" in the brain that essentially reproduce the feelings we see in others.[72] The mirror neurons of a monkey who is observing somebody else fire in the monkey's brain as if it were performing those very actions itself, thereby creating an empathic experience physiologically with whomever is being observed.[73]

Empathy has long been associated with workplace success.[74] In a 2015 Global Empathy Index, the top ten businesses generated 50 percent more net income per employee than the bottom ten.[75] President Obama famously said being empathic was one of his criteria for a Supreme Court justice.[76] Managers who demonstrate empathy have employees who are sick less often and who report greater happiness, and a large-scale study found that doctors high in empathy have patients who enjoy better health.[77] Those higher in empathy also have been shown to be more ethical, more giving (even if it is against their own personal interest), less biased, less bullying, and more likely to engage in heroic acts.[78]

Empathy increases our ability to foster collegiality, collaboration, and harmony in interpersonal relationships by allowing us to participate in the emotional currents of others. The verbal expression of emotional empathy—"I know how you feel"—is a powerful bonding tool and is particularly useful in settings that involve building or maintaining close relationships, which is critical to effective leadership, teamwork, and counseling.

Through empathy, we can both share in and contribute to a group's emotional experience, good and bad, whether we intend to or not. Tapping into others' emotions, we can make choices that promote their well-being, and mirroring those more positive emotions, in turn, gives us a more positive feeling ourselves. Of course, that can work for the worse, as well. While ignoring or denying the emotions around us may shield us in some cognitive way, ultimately those emotions are still being mirrored and felt, even if subconsciously. This is the basis of a phenomenon known as emotional contagion, in which emotions spread throughout groups.[79]

Empathy is apparently in decline. Compared to previous generations, more recent University of Michigan graduates are less able to exhibit empathy, registering a 48 percent drop in 2009 compared to 1979, which may account for a reported rise in employees in the services industries who are unable to show empathy and connect with colleagues.[80] Similarly, an evaluation of thousands of supervisors found that only 40 percent were proficient or strong in empathy. Of the eight leadership interaction skills measured, listening and responding with empathy was one of the weakest.[81]

Research has uncovered evidence of a genetic basis to how much empathy we have, so we may all start with different set points as to what triggers our empathic feelings.[82] As a general matter, women tend to be more emotionally empathic than men as measured by most EI assessments.[83] Most psychologists agree that psychopaths have no or very low levels of emotional empathy, although they may be able to use cognitive empathy to mimic emotions they can't feel or to manipulate others' emotions to take advantage of them.[84]

A flawed mirroring process may undercut our ability to feel empathic. A dysfunctional mirror neuron system may underlie the social deficits in autism, for example, in effect disconnecting the autistic individual from tapping into the emotions of others.[85] Also, the power of mirroring can be subverted if we don't consciously recognize the emotions in ourselves that the mirroring tries to prompt.[86]

One's empathy may also be low because of a simple lack of exercise.[87] In one study, upper-class people with higher educations and greater wealth exhibited lower empathy simply because, researchers theorized, they weren't as dependent on others and their emotions and therefore tapped in to them less often.[88]

Empathy can be increased through training.[89] Doctors, for example, have been trained to be more empathetic, resulting in improvements in both patient satisfaction and the doctors' own emotional well-being.[90] Companies like Cisco Systems, Breakthru Beverage Group, Ford Motor Co., and Aston Martin Lagonda Ltd., are offering crash empathy training to help better connect with clients.[91] Roman Krznaric, a popular British philosopher and author of *Empathy*, runs empathy training for Britain's top judges and is also opening the world's first "interactive" Empathy Museum in London.[92] There is even some evidence that psychopaths might be trained to have more empathy.[93]

Sympathy or compassion—kind feelings or behaviors in response to others' plights—is related to and often confused with empathy, but research distinguishes them. Empathy is a transiently shared emotional experience between an observer and a subject, while compassion is sympathy for someone's plight. While those high in emotional intelligence do demonstrate higher levels of compassion, having emotional empathy doesn't necessarily mean we want to or will help someone in need.[94]

Having a high level of empathy could pose challenges. For example, leaders with high empathy who must make difficult decisions risk being paralyzed by their concern for those disadvantaged by the decision, if the EI skill of emotional regulation is not well developed.[95]

A successful California "lawyer to the stars" was known for her personal interest in and care of her clients and their often highly emotional concerns over privacy, publicity and the like. In return, her celebrity clients were fiercely loyal and gratefully referred others to her thriving practice. Unfortunately, she was frequently in her office with the door closed and the lights off, suffering with a migraine. While her emotional empathy was highly developed and paid off professionally, her ability to manage the emotions she was bombarded with was less so.

3. Emotional Understanding

Any fool can know, the point is to understand.[96]

—Albert Einstein

Emotional understanding rests on examining the information gleaned from accurately perceived emotions in ourselves and others and our experiences of emotional empathy. Why and how do these emotions arise, how do they combine with other emotions, what happens to them over time, and what makes them morph up or down in intensity?

When we understand the rise and flow of emotions, we can assess the origins of our own and others' emotions and their likely course, predict outcomes of emotion-producing events and behavior, and plot a best course of action to accomplish our goals.

Too often people provoke and escalate bad feelings, their own or those of others, by repeating behaviors—disparaging themselves to supervisors, humiliating associates in public, taking credit for other partners' work—without any apparent understanding of the emotional impact their actions might make on themselves or others. They are genuinely unclear why they or others are feeling down. They didn't mean any harm, many will say when questioned. How could they know that their behavior would prompt such personal, such emotional, such irrational responses?

Learning the triggers that set off emotions, the consequences of our emotional expressions on others, and how best to use or defuse our own and others' emotions is an excellent example of how the emotional and cognitive parts of our brains can work together to improve overall intelligence.[97]

In EI assessments, lawyers' average score on emotional understanding approaches that of the general population, making it our highest subscore. Abstract thinking and analytic skills common in lawyers are highly useful to emotional understanding.[98] "Why did I fly into a fit of anger? Was it what was said or the situation? Did I feel disrespected, humiliated in front of others, or unfairly treated? Did the expression of anger help my cause? What could I have done to produce a better outcome?" These are inquiries comfortably made by lawyers in other realms that they can also use to better understand emotions.

Unfortunately, any benefit lawyers get from their above-average scores in emotional understanding may well be undercut by their below-average scores in emotional perception. Nearly all formulations of emotional intelligence are "garbage in/garbage out" scenarios, whereby good analytical skills are of limited use if the initial data we perceive about our own or others' emotions are incorrect.

Developing an understanding of emotions is a critical step toward managing our emotional experiences and relationships.[99]

One senior partner had the reoccurring and unsettling experience of having his associate walk into his office and quit. He was baffled because he worked hard to maintain friendly relations with those he supervised, and it appeared that each of the quitters had different, and he thought unique, complaints when they were ultimately interviewed at their exit.

It became apparent that each of these associates had expressed to the partner early on their annoyance with some aspect of their work with him. His response was usually to inquire about their families and monitor their workload, assuring them of how much he valued them. What the partner failed to understand was how each associate's initial annoyance, as it continued to go unaddressed, over time had developed into frustration, then progressed to irritation, anger, and ultimately rage. Being "nice" was not a sufficient strategy to interrupt the progression.

4. Emotional Regulation

Any one can get angry—that is easy . . . but to do this to the right person, to the right extent, at the right time, with the right motive, and in the right way, that is not for every one, nor is it easy.[100]

—Aristotle

[L]et's not forget that small emotions are the great captains of our lives, and that these we obey without knowing it.[101]

—Vincent van Gogh

In "Mork's Mixed Emotions," named by TV Guide as one of the greatest episodes in television history, Mork, an alien played by comedian Robin Williams, is traumatized by his first vivid nightmare, so he decides to shut down all of his emotions. A kiss from his friend Mindy brings all those emotions back but also causes Mork to lose his ability to control them, an illustration of a failure of emotional regulation.[102]

The word "emotion" derives from "exmovere," the Latin verb "to excite," or "set in motion." Emotions excite us: they set in motion internal and behavioral responses that are a product of our genetics and our cumulative experiences.[103] We can learn to regulate our internal emotional experiences and also our emotionally driven behaviors in order to better manage the emotions in our relationships.[104]

In emotional dilemmas, the other components of emotional intelligence—recognizing our emotions, feeling others' pain, understanding emotions—are of limited use if we are not able to implement what we learn to be the best approach to deal with those emotions. It's not enough to KNOW about emotions through the skill of emotional understanding, we also have to DO something about those emotions—to be able to "operate the machinery of emotional regulation."[105] How do I turn my embarrassment at dropping my papers into the confidence I need to make my presentation? What can I do instead of flying off the handle when my assistant keeps making the same mistake in order to change his behavior? What would be the best approach to smooth our relationship when I have forgotten my significant other's birthday?

Being able to regulate emotions translates into several positive outcomes, including high levels of well-being, disposable income, and socioeconomic status.[106]

As a simple matter, emotional regulation skills help us pay attention by recognizing and ignoring emotional distractions.[107] The ability to regulate emotions also means being able to increase our experience of positive emotions, which itself is correlated with success.[108] But regulating one's emotions sometimes means accessing an unpleasant emotion, such as anger, rather than a pleasant one, like calm, in order to accomplish a desired goal in a particular situation, like succeeding in a confrontation.[109]

Using emotional regulation to move at will from one emotion to another, called "emotional agility," can get us out of an emotional ditch, regardless of whether that is a negative or positive feeling, and thereby "alleviate stress, reduce errors, become more innovative, and improve job performance."[110]

Supreme Court Justice Sonia Sotomayor testifies to the importance of emotional regulation for judges: "You have to be aware that you might be angry with a defendant and then acknowledge and deal with that anger as a person—and consciously set it aside."[111] Young lawyers also benefit from being able to regulate their emotions. A study of successful Am Law 100 associates by the Center for the Study of the Legal Profession at Georgetown Law School found they could, among other things, keep appropriate emotional boundaries. This allowed them to maintain some "emotional independence" and avoid becoming "overly involved in colleagues' feelings and intimate emotions," both signs of emotional regulation skills.[112]

Since emotional regulation draws on cognitive ability in some of the same ways that emotional understanding does, lawyers often score reasonably well on it, though again, their scores are lower than those of the general population.[113] The conscious engagement of our analytical skills helps in plotting the best course and could make us more accountable for taking the appropriate steps.

A senior lawyer with young children was torn between her obligations on the home and professional fronts, a common dilemma. Her emotions (guilt, frustration, fear, anger) and those of her children and coworkers (resentment, frustration, fear, anger) were identifiable and fully felt, and she well understand why they arose and intensified. The issue was how to manage her own feelings and the emotions of others that often burst to the surface in unproductive ways, so that she could be most effective in both realms.[114]

She made several changes to her schedule: meditating, decompressing before entering each realm, and dedicating a few minutes to each child individually every evening. She brought her kids to the office, and explained matters she was working on, involved friends/relatives in child events, made a standing arrangement with an emergency backup, and committed one night a week to family time. At work, she dedicated time to managing her schedule and checked in more frequently with colleagues and clients. She also participated several times a month in a networking program that she enjoyed with clients and colleagues.

This lawyer regularly reviewed the effects these moves had on her and others' emotions, and then recalibrated. She monitored her reactions to others' emotional states, actively listened to her children's and colleagues' emotions, expressed warmth and optimism to both, and periodically gave herself a pep talk and an emotional treat. These changes, coupled with her consciously practicing better emotional responses, helped her and others experience emotions that she recognized improved her own equilibrium and her relations at home and work.

Again, however, as with emotional understanding, our emotional regulation strategies can be doomed from the start if our take on the emotions we are responding to is incomplete or simply inaccurate. We lawyers also have a certain competence in a couple of approaches to emotional regulation which more often prove troublesome rather than helpful:

Suppression
Rumination

Suppression

Stifle it!

—Archie Bunker in the 1970s TV sitcom *All in the Family*

A workplace whose professionals were chosen and are valued for their cognitive skills and not their emotional ones and that puts a high premium on staying "rational" is a workplace that likely prizes suppression.

In suppressing emotions, we stuff them down deep and try to pretend they don't exist. We don't know what to do with them and fear they threaten our best functioning, or we consider those feelings simply unprofessional—less than totally rational. Yet ignoring emotions risks their evolving into more intense, and therefore even more unmanageable, versions of themselves and carries a high cognitive and physical cost.

Research has identified a few advantages in suppressing emotion. Some displays of emotion, such as gloating after winning, which may seem quite satisfying after a battle royale, damage relationships and lower the likability and influence of the winner. So if tempted to gloat, it's better to simply suppress it.[115] Also, momentary suppression of emotions rather than impulsive action may give everyone time to consider cognitively the best way to proceed. Six Seconds, an organization that promotes EI, is named after research showing that using emotional regulation to wait six seconds before acting on emotions produces better, more cognitively engaged results.[116]

Selectively suppressing certain emotions can demonstrate good emotional regulatory skills. Suppressing negative emotions can be strategically useful to leaders, for example, who are better able to lead through positive emotions than negative ones, so if you are having a bad day, it might be best for the office if you just suck up those negative feelings and put a smile on your face.[117]

But in most situations and particularly when used reflexively, suppression is a lose/lose proposition. Research shows that the effort of constantly pushing down emotions, called "emotional labor," takes up cognitive resources and reduces our functioning.[118] And conscious suppression may actually backfire by reinforcing through our focused effort what we are attempting to suppress.[119] The irony, therefore, is that often people work at putting aside emotions because they think it will help them get on with their work when, in fact, that strategy hinders their ability to do so. People who suppress emotion are worse at problem solving, completing tasks, memory and interpersonal relationships, and also have lower personal well-being.[120] By consciously bringing to light our feelings, we can reduce the emotional labor of suppression and bring both emotional and cognitive resources to bear on the problem.

The son of a senior executive I was consulting with died suddenly of an accidental drug overdose. The executive didn't miss a beat, showing up at work as usual and assuring everyone that he had reconciled himself to his loss. But it was clear that his response time had slowed, his memory was much worse, and he had trouble making decisions—all in contrast to his usual behavior. There is no happy ending here—he was eventually retired because of his inability to fully function. His repeated attempts to convince everyone that everything was fine were not sufficient to overcome the cognitive effects of what must have been massive suppression of grief and other emotions.

Suppression also has serious negative consequences in our interactions with others. For starters, suppressing or faking emotions undercuts our efforts at communication. A UK survey determined that while it occurred in almost two-thirds of workplace communications, the more suppression or faking involved, the less successful that communication was perceived to be by the recipient.[121] Being emotionally suppressed also reduces our influence and ability to lead.[122]

Suppression, often a strategy we employ when under stress, ratchets up stress and its debilitating effects for as long as four hours after the act of suppression.[123] In addition to cognitive effects, physical reactions to suppression can be significantly debilitating—even undercutting the ability to maintain a strong grip and to withstand sustained muscle contraction—making sufferers more likely to give up.[124] These debilitating effects of suppressing emotions may contribute to the low resilience we see in attorneys.[125] The mental energy lawyers use to suppress emotions may reduce their capacity both mentally and physically to persevere through a trying period and bounce back with renewed energy.

During a discussion with a managing partner, he suddenly fainted and was taken to the hospital in an ambulance. The diagnosis was that he had internal bleeding from ulcers that were caused by stress and that had developed over many months, if not years. I had been discussing with him what he insisted were not indications of contention within his firm, despite what had been described to me as a highly contentious workplace where partners had come to physical blows and an associate was suing a partner. This gentleman came across as courtly and was described as "of the old school," who could not tolerate conflict and therefore ignored it, suppressing any related negative feelings. Unfortunately, his body hadn't bought into the strategy—he was literally being eaten up by the toll suppression was taking.

Rumination

The second approach to regulating emotions that many lawyers take, whether consciously or unconsciously, is to ruminate, or to reexperience our negative emotions like a cow repeatedly chewing her cud.[126]

The critical downside of rumination is the negative nature of the emotional overload. Because of the mounting anxiety and stress, levels of the hormones adrenaline and cortisol chronically elevate, with accompanying physical and mental debilitation.[127] Ruminators also are less productive because they are mentally trapped in endless loops, with no way to move forward. As the Center for Creative Leadership (CCL), a well-respected research and services provider, points out, "There is no benefit to rumination."[128]

On the other hand, "planning for the future, or reviewing the past without negative emotion, is what we call reflection. It is a positive and important thing to do."[129] The key is eliminating the negative emotional aspects associated with those reflections, which requires emotional regulation skills.

Lawyers no doubt assume that if they think hard and long enough about a difficult situation, they will be able to successfully decipher it. However, the focused repetition can reinforce and magnify the unpleasant feelings involved. This excessive ruminating, coupled with the typical lawyer tendencies toward introverted analysis and pessimism, generates plenty of "what if" and "if only" anxiety. Dwelling on negative emotions ratchets up stress, makes it difficult to take others' perspectives into consideration, and increases the chances we'll lash out. Further, the negative reinforcement may exacerbate lawyers' typically low resilience and high-risk aversion professionally and make it even harder to recover from personal distress. We can become so consumed with our distressing feelings that we can't move on to solving the problem.[130]

Lawyers' reliance on these two extremes of emotion regulation—suppression and rumination—on one hand ignoring emotion and on the other marinating in it, illustrate their limited skills in this area. Both responses deplete cognitive and emotional resources and result in poor outcomes in terms of stress, problem solving, memory, interpersonal relationships, and well-being.[131]

THE FOUR COMPONENTS OF EMOTIONAL INTELLIGENCE AND WHERE WE LAWYERS FALL SHORT

1. Emotional Perception—accurately being aware of our own and others' emotions
   - Lawyers' weakest skill of the four, and one that the other three depend on

(Continued)

2. Emotional Empathy—transiently experiencing another's accurately identified emotional state based on various cues and our own emotional history
   - A skill rainmakers and managing partners employ more than other lawyers
3. Emotional Understanding—discerning why and how emotions are generated, combine, and evolve
   - Lawyers' strongest skill because of its cognitive and analytical aspects, if not undermined by weak perception
4. Emotional Regulation—managing our internal experience of emotion, our behavioral expressions of emotion, and the emotional aspects of relationships
   - A fairly strong skill for lawyers if not undermined by weak perception, although a tendency to overuse suppression and rumination

Chapter Endnotes

1. Gaston Kroub, "Are You Smart Enough To Be a Good Lawyer?" *Above the Law,* November 18, 2014; Richard, "Herding Cats," *Altman Weil Report to Legal Management,* 1–12.
2. Matthew Todres et al., "The Emotional Intelligence of Medical Students; An Exploratory Cross-Sectional Study," *Medical Teacher* 32 (2010): e42–e48; Nicole J. Borges et al., "Emotional Intelligence and Medical Specialty Choice: Findings from Three Empirical Studies," *Medical Education* 43 (2009): 565–72. Ramzan Shahid, Jerold Stirling, and William Adams, "Assessment of Emotional Intelligence in Pediatric and Med-Peds Residents," *Journal of Contemporary Medical Education,* Vol 4, Issue 4, January 26, 2017, which showed higher than average EI scores for first year pediatric residents than for the general population.
3. J. Randolph Evans and Shari L. Klevens, "Sex with Client Is Flirting with Disaster," *Daily Report,* September 24, 2013, http://www.dailyreportonline.com/id=1202620431509?slreturn=20150802162633: an unhappy client/husband was awarded $1.5 million against the Mississippi lawyer who had an affair with the client's wife; a Minnesota lawyer was barred from practicing law for fifteen months after a two-day affair with his client; Pennsylvania enforced for the first time its prohibition against sex with clients with a one-year suspension, and Ohio suspended a lawyer for one year for simply proposing the arrangement. Marlise Silver Sweeney, "Ex-Bryan Cave Lawyer Charged with Making Death Threat," *The Am Law Daily,* July 3, 2013. Ross Todd, "Attorney Caught in Wiretapping

Scandal Loses Appeal," *The Recorder,* August 25, 2015, http://www.therecorder.com/id=1202735687499/Attorney-Caught-in-Wiretapping-Scandal-Loses-Appeal?slreturn=20170024163001; Zoe Tillman, "Former White House Lawyer Disbarred in D.C.," *The Blog of Legal Times,* July 1, 2015, http://www.nationallawjournal.com/legaltimes/id=1202731098423/Former-White-House-Lawyer-Disbarred-in-DC?slreturn=20170102125116; Joe Patrice, "Federal Judge Retires Amid Rape Allegations," *Above the Law,* March 17, 2016.

4. Joseph A. Corsmeier, "Lawyer Who Dissed Client Online Suspended," *Today's General Counsel,* September 9, 2015, http://www.todaysgeneralcounsel.com/lawyer-who-dissed-client-online-suspended/?utm_source=afternoonnewsletter; Rafael Olmeda, "Supreme Court Suspends Former Prosecutor Over Relationship with Judge," *Sun-Sentinel,* June 25, 2013. Wisconsin Judicial Commission v. Prosser, 2012AP566-J (2013), cited in Dan Defoe, "Law Student Emotional Intelligence, Personality and Psychological Health: An Initial Understanding of Well-Being Indicators and Challenge to Educators," *Psycholawlogy Blog,* March 31, 2013, http://www.psycholawlogy.com/2013/03/31/emotional-intelligence-psychological-health-and-law-student-personalities-an-initial-understanding-of-well-being-indicators/.
5. An ill-advised firm-wide email rant sent by a frustrated partner generated hundreds of angry responses. David Law, "Did This Biglaw Partner Act Like a Big Tool? Let's Discuss," *Above the Law,* May 15, 2014. A General Counsel's public castigation of his staff, in a display of emotional pique, backfired. Max Taves and Cheryl Miller, "CPUC's Top Lawyer Blasted by Staff During, and After, Keynote Speech," *The Recorder,* June 18, 2013, http://www.law.com/jsp/ca/PubArticleCA.jsp?id=1202607089628&CPUCs_Top_Lawyer_Blasted_by_Staff_During_and_After_Keynote_Speech#ixzz2d0zZLJ5Q. Tillman, "Ex-Judge Who Sued Dry Cleaners Over Lost Pants Faces Ethics Charges," *Law.com,* June 7, 2016, http://www.law.com/sites/almstaff/2016/06/07/ex-judge-who-sued-dry-cleaners-over-lost-pants-faces-ethics-charges/.
6. Daicoff, "Expanding the Lawyer's Toolkit of Skills and Competencies," 804, citing Hart Research Associates, *supra* note 3 (reporting that a majority of the public held negative perceptions of lawyers as not honest or ethical, greedy, etc.); Hengstler, *supra* note 3, at 63–64 (reporting on the discouraging results of a poll on public opinion of attorneys, whose ethical and honesty standards were perceived as much lower than other professions).
7. After reviewing the lawsuit in Spain against US officials, including William J. Haynes II, former Pentagon general counsel, for the torture of Spanish citizens at Abu Ghraib, English barrister Philippe Sands concluded that: "If not for lawyers, none of these abuses would have ever occurred." Jane Mayer, "The Bush Six," *The New Yorker,* April 13, 2009. Lawyer Philip Howard suggests in his book *Life Without Lawyers* that everyone might be better off without "a little lawyer on their shoulder whispering in their ear all day long." Philip K. Howard, *Life Without Lawyers: Restoring Responsibility in America* (New York: W.W Norton and Co., 2009).
8. Jill Breslau and Daicoff, "The Illicit Relationship of Lawyers and Emotion," *Cutting Edge Law,* September 1, 2008, http://cuttingedgelaw.com/content/illicit-relationship-lawyers-and-emotion. "[These] do not have emotional

brains . . . we are talking about someone with instant reflexes and a narrowly focused instinct, without feelings or conscience, with only a reptilian brain . . . no wonder we are unpopular. Sadly, the process of legal education and the practice of law, both explicitly and implicitly, foster this perception."

9. The lawyer who drunkenly tossed her panties at the police (Staci Zaretsky, "Lawyer Gets Wasted, Throws Panties at Police," *Above the Law,* June 3, 2013, http://abovethelaw.com/2013/06/lawyer-gets-wasted-throws-panties-at-police/; the criminal defense attorney found naked with an adolescent in the court's conference room, the lawyer who allegedly masturbated on a coworker's dress (Christopher Danzig, "Lawsuits of the Day: Ewwww. OMG, OMG. Gross," *Above the Law,* June 5, 2012, http://abovethelaw.com/2012/06/lawsuits-of-the-day-ewwww-omg-omg-gross/2/).
10. One nationwide poll "found deep distrust of the legal system across the board," with only 26 percent of voters believing our civil justice system provides timely and reliable resolution of disputes and 92 percent wanting it to change. A Gallup poll showed that only 29 percent of Americans have a "great deal" or "quite a lot" of confidence in the criminal justice system. Ron Faucheux, "By the Numbers: Americans Lack Confidence in the Legal System," *The Atlantic,* July 6, 2012.
11. In a DRI-The Voice of the Defense Bar poll, 41 percent of respondents indicated they were not confident that the civil law system produces just and fair results. A whopping 83 percent indicated that "the side with the most money for lawyers usually wins." About two-thirds said that they preferred juries over judges to decide disputes, showing even distrust of the legal system's designated presiding officer. Gary Long, Greg Fowler, and Simon Castley, "DRI National Poll Uncovers Perceptions of Flaws in U.S. Civil Justice System," *Lexology,* September 27, 2012. http://www.lexology.com/library/detail.aspx?g=f64d5c01-d85b-4428-b65f-b996479144d3.
12. While confidence in the leaders of most institutions slipped by one or two points since 2010, "confidence in the Supreme Court fell 7 points from 31 percent to 24 percent . . . and confidence in the courts and the justice system fell 5 points from 24 percent to 19 percent." Humphrey Taylor, "Confidence in Congress and Supreme Court Drops to Lowest Level in Many Years," *Harris Polls,* May 18, 2011, http://www.harrisinteractive.com/NewsRoom/HarrisPolls/tabid/447/mid/1508/articleId/780/ctl/ReadCustom%20Default/Default.aspx.
13. "Honesty/Ethics in Professions," *Gallup,* December 7–11, 2016, http://www.harrisinteractive.com/vault/Harris-Interactive-Poll-Research-Trust-in-Priests-and-Clergy-Falls-26-Points-in-Twelve-Months-2002-11.pdf; Deborah L. Rhode, *Lawyers as Leaders* (Oxford: Oxford University Press, 2013), 2.
14. Top of the list were members of the armed services who, 78 percent say, contribute "a lot" to society's well-being. Close behind were teachers, medical doctors, scientists, and engineers, with the support of more than a majority. The bottom dwellers were business executives at 24 percent and, yes, in last place, lawyers at 18 percent. While we might bask in 18 percent of the public thinking, we contribute "a lot" to society; 34 percent of Americans rank lawyers' contribution as "not very much" or "nothing." Zaretsky, "Lawyers: The

Most Despised Profession in America," *Above the Law,* July 15, 2003, http://abovethelaw.com/2013/07/lawyers-the-most-despised-profession-in-america/.

15. "The list of arrogant firms has more than doubled since the legal industry escaped the depths of the recession, but has grown two times as fast as BTI's list of firms praised for excellent client service." The list published in 2016 includes some of the most profitable BigLaw firms, and also those ranked high in client service. Aebra Coe, "GCs Say This Firm Is the Most Arrogant," *Law360,* November 28, 2016, http://www.law360.com/articles/866039/gcs-say-this-firm-is-the-most-arrogant. See also Staci Zaretsky, "The Most Arrogant Biglaw Firms? There's a Ranking for That!" *Above the Law,* November 19, 2013.
16. According to researchers at the University of Akron and Michigan State University who developed the Workplace Arrogance Scale. "Identifying the Arrogant Boss," *Science Daily News,* June 25, 2012, https://www.sciencedaily.com/releases/2012/07/120725105311.htm.
17. Gary A. Hengstler, "Vox Populi: The Public Perception of Lawyers: ABA Poll," *ABA Journal,* 60, 62 (1993): 60. The study was conducted by Peter D. Hart Research Associates Inc.
18. A. Cotti et al., "Road Traffic Accidents and Secondary Victimisation: The Role of Law Professionals," *Medicine and Law* 23 (2004): 259–68.
19. Daicoff, *Lawyer, Know Yourself,* 101.
20. Cicero, quoted in Walter R. Fisher, *Human Communications as Narration: Toward a Philosophy of Reason, Value and Action* (Columbia, SC: University of South Carolina Press, 1987), 37.
21. Mary E. Clark, *In Search of Human Nature* (London: Routledge, 2002), 155.
22. Sir Henry Sumner Maine, *Ancient Law, Its Connection with the Early History of Society and Its Relation to Modern Ideas.* 4th American from the 10th London edition (New York: Henry Holt and Co., 1906), http://oll.libertyfund.org/titles/2001.
23. Melissa Nelken, "If I'd Wanted to Learn about Feelings, I Wouldn't Have Gone to Law School," *Journal of Legal Education,* 46 (1996): 421. Melissa Nelken is Faculty Chair of the Hastings Center for Negotiation and Dispute Resolution.
24. Dirk Baltzly, "Stoicism," *The Stanford Encyclopedia of Philosophy,* ed. Edward N. Zalta, 2012, quoting Plato, *Phaedrus,* http://plato.stanford.edu/archives/win2012/entries/stoicism/, sections 246a–254e; Publilius Syrus, "Sententiae," in J.W Duff and A.M Duff (eds), *Minor Latin Poets* (Cambridge: Harvard University Press, 1934).
25. Paul Thomas Young, *Emotion in Man and Animal: Its Nature and Relation to Attitude and Motive* (New York: John Wiley & Sons, 1943), 263; Mayer and Salovey, "Emotional Intelligence," *Imagination, Cognition, and Personality,* 185.
26. Max Meyer, "That Whale Among the Fishes—The Theory of Emotions," *Psychological Review,* 40 (1933): 292–300.
27. Edward L. Thorndike, "Intelligence and Its Uses," *Harper's Magazine,* 140 (1920): 227–335.
28. Harold Anthony Lloyd, "Cognitive Emotion and the Law," August 1, 2016, *Law & Psychology Review,* https://poseidon01.ssrn.com/delivery.php?ID=12300301706802912006900309700709300203500500007406608709012100700412309003002501811910002804301410306102101101202406900907609100 00053057

0800860280300641091070730050910630280370250800840921260650751021 19 1260720 8300311112706710109 1127122108111002 003106124&EXT=pdf.

29. John L. Diamond, Lawrence C. Levine, and Anita Bernstein, *Understanding Torts,* 4th ed. (Danvers, MA: Matthew Bender & Co., 2010), 26, 214; Beau Baez, *Tort Law in the USA* (Leiden: Kluwer Law International, 2010), 166.
30. For more, including resources on the differing treatment of insanity by individual states, see Public Broadcasting Service, "A Case of Insanity," *Frontline,* 1995, http://www.pbs.org/wgbh/pages/frontline/shows/crime/trial/faqs.html#3.
31. D.E. Smee et al., "Critical Concerns in Iraq/Afghanistan War Veteran-Forensic Interface: Veterans Treatment Court as Diversion in Rural Communities," *The Journal of the American Academy of Psychiatry and Law,* 41 (2013): 258. As of June 2016, over 200 were in existence nationally.
32. William H. McMichael, "The Battle on the Home Front: Special Courts Turn to Vets to Help Other Vets," *ABA Journal,* November 1, 2011, 42.
33. Kevin Davis, "Brain Trials," *ABA Journal,* November, 2012, 37.
34. The annual average of cases using neuroscientific evidence nearly doubled from 17 in 2005–2008 to 34 in 2009–2012. Paul Cately and Lisa Claydon, "The Use of Neuroscientific Evidence in the Courtroom by Those Accused of Criminal Offenses in England and Wales," *Journal of Law and Biosciences,* 2 (2015): 510–49.
35. Neil Feigenson, Jaihyun Park, and Peter Salovey, "Effect of Blameworthiness and Outcome Severity on Attributions of Responsibility and Damage Awards in Comparative Negligence Cases," *Law and Human Behavior* 21 (1997): 597–617.
36. Nelken, "If I'd Wanted to Learn About Feelings, I Wouldn't Have Gone to Law School," *Journal of Legal Education,* 422.
37. Breslau and Daicoff, "The Illicit Relationship of Lawyers and Emotion," *Cutting Edge Law.*
38. Goleman, *Working with Emotional Intelligence* (New York: Bantam, 2011), 52.
39. This film was based on Philip K. Dick's 1968 novel, *Do Androids Dream of Electric Sheep?*
40. Antonio Damásio, *Descartes' Error: Emotion, Reason and the Human Brain* (New York: Avon Books, 1994), 3–19. Damásio is the David Dornsife Professor of Neuroscience at the University of Southern California, where he heads USC's Brain and Creativity Institute, and is an Adjunct Professor at the Salk Institute.
41. Phineas Gage, a 25-year-old railroad foreman, had been studied in the 19th century after a 13-foot, 3.5-pound rod went through his head in 1848 in a construction accident in Vermont. Astonishingly, Gage was walking and talking within minutes, and one of his doctors wrote: "Mr. Gage . . . talked so rationally and was so willing to answer questions . . . that neither at that time nor on any subsequent occasion, save once, did I consider him to be other than perfectly rational." Damásio, *Descartes' Error,* 12. Damasio went on to study many modern patients with similar brain damage, including "Elliott," who has been identified as the lawyer described but may be a composite of several of his patients, including a lawyer. Goleman, *Emotional Intelligence: Why It Can Matter More Than IQ*
42. Damásio, *Descartes' Error,* 38.
43. Descartes, writing in 1649, contended that emotions "agitate and disturb" the soul and render judgment "confused and obscure," but that they can

be controlled through rationality. René Descartes, *Discourse on the Method of Rightly Conducting the Reason and Seeking the Truth in the Sciences,* Charles W. Eliot ed. (New York: P.F. Collier & Son, 2001).

44. Dana L. Joseph and Daniel A. Newman, "Emotional Intelligence: An Integrative Meta-analysis and Cascading Model," *Journal of Applied Psychology,* 95 (2010): 54–78. Individuals have a broad range of "normal" ability in each of these areas, although significantly low abilities may signal serious psychiatric conditions. James A. McCubbin et al., "Cardiovascular-Emotional Dampening: The Relationship Between Blood Pressure and Recognition of Emotion," *Psychosomatic Medicine: Journal of Biobehavioral Medicine,* 73 (2011): 743–50.
45. Kathleen Megan, "Yale Expert Says Teaching About Emotions Reduces Bullying," *Hartford Courant,* November 22, 2013.
46. Bradberry and Greaves, *Emotional Intelligence 2.0,* 13.
47. Richard, "Herding Cats," *Altman Weil Report to Legal Management,* 1–12.
48. Bradberry, Nick Tasler, and Lac D. Su, "Lawyers with Personality?" *TalentSmart,* 2011, 1, http://www.talentsmart.com/articles/Lawyers-With-Personality—653256185-p-1.html.
49. John D. Mayer, Richard D. Roberts, and Sigal G. Barsade, "Human Abilities: Emotional Intelligence," *Annual Review of Psychology,* 59 (2008): 507–36.
50. W. Gerrod Parrott, "The Nature of Emotion," in Abraham Tesser and Norbert Schwarz, ed., *The Blackwell Handbook of Social Psychology: Intraindividual Processes* (London: Blackwell Publishers, 2001), 375–90.
51. Most researchers discuss seven primary emotions—anger, sadness, fear, surprise, disgust, shame, and happiness, but Goleman suggests eight—or the "blue, red, and yellow of feeling from which all blends come"—by replacing happiness with enjoyment and love. Daniel Goleman, *Emotional Intelligence* (New York: Bantam Books, 1995), 289. Other theoreticians talk about emotional families, such as the four basic emotional families of anxiety, anger, depression, and contentment. Bradberry and Greaves, *Emotional Intelligence 2.0,* 48. See also Robert Plutchik, "The Nature of Emotions," *American Scientist,* 89 (2001): 344–50.
52. Goleman, *Working with Emotional Intelligence,* 289; Theodore D. Kemper, "How Many Emotions Are There? Wedding the Social and the Autonomic Components," *American Journal of Sociology* 93 (1987): 263–89. Thousands of students nationwide reported to the Yale Center's Emotion Revolution online survey, supported by Lady Gaga's Born This Way Foundation, that four out of the top five emotions they experience at school are predominantly negative. "Lady Gaga Speaking to the Yale Emotion Revolution Summit," YouTube video, 1:00:26, 2015, https://www.youtube.com/watch?v=gSwxK4pFF1o&ebc=ANyPxKqHBfT_nrRaOCis9NV0VrlQNpSijPIDjRMH1Z59FSz5DLHeBGCCXKcPSxk1GDuyJMvWJLzjqCEd8tqs3VXykDNBAVIAag
53. Yasemin Erbas et al., "Negative Emotion Differentiation: Its Personality and Well-Being Correlates and a Comparison of Different Assessment Methods," *Cognition and Emotion,* 28 (2014): 1196–1213; J. D. Mayer, Maria DiPaolo, and Peter Salovey, "Perceiving Affective Content in Ambiguous Visual Stimuli: A Component of Emotional Intelligence," *Journal of Personality Assessment* 54 (1990): 772–81; Salovey et al., "Emotional Attention, Clarity, and Repair:

Exploring Emotional Intelligence Using the Trait Meta-Mood Scale," in James W. Pennebaker ed., *Emotion, Disclosure, and Health* (Washington, DC: APA, 1999), 125–54.

54. Michael Hoerger et al., "Emotional Intelligence: A Theoretical Framework for Individual Differences in Affective Forecasting," *Emotion,* 12 (2012): 716–25; David Rosete and Joseph Ciarrochi, "Emotional Intelligence and Its Relationship to Workplace Performance Outcomes of Leadership Effectiveness," *Leadership and Organization Development Journal*; Karen Gasper and Gerald L. Clore, "Do You Have to Pay Attention to Your Feelings to Be Influenced by Them?" *Personality and Social Psychology Bulletin,* 26 (6): 1.
55. Bradberry and Greaves, *Emotional Intelligence 2.0,* 26.
56. Richard Boyatzis, lecture at Case Western Reserve University, 2012, https://class.coursera.org/lead-ei-002/lecture/19.
57. Bradberry and Greaves, *Emotional Intelligence 2.0,* 13.
58. Deborah Serani, "The Emotional Blindness of Alexithymia," *Scientific American,* April 3, 2014. Damage to the amygdala can destroy the ability to discern negative emotions, particularly fear and anger, and those affected by alexithymia may not be able to decipher others' emotions any better than their own. Sarah-Neena Koch, "Subcortical Brain Structures, Stress, Emotions, and Mental Illness," *MyBrainNotes.com,* 2013, http://mybrainnotes.com/memory-brain-stress.html; John Allman, *Evolving Brains* (New York: Scientific American Library, 2000). Amygdalar damage made a person with normal vision unable to see negative emotional content, such as fear and anger, in facial expressions. Ralph Adolphs et al., "Neuropsychological Approaches to Reasoning and Decision-Making," in Antonio R. Damasio, Hanna Damasio, and Yves Christen ed., *Neurobiology of Decision-Making* (New York: Springer-Verlag, 1996), 157–79. Amygdalar damage can also disrupt the ability to perceive the emotional content of speech, particularly auditory expressions of fear and anger, even when the person has normal hearing abilities. Sophie K. Scott et al., "Impaired Auditory Recognition of Fear and Anger Following Bilateral Amygdala Lesions," *Nature,* 385 (6613): 254–57.
59. Susan David, "Recovering from an Emotional Outburst at Work," *Harvard Business Review,* May 8, 2015, https://hbr.org/2015/05/recovering-from-an-emotional-outburst-at-work.
60. William Shakespeare, *The Tragedy of Othello: The Moor of Venice,* eds. Tucker Brooke and Lawrence Mason (New Haven: Yale UP, 1947). The term "Othello's Error" was coined by Paul Ekman in his 1985 book, *Telling Lies.*
61. Robert Rosenthal et al., "The PONS Test: Measuring Sensitivity to Nonverbal Cues," *Advances in Psychological Assessment,* ed. Paul McReynolds (San Francisco: Jossey-Bass, 1977). Evidently only minor disadvantages arise from this ability. Reading nonverbal cues meant to be hidden can be intrusive and raise conflict in the workplace if negative emotions, like envy, anger or resentment, are recognized and acknowledged. Elfenbein and Ambady, "Predicting Workplace Outcomes from the Ability to Eavesdrop on Feelings," *Journal of Applied Psychology,* 87 (2002): 963–71. See Defoe, "Eavesdropping on Feelings, Emotional Intelligence, and Workplace Interventions." *Psycholawlogy,* August 28, 2012, http://www.psycholawlogy.com/2012/08/28/

eavesdropping-on-feelings-emotional-intelligence-and-workplace-interventions/. One study also raised the possibility that people with emotional perception skills may under some conditions be less able to detect deception in others. Alysha Baker, Leanne ten Brinke, and Stephen Porter, "Will Get Fooled Again: Emotionally Intelligent People Are Easily Duped by High-Stakes Deceivers," *Legal and Criminological Psychology* 18 (2): 300–313. Another study found that males with high emotional perception, particularly if they are status-conscious, are more likely to be stressed out by perceived expressions of negative emotions. Myriam N. Bechtoldt and Vanessa K. Schneider, "Predicting Stress from the Ability to Eavesdrop on Feelings: Emotional Intelligence and Testosterone Jointly Predict Cortisol Reactivity," *Emotion*, 16 (6), Sep. 2016, 815–25. A study of high-EI women also found high stress. "Relation between emotional intelligence and perceived stress among female students," Nasrin Zamani Forushani. Mohammad Ali Besharat, *Procedia—Social and Behavioral Sciences*, 30 (2011), 1109–12. Yet clearly high emotional understanding and management skills are effective in coping with the fallout that comes from stress, like depression, hopelessness, and suicidal ideation. Joseph Ciarrochi, Frank P. Deane, and Stephen Anderson, "Emotional Intelligence Moderates the Relationship between Stress and Mental Health," *Personality and Individual Differences*, 32 (2), 19 January 2002, 197–209.

62. "SEEC Research," *UC San Diego Empathy Center*, 2017, http://empathy.ucsd.edu/research/index.html; Daniel J. Siegel, "Mindfulness Training and Neural Integration: Differentiation of Distinct Streams of Awareness and the Cultivation of Well-Being," *Social Cognitive and Affective Neuroscience*, 2 (4): 259–63.
63. Charles Darwin, *The Expression of Emotions in Man and Animals*, ed. Joe Cain and Sharon Messenger (New York: Penguin Classics, 2009).
64. Paul Ekman ed., *Darwin and Facial Expression: A Century of Research in Review*, 2nd ed. (Los Altos, CA: Malor Books, 2006).
65. Goleman, *The Brain and Emotional Intelligence: New Insights*.
66. Ekman ed., *Darwin and Facial Expression: A Century of Research in Review*.
67. Lisa F. Barrett, Batija Mesquita, and Maria Gendron, "Context in Emotion Perception," *Current Directions in Psychological Science*, 20 (2011): 286–290.
68. Peter Frampton, "Do You Feel Like We Do?" *Frampton's Camel* (New York: A&M Records, 1973).
69. Richard, "Herding Cats," *Altman Weil Report to Legal Management*, 1–12; Richard, personal communication.
70. Richard, "Hiring Emotionally Intelligent Associates," *Bench & Bar of Minnesota*.
71. "What Is Empathy?" *Greater Good: The Science of a Meaningful Life*, 2013, http://greatergood.berkeley.edu/topic/empathy/definition#what.
72. Adam Gopnik, "Mindless: The New Neuro-skeptics," *The New Yorker*, September 9, 2013, 86–88.
73. Marco Iacoboni et al., "Cortical Mechanisms of Human Imitation," *Science* 286 (5449): 2526–28.
74. Goleman, "An EI-Based Theory of Performance," in Daniel Goleman and Carey Cherniss (eds.), *The Emotionally Intelligent Workplace: How to Select for, Measure, and Improve Emotional Intelligence in Individuals, Groups, and Organizations* (San Francisco, CA: Jossey-Bass, 2000).

75. Belinda Parmar, "The Most (and Least) Empathetic Companies," *Harvard Business Review,* November 27, 2015.
76. Peter Baker, "In Court Nominees, Is Obama Looking for Empathy by Another Name?" *New York Times,* April 25, 2010.
77. Bernie Wong and Neha John-Henderson, "Does Your Manager Feel Your Pain?" *Greater Good: The Science of a Meaningful Life,* May 13, 2013, http://greatergood.berkeley.edu/article/research_digest/does_your_manager_feel_your_pain; Resnik and Dinse, "Do U.S. Research Institutions Meet or Exceed Federal Mandates for Instruction in Responsible Conduct of Research? A National Survey," *Academic Medicine,* 1237–42.
78. Daniel C. Batson et al., "Is Empathic Emotion a Source of Altruistic Motivation?" *Journal of Personality and Social Psychology,* 40 (2): 290–302; Nancy Eisenberg and Paul A. Miller, "The Relation of Empathy to Prosocial and Related Behaviors." *Psychological Bulletin,* 101 (1): 91–119. See also *Bullied: Why You Feel Bad Inside and What to Do About It,* a 2013 book by Katherine Mayfield on raising EI of young people to help them defuse and deal with bullying. "What's missing is emotional intelligence . . . Until the emotional side of the issue is addressed, the epidemic will most likely continue." Mayfield, quoted in "New Book by Award-Winning Author Offers an Innovative Approach to Bullying Epidemic," *Digital Journal,* December, 2013, http://www.digitaljournal.com/pr/1650921#ixzz2oWCUnJjE.
79. Amanda Enayati, "Don't Let Others Stress You Out," *CNN: The Chart,* September 7, 2011, http://thechart.blogs.cnn.com/2011/09/07/dont-let-others-stress-you-out.
80. Na'amah Razon and Jason Marsh, "Empathy on the Decline," *Greater Good,* January 28, 2011, http://greatergood.berkeley.edu/article/research_digest/empathy_on_the_decline/.
81. "What's the Number 1 Leadership Skill for Overall Success?" February 23, 2016, *Development Dimensions International,* February 23, 2016, http://www.ddiworld.com/global-offices/united-states/press-room/what-is-the-1-leadership-skill-for-overall-success.
82. Marsh, "The Unselfish Gene," *Greater Good,* November 20, 2009, http://greatergood.berkeley.edu/article/item/the_unselfish_gene/.
83. Goleman, "Are Women More Emotionally Intelligent Than Men?" *Psychology Today,* April 29, 2011; Reuven Bar-On, "Emotional and Social Intelligence: Insights From the Emotional Quotient Inventory," in *The Handbook of Emotional Intelligence,* eds. Reuven Bar-On and James Donald Alexander Parker (San Francisco: Jossey-Bass, 2000), 363–88. In his analysis of 7700 administrations of the EQ-i, Bar-On found that women scored higher than men in the broad "interpersonal" category overall and in each of its subcategories: Empathy, Interpersonal Relationships, and Social Responsibility. Men did not demonstrate strength in any of the five major categories but scored higher than women in a variety of subcategories: Actualization, Assertiveness, Stress Tolerance, Impulse Control, and Adaptability.
84. Scott A. Bonn, "How to Tell a Sociopath From a Psychopath," *Psychology Today,* January 22, 2014.

85. Mirella Dapretto et al., "Understanding Emotions in Others: Mirror Neuron Dysfunction in Children with Autism Spectrum Disorders," *Nature Neuroscience* 9 (1): 7.
86. Goleman, *The Brain and Emotional Intelligence: New Insights.*
87. Marsh, "You Can't Buy Empathy," *Greater Good: The Science of a Meaningful Life,* December 14, 2010, http://greatergood.berkeley.edu/article/item/you_cant_buy_empathy.
88. Grewal, "How Wealth Reduces Compassion: As Riches Grow, Empathy for Others Seems to Decline," April 10, 2012, *Scientific American.*
89. Marsh, "You Can't Buy Empathy," *Greater Good.*
90. "News Release: Brief Training Program Improves Resident Physicians' Empathy with Patients," *Massachusetts General Hospital,* May 7, 2012, http://www.massgeneral.org/about/pressrelease.aspx?id=1461; Michael Krasner et al., "Association of an Educational Program in Mindful Communication with Burnout, Empathy, and Attitudes Among Primary Care Physicians," *The Journal of the American Medical Association,* 302 (12): 1284–93.
91. Joann S. Lublin, "Companies Try a New Strategy: Empathy Training," *Wall Street Journal,* June 21, 2016.
92. Roman Krznaric, *Empathy: Why It Matters, and How to Get It* (New York: Perigee, 2014). Empathy Museum, n.d., http://www.empathymuseum.com/.
93. Melissa Hogenboom, "Pyschopathic Criminals Have Empathy Switch," *BBC News,* July 24, 2013, http://www.bbc.co.uk/news/science-environment-23431793.
94. Elliot M. Hirsch, "The Role of Empathy in Medicine: A Medical Student's Perspective," *Virtual Mentor* 9 (6): 423.
95. "Caregivers Also Risk Feeling Emotionally Overwhelmed If They Can't Manage Their Feelings of Empathy." From Olivia Solon, "Compassion Over Empathy Could Help Prevent Emotional Burnout," *Wired,* July 12, 2012. High emotional understanding and management skills are effective in coping with the stressful fallout that might come to those with keen emotional perception and empathy. Joseph Ciarrochi, Frank P. Deane, Stephen Anderson, "Emotional Intelligence Moderates the Relationship Between Stress and Mental Health," *Personality and Individual Differences,* 32 (2), January 19, 2002, 197–209.
96. Commonly attributed to Albert Einstein (1879–1955).
97. For more on contribution of cognitive appraisal of situations and its potential role in reducing emotional stress, see R.S Lazarus, "From Psychological Stress to the Emotions: A History of Changing Perspectives," *Annual Review of Psychology,* 44 (1993): 1–21.
98. Richard, "The Lawyer Types," *ABA Journal,* July, 1993, 74–78; Richard, "Herding Cats," *Altman Weil Report to Legal Management,* 1–12. These attributes are high for lawyers on both the MBTI and the Caliper Profile.
99. David, "Recovering from an Emotional Outburst at Work," *Harvard Business Review.*
100. Book II, 1109a.27
101. Letter 790 from Vincent van Gogh to Theo van Gogh dated Saint-Rémy-de-Provence, Sunday, 14 or Monday, 15 July 1889Br. 1990: 791 | CL: 603 http://www.vangoghletters.org/vg/letters/let790/letter.html#translation.

102. Episode 20, aired February 22, 1979. TV.com, http://www.tv.com/shows/mork-and-mindy/morks-mixed-emotions-29177/. There are few disadvantages to being skilled in emotional regulation, particularly if other components of EI are in place. Those able to regulate emotions may reduce their feelings of compassion rather than be overwhelmed by their empathic reactions to needy children, for example. Emma Seppala, "Compassionate Mind, Healthy Body," *Greater Good,* July 24, 2013, http://greatergood.berkeley.edu/article/item/compassionate_mind_healthy_body.
103. Philip A. Vernon et al., "A Behavioral Genetic Study of Trait Emotional Intelligence," *Emotion,* 8 (5): 635–42.
104. Some researchers have found that those high in emotional understanding are often also high in the ability to manage emotions, although they remain separate abilities. Bradberry and Greaves, "Heartless Bosses?" *Harvard Business Review* 83 (12): 24.
105. Stephane Côté et al. "Emotional Intelligence and Leadership Emergence in Small Groups," *Leadership Quarterly* 21 (2010): 496–508.
106. Ibid.
107. Thu-Huong Ha, "Study: Emotionally Aware Children Are also More Focused and Pay Better Attention," *Quartz,* July 15, 2015, http://qz.com/453631/understanding-emotions-helps-children-to-focus-and-pay-attention/.
108. Donald A. Saklofske et al., "Relationships of Personality, Affect, Emotional Intelligence and Coping with Student Stress and Academic Success: Different Patterns of Association for Stress and Success," *Learning and Individual Differences* 22 (2012): 256.
109. Defoe, "The [Lawyer's] Smart Use of Unpleasant Emotions–Emotionally Intelligent Emotion Regulation," *Psycholawlogy,* June 7, 2013, http://www.psycholawlogy.com/2013/06/07/the-lawyers-smart-use-of-unpleasant-emotionsemotionally-intelligent-emotion-regulation/.
110. Susan David and Christina Congleton, "Emotional Agility," *Harvard Business Review,* November, 2013.
111. "Oprah Interviews Sonia Sotomayor," *O Magazine,* February, 2013, 146.
112. Lori Berman and Heather Bock, "Developing Attorneys for the Future: What Can We Learn from the Fast Trackers?" *Santa Clara Law Review* 52 (2012): 896–97.
113. Richard, "Herding Cats," *Altman Weil Report to Legal Management,* 1–12.
114. David and Congleton, "Emotional Agility," *Harvard Business Review.*
115. DeFoe, "Don't Grin When You [Lawyers] Win: The Social Benefits of Appearing 'Humble in Victory,'" *Psycholawlogy,* May 23, 2015, http://us9.campaign-archive1.com/?u=3d1a3948dc9d24fb867494685&id=45d515b7ac&e=c35e23051d.
116. "Six Seconds," *SixSeconds.org,* http://www.6seconds.org/.
117. Goleman, "Leadership That Gets Results," *Harvard Business Review,* March–April, 2000.
118. Debora Cutuli, "Cognitive Reappraisal and Expressive Suppression Strategies Role in the Emotion Regulation: An Overview on Their Modulatory Effects and Neural Correlates," *Frontiers in Systems Neuroscience,* 8 (175).
119. David and Congleton, "Emotional Agility," *Harvard Business Review.*

120. James J. Gross, "Emotion Regulation: Affective, Cognitive, and Social Consequences," *Psychophysiology* 39 (3): 281–91.
121. Sandi Mann, "Emotion at Work: To What Extent Are We Expressing, Suppressing, or Faking It?" *European Journal of Work and Organizational Psychology* 8 (3): 347–69.
122. Amy J.C Cuddy, Matthew Kohut, and John Neffinger, "Connect, Then Lead," *HBR Magazine Online*, July–August, 2013, http://hbr.org/2013/07/connect-then-lead/ar/.
123. Joyce E. Bono et al., "Workplace Emotions: The Role of Supervision and Leadership," *The Journal of Applied Psychology*, 92 (5): 1357–67.
124. Daniel Kahneman, *Thinking Fast and Slow* (New York: Farrar, Straus and Giroux, 2011), 42. Physical impacts of stress include a pounding heartbeat, sweating, rapid breathing, fatigue, restlessness, tension, aching muscles and headaches, nearly all in response to the amygdala sending shots of cortisol. See Mayo Clinic Staff, "Stress Symptoms: Effects on Your Body and Behavior," *Mayo Clinic*, http://www.mayoclinic.org/healthy-lifestyle/stress-management/in-depth/stress-symptoms/art-20050987.
125. Richard, "Herding Cats," *Altman Weil Report to Legal Management*, 1–12.
126. Rumination "is the mental process of thinking over and over about something, which happened either in the past or could happen in the future, and attaching negative emotion to it." Nick Petrie, "Wake Up! The Surprising Truth About What Drives Stress and How Leaders Build Resilience," *Center for Creative Leadership*, August, 2013, last accessed October 16, 2013, http://www.ccl.org/leadership/pdf/research/WakeUp.pdf, 5. "Rumination" comes from the term used to describe how cows chew on their cud, swallow, regurgitate, then repeat that cycle with the same cud six more times.
127. D.K. Thomsen et al., "Negative Thoughts and Health: Associations Among Rumination, Immunity, and Health Care Utilization in a Young and Elderly Sample," *Psychosomatic Medicine*, 66 (2004): 363–71.
128. Petrie, "Wake Up! The Surprising Truth About What Drives Stress and How Leaders Build Resilience," *Center for Creative Leadership*, 7.
129. Ibid., 8.
130. Richard, "We Need a Chief Resilience Officer," *Lawyer Brain Blog*. For further information on typical lawyer attributes, see the statistics in endnote 106 of Chapter 3.
131. David, "Recovering from an Emotional Outburst at Work," *Harvard Business Review*.

Chapter Three

The Business Case for Emotionally Intelligent Lawyers: Four Advantages Emotional Intelligence Brings to Your Practice

An attorney can master a particular area of law and know it inside-out, but practicing lawyers are continually dealing with people. On a daily basis, attorneys must deal with clients, paralegals, coworkers, support staff, adversaries, civil servants, judges, business development sources, family, and friends. With rare exception, the ability to manage those personal relationships determines how successful and satisfied an attorney will be.[1]

—Arnie Herz, speaker, mediator, lawyer, and professional blogger

Although we don't have much research relating to the emotional intelligence of lawyers specifically, we do have persuasive indications from EI assessments, research on other professional groups, and observations by lawyers themselves that emotional intelligence (EI) is a significant factor in a successful legal practice.

Those lawyers who score higher in emotional intelligence, as well as in other attributes that indicate EI, are more successful practitioners than their colleagues with lower EI. Researchers concluded from reviewing the assessments of 130 criminal and corporate practitioners and judges that those few who scored above average in emotional intelligence were "the star performers—stood out from the rest." They also found that among a small group of lawyers, high scores in five EI factors distinguished those attorneys who felt themselves to be successful at work from those who didn't.[2]

In several different groups of Canadian attorneys, those who were ranked as the highest performers also scored higher in emotional intelligence than their less outstanding peers. Of 150 Canadian lawyers, the 15 attorneys identified as the top performers had higher overall levels of EI than the rest.[3] Four other Canadian groups—(1) top corporate litigators, (2) top corporate dealmakers, (3) top women lawyers, and (4) top lawyers forty years old and younger—all had EI scores higher than less-distinguished lawyers in their categories and higher than the general population.[4]

In his early work, consultant Dr. Larry Richard identified personal characteristics of successful rainmakers and managing partners that included several attributes, such as higher empathy and resilience, correlated with emotional intelligence.[5] A limited study of the EI assessments of a small group of lawyers listed in "The Best Lawyers in America" (as judged by their peers) found that these "excellent" lawyers were on a higher EI plane than their colleagues, on average scoring almost 20 percent higher.[6]

Observers of legal practitioners have long noted that those lawyers who are most successful exhibit attributes associated with emotional intelligence. Randall Kiser's survey of seventy-eight successful litigators, discussed in *How Leading Lawyers Think: Expert Insights into Judgment and Advocacy*, identified several traits of successful litigators that are critical to their success and that he considered to be indicative of EI, such as empathy, relationship-building skills, and self-management.[7]

Another way of determining what makes lawyers successful is to ask lawyers themselves. When asked over the last twenty years what attributes they believe to be important to the practice of law, lawyers have consistently listed nontraditional skills that imply emotional intelligence, such as self-knowledge, self-awareness, self-management, and certain interpersonal skills like attentive listening and strong verbal and nonverbal communication.[8]

The most extensive study using that methodology to delve into the personal attributes that make for successful attorneys was completed in 2011 by Law Professor Marjorie Shultz and Psychology Professor Sheldon Zedeck of the University of California at Berkeley. They used a multistep assessment process over six years with the aim of recommending to law schools how to shape curriculum for skills necessary for effective lawyering. From interviews with alumni, clients, faculty, students, and judges associated with Berkeley Law School, they developed a "job analysis" consisting of twenty-six "Effectiveness Factors" of successful practitioners. Skills such as empathy, relationship building, and listening were included with the more traditional analysis and reasoning, problem-solving, and research abilities. They then gathered more than 800 specific examples of attorney behaviors "to represent poor, below average, average, good, and outstanding behaviors across the 26 factors."[9]

Using that data, the authors administered attorney effectiveness questionnaires to 1,148 alumni of Berkeley Law and Hastings College of the Law and asked them, their supervisors, and peers to rate the participants on the Effectiveness Factors. Finally, traditional benchmarks, like LSAT scores, undergraduate grade point average (UGPA), and first-year law school grades, were correlated with the ratings on those factors.

The conclusion of Shultz and Zedeck's study was that "other elements of intelligence—traditionally labeled 'noncognitive' predictors but often referred to as 'nonscholastic or nonacademic'" are also valid predictors of performance for lawyers. In fact, the authors found that noncognitive constructs (including personality, dispositional optimism, self-monitoring, and emotional recognition) "correlated at a higher level of significance with lawyer performance factors than did LSAT, UGPA, or Index [combinations of those factors]," which form the bases of most law school admissions.[10]

The most striking insight from the Shultz/Zedeck study is that applicants chosen for their ability to excel at those few cognitive skills that law schools teach and measure are "unlikely to exhibit

[the] strong emotional development" that the researchers found necessary to practice law well.[11]

Even the youngest lawyers have been found to benefit from emotional intelligence in their practices. The Center for the Study of the Legal Profession at Georgetown Law School identified three behavioral competencies "especially critical in predicting performance" in successful Am Law 100 associates, which "capture a specific set of interpersonal skills not captured in technical or individual work competencies." These interpersonal competencies produce strong performance in three areas: (1) associates' work mindset and philosophy, including emotional health, motivation, and drive; (2) managing individual work tasks and the work environment; and (3) working and collaborating with others, including "interpersonal abilities and influence."[12]

These high performers were able to maintain "equanimity," that is, rise above pressure and anxiety, to persist in the face of challenges, "to acknowledge and accept their own strengths, weaknesses, boundaries, preferences and sphere of control," and to deal well with "unforeseen demands or setbacks."[13]

They were also found to build and use social networks, developing professional relationships as resources for the future. "[High-performers] are aware of what others can do for them, as well as what effect they might have on others . . . [They] use their interpersonal understanding of others to influence and impact them, rather than using generic tactics." They deal with conflict directly, "while still maintaining a positive impression with others." Importantly, they also maintain some "emotional independence," not becoming "overly involved in colleagues' feelings and intimate emotions." The study concluded that, "A key part of being a high-performing attorney may [be] the ability to accept and work through personal concerns, apprehensions or fears."[14]

These descriptions of successful associates read like a playlist for the virtues of EI. High EI associates recognize and appropriately cope with the emotional aspects of practicing law—managing their own stress with resilience and addressing conflict while maintaining productive interpersonal relations.

So exactly how does emotional intelligence make us better lawyers? Discussed below are the following four advantages emotional intelligence brings to our success in practicing law:

1. *Emotionally Intelligent Lawyers Are Smarter*
2. *Emotionally Intelligent Lawyers Are Stronger Practitioners: Negotiators, Case Managers, Litigators, and Judges*
3. *Emotionally Intelligent Lawyers Make More Money*
4. *Emotionally Intelligent Lawyers Are Healthier and Happier*

Thereafter, these advantages of individual lawyers with emotional intelligence culminate in Chapter 4's *Four Ways Emotional Intelligence Builds More Successful Law Firms and Law Departments.* To raise a firm's or department's EI, Chapter 5 discusses *Four Steps to Achieving an Emotionally Intelligent Workplace.*

In Chapter 6, you can find out your own personal EI level in *What's My Emotional Intelligence?* and then leverage that level up by following the advice in Chapter 7's *How Do I Raise My Emotional Intelligence?*

Let's start with the four major advantages emotional intelligence brings to your personal practice.

Advantage 1: Emotionally Intelligent Lawyers Are Smarter

Stupidity is not a lack of intelligence, it is a lack of feeling.[15]

—Robert Musil, Austrian novelist

How does emotional intelligence make us smarter lawyers?

IQ (Intelligence Quotient) has long been the accepted measure in the United States of "smart." The sufficiency of IQ as a predictive tool of success, however, has long been disputed. One of the enduring conundrums is that people with average IQs outperform those with the highest IQs 70 percent of the time.[16] David Wechsler himself, who developed the Wechsler Adult Intelligence Scale, the most widely used IQ test, firmly believed that there were "non-intellective" factors that influenced "intelligent behavior," and that, even though he knew of no way to measure them accurately, these factors should be considered when assessing intelligence.[17]

Lawyers on average enjoy a high IQ, usually cited as one to two standards of deviation (i.e., 15 to 30 points) above the average 100. If a high IQ is all we need to be a successful lawyer, then why do so many smart lawyers fail? The resounding answer has been a lack of emotional intelligence.[18]

Evidence of how much "smarter" the emotionally intelligent are has been amassed in extensive research.[19] A meta-analysis reviewing hundreds of studies found greater EI correlated with higher achievement "in domains such as academic performance, job performance, negotiation, leadership, emotional labor, trust, work-family conflict, and stress," and concluded that EI was the factor that "predict[s] job performance over and above cognitive intelligence and [personality]."[20] High EI has been found to make us even smarter than experience in our field.[21]

High emotional intelligence makes us smarter lawyers for two reasons:

1. EI gives the cognitive brain access to emotional data valuable to our practices.
2. EI helps manage the flood of emotions that can undercut optimal cognition.

First, recognizing emotional cues in ourselves and others provides us with information that can be critical to fully understanding the complexities of a situation, such as a job interview, a negotiation, a partner's complaint, or a witness's testimony. Those emotional cues may also be available to us sooner than our rational thoughts, helping us reach the correct conclusion more quickly.

A famous study called the Iowa Gambling Task, conducted by the neuroscientist Antonio Damásio, illustrates the advantage of being aware of our own emotional cues. Participants were presented with four virtual decks of cards on a computer screen. Each time they chose a card they would either win or lose money, with the goal being to win as much as possible in the shortest time. The decks differed in their rates of wins and losses, so that over time some decks were "losing decks" and others were "winning decks."

Most participants identified the winning decks after about forty or fifty selections. However, measurements of galvanic skin response made during the experiment showed that after only ten selections, long before they were cognitively aware whether decks were winning or losing, participants registered a physical "stress" reaction when approaching the losing decks. In other words, their emotions were accurately signaling the losing decks well before their cognitive brains could. Not only were these "gut feelings" accurate, but they were accurate very early on, giving participants who were attuned to their own emotional cues a significant advantage.[22]

Second, being able to manage our own or others' emotional noise can improve the speed and clarity of our cognitive thinking.[23] We have probably all had the experience of finding it difficult to solve a perplexing problem right before, during, or after a strongly emotional interchange with our colleague, spouse, or child. But we don't always recognize the extent to which unbridled emotion is undercutting our cognitive abilities.

In my practice, I have repeatedly seen the deleterious effects of unmanaged emotions on lawyers' performance. In one case, a middle-aged lawyer was exhibiting what some of his partners feared was early onset Alzheimer's. A trusts and estates lawyer, his work seemed to continue to be satisfactory, but those who worked with him noticed he was taking a very long time to reach conclusions, often repeatedly reviewing his work, and was relying heavily on associates' input. A neurological assessment did in fact show significant impairment in memory and processing speed. The lawyer seemed as mystified as others by this development, but he remained confident that he could continue to give good legal advice. His wife then confided that a year earlier she had been diagnosed with cancer and given an uncertain prognosis, a frightening situation for their family, which included three young children.

This is a dramatic example of cognitive impairment caused by emotional stress, and perhaps it seems obvious that this highly charged emotional situation would impact the trusts and estates lawyer's ability to think clearly. Yet he had not spoken of it to the firm and wasn't conscious of it as a possible cause of his memory lapses and fogginess. Nor, evidently, could he manage those unrecognized emotions sufficiently so as not to compromise his competence. He was simply soldiering on. Happily, after learning coping skills, he returned to his work fully functional.

Even strong positive emotions that are unmanaged can undercut cognitive functioning. Admittedly, I don't often find that to be an issue for attorneys, but I did counsel a senior associate because of a sudden dip in performance at a critical juncture in a case. He came to realize that his "distraction" was largely elation over his girlfriend unexpectedly saying "Yes" to his proposal to marry. Through coaching, he learned how to contain his positive emotional overload so as to be able to continue to focus fully on his demanding cognitive tasks.

It is not that IQ doesn't matter. Daniel Goleman acknowledges the role of IQ in many professions, but reiterates the value that EI adds: "It typically takes an IQ about 115 or above to be able to handle the cognitive complexity facing an accountant, a physician or a top executive. But here's the paradox: once you're in a high-IQ position, intellect loses its power to determine who will emerge as a productive employee or an effective leader. For that, how you handle yourself and your relationships—in other words, the emotional intelligence skill set—matters more than your IQ. In a high-IQ job pool, soft skills like discipline, drive and empathy mark those who emerge as outstanding."[24]

As consultant Dr. Larry Richard has written: "Being an *intellectually* smart lawyer is the mere table stakes to get into the game of BigLaw. To succeed on a sustained basis, today's lawyer needs to develop EI skills."[25]

The evidence for emotional intelligence making us smarter is documented, among other places, in the research on how:

Emotionally Intelligent Lawyers Make Better Decisions
The Emotionally Intelligent Are "Smartest" Over a Lifetime
Even Smart Artificial Intelligence Requires Emotional Intelligence

Emotionally Intelligent Lawyers Make Better Decisions

> *A full 70% of male leaders who rank in the top 15% in decision-making skills also score the highest in emotional intelligence skills. In contrast, not one single male leader with low E[motional] Q[uotients] was among the most skilled decision makers.*[26]
>
> —Travis Bradberry, author and emotional intelligence expert, and Dr. Jean Greaves, author and CEO of TalentSmart

While we pride ourselves on our intellectual acumen, many of our decisions, especially those involving complex factors, are not simply rational. Brain scans have emphatically demonstrated that decisions are often prompted by emotions—emotions that we may or may not recognize.[27] Further, as Damásio and others have found, weighing emotions inextricably woven into our thoughts and experiences over the years allows us to make decisions that are better than ones reached through sheer cognitive analysis. Re-experiencing, whether consciously or subconsciously, the emotional states associated with prior decisions helps us more accurately evaluate current choices.[28]

Confirmation and expansion of Damásio's and others' conclusions has come from Dr. Daniel Kahneman, an Israeli psychologist and professor at Princeton whose work in the emerging field of behavioral economics won him the Nobel Prize in Economics in 2002. His 2011 *New York Times* bestseller *Thinking, Fast and Slow* views decision making as a constant, if often unrecognized, interplay between cognitive analysis and the processing of emotional information.[29]

To illustrate this point, Dr. Kahneman describes the brain as composed of two systems: System 1 is the "emotional" part of the brain that is extremely fast and intuitive and is particularly important in skill acquisition and in making certain types of judgments and decisions. System 2 is the more logical side of the brain that works more slowly than System 1 and is responsible for completing cognitive tasks, such as computation and logical thought, and also for self-awareness and self-control. These two systems are not, in fact, truly divided, but are part of a single interrelated process, with System 1 quickly accessing stored responses and generating complex patterns of ideas, while the slower System 2 constructs thoughts and analyzes in an ordered series of steps the assumptions and responses of System 1. But System 1 is more powerful and typically dominates when the two are at odds.[30]

To return to Damasio's Gambling Task experiment, System 1 could be said to quickly sense which decks are the "losing" decks in the Gambling Task, but participants can only become consciously aware of that fact through the slower interpretive and analytic work of System 2. Emotional intelligence indicates a System 2 that is consciously sensitive to and responsive to System 1 data.

Emotional intelligence improves every aspect of decision making. For starters, EI helps us assemble the best participants for making a decision: being aware of our own and others' emotional biases and emotional management skills gives us clues as to who will work well together and best move the process forward. The ability to recognize and regulate emotions that may arise during the decision-making process reduces results tainted by extraneous or damaging emotions like jealousy or fear or pride.[31] Putting those emotions aside frees up our cognitive resources so we can be more creative in our problem solving: "When you unhook yourself from your difficult thoughts and emotions, you expand your choices."[32] Emotional intelligence empowers people to work well together as teams and to resolve interpersonal conflicts. It also improves the ultimate decision by expanding participants' information-gathering abilities and increasing their motivation and perseverance during the decision-making process.[33]

Emotional intelligence comes into play again when explaining and implementing a decision. No strategic plan or change management decision can succeed, as any executive committee knows, if the emotional responses that it is likely to generate aren't considered and appropriately handled.

In sum, making the best decisions in the most efficient manner involves being able to accurately assess the various emotional aspects involved, remediate or at least factor in the possible effects that unproductive emotions may have on the decision-making process and on the decision itself, promote emotions that are productive, and manage the emotional responses of the various parties to, and of those affected by, the decision. As one researcher concluded, "it turns out that paying attention to your emotions is the most *logical* way to make good decisions."[34]

The Emotionally Intelligent Are "Smartest" Over a Lifetime

Longitudinal studies bear out the greater importance of EI over IQ in achieving success over an entire lifetime. In the 1950s, eighty Ph.D. candidates at the University of California at Berkeley "underwent a battery of personality tests, IQ tests, and interviews . . . Forty years later, when they were in their early seventies, the same people were tracked down and . . . [their success was evaluated] based on resumes, opinions of experts in their own fields," and recognition by professional groups. Social and emotional abilities were found to be four times more important than IQ in accounting for professional success.[35]

Even earlier, in 1938, 268 Harvard undergraduate students were chosen for what was anticipated to be a longitudinal study of the impact of IQ and body type on success. As George Vaillant, the current study director, sums up in his review of more than seventy years of research, *Triumphs of Experience: The Men of the Harvard Grant Study*, both of those factors were eventually discarded as irrelevant. Rather, "It was the capacity for intimate relationships that predicted flourishing in all aspects of these men's lives."[36] That capacity is a reflection of emotional intelligence.

Similar results were found in experiments involving less privileged populations. In a forty-year investigation of 450 boys who grew up in Somerville, Massachusetts, two-thirds of the boys were from welfare families, and one-third had IQ scores below ninety, or materially below average. Yet IQ was determined to have little relation to how well they did at work or in other areas of their lives. What researchers found to have made the biggest difference were abilities such as being able to handle frustration, manage emotions, and get along with other people, traits that are now recognized as attributes of EI.[37]

Even Smart Artificial Intelligence Requires Emotional Intelligence

In another testament to the importance of emotions in working smart, researchers at MIT's Artificial Intelligence Laboratory include emotions in their computerized platform for artificial intelligence, because they have found that, "intuition and emotions play crucial roles in the ability to make smart, rational decisions."[38]

Google also believes that reading and understanding feelings makes artificial intelligence more intelligent. At the 2012 Demo Conference in Silicon Valley, Ray Kurzweil, the technology director at Google, said that the most difficult challenge in its effort to develop computers that match the full range of human intelligence by the year 2029 is programming "emotional intelligence, being funny, getting the joke, being sexy, being loving, understanding human emotion. That's actually the most complex thing we do."[39]

EMOTIONALLY INTELLIGENT LAWYERS ARE SMARTER

Emotional intelligence helps us work smarter by:

- recognizing important emotional data, and
- effectively managing emotions that could undercut optimal cognition, thereby
- improving the decision-making process and the decisions themselves—assembling those who are most emotionally intelligent, recognizing and regulating inappropriate emotions, improving teamwork and conflict resolution, expanding information-gathering capabilities, freeing creative problem solving, increasing motivation and perseverance, and selling the decision to those it impacts, and
- maximizing lifetime likelihood of success.

The artificial intelligence scientific community recognizes that emotional intelligence is necessary to make artificial intelligence truly "smart."

Advantage 2: Emotionally Intelligent Lawyers Are Stronger Practitioners

The advantages of emotional intelligence translate into specific benefits for practitioners:

At the Negotiating Table
In the Courtroom (as case managers, litigators, or judges)

At the Negotiating Table

> *In a negotiation, particularly in a bitter dispute, feelings may be more important than talk.*[40]
>
> —William L. Ury, Roger Fisher, Bruce M. Patton, master negotiators and authors of *Getting to YES*

Emotions play a critical role in negotiation: conflict of any sort is riddled with emotion. Individual parties and organizational representatives on both sides bring their personal emotions to the negotiating table, and the negotiators themselves have emotional stakes in the outcome.[41]

During the high-stakes, protracted negotiations over Viacom International's ultimately successful 1993 takeover of Paramount Communications, investment banker Felix Rohatyn was quoted as saying, "most deals are 50% emotion and 50% economics."[42] Using emotional intelligence can give a negotiator an edge in navigating the half of negotiation challenges that are emotional.

In his article, "Further Beyond Reason: Emotions, the Core Concerns, and Mindfulness in Negotiation," Leonard Riskin acknowledges that negotiators may come to the table with no conscious awareness of their own emotions, or they may ignore their emotional reactions in order to avoid discomfort or feel overwhelmed. He especially bemoans lawyers' no-emotions approach: "Negotiators—especially those trained in law—[who] commonly address this problem by trying to exclude emotions from negotiation and to focus solely on so-called objective, rational factors, such as money."[43]

Anxiety is the most dominant emotion that experienced negotiators contend with in themselves, whether or not they recognize it: they are anxious about whether any agreement, let alone an acceptable one, can be reached, whether the other side is trustworthy or intentionally cutthroat, and whether their own abilities are sufficient to produce the best deal.[44]

If anxiety isn't properly recognized and then managed, it can make us defensive and therefore less effective. We may close down for fear of the other side exploiting our honesty; we may interpret innocent questions as manipulative ploys or threats; and our defensiveness may be read across the table as deception or hostility. Those reactions can prompt the other side to be defensive themselves, in turn escalating tensions over time.

What should be done with emotions that surface in negotiations? There is abundant advice in the business press. In *Getting to YES*, the authors suggest that the parties' emotions should be made explicit and acknowledged as legitimate. They also encourage letting the other side let off steam, but discourage reacting to emotional outbursts.[45]

Business lawyers often say they are hesitant to express goodwill or reach an emotional rapport with opposing counsel or parties for fear that their clients or others will consider them too "soft" to forge the best deal. Authors Daniel Shapiro and Roger Fisher in *Beyond Reason: Using Emotions as You Negotiate* think expressing negative emotions impedes the process of negotiation, while expressing positive emotions fosters it; they advocate making the other side feel appreciated and affiliated to help build a cooperative relationship that is more likely to resolve the substantives issues.[46]

A study analyzing relative power positions in a negotiation has refined the cost/benefit of displays of anger: high-power negotiators may benefit from such a display, whether it is appropriate or not, as an intimidation, but low-power negotiators usually do not. At best, their high-power counterparts may ignore the anger if they think it is appropriate; at worst, they may retaliate by increasing their demands if they deem the anger inappropriate.[47]

One study found it's better to start a short-term negotiation in a good mood and then get angrier, rather than start out tough and then soften up. Those starting out more pleasant were able to realize all of the monetary benefits of an angry negotiating style but also keep their negotiating partner from disliking them so much so as to retaliate on terms, in part because the initial happy mood was contagious.[48]

The components of EI each bring specific advantages to negotiators. Those who score high in perceiving emotions have been found more likely to successfully analyze the issue to be negotiated.[49] Higher levels of emotional perception on the part of sellers have been linked to an increase in the amount of money gained overall and are marginally related to the proportion of money the seller individually receives.[50]

High scores in understanding emotions correlate with the negotiation opponent not only feeling positively about the negotiation outcome, irrespective of the financial terms, but also liking the other negotiator and preferring to negotiate with him or her in the future.[51]

The ability to regulate emotions helps negotiators realize the attractiveness of an offer by being able to consciously eliminate the distracting emotions that aren't relevant or are counterproductive. In an interesting experiment, participants could share $1 to $20 with a second player, but only if both subjects agreed on the amount. When offered small amounts, the second subject often became so annoyed at the other player that he or she refused the offer, even though he or she lost whatever little amount the other player might give. A functional brain magnetic resonance image during these negotiations showed that both the emotional center, the amygdala, and the neocortex (the thinking brain) were activated. The scenario provoked an internal negotiation: Take the money and run? Or punish the stingy bastard by refusing to accept his or her offer? Those participants with high emotional regulation scores could choose to take the money in spite of their annoyance at how small the amount was.[52]

Mediation requires similar skills as negotiation, but with less emphasis on advocacy and more on consensus building. As in other types of negotiation, reading, understanding, and regulating emotions is critical to achieving agreement, and empathy that taps into others' perspectives plays an important role in reaching consensus. Yet once again emotion is often not given appropriate consideration by mediators.[53] "Conflict-resolution training, by and large, teaches us to mediate 'from the neck up.' The topic of emotions is dealt with superficially, if at all," as one mediation professor puts it.[54]

EMOTIONAL INTELLIGENCE BUILDS BETTER NEGOTIATORS
• More successful analysis of the issues • More insightful evaluation of offers • Better financial outcomes • Greater satisfaction with the results regardless of the financial outcome • Improved relationships with opposing negotiators

In the Courtroom

> *When lawyers lack self-awareness and emotional intelligence, they unwittingly overlook key factors in case evaluation, mismanage pretrial preparation and fail to achieve optimal trial results.*[55]
>
> —Randall Kiser, author of *How Leading Lawyers Think* and *Beyond Right and Wrong*, and principle analyst at DecisionSet®

With respect to matters headed for the courtroom, all of the legal personnel involved can benefit from emotional intelligence, including case managers, litigators, and judges.

Case Managers

Lawyers have surprisingly poor track records in choosing case strategies and predicting case outcomes. Emotional intelligence can improve our abilities in this area.

In *Beyond Right and Wrong: The Power of Effective Decision Making for Attorneys and Clients*, Randall Kiser evaluated litigators' ability to accurately assess upcoming cases and discovered that decisions to go to trial were often misguided. An extensive analysis of 11,306 decisions in actual litigation matters found that in 61 percent of cases settlement offers that had been refused were more lucrative for plaintiffs than what they ended up getting at trial.[56]

Factors like the extent of the lawyer's experience, rank of the lawyer's law school, and size of the law firm did not improve the soundness of advice about whether to settle or go to trial. In fact, over the forty years that Kiser reviewed, the ratio of poor case evaluation increased.[57]

Another survey reached a similar conclusion: lawyers are often overconfident, men more so than women, in predicting the outcome of both civil and criminal cases. As set forth in "Insightful or Wishful: Lawyers' Ability to Predict Case Outcomes," 481 lawyers representing plaintiffs and defendants expecting to go to trial within a year were asked their "win situation in terms of your minimum goal" and then how confident they were on a scale of 0 to 100 of achieving that goal.[58]

Following up after the trials, the researchers determined that 32 percent of lawyers met their goals, 24 percent exceeded their goals, and 44 percent were not as successful as they had predicted. Surprisingly, those lawyers who were the most confident were also the most likely to fail to reach their goal. Again, the accuracy of lawyers' predictions was found not to be enhanced by length of litigation experience.[59] The fact that almost half these lawyers were not able to meet the minimum goal that they themselves set, despite high levels of confidence and often many years of experience, amounts to glaring misjudgment, as well as a disservice to clients.

A striking collection of studies demonstrates that being able to recognize emotional cues makes us better at predicting outcomes of all kinds. Dubbed "the emotional oracle effect," high EI has been shown to enhance our predictive abilities in such widely diverse contests as presidential elections, the box-office success of movies, the winners of American Idol, movements of the Dow Jones Index, college football championship games, and even the weather.[60]

How does emotional intelligence increase our accuracy in making predictions? According to the lead researcher studying the phenomenon: "[W]hat feels 'right' or 'wrong' summarizes all the knowledge and information that we have acquired consciously and unconsciously about the world around us . . . In a sense, our feelings give us access to a privileged window of knowledge and information—a window that a more analytical form of reasoning blocks us from."[61]

It is difficult to determine where the breakdown in our forecasting of cases is occurring—are lawyers really not able to accurately assess the likely results of trial even after years of experience, are they unable to acknowledge to themselves or to their clients the true odds, or are they unable to convince their clients of the preferred course?

All of these aspects of case management would benefit from higher EI: being able to access the "gut feelings" that years of experience have built, having the emotional resources to honestly face the odds of success/failure, and being able to communicate persuasively with clients, which often requires an emotional rapport.

A personal trait contributing to this case-analysis deficit may be lawyers' low resilience, which makes them less able than most people to recover emotionally from setbacks, such as a loss at trial.[62] The fear of having to deal with a setback may encourage lawyers to give a more optimistic forecast than is realistic—one that the client is happy to hear and the lawyer is personally more comfortable contemplating.

Case analysis may also be shaped consciously or unconsciously by feelings about financial matters. Lawyers with contingency fee arrangements may be incentivized to try for a higher court award than the settlement offer, there may be a higher percentage fee for awards won in court, or cases that go to trial may simply allow lawyers to bill more hours. These factors may be more or less conscious and carry more or less weight depending on the individual lawyer's emotional connections with money and prestige and his or her awareness of those emotions.[63]

Research on doctors may provide another clue to emotion's role in prediction. When Harvard researcher Nicholas Cristakis asked doctors how long their terminally ill patients would survive, the better the doctors knew their patient, the more likely they were to overestimate survival by a large margin.[64] A similar distortion in legal case analysis may occur when the lawyer has a strong emotional attachment to a client, which the lawyer may not even be unaware of. That attachment may elevate the stakes of a disappointing failure even higher.

As one of the lawyers interviewed by Kiser said: "[C]ase evaluation. It's a people skill. If you don't have a feel for people you won't make it . . . This has so many facets it's like a symphony."[65]

Law schools do not teach how to handicap trials, nor do they help develop the important skills of accounting for one's own emotional biases, for example, or telling a client that a case is not a winner, a message that requires both judgment and diplomacy.[66] And evidently years of trial experience isn't sufficient to give lawyers much advantage in these areas either. So lawyers evaluating cases are left to rely on whatever emotional intelligence they have. Thankfully, that can be increased and along with it the accuracy of a lawyer's case analysis.

EMOTIONALLY INTELLIGENT LAWYERS MAKE BETTER CASE MANAGERS

- Emotional intelligence, more than education or length of experience, allows lawyers to make better case predictions by being able to access "gut" emotional data relating to past cases and by recognizing and managing all the emotional factors that impact case management.
- An emotionally intelligent lawyer can recognize and manage his or her own emotional biases, like pride, fear of failure, feelings about money, competition, approval and prestige, and his or her personal attachment to the client, as well as the client's anger, fears, and doubts and the opposing parties' and counsels' emotional demands, all without impairing effective case management.

Litigators

The role of a litigator these days is not simply to shout loudest, but to use one's emotional intelligence and intuition to deliver the results a client is seeking.[67]

—Sonita Hayward, solicitor and business director at British firm Bolt Burden Kemp

Trial attorneys can be challenged by the emotional currents that an environment of confrontation, ambition, and personal risk presents to all litigation participants. Accurately perceiving and understanding the emotions at play, and then regulating their own and others' emotions appropriately gives litigators a tremendous advantage. This is particularly true when we know that counsel on the other side is likely not to have the benefit of high EI.

To start with, clearly understanding the client's objectives sets the stage for a successful litigation approach. An insurer may wish to avoid setting a precedent, or the parties' disagreements may relate primarily to damages, or preservation of the business relationship may be the primary goal. In each case an "all-guns-blazing" approach would be unsuitable and even counterproductive. The successful litigator will effectively discern from emotional cues not only the spoken objectives but also the unspoken ones.

As one litigator opined, "A litigator can use their emotional intelligence to read between the lines and . . . help to shape and inform their client's views and manage expectations. Regulating one's own emotions is also a very valuable skill . . . Equally important is having the ability to take a step back and look objectively at your own client's case, to counter-act any own client bias that you may develop."[68]

EI skills are also valuable in evaluating and influencing witnesses, honing the roles of supporting lawyers and staff, and building a persuasive presentation to a judge or jury. During both preparation and trial, knowing the difference between emotional tactics that produce reliable results and those that result in undesirable emotional reactions too difficult to manage is an important tool.[69]

Litigators then have to assess and respond to the emotions in the courtroom. Randall Kiser studied seventy-eight leading litigators who were selected from 8,114 attorneys in New York and California and who had extensive trial experience and superior performance in predicting case outcomes. These superior litigators testified to the importance of emotions in the courtroom—the emotions of lawyers, clients, witnesses, and judges, with their comments reading like a playbill for the benefits of having emotional intelligence.

They attribute errors in the courtroom to failing to take into account emotional components of the case (saying "the soft stuff is important")—being book smart, but not people smart,[70] or being either overemotional or too detached from emotions, including the jurors' emotions ("Juries are primarily emotional").[71] These lawyers say they "listen to my gut . . . It's better than my analytical ability," and found success by knowing themselves, their emotions, and how to "stop that emotional train."[72] So they advocate going with your heart and "feeling the emotion of the case . . . Letting oneself feel the emotion, without being overcome by it."[73]

One author examines in detail aspects of three highly publicized cases that demonstrate the importance of EI, or lack thereof, in the courtroom: the O.J. Simpson trial, a case from the Vioxx pharmaceutical litigation, and the Triangle Shirtwaist disaster case. In both the Simpson and Vioxx cases, "non-empathetic" litigators made poor decisions "as a result of their failure to calibrate their trial strategies to the actual, as opposed to logical, responses of the non-lawyer juries."[74] The author contends that the prosecution's strategy in Simpson failed to take into account the emotional orientation of the jury regarding race relations in the city. The defense in Vioxx presented an "object lesson in a familiar logical, non-empathetic, and failed, strategy—that a dry emphasis on the failure of the plaintiff's case to establish causation, a necessary but technical element in tort liability, would be a sufficient defense to a highly emotional case."[75] On the other hand, in the Triangle Shirtwaist trial, "Max Steuer, counsel for the defendants . . . gives us a flawless example of situational, or tactical, empathy, both in his immediate understanding of the possible advantages offered to his case by the prosecution's star witness and in his sensitive handling of the witness to achieve the best result for his clients."[76]

One of the subscores of Emotional Perception on the Mayer-Salovey-Caruso-Emotional Intelligence Test (MSCEIT) relates directly to a person's ability to "read a room" emotionally. That score identifies strengths and weaknesses in accurately assessing the emotional tone of an audience in the case of speakers and professors, or of a judge and jury in the case of litigators.

Litigation lawyers place great emphasis on their analytic legal skills, but regardless of how expertly a case is presented, verdicts are often influenced by individual personality attributes, ways of organizing and processing information, and group dynamics. And research clearly shows, not unsurprisingly, that juries, like people in other arenas, are often more influenced by their emotions than by the clear instruction of the law.[77]

Randall Kiser concludes from his study of leading litigators: "it is a perpetual challenge to exploit the benefits of emotional commitment and enthusiasm while avoiding the damage of emotional biases and extremism. What seems to distinguish the study attorneys from some of their colleagues is not that they avoid this conundrum altogether but that they are thinking about it regularly."[78] These are hallmarks of emotional intelligence: being emotionally aware and actively engaged in reading and regulating emotions.

EMOTIONALLY INTELLIGENT LAWYERS MAKE BETTER LITIGATORS

- Employing the emotional intelligence skills of accurate emotional perception, emotional empathy, emotional understanding, and emotional regulation gives litigators a decided advantage over those less skilled when approaching, preparing, and presenting cases in typically emotionally charged, confrontational situations.
- Emotionally intelligent litigators who can read and manage their own emotions, their clients'/witnesses'/staff's emotions, and those of opposing parties and counsel can fashion an emotionally compelling story for the judge or jury.

Judges

The righteously angry judge is aware of both the benefits and dangers of anger, and seeks to maximize the former and minimize the latter.[79]

—Terry A. Maroney, Professor of Law,
Vanderbilt University Law School

Judges are regularly exposed to highly charged situations that involve confrontation, and they are also held to a high standard of conduct. Working under intense public scrutiny, for high stakes, and in relative isolation has emotional fallout for judges that, among other things, challenges them to make good decisions. The rising incidence of depression and suicide among judges testifies to the emotional strain inherent in their position.[80]

As is true for litigators, a judge's emotional incompetence can cost a litigant his or her case. For example, the plaintiff's lawyer in a medical malpractice case appealed the judge's decision against him on the basis of the judge's tendency to "interrupt, patronize, and admonish" him for his "emotional tantrums." The appellate panel vacated the decision, citing the judge's "excessive intervention" and the "cumulative effect" of her "improper conduct": "Our review of the record convinces us that the repeated conflict between the court and the plaintiff's counsel, at all phases of the trial—and often times in the presence of the jury—unnecessarily injected personality issues into the case, which militated against a fair trial."[81]

Sonia Sotomayor, who has reached the pinnacle of our legal system as a US Supreme Court Justice, has this to say about judicial emotions during trial: "You can't be emotionless. No one can . . . You can't be a judge if you try to be a robot. Because then you're not going to be able to look at both sides, and hear both sides. At the same time, if you're being ruled by emotion, then you're not being fair and impartial. So what do you do with your emotions? My feeling is that you have to be aware. You have to be aware that you might be angry with a defendant and then acknowledge and deal with that anger as a person—and consciously set it aside."[82]

While there are limited data on judges' level of overall emotional intelligence and its components, there are a few studies that give us some insight into how emotional intelligence can support a judge's optimal performance.

In a study published in the *Proceedings of the National Academy of Sciences,* researchers measured the effect on judicial decision making of efforts by eight parole judges in Israel to suppress their emotions. These judges approved on average 35 percent of cases requesting parole at a clip of six minutes per case during their day, which included three food breaks. But, "[t]he proportion [of approved cases] spikes after each meal, when about 65% of requests are granted," while during the two-hour period before a food break, "the approval rate drops steadily, to just about zero before the meal."[83] The judges' (perhaps unconscious) efforts to suppress feelings of hunger and fatigue appear to negatively impact their fairness in their hearings. Lawyers' generally low levels of resilience may well have contributed to the judges being unable to overcome the effects of physical and emotional depletion.[84]

Anger is evidently one of the more common emotions that judges experience in their work. Judges are more likely to express anger than other emotions in part because anger may be the least stigmatizing and may even increase their status because of its association with power. Further, "At sentencing, judges may perceive that it is part of their role to express anger—not just on their own behalf, but on behalf of the victims and the public."[85]

Anger has some advantages—it helps give the energy to engage in confrontation, which can be a large part of a judge's work, and a sense of empowerment. Anger has also been found to "facilitate judgment" by "narrowing and focusing attention."[86]

At the same time, anger poses some dangers to a judge's ability to make sound judgments. Angry people tend to revert to stereotypes in making judgments. Anger is also self-reinforcing: angry people tend to be more receptive to angry arguments, as well as to arguments that confirm their initial assessment of a situation. So they may reach a decision prematurely, or make an overly punitive decision.

Judges may also bring to the courtroom emotions and moods that, if they are not astute in reading, understanding, and managing, may inappropriately influence their decisions. For example, we tend to hear and remember facts consistent with our mood—positive facts when we are feeling positive and negative facts when we are feeling negative.[87] In mock-jury studies, researchers found that "experimentally induced, irrelevant anger" was correlated with "more punitive judgments of tort defendants, as well as with greater levels of punishment."[88] Similarly, teachers in a positive mood gave the same paper one to two grades higher than they did when they were in a negative mood. Perhaps most striking was that 85 percent of the teachers said that their mood had no impact on their judgment, a colossally high level of lack of awareness.[89]

Judges are lawyers, after all, and are subject to the same negativity that lawyers often experience, but according to one study, "temporary, mild negative feelings have important benefits" that lawyers, and specifically judges, might take advantage of. During short-term bouts of negativity, people were more skeptical, less gullible or incorrectly inferring causation, more likely to pay attention to and remember details, more able to detect deception, more persevering on difficult cognitive tasks, more concerned with fairness, and able to make higher-quality and more persuasive arguments.[90]

The author of the study notes that these are not benefits of being in a prolonged depression but are ones that a good manager of emotions might make use of on a short-term basis for a specific reason. Being steeped in negativity not only impairs judgment but also exposes judges to the pernicious health effects of long-term exposure to stress hormones and produces poor performance from those around them. It may also underlie increasing incidences of depression and suicide in judges.[91] Having the emotional intelligence to regulate their emotions, including being able to temporarily enter into a slightly negative mindset and then recover, would allow judges to selectively experience the emotion that would best serve justice and themselves.

EMOTIONAL INTELLIGENCE IMPROVES JUDGES' FAIRNESS AND HEALTH

Emotional intelligence improves judicial judgment, fairness, health, and well-being by giving judges the skills to be aware of, understand, and regulate their own emotions (such as anger and feelings of isolation), as well as the emotions present in a highly confrontational environment.

Advantage 3: The Bottom Line: Emotionally Intelligent Lawyers Make More Money

> *[P]eople with high EQ make more money . . . The link between EQ and earnings is so direct that every point increase adds $1,300 to an annual salary . . . We haven't yet been able to find a job in which performance and pay aren't tied closely to EQ.*[92]
>
> —Travis Bradberry, author and emotional intelligence expert, and Dr. Jean Greaves, author and CEO of TalentSmart

For most lawyers, talk about emotional intelligence is likely to fall on deaf ears unless the advantages drop to the bottom line. They do: there are demonstrable correlations between EI and financial gain that hold across industries. Those who are best able to manage their emotions and emotional behavior, for example, are also those with the highest disposable income and highest socioeconomic status.[93]

Income is likely correlated with EI because in a broad range of US industries, higher EI correlates with significantly higher productivity. The emotionally intelligent have higher performing accounts, departments, and divisions; perform better militarily; sell more products and services; and even make more touchdowns than their lower-EI colleagues.[94] The performance premiums attributed to high emotional intelligence range from 15 percent to over 100 percent.[95] EI scores even predict who in organizations will get merit salary increases and promotions.[96]

The studies examining this correlation in professionals whose performance standards relate most closely to legal practices, particularly to partners who are compensated on volume of revenue, are those of consultants, accountants, and salespeople.

Consultants. A multinational consulting firm that measured the EI of senior partners found that partners high in EI were each generating an average of $1.2 million, or 139 percent, more in profit than their low EI partners.[97]

Accountants. In a large, multinational professional services firm with over 65,000 accountants, senior managers who had been with the firm an average of nineteen years and a partner an average of ten years were drawn from both those recognized as exceptional, and those who were not. The correlation between their annual revenue and profit performance and their EI scores was striking: "93% (i.e., 13/14ths) of the competencies predicting [financial] performance were from the emotional intelligence clusters."[98] Further, those high in EI competencies produced profits almost five times greater than those low in those competencies, compared to an increase of only 50 percent for those with high cognitive competencies.

Sales. Insurance agents who scored high on at least five of eight emotional competencies sold twice as much in policy premiums as agents who scored lower; sales staff with higher EI in a greeting card company produced 25 percent more sales than their low EI counterparts; and Coca-Cola division leaders with EI competencies outperformed their sales targets by 15–20 percent, while division leaders who didn't have those competencies missed targets by approximately the same margin.[99]

These highly persuasive data indicate that emotionally intelligent lawyers are also likely to perform at significantly higher levels than their lower EI colleagues, making them materially more financially successful. Heidi Gardner, Distinguished Fellow at Harvard Law School's Center on the Legal Profession, a Lecturer in Law, and Faculty Chair of its Accelerated Leadership Program, agrees, concluding in her extensive review of law partners that personal revenue is greatly increased by those lawyers who master collaboration, a skill dependent on emotional intelligence: "Partners who collaborate realize the benefit of generating more sophisticated, innovative and lucrative work."[100]

For those lawyers who question how such "soft skills" can bring in more money, the following discusses how emotionally intelligent lawyers make more money because:

Emotionally Intelligent Lawyers Get and Keep More Clients
Emotionally Intelligent Communication Cements Client Relationships
Emotionally Intelligent Client Service Reaps Revenues

Emotionally Intelligent Lawyers Get and Keep More Clients

The purpose of business is to create and keep a customer.[101]

—Peter Drucker

Among lawyers, making money starts and often ends with getting and keeping clients. Many lawyers mistakenly believe that both depend entirely on their legal expertise.

A firm asked that I work with their well-known antitrust partner on client service skills. The results of several assessments pointed to the same personality profile I encountered in person. The gentleman was confident, aggressive, independent, and a perfectionist. He talked at me more than with me. He resented having a non-antitrust litigator try to "help" him with something he didn't need help with. As he pointed out several times to me, he was one of the "winningest" antitrust litigators in the country. That should be sufficient for any client.

Perhaps the most difficult discussion we had was about emotional intelligence. This litigator had scored poorly on the assessment, unlike his SAT, LSAT, and other assessments, and he was quite disdainful of the measure's validity or usefulness. What on earth could such squishy topics tell him about being a better antitrust litigator?

The problem was that this lawyer's well-respected firm was losing cases to other antitrust litigators because of the reputation their star had gained as being unpleasant to work with. Few new clients were asking for him. No past client wanted to work with him again, and even other non-antitrust matters of his past clients seemed to be making their way to other firms. In addition, his conduct in the firm—his treatment of associates, open warfare with other partners, and unwillingness to submit to firm protocols—was alienating him from any supporters in the firm he might once have had. After several requests to address their concerns proved unsuccessful, the firm was considering asking him to leave.

I tried to explain to this gentleman that emotional intelligence is a valuable tool to both get and keep clients, referencing an early survey that found successful rainmakers exhibited higher levels of certain emotional intelligence skills, such as empathy, than the average lawyer.[102] *We must "show an interest in the client as a person," as one rainmaker said, an "intimacy" that many lawyers are uncomfortable with or simply don't know how to achieve.*[103]

Unfortunately, this lawyer did not find my suggestions or his firm's concerns worth acting on. He said in our last session that he thought the firm was being "silly" about client feedback on these issues, and his only concession would be to employ new software, which he thought would resolve any criticisms of his responsiveness. I heard within the year that he was leaving the firm.

Accurately perceiving our own and others' emotions, empathically engaging with our clients, and regulating our emotions and relationships based on an understanding of emotions—these EI skills together propel us toward the epitome of client service.[104] Given the increasing number of businesses that recognize and value emotional intelligence, it may even be that, as the general counsel on a legal marketing panel unanimously said, not only does your client or potential client "prefer to like someone they hire," they also "look at outside counsel's emotional IQ as much as their legal IQ."[105]

Unfortunately, lawyer personal attributes can complicate getting and keeping clients. Low emotional perception together with other common lawyer tendencies like high pessimism, introversion, skepticism, autonomy, abstraction and urgency, and low sociability and resilience, while useful in some contexts, can all weigh against delivering good client service.[106] Thus, it is often harder for lawyers to initiate and build relationships with clients, and they are likely to project a protective defensiveness that can alienate clients who want to build a relationship. While these attributes may pose daunting challenges, they can also be offset or compensated for by building strong EI skills.

Getting Clients

Ultimately, hiring a [lawyer] is about confidence and trust. It is an emotional act.[107]

—David Maister, author and professional services guru

Prospective clients of professional services cite four recurring objections to the way professionals sell their services: failure to understand the client's needs, failure to listen to the client, failure to persuasively present their value to the client, and failure to tailor solutions to the client's needs.[108]

Client service starts, therefore, with being able to forge in a fairly short time an initial relationship with a prospective client that they perceive as offering a customized benefit/solution "that appeals to the customer's emotions," as one rainmaking consultant advises.[109] Truly understanding the client's viewpoint involves the EI skills of emotional perception and emotional empathy. These skills, as well as understanding and regulating emotions, will be what guides you through the relationship-building process.

An attractive pitch demonstrates how well we understand our prospective client, an understanding gained through careful listening, and it also presents a value proposition *in terms of what the client is looking for.* Meeting the *client's* objectives is critical. Maybe the client doesn't want to win but wants to maintain the relationship with the other side through a mutually satisfactory resolution. Maybe the client is more concerned about making sure all avenues have been evaluated with respect to how to approach an acquisition, rather than having someone else complete it. Maybe the client is most interested in the impact of a deal on his or her career—succession, promotion, and so on.

According to lawyer Daniel Pink's *To Sell Is Human: The Surprising Truth About Moving Others,* workers in every type of job today spend at least 41 percent of their time in "sales-mode," which he believes requires exhibiting understanding and empathy with each prospective client.[110] However, as has been noted by legal marketing specialists, lawyers have traditionally not been great at "sales." In fact, 25 percent of 150 chief marketing officers in law firms across the country identified the biggest obstacle to firm revenue growth as the lawyers themselves, with law firm culture close behind.[111] "In part, it is because lawyers place a premium on their own expertise and credentials, not realizing that successful selling is more about building trust and connecting. There also are personality traits that impede selling."[112]

Despite lawyers' inclination to introversion, which has been cited as a common obstacle to selling themselves to clients, emotionally intelligent strategies can compensate for its disadvantages.[113] Research is now confirming that the most effective salespeople are those who can modulate their approach, whatever it is, in responses to the personality and preferences of the prospective client. Firms hiring sales professionals who aren't lawyers look primarily for those same traits: emotional intelligence and, particularly, empathy.[114]

> *I was asked to work with a new partner who was considered by her firm to be an intellectual "star" in a rising area. Her shyness, however, posed obstacles to getting clients. When I asked to assess her personal attributes, the lawyer confided that she realized she was off the charts for introversion, and that the sales "dance" terrified her. Luckily, she tested high in several very useful emotional intelligence skills, including being able to accurately survey a room for emotions. Speaking, which requires little interaction, became her primary pitch tool, where she could moderate her presentations to elicit interest and then use a play card to follow up, sometimes referring potential clients to her more voluble colleagues.*

Here are some tips for how to use emotional intelligence in preparing to meet with a prospect and in understanding what your prospect really wants.

Preparing to Meet with a Prospect. The first meeting with a prospect is a critical point, and perhaps the only shot you get, in initiating a trusting professional relationship.

Preparation is important. It's often difficult to determine a potential client's preferences before working with them. Debriefing someone who knows them or their company's culture ahead of time is always helpful. Googling them and their company and setting alerts on relevant news must be *de rigor* by now. You should also ask the prospect directly ahead of time about their thoughts on as many issues as they are willing to give. Simply inquiring as to your prospect's preferences on various matters can itself be a distinguishing gesture, setting you apart from the "this is how we do it" crowd. Regardless of the information you walk into the room with, being emotionally intelligent enough to be deft in recognizing, and agile in responding to, the cues you get when you meet is ultimately the best preparation.

Here are some emotionally attuned questions useful to consider about that first meeting, even if not all of them can be answered:

- Where does the prospect want a first meeting? Do they prefer to discuss initial business issues at the office, over lunch or a drink, or during a game of golf?
- How long do they want this encounter to last? Short introduction or extensive delving into the intricacies of a matter?
- How many people are they expecting? Do they prefer a broad show of force or a quiet interchange? Is it the expanse of expertise or the total hourly rates that they will note?
- What role should a reference or other middle person play? Only make the introduction or attend?
- What kind of "promotional" material do they prefer? A list of your relevant experience? Discussion of a recent case? A recitation of the various complications/factors that their industry/matter may encounter? Your personal approach to a matter of this kind?
- Do they want an agenda and material in advance of a meeting (which they can alter), prefer to brainstorm and review the material once you meet, or rather ask questions after they've had a chance to digest everything?
- What information about your firm and office procedures does the potential client consider relevant to determining whether to proceed with this engagement? How critical is hourly rate/cost? Billing and origination policies? Team structure and diversity? Cyber-security measures?

Understanding What Your Prospect Really Wants. Empirical evidence shows that this first meeting can be a crucial time (and perhaps the only time) for attorneys to learn vital information about the engagement. A review of videotaped and transcribed "first interviews" between attorneys and their potential clients concluded that "'clients reveal critical self-information in their opening words . . .' This information usually is not acknowledged by legal interviewers, with negative consequences. Failure to hear and see affects the legal interviewer's ability to form a relationship with a client, to comprehend the full range of information the client needs to share, and to collaborate with the client in telling their story in 'legally and emotionally effective language.'"[115]

Asking emotionally intelligent questions during your initial conversations can lead lawyers not only to successfully complete the stated job that they are hired to do but also to discover and understand the unstated objectives. As Chip Conley, the founder of the hotel chain Joie de Vivre and now Head of Hospitality at AirBnB, said, EI allows you to recognize "the needs [clients] may not even know they have."[116]

Here are some emotionally attuned questions that lawyers should be able to answer about their first interchanges with a prospective client:

- What are the client's primary business objectives? Winning at all cost? Exploring alternative approaches to the matter? Setting precedent? Achieving cost savings? Speed? Preserving relationships?
- What is the measure of success? What metrics should be tracked?
- What are the client's primary personal objectives? Selling themselves internally? Preserving their personal reputation in the industry? Showcasing a successful endeavor? Peace of mind while not having to personally deal with the matter? Team building with others to produce a group result?

Keeping Clients

> *Many lawyers never do seem to understand that they are dealing with people and not solely with the impersonal law.*[117]
>
> —Erin N. Griswold, former Dean of Harvard Law School

> *There are many clients that say, this particular lawyer was very brilliant, had all the good negotiating points, but by the end of the transaction, I didn't want to have anything more to do with this lawyer . . . sadly, many lawyers are completely blind and oblivious to this human impact that they have on clients.*[118]
>
> —Bee Leay Teo, lawyer and executive consultant, Baker & McKenzie

> *No one cares how much you know, until they know how much you care.*[119]
>
> —Theodore Roosevelt

Once you get a client, the next challenge is to keep them. Keeping a client produces a geometric return financially, and emotional intelligence plays a vital role in achieving that return.

A well-known study by three Harvard Business School professors provides some metrics on the financial impact of satisfying customers. According to their research, completely satisfied customers—those who rate a service provider 4.5 or 5 out of 5—are far more loyal than those customers who are merely satisfied, giving ratings of 3 to 4.5.[120]

Typically, only 25–30 percent of law firms' clients rate themselves as completely satisfied (4.5 to 5) with all aspects of a firm's services.[121] Therefore, as many as 70–75 percent of a firm's clients, including even some of your clients with whom you think you have a solid relationship, may be open to being courted by competitors.[122]

Hotel companies, whose clients walk out the door every day and must be convinced to return after a short experience, are customer satisfaction experts. Predictably, a study of professionals in hospitality management found them to be above average in emotional intelligence.[123] Other industries of various stripes, including some law firms, have taken advantage of hospitality's expertise by sending employees to companies like Ritz-Carlton for training in leadership and customer service.[124]

According to Symon Bridle, Chief Operating Officer of the Rosewood Hotel Group, a global luxury hotel management company, client satisfaction is a function of the "emotional connection" that is made, which comes down to the client's interactions with individuals on the front lines.[125] This should be kept in mind in your management of associate and staff interactions with your clients.

How do hotels sculpt their interactions so as to satisfy customers? For one thing, they ask them directly about their experience. "The Dorchester Collection of hotels in the US and Europe uses 10,000 surveys annually to determine its customers' emotional attachment and loyalty," according to Ann Brant, director of organizational performance. Similarly, Heather Briggs, Hyatt Hotels' VP for consumer insights and market research, says, "We live and die by guest feedback."[126]

Hotels also regularly take steps to make sure a client's emotional situation at the hotel is quickly and accurately assessed. The industry maintains that even small changes in employees' expressions toward guests can make a difference in that person's emotional attachment. In the Affinia boutique chain, everyone from housekeeping to management is trained to tailor his or her interactions with guests to the guest's emotional cues and body language. For example, staff is taught to mirror a guest's volume and rhythm of speech to put him or her at ease, to recognize that a guest touching their face or pulling on their ear is a sign of stress or anxiety, and to take steps to soothe an angry patron without face-to-face confrontation.

Small gestures matter. Changing the twenty-five-year tradition at Hilton's DoubleTree Hotels from simply having warm chocolate chip cookies available at check-in to personally handing the cookie to the guest resulted in markedly higher customer satisfaction scores on the "overall arrival experience." Similarly, Ritz Carlton doormen are trained to look for names on luggage tags so that guests can be greeted by name as soon as possible after arrival.[127]

What exactly makes for satisfied legal clients? It is often difficult for clients to gauge how good their lawyers are—clients can look at their objectives compared to the results, they can look at the fees and then they can tap into how the experience "felt." But none of these avenues may tell the "true" story, in the view of their lawyers, of how well a matter was handled.[128]

In litigation, one would think, the client who "wins" would invariably be satisfied. But research has established that litigants may be dissatisfied despite "winning" if they feel they were not adequately given a voice and a chance to participate.[129] Note that this research points out that clients evaluate their lawyers on how they *feel*—they want to feel heard and included.

What we do know is that there is widespread evidence of client dissatisfaction with their legal providers that has been mounting over the last decade. Even clients of lawyers who have successfully concluded transactions and trials for them increasingly are complaining and pressuring their lawyers to be more economical, efficient, responsive, and accountable. An *Outside Counsel* survey reported that the percentage of in-house counsel who ended relationships with their law firms during the multiyear period reviewed ranged from a low of 41.5 percent to a high of 55.6 percent, with "communication/personality issues" cited by a third to half of respondents for the reason for the firing.[130] The *National Law Review* article "What GCs Really Want in a Law Firm" identified "responsiveness" and a "good working relationship" as two of the four things that general counsel primarily want.[131] One survey of corporate counsel concluded that: "The good news is that only a small minority of respondents cited incompetence among their law firms as problem areas . . . [but] law firms can best serve their litigation clients as true service providers, not merely specialists in the law."[132]

What is disconcerting is the evidence that lawyers are often oblivious to the extent of client discontent. The 2015 Lexis Nexis Bellweather Report reported that 80 percent of lawyers surveyed responded that they are above average at client service, while only 40 percent of clients surveyed identified service from their lawyers as being above average.[133]

So in addition to being a good lawyer—a good negotiator or dealmaker or case manager or litigator—in order to be successful, lawyers also need to deliver their services in a way that feels good to that particular client. That requires ongoing reading of a client's emotional cues and the ability to produce the feeling the client wants. Those skills require emotional intelligence.

Clients are clearly attuned to the importance of having an emotional connection with their lawyers. Twice a year Pfizer grades each law firm in its Preferred Lawyer Alliance (PLA) on performance issues ranging from substantive knowledge to responsiveness and willingness to collaborate to how well they take the feedback they are given. Amy Schulman, former executive vice president, general counsel, and president of nutrition, says making the PLA relationships work was like developing other intimate relationships: "Relationship-building requires a certain kind of emotional courage and confidence."[134] Jacqueline Barrett, Group Compliance Director at Vodafone, finds that "[Lawyers'] emotional intelligence skills are often underdeveloped in comparison with their technical skills."[135]

According to Susie Lees, Executive Vice President and General Counsel at Allstate: "A trusted adviser is someone who knows how to get along with their clients, who knows how to respond instinctively to their clients' needs. This requires not just the ability to read a client's needs, but self-awareness and, in particular, an awareness of the impact you are having on those around you."[136]

Another commentator noted: "Attorneys who fail to acknowledge and address [the significant emotional investment by clients] . . . may be cultivating negative situations for both parties. At the very least, they may create a situation where the client is less likely to hire them or refer others to them in the future. Often, clients are looking for empathy and a sense of justification." As a Harvard law professor said: "The general public perception is that lawyers are more unfeeling than they ought to be . . . sometimes lawyers may be a little tone-deaf when it comes to what a client really wants . . . [and] overemphasize legal remedies."[137]

Providing the type of emotional connection that clients clearly want can be the distinguishing factor that raises your performance above the less emotionally aware competition. "With so many competing products and services that look alike in the mind of the customer, it will be the emotional intelligence embedded in the experience that will become the final differentiator."[138]

Harvard Business School did two widely reviewed and award-winning case studies of Baker & McKenzie in 2007 and 2008 at a time when clients were winnowing the number of law firms they used. According to the HBS analysis:

"[T]hat customers of legal services were looking to significantly reduce the number of law firms they used based largely on firms' ability to deliver a dynamic service relationship was startling to many . . . 'Now more than ever,' [John] Conroy [chairman of Baker & McKenzie] explained, 'there are many law firms that have the legal expertise that clients need; far fewer have the relationship development and "value-added" service that clients are increasingly demanding.' Added an internal Baker & McKenzie document: 'The unfortunate truth [about the legal profession] is that clients, in the main, are not particularly happy with the service [their] lawyers provide them. It is one of the ironies of the [legal service] business that [many lawyers] are often poor at client service . . . there is an urgent focus on improving the soft skills and *emotional intelligence* that are so important to true "counsel of choice" relationships'"[139] (emphasis added).

One study illustrates the advantage emotional intelligence gives to a service provider who recognizes and manages the emotional aspects of its client. The claims adjustment process, like the delivery of legal service, is often loaded with highly emotional aspects—feelings of anger, resentment, violation, and fear. A study of twenty-six claims adjustment teams found that the average EI of the team members—not the amounts in contest or the difficulty of the issues or the extent of the delay or the ultimate settlements received, but the team's EI alone—predicted customer satisfaction.[140]

Given that excellent client service should be the holy grail of our industry, there appears to be little direct instruction, either in our law schools or workplaces, as to what behaviors that involves. Many new partners don't feel they have been taught client development skills,[141] and neither do law students: in an informal survey of forty-five graduating law students, "the majority of the student respondents felt that they had little or no meaningful education about clients, their needs and expectations, how to relate with clients and others, the importance of compassion and empathy and the public's perception of lawyers and the law. . . . Some students reported that they learned about clients' needs by observing the attorneys with whom they worked, primarily in externships. Sometimes the examples were not positive, but they were still instructive."[142]

As one litigator and former prosecutor acknowledged, "As analytical professionals, our job frequently requires us to analyze dispassionately a complicated problem and provide sober counsel about how to proceed. We seem to expect clients to act the same way . . . However, clients are not supposed to be dispassionate. If they're in a litigation, they're in some kind of mess. And in my experience everyone is emotional—plaintiffs who feel like they're wronged, defendants who feel like they're unfairly attacked, parties of all stripes who are appalled at the conduct of the other side, or the other side's lawyers, or the judges or arbitrators, or the expert witnesses, or who knows who else . . . You will serve the client—and gain the client's trust—if you acknowledge their emotional investment and your role as not simply a tactician or fighter, but as a service professional."[143]

Professional services guru David Maister summed it up this way, "Stated bluntly, professionals say that they want the benefits of romance, yet they still act in ways that suggest that what they are really interested in is a one-night stand . . . Moving from a one-night-stand (transactional) mentality to a romance (relationship) mindset is not about incremental actions, but requires a complete reversal of attitudes and behaviors."[144]

Lawyers' failure to connect with clients emotionally not only reduces their grasp of the issues[145] but may even be doing clients emotional damage. Studies have found that those who go through legal proceedings to get compensation for personal injuries have a worse physical and psychological recovery than those who do not,[146] possibly suffering from a condition called "legal abuse syndrome."[147] A related condition referred to as "secondary victimization" is the result of clients suffering additional emotional harm at the hands of their own lawyers who fail to take into account their clients' emotional needs.[148]

In one of the studies, clients specified communication and empathy as what they most needed to avoid feeling reinjured. They wanted to feel "involved," that their lawyer listened to their story and their opinions and responded to issues they raised. Clients wanted information in advance and preferably face-to-face to start, with a telephone call at least once every two months, even if nothing was happening. Personal contact gave them a feeling of being taken seriously and was seen as an efficient way to communicate. Some were indignant that their lawyer had never reached out or invited them to come to the office. In short, clients wanted a show of empathy, at least in the beginning when the client was most shaken, "even if later on the lawyer was more business-like."[149]

While these instructions may not always generalize to all legal relationships, the universal value of this study is that it homes in on specific ways that emotionally intelligent lawyers can better serve clients, by providing emotional, empathic support, and regular, clear communication.[150]

A gentleman who had served as general counsel for several large public companies relayed a story about a preeminent intelligent property lawyer to whom he had brought a bet-the-company lawsuit. The GC initially spoke to the lawyer over the phone and then sent on all the relevant documents. After a silence of several days, the GC left a message with the lawyer that he was looking forward to discussing the case. After several more silent days, the GC called again and asked the lawyer's assistant to schedule a meeting appointment. After a few more days, the GC phoned again and insisted on speaking to the lawyer at that moment.

The lawyer explained that he had little time to talk, because he was involved in hearings on a complex matter but had gotten all the documents he needed. He assured the GC that he was accomplished at evaluating and pursuing these types of cases, and he would contact the GC if he needed any further information.

By that time, the GC had become quite exorcised and made it clear to the lawyer that he would not hire anyone, including someone as preeminent as he was, to handle this matter whom he hadn't looked in the eye and informed of the massive stakes in the offing. When they had that meeting, the GC insisted that he be contacted at least every week regardless of developments in order to reassure himself and his business clients that all was on track.

In a talk to the 2008 graduating class of Harvard Law School, Arnie Herz, an attorney, commentator, and author of the then hugely popular blog "Legal Sanity," acknowledged what had gotten these students to that auspicious point, while cautioning them against relying on it too much as they progressed through their careers:

> *[Y]our entire life, intelligence has been king . . . [But] intelligence is not the distinguishing characteristic between those law students who are hugely successful and those who are not . . . So what is the distinguishing characteristic? . . . The paradigm shift is that intelligence is no longer king, relationships are . . . Relationships must accommodate feelings and meet needs: this helps us connect as human beings and distinguishes us from the competition. By becoming relationship savvy, you will gain a most valuable tool that will help you achieve the success and satisfaction you want and deserve in your career.*[151]

Here are some emotionally attuned tactics that can help build a lasting relationship with your client:

How Much Contact Is Just Enough? Determine up front what kind of interface with their lawyer the client wants and check in regularly to see if their preferences have changed. Does the client want scheduled reviews over the course of the matter or prefer an as-issues-develop approach? By email, phone, or in person? Would they welcome an occasional informal drink or meal to allow candid in-person feedback?

Build a Personal Relationship. Verbally acknowledge the client's personal and business situation—the difficulties and risks, including the emotional ones. Make sure you understand the hierarchy the client is in and who and what is most important to his or her progress in the company. Among lawyers, self-deprecation is hard to find, so putting away the braggadocio comments can be refreshing. Don't forget to verbally praise the client's expertise and judgment where appropriate. Abstaining from criticism is not a compliment. Picking up on the names and activities of the spouse and kids shows an interest in the whole client. Simply taking the time for a short chat about vacations/golf/sailing is a relationship builder.

Does Your Client Need More Than Legal Advice? Has there been a recent move or divorce? Is he or she single parenting? Attending to a disabled or problemed child or an elderly or ill parent? These count as some of the highest stress factors we can face. You don't want to be perceived as nosy or gossipy, but you can be sensitive, sympathetic, and supportive regarding the nonlegal challenges your client is facing.

Producing the Best Product for Your Client. The client's desires should shape the product you deliver. Do you produce a memo or is a telephone conversation sufficient? How broad is the advice—do you spell out all or only particular risks? Include all possible steps to defuse them or only preferred ones? Include cost analyses and ramifications for company relationships? The long version or the executive summary?

Knowing How Best to Deliver to Your Client. Who should be addressed directly on various aspects of a matter and who gets copied on emails? And in which order? Does the client need to review and revise before anything is distributed for comment, or does he or she prefer that teammates weigh in before he or she is sent a "finished" product? Should it be sent electronically or as a hard copy? With comments/changes noted?

Being a Trusted Advisor. Coming up with a long list of legal points, no matter how brilliant some of them are, may not be the kind of advice your client ultimately needs. Use empathy to bring your client through what can seem like a trade-off maze to what your legal experience and your deep understanding of your client professionally and personally tells you is the best solution. And don't fail to say you will be there until you both are comfortable with how to proceed.[152]

Following Up with Your Client. After the matter is concluded, what sort of postmortem and follow-up documentation or meetings should there be? Are there any guidelines on preferred document disposal? Should there be a meeting/memo for individual or team feedback? From both sides? A post-matter budget analysis and review of potential savings for the future? Do continuing periodic status reports on current industry matters help or just fill up their in-box?

EMOTIONALLY INTELLIGENT LAWYERS GET AND KEEP MORE CLIENTS

- Emotional intelligence skills propel the epitome of client service.
- Hiring a lawyer is an emotional act: potential clients prefer to like you and are concerned about your emotional intelligence.
- Typical lawyer personal attributes like low emotional perception, emotional empathy, and emotional regulation, combined with high pessimism, introversion, skepticism, autonomy, abstraction, and urgency, and low sociability and resilience can all weigh against delivering good client service but can also be offset or compensated for by building strong emotional intelligence skills.
- Lawyers increasingly spend a significant amount of time in "sales mode," which they have traditionally not been great at because of their approach, prioritizing expertise and credentials over establishing a connection.
- Use emotionally attuned tips in preparing to meet with a prospect and to understand what your prospect really wants.
- Keeping a client produces a geometric return financially, and emotional intelligence plays a vital role in achieving that return.
- There is widespread evidence of client dissatisfaction; only 25–30 percent of law firm clients rate themselves as completely satisfied.
- Client satisfaction is a function of the "emotional connection" that is made, which comes down to how clients *feel* about their interactions with individual providers, which can be a significant distinguishing factor.

(Continued)

- Lawyers' failure to connect with clients emotionally may even be a factor causing clients emotional damage, reflected in the concepts of "legal abuse syndrome" and "secondary victimization."
- Little instruction is provided, either in law schools or workplaces, as to what behaviors great client service involves.
- Clients identify communication and empathy as the behaviors they most need.
- Use emotionally attuned tactics that can help build a lasting client relationship.

Emotionally Intelligent Communication Cements Client Relationships

What we've got here is failure to communicate.

—"The Captain" (played by Strother Martin) in *Cool Hand Luke* (1967)

Communication is such an important ingredient of good client service, and one that lawyers so often get wrong, that it deserves its own discussion.

Long-standing research makes it clear that the best communication is founded on accurately reading and understanding emotional cues, however they are communicated, and then responding (using appropriate emotional cues) to the emotional needs that were expressed.[153] Communication that fails to convey any emotion can cause problems. Email is a perfect example. People constantly misread the intent of email because they can't tell the emotional state of the sender.

Communication permeates all aspects of legal practice—communication with staff, associates and partners, "non-lawyer" colleagues like investigators, experts, and witnesses, as well as with clients. Communication styles and skills influence court interactions and can give evidence of upcoming decisions, even at the Supreme Court level, and often without the parties' awareness.[154] How a jury votes depends at least in part on the communication abilities and styles of the lawyers involved.[155] So simple awareness of communication style and its emotional content can improve the effectiveness of efforts to communicate in the legal arena.

Clients everywhere complain repeatedly about their lawyers' communication. In the latest survey by Acritas of 968 senior in-house lawyers in companies in a variety of industries with more than $50 million in revenue, the 17 percent who fired their law firm for poor service (up from 15 percent the year before) cited poor communication as the primary failing. "Many respondents expressed frustration that firms did not use preferred communication channels, giving the impression of disinterest."[156] The tone of some of the clients' comments made these frustrations clear: their comments went from "we were 'dissatisfied'" to "[the firm's] attitude toward us was very disappointing" to "we came to despise the firm."[157]

Communication is overwhelmingly the most common complaint about lawyers made to bar associations: in Florida, lack of communication is the number one complaint; in Virginia, the most common complaints are failure to communicate and general neglect. Kentucky is even more specific: "bar complaints in Kentucky follow the same pattern as they do elsewhere . . . deficits in EI underlie most concerns."[158] Communication has also become the primary basis of both Canadian and US malpractice claims.[159] "The number-one complaint is, 'My lawyer isn't talking to me.'"[160]

Communication can be improved. The medical field has become quite effective in improving physician communication with patients, and EI training (provided in all UK medical schools) has become the preferred route to that improvement.[161]

Emotionally intelligent practitioners can improve their communication by learning the EI skills associated with:

The Art and Science of Listening
Reading Nonverbal Communication

The Art and Science of Listening

Listening is the ability to hear what people are saying or not saying, as distinguished from the words they enunciate.[162]

—Gerry Spence, member of the American Trial Lawyers Hall of Fame, who claims to have never lost a criminal case as either a prosecutor or defense lawyer, nor any civil case since 1969

Communication is at the heart of client satisfaction, and listening, not speaking, is the foundation of communication. Achieving good listening is one of the most direct, inexpensive ways of improving client service.[163] Improvements in listening have been demonstrated to elevate individual performance and contribute to individual and organizational profitability.[164] An assessment of 15,000 leaders in 18 countries found that the number one leadership skill over all other skills is listening and responding to others.[165]

Listening well is an exercise in emotional intelligence—accurately perceiving the emotions that are in play, understanding how those emotions have developed, and managing our own and others' emotions so that they enhance rather than interfere with or undercut the message that we are trying to convey.

What Jack Welch, Chairman of GE from 1981 to 2000, said he valued most about his favorite lawyer was that he was the best listener he'd ever met.[166] Listening is a high priority in GE's corporate culture: "General Electric—long considered the preeminent company for producing leaders . . . places 'listening' among the most desirable traits in potential leaders," and "'humble listening' is among the top four most important characteristics that GE Chairman of the Board Jeff Immelt thinks leaders should have.[167] Humble listening is the ability to really hear and appreciate what someone else is saying without advocating one's own, more insightful, opinions.

Good listening is a skill that is not often mastered, however. One consultant estimates that *one out of four* Fortune 500 managers has a listening deficit—"the effects of which can paralyze cross-unit collaboration, sink careers, and if it's the CEO with the deficit, derail the company . . . Conventional advice for better listening is to be emotionally intelligent."[168]

Careful listening is confounded by the "down time" that our physiology presents. Although we talk at a rate of 120 to 150 words per minute, the brain can process 400 to 800 words per minute.[169] So listening absorbs only a small part of our language-processing capacity at any moment, tempting many of us, and particularly lawyers, to talk to ourselves during the downtime while we are listening to others: we silently argue with the speaker or ourselves, arrange and rearrange our points, and hunt for the nearest opening to allow us to demonstrate our expertise. By being so preoccupied, we can miss out on much of what is being conveyed.

Low EI, including in the critical component of perceiving emotions, in which lawyers most frequently have deficits, can preclude us from hearing the client's emotional message, which can reveal valuable information about the client's professional and personal priorities, and his or her reaction to our advice. Lawyers' tendency toward high urgency further promotes poor listening, prompting us to supply a missing word, interrupt, close any silent gaps, and direct the conversation to the wrap-up we've been mentally preparing.[170] Unfortunately, building client relationships is not always an efficient process, and listening is often a slow undertaking that requires patience.

Poor listening not only misses out on important information but also conveys negative impressions to our clients. Kevin O'Keefe, whose company LexBlog publishes hundreds of law blogs, found that over 90 percent of his lawyer audience uses some form of social media, but less than 10 percent use one that is a "listening tool" for others' input. O'Keefe calls what most lawyers do—using social media just to spread the word about their organizations and themselves—the "bullhorn approach." "[L]istening is the most important aspect of social media. More important than content. More important than sharing. More important than likes and comments. And much more important than traffic." If you use the bullhorn approach, "At best you'll be as ineffective in your use of social media as most other legal professionals. At worst, you'll be perceived as placing yourself before others."[171]

Since "[m]ost lawyers don't do it very well," being a good listener can be what distinguishes you from the herd.[172] As one trial lawyer opined: "I know lawyers who have never successfully cross-examined a witness, never understood where a judge was coming from, and never ascertained what those around them were saying . . . all because they do not listen."[173]

"Listen Well" in Chapter 7 lists tips for becoming a more emotionally intelligent listener.

Reading Nonverbal Communication

> *There was speech in their dumbness, language in their very gesture.*[174]
>
> —Shakespeare, *The Winter's Tale*

A sizable part of listening involves "hearing" nonverbal communication, which constitutes a much greater part of our communication than does verbal communication. One study found that only 8 percent of communication is verbal, while 7 percent is tonality and 85 percent is expressed through body movement.[175]

Nonverbal communication is so pervasive and complex that several specialized areas of academic study concentrate on a single type. "Proxemics" is the study of a culture's personal sense of appropriate physical space. Unfamiliar closeness, for example, can raise questions about intentions and bring anxiety to an uncomfortable level, whether in an elevator or a witness box. The science of "kinesics" is the study of messages sent through body movement, commonly called "body language." "Vocal chronemics" is the study of the rate of speech patterns and their changes, while "paralinguistics combines the studies of pitch, intensity, tone, timbre, tempo, stress and volume of the voice."[176]

People tend to trust nonverbal communication over verbal communication—relying on what is expressed, not what is said—in part because they believe that nonverbal communication is more likely to convey a person's true emotions, that our genuine feelings "leak out" through our nonverbal expressions, a belief supported by research.[177] That makes both our ability to read those nonverbal emotional cues and to give back the nonverbal cues that will engender trust crucial to providing sound legal advice.

A meta-analysis of courtroom communication determined that nonverbal communication can be extremely important in the outcome of litigation, with a judge's nonverbal communication, for example, affecting how a jury votes.[178] One law firm has explicitly made their expertise in nonverbal communication a selling point for their litigation services, writing: "[O]ver 60% of the impact of meaning of the communicated message resides in the non-verbal behavior accompanying the oral message. The ability to read and decode this leakage is of invaluable aid to the trial lawyer. It can be used in detecting deception during the interview or interrogation; it can be used in orchestrating your conduct and your witness's conduct during the course of the trial; it can be used to enhance your ability to communicate to the jury or to the court."[179]

Lawyers need to have well-developed emotional perception, emotional understanding, and emotional regulation to accurately read and influence clients, opposing counsel and parties, experts, witnesses, jurors, and judges, and to convince them all to put their trust in us. The Appendix lists some resources for learning how to better read nonverbal communication.

EMOTIONALLY INTELLIGENT COMMUNICATION CEMENTS CLIENT RELATIONSHIPS

- Communication is a critical ingredient of good client service, and one that lawyers often get wrong.
- The best communication is founded on accurately reading and understanding emotional cues, however they are communicated, and then responding (using appropriate emotional cues) to the emotional needs that were expressed.
- The No. 1 leadership skill—not often mastered—is listening and responding.
- Communication permeates all aspects of legal practice, influencing court interactions, how a jury votes, and giving evidence of upcoming decisions.

(Continued)

- Clients everywhere complain repeatedly about their lawyers' communication, making it the number one complaint to bar associations and the primary basis of malpractice claims.
- Our brains listen at a slower pace than we can think, requiring concentration and patience.
- Low EI and high urgency challenge lawyers to be good listeners.
- A sizeable part of listening involves "hearing" nonverbal communication, which constitutes over 80 percent of communication, and is more trusted than verbal communication.

See the "Listen Well" section in Chapter 7 and the Appendix for tips and resources for becoming a more emotionally intelligent communicator.

Emotionally Intelligent Client Service Reaps Revenues

The ultimate benefit that better client service gives lawyers is higher income. A study of marketing professionals determined that those with higher emotional intelligence are not only better at retaining customers but also, as we would expect, are superior revenue generators. The proof is in the numbers. Just a 5 percent increase in client retention is estimated to produce a 25 percent to 85 percent increase in profits over the lifetime of the client through repeat business, less sensitivity to pricing, cross-selling/expansion, and new client referrals.[180]

Emotionally attuned client-centered legal service keeps clients coming back to the firm, but that kind of service can also support higher rates even in an extremely competitive marketplace. As one law firm consultant points out: "Markets reward scarcity. Great client experience in the legal market is scarce . . . in fact, it's such a huge differentiator that you can probably charge a lot for it . . . The price of almost every lawyer product . . . will decrease over the coming decade. But the price of a lawyer's service—the personal, customized, convenient, anticipatory, strategic, counseling, caring way in which the client is treated and their interests looked after—will hold steady and will very probably rise."[181]

BIT Consulting, a research group, offered these statistics on the financial edge that professional services firms that deliver consistently superior client service can enjoy:

- "8% hourly rate premiums,
- 33% higher profits per partner equivalent, and
- 39% higher client retention."[182]

A survey conducted by BTI showed a striking 25 percent increase in 2015 in top hourly legal rates—reaching over $2,000 an hour, indicating that clients continue to pay "their most trusted senior lawyers" a high premium for the best service. These preferred lawyers "treat the client with overarching commitment to understanding their business, and to being in a constant dialogue with them."[183]

Having clients more satisfied with our service not only pays well but can make us feel better, too, as researchers found to be the case with physicians.[184]

EMOTIONALLY INTELLIGENT LAWYERS MAKE MORE MONEY

- Emotionally intelligent lawyers are more productive, as are emotionally intelligent consultants, accountants, and sales personnel.
- Emotionally intelligent lawyers get and keep more clients.
- Emotionally intelligent lawyers build strong relationships by being more effective listeners and communicators, both verbally and nonverbally.
- Emotionally intelligent lawyers reap the revenues generated by better client service.

Advantage 4: Emotionally Intelligent Lawyers Are Healthier and Happier—Rescuing Lawyers in Distress

There is no such thing as a separation of mind and body—the very molecules in our bodies are responsive to our psychological environment.[185]

—Denis Novack of Drexel University College of Medicine, who studies the connection between emotions and health, stress and premature aging

It is not stress that kills us. It is effective adaptation to stress that allows us to live.[186]

—George Vaillant, Professor of Psychiatry at Harvard Medical School

Emotional intelligence not only improves career performance but also enhances other aspects of a person's life, such as his or her physical health, social and family relationships, and mental well-being, resulting in lower levels of anxiety, stress, depression, and other signs of distress.[187]

After a large meta-analysis found that those with higher EI have better mental, psychosomatic, and physical health, a follow-up meta-analysis reviewing another 150 studies and an additional 19,815 participants again concluded that there was an overall positive association between EI and physical health and an even stronger association between EI and mental health.[188]

This chapter discusses how this and other research offers hope to lawyers that emotional intelligence can help them face the deep and long-standing challenges to their physical and mental health that they are subject to throughout their careers, and explores theories as to why lawyers are so vulnerable to distress:

Emotional Intelligence Reduces the Plague of Anxiety, Stress, Burnout, Substance Abuse, Depression, and Suicide
Why? Accounting for Lawyer Debilitation

Emotional Intelligence Reduces the Plague of Anxiety, Stress, Burnout, Substance Abuse, Depression, and Suicide

[Lawyers] are the best-paid professionals, and yet they are disproportionately unhappy and unhealthy. And lawyers know it; many are retiring early or leaving the profession altogether.[189]

—Martin Seligman, University of Pennsylvania Psychology Professor and author of *Authentic Happiness*

The American Institute of Stress reports job-related pressure is the top source of stress for Americans, and has been skyrocketing in recent decades, exacerbated by the 2008 recession and subsequent attempts to keep costs down. From two-thirds to 80 percent of workers report high levels of stress, which they are "totally dissatisfied" with.[190] The American Institute of Stress reports that stress is the main cause underlying 40 percent of workplace turnovers and 80 percent of work-related injuries.[191]

While short bursts of stress can be energizing and produce higher performance, stress that becomes a constant companion, as it does in professions like law, lowers performance if it isn't managed well. Even small daily doses of stressful events have profound and long-term impacts on our functioning.[192]

The top two issues that leaders worldwide wrestle with are stress and burnout. "Burnout" is the result of excessive stress that produces physical, emotional, and mental exhaustion, dramatically reducing personal performance and often resulting in disengagement, substance abuse, and depression.[193]

Unmanaged emotions are one of the primary culprits that place us under debilitating stress. In stressful situations, automatic emotional reactions ratchet up the volume of our anxiety and other distress emotions, which then can intensify each other, spiraling up into greater and greater stress on our bodies and our minds. The emotional pain of stress is felt and processed in the brain just as physical pain is and in the same area, the anterior cingulate cortex.[194] So to the same extent as physical pain, the emotional pain of stress is also physically, intellectually, and emotionally debilitating, as if we were walking around on a broken leg.

Physically, ongoing stress actually reshapes the brain, causing neurons to shrink. Prolonged stress deteriorates and shortens telomeres (a piece of DNA) that are found at the tip of chromosomes in each cell of the body, accelerating aging and declining health as they repeatedly reproduce.[195] The high levels of the fight-or-flight hormone cortisol bathing our bodies put us at higher risk for coronary disease: abdominal fat builds up, we become insulin resistant, our arteries stiffen and blood pressure rises, and heart rates and blood flow increase, often damaging and eventually blocking vessel walls. In addition, white blood cell production and therefore immune functioning is impaired, making us more likely to succumb to all sorts of illness.[196]

Unmanaged stress unequivocally reduces our intellectual functioning also. "Stressed people don't do math very well. They don't process language very efficiently, and they have poorer memories, both short- and long-term."[197] Math and language abilities drop as much as 50 percent; decision making becomes compromised.[198] One neuropsychologist compares chronic stress to "fine sand being drizzled into the brain. It might keep working, but if you dump enough sand in there, it'll freeze up at some point."[199] Those suffering from such high stress may not even realize the seriousness of their condition, which can easily tip into clinical conditions like extreme anxiety and clinical depression.[200]

Raising emotional intelligence is a key strategy to significantly improve stress management. That link was established in 1908 and has been consistently confirmed since.[201] Those with higher overall EI can lower their anxiety and distress at the prospect of a challenging task; those with the ability to accurately identify emotions are at less risk of suffering from depression; and those able to regulate their emotions have been determined to experience the highest level of well-being.[202]

Important research published in 2013 found that, as with doctors,[203] lawyers gain significant protection against burnout and job dissatisfaction with higher EI.[204] Using emotional regulation skills to overcome negative feelings with more positive ones can significantly reduce both stress and distress levels, which pays off in greater cognitive functioning and financial results,[205] even lowering blood pressure and raising immunity.[206]

It is no wonder then that the employers in the CareerBuilder survey mentioned earlier give as the number one reason for preferring the emotionally intelligent that "employees with high EI are more likely to stay calm under pressure"—that is, they are better able to manage stress.[207]

Unfortunately, by nearly every measure the legal profession suffers from outsized distress, starting in law school.

Lawyers in Distress

While the nation experiences high levels of stress, perhaps no other profession is as stressed as lawyers. The current marketplace poses rising competition for clients, slower growth, declining profitability, increasing layoffs, and the specter of lost jobs. Further, lawyers often view their role as taking on the stressful problems of their clients, often very complex issues on fast-track timeframes and frequently involving individual or corporate life-or-death situations.

As a therapist who specializes in lawyers puts it: "Paid worriers, lawyers are expected to predict the future, to anticipate threats and guard against anything that could arise. So they learn to see problems everywhere, even when they don't exist. And they start to perceive threats as if they're life-or-death matters. That's the very definition of anxiety."[208] It is not surprising, then, that studies have found higher levels of occupational stress and burnout rates in lawyers relative to other occupations and that these profoundly affect attorneys' daily functioning.[209]

The behavioral manifestations of anxiety and stress include irritability, obsessive thoughts, feelings of inadequacy, difficulty concentrating, a sense of worry and impending danger, sleep deprivation, heart palpitations, sweating, fatigue, and muscle tension. Some attorneys withdraw from peers, friends, and family or engage in "maladaptive coping behaviors," such as self-medicating with alcohol and other substances. "[W]ithout a doubt, every lawyer I see has anxiety greater than the average population," a lawyer-turned-therapist says, who sees such "strange compensatory behavior" among lawyers as "hair pulling, hand washing, food disorders and gym anorexia . . . [and other] weird stuff—lawyers who stay up all night playing video games, guys who use prostitutes."[210]

These concerns are not a new phenomenon. For decades lawyers have reported high levels of distress. In 1991, the American Bar Association (ABA) issued a report on the unusually high levels of health problems experienced by lawyers.[211] In the late 1990s, an extensive study found above-average incidences of substance abuse, depression, and other signs of psychological distress among lawyers, who were suffering from alcoholism and other maladaptive behaviors at rates twice that in the general population, as well as elevated levels of hostility, anger, and marital dissatisfaction.[212]

As one state Lawyer Assistance Program recounted in 1996: "Estimates of the number of lawyers affected by substance abuse, psychological disorders, or other impairments vary greatly, from a low of 15 percent to a high of 50 percent . . . Suicide currently ranks as one of the leading causes of premature death in the legal profession."[213] In 2004, one of the first comprehensive looks at lawyer personalities, *Lawyer, Know Thyself: A Psychological Analysis of Personality Strengths and Weaknesses,* drew attention to the growing crisis of distress among lawyers.[214]

Startled by the statistics, bar associations across the United States started lawyer assistance programs or bolstered existing ones, and instituted continuing legal education to address substance abuse and mental illness.[215] The ABA became increasingly active in providing support for distressed lawyers. Its Commission on Impaired Attorneys, created in 1988, was renamed the Commission on Lawyer Assistance Programs to avoid any implied stigma and to better describe its expanded mental health services, which were extended internally throughout the ABA, as well as to state programs. Whereas only four state bar lawyer assistance programs existed in 1980, today all fifty states (and Canada and Great Britain) have developed bar programs or committees focused on these issues.[216]

We now know that these indications of distress are already evident when students enter law school and deepen even further as they enter law practice.

Starting in Law School

> *It is well known that lawyers suffer higher rates of depression, anxiety and other mental illness, suicide, divorce, alcoholism and drug abuse, and poor physical health than the general population or other occupations, [but what is less well-known is that] these problems begin in law school. Although law students enter law school healthier and happier than other students, they leave law school in much worse shape.*[217]
>
> —Roy Stuckey, law professor and principal author of *Best Practices of Legal Education*

Students appear to enter law school with a mental health profile typical of or better than most Americans. However, it has been long documented that during the course of law school and then throughout their legal careers, these same people manifest unusually high levels of distress.

In the 1990s, while only 10 percent of pre-law students were found to suffer from depression, it was determined that "psychiatric distress increases significantly during law school, with 17%–40% of students reporting significantly elevated levels of depression and 20%–40%" reporting "other significantly elevated symptoms, including obsessive compulsive, interpersonal sensitivity, anxiety, hostility, paranoid ideation, and . . . social alienation and isolation."[218]

Of more than 3,000 law students from fifteen law schools surveyed in 2014, 18 percent had been diagnosed with clinical depression and 37 percent were screened positive for anxiety, more than twice the percentage among other graduate students, with 14 percent of law students qualifying as severely anxious. The percentages of those binge drinking were also high.[219]

A 2014 survey of Yale Law School students found that 70 percent of respondents struggled with mental health issues during their time at law school, and 50 percent indicated that mental health challenges affected their ability to perform academically. Thirty percent of those with mental health concerns were unable or unwilling to seek help out of fear of repercussions from faculty, administrators, and peers, and from state bar associations and the government.[220] Despite the ABA's House of Delegates passing an advisory resolution discouraging bar admissions authorities from investigating applicants' mental health, forty-one states include questions about a candidate's mental health history, diagnosis, or treatment, opening the door to disclosure of medical records. In recognition of this growing concern, the ABA's Law Student Division has instituted an annual Mental Health Day.[221]

These elevated levels of distress are evidently not limited to law students in the United States. Researchers in Australia found that, as in the United States, "Australian law students have higher rates of psychological distress and depression than community members of similar age and sex and that the deterioration in mental health may begin in the 1st year of study."

The Australian study points specifically to a lack of emotional intelligence as a determining factor in higher rates of distress: among Australian law students, those with higher EI have a lower incidence and severity of psychiatric symptoms, use less alcohol, and enjoy greater life satisfaction.[222]

Lawyers at Their Weakest

> *Lawyers are in remarkably poor mental health . . . Lawyers are trained to be aggressive, judgmental, intellectual, analytical and emotionally detached. This produces predictable emotional consequences for the legal practitioner: he or she will be depressed, anxious, and angry a lot of the time.*[223]
>
> —Martin Seligman, University of Pennsylvania Psychology Professor and author of *Authentic Happiness*

Once those increasingly distressed law students become practicing attorneys, the statistics on how badly they fare in terms of mental and physical health in comparison to other professions are quite astonishing. Reports over the years have unfortunately telling titles: "Those Unhappy, Unhealthy Lawyers," "Alcoholism, Drug Abuse and Lawyers: Are We Ready to Address the Denial?" "Being a Happy, Healthy, and Ethical Member of an Unhappy, Unhealthy and Unethical Profession," "The Depressed Lawyers—Why Are So Many Lawyers So Unhappy?" and "Why Are Lawyers Killing Themselves?"[224]

While the World Health Organization considers depression a global epidemic with 10 percent of the population suffering from it, Dan Lukasik, founder of the website "Lawyers with Depression,"[225] contends that in the legal industry depression specifically, but also other mental health issues, are at "catastrophic" and "pandemic" levels, and the numbers collected over the years bear him out, with reports of practicing lawyers exhibiting "clinical anxiety, hostility and depression at rates that range from 8–15 times the general population."[226] The subject of depression among lawyers, outpacing all other professions, is alone so troublesome as to have an extensive library.[227]

The most recent and comprehensive study on lawyer distress, conducted in 2016 and funded by the Hazelden Betty Ford

Foundation and the ABA's Commission on Lawyer Assistance Programs, found that lawyer mental health distress continues to be significant and growing. Substantial rates of behavioral health problems were reported among 12,825 licensed, employed attorneys, with 36.4 percent screening positive for "hazardous, harmful, and potentially alcohol-dependent drinking," a rate substantially higher than among the general population and among physicians and surgeons, who exhibit substance use and mental health disorders at a rate similar to the general population. Levels of depression at 28 percent, anxiety at 19 percent, and stress at 23 percent among attorneys were also significant, and markedly increased from older reports.

Attorney and clinician Patrick R. Krill, Hazelden's architect of the project, concluded: "Any way you look at it, this data is very alarming, and paints the picture of an unsustainable professional culture that's harming too many people. Attorney impairment poses risks to the struggling individuals themselves and to our communities, government, economy and society." The report concluded that "although the consequences of attorney impairment may seem less direct or urgent than the threat posed by impaired physicians, they are nonetheless profound and far-reaching."[228]

A memoir published in 2016 by a New York City lawyer—who practiced for years in prominent firms while drinking a bottle of wine a night and "waking up" with cocaine in the mornings without, in her opinion, her colleagues being the wiser—testifies to the silence in which many distressed lawyers suffer.[229]

Although not often publicly discussed and not consistently tracked, the public reports, if not the overall number, of lawyers who relieve themselves of their distress through suicide appear to have increased significantly.[230] "In 1996, lawyers overtook dentists as the profession with the highest rate of suicide."[231] While men have a higher suicide rate than women generally, a National Institute for Occupational Safety and Health study found that male lawyers in the United States are two times more likely to commit suicide than men in the general population.[232] Even a high level of tolerance for distressing negative emotions, which lawyers may more likely have, has been found not sufficient to shelter sufferers from higher suicide rates.[233] In the 2016 Hazelden/ABA study, "11.5% of the participants reported suicidal thoughts at some point during their career, 2.9% reported self-injurious behaviors."[234]

While not often reported, public acknowledgments of suicides by judges are also becoming more common.[235] They are possibly even more vulnerable to mental health issues because of their isolation, public standing, and the expectation that they will be strictly rational at all times.

In the documentary *A Terrible Melancholy: Depression in the Legal Profession,* Judge Michael Miller talks about the loneliness of being a judge.[236] Psychiatrist Isaiah Zimmerman culled quotes from twenty years of notes he accumulated while treating state and federal judges that attest to that loneliness. His assessment is that personality traits, such as introversion, less "emotional access," and less "emotionally nuanced intellectuality" contribute to feelings of isolation, which, if unmanaged, can easily evolve into depression and other types of emotional distress.[237]

In recognition of these escalating problems, suicide awareness and prevention programs for and by lawyers have become increasingly common.[238] As a direct result of the Hazelden/ABA study, on February 6, 2017, the ABA's House of Delegates approved changes to the Model Rule for Minimum Continuing Legal Education, passed without any opposition or debate, requiring regular minimal education in mental health and substance abuse.[239]

THE PLAGUE OF LAWYER DISTRESS

- National stress levels are at an all-time high.
- Lawyers have for decades displayed high levels of distress compared to other professions—evidenced by high rates of anxiety, stress, burnout, substance abuse, depression, and suicide.
- Indications of distress start in law school and climb during law practice, with recent statistics showing the problem at an all-time high.
- Judges also appear to be vulnerable to these mental health challenges.

Why? Accounting for Lawyer Debilitation

There is plenty of speculation—ranging from the nature of our jobs to pervasive career dissatisfaction to the personality attributes we have—as to why lawyers suffer so disproportionately.[240] What is common to these attempts at explaining lawyer distress is the recognition that many lawyers are ultimately ineffective at coping with their emotions, regardless of how and why they arise.[241]

Work Profile. Martin Seligman, the Zellerbach Family Professor of Psychology at the University of Pennsylvania, suggests that the emotional costs of "low decision latitude in high-stress situations" and the win-lose zero-sum aspect of law practice contribute to the poor physical and mental health of lawyers. "Low decision latitude," or the lack of power to determine and control how we solve problems at work, is correlated with both depression and coronary artery disease. "[J]unior associates in major firms . . . often fall into this cusp of high pressure accompanied by low choice . . . [with] little voice about their work, only limited contact with their superiors, and virtually no client contact. Instead, for at least their first few years of practice, many remain isolated in a library, researching and drafting memos on topics of the partners' choosing."[242]

Win-lose zero-sum contests, the all-or-nothing model that American law is founded on, provoke the highest degree of aggression and emotional detachment, in Seligman's opinion, necessarily resulting in lawyers who are "depressed, anxious, and angry a lot of the time."[243]

An important 2012 study identified the way lawyers think and reason as "the main and deeper source of their susceptibility to stress and burnout," because it "underestimates emotions, interpersonal relations and social context."[244] As the authors of *The Illicit Relationship of Lawyers and Emotions* concluded: "We are not suffering, as a profession, from our inability to think clearly or analyze properly, we are suffering because we have been trained to ignore our emotional dimension."[245]

Career Dissatisfaction. Many point to the outsized career dissatisfaction that lawyers report as either a cause or a consequence of their distress. A CareerBliss survey determined from over 65,000 employee reviews that of all careers surveyed, law associates were the unhappiest in their jobs, with legal assistants coming in as the third unhappiest.[246] Former Supreme Court Justice Sandra Day O'Connor once acknowledged that "job dissatisfaction among lawyers is widespread, profound and growing worse,"[247] which a series of studies has confirmed.[248] A 2016 survey found the percentage of lawyers who wouldn't go to law school again is steadily rising, from a third among those who graduated between 1906 and 1979 to two-thirds among graduates since 2000.[249]

One indicator of how dissatisfied lawyers are is the astronomic rate of attrition, one of the banes of the legal industry, which has continued unevenly but persistently even into the era when jobs are few and precious.[250] In 2012, a whopping 57 percent of associates left the profession of law entirely, not just their jobs, before their fifth year of practice.[251]

Unhappiness. Studies conclude that raising career satisfaction does indeed help lower the stress that lawyers report, but that alone is insufficient to significantly reduce their distress levels.[252] So some commentators attribute the distress more to a general disposition toward glumness. As Benjamin Cardozo once said many years ago, "I fear that happiness isn't in my line . . . all trouble is in the disposition that was given to me at birth, and so far as I know, there is no necromancy in an act of Congress that can work a resolution there."[253] Or, as a more contemporary lawyer put it, "We might like to feel happy, but we have been trained not to feel anything."[254]

The time when Baker & McKenzie was developing their new client service program (the early 2000s) was arguably the heyday of lawyering satisfaction in terms of demand and profits, yet the authors of the HBS case study noted an internal memo advocating professional development programs because "'[These associates] suspect that many partners are unhappy, and they do not want to be.'"[255] Confirming those suspicions, when seventy-five managing partners of midsize firms were asked, "What film best describes your firm?" 35 percent of those answering responded: *Grumpy Old Men.*[256] And in another survey, 40 percent of managing partners reported that partner morale at their firms was lower than during the market collapse in 2008.[257] When one Wall Street law firm's entire Mannheim office packed up and reverted back to its pre-merger form, one former partner was reported to have explained his leaving as follows: "There are some great lawyers at [the Wall Street firm]. I just don't think they are particularly happy."[258]

The emotion of happiness, under various definitions, has become a booming research topic and the subject of over 35,000 books published in the last ten years. Happiness is at least partially set at birth, with one estimate that 44–52 percent of happiness levels are genetic.[259] While there are studies as to relative happiness quotients among countries, once out of poverty levels there is no evidence of happiness being associated with income. Surveys have found no difference, for example, in happiness levels between those on the Forbes 400 and Maasai Mara herdsmen in East Africa.[260]

While some of the Big Five personality traits are correlated with happiness,[261] EI is not only more associated with happiness than any of those traits, but unlike traits, EI actually produces happiness, rather than just being a by-product of happiness: being happy doesn't mean you are emotionally intelligent, but if you are emotionally intelligent, you are more likely to be happy.[262]

Research over the years has established that it is better to be happier than not, and not just for feel-good reasons. "Happiness not only feels good, it is good. Happier people have more stable marriages, stronger immune systems, higher incomes, and more creative ideas than their less happy peers. Furthermore, cross-sectional, longitudinal, and experimental studies have demonstrated that happiness (i.e., long-term positive affect or well-being) is not merely a correlate or consequence of success but a cause of it." People who are happy are more successful in work, school, and sports, are less depressed, have fewer physical health problems, and have better relationships with other people, all contributing to better functioning.[263]

In law, too, greater happiness accomplishes more than making us feel good. Happier lawyers are arguably better lawyers because of the interplay of happiness with performance, collaboration, and professionalism—valuable practice assets—and the way that interplay contributes to more congenial workplaces and more satisfied clients.[264]

Yet lawyers as a population may be primed for unhappiness, and also depression. When Yale psychologist Peter Salovey was still formulating his theory of emotional intelligence, he studied whether mood affects deductive or inductive reasoning abilities by using questions from the LSAT as examples requiring deductive reasoning. He concluded that a depressed mood produced significantly better performance in deductive reasoning (which starts from a general premise and analyzes whether specific instances are included within that premise), while an elevated mood produced better performance in inductive reasoning (which arrives at a general premise from specific instances). Therefore, those who did well on the LSAT, making them more likely to be accepted into law school, were also more likely to be feeling somewhat "down," and more susceptible to depression.[265]

While this is not the only study to recognize some value in occasional negative moods—one found that "temporary, mild negative feelings have important benefits" that lawyers might want to take advantage of—there are no benefits to being in a prolonged depression.[266] So it is only with good emotional regulation skills that we can make use of a slightly depressed mood on a short-term basis for a specific reason, and then pull ourselves out of it before it turns dangerous.

Lawyers' Other Personal Attributes. "Lawyer personalities aren't interchangeable with those of other professionals," and our typical personal attributes, besides emotional intelligence, that are unusually high or low compound our tendency toward distress and make it harder to recover.[267] High pessimism, introversion, skepticism, autonomy, abstraction and urgency, low sociability and resilience, and limited conflict resolution strategies all tend to isolate lawyers and feed their distress.[268] These traits in some respects both reflect and exacerbate low EI, but they also can be moderated with greater EI.

Pessimism is so high and pervasive among lawyers, and it impacts EI and attempts to cultivate EI so much, that it deserves a separate discussion. Professor Seligman, founder of the school of Positive Psychology that focuses on personal attributes that produce success, concluded after studying 104 professions that only one profession—lawyers—has a personal attribute that promotes success, and that is pessimism. Pessimism was so highly correlated with success in law that the more pessimistic the law student, the more successful they were on "the traditional measures of achievement, such as grade point averages and law journal success."[269]

In *Authentic Happiness,* Seligman points to pessimism as the primary source of the physical and emotional ravages that the legal profession suffers: pessimism can be useful in a legal career but does not always make for a happy or successful human being. "Lawyers who can see clearly how badly things might turn out for their clients can also see clearly how badly things might turn out for themselves. Pessimistic lawyers are more likely to believe they will not make partner, that their profession is a racket, that their spouse is unfaithful, or that the economy is headed for disaster."[270]

Given all these tendencies, lawyers are more likely to find it challenging to effectively lead and mentor others, work in teams, maintain collegial partnerships, attract and retain clients, and develop loyal staff. Further, their social lives may suffer due to difficulties maintaining personal social support. A hesitancy to seek help further compounds their difficulties.[271] All of this can leave lawyers feeling isolated, disconnected, and unsuccessful in their work and personal lives—feelings that can exacerbate distress into a dangerous, downward spiral.[272]

ACCOUNTING FOR LAWYER DISTRESS

- The zero-sum winner-take-all litigation model, low decision latitude, and fierce rationality that underpin law practice all promote distress.
- Lawyers register high levels of career dissatisfaction and unhappiness, evidenced in attrition rates.
- Lawyers may have a predisposition to a negative mood, correlated to higher scores on the LSAT, which could prime them for unhappiness and depression.

(Continued)

- Lawyers' distinctive personal attributes magnify the likelihood of distress: high pessimism, introversion, skepticism, autonomy, urgency, abstraction, and low sociability and resilience, coupled with limited conflict resolution skills.
- An aversion to seeking aid exacerbates lawyers' suffering.
- Low emotional intelligence both gives rise to lawyers' distress and leaves them less equipped to identify and resolve emotional stressors.

This profile doesn't mean that lawyers are doomed.[273] But it does require building EI skills to effectively turn these attributes into advantages that support instead of sabotage a practice.

Both the Shultz and Zedeck and Georgetown studies of successful lawyers confirmed the performance value of managing distress with EI skills. Shultz and Zedeck concluded that personal attributes, such as optimism and the ability to recognize and regulate emotions, are more significant in accounting for effective lawyer performance than cognitive factors.[274] Georgetown found that the highest-performing associates were able to maintain "equanimity" in the face of pressure and anxiety, deal well with "unforeseen demands or setbacks," and build and use social networks while maintaining some "emotional independence."[275]

Lawyers can muster their highly tuned intelligence, ambition, competitiveness, and winner-take-all mindset in the service of building EI skills.

EMOTIONALLY INTELLIGENT LAWYERS ARE HEALTHIER AND HAPPIER

Despite high stress and personal vulnerabilities specific to lawyers, raising emotional intelligence produces:

- Better physical health with
  - Less incidence of coronary disease and other illness, lower blood pressure, stronger immunity, and better cognitive performance under pressure.

(Continued)

- Better mental health with
  - Greater happiness and well-being, more social connectedness, higher rates of job satisfaction, and lower anxiety, stress, burnout, depression, substance abuse, and suicide.

Of course, if you're already quite satisfied with your work and personal life, you might be asking yourself why you should care about your emotional intelligence. Psychology Professor Jack Mayer, one of the original theorists of EI, concedes that people with low EI can still be highly successful due to other strengths that they adapt. Certainly, in law relatively low average EI compared to other professions has obviously not been a bar to certain types of success.

Nonetheless, Professor Mayer and others insist that anyone with less than an optimal EI would perform at a higher level, feel mentally and physically better, and enjoy work, colleagues, friends and family more if they were better able to recognize and handle emotions—both their own and those of others.[276]

This is how Mayer describes what high EI looks like in the real world: "The high EI individual, most centrally, can better perceive emotions, use them in thought, understand their meanings, and manage emotions than others. Solving emotional problems likely requires less cognitive effort . . . The person also tends to be somewhat higher in verbal, social, and other intelligences, particularly if the individual scored higher in the understanding emotions portion of EI . . . tends to be more open and agreeable . . . is drawn to occupations involving social interactions such as teaching and counseling more so than to occupations involving clerical or administrative tasks . . . is less apt to engage in problematic behaviors, and avoids self-destructive, negative behaviors such as smoking, excessive drinking, drug abuse, or violent episodes . . . is more likely to have possessions of sentimental attachment around the home and to have more positive social interactions, particularly if the individual scored highly on emotional management. Such individuals may also be more adept at describing motivational goals, aims, and missions."[277]

FOUR ADVANTAGES EMOTIONAL INTELLIGENCE BRINGS TO YOUR PRACTICE

1. Emotionally intelligent lawyers are smarter.
2. Emotionally intelligent lawyers are stronger practitioners: negotiators, case managers, litigators, and judges.
3. Emotionally intelligent lawyers make more money.
4. Emotionally intelligent lawyers are healthier and happier.

Chapter Endnotes

1. Arnie Herz, "Relationships Are King," *Touro Law Review* 24 (2008): 4.
2. Those factors were Self-Actualization, Happiness, Stress Tolerance, Assertiveness, and Social Responsibility. Stein and Book, *The EQ Edge,* 317.
3. Irene E. Taylor, "Top 40: 40 and Under 40," *Lexpert,* November/December, 1–13, 92. These high EI lawyers also had stronger interpersonal skills, such as empathy, were more self-actualized, managed stress more effectively, were more optimistic, and were older than their less distinguished colleagues.
4. Daicoff, "Expanding the Lawyer's Toolkit of Skills and Competencies: Synthesizing Leadership, Professionalism, Emotional Intelligence, Conflict Resolution, and Comprehensive Law," *Santa Clara Law Review* 52 (2012): 818–19.
5. Richard, "Herding Cats," *Altman Weil Report to Legal Management,* 1–12; Richard, personal communication.
6. They scored 102 on the MSCEIT, higher than the averages we have for lawyers. R. Muir, L. Richard, unpublished data, 2005. Like most lawyers, these excellent lawyers were weakest at recognizing emotions and best at analyzing emotions. Their highest average score was in Understanding Emotions (112), with a relative strength in Managing Emotion (104).
7. Randall Kiser, *How Leading Lawyers Think: Expert Insights into Judgment and Advocacy* (New York: Springer-Verlag, 2011), 11–19, 92, 100–103. Most of those selected had tried between 30 and 175 cases. Their clients obtained better, rather than worse, financial results at trial by rejecting their adversary's settlement proposals, and their demands/offers were within 20 percent of the ultimate trial award.
8. Daicoff, "Expanding the Lawyer's Toolkit of Skills and Competencies," *Santa Clara Law Review,* 818–19, 824–25.
9. Marjorie M. Shultz and Sheldon Zedeck, "Predicting Lawyer Effectiveness: Broadening the Basis for Law School Admission Decisions," *Law & Social Inquiry* 36 (2011): 629.
10. Ibid., 625, 654.
11. Ibid., 654.

12. Berman and Bock, "Developing Attorneys for the Future: What Can We Learn from the Fast Trackers?" *Santa Clara Law Review,* 891, 895.
13. Ibid., 895.
14. Ibid., 895–97.
15. Robert Musil, "On Stupidity," lecture, delivered in Vienna, March 1937.
16. Bradberry, "Habits of Highly Emotionally Intelligent People," *PS News.*
17. The Wechsler Adult Intelligence Scale, the most widely used IQ test, was developed in 1939 by David Wechsler. "David Wechsler," in *Encyclopædia Britannica,* 2016, retrieved from https://www.britannica.com/biography/David-Wechsler-American-psychologist.
18. Richard, "Why Smart Lawyers Fail," presentation to the American Bar Association, 2007.
19. There is some evidence that high EI is primarily a benefit in work that involves "emotional labor" (i.e., work that invokes our emotions). Lawyering, while often emotion-averse, nonetheless regularly engages our emotions. Dana L. Joseph and Daniel A. Newman 2010, "Emotional Intelligence: An Integrative Meta-analysis and Cascading Model," *Journal of Applied Psychology* 95 (1): 54–78.
20. Ernest H. O'Boyle et al., "The Relation Between Emotional Intelligence and Job Performance: A Meta-Analysis," *Journal of Organizational Behavior* 32 (5): 789, 806.
21. Cary Cherniss, *The Business Case for Emotional Intelligence* (New Brunswick, NJ: Consortium for Research on Emotional Intelligence in Organizations, Rutgers University, 1999).
22. Antoine Bechara et al., "Insensitivity to Future Consequences Following Damage to Human Prefrontal Cortex," *Cognition* 50 (1994): 1–3, 7–15.
23. Kahneman, *Thinking Fast and Slow.*
24. Daniel Goleman, "They've Taken Emotional Intelligence Too Far," *TIME,* November 1, 2011.
25. Richard, "The Psychologically Savvy Leader," *LawyerBrain Blog,* November 11, 2013, http://www.lawyerbrainblog.com/2013/11/the-psychologically-savvy-leader/.
26. Bradberry and Greaves, *Emotional Intelligence 2.0,* 234.
27. Dan Ariely, *Predictably Irrational: The Hidden Forces That Shape Our Decisions* (New York: Harper Collins, 2008); Benedetto De Martino et al., "Frames, Biases, and Rational Decision-Making in the Human Brain," *Science* 313 (5787): 684–87.
28. Damásio, *Descartes' Error,* 165–201.
29. Kahneman, *Thinking Fast and Slow.* See also Gigerenzer, G. *Gut Feelings: The Intelligence of the Unconscious.* New York: Viking. (2007). A director at the Max Planck Institute for Human Development, whose breakthrough research was a major source for Malcolm Gladwell's *Blink,* goes step-by-step through the science of good decision-making. "The trick is not to amass information, but to discard it: to know intuitively what one doesn't need to know" by drawing on a collection of "cognitive, emotional and social" data. https://www.mpib-berlin.mpg.de/en/research/adaptive-behavior-and-cognition/publications/books/gut-feelings
30. Ibid., 21.

31. Bradberry and Greaves, *Emotional Intelligence 2.0,* 234. "A full 70 percent of male leaders who rank in the top 15 percent in decision-making skills also score the highest in emotional intelligence skills. In contrast, not one single male leader with low EQ was among the most skilled decision makers." Jeremy Yip and Stephane Côté, "The Emotionally Intelligent Decision Maker: Emotion-Understanding Ability Reduces the Effect of Incidental Anxiety on Risk Taking," *Psychological Science* 24 (1): 48–55.
32. David and Congleton, "Emotional Agility," *Harvard Business Review.*
33. Moira Mikolajczak et al. "Sensitive but Not Sentimental: Emotionally Intelligent People Can Put Their Emotions Aside When Necessary," *Personality and Individual Differences* 52 (4) (2012): 537–40; Corey K. Fallon et al. "Emotional Intelligence, Cognitive Ability and Information Search in Tactical Decision-Making," *Personality and Individual Differences* 65 (2014): 24–29.
34. Bradberry and Greaves, *Emotional Intelligence: 2.0,* 234, emphasis in original. See also James D. Hess and Arnold C. Bacigalupo, "Enhancing Decisions and Decision Making Processes Through the Application of Emotional Intelligence Skills," *Management Decision* 49 (5): 710–21.
35. Cherniss, "Emotional Intelligence: What It Is and Why It Matters," paper presented at the Annual Meeting of the Society for Industrial and Organizational Psychology, New Orleans, LA, April 15, 2000.
36. George E. Vaillant, *Triumphs of Experience: The Men of the Harvard Grant Study* (Cambridge, MA: Belknap Press, 2012).
37. "Cambridge-Somerville Youth Study," *ChildTrends,* 2007, http://childtrends.org/?programs=cambridge-somerville-youth-study.
38. Hess and Bacigalupo, "Enhancing Decisions and Decision Making Processes Through the Application of Emotional Intelligence Skills," *Management Decision,* 711.
39. Douglas Okasaki, "You Can No Longer Hide Your Emotions," *Gulf News,* January 28, 2014, http://gulfnews.com/business/media-marketing/you-can-no-longer-hide-your-emotions-1.1283230.
40. William L. Ury, Roger Fisher, and Bruce M. Patton, *Getting to YES: Negotiation Agreement Without Giving In* (New York: Houghton Mifflin, 1981), 29.
41. Clark Freshman, Adele Hayes, and Greg Feldman. "The Lawyer-Negotiator as Mood Scientist: What We Know and Don't Know about How Mood Relates to Successful Negotiation." *Journal of Dispute Resolution* 1 (2002): 1–79.
42. James K. Sebenius, "Six Habits of Merely Effective Negotiators," *Harvard Business Review,* April, 2001, 89.
43. Leonard L. Riskin, "Annual Saltman Lecture: Further Beyond Reason: Emotions, the Core Concerns, and Mindfulness in Negotiation," *Nevada Law Journal* 10 (2009): 294.
44. Michael Wheeler, "Get in the Right State of Mind for Any Negotiation," *Harvard Business Review,* May 5, 2015.
45. Ury, Fisher, and Patton, *Getting to YES.*
46. Roger Fisher and Daniel Shapiro, *Beyond Reason: Using Emotions as You Negotiate* (New York: Viking, 2005), 5–8.
47. Gerben Van Kleef and Stephane Gote, "Expressing Anger in Conflict: When It Helps and When It Hurts," *Journal of Applied Psychology* 92 (6): 1557–69.

48. Alan Filipowicz, Barsade, and Shimul Melwani, "Understanding Emotional Transitions: The Interpersonal Consequences of Changing Emotions in Negotiations," *Journal of Personality and Social Psychology* 101 (3): 541–56.
49. David Matsumoto et al., "Unraveling the Psychological Correlates of Intercultural Adjustment Potential," *International Journal of Intercultural Relations* 28 (3): 281–309.
50. Hilary Anger Elfenbein et al., "Reading Your Counterpart: The Benefit of Emotion Recognition Accuracy for Effectiveness in Negotiation," *Journal of Nonverbal Behavior* 31 (4): 205–23.
51. These results held even after controlling for the opponent's personality and how much he or she eventually received in the negotiation. The negotiator's IQ was found not to play a role in the outcome. "Practical implications of these findings are clear; when negotiations require a future relationship or future cooperative interaction, it is better to assign a person to the negotiation who understands emotions." Jennifer S. Mueller and Jared R. Curhan, "Emotional Intelligence and Counterpart Mood Induction in a Negotiation," *International Journal of Conflict Management* 17 (2): 122.
52. Lynn Imai and Michele J. Gelfand, "The Culturally Intelligent Negotiator: The Impact of Cultural Intelligence (CQ) on Negotiation Sequences and Outcomes," *Organizational Behavior and Human Decision Processes* 112 (2): 83–98.
53. Elyse Glickman, "Work/Life: Mark Baer," *Los Angeles Business Journal*, August 28, 2015, http://www.labusinessjournal.com/news/2015/aug/28/worklife-mark-baer/. A growing body of literature on emotions and mediated conflict resolution is reviewed in Tricia S. Jones, "Emotion in Mediation: Implications, Applications, Opportunities, and Challenges," in Margaret S. Harman ed., *Handbook of Mediation: Bridging Theory, Research and Practice* (Hoboken, NJ: Wiley-Blackwell, 2006).
54. Charlie Irvine, "Building Emotional Intelligence," in *Choreography of Resolution*, eds. Michelle LeBaron, Carrie MacLeod, and Andrew Floyer Acland (New York: American Bar Association, 2013), 108. Professor Irvine teaches a master's program in Mediation and Conflict Resolution at Strathclyde Law School, Glasgow, Scotland, is chairman of the Scottish Mediation Network, and is adjunct professor at John Marshal Law School, Chicago.
55. Kiser, "The Emotionally Intelligent Lawyer: Balancing the Rule of Law with the Realities of Human Behavior," *Nevada Law Journal* 15 (2): 52.
56. Cases in which plaintiffs had contingency fee arrangements and those in which defendants did not have insurance coverage both more often mistakenly went to trial. Kiser, *Beyond Right and Wrong: The Power of Effective Decision Making for Attorneys and Clients* (Berlin: Springer-Verlag, 2010), 52, 119.
57. Ibid., 55.
58. Jane Goodman-Delahunty et al., "Insightful or Wishful: Lawyers' Ability to Predict Case Outcomes," *Psychology, Public Policy, and Law* 16 (2): 139.
59. Ibid., 144.
60. Michel Pham et al., "Feeling the Future: The Emotional Oracle Effect," *Journal of Consumer Research* 29 (3): 461–77.

61. "The Emotional Oracle Effect," *Columbia Business School Newsroom*, February 24, 2012, https://www8.gsb.columbia.edu/newsroom/newsn/1957/the-emotional-oracle-effect.
62. Richard, "Resilience and Lawyer Negativity," *LawyerBrain Blog*, September 19, 2012, http://www.lawyerbrainblog.com/2012/09/resilience-and-lawyer-negativity/.
63. People are more averse to taking a risk when they expect to gain something, but are more willing to take a risk when they have something to lose, so both attorney and client decisions may be affected by whether they perceive they have something to win or something to lose. Behavioral economist and University of Pennsylvania finance professor Martin Asher notes that when given the choice to receive $200 or flip a coin to receive either nothing or $500, most people take the $200 rather than risk getting nothing. But if they become the payor, they choose to flip the coin, risking a bigger loss in hopes of not having to pay anything. Randall L. Kiser, Martin A. Asher, and Blakely B. McShane, "Let's Not Make a Deal," *Journal of Empirical Legal Studies* 5 (3): 551–91; Jonathan D. Glater, "Study Finds Settling Is Better Than Going to Trial," *New York Times*, August 7, 2007.
64. Atul Gawande, "Letting Go," *The New Yorker*, August 2, 2010, 6.
65. Kiser, *How Leading Lawyers Think*, 82.
66. Ibid.
67. Sonita Hayward, "Emotional Intelligence in Litigation," *The Law Society Gazette*, July 31, 2015, http://www.lawgazette.co.uk/law/practice-points/emotional-intelligence-in-litigation/5050357.article
68. Ibid.
69. Howard Scher, "Litigation: The 5 Traits of Highly Effective Trial Lawyers: Experience and Specialization Aren't Always the Most Important Qualities for a Successful Lawyer," *Inside Counsel Magazine*, August 30, 2012.
70. Kiser, *How Leading Lawyers Think*, 82, 84.
71. Ibid., 80.
72. Ibid., 109–10.
73. Ibid., 85.
74. Ian Gallacher, "Thinking Like Non-Lawyers: Why Empathy Is a Core Lawyering Skill and Why Legal Education Should Change to Reflect Its Importance," *Journal of the Association of Legal Writing Directors*, October 16, 2010, 25.
75. Ibid., 19.
76. Ibid., 28.
77. Kiser, *How Leading Lawyers Think*. See also Neil Feigenson, Jaihyun Park, and Peter Salovey, "Effect of Blameworthiness and Outcome Severity on Attributions of Responsibility and Damage Awards in Comparative Negligence Cases," *Law and Human Behavior* 21 (6): 597–617.
78. Ibid., 85.
79. Terry A. Maroney, "Angry Judges," *Vanderbilt Law Review* 65 (2012): 59.
80. Mark Baer, "Empathy and Decision Making," *Huffington Post*, August 17, 2015, http://www.huffingtonpost.com/mark-baer/empathy-and-decision-maki_b_7992786.html; Daniel Lukasik, "Judges and Depression," 2011, http://www.in.gov/judiciary/center/files/jedu-lib-social-dark-side-judging-depression-article.pdf.

81. Andrew Keshner, "Trial Founders on 'Personality Issues' Between Judge, Counsel," *New York Law Journal*, May 17, 2013, http://www.newyorklawjournal.com/PubArticleNY.jsp?id=1202600442171&Trial_Founders_on_Personality_Issues_Between_Judge_Counsel#ixzz2Yg5ziBFr.
82. "Oprah Interviews Sonia Sotomayor," *O Magazine*, February, 2013, 146.
83. Kahneman, *Thinking Fast and Slow*, 44.
84. Richard, "Herding Cats," *Altman Weil Report to Legal Management*, 1–12.
85. Maroney, "Angry Judges," *Vanderbilt Law Review*, 1218, 1262.
86. Ibid., 1263, 1262.
87. Peter Salovey and Dennis C. Turk, *Reasoning, Inference, and Judgment in Clinical Psychology* (New York: Free Press, 1988), 107–23.
88. Maroney, "Angry Judges," *Vanderbilt Law Review*, 1267.
89. Marc A. Brackett et al., "The Influence of Teacher Emotion on Grading Practices: A Preliminary Look at the Evaluation of Student Writing," *Teachers and Teaching: Theory and Practice* 19 (6): 634–46.
90. Joseph P. Forgas, "Don't Worry, Be Sad! On the Cognitive, Motivational, and Interpersonal Benefits of Negative Mood," *Current Directions in Psychological Science* 22 (2013): 225–32.
91. Maroney, "Angry Judges," *Vanderbilt Law Review*.
92. Bradberry and Greaves, *Emotional Intelligence 2.0*, 21–22.
93. Côté et al., "Emotional Intelligence and Leadership Emergence in Small Groups," *Leadership Quarterly* 21 (2010): 496–508.
94. John Bachman et al., "Emotional Intelligence in the Collection of Debt," *International Journal of Selection and Assessment* 8 (2000): 176–82; David C. McClelland, "Identifying Competencies with Behavioral-Event Interviews," *Psychological Science* 9 (5): 331–39; Bar-On et al., "The Bar-On Model of Emotional-Social Intelligence (ESI)," *Psicothema*, 18 (2006), suppl. 13–25; Arthur H. Perlini and Trevor R. Halverson, "Emotional Intelligence in the National Hockey League," *Canadian Journal of Behavioural Science* 38 (2): 109–19.
95. The exact extent to which EI accounts for performance is difficult to quantify, although several researchers have attempted it. Goleman originally estimated 80 percent of performance was due to EI (Goleman, *Emotional Intelligence*), but later revised that down to two-thirds. Goleman, *Working with Emotional Intelligence*, 31. A 2006 meta-analysis concluded "that roughly 29% of the variance in occupational performance is accounted for by EI." Perlini and Halverson, "Emotional Intelligence in the National Hockey League," *Canadian Journal of Behavioural Science*. A proprietary study found that EI "accounts for 58% of performance in all types of jobs," and that "90% of high performers are high in EQ. On the flip side, just 20% of low performers are high in EQ." Bradberry and Greaves, *Emotional Intelligence 2.0*, 20–21. Some still question EI's role, particularly in jobs that do not require emotional labor. In one comprehensive analysis, researchers concluded that cognitive ability accounted for more than 14 percent of job performance and EI accounted for less than 1 percent. Dana L. Joseph and Daniel A. Newman, "Emotional Intelligence: An Integrative Meta-analysis and Cascading Model," *Journal of Applied Psychology* 95 (1): 54–78.

96. Paulo N. Lopes, Peter Salovey, and Rebecca Straus, "Emotional Intelligence, Personality and the Perceived Quality of Social Relationships," *Personality and Individual Differences* 35 (3): 641–58.
97. Boyatzis, "Presentation at the Linkage Conference on Emotional Intelligence," Chicago, IL, September 27, 1999.
98. Boyatzis, "Using Tipping Points of Emotional Intelligence and Cognitive Competencies to Predict Financial Performance of Leaders," *Psicothema* 18 (2006): 130.
99. Ibid. Cary Cherniss, "Business Case for Emotional Intelligence," 1999, http://www.eiconsortium.org/reports/business_case_for_ei.html. Bradberry and Greaves, "Self Scores of Emotional Intelligence and Job Performance: An Analysis across Industry and Position," *TalentSmart,* 2003, http://www.talentsmart.com/media/uploads/pdfs/Technical_Manual.pdf; McClelland, "Identifying Competencies with Behavioral-Event Interviews," *Psychological Science.*
100. Heidi Gardner, "When Senior Managers Won't Collaborate," *Harvard Business Review,* March 10, 2015, 11, 20. Gardner released a book in 2016 entitled *Smart Collaboration: How Professionals and Their Firms Succeed by Breaking Down Silos.* Boston, Mass; Harvard Business Review Press.
101. Peter Drucker, "Are Your Clients Turning into Customers?" *InFocus,* 2014, http://us5.campaign-archive2.com/?u=7e4e5944cae60e106511e4739&id=782f09508b&e=eb7993ca93.
102. Richard, "Herding Cats," *Altman Weil Report to Legal Management,* 1–12.
103. Quoted in David Maister, "Are Law Firms Manageable?" *DavidMaister.com,* 2006, http://davidmaister.com/articles/are-law-firms-manageable/.
104. The advent of sophisticated software that lawyers can use to manage their caseloads and clients does not mean that personal skills are or will become less valuable. In fact, they may become more valuable. Michael Mills, "What Are Good Humans for . . . in Legal Services?" *3 Geeks and a Law Blog,* September 21, 2015, http://www.geeklawblog.com/2015/09/what-are-humans-good-for-in-legal.html?m=1.
105. John O Cunningham, "Chief Legal Officers Tell Outside Counsel What They Want . . . and Don't," *C3,* June 20, 2013, https://johnocunningham.wordpress.com/2013/06/20/chief-legal-officers-tell-outside-counsel-what-they-want-and-dont/; see also the 16th Annual BTI Client Service All-Stars 2017, *BTI Consulting Group,* http://www.bticonsulting.com/client-service-all-stars-law.
106. While sometimes a useful career tool, pessimism, which lawyers are high in, undercuts trust and relationships. Seligman, *Authentic Happiness* (New York: Free Press, 2002), 179. The majority of lawyers are introverts, unlike the general population. Richard found that lawyers score exceedingly high on the Caliper Profile in "skepticism"—in the 90th percentile, meaning nearly all the lawyers were highly skeptical. Skeptics are cynical, judgmental, questioning, argumentative, and self-protective, and being skeptical makes it hard to trust others and to earn others' trust. Lawyers score in the 89th percentile in autonomy, indicating they prefer working alone, without much supervision. They score in the 81st percentile in "abstract thinking," clearly helpful in some aspects of work, but may also limit the ability

to recognize and take concrete steps. Lawyers score in the 78th percentile in "urgency"—a sense of immediacy, which can make them impatient and more prone to mistakes. They score in the 19th percentile in sociability, which means they are likely uncomfortable initiating social interactions, building relationships of all kinds, and "participating in activities requiring emotional rather than analytic intelligence." They score in the 30th percentile in resilience, which indicates difficulties in recovering from setbacks and raises one's defensiveness. Richard, "The Lawyer Types," *ABA Journal*; Richard, "Herding Cats," *Altman Weil Report to Legal Management,* 1–12. See also Deborah L. Rhode, "Developing Leadership," *Santa Clara Law Review* 52 (3): 695.

107. Maister, "Are Law Firms Manageable?" *DavidMaister.com.*
108. Mike Schultz and John Doerr, "How Clients Buy: 2009 Benchmark Report on Professional Services Marketing and Selling from the Client Perspective," *RainToday.com Research,* 2009.
109. Drucker, "Are Your Clients Turning into Customers?" *InFocus.*
110. "Daniel H. Pink: 7 Questions in 10 Minutes—The New World of Sales and Selling," *The Arts and Business Council of Greater Philadelphia,* January 28, 2013, YouTube Video [10:00], http://www.youtube.com/watch?v=O1bSwewzyjQ#t=145.
111. "Attorneys Pose Biggest Obstacle to Law Firm Growth," *BTI Consulting Group,* January 18, 2017, http://www.bticonsulting.com/themadclientist/2017/1/18/attorneys-pose-biggest-obstacle-to-law-firm-growth. Culture is second, with 23.9 percent of CMOs blaming it this year. Percent blaming attorneys is up from 18.6 percent in 2014.
112. Susan Saltonstall Duncan, "How to Sell: Stop Pitching and Start Listening and Relating," *InFocus: Insights on Legal Practice Strategies and Innovations,* February 7, 2013, http://www.rainmakingoasis.com/wp-content/uploads/2016/08/How-to-Sell_Stop-Pitching-and-Start-Listening-and-Relating.pdf.
113. Over 57 percent of lawyers tested are introverts, compared to only 25 percent of the general population. Richard, "The Lawyer Types," *ABA Journal.* Other later studies have found up to 60 percent of lawyers to be introverts. Leslie A. Gordon, "Most Lawyers Are Introverted, and That's Not Necessarily a Bad Thing," *ABA Journal,* January 1, 2016.
114. "Daniel H. Pink: 7 Questions in 10 Minutes," *The Arts and Business Council of Greater Philadelphia;* Greg Fleischmann, Kevin Iredell, and Kevin McMurdo, "Sales Professionals in Law Firms—Are We Finally Ready?" *LMA International,* September 9, 2015, http://blog.legalmarketing.org/sales-professionals-in-the-law-firm-are-we-finally-ready.
115. Peter Reilly, "Teaching a Law Student How to Feel: Using Negotiations Training to Increase Emotional Intelligence," *Negotiation Journal* 21 (2005): 301–14.
116. Patrick Mayock, "Conley Talks Jobs, Careers, Callings," *HotelNewsNow,* February 28, 2012, http://www.hotelnewsnow.com/articles/14304/Conley-talks-jobs-careers-callings
117. Erin N. Griswold, "Law Schools and Human Relations," *Chicago Bar Record* 37 (1956): 199–208.

118. Boris Groysberg and Eliot Sherman, "Baker & McKenzie (B): A New Framework for Talent Management," *Harvard Business School Review*, 2007, 1.
119. Attributed to Theodore Roosevelt, Michael F. Andrew, "People Don't Care How Much You Know Until They Know How Much You Care," *LinkedIn.com*, February 19, 2015, https://www.linkedin.com/pulse/show-how-much-you-care-michael-f-andrew.
120. James L. Heskett, Thomas O. Jones, Gary W. Loveman, W. Earl Sasser, Jr., Leonard A. Schlesinger, "Putting the Service-Profit Chain to Work," *Harvard Business Review*, July–August 2008
121. "InHouse Counsel Magazine ACC/Serengeti Managing Outside Counsel Survey," *InHouse Magazine*, 2006. In 2006, chief legal officers in the top 250 corporations said that during the prior year they recommended only a quarter of their outside firms, and two-thirds fired as many as half their primary firms. One survey showed that nationally 70 percent of Fortune 1000 companies do not recommend their primary law firm. Marcie Borgal, "How to Prevent the Dreaded 'Dissatisfied Client Syndrome,'" *Complete Lawyer*, 2 (2006).
122. Susan Saltonstall Duncan, "In 2013, Will More Firms Finally Understand that Client Feedback = Better Revenue and Profitability?," *InFocus Blog*, January 3, 2013, http://www.rainmakingoasis.com/in-2013-will-more-firms-finally-understand-that-client-feedback-better-revenue-and-profitability/.
123. Sheila A. Scott-Halsell, Shane C. Blum, and Lynn Huffman, "A Study of Emotional Intelligence Levels in Hospitality Industry Professionals," *Journal of Human Resources in Hospitality and Tourism* 7 (2): 149–50. For a case study of improving guest satisfaction in the hospitality space by using EI, see "Case: Emotional Intelligence for Hospitality at Restaurant Sunndays," *Six Seconds*, Apr 24, 2017, http://www.6seconds.org/2017/04/24/case-emotional-intelligence-hospitality-restaurant-sunndays/
124. Jeff Blumenthal, "Lawyers Take Lessons on Leadership," *Philadelphia Business Journal*, October 2, 2006.
125. Symon Bridle quoted in Julie Weed, "Checking In After Checkout," *New York Times*, May 27, 2013.
126. Andrea Petersen, "Checking In? Hidden Ways Hotels Court Guests Faster," *The Wall Street Journal*, April 11, 2012.
127. Ibid.
128. "Professional services are notoriously opaque: It's hard for clients to judge their value, even after the fact." Gardner, "When Senior Managers Won't Collaborate," *Harvard Business Review*.
129. Tom R. Tyler, "The Psychological Consequences of Judicial Procedures: Implications for Civil Commitment Hearings," in *Law in a Therapeutic Key: Developments in Therapeutic Jurisprudence 3*, ed. David B. Wexler and Bruce J. Winick (Durham, NC: Carolina Academic Press, 1996), 433–38.
130. "Managing Outside Counsel Study," *InHouse Counsel Survey*, 2010, 26.
131. Seth Apple, "What General Counsel Really Want in a Law Firm," *National Law Review*, January 14, 2013.
132. Helen Duncan and Peter H. Mason, "In-House Counsel Offer Their Advice to Law-Firm Litigators," *San Francisco Daily Journal*, September 27, 2004, 5.

133. *Lexis Nexis Business of Law Blog*, http://businessoflaw.lexisnexis.co.uk/download-the-bellwether-report-2015/.
134. Aric Press, "Don't Look Down," *American Lawyer*, July 14, 2011.
135. Jonathan Middleburg and Lucy Butterworth, "Emotional Intelligence: What Can Learned Lawyers Learn from the Less Learned?" *The Barrister Magazine*, 2013.
136. Ibid., 5.
137. Todd Rakoff quoted in Robert A. Mines, Rachel A. Meyer, and Michael R. Mines, "Emotional Intelligence and Emotional Toxicity: Implications for Attorneys and Law Firms," *The Colorado Lawyer* 33 (4): 91–96.
138. Chris Frawley, "The Emotionally Intelligent Organization and the Customer Experience," November 3, 2013, http://www.beyondphilosophy.com/blog/the-emotionally-intelligent-organization-and-the-customer-experience/.
139. Groysberg and Sherman, "Baker & McKenzie (A): A New Framework for Talent Management," *Harvard Business School Review*, September 12, 2008, 3.
140. Salovey et al., "Emotional Intelligence in Practice," in *Positive Psychology in Practice*, ed. Alex Linely and Stephen Joseph (Hoboken, NJ: Wiley, 2004), 447–63.
141. Claire Zillman, "Survey: Generally Content, New Partners Fear Lack of Training Will Hamper Ability to Win Clients," *The Am Law Daily*, October 22, 2012.
142. Kristen B. Gerdy, "Clients, Empathy, and Compassion: Introducing First-Year Students to the 'Heart' of Lawyering," *Nebraska Law Review*, February 2008, 41–42.
143. John G. Balestriere, "In the Attorney-Client Relationship, You Are the Service Professional," *Above the Law*, February 5, 2016, http://abovethelaw.com/2016/02/in-the-attorney-client-relationship-you-are-the-service-professional/.
144. Maister, "Do You Really Want Relationships?" *DavidMaister.com*, 2005, http://davidmaister.com/articles/2/80/.
145. The value of the emotional connection in healthcare goes far beyond providing patients with simple comfort. Halpern, "What Is Clinical Empathy?" *Journal of General Internal Medicine*, 670–74. Empathy can be directly therapeutic by reducing patient anxiety and prompting more frank disclosure. Herbert M. Adler, "The History of the Present Illness as Treatment: Who's Listening, and Why Does It Matter?" *Journal of the American Board of Family Practice* 10 (1997): 28–35; William Zinn, "The Empathic Physician," *Archives of Internal Medicine* 153 (1993): 306–12. The emotional connection also helps uncover psychosocial concerns, which account for as much as 30 percent of physical illnesses. Elam and Stratton, "Should Medical School Applicants Be Tested for Emotional Intelligence?" *American Medical Association Journal of Ethics*.
146. B. Gabbe et al., "The Relationship Between Compensable Status and Long-Term Patient Outcomes Following Orthopaedic Trauma," *Medical Journal of Australia* 187 (2007): 14–17. A 2012 study in Holland also found that for personal injury clients "[o]ne predictor for worse recovery is lawyer engagement." N.A Elbers, "Exploring Lawyer-Client Interaction: A Qualitative Study of Positive Lawyer Characteristics," *Psychological Injury and Law* 5 (1): 89.

147. EAA, "Legal Abuse Syndrome," http://www.equalaccessadvocates.com/product/las/
148. A. Cotti et al., "Road Traffic Accidents and Secondary Victimisation: The Role of Law Professionals," *Medicine and Law* 23 (2004): 259-268. Practice group leader Ruth Hudson explains how EI makes her a better lawyer. Ruth Hudson, "The Importance of Emotional Intelligence for Lawyers," *Lawyers Weekly*, December 20, 2016, http://www.lawyersweekly.com.au/opinion/20258-the-importance-of-emotional-intelligence-for-lawyers.
149. Elbers et al., "Exploring Lawyer-Client Interaction," *Psychological Inquiry and Law*, 93.
150. Ibid., 93.
151. Herz, "Relationships Are King," *Touro Law Review*, 4.
152. Ilina Rejeva, "How Can Empathy Help You Differentiate Your Law Firm?" *Legal Trek.com*, September 28, 2014, https://legaltrek.com/blog/2014/09/how-can-empathy-help-you-differentiate-your-law-firm/.
153. "Reading Facial Expressions of Emotion," in *Psychological Science Agenda*, 2011.
154. Cristian Danescu-Niculescu-Mizil et al. "Echoes of Power: Language Effects and Power Differences in Social Interaction," paper presented at the International World Wide Web Conference, Lyon, France, April 16–29, 2012. An examination of the linguistic styles in oral argument in 204 Supreme Court cases found that people tended to "unconsciously mimic" the word usage of those who had higher status or power, and "when trying to convince someone of an opposing view." Female lawyers "coordinated" their word usage with justices more than male lawyers, but justices "coordinated" more with male lawyers than female lawyers. Karin Aronsson, Linda Jõnsson, and Per Linell, "The Courtroom Hearing as a Middle Ground: Speech Accommodation by Lawyers and Defendants," *Journal of Language and Social Psychology* 6 (1987): 99–115. In 2009 and 2010 Supreme Court cases, interruptions and questions by the justices signaled a likelihood of voting against the side they were questioning. Christopher M. Kimmel, Patrick A. Stewart, and William D. Schreckhise, "Of Closed Minds and Open Mouths: Indicators of Supreme Court Justice Votes during the 2009 and 2010 Sessions," *The Forum* 10 (2). Similarly, before becoming Chief Justice of the Supreme Court, John Roberts found the party who received the most questions during the 1980 and 2003 Supreme Court sessions lost the case 86 percent of the time. John G. Roberts, Jr. "Oral Advocacy and the Re-emergence of a Supreme Court Bar," *Journal of Supreme Court History* 30 (2005): 75. A study of the 202nd term found that justices played devils' advocate with parties with whom they disagreed much more than they did with parties with whom they agreed. Sarah Shullman, "The Illusion of Devil's Advocacy: How the Justices of the Supreme Court Foreshadow Their Decisions during Oral Arguments," *Journal of Appellate Practices and Processes* 6 (2004): 271. Similarly, with respect to Supreme Court oral arguments from 1979 to 1995, see Timothy R. Johnson, Ryan A Black, Jerry Goldman, and Sarah Treul, "Inquiring Minds Want to Know: Do Justices Tip Their Hands with Questions at Oral Argument in the U.S. Supreme Court?" *Washington University Journal of Law and Policy*, 29 (2009): 241–61. For cases in 1969–1970, see Glendon Schubert, "Oral Arguments in

Supreme Court Decision Making: Ethological and Paralinguistic Analysis of Psychophysiological Biosocial Political Behavior," in Albert Somit and Steven A Person, eds., *Research on Biopolitics*, Vol 5 (Greenwich, CT: JAI Press, 2007), 3–56.

155. Margaret T. McLaughlin et al., "Juror Perceptions of Participants in Criminal Proceedings," *Journal of Applied Communication Research* (1979), 91–102.
156. Rich Steeves, "Price, Service among Key Reasons Why Clients Fire Law Firms," *Inside Counsel*, September 12, 2013, http://www.insidecounsel.com/2013/09/12/price-service-among-key-reasons-why-clients-fire-l.
157. Aric Press, "Why Clients Hire and Fire Law Firms," *American Lawyer*, September 10, 2013.
158. Gary Steedly and Paula Raines, "Emotional Intelligence: The Secret Ingredient in Effective Leadership," February, 18, 2007 (Powerpoint), slide 45.
159. Kara MacKillop and Neil Vidmar, "Legal Malpractice: A Preliminary Inquiry," *First Annual Conference on Empirical Legal Studies Paper*, 2006.
160. "Ways to Avoid Legal Malpractice, as Claims Rise Industry-Wide," *YourABA*, December, 2016, http://www.americanbar.org/publications/youraba/2016/december-2016/legal-malpractice-claims-are-on-the-rise—but-you-can-take-steps.html.
161. The training and coaching program provided to WellStar Health System's five hospitals and more than 550 doctors increased patient reports of clear communication from 77.5 to 86.2 percent after only a few months. "Communication is increasingly understood to be at the root of many of healthcare's failures—and a leading culprit in rising costs. Research shows that when doctors don't listen to patients, they miss important health cues and misdiagnose illness. Meanwhile, patients who don't understand what their doctors say fail to follow their regimens, leading to preventable hospitalizations, complications and poor outcomes." Patients at the University of Missouri School of Medicine medical center increased their satisfaction ratings from the lowest quarter of hospitals in the country to over 90 percent after physician training. Lisa Landro, "The Talking Cure for Health Care: Improving the Ways Doctors Communicate with Their Patients Can Lead to Better Care—And Lower Costs," *The Wall Street Journal*, April 8, 2013. See also Cherry et al., "Emotional Intelligence in Medical Education," *Medical Education Journal*, 468–78.
162. Gerry Spence, *How to Argue and Win Every Time* (New York: Macmillan, 1995), 67.
163. The Canadian Bar Association's Task Force on Legal Literacy identified improving lawyers' listening skills as more effective in improving lawyers' public image than public relations efforts. "Reading the Legal World: Literacy and Justice in Canada: Report of the Canadian Bar Association Task Force on Legal Literacy" (Ottawa, Canada: Canadian Bar Association, 1992).
164. After the supervisors in a manufacturing plant received training in the emotional competency of how to listen better, lost-time accidents decreased by 50 percent, grievances went down from fifteen per year to three, and the plant significantly exceeded productivity goals. A. Pesuric and W. Byham, "The New Look in Behavior Modeling," *Training and Development* (1996): 25–33.

In another plant where supervisors received similar training, production increased 17 percent, compared to no increase for a group of matched supervisors who were not trained. Jerry I. Porras and Brad Anderson, "Improving Managerial Effectiveness Through Modeling-Based Training," *Organizational Dynamics* 9 (4): 60–77.

165. "What's the Number 1 Leadership Skill for Overall Success?" February 23, 2016, Development Dimensions International.
166. Comments made by GE Chairman and CEO Jeff Immelt in a speech at a conference in spring 2011 at the Georgetown Law School Center for the Study of the Legal Profession. Cited in Maister, Charles Green, and Robert Galford, *The Trusted Advisor* (New York: Touchstone, 2000), 97.
167. Ram Charan, "Why Leaders Cannot Afford to Turn a Deaf Ear to Their Stakeholders," *The Economic Times,* August 24, 2012.
168. Ibid. Also, Ram Charan, "The Discipline of Listening." *Harvard Business Review,* June 21, 2012.
169. Stephen E. Lucas, *The Art of Public Speaking* (New York: McGraw-Hill, 2012), 50.
170. Richard, "Herding Cats," *Altman Weil Report to Legal Management,* 1–12.
171. He names Feedly, Zite, and Flipboard as social media listening tools. Kevin O'Keefe, "Legal Professionals Missing the Most Important Aspect of Social Media: Listening," *Real Lawyers Have Blogs,* August 7, 2013, http://kevin.lexblog.com/2013/08/07/legal-professionals-missing-most-important-aspect-of-social-media-listening/.
172. Cordell Parvin, "One Great Differentiator: Become Your Clients' Best Listener," *Cordell Parvin Blog,* July 10, 2012, http://www.cordellblog.com/client-development/one-great-differentiator-become-your-clients-best-listener/.
173. Spence, *How to Argue and Win Every Time.*
174. William Shakespeare, *The Winter's Tale* (New York: Dover, 2000), Act V, scene V.2, lines 3119–3120.
175. Elizabeth LeVan, "Nonverbal Communication in the Courtroom: Attorney Beware," *Law and Psychology Review,* 83 (1984). Another study found that 10 percent of communication is verbal and as much as 90 percent is nonverbal. A. Mehrabian, *Silent Messages* (Belmont, CA: Wadsworth, 1971).
176. "Non-verbal Communication: Non-verbal Communication in the Courtroom," *Tolmage, Peskin, Harris, Falick Law Firm,* 2013, http://www.stephanpeskin.com/NY-Injury-Resources/Resources-for-Attorneys/Non-Verbal-Communication.shtml.
177. Tony Schwartz, *The Way We're Working Isn't Working: The Four Forgotten Needs that Energize Great Performance* (New York: Simon and Schuster, 2010).
178. Kathyrn Meagan Cowles, "Communication in the Courtroom," Bachelor's Thesis, 2011, 14; "Legal Beat: Judges Try Curbing Body-Language Antics," *The Wall Street Journal,* September, 1997.
179. "Non-verbal Communication," *Tolmage, Harris, Falick Law Firm.*
180. Duncan, "In 2013, Will More Firms Finally Understand That Client Feedback = Better Revenue and Profitability?" *InFocus Blog.* See Blair Kidwell et al., "Emotional Intelligence in Marketing Exchanges," *Journal of Marketing* 75 (2011): 78–95.

181. Jordan Furlong, "Pricing to the Client Experience," *Law 21 Blog,* March 1, 2012, http://www.law21.ca/2012/03/pricing-to-the-client-experience/.
182. "Client Feedback and Satisfaction," *BTI Consulting Group, Website,* 2013, http://www.bticonsulting.com/client-feedback-evaluation/.
183. Julie Triedman, "Billing $2K an Hour? Study Says Clients Will Pay if Lawyers Deliver," *American Lawyer,* May 12, 2016.
184. Grewal and Davidson, "Emotional Intelligence and Graduate Medical Education," *Journal of the American Medical Association.*
185. Denis Novack, quoted in, "Study Is First to Confirm That Stress Speeds Aging," *The Washington Post,* November 11, 2004.
186. George Valliant quoted in Steven J. Stein, Howard E. Book, and Korrel Kanoy, *The Student EQ Edge* (San Francisco, CA: Jossey-Bass, 2013), chapter 16.
187. Corina Greven, Tomas Chamorro-Premuzic, Adriane Arteche, and Adrian Furnham, "A Hierarchical Integration of Dispositional Determinants of General Health in Students: The Big Five, Trait Emotional Intelligence and Humor Styles," *Personality and Individual Differences* 44 (2008): 1562–73; Mayer, Roberts, and Barsade, "Human Abilities: Emotional Intelligence," *Annual Review of Psychology,* 507–36; Carol L. Gohm, Grant C. Corser, and David J. Dalsky, "Emotional Intelligence Under Stress: Useful, Unnecessary, or Irrelevant?" *Personal Individual Differences* 39 (2005): 1017–28; Gerald Matthews et al. "Emotional Intelligence, Personality, and Task-Induced Stress," *Journal of Experimental Psychology: Applied* 12 (2005): 96–107; Alexandra Martins, Nelson Ramalho, and Estelle Morin, "A Comprehensive Meta-analysis of the Relationship Between Emotional Intelligence and Health," *Personality and Individual Differences* 49 (6): 554–64.
188. Nicola S. Schutte et al. "A Meta-analytic Investigation of the Relationship between Emotional Intelligence and Health," *Personality and Individual Differences* 42 (6): 921–33; Martins, Ramalho, and Morin, "A Comprehensive Meta-analysis of the Relationship Between Emotional Intelligence and Health," *Personality and Individual Differences,* 561.
189. Martin Seligman, *Authentic Happiness,* 177.
190. Judy Martin, "Workplace Stress Is Curveball Lobbed at Employee Emotional Intelligence," *Forbes Online,* November 19, 2012, http://www.forbes.com/sites/work-in-progress/2012/11/19/workplace-stress-is-curveball-lobbed-at-employee-emotional-intelligence/.
191. Tomas Chamorro-Premuzic, "Can You Really Improve Your Emotional Intelligence?" *Harvard Business Review,* May 29, 2013.
192. "Stress in America: Missing the Healthcare Connection," *American Psychological Association,* 2012, https://www.apa.org/news/press/releases/stress/2012/full-report.pdf.
193. Petrie, "Wake Up! The Surprising Truth About What Drives Stress and How Leaders Build Resilience," *Center for Creative Leadership.*
194. Vivienne Parry, "How Emotional Pain Can Really Hurt," *BBC News,* July 19, 2008, http://news.bbc.co.uk/2/hi/health/7512107.stm.
195. Elissa Epel et al., "Can Meditation Slow Rate of Cellular Aging? Cognitive Stress, Mindfulness, and Telomeres," *Annals of the New York Academy of Sciences* 1172 (2009): 34–53.

196. Bruce McEwan, *The End of Stress as We Know It* (Washington, DC: Joseph Henry Press, 2002); D.K Thomsen et al., "Negative Thoughts and Health: Associations Among Rumination, Immunity, and Health Care Utilization in a Young and Elderly Sample," *Psychosomatic Medicine.*
197. Diane Coutu, "The Science of Thinking Smarter: A Conversation with Brain Expert John J. Medina," *Harvard Business Review,* May, 2008, 51-52.
198. "How Does Stress Influence Bad Decision-Making?" *European Commission: Community Research and Development Information Service,* http://cordis.europa.eu/news/rcn/31097_en.html.
199. Judy Martin, "Workplace Stress Is Curveball Lobbed at Employee Emotional Intelligence," *Forbes Online,* November 19, 2012, http://www.forbes.com/sites/work-in-progress/2012/11/19/workplace-stress-is-curveball-lobbed-at-employee-emotional-intelligence/.
200. Goleman, "Are Women More Emotionally Intelligent Than Men?" *Psychology Today.*
201. Robert M. Yerkes and John D. Dodson, "The Relation of the Strength of Stimulus to Rapidity of Habit Formation," *Journal of Comparative Neurology and Psychology* 18 (1908): 459–82.
202. Veneta A. Bastian, Nicholas R. Burns, and Ted Nettelbeck, "Emotional Intelligence Predicts Life Skills, but Not as Well as Personality and Cognitive Abilities," *Personal Individual Differences* 39 (2005): 1135–45; Gerald Matthews et al., "Emotional Intelligence, Personality, and Task-Induced Stress," *Journal of Experimental Psychology: Applied* 12 (2006): 96–107; John S. Carton et al., "Nonverbal Decoding Skills and Relationship Well-Being in Adults," *Journal of Nonverbal Behavior* 23 (1999): 91–100; Côté et al., "Emotional Intelligence and Leadership Emergence in Small Groups," 25.
203. For physicians, participating in emotional awareness training programs increases their patients' satisfaction, results in more patient-centered care, improves physicians' well-being, and reduces burnout. Krasner et al., "Association of an Education Program in Mindful Communication with Burnout, Empathy, and Attitudes Among Primary Care Physicians," *Journal of the American Medical Association* 302 (2009): 1284–93.
204. Maria Platsidou and Layla Salman, "The Role of Emotional Intelligence in Predicting Burnout and Job Satisfaction of Greek Lawyers," *International Journal of Law, Psychology and Human Life* 1 (2012): 13–22. Leanne Mezrani, "Fear of Failure Holding Back Young Lawyers," *Lawyers Weekly,* September 24, 2013, http://www.lawyersweekly.com.au/news/14721-fear-of-failure-holding-back-young-lawyers.
205. In some limited situations, negative thinking may lead to more accuracy, and optimistic thinking may underestimate risks. Christopher Peterson and Robert S. Vaidya, "Optimism as Vice and Virtue," in Edward C Chang, Lawrence J. Sanna eds., *Virtue, Vice, and Personality: The Complexity of Behavior* (Washington, DC: APA, 2003), 23–37. "Predicting Academic Strength Emotionally," *InderScience Publishers,* June, 28, 2011, http://www.alphagalileo.org/ViewItem.aspx?ItemId=106682&CultureCode=en. Saklofske et al., "Relationships of Personality, Affect, Emotional Intelligence and Coping with Student Stress and Academic Success: Different Patterns of Association

for Stress and Success," *Learning and Individual Differences,* 256. Cherniss, "Emotional Intelligence."

206. Seligman, *Authentic Happiness.*
207. "Seventy-One Percent of Employers Say They Value Emotional Intelligence Over IQ, According to CareerBuilder Survey," *CareerBuilder.com,* August 18, 2011.
208. Gordon, "How Lawyers Can Avoid Burnout and Debilitating Anxiety," *ABA Journal,* July 1, 2015.
209. Tsai Feng-Jen, Wei-Lun Huang, and Chang-Chuan Chan, "Occupational Stress and Burnout of Lawyers," *Journal of Occupational Health* 51 (2009): 443–50; Platsidou and Salman, "The Role of Emotional Intelligence in Predicting Burnout and Job Satisfaction of Greek Lawyers," *International Journal of Law, Psychology and Human Life;* Susan E. Jackson, Jon A. Turner, and Arthur P. Brief, "Correlates of Burnout Among Public Service Lawyers," *Journal of Occupational Behaviour* 8 (4): 339–49.
210. Gordon, "How Lawyers Can Avoid Burnout and Debilitating Anxiety," *ABA Journal.*
211. American Bar Association, Section of General Practice, *The Report of At the Breaking Point: A National Conference on the Emerging Crisis in the Quality of Lawyers' Health and Lives and Its Impact on Law Firms and Client Services* (Chicago: American Bar Association, 1991).
212. Daicoff, "Other, Expanding the Lawyer's Toolkit of Skills and Competencies," *Santa Clara Law Review,* 818–19, 807; Connie Beck, Bruce D. Sales, and G. Andrew H. Benjamin, "Lawyer Distress: Alcohol-Related Problems and Other Psychological Concerns Among a Sample of Practicing Lawyers," *Journal of Law and Health* 10 (1996): 1–50; G. Andrew H. Benjamin, E.J. Darling, and B.D. Sales, "The Prevalence of Depression, Alcohol Abuse, and Cocaine Abuse Among United States Lawyers," *Journal of Law and Psychiatry* 13 (3): 233–46.
213. Myer J. Cohen, "The Impaired Lawyer," *American Bar Association Experience,* 12 (2).
214. Daicoff, "Lawyer, Be Thyself: An Empirical Investigation of the Relationship between the Ethic of Care, the Feeling Decision-Making Preference, and Lawyer Wellbeing," *Virginia Journal of Social Policy of Law* 16 (87); Daicoff, "Expanding the Lawyer's Toolkit of Skills and Competencies," *Santa Clara Law Review,* supra note 20 at 6–7.
215. Benjamin, Darling, and Sales, "The Prevalence of Depression, Alcohol Abuse, and Cocaine Abuse among United States Lawyers," *Journal of Law and Psychiatry* 13 (3).
216. Cohen, "The Impaired Lawyer," *American Bar Association Experience.*
217. Roy Stuckey, *Best Practices for Legal Education* (New York: Clinical Legal Association, 2007), 22.
218. Kahneman, *Thinking Fast and Slow,* 233–46; Greg K. McCann, David J. Tarbert, and Michael S. Lenetsky, "The Sound of No Students Clapping: What Zen Can Offer Legal Education," *University of San Francisco Law Review* 29 (6): 313–14.
219. Karen Sloan, "Law Schools Tackle Mental Health," *National Law Journal,* May 9, 2016. This is consistent with a significant portion of practicing attorneys

who reported in the 2016 Hazelden Betty Ford/ABA study that their drinking problem began in law school.

220. Brianna Pena, *Falling through the Cracks: A Report on Mental Health at Yale Law School* (New Haven, CT: Yale Law School Mental Health Alliance, 2014); Sloan, "Yale Law Students Lobby for Better Services," *National Law Journal*, May 9, 2016; Gordon, "How Lawyers Can Avoid Burnout and Debilitating Anxiety," *ABA Journal*.
221. Sloan, "Law Schools Tackle Mental Health," *National Law Journal*.
222. Defoe, "Law Student Emotional Intelligence, Personality, Psychological Health: An Initial Understanding of Well-Being Indicators and Challenge to Educators," *Psycholawlogy Blog*, March 31, 2013, citing Colin James, Miles Bore, and Susanna Zito, "Emotional Intelligence and Personality as Predictors of Psychological Well-Being," *Journal of Psychoeducational Assessment* 30 (4): 425–38.
223. Seligman, *Authentic Happiness*, 177, 181.
224. Among those cited in Kiser, *Beyond Right and Wrong*, 184, and more recently "Why Are Lawyers Killing Themselves" (2014), *CNN*, http://www.cnn.com/2014/01/19/us/lawyer-suicides/.
225. Dan Lukasik, "Lawyers with Depression," http://www.lawyerswithdepression.com/.
226. See endnote 224 above. One-third of all lawyers "suffer from either depression, alcohol or drug abuse"; about 20 percent of attorneys, almost twice the rate in the general population, abuse alcohol; 30 percent of male lawyers and 20 percent of female lawyers meet the clinical criteria for anxiety disorder (compared to only 4 percent of the general population); and 21 percent of male lawyers and 15 percent of female lawyers meet the clinical criteria for a diagnosis of obsessive-compulsive disorder (compared to only 1.4–2 percent of the general population). See also *Out of the Darkness: Overcoming Depression among Lawyers* (ABA, 2015), http://www.americanbar.org/publications/gp_solo/2015/march-april/out_the_darkness_overcoming_depression_among_lawyers.html.
227. Sue Shellenbarger, "Even Lawyers Get the Blues: Opening Up About Depression," *The Wall Street Journal*, December 13, 2007, 1. In a review of 801 lawyers in the state of Washington, 19 percent suffered from depression. Benjamin et al., 1990. 25 percent of 2,570 lawyers surveyed in North Carolina reported experiencing clinical symptoms of depression, such as loss of appetite, lethargy, suicidal thoughts, or insomnia, at least three times a month during the prior year. Michael J. Sweeney, "The Devastation of Depression," *Bar Leader*, March–April, 1998, 11–13. See also Dan Lukasik, "Lawyers with Depression," http://www.lawyerswithdepression.com/.
228. "Attorneys working in private firms or for the bar association registered higher distress than those in other environments, as did those at the junior or senior associate level compared with other positions." While men had significantly higher levels of depression, women had higher levels of anxiety and stress, and anxiety, depression, and stress scores decreased as participants' age or years worked in the field increased. "The most common mental health conditions reported were anxiety (61.1%), followed by depression (45.7%), social anxiety (16.1%), attention deficit hyperactivity disorder (12.5%), panic

disorder (8.0%), and bipolar disorder (2.4%). In addition, 11.5% of the participants reported suicidal thoughts at some point during their career, 2.9% reported self-injurious behaviors, and 0.7% reported at least 1 prior suicide attempt." The most common barriers for attorneys to seek help were fear of others finding out. Patrick R. Krill, Ryan Johnson, and Linda Albert, "The Prevalence of Substance Use and Other Mental Health Concerns Among American Attorneys," *Journal of Addiction Medicine* 10 (1): 46–52.

229. Lisa Smith, *Girl Walks Out of a Bar* (New York: SelectBooks, 2016).
230. One of the latest casualties is a senior partner of a major firm who threw himself in front of a train not long after a demotion from his management position. Roy Strom, "Bad Drugs or Big Law Stress? Jury to Decide," *American Lawyer*, March 19, 2017.
231. Tyger Latham, "The Depressed Lawyer—Why Are So Many Lawyers So Unhappy?" *Psychology Today*, May 2, 2011.
232. C. Stewart Mauny, "The Lawyers' Epidemic: Depression, Suicide and Substance Abuse," *South Carolina Lawyer*, January, 2012, 3.
233. Michael D. Anestis et al., "Sex and Emotion in the Acquired Capability for Suicide," *Archives of Suicide Research* 15 (2011): 172–82.
234. Krill, "The Prevalence of Substance Use and Other Mental Health Concerns among American Attorneys," *Journal of Addiction Medicine*. Men and respondents 30 years old or younger who took the entire survey had a higher proportion of problematic drinking, while women outpaced men among those not taking the full survey. A majority of those testing positive for alcohol abuse reported excessive use started after law school.
235. Debra Cassens Weiss, "Emphasis on Money Can Be Source of Depression in Law School," *ABA Journal*, March 13, 2008.
236. Daniel T. Lukasik, *A Terrible Melancholy: Depression in the Legal Profession*, YouTube video [31:58], June 24, 2013, https://www.youtube.com/watch?v=B17-G8aoEa8.
237. Isaiah M. Zimmerman, "Isolation in the Judicial Career," *Court Review*, Winter, 2000.
238. More than 150 lawyers attended a special program at Loyola School of Law in April 2013, on the topic of "Lawyers and Suicide: What We Can Do," co-sponsored by the Illinois Lawyers' Assistance Program and the Illinois Chapter of the American Foundation for Suicide Prevention. See Daniel Lukasik, *Lawyers with Depression Blog*, http://lawyerswithdepression.wordpress.com/.
239. Karen Sloan, February 6, 2017, "ABA Calls for Substance Abuse and Mental Health CLE," *National Law Journal*.
240. Other suggestions of factors that might account for the high levels of distress among lawyers include a law school admissions process that unintentionally favors those with latent mental illness, ambivalence about what career lawyers really want (which usually predates law school), dashed expectations of those who went to law school to have "meaningful work," pervasive feelings of isolation and a destructive emphasis in law on money and prestige over other indicators of success. Daicoff, *Lawyer, Know Yourself*. Kiser, *How Leading Lawyers Think*, 183; Weiss, "Emphasis on Money Can Be a Source of Depression in Law School," *ABA Journal*. Lawrence S. Krieger and Kennon M. Sheldon, "What

Makes Lawyers Happy?: A Data-Driven Prescription to Redefine Professional Success," 83 *George Washington Law Review* 554 (2015).

241. James, Bore, and Zito, "Emotional Intelligence and Personality as Predictors of Psychological Well-Being," *Journal of Psychoeducational Assessment,* 425–38.
242. Seligman, *Authentic Happiness,* 179.
243. Ibid., 181.
244. Platsidou and Salman, "The Role of Emotional Intelligence in Predicting Burnout and Job Satisfaction of Greek Lawyers," *International Journal of Law, Psychology and Human Life,* 13–22.
245. Breslau and Daicoff, "The Illicit Relationship of Lawyers and Emotion," *Cutting Edge Law.*
246. Jacquelyn Smith, "The Happiest and Unhappiest Jobs in America, *Forbes,* March 22, 2013.
247. John Monahan and Jeffrey Swanson, "Lawyers at Mid-Career: A 20-Year Longitudinal Study of Job and Life Satisfaction," *University of Virginia Law School Public Law and Legal Theory Working Paper Series,* 2008, 3.
248. There is a "considerable consensus" that at least 20 percent of lawyers are extremely dissatisfied with their jobs. Richard, "Herding Cats," *Altman Weil Report to Legal Management,* 1–12. See also Ronit Dinovitzer and Bryant G. Garth, "Lawyer Satisfaction in the Process of Structuring Legal Careers," *Law and Society Review* 41 (1): 1–52. A survey of Stanford University law grads found that more than half of them would not enter the profession if they had it to do over. Nancy Levitt and Douglas Linder, "Happy Law Students, Happy Lawyers," *Syracuse Law Review* 58 (2008). Even before the 2008 recession, six out of ten attorneys who had been practicing ten years or more who were surveyed by the ABA said they would not recommend a legal career to a young person. Stephanie Francis Ward, "Pulse of the Legal Profession," *ABA Journal,* October 1, 2007.
249. Sloan, "Would You Do Law School Again? 67% of Grads Said Yes," *National Law Journal,* March 23, 2016.
250. "Seven in ten lawyers responding to a California Lawyers magazine poll said they would change careers if the opportunity arose." Latham, "The Depressed Lawyer—Why Are So Many Lawyers So Unhappy?" *Psychology Today.* In 2006, 37 percent of associates at BigLaw firms (more than 500 lawyers) quit their firms by the end of their third year of practice. Ashby Jones, "The Third Year Dilemma: Why Firms Lose Associates," *Wall Street Journal,* January 4, 2006. Long before the recession, while a majority of lawyers reported at least moderate satisfaction with their careers, a similar majority claimed nonetheless to be looking for a different job. Dinovitzer and Garth, "Lawyer Satisfaction in the Process of Structuring Legal Careers," *Law and Society Review* 41 (1); some take the view that unhappiness in the profession has been exaggerated. See "The 2015 Associates Survey: Happier Than Ever," *American Lawyer,* August 31, 2015. But the scant evidence for happiness doesn't hold up well to the avalanche of indications of dissatisfaction. For examples, see Dinovitzer and Garth, "Lawyer Satisfaction in the Process of Structuring Legal Careers," *Law and Society Review.*
251. Sweeney, citing NALP survey results, "The Female Lawyer Exodus," *The Daily Beast,* July 31, 2013, http://www.thedailybeast.com/witw/articles/2013/07/31/the-exodus-of-female-lawyers.html.

252. Platsidou and Salman, "The Role of Emotional Intelligence in Predicting Burnout and Job Satisfaction of Greek Lawyers," *International Journal of Law, Psychology and Human Life.*
253. Seligman, *Authentic Happiness,* 177.
254. Breslau and Daicoff, "The Illicit Relationship of Lawyers and Emotion," *Cutting Edge Law.*
255. Groysberg and Sherman, "Baker & McKenzie (A)," *Harvard Business School Review,* 16.
256. "The MPF 2013 Leadership Conference," *Managing Partner Forum,* May 9, 2013.
257. "Firms in Transition: An Altman Weil Flash Survey," *Altman Weil,* 2013, http://www.altmanweil.com/dir_docs/resource/2d831a80-8156-4947-9f0f-1d97eec632a5_document.pdf.
258. Quoted in Ronda Muir, "Coda: Happiness Hits the Bottom Line," *Law People Blog,* May 10, 2008, http://www.lawpeopleblog.com/2008/05/coda-happiness-hits-the-bottom-line/; Sofia Lind, "Shearman Parts with 30-Lawyer German Office," *Legal Week,* April 22, 2008.
259. David Lykken and Auke Tellegen, "Happiness Is a Stochastic Phenomenon," *Psychological Science* 7 (3): 186–89.
260. Matthew Herper, "Now It's a Fact, Money Doesn't Buy Happiness," *Forbes,* September 23, 2004, http://moneycentral.msn.com/content/invest/forbes/P95294.asp.
261. Chamorro-Premuzic, Adrian Furnham, and Martin Lewis, "Personality and Approaches to Learning Predict Preference for Different Teaching Methods," *Learning and Individual Differences* 17 (2007): 241–50. Individuals high in Agreeableness, high in Conscientiousness and low in Neuroticism tend to be happier. Another study reported that "Agreeableness and Conscientiousness . . . increas[ed] the probability of positive experiences in social and achievement situations, respectively, and these experiences in turn increase subjective well-being." Dr. Reena Singh Rajput, *Impact of Personality, Emotional Intelligence, Intrinsic Motivation and Wellbeing among Students* (New Delhi: Laxmi Books Publications), 8.
262. Bar-On, "The Bar-On Model of Intelligence: A Valid, Robust and Applicable EI Model," *Organisations and People* 14 (2): 27–34.
263. Sonja Lyubomirsky and Kristin Layous, "How Do Simple Positive Activities Increase Well-Being?" *Current Directions in Psychological Science,* 22 (1): 57–62.
264. Levit and Linder, "Happy Law Students, Happy Lawyers," *Syracuse Law Review.* Krieger and Sheldon, "What Makes Lawyers Happy?", *George Washington Law Review.*
265. Tibor P. Palfai and Peter Salovey, "The Influence of Depressed and Elated Mood on Deductive and Inductive Reasoning," *Imagination, Cognition and Personality* 13 (1): 57–71.
266. Bruce Bower, "The Bright Side of Sadness," *ScienceNews,* October 18, 2013, https://www.sciencenews.org/article/bright-side-sadness.
267. "'Lawyer traits contribute to an uneven development of skills . . .a tendency to overemphasize logic, rationality, and . . .overlook interpersonal and emotional concerns." Press, "Don't Look Down," *American Lawyer.*

268. Richard, "The Lawyer Types," *ABA Journal*; Jeff Foster et al., "Understanding Lawyers: The Personality Traits of Successful Practitioners—Results from the Hogan Assessment Project on Lawyer Personality," *Hildebrandt Baker Robbins,* 2010, 1–6, http://www.thresholdadvisors.com/wp-content/uploads/2011/04/Understanding-Lawyers-White-Paper-Oct-2010-revised.pdf.
269. Seligman, *Authentic Happiness,* 178.
270. Ibid., 179.
271. Gordon, "How Lawyers Can Avoid Burnout and Debilitating Anxiety," *ABA Journal.*
272. "Social connectedness . . . generates a positive feedback loop of social, emotional, and physical well-being. Unfortunately, the opposite is true for those who lack social connectedness." Emma Seppala, "Compassionate Mind, Healthy Body," *Greater Good: University of California, Berkeley,* July 24, 2013, http://greatergood.berkeley.edu/article/item/compassionate_mind_healthy_body. Since clinically depressed people have less ability to recognize negative emotions, they may not see and therefore not regulate their own and others' negative feelings, including the very feelings that are fueling their depression. People with and without diagnosed clinical depression were equally able to differentiate between positive emotions. "Press Release: Feeling Guilty Versus Feeling Angry—Who Can Tell the Difference?" *Association for Psychological Science,* September, 24, 2012, https://www.psychologicalscience.org/index.php/news/releases/feeling-guilty-versus-feeling-angry-who-can-tell-the-difference.html. Lawyers' resistance to seeking outside help prolongs their suffering. Gordon, "How Lawyers Can Avoid Burnout and Debilitating Anxiety," *ABA Journal.*
273. Rhode, "Developing Leadership, *Santa Clara Law Review,* 695.
274. Shultz and Zedeck, "Predicting Lawyer Effectiveness," *Law and Social Inquiry,* 654.
275. Berman and Bock, "Developing Attorneys for the Future," *Santa Clara Law Review,* 896–97.
276. Mayer et al., "Emotional Intelligence," *Psychological Inquiry,* 197–215.
277. "Emotional Intelligence," *The Personality Laboratory at the University of New Hampshire,* 2014, https://pages.unh.edu/jdmayer/home.

Chapter Four

Four Ways Emotional Intelligence Builds More Successful Law Firms and Law Departments

Emotional intelligence (EI) not only gives lawyers a personal edge, it also empowers practice groups and organizations. Emotional intelligence builds more successful law firms and law departments in four ways:

1. *Emotionally Intelligent Leaders Are More Effective*
2. *Emotional Intelligence Builds a More Productive Culture*
3. *Emotional Intelligence Lowers the Risk of Liability*
4. *Emotionally Intelligent Practices Are More Profitable*

1. Emotionally Intelligent Leaders Are More Effective

> *A leader's intelligence has to have a strong emotional component. He has to have high levels of self-awareness, maturity and self-control. She must be able to withstand the heat, handle setbacks and when those lucky moments arise, enjoy success with equal parts of joy and humility. No doubt emotional intelligence is more rare than*

book smarts, but my experience says it is actually more important in the making of a leader. You just can't ignore it.[1]

—Jack Welch, former CEO of General Electric

Research shows convincingly that EQ is more important than IQ in almost every role and many times more important in leadership roles.[2]

—Dr. Stephen Covey, author of *The 7 Habits of Highly Effective People*

In the fields I have studied, emotional intelligence is much more powerful than IQ in determining who emerges as a leader. IQ is a threshold competence. You need it, but it doesn't make you a star. Emotional Intelligence can.[3]

—Warren Benis, author and researcher

Without emotional intelligence, a person can have the best training in the world, an incisive, analytical mind and an endless supply of smart ideas, but he still won't make a great leader.[4]

—Daniel Goleman, in "What Makes a Leader"

At its root, then, the primal job of leadership is emotional.[5]

—Daniel Goleman, Dr. Richard Boyatzis, and Dr. Annie McKee, authors of *Primal Leadership: Learning to Lead with Emotional Intelligence*

Leadership is "the single largest determinant of business success," and as years of research and those quoted above all attest, emotional intelligence is the cornerstone of great leadership—throughout the world and with respect to all different types of work.[6] Presidential historian Fred I. Greenstein argues in *The Presidential Difference: Leadership Style from FDR to Barack Obama* that emotional intelligence is the most important predictor of even a US president's success.[7] High EI raises a leader's ability to manage specific challenges and also makes those challenges feel less difficult to address.[8]

Emotional intelligence is more relevant to success than a leader's cognitive intelligence or personality traits.[9] The Center for Creative Leadership found that the most effective leaders outscore low performers on each of fifteen EI factors, with only eight EI strengths—including self-awareness, stress tolerance, and empathy—predicting high performers 80 percent of the time.[10] Another study found two EI abilities—emotional perception and emotional regulation—the most highly correlated with leadership effectiveness. The level of a leader's emotional awareness has been demonstrated to predict both how well steps are planned to accomplish goals and also how well those goals are ultimately accomplished.[11]

The bottom line is that, when it comes to leadership, "EQ skills are more important to job performance than any other leadership skill."[12]

Emotional intelligence is a measure of the extent of influence wielded by both formally designated leaders and unofficial leaders.[13] It is also the most accurate indicator of who will emerge as a leader—again more predictive than personality traits, gender, or cognitive intelligence: "transformational leaders" (those leaders who dramatically impact an organization) can be predicted from their EI scores alone.[14]

Old distinctions between leadership and management have narrowed. In the new knowledge economy, as Drucker points out: "with the rise of the knowledge worker, one does not 'manage' people . . . The task is to lead people. And the goal is to make productive the specific strengths and knowledge of every individual."[15] Perhaps nowhere is this confluence of leadership and management expertise more evident than in legal workplaces, where often the same person or people perform both roles—inspiring a vision and making it happen operationally—and also where the highly independent troops are resistant to both being led and being "managed."

How do we recognize high EI leaders? Maister's survey of 139 offices of 29 professional service firms in 15 countries determined some emotion-specific attributes of successful managers: "even-keeled and even-tempered," "good at reading people," "sensitive to personal issues," "caring about things happening in your people's lives," "real concern for people as individuals," "emotional courage," "upbeat personal style," "concentrate on the positive."[16] Being open to feedback and not defensive, recognizing and understanding their own emotions and those of others, being available to their direct reports and sharing the credit for successes are other noted hallmarks of emotionally intelligent leaders.[17] In the six emotionally intelligent leadership styles Daniel Goleman has identified,[18] each share the characteristics of being "exquisitely sensitive to the impact they are having on others" and "able to adjust their styles accordingly."[19]

Low EI leaders, on the other hand, typically don't welcome feedback, are rigid and resistant to change, are either overly emotionally reactive or too distant emotionally, and often handle issues inconsistently or unpredictably, shortcomings that lower morale, retention, and an organization's performance.[20] Dr. Annie McKee, author of *Resonant Leadership: Renewing Yourself and Connecting with Others through Mindfulness, Hope, and Compassion*, found that the reason leaders become derailed is because of deficits in emotional competence, evidenced by difficulty in handling change, not being able to work well in a team, and poor interpersonal relations—all tendencies that lawyer leaders are likely to grapple with, both in themselves and in their charges.[21]

Emotional intelligence will play an even greater role in successful leadership through the 21st century. Chief psychologist for the Australian Olympic Team and best-selling author Graham Winter asked public-sector leaders what leadership capabilities would be most important in the new century: "they [all] saw the challenges through the lens of emotional intelligence. Those challenges were about leading through ambiguity, engaging diverse stakeholders, tackling wicked problems and delivering more with less."[22]

The author of *Great People Decisions* notes that, in a world that is "increasingly complex—uncertain and volatile, global and diverse . . . experience and knowledge are less relevant . . . whereas emotional intelligence-based competencies—such as flexibility, empathy, organizational awareness, and relationship management . . . differentiate stars from average performers at the top."[23]

As in the business world, legal expertise is not what qualifies our most successful leaders. Building and nurturing relationships does. A study of leaders of professional service firms (including law firms) found only one quality requiring technical skill—business understanding—among the most important leadership qualities, while EI skills, like the ability to engage colleagues, especially in times of stress, around a vision that was emotionally compelling and attainable, were key.[24]

Lawyer leaders ignore at their peril the ineluctable ingredient that emotional intelligence contributes to successful leadership. Alliances, personal and organizational, are initiated, built, and sustained; clients are gained and retained; warring partners are reconciled; messy, independent-minded groups of lawyers are led to consider and reach a consensus on difficult decisions, and then are motivated to follow through, all through the exercise of emotional intelligence.

As we move forward through a challenging 21st century, emotional intelligence empowers leaders to tackle:

External Challenges: Meeting the Marketplace Mandate
Internal Challenges: Innovating, Achieving Influence, and Motivating and Effectuating Change

THE EMOTIONAL INTELLIGENCE EDGE FOR LEADERS

- The most effective leadership is correlated with emotional intelligence, not IQ or personality traits.
- "Transformational leaders," or those who can affect significant change, can be identified by their high emotional intelligence alone.
- Emotional intelligence is the most accurate indicator of who will emerge from a group as a leader.
- Emotional intelligence has the greatest impact both on how well steps are planned to accomplish goals and how well those goals are in fact accomplished.
- Emotional intelligence, and specifically the ability to engage in and sustain relationships within the workplace and with clients, will have a greater role in successful leadership through the 21st century.

External Challenges: Meeting the Marketplace Mandate

> *[There is] a shift towards the buyer's market, the emergence of clients as major agents of change, downward pressure on fees, new efficiencies being driven by the recession and the uptake in novel ways of sourcing legal work.*[25]
>
> —British Law Professor Richard Susskind, OBE, IT Adviser to the Lord Chief Justice of England and Wales, and author of *The End of Lawyers? Rethinking the Nature of Legal Services*

> *[L]aw firms need a new style of leadership if they are to be effective in achieving their goals and delivering legal services in the future.*[26]
>
> —Simon Tupman, author of "The Leadership Imperative—A Study into Law Firm Leadership"

The legal marketplace is changing, and demand for traditional legal services is down.[27] Several trends are posing daunting challenges, including the following:

Globalization
Advancing Technology
The End of Lawyers?
Mounting Financial Pressures

Coupled with the low enthusiasm our clients appear to have for dealing with lawyers, these drags on demand are increasingly impacting our finances, and over 60 percent of law firm leaders believe the trend of eroding demand is permanent.[28]

Globalization

The reach and instantaneity of the Internet has put law firms and law departments in a new world in which our clients and colleagues are further and further away, our competition is geometrically expanding, and the demands on our collaborative skills are ratcheting up.

Clients are increasingly from emerging markets, rather than the industrial nations we are more familiar with, and they often already have lawyers by their side. McKinsey & Co. is forecasting that by 2025, the emerging economies' share of Fortune Global 500 companies will jump to more than 45 percent from just 5 percent in 2000, generating 70 percent of the new $1 billion+ companies.[29]

New providers from around the world are entering the legal services business, some of whom enjoy substantial advantages over US law firms, and existing providers are consolidating.[30] The four major accounting firms are offering increasingly sophisticated cross-disciplinary legal services globally.[31] Rapidly expanding Chinese law firms, who only a few years ago were not in our competitive universe, now boast eight firms of more than 1,000 lawyers, are the top firms in the Asia-Pacific region in terms of size, and are among the largest firms globally.[32] They are also enjoying phenomenal growth: the top 30 Chinese firms' revenue in 2015 grew 55 percent compared to 2013 and lawyer headcount was up 36 percent.[33] And they are aiming for the United States.[34]

Nonlegal entities like LegalZoom, RocketLawyer, and Nolo provide low-cost legal documents in every state, while others offering high-end litigation, cybersecurity, and other legal management services—like Axiom, Pangea3, QuisLex, and UnitedLex—are included in the top band of Chambers annual ratings. Consulting firms providing services that overlap with legal services, such as the Mintz Group, Navigant, and Marsal and Alvarez, are also aggressively pursuing work outside the oversight of a law firm.[35]

At the same time, corporate counsel are shifting outside legal work in-house at a quickening pace.[36] The number of in-house lawyers has roughly doubled in the last 40 years, and their plans are to further reduce reliance on outside law firms.[37] So there is simply less traditional outside legal business to go around, as evidenced by the drop in the number of total hours billed by law firms.[38]

Australia and the United Kingdom put their law firms at a decided advantage years ago by allowing them to consolidate with other professional services under an alternative business structure umbrella, obtain non-lawyer investors, and make public offerings.[39] In the meantime, an American Bar Association (ABA) resolution allowing non-lawyers to provide low-cost legal services[40] in the United States has passed despite a strong backlash,[41] while the ABA's Commission on the Future of Legal Services[42] is still asking for comments (for the third time) on allowing non-lawyer investors in US law firms.[43]

As the reach of business clients and the spread of competition grow, law firms are banding together in Swiss Verein–type international associations, limited guarantee companies,[44] and other far-flung alliances. Dentons, a Swiss Verein, was formed only a few years ago in a three-way merger between US-based SNR Denton, Salans of France, and Fraser Milner Casgrain of Canada, and then merged in 2015 with China's Dacheng Law Offices, at the time the largest Chinese law firm, to make the largest law firm in the world, with more than 7,300 lawyers.[45]

Advancing Technology

The broadest impact of advancing technology has been the generation of entire new industries that offer alternatives to traditional legal providers and that can digitally manage and efficiently deliver services from low-cost zones around the world, a development that is welcomed by the majority of corporate legal departments and that puts further pressure on traditional demand.[46]

Alternative legal providers (ALPs) currently account for only 1 percent of US legal services revenue, but rising demand is helping them realize 20 percent growth annually, projected to reach 50 percent or higher per annum over the short term.[47] Thomas Reuters' "2017 Alternative Legal Service Study: Understanding the Growth and Benefits of These New Legal Providers" reports on "a seismic shift that has already happened with 51% of law firms and 60% of corporate legal departments currently using Alternative Legal Service Providers for at least one type of service. And those numbers are expected to grow."[48] The ALPs siphon off through technology work that lawyers used to do at a decent profit, including legal research, discovery, deposition summaries, trial prep, and trial support, making a legion of young lawyers and support staff unnecessary.[49] Because of these competitors, "Today, 25% to 50% of the revenue of most large law firms is already squarely under attack."[50] Yet law firms appear uninterested in considering offering services that compete with the ALPs.[51]

Although certainly not tech forward as an industry,[52] lawyers are using more sophisticated technology-based processes[53] for client relationship management, knowledge management, and e-discovery.[54] ROSS, a natural language legal research program built on IBM's Watson technology, was first trained in Canadian employment law and then American bankruptcy law.[55] It mines facts and conclusions from a billion text documents a second, assesses legal precedents, and predicts court case outcomes with a confidence rating. Several American law firms have signed up to try it.[56]

DLA Piper and Deloitte have both rolled out to their corporate lawyers worldwide new advanced document review software developed by Kira Systems Inc.[57] Magic Circle firm Linklaters signed with RAVN Systems to use its software, and both law firms and law departments are using Neota Logic's innovative interactive expert systems that guide regulatory and compliance advice.[58] Baker McKenzie has set up a global innovation committee of senior partners to track emerging legal technology and set firm strategy on its uses and perils,[59] and a firm in the United Kingdom is using proprietary software to advise clients regarding Brexit issues in a number of "multi-billion dollar transactions."[60]

These technological developments are already making profound changes in legal practices. Kira reports that its products reduce lawyer time spent on contract review by 20 to 60 percent. A 2016 report by a University of North Carolina School of Law professor and a Massachusetts Institute of Technology labor economist concludes that only 4 percent of lawyers' time is now spent on basic document review and that the immediate implementation of all new legal technology would result in an estimated 13 percent decline in lawyers' hours, although a more realistic adoption rate would cut hours by 2.5 percent annually over five years.[61] In January 2017, the McKinsey Global Institute report estimated that 23 percent of a lawyer's job could be automated with current technology.[62]

More developments in technologically assisted lawyering are on the horizon. More than 280 legal technology start-ups have raised over $750 million since 2012, according to the research firm CB Insights.[63] One of ROSS's investors is Dentons' Nextlaw Labs, whose mission is to "transform the practice of law" through new technology.[64] Thomson Reuters, in partnership with IBM, announced in 2015 the creation of a center of excellence for cognitive computing that will promote the commercialization of artificial intelligence across several industries, including law.[65] The International Association of Artificial Intelligence and Law, devoted exclusively to the study of artificial intelligence in law, celebrated its twenty-five-year mark with announcements of new developments in the works,[66] and the UK's First Legal Innovation Centre was launched in February 2017 at Ulster University in collaboration with Allen & Overy and Baker McKenzie.[67]

The End of Lawyers?

> *[What] make[s] people valuable as technology advances is . . . empathy. Yes, empathy. Discerning what some other person is thinking and feeling, and responding in some appropriate way.*[68]
>
> —Lawyer Michael Mills, Co-Founder and Chief Strategy Officer of Neota Logic, a technology platform for legal services

In March 2016, a Google computer program thoroughly beat one of the world's top players in Go, the most complex board game ever created, which requires multilevel strategic thinking and judgment.[69] So is an automated lawyer much further behind?[70]

Lawyers have been warned for years of their demise. British Law Professor Richard Susskind—since 1998 the IT Adviser to the Lord Chief Justice of England and Wales—asked that question in his book *The End of Lawyers?*[71] He answered the question in his latest book, *The Future of the Professions.* There he predicts that within a few decades "the traditional professions will be dismantled, leaving most (but not all) professionals to be replaced by less expert people and high-performing systems . . . there will not be sufficient growth in the types of professional tasks in which people, not machines, have the advantage to keep most professionals in full employment."[72]

Already "The World's First Robot Lawyer" is being touted for having processed hundreds of thousands of parking tickets to save clients millions of dollars.[73] The brainchild of a Stanford University student, the artificial intelligence–driven chatbot first works out whether an appeal is possible, and then guides users through the appeals process. The next applications being developed are processes for getting flight delay compensation, explaining the legal rights of those who are HIV positive, and guiding immigrants through the legal system.

An important study announced in 2016 that, as predicted over fifty years ago, a robot using artificial intelligence reached the same conclusions as the judges did in almost 80 percent of the court cases presented to it, raising the question not only of whether machines may be able to more accurately predict the outcome of court proceedings than our litigators, but also whether at some point a human judge is going to be unnecessary.[74]

We are starting to acknowledge the impact of technology on the profession. Over 80 percent of law firm leaders recognize that nontraditional service providers are here to stay, and more than 88 percent believe technology will continue to replace human resources.[75] A majority of general counsel expect technology to reduce a significant number of their in-house attorneys within the next five years, according to a 2016 Deloitte survey.[76]

Is there a way we human lawyers can outrun technology so as not to become the next elevator operators?[77] Many experts agree that emotional intelligence can inoculate human lawyers from obsolescence, making them valuable despite technological advances. In *Humans Are Underrated*, the author contends that as "the skills that have been the basis of progress for most of human history: Logic, knowledge and analysis . . . [are] being commoditized by advancing technology, . . . the skills of deep human interaction" will only become more valuable.[78] With the growing involvement of smart machines, clients will want relationships with human lawyers they trust.[79] As one *Harvard Business Review* article proclaims: "The Rise of AI Makes Emotional Intelligence More Important."[80]

Law Professor Daicoff pointed out early on: "Our clients may believe they only need our intellectual dexterity and our legal knowledge. But they actually want and deserve more: to have the feeling that we are really present to them, we are connecting with them, we are interested, we are not judging them, and that they are more than their cases."[81]

Emotionally intelligent lawyers offer clients the opportunity to connect with a person who hears, understands, and empathizes with his or her issues, someone to air dilemmas with, someone who can see the gray, who can help make the difficult judgment calls and then sympathetically explain what's happening and why. SimSensei's star virtual therapist Ellie is making inroads against her human counterparts by using technologically generated emotion recognition, empathy, and emotional understanding in a non-judgmental way.[82] As machines improve these EI skills, lawyers are well-advised to at least keep up.

The future may accommodate both lawyers and machines. After being defeated by IBM's DeepBlue, Garry Kasparov invented Centaur Chess with the belief that by pairing humans *together with* computers, their combined performance is amplified.[83] ROSS's co-founder agrees: "When you pair the computer with the human, you get something way better than either the human or the computer. If you look at it from that formula, humans will always be on the winning side."[84]

So, no, thankfully, HAL from *2001: A Space Odyssey*, or even some Google-updated Go-competent version, is not likely to replace us as the perfect lawyer.[85] But a human lawyer who can reliably bring empathy and other EI skills to the table might well.

Mounting Financial Pressures

Given these competition and technology headwinds, the prospect of a return to the double-digit law firm growth of years past remains dim: in 2014, Citibank's Law Firm Group acknowledged "a fundamental shift in the market for legal services, resulting in a changed and more muted demand environment," projecting no return "to pre-2008 levels of performance," a prediction that holds true into 2017.[86]

Clayton Christensen, a professor at Harvard Business School and author of the best-selling book *The Innovator's Dilemma*, which articulates the concept of disruptive innovation, argues in *Harvard Business Review*, "that a disruptive transformation in the legal market may well already be underway." He also warns that, "The temptation for market leaders to view the advent of new competitors with a mixture of disdain, denial, and rationalization is nearly irresistible . . . there may be nothing as vulnerable as entrenched success."[87]

Several spectacular law firm closings over the last few years testify to the difficulty of traditional legal institutions maneuvering in a changing market. Martin Bienenstock, a senior partner at Dewey & LeBoeuf with a Wharton School MBA and a University of Michigan JD who taught corporate reorganization at Harvard Law School, said of the collapse of his firm in 2012: "The world changed and we didn't see it coming."[88]

There is evidence that further firm closings are on the horizon. Heavy lateral churn, high bank debt, weak leadership, significant excess capacity, and cracks in firm culture are all warning signs that Citibank points to in developing a "somewhat robust" watch list of law firms they believe may fail in the near future.[89]

Addressing these marketplace trends is urgent. Deloitte UK's 2016 report on the legal profession, entitled "Developing Legal Talent: Stepping into the Future Law Firm," warns that "by around 2020 we expect a tipping point for firms."[90] Law firms that fail to address "the quickening pace of technological development, shift in workforce demographics, and need to offer clients more value for money" could well be out of the competition by 2025, a risk that is particularly high for midsized firms.[91]

These massive currents in our marketplace demand changes in how we lead. While 86 percent of executives surveyed by the Center for Creative Leadership believe the ability to work through this increasingly complex 21st-century landscape is "extremely important," just 7 percent describe themselves as being "very effective" at it.[92] The "increased level of complexity and interconnectedness" has prompted CCL to name emotional intelligence as the critical leadership quality.[93]

As Roger Enrico, once CEO and Chairman of PepsiCo and Chairman of DreamWorks, puts it, "the 'soft stuff' is always harder than the hard stuff."[94] And the greater the stress an organization is facing, the more important a leader's soft skills become.[95]

EXTERNAL CHALLENGES THAT REQUIRE EMOTIONALLY INTELLIGENT LEADERSHIP

- Decreasing demand for traditional legal services
- Increasing globalization that facilitates the entry of more competitors around the world and that requires collaborative, cross-boundary relationship skills
- The movement of legal work in house
- Advancing technology that empowers new competitors and continues to encroach on the human role in providing traditional legal services
- Mounting financial pressures caused by these market conditions and the failure to acknowledge and respond to them

Internal Challenges: Innovating, Achieving Influence, and Motivating and Effectuating Change

The domain of the leader is the future. The most significant contribution leaders make is not simply to today's bottom line; it is to the long term development of people and institutions so that they can adapt, change, prosper and grow.[96]

—James Kouses and Barry Posner, authors of *The Leadership Challenge*

It is not the strongest of the species that survive, nor the most intelligent, but the one most responsive to change.[97]

—Leon C. Megginson, Professor of Management at Louisiana State University, paraphrasing Charles Darwin's *On the Origin of Species*

Leadership is about producing change . . . Future success will be based not only on the historic practice and transactional skills that make attorneys important but will also depend on the lawyer-leader to transform their firms and inspire the people within them.[98]

—Roland B. Smith, Ph.D., Centre for Creative Leadership

> *Frans de Waal, a primatologist at Emory University, has observed that the size and strength of male chimps is an extremely poor predictor of which animals will dominate the troop. Instead, the ability to forge social connections and engage in 'diplomacy' is often much more important.*[99]
>
> —Jonah Lehrer, author

It is into this market maelstrom that lawyer leaders must navigate.[100] Firms around the world are facing the urgency of change,[101] but how do we generate creative approaches to difficult circumstances, convince our workforce to embrace change, and then actually move them forward?

The current questioning of our business models illustrates the dilemmas before us. Do law firms continue along the billable hour revenue model?[102] Move with the times toward alternative or fixed-fee arrangements?[103] Divide our firms into closed-end contract workers on one side and the traditional service professionals climbing the management ladder on the other? Eliminate tiers? Add them? Retain or revisit the old lock-step compensation format? Let lawyers eat what they kill or share the spoils? Establish new offices? Expand internationally? Rework our targeted client list or practices offerings? Making and implementing these tough decisions requires keen leadership that can influence and motivate the people at the core of success.

Emotional intelligence gives leaders valuable strategies for:

Inspiring Innovation
Achieving Influence
Motivating and Effectuating Change

Inspiring Innovation

The strategy employed by most law firms today seems to be to ignore the dramatic evolutions in the marketplace[104] rather than re-think the old mergers and laterals tacks,[105] but emotionally intelligent leadership can help firms better meet these challenges through innovation.[106] Creativity does not just promote the arts. "[M]ost creativity comes from solving the zillions of problems we all encounter every day. Ironically, when we most need creativity, we tend to be in an emotional state where creativity is least accessible. Fear and distress . . . shut off the cerebral cortex, where creativity and problem-solving live."[107] Emotional intelligence empowers us to shelve those inhibiting emotions and access constructive feelings that can generate creative solutions.[108]

EI can also get us out of a dead-end emotional ditch that blocks creativity. "Leaders stumble not because they *have* undesirable thoughts and feelings—that's inevitable—but because they get *hooked* by them, like fish caught on a line . . . When you unhook yourself from your difficult thoughts and emotions, you expand your choices."[109]

The leader's EI fuels his or her own innovation and creative problem solving, but also "plays a critical role in enabling and supporting the awakening of creativity" in workers and managing the "tension, conflict, and emotionally charged debates and disagreements" that "engaging in creativity in organizations inevitably creates."[110]

A deputy general counsel was known for requiring that lawyers collate and present on a biweekly basis various metrics he felt were important to the legal department's success, such as hours worked by outside attorneys, composition of department teams, and type, geographical location, and budget status of legal matters, among other factors. While these data were certainly of some value, the reporting obligations were breeding complaints and frustration because of the amount of effort needed to gather, analyze, and convey the information, with what the lawyers saw as limited payoff. Yet the deputy GC was insistent that they continue to compile it.

There is often an emotional context to repetitive or obsessive thinking or behavior. By repeatedly exercising some control over what we can control, we hope to allay the anxiety associated with the fear of what we can't control. Unfortunately, that repetition can crowd out other valuable thoughts. In this case, the deputy GC was haunted by a competitor's comparably lower legal spend that he feared could eventually cost him his job. He believed that the reason for the competitor's better numbers was a more sophisticated work management approach.

He repeatedly gathered and poured over data that he thought would help him build a more competitive model. It was when he acknowledged and surrendered the grip of his outsized fear that he could openly and creatively discuss with his lawyers what the department could do to reduce their legal spend. The time that had been spent on data collection was used instead to brainstorm, with a third party occasionally accumulating data deemed useful.

Even when we are armed with more innovative strategies, we often don't think we have the leadership muscle to make change happen. While most of the 238 managing partners of US law firms acknowledge that the legal market has fundamentally and permanently transformed and the pace of change is likely to accelerate, they give themselves a five out of ten rating on their seriousness in making changes, with only a minority saying they have undertaken anything significant.[111] Even lower than their scores on their seriousness in making changes is the average three out of ten rating their chief legal officer clients gave them, evidencing little success just in convincing their clients of their commitment to change, let alone actually producing it. It is no wonder that competitors are making inroads.[112]

Achieving Influence

Leadership, especially of a business whose assets walk out the door every night, is largely a matter of influence. "As former General Electric General Counsel Ben Heineman notes, 'leadership [in law] today is often not command and control but persuasion, motivation, and empowerment of teams around a shared vision.'"[113]

"Matrixed organizations," a structure where authority flows sideways across departments as well as up and down the ladder, is already common among law firms and is predicted to be increasingly common in the 21st century. Leadership EI traits like empathy, conflict management, and self-awareness are consistently tied to successful business outcomes within these organizations because "individuals are required to lead by influence" rather than authority.[114]

The degree of lawyers' success in influencing our organizations is so far not encouraging. A 2017 study finds that while Canadian law firms talk a good "innovation" game, little innovation is actually taking place, with a stark divide between associates and partners in their perceptions of and efforts toward innovation. For instance, 89 percent of partners agreed that, "innovation was one of the firm's highest strategic priorities," while fewer than half of associates agreed.[115]

What should we do differently? An important first step is to be able to project the emotions that give a person influence. According to a Harvard psychology professor, we make judgments about our leaders based primarily on two characteristics: first their warmth, which we believe indicates their trustworthiness, and then their strength or competence, in that order. Moreover, "[T]hese two dimensions account for more than 90% of the variance in our positive or negative impressions." So, "the way to influence—and to lead—is to begin by expressing emotional warmth." Suppressing warmth and banking on an impression of competence, which lawyers often naturally do, can actually lower our influence.[116]

How many lawyer leaders are known for their warmth? This is not a common characteristic. Lawyers usually elevate their most "competent" peers into management, yet, as a study of 51,836 leaders found, the chance that a manager who is strongly disliked will be considered by his or her organization as a good leader is only about one in 2,000.[117] Is likability or warmth on your performance review checklists?

My experience with a department chair illustrates this point well. The woman was a well-known authority and thought leader in a highly complex niche. Members assigned to her department clearly respected that expertise, but to the person they did not want to work with her. She was insular, highly critical, and unresponsive to interpersonal conflicts, time management issues, and other concerns. When she was criticized by subordinates, the firm and she both reiterated her high standing in her legal area. But this leader, who was so well credentialed and attracted clients, was unable to personally connect with those in her group. Many left the department. Those who couldn't often left the firm. The firm's eventual response was to make her a department of one partner with constantly rotating subordinates, and the lack of stability, coupled with her poor interpersonal skills, eventually turned off many of her clients. People simply didn't like her. She was furious that the firm wasn't "backing" her by forcing associates and staff to stay in her department and by pushing back against client dissatisfaction. Eventually she decamped for another firm, which no doubt had to wrestle with these issues again.

Motivating and Effectuating Change

Change is a highly emotional prospect and process. William Bridges's Transition Model describes the progression of internal emotions that those in transition experience and that slows real change. That progression starts with the emotional upheaval of shock, anger, fear and resistance at the prospect of change, moving to skepticism, resentment, frustration and low productivity while internally holding on to the old but trying to adapt to the new, ending in excitement and hope in experiencing early gains from the change.[118] Those with low emotional intelligence, as are many lawyers, suffer higher levels of stress and other negative emotional reactions in the face of change and job insecurity and are also more likely to engage in negative coping behaviors compared to their high EI colleagues.[119]

Change management requires someone with "'the right people skills,'"[120] someone who can access and manage his or her own emotions and also the full range of emotions being experienced by others. Leaders must first persuasively present a direction and then "motivate people to give of their best," in each case by wielding influence the hard, old-fashioned way—through personal relationships.[121]

Up to 70 percent of all change initiatives fail, primarily due to "people issues."[122] One of the most common complaints of managing partners worldwide is the difficulty of getting partners to work well together,[123] and they rate resistance to change as one of the major obstacles in making appropriate responses to the marketplace.[124] Altman Weil's Law Firms in Transition 2016 study of over three hundred firms agreed: "It's not so much firm leaders, it's their partners who don't feel a sense of urgency to evolve and adapt."[125] Managing partners in New Zealand, Australia, and the United Kingdom also claim their greatest barriers to delivering on change are their partners' "reluctance to change" and "personalities."[126]

Lawyers' typical personal attributes profoundly complicate the job of those trying to lead lawyers to embrace change and persevere through its dislocations.[127] Lawyers who in addition to being low EI are risk-averse, untrusting, supremely pessimistic about outcomes, and hesitant to put themselves in what could be a failing situation are well prepared to challenge authority and aggressively counter management's recommendations for change.[128] Given these attributes, lawyer leaders will be confronted again and again with roadblocks and dissension, and a leader who is himself or herself low in resilience or in conflict resolution skills is handicapped. As one expert says, "to convert the vision into reality, one faces incredible amounts of resistance . . . Only a few are able to find the requisite emotional energy to keep going. It is such energy that makes one a leader."[129]

A leader's proactive use of emotional intelligence can help cope with these escalating demands and tensions from both the outside marketplace and inside our workplaces. EI skills are instrumental in building collaborative, cross-boundary relationships, outperforming machines, generating trust, promoting innovation, and energizing lawyers to move forward through change.[130]

INTERNAL CHALLENGES THAT REQUIRE EMOTIONALLY INTELLIGENT LEADERSHIP

- Emotional intelligence helps leaders be innovative problem solvers and encourage creativity in their workplaces.
- Emotional intelligence raises a leader's ability to influence, persuade, and motivate.
- Emotional intelligence is particularly valuable in matrixed organizational structures, such as law firms, which rely on influence and are likely to become increasingly common during the 21st century.

(Continued)

- Emotional regulation empowers leaders to project the warmth that is a first step in gaining influence.
- The prospect and process of change engenders an array of difficult-to-manage emotions, and lawyers typically suffer high stress and exhibit strong resistance to change.
- Emotional intelligence better equips leaders to rally lawyers through change, one of the most difficult undertakings lawyer leaders face.
- Emotional intelligence helps bolster some of a lawyer leader's personal attributes, such as low resilience, when faced with continuing resistance to change.

2. Emotional Intelligence Builds a More Productive Culture

> *A law firm's culture is the daily manifestation of its explicit performance expectations and implicit behavioral norms—what is encouraged and what is tolerated. And the culture that a law firm develops and sustains has an impact on its productivity, retention rates, and morale—positive or negative, as the case might be.*[131]
>
> —Jordan Furlong, law firm consultant and commentator

> *It is hard to unbundle which is the cause and which is the effect, but the combination of a desire for autonomy and high levels of skepticism make most law firms low-trust environments.*[132]
>
> —David Maister, "Are Law Firms Manageable?"

An article entitled "Firm Culture Matters Most" maintains that the success of individual lawyers is a direct function of the culture or the "personality of the firm."[133] One reason that emotional intelligence is so pivotal to effective leadership is the decisive role leaders have in shaping the culture of their workplaces, whether by intention or not.[134] Leaders' competence in emotional intelligence sets an example, is projected throughout the workplace, and builds and sustains the kind of emotionally supportive culture that produces excellence, loyalty, productivity, and profitability.[135]

On the other hand, stated expectations and implicit norms that can develop in a low EI environment can lead to an excoriating climate. The "five top amygdala triggers" that ratchet up stress in cultures are (1) condescension and lack of respect, (2) being treated unfairly, (3) being unappreciated, (4) feeling that you're not being listened to or heard, and (5) being held to unrealistic deadlines.[136] Incivility can rage through an organization, resulting in what has been demonstrated to be depressed performance, reduced collaboration, and higher attrition, with frustration and anger eventually turned toward clients.[137]

These factors and incivility are perceived to exist in many legal workplaces. Law firms are legendary for their cultural emphasis on individualism, competition among colleagues, prioritizing achievement over personal well-being, and an adversarial subtext to relationships. Firms' willingness to indulge powerful or profitable "assholes" has long been a topic of discussion: practices often overlook what in other environments might be dubbed emotional or verbal abuse, particularly by rainmakers.[138] Legal workplaces also frequently treat "non-lawyers" worse than lawyers. Too often poor behavior is "met with a wall of silence."[139]

These low EI law practices can become "emotionally toxic," a term that describes one of the unhealthiest states of workplaces,[140] characterized by deficiencies in self- and other-awareness and empathy.[141] "[I]n law practices with high emotional toxicity, the damage of 'lower production, decreased morale, poor attitudes, and . . . [the loss of] valued employees'" decimates their profitability and exposes them to serious liabilities.[142]

Although there are little data on how pervasive these toxic cultures are in our profession, we do have a litany of anecdotes and surveys from around the world that testify to their presence.[143] As a midlevel associate at a New York firm said, "The general sentiment when people leave is, 'thank god I don't have to deal with this abuse anymore.' Because at the end of the day, it's constant abuse or fear of abuse."[144]

The recent spotlight on bullying, characterized by low emotional empathy,[145] puts pressure on cultures to actively oppose insensitivity to others.[146] Tensions in legal workplaces may become more strident when incoming Millennials marinated in sensitivities to micro-aggressions find themselves in cultures that harbor or ignore behaviors they consider unfair or offensive.[147]

I am often asked whether we are hiring low emotional intelligence or we are molding it through the cultures in our workplaces. Since there is a low average EI among lawyers, the likelihood of any random hire being low in EI is high. But one client has given additional insight into that question. A small West Coast firm had, unusually, administered personal style assessments regularly for several decades to its attorneys. By reviewing them, I could see that their EI and other characteristics were quite diverse when they first arrived, but became increasingly similar over the course of time, resulting in a fairly uniform profile. This is a testament not to the mini-me approach that lawyers are often accused of in hiring, but to the power of culture in shaping our workforce despite initial diversity. Yes, we probably hire more professionals with lower EI than many other industries, but we also make them ourselves.

It's not that lawyer workplaces should be "nicer" just so we all play better together: there are real business reasons for making our cultures more emotionally intelligent.[148] Primary among the many benefits of a higher EI workforce are four that law firms and law departments throughout the country aspire to:

1. *Lower Attrition*
2. *Reduced Conflict and Better Conflict Management*
3. *Higher-Functioning Teams*
4. *Greater Personal Well-Being*

Lower Attrition

Law firms suffer from exceedingly high rates of attrition, and the loss of lawyers wastes valuable time and expense, estimated to approach hundreds of thousands of dollars per lawyer. Fortune 100 companies have an average attrition rate of less than 5 percent, while half of all law firm associates are gone within three years.[149]

This loss is likely to get worse over time. Millennials are almost three times more likely than older workers to leave their jobs in the next six months, in part because they are twice as likely as GenXers and four times more likely than Baby Boomers to find their work unfulfilling. The very things that Millennials say they want more of at work—feedback and collaboration—are best provided by building workplace emotional intelligence.[150]

Numerous studies over the years have established that building a more emotionally intelligent workforce dramatically lowers attrition rates: hiring for EI resulted in a 63 percent lower attrition rate at L'Oreal, a drop from 35 to 5 percent annual turnover in recruiters at the US Air Force, and 6 percent compared to 50 percent loss within two years of division presidents at a large beverage firm.[151]

High EI employees are, in psychological jargon, more "employable," meaning they stay longer and enjoy higher career success because they are "more rewarding to deal with" and more often meet employers' goals.[152] They also have greater resilience after setbacks and more persistence through difficult times, all of which promotes more personal satisfaction at work, as well.

Reduced Conflict and Better Conflict Management

> *The lack of detailed attention to emotions and relationships is the biggest gap in our understanding of conflict.*[153]
>
> —Suzanne Retzinger and Thomas Scheff, "Emotion, Alienation, and Narratives: Resolving Intractable Conflict"

> *[L]awyers' conflict resolution capabilities are enhanced by emotional skills like self-observation and awareness of the assumptions, anxieties and conflicts that are part of who one is.*[154]
>
> —Professor Melissa Nelken, Faculty Chair of the Hastings Center for Negotiation and Dispute Resolution

> *I sense a new moment emerging in the dispute resolution field when those of us committed to managing conflicts on the outside will increasingly understand that we must focus intently on the inside.*[155]
>
> —Erica Fox, negotiation lecturer at Harvard Law School

Dealing with destructive, entrenched conflict is one of the steepest challenges for law firms and law departments, to which survey after survey of managing partners attests.[156] In one, 40 percent of managing partners of midsize US law firms said that "managing conflict" and 23 percent said managing "partner revolt or upheaval" had been what most put them to the test during the prior year.[157] As one expert says, "Effectively addressing conflict is a key leadership attribute and most of us don't do it very well."[158]

Conflict invariably is accompanied by strong emotion. "Since the triggers of emotion and the triggers of perceived conflict are the same, to recognize that someone is in conflict is to acknowledge that he has been triggered emotionally."[159]

As Jack Mayer, one of the original theorists of EI, noted, "If people could always stay perfectly rational and focused on how to best meet their needs and accommodate those of others . . . then many conflicts would either never arise or would quickly de-escalate."[160] But this is fanciful thinking. Emotions are often inextricable from the factors that created the conflict in the first place, and the inability or unwillingness to recognize and deal with those emotions enflames and complicates those conflicts further. Resolving conflicts requires fully addressing three dimensions—emotional, cognitive, and behavioral.[161]

One complication of trying to manage emotions while engaged in conflict lies in the physiological reactions that emotions produce. The amygdala, the emotional center of the brain, responds very quickly to perceived attacks and long before the cognitive brain adds its analysis to the situation, producing a "refractory state" "during which time our thinking cannot incorporate information that does not fit, maintain, or justify the emotion we are feeling."[162] This supports the long-standing concept of "confirmation bias," our tendency to only pay attention to facts that confirm, while ignoring information that might challenge, our preconceived notions. This tendency is attributed to low emotional perception and emotion regulation.[163] Locked into an emotional knee-jerk, we become even more entrenched in our position.[164] Dr. Kahneman believes we often have a similar bias toward those advisors "who offer highly favorable estimates of the outcomes . . . Such a predisposition, often shared by leaders on both sides of a conflict, is likely to produce a disaster."[165]

Not surprisingly, then, studies have concluded that "higher EI scores are related to improved . . . conflict management."[166] The most telling research found that simply focusing on the emotions rather than the details of the conflict reduces amygdala activity and emotional arousal, thereby increasing the likelihood of a resolution.[167] Various conflict resolution models have been proposed that promote explicitly identifying and acknowledging the emotions involved.[168]

Both the high incidence of conflict implicit in practicing law and the emotional fallout from it may be below the radar of those entering or even practicing law. As Herz expressed it to a Harvard Law class: "Most law students and practitioners were probably not inspired to go to law school to deal with difficult people in crisis and others who are impossible to please. Even if you are completely successful in helping them, those same people often are not pleased about paying you."[169]

But is conflict endemic not only to our work but to our organizational model as well? Hire many more lawyers than are expected to make partner so even at the outset any reasonable chance of career success is low. Pit associates against each other to perform, encouraging self-promotion and undercutting. Play partners off against each other in the race to bag and keep clients. Make everyone compete to rise in firm or department management as the organization grows increasingly hierarchical. And of course, make all the stakeholders—associates, senior associates, nonequity partners, equity partners, rainmakers—vie for a share of the compensation pie. Are we structuring our workplaces to produce shoulder-to-shoulder colleagues or knife-in-the-teeth gladiators?

Add to this environment the personal styles of the professionals involved and the legal workplace becomes even more rife with unresolved conflict. Low EI is itself a harbinger of conflict. Lawyers are typically weak in perceiving emotions, and misperceived emotion is a common driver of conflict.[170] One party attributes an action by another party to his or her negative emotion—such as disrespect, greed, hatred, envy, or revenge—even if that attribution turns out to be entirely incorrect. The accused—a low resilience, defensive lawyer—is likely to respond to any hint of accusation by counterpunching to defend himself or herself first and determining the facts later, only after the destructive fallout has already occurred. Combined with impaired information gathering—our viewpoint narrowed and often biased—the conflict becomes even harder to resolve.[171]

Deficits in empathy, emotional understanding, and emotional regulation also add to the fracas. We don't "get" what the other person is feeling—the resentment or jealousy or fear, we don't understand how those emotions we can't even identify are likely to evolve under the pressure of all the influences at play, and we have little ability to change our own or others' emotional displays, which can deepen or expand the conflict.

Other typical lawyer attributes, and the responses those attributes usually prompt lawyers to make when they are under stress, induce and prolong conflicts. Stressors that trigger problematic reactions in Myers-Briggs Type Indicator (MBTI) "Thinkers," for example, which most lawyers are according to this widely used personal style assessment, include incompetent people, anything illogical, unjust, or unfair, lack of control, and being confronted with strong emotions. Likely reactions include extremely strong emotional outbursts—usually of anger, a profound sense of alienation, fear of permanently losing control, passive-aggressiveness, hypersensitivity, inflexibility, and domineering, demanding stances.[172] Thinkers with EI are explicitly acknowledged by MBTI research to be best equipped to moderate these reactions.[173]

Similarly, using the Hogan assessments, lawyers were found under stress to "become argumentative and critical of others" and then "to physically or emotionally distance themselves from others and become uncommunicative," called "Moving Away" from conflict, in marked contrast to other professionals who favor the more successful "Moving Against" the conflict to solve or remove it.[174]

Results from the *Thomas Kilmann Instrument* (TKI) find the most frequently used conflict resolution strategy by senior management executives is collaboration, which one study reports "individuals with high emotional intelligence prefer."[175] Scattered TKI results indicate, however, that, consistent with low EI, lawyers are not typically comfortable with collaboration or the two other cooperative resolution styles (compromise and accommodation). They prefer two uncooperative styles—avoiding conflict altogether (interestingly enough) or fighting to win.[176]

Unfortunately, both these strategies have major pitfalls. Avoidance not only doesn't solve most conflicts but also carries a cost. "Whatever its short-term advantages in minimizing stress and unpleasantness, experts suggest that conflict avoidance should be avoided. Unaddressed problems generally fester, impair performance, and lead to more costly confrontations later on."[177]

Avoidance of conflict is, in my estimation, the Achilles heel of many legal practices. Conflict can be a mechanism to provide valuable information to better the functioning of our organizations. But time and again, lawyers simply turn away. Maybe we don't see the signs in the first place, being low in awareness. Or maybe we strategize that it's better to just ignore conflict and see if it goes away by itself, steeling ourselves to any intimations of problems. Perhaps we fear that acknowledging conflicts would reflect poorly on our leadership or that trying to address them would expose our lack of skills or rupture important alliances. For whatever reasons, this is one of the few circumstances when leaders can sound downright optimistic, saying that "everything is fine."

One managing partner, whom I pointedly questioned, repeatedly assured me that any conflicts within the firm were minor and typical and would certainly not be debilitating over the long run. I came to interview him after being asked by several of his partners to help address what they considered to be a crisis—after several vigorous altercations, many lawyers had their resumes out and neither hints nor confrontations had brought the managing partner to acknowledge, let alone deal with, the issues. His denial of any trouble magically eliminated any concern he would have otherwise had—until the whole thing blew up around him. That firm no longer exists.

Brian Scudamore, founder and CEO of O2E Brands, the banner company for 1-800-GOT-JUNK, advocates a "race to the conflict." Employees are encouraged to quickly acknowledge a conflict in order to get it resolved rapidly and thereby preserve good working relationships.[178] "Delivering a difficult message is like throwing a hand grenade," as one commentator asserts, but "Choosing not to deliver a difficult message is like hanging on to a hand grenade once you've pulled the pin."[179]

Even if racing to the conflict is a reaction we could instill in legal workplaces (one that those intent on winning might entertain), once there, lawyers are not likely to have the interpersonal skills to resolve the conflict. Parties may well be antagonized into new conflicts by their treatment during the "resolution." So our speed to recognize conflict must be accompanied by skills that emotional intelligence provides in managing the resolution.

Yet lawyers' other preferred alternative—"wins," often realized through a scorched earth assault—can produce long-abiding resentments on all sides that give birth to the next round of conflicts. These highly charged contests also prove mentally and physically debilitating over time.[180] So lawyers are often left with ineffective conflict management.

Here are some practical tips for spotting and managing conflict:

- **Ask If There's a Conflict.** If there is uncertainty as to what a person intends, ask them. A growl or a stare doesn't necessarily mean a conflict exists. Assuming that someone is motivated by malice or other bad intent can be energizing and raise your combative hackles, which may produce a fast reaction. But it is a disservice to all if that reaction needlessly produces or exacerbates conflicts.
- **Acknowledge Emotions.** Yours, theirs, a third party's. You don't have to agree that those emotions are justified, only that they exist. Focusing on the emotions rather than the details of the conflict can itself reduce amygdala activity and therefore problematic emotional arousal.[181]
- **Listen to Your Approach to Addressing Conflict.** Here is where empathy is very useful. How loaded are your words? What is the other person likely to feel when they hear what you are saying? Are you trying to understand the other's viewpoint and be fair? Or are you trying to win by innuendo or accusation? If so, might you do more damage than even losing on the merits?

- **Modulate Your Tone and Body Language.** A factor that sometimes outshines the content of a conflict is 'how" it is discussed (i.e., the vocal tone and body language used). Negative feedback given in a warm, positive tone makes the receiver of the feedback feel good about the interaction, and positive feedback given in a cold, critical tone makes the receiver feel negative, even with respect to the positive points made.[182] Doctors most susceptible to being sued can be identified by their intonation, pitch, and rhythm.[183] In other words, the emotional content of our communication, even more than the substantive content, can build rapport and defuse conflict or exacerbate it.
- **Consider a Range of Resolutions.** Are there any resolutions that avoid making one person the winner and the other the loser? Ask your rival what he or she suggests to ameliorate the situation and look for ways to incorporate those suggestions into a resolution. That is collaboration.
- **Give Credit Away.** Harry Truman, Ronald Reagan, and a number of others are all credited with saying essentially that much can be accomplished if we are willing to give someone else the credit.[184] So it is with conflicts. This is again a hard one for lawyers, because they so value a "win" with attribution. Try giving that kudo away in exchange for greater trust and collegiality, and possibly even a greater win down the road.

Higher-Functioning Teams

> *Those who have learned to collaborate and improvise most effectively have prevailed.*
>
> —attributed to Charles Darwin

After Tom Peters' information and technology revolution,[185] the next revolution coming to professional services firms is the ascendance of teams—management, client, industry, marketing, and other types of teams. Particularly in a "world being eaten by software," groups are essential to our economic survival because "what humans will continue to do . . . is **what we do best in groups**: 1. Idea-generation, problem-solving, strategy, 2. Persuasion, argument, storytelling, and 3. Collaboration."[186] Even leadership is now best realized in teams, or what the Center for Creative Leadership calls "collective leadership."[187] In a survey of leaders of 78 large law firms, 71 percent expected to increase their use of teams.[188]

Harvard Law Professor Heidi Gardner finds that collaboration and teamwork are the most critical elements of organizational design that support high-quality client service and drive greater profitability in law firms.[189] Team effort responds to the complexities of today's legal practice by producing more comprehensive expertise and greater innovation due to the cross-fertilization of minds, a higher likelihood of someone connecting with the client on a personal level and therefore better client service, greater loyalty, and ultimately higher revenues.[190] A team that builds a close relationship with a client also helps retain the client when a single attorney leaves.[191] In short, teams are the hands and feet of successful law practices in the 21st century.[192]

The Georgetown study of successful Am Law 100 associates found the ability to work well in teams is "especially critical in predicting performance" because good teamwork "captures a specific set of interpersonal skills not captured in technical or individual work competencies," including the ability to resolve conflicts.[193]

In an extensive review of how best to structure the most effective teams, Google determined in 2016 that IQ is much less relevant than "members [who] listen to one another and show sensitivity to feelings and needs."[194] This emotional sensitivity makes the team a "safe place" for collaboration and free-form brainstorming, and therefore more likely to succeed.

Decades of research agrees that higher EI is positively linked with team performance, effective conflict resolution within the team, and faster problem solving, significantly undercutting the value of a team's IQ.[195] Just "the ability to understand one another's emotional expressions explained 40% of the variance" in the higher performance achieved by high EI teams.[196] High EI teams have higher levels of intra-team trust,[197] are more creative[198] and have stronger "strategic vision."[199] Simply knowing the average EI of the team handling a matter, and that alone, predicts customer satisfaction.[200] As one researcher said, the hallmarks of high EI—"constructive communication, empathy, self-awareness—are simply inconsistent with the attributes of a dysfunctional team."[201]

Emotionally intelligent teamwork also is good for the individual team members: it provides support in times of setback, gives opportunities to develop leadership skills and to form close work relationships, and ultimately improves team members' personal well-being, in turn making them more likely to stay.[202]

Lawyers, independent as they are, may look for reasons not to work in teams. Gardner notes that, "[F]or people who have strong autonomy preferences, group work can be constraining and frustrating, and that may undermine their satisfaction with their work. They may . . . concentrate on aspects of the task that allow them to work alone, free of the obligations and constraints that come from working with others. Because they avoid collaboration, they tend not to build the kinds of skills and knowledge that enable smooth cross-practice working and thus continue to perceive the costs of collaboration as high." She believes, however, that "as people gain experience of interdependence, they grow more accepting of it and even come to prefer it to solo working."[203]

The goal should be obvious. It is the mechanism for getting there that legal workplaces have the most problem with. Law firms remain the habitat of siloed lone wolves whose interactions are largely virtual because of lawyer attributes, the ease and pervasiveness of technological communication, and the typical legal organizational structure and culture.[204] A change of attitude and culture to one that values and promotes emotional intelligence is the beginning of building emotionally intelligent teams.[205] As pointed out in *Harvard Business Review's* "Building the Emotional Intelligence of Groups," "For organizations with long histories of employees checking their emotions at the door, change will occur, if at all, one team at a time."[206]

Greater Personal Well-Being

> *[T]he psychological climate of the workplace plays a much more important role in the ultimate level of profitability, productivity, and client satisfaction than previously believed . . . In short . . . happy people generate higher profits.*[207]
>
> —Dr. Larry Richard, consultant

As organizational EI rises, there is a corresponding increase in personal well-being.[208] That well-being translates into higher retention, fewer illnesses, and less depression and other indications of distress—in short, greater productivity.[209] Even cognitive analysis improves: doctors who are optimistic and in a good mood reach the right diagnosis 19 percent faster than doctors who are in an unhappy mood.[210]

Harvard Business Review's January/February 2012 cover trumpeted "The Value of Happiness: How Employee Well-Being Drives Profits," citing research that happiness precedes success; it doesn't follow from it.[211] So a legal workplace whose culture promotes personal well-being has a significant business asset.

Contrary to what many legal workplaces appear to assume, lawyer well-being is more a factor of internal feelings than of external factors. Drawing from data from several thousand lawyers in four states, the first research to identify contributors to the well-being of lawyers found that external factors (i.e., class rank, law review membership, law school rank, law school debt, earnings, attaining partnership) showed "nil to small associations with lawyer well-being." Rather, internal psychological factors—feelings of autonomy, relatedness to others, and competence, shown in previous research to actually erode during law school—appear to be the most important contributors to lawyers' happiness, followed by choices regarding family and personal life. These internal factors were approximately 5 times stronger than that of class rank and 3.5 times stronger than that of income or school debt with respect to well-being. The authors felt compelled to conclude that the data demonstrate "that lawyers are very much like other people, notwithstanding . . . the common perception that lawyers are different from others in fundamental ways."[212]

Of course, much of our well-being is under our own personal control, and there are demonstrated ways, large[213] and small,[214] for us to experience more positive feelings.[215] People who consciously engage in intentionally positive activities, such as thinking gratefully, optimistically, or mindfully, for example, become significantly happier.[216]

Our organizations also have a role in cultivating positive feelings.[217] We can set in place policies and educational opportunities to promote emotional intelligence, which supports those feelings that generate well-being and empowers workers to choose their emotions, including the positive ones, more reliably.[218]

But Dr. Richard acknowledges the same resistance in legal workplaces to adopting policies that promote personal well-being that I have repeatedly encountered. "Many lawyers will dismiss this . . . out of hand, or marginalize it by sarcastically labeling it as 'Kumbayah management' or complaining that 'now you want to create a hugfest.' But smart leaders know better than that. These ideas are backed up by extensive empirical science . . . Law is a people business—our assets are our people. So it stands to reason that bringing out the best in our people is a surefire formula for success."[219]

A small California firm asked me to help address an underperforming department, which it was considering "cutting loose." It was a small department of three partners, five associates, and two paralegals. The financial statements showed that the department was in fact quite profitable, although at a slightly lower margin than the two other, larger departments in the firm. The clients were very loyal, billable hours were high, and the department members seemed quite satisfied working together. What was prompting the firm to consider dumping a profitable group?

It turned out that the charge against the department was that it was "unprofessional." Its members did not socialize with the rest of the firm, did not organize and distribute its work, and did not respond to clients or even to partners in other departments in the manner that the other departments did. Further, the other partners considered these wayward ways to be an intentional affront to them and how they ran their departments, challenging or mocking them. An impasse had been reached, where the exasperation of both sides precluded discussion between them.

Using assessments, I found that all members of the "unprofessional" department had a strikingly similar personal style—quite introverted and preferring to conclude their work late in the cycle—a style that was at odds with the members of the other two departments, who were more extroverted and longer-range planners. This one department felt unprofessional to the other two departments because they did things differently.

When we together reviewed this information, it became apparent that the work of the detail-oriented, fast-paced regulatory practice of the "unprofessional" department benefitted from a different type of approach than was used elsewhere in the firm and that its lawyers' personal style was well suited to that work.

The other findings that showed up in the assessments were that nearly all the attorneys valued harmony and collegiality, yet most of them had EI deficits. I believe those deficits hampered them from recognizing initially the resentments that were building, from empathizing with lawyers who had practice demands different from their own, from understanding why they felt animosity, and from addressing a situation that had been developing over years, one that threatened their valued harmony.

In this case, there is not a rosy ending. Intellectually, everyone at the firm undoubtedly came to understand the dynamics at work: the one group had a different type of practice that benefitted from a different work style and that they enjoyed. But the emotionally charged reactions persisted—the other two departments were not able to modulate their judgments or resentments and the unwelcome department retreated even more under the glare of disapproval—so all sides felt uncomfortable and productivity plummeted. The wayward department eventually picked itself up and left for the arms of a firm that welcomed its style and profitability.

EMOTIONAL INTELLIGENCE BUILDS A MORE PRODUCTIVE CULTURE

- Low emotional intelligence cultures are likely to become "emotionally toxic" with high stress and low performance.
- Emotionally intelligent cultures can accomplish the following:
    1. Lower the high attrition among associates and laterals that costs legal workplaces hundreds of thousands of dollars in time and resources.
    2. Reduce the conflict inherent in the structure of many legal workplaces, reduce the personal conflict that is common among lawyers, and improve management's approaches to conflict resolution.
    3. Produce higher-functioning legal teams that are key to greater collaboration and better performance in the 21st century.
    4. Raise personal well-being, which produces increased productivity.

3. Emotional Intelligence Lowers the Risk of Liability

[Ethics] entails not only compliance with formal ethical rules, but also adherence to widely accepted norms of honesty, fairness, civility and respect for societal interests.[220]

—Deborah L. Rhode, Stanford University Law School Professor of Law and Director of their Center on the Legal Profession

My mind seems to have become a kind of machine for grinding general laws out of large collections of facts . . . . [resulting in] a loss of happiness, and may possibly be injurious to the intellect, and more probably to the moral character, by enfeebling the emotional part of our nature.[221]

—Charles Darwin

In a law practice setting, the emotional deficiencies of the partners have the most impact [on liability].[222]

—Robert A. Mines, Rachel A. Meyer, and Michael R. Mines, "Emotional Intelligence and Emotional Toxicity: Implications for Attorneys and Law Firms."

> *Because contemporary attorneys are more likely to face a malpractice claim regarding their relationship skills than their calendaring systems, attorneys who lack emotional intelligence are a swelling financial risk for law firms and malpractice insurers.*[223] *At the most elemental level of law practice, emotional intelligence appears to be necessary for attorneys to avoid malpractice liability.*[224]
>
> —Randall Kiser, author of *How Leading Lawyers Think* and *Beyond Right and Wrong,* and principal analyst at DecisionSet®

There is no question that charges of lawyer misconduct are on the rise. The incidence and costs of malpractice claims have risen dramatically, with trends showing increasingly larger claims as well.[225] The number of complaints and disciplinary actions are also increasing nationwide.[226]

Commentators have remarked for years on the decline in ethical standards among lawyers: not the least of whom was Warren Burger in an article published over 20 years ago entitled, "The Decline of Professionalism."[227] In a 2016 survey, 37 percent of respondents rated the honesty and ethical standards of lawyers low or very low, a rating worse than medical professionals, police, clergy, accountants, building contractors, journalists, bankers, real estate agents, and business executives.[228] Even lawyers think lawyers should be behaving better: in one instance, 62 percent of the lawyers surveyed thought lawyers were inadequately policing lawyer misconduct.[229]

Widespread reports of significant lawyer misconduct reinforce these impressions of lawyers' vulnerability to wrongdoing and may encourage people to press disciplinary charges or sue.[230] Among many others, a federal judge ruled in 2016 that Department of Justice prosecutors who appear in 26 states must attend ethics training in light of their repeated misconduct in thousands of migrant lawsuits, and another 2016 decision vacated a $200 million infringement award because of the misconduct of the awardee's in-house counsel.[231]

Lawyers are intelligent, cognizant of the elements of misconduct and of the personal and professional fallout, and they are risk averse. So why are these claims on the rise? Why aren't we better able to monitor and control the precedents of censure and liability?

August bodies have weighed in on what bedevils our profession, ethically speaking. The Carnegie Foundation's 2007 report on legal education found one of its primary deficits to be a failure to produce graduates who have "ethical and social skills," noting that "law students' moral reasoning does not appear to develop to any significant degree during law school," nor, tellingly, later during practice.[232] There is some evidence that students' ethics actually decline during law school.[233]

With all the professionalism and ethics classes blooming in law school and continuing legal education (CLE) curricula,[234] what are we still missing in producing more ethical lawyers? A Louisiana judge recently named the problem while holding an assistant district attorney in contempt, saying his "emotional intelligence needs strengthening."[235]

Emotional intelligence can't compensate for willful misconduct, which accounts for an unknown proportion of sanctions and liability, but for those who are not intentionally unethical, who find themselves the victim of good intentions gone wrong, raising emotional intelligence may well be key to improvement.

We have been educating our minds without educating our emotions. According to Hebrew University economics professor Eyal Winter, author of *Feeling Smart: Why Our Emotions Are More Rational Than We Think* (PublicAffairs, 2014), "we know that the types of decisions that invoke perhaps the most intensive collaboration between rationality and emotions are ethical or moral considerations."[236] An attorney whose practice is devoted entirely to defending disciplinary actions confirms that unmanaged emotions like anger and frustration, and the habit of avoiding dealing with those emotions, are what put lawyers most at risk for not only a single disciplinary procedure but multiple ones.[237]

Putting our personal feelings aside to vigorously represent "personally repugnant clients and causes" can dull our sensitivity to the emotional discomfort of misconduct.[238] Dr. Kahneman says we court danger by believing we make decisions rationally, when in fact we are nonetheless influenced by intuition, emotions, and biases we do not recognize.[239] So trying to detach ourselves from emotions doesn't stop them from influencing our behavior, or more precisely our misbehavior. Awareness of our "gut feelings," which embody past responses to ethical decisions, guides us as to how decisions being made today might make us feel,[240] thereby leading us to avoid what we have learned makes us feel guilty, for example.[241]

Emotional intelligence reduces risks of liability in several ways: the emotionally intelligent can more accurately assess the risks involved,[242] better understand which ethical standards are appropriate in the situation,[243] and recognize and deal better with the emotional fallout from their ethical choices, especially when they are ignoring or acting against their personal values.[244] Empathy in particular gives us a clear edge in making ethical decisions—people act more ethically when they can put themselves in someone else's shoes.[245] Empathy also gives us the insight to recognize when and how others are making ethical decisions, an ability which in turn motivates peer pressure and empowers whistleblowing.[246]

The following factors that impact lawyers' risk of liability can improve with greater emotional intelligence: risk appraisal, communication, "arrogance," power, high distress levels, and both typical lawyer personal attributes and the uniformity of those attributes.

Risk Appraisal. As pointed out before, researchers have demonstrated the "oracle effect" of emotional intelligence in predicting outcomes.[247] EI also empowers us to rightly ignore extraneous emotional reactions that could muddle our appraisal of risk. In an important study, participants with higher emotional perception and emotional understanding appropriately ignored incidental emotions that were irrelevant to evaluating the risk, in some cases taking on even more risk as a result.[248] As the lead author explained: "People who are emotionally intelligent don't remove all emotions from their decision-making . . . They remove emotions that have nothing to do with the decision."[249] In a double whammy, lawyers' low EI may not only limit our risk assessment abilities, but knowing that deficit, even unconsciously, we may unnecessarily steer away from all risks.

Communication. Being out of touch with our and our clients' emotions can make it hard to communicate effectively, which has major liability implications. In healthcare, "an empirical link between communication behaviors and subsequent malpractice litigation"[250] has prompted industry-wide instruction in emotionally intelligent communication.[251] Given that "My lawyer isn't talking to me"[252] is the number one complaint being made to bar associations [253] and is the primary underlying cause of malpractice claims in Canada and the United States,[254] improving lawyers' communication by raising their EI can dramatically reduce their liability exposure.

Passing the Critical Malpractice Test: Arrogance. The most interesting study relevant to risk management for professional service providers is one that accurately identified surgeons who had been sued for malpractice using only forty-second sound clips. In these recordings of conversations between a doctor and his or her patients, the spoken content was filtered out, leaving only intonation, pitch, and rhythm. The clips were then evaluated for various perceived attributes of the doctors. Those doctors rated highest in a single attribute—"dominance," also described as arrogance—were also the ones who had been sued.[255]

The unavoidable conclusion was that many medical malpractice claims don't arise because of technical incompetence or malfeasance, but rather because of deficits in relationship building. "'If a doctor and patient have a strong relationship, even if something goes wrong, they are less likely to sue,' confirms Robin Diamond, chief patient safety officer at Doctors Co., which provides malpractice insurance for 73,000 physicians."[256] I have personal experience of a client who wanted to sue a doctor involved in his care but who refused to sue another physician instead, against whom the case was much stronger, simply because he liked her.

Shouldn't we lawyers be aiming for that same type of relationship with our clients? The one that makes us "right" or at least "all right" from a liability standpoint?

Yet BTI reports annually on the lawyers whom Fortune 1000 clients consider arrogant,[257] and public surveys reflect a distrust of lawyers and their ethics. Deficits in EI lead us to miss or misread emotional cues in ourselves and others and insufficiently manage or mismanage emotional responses, thus impeding our ability to build trusting professional relationships. The MBTI "Thinker" preference, together with introversion, high skepticism, and low sociability common to many lawyers, can come across as cold or uncaring. That combination of attributes, as doctors have found, can fuel malpractice claims.

Coping with Power. Another factor that can corrupt good ethical judgment is power, which one University of California, Berkeley psychologist compares "to brain damage . . . [to] a brain area that's crucial for empathy and decision-making." Coinciding with feelings of power are "deficits in emotional awareness," difficulties in reasoning about emotions, and an increased cognitive override of emotions, all of which can corrupt moral decision making and often lead to rationalizing harmful actions, particularly in "high-conflict, personal moral dilemmas,"[258] a common situation for lawyers. Ethical problems mount when people "believe they will never get caught and feel smart enough to worm their way out of it."[259] Furthermore, "people in power tend to reliably overestimate their moral virtue, which leads them to stifle oversight . . . The end result is sometimes power at its most dangerous."[260]

The Risk of High Distress. The astronomically high level of distress among lawyers is itself sufficient to raise significantly the incidence of legal malpractice.[261] Attributes of emotional distress like reduced cognitive functioning, poor memory, and depression prime a lawyer for malpractice, and his or her workplace also risks being disciplined or sued for the failure to identify and correct the problems caused by an attorney essentially missing in action.[262]

Other Typical Lawyer Attributes. Again, other typical lawyer attributes, besides low EI, make us susceptible to liability, attributes that could be assuaged with higher emotional intelligence.[263] A strong sense of urgency can push us to both communicate poorly and make decisions too quickly, a tendency reinforced by busy, deadline-driven clients. Greater awareness of the internal emotional cues that drive urgency could help slow us down to review other considerations, including those "out of the box," which to a harried lawyer can seem unnecessarily time consuming. Lawyers' introversion, high autonomy, and low sociability usually keep us from voluntarily involving or consulting with others who might spot problematic behavior or decisions, an easier prospect if one has the confidence of being able to emotionally handle relationships.

Similarly, the low-resilience lawyer who knows he or she is caught in a situation with potential liability is unlikely to affirmatively reach out, fearing an imbroglio that he or she can't recover from, yet resilience can be raised through effective emotional regulation. Lawyers' preferred conflict resolution styles also expose us to greater liability. When used with clients, even if unintentionally, both all-out winning and avoiding conflict altogether can stoke the perception of our being arrogant and cold on one hand, or, on the other, result in greater exposure. Raising our emotional intelligence gives us the ability to work through conflict with clients and colleagues more collaboratively.

Uniformity of Lawyer Attributes. In fact, one of the most glaring risks for liability in our legal organizations is the uniformity in attributes that lawyers exhibit. A diversity of opinions and skills indisputably produces the best analyses and decisions, and therefore those most resistant to charges of misconduct or malpractice.[264] The lack of diversity in how our legal professionals think and feel presents an enormous concern from a risk management perspective.

These various factors all exacerbate the liability risk for lawyers, and that exposure is not likely to abate. For example, lawyers have proven themselves vulnerable to the explosion of sexual harassment suits,[265] often arising because of failure to read emotional cues, understand emotions, and/or manage them. These lawsuits exact financial and reputational costs that can be devastating to both individuals and organizations and will particularly adversely impact a firm's or department's desirability as a workplace and service provider among Millennials, who are highly sensitized to micro-aggressions.[266]

Rule 8.4(g) of the American Bar Association Model Rules of Professional Conduct was amended in August 2016 to prohibit lawyers from engaging in conduct that they know or reasonably should know constitutes harassment or discrimination with respect to several protected classes.[267] It is clearly intended to have wide application in the legal profession, including in the operation and management of law practices.[268] As amended, the Rule could significantly broaden the legal profession's exposure to liability, since many legal cultures are both conducive to harassment and suffer from chronic underrepresentation and underpromotion of women and minorities.[269]

The healthcare industry actively promotes emotional intelligence to reduce the incidence of misconduct that engenders liability.[270] Studies undertaken to raise ethical behavior in a healthcare setting conclude that, "[o]verall emotional intelligence of hospital employees had a significant impact on their ethical behavior," and that, "higher EQ scores predict higher performance in ethics"—specifically the ability to regulate emotions.[271]

The major accounting firms also are attentive to the role of emotions in liability: KPMG's US partners took personal style assessments so that its teams could be organized to respond to all aspects of an engagement, including ensuring that someone on each team had the EI to build and cement relationships, thereby reducing the risk of liability.[272]

Recognizing the importance of emotional intelligence is a start to reducing lawyers' exposure to professional sanctions and liability. The question remains whether we will do what needs to be done "in light of existing, countervailing, long-ingrained lawyer characteristics and decision-making approaches."[273]

Troublesome Outliers: Moral Disengagement, Narcissism, Machiavellianism, Sociopathy, and Psychopathy

It's mercy, compassion, and forgiveness I lack; not rationality.
—Beatrix Kiddo (played by Uma Thurman) in *Kill Bill*

A discussion of liability risks that emotional intelligence can ameliorate is not complete without pointing to the high incidence of social outliers who are attracted to the practice of law and pose serious ethical challenges: those morally "disengaged," narcissists, Machiavellians, sociopaths, and psychopaths.

Moral Disengagement. Albert Bandura, a psychology professor at Stanford University, focuses on what makes some people "disengage" from what they know to be morally appropriate, an inquiry "highly relevant to understanding unethical behavior in 21st century organizations."[274] Moral disengagement occupies the place between normal ethical behavior and the more extreme lack of ethical restraints exhibited by the personality disorders discussed below.

Bandura has identified "eight cognitive tactics"[275] centered on compartmentalization and justification that deactivate our ethics. We lawyers are, of course, by both training and practice, particularly good at cognitively compartmentalizing and justifying actions, including our most suspect ones.[276] According to Bandura, people with one or more of the following four personal attributes will be most predisposed to moral disengagement[277]: low empathy, high cynicism, lack of control, and weak moral identity.

Of these predispositions, some lawyers likely fall into all four, exhibiting low empathy, high cynicism (also known as skepticism), feelings of lack of control over their professional work (similar to Seligman's identification of low decision latitude), and a weak moral identity (as flagged by the Carnegie Foundation report).

Narcissism, Machiavellianism, and psychopathy (and sociopathy), together referred to as the "dark triad,"[278] are personality disorders that occur relatively frequently among lawyers[279] and exhibit, among other things, unethical acts at a much higher order of magnitude than other populations.

Narcissism. Researchers define narcissistic behavior "as remorseless, without conscious or concern for others, lacking empathy and human values, self-involved with an inflated self-image, cold and exploitative, with a strong need to be in control and not criticized. As such, it is associated with decisions that are not in the best interests of organizations, their members, stakeholders, clients or the wider community."[280] These people are often initially liked and respected. As Stanford Law Professor Rhode has noted in discussing law firms, "narcissistic individuals are often selected for leadership positions because they project the confidence and charisma that makes a positive impression. Yet over time, those characteristics can translate into a sense of entitlement, overconfidence, and an inability to learn from mistakes."[281]

Machiavellianism. Machiavellianism is named after the Italian political philosopher Niccolo Machiavelli, famous for his classic 1513 treatise *The Prince,* in which he advocates instilling fear through manipulation and occasional cruelty in order to gain power.[282] Machiavellians tend to be unemotional and able to detach from conventional morality in order to deceive and manipulate at the expense of (or at least without regard to) others. While Machiavellianism is not correlated with any particular personality trait or IQ, it is characterized by low EI.[283] However, Machiavellians can make use of isolated EI skills, like emotional perception, to "demean and embarrass their peers for personal gain."[284]

Antisocial Personality Disorder. The terms *sociopathy* and *psychopathy* are common terms often used interchangeably for antisocial personality disorder.[285] Approximately 4 percent of people in senior workplace positions are estimated to be psychopaths, and CEOs and lawyers are the careers with the highest concentration of them.[286] Although they are charming and friendly in interviews, they can display an array of troubling behaviors, including a disregard for the feelings of others; a lack of remorse or shame; the intention to sabotage, manipulate; and humiliate; egocentricity; deceptiveness; and the failure to follow through.[287]

Psychopaths have been definitively demonstrated to suffer significant deficits in one or more components of EI,[288] critically a lack of emotional empathy. Studies show that even having high levels of cognitive empathy or emotional understanding when coupled with low levels of emotional empathy allows these people to expertly manipulate others without regret.[289]

The historic sentiment is that "there's virtually no known treatment for ruthless, manipulative, law-abiding citizens who lack empathy," although some promising research suggests that psychopaths are simply set at a no-empathy default that might be turned on consciously or through suggestion.[290]

The book *Snakes in Suits: When Psychopaths Go to Work* specifically deals with "successful" psychopaths who are attracted to today's corporate work environment, where taking big risks can lead to equally high profits. While these people are often initially mistaken for superstars, their lack of emotional capabilities can create hostile work environments that end by alienating employees and, in some cases, destroying companies.[291]

The high concentration of psychopaths among lawyers is attributed by one consultant to "an often cold, impersonal, non-humane, self-aggrandizing and power-driven profession."[292] The prize of "power, status, admiration and financial reward" is highly attractive to low-empathy, arrogant personalities who are less likely to make good decisions or to act for the good of the group, the profession,[293] or society in general.[294] "Deep inside me there's a serial killer lurking somewhere," one successful lawyer admitted. "But I keep him amused with cocaine, Formula One, booty calls, and coruscating cross-examination."[295]

In *Confessions of a Psychopath: A Life Spent Hiding in Plain Sight,* diagnosed psychopath M.E. Thomas describes herself "as a cut-throat attorney who sailed through law school without much effort, landed a position at a prestigious law firm, and then became a law professor. She also claims to fantasize about murder, drops friends when their personal problems get in the way of her fun, and plots ways to 'ruin people' in her spare time," her favorite pastime.[296]

Thomas acknowledges that these traits have both contributed to her success, and held her back. "Her book details the time she has spent going out of her way to toy with other people's emotions . . . 'I think one of the things that's been my downfall in the past is when I start thinking that I'm normal and fine and that when something happens it's someone else's fault. I have to remind myself that I am this way. I am naturally manipulative. I have a tendency to indulge in self-deception.'"[297]

Of course, having EI skills doesn't guarantee that someone is nice, sympathetic, compassionate, sentimental, or ethical, because those skills can be used to achieve both good and bad ends.[298] Much depends on the person's values, morals, and goals—"[e]mpathic ability is value neutral, sometimes helping and other times hurting people,"[299] if, for example, it's used to manipulate others to their detriment. Similarly, "emotion-regulation knowledge is itself neither positive nor negative, but can facilitate the objectives of individuals whose interests are in doing harm as well as those interested in benefitting the greater good."[300] Those who value harmonious relationships may use EI skills to achieve those goals. Psychopaths, on the other hand, may use those same EI skills to take advantage of others.[301]

What is relevant to the incidence of legal misconduct is the high concentration among lawyers of narcissism, Machiavellianism, sociopathy, and psychopathy—people who either have low overall emotional intelligence or have EI skills that they use to knowingly promote their own unethical agendas.[302] Whatever benefits their charisma and brashness may bring to organizations will be far outweighed by the ultimate extent of the liability, to say nothing of the damage their outsized presence does to organizational functioning and culture. Leaders and recruiters must pay attention to signs of these conditions if they are trying to build a more emotionally intelligent, and successful, workplace.

In the 1985 movie Jagged Edge, *Glenn Close plays a glamorous lawyer who falls for her intelligent and charming client, Jeff Bridges, a successful newspaper publisher accused of murdering his wealthy wife. The two become lovers, and while Close is confronted with ambiguous evidence throughout the trial, he convinces her that he is innocent and she succeeds in getting him cleared. Afterwards, Bridges tries to kill Close, and she realizes that she has been expertly deceived.*

A classic psychopath, Bridges' character displays certain EI skills, even though he lacks empathy. He reads emotional cues well, seems to understand the way emotions influence behavior, can regulate his own emotions appropriately under difficult circumstances, and knows how to manage emotional relationships in order to achieve the results he wants. In fact, it is his emotional intelligence *that make him successful not only in his work but also in achieving his morally reprehensible ends.*

EMOTIONAL INTELLIGENCE LOWERS THE RISK OF LIABILITY

- The rise in disciplinary actions and malpractice claims as a result of unintentional misconduct may be associated with low emotional intelligence.
- Widespread reports of lawyer misconduct may encourage complaints and suits.
- Law schools fail to educate law students about the emotional aspects of ethics, with some research showing that moral reasoning actually declines during law school.
- Emotional intelligence helps draw on "gut feelings" about past ethical decisions to inform current behavior.
- Trying to detach from emotions in morally repugnant situations can dull our sensitivity to ethical issues, yet doesn't eliminate their influence on our decisions and behavior, whether conscious or unconscious.
- Among other advantages, emotional intelligence raises awareness that ethical issues are being presented and which ethical standards are appropriate.
- People act more ethically when they have the empathy to put themselves in someone else's shoes. Empathy also helps recognize others' ethical decisions, which can motivate peer pressure and whistleblowing.
- Emotional intelligence helps recognize and deal with the personal emotional fallout from taking legal positions that are morally repugnant.
- Emotional intelligence aids in making accurate risk assessments by recognizing and discounting irrelevant emotions.
- Emotional intelligence may inoculate lawyers from some malpractice suits, as it appears to do with doctors, by improving communication and building strong client relationships.
- Emotional intelligence can address some of the negative consequences of gaining power.
- Emotional intelligence reduces the lawyer distress that poses a high risk of liability.
- Emotional intelligence builds awareness of and helps manage typical lawyer tendencies that can lead to liability, such as being hasty, appearing arrogant, working alone, failing to constructively manage adversity and conflict, and lacking diverse perspectives.

(Continued)

- Emotional intelligence reduces the likelihood of misconduct arising from deficits in emotional intelligence that figure frequently in sexual harassment lawsuits.
- Emotional intelligence helps reduce lawyer predispositions toward "moral disengagement."
- While having emotional intelligence does not preclude intentional misconduct, high overall emotional intelligence is generally inconsistent with the "dark triad" personality disorders of narcissism, Machiavellianism, and antisocial disorder that are disproportionately represented among lawyers who exhibit high levels of actionable behavior and are organizationally destructive.

4. Emotionally Intelligent Practices Are More Profitable

> *[A]ttitudes cause (yes, cause) a demonstrable, measurable improvement in financial performance.*[303]
>
> —David Maister, author and professional services guru, from his study of professional service firms worldwide

Study after study has confirmed that organizations "with higher EI scores are more likely to be highly profitable."[304] A review of senior executives in a large, multinational professional services firm, for example, found those executives high in EI competencies produced profits almost five times greater than those low in those competencies,[305] so accumulating higher revenue from emotionally intelligent individuals produces higher organizational revenue.[306] Closer to home, Baker & McKenzie managers attributed years of double-digit growth in profitability to a professional development program for its lawyers grounded in emotional intelligence,[307] and reports from clients continuing into 2016 place the firm at the pinnacle of customer service.[308]

In addition, emotionally intelligent leadership alone "can have a dramatic effect on a law firm's economic prospects."[309] Over a decade ago Jim Collins in *Good to Great* cited "Level 5" leaders who exhibit what today we would call emotional intelligence as the distinguishing trait of companies that dramatically outperform the market.[310] Emotionally intelligent leadership both optimizes individual performance and engenders more emotionally intelligent cultures, cultures that, as we have seen, lower attrition, manage conflict better, empower teams, embrace innovation, follow through on change, have healthier, happier professionals, and serve clients better, all of which fuels profitability.[311]

The author of *Nice Companies Finish First: Why Cutthroat Management Is Over—And Collaboration Is In* reviews a list of companies like Jet Blue, Zappos, Apple, Amex, Pepsi, and Patagonia who have harnessed EI traits to build more collaborative, productive workplaces that benefit the bottom line.[312] But the value of collaboration is not just for companies hawking consumer products.

According to Harvard Law Professor Gardner, collaboration is crucial to increasing profitability in legal organizations, and it is emotional intelligence that informs collaboration. In "the first empirical confirmation" of the financial benefits of collaboration, Gardner cites actual results achieved by a global law firm,[313] showing that individual law partners who collaborate within the firm realize greater personal revenue, and so does the whole firm.

"Simply put, the more disciplines that are involved in a client engagement, the greater the annual average revenue the client generates," because work across disciplines carries a premium, is less price sensitive, and promotes interactions with the highest client decision makers, making that client "more likely to become 'institutionalized'" (i.e., less vulnerable to any individual lawyer spiriting the client away). Gardner notes the added advantages that collaboration-generated revenue recovers more quickly after a downturn, and reduces the risk of misconduct because of the involvement of more lawyers.[314] She finds that collaborative workplaces also likely have increased revenues generated from innovation.[315]

Emotionally intelligent law practices generate higher revenues and have lower expenses for mental and physical debilitation, early burnout, attrition, and malpractice claims.[316] Further, high EI firms enjoy the decided advantage of competing largely against lawyers with low EI.[317] The bottom line is increased profits.

EMOTIONALLY INTELLIGENT PRACTICES ARE MORE PROFITABLE

Emotionally intelligent organizations are more profitable because of

- the accumulation of higher revenue generated by emotionally intelligent individuals;
- more effective leadership that optimizes individual performance and builds emotionally intelligent cultures that are more productive;
- greater productivity, stronger client relationships and loyalty, greater innovation, less conflict and better management of conflict, more collaboration, better functioning teams, and more satisfied professionals;
- lower expenses due to less mental and physical debilitation, reductions in early burnout and attrition, and lower liability costs; and
- competitors in the field with typically lower emotional intelligence.

Chapter Endnotes

1. Jack Welch, "Four E's (a Jolly Good Fellow)," *The Wall Street Journal,* January 23, 2004.
2. Covey, review of Bradberry and Greaves, *The Emotional Intelligence Quick Book* (New York: Simon & Schuster, 2005).
3. "Sometimes, EQ is more important than IQ," *CNN.com,* February 2, 2005, http://www.cnn.com/2005/US/Careers/01/13/emotions/.
4. Goleman, "What Makes a Leader," *Harvard Business Review,* 1998.
5. Goleman, Boyatzis, and Annie McKee, *Primal Leadership: Learning to Lead with Emotional Intelligence* (Cambridge: Harvard Business Press, 2002), ix.
6. Simon Tupman, "The Leadership Imperative: A Study into Law Firm Leadership," *Law Management Group and Simon Tupman,* March 2012, 19. In "Good to Great," Jim Collins concluded that what it takes for a good company to become a great one, using Collins' bottom-line standard of cumulated stock returns of 6.9 times the stock market in 15 years, is simply great leadership. The former Australian Prime Minister Julia Gillard's department provided emotional training workshops and personal coaching to her cabinet and staff "to foster enlightened and responsible leadership." Natasha Bita, "PM's Department Spends $650,000 'To Put the Lights On,'" *The Australian,* September 19, 2011.
7. Fred I. Greenstein, *The Presidential Difference: Leadership Style from FDR to Barack Obama* (Princeton: Princeton University Press, 2009).

8. Stein et al., "Emotional Intelligence of Leaders: A Profile of Top Executives," *Leadership and Organization Development Journal,* 30 (2009): 87.
9. In a study of 120 top Australian business executives, variations in IQ did not predict performance, leading the researchers to speculate that after a certain level of cognitive intelligence, higher IQ makes little difference. David Rosete and Joseph Ciarrochi, "Emotional Intelligence and Its Relationship to Workplace Performance Outcomes of Leadership Effectiveness," *Leadership and Organization Development Journal.* Although EI's role with respect to leadership is not without controversy. Frank Walter, Ronald H. Humphrey, and Michael S. Cole, "Unleashing Leadership Potential: Toward an Evidence-Based Management of Emotional Intelligence," *Organizational Dynamics* 41 (3): 212–19.
10. "Emotional Intelligence & Return on Investment: Return on Your EQ-i investment," *MHS,* n.d, 1–12, http://downloads.mhs.com/ei/MHS_Brief_ROI.pdf.
11. Rosete and Ciarrochi, "Emotional Intelligence and Its Relationship to Workplace Performance Outcomes of Leadership Effectiveness," *Leadership and Organization Development Journal.*
12. Bradberry and Greaves, *Emotional Intelligence 2.0,* 236.
13. Rhode, "Developing Leadership," *Santa Clara Law Review,* 690–91.
14. B. Mandell and S. Pherwani, "Relationship between Emotional Intelligence and Transformational Leadership Style: A Gender Comparison," *Journal of Business and Psychology* 17 (3): 397–98. Another study found less significant correlations between EI and transformational leadership. Peter D. Harms and Marcus Credé, "Emotional Intelligence and Transformational and Transactional Leadership: A Meta-Analysis," *Journal of Leadership and Organizational Studies* 17 (1): 5–17. See also Côté et al., "Emotional Intelligence and Leadership Emergence in Small Groups," *Leadership Quarterly,* 496–508.
15. Alan Murray, "What Is the Difference Between Management and Leadership?" *The Wall Street Journal,* n.d.
16. Maister, *Practice What You Preach: What Managers Must Do to Create a High Achievement Culture* (New York: Free Press, 2001).
17. Harvey Deutschendorf, "5 Ways to Spot an Emotionally Intelligent Leader," *Business 2 Community,* November 6, 2013, http://www.business2community.com/leadership/5-ways-spot-emotionally-intelligent-leader-0673416#cPWBvzCAIDjYzzul.97.
18. Rhode, "Developing Leadership," *Santa Clara Law Review,* 701. Goleman, Boyatzis and McKee's *Primal Leadership* is grounded in EI research. Drawing on Hay data on over 20,000 leaders worldwide, Goleman identified six leadership styles: Coercive leaders demand immediate compliance; "Authoritative leaders mobilize people toward a vision. Affiliative leaders create emotional bonds and harmony. Democratic leaders build consensus through participation. Pace-setting leaders expect excellence and self-direction. Coaching leaders develop people for the future." Goleman, "Leadership That Gets Results," *Harvard Business Review,* March–April, 2000.
19. Goleman, *Working with Emotional Intelligence,* 78–80. Rhode, *Lawyers as Leaders* (Oxford: Oxford University Press, 2013), 7. In the summer of 2013, Deborah L. Rhode, a professor at Stanford Law School, published a book entitled *Lawyers*

as Leaders, expanding on her oft-cited 2012 article, "Developing Leadership," which focused on the challenges of the modern lawyer leader. As Rhode has pointed out, no clear profile of the ideal characteristics of an effective leader has been developed. She concludes that, as Goldman believes, the ideal leader is a moving target because "successful leadership requires a match between what the circumstances demand and what an individual has to offer." Rhode, "Developing Leadership," *Santa Clara Law Review,* 691.

20. Deutchendorf, "5 Ways to Spot an Emotionally Intelligent Leader," *Business 2 Community.*
21. Abhijit Bhaduri, "How to Develop Emotional Intelligence: An Interview with Annie McKee," *The Times of India,* April 12, 2013, http://blogs.timesofindia.indiatimes.com/just-like-that/entry/how-to-develop-emotional-intelligence?sortBy=AGREE&th=1. Boyatzis and McKee, *Resonant Leadership: Renewing Yourself and Connecting with Others Through Mindfulness, Hope, and Compassion* (Cambridge: Harvard Business Review Press, 2005).
22. "Strategic Leadership Resources Announces How and Why to Improve Emotional Intelligence," *BWW Geeks World,* June 27, 2013, http://m.bwwgeeksworld.com/article/Strategic-Leadership-Resources-Announces-How-and-Why-to-Improve-Emotional-Intelligence-20130627.
23. Whitney Johnson, "Disrupt Yourself," *Harvard Business Review,* July–August, 2012, 149.
24. Fulbright & Jaworski's 2004 annual survey of corporate counsel reported that, "only a small minority of respondents cited incompetence among their law firms," but that in light of "the real issues . . .unpredictable costs, poor communication and inadequate preparation . . .law firms should refocus their efforts . . .as true service providers, not merely specialists in the law." Duncan and Mason, "In-House Counsel Offer Their Advice to Law-Firm Litigators," *San Francisco Daily Journal.* Of the four reasons companies fire outside counsel, an ACC/Serengeti Managing Outside Counsel Survey reported, two are for deficiencies in "soft" skills—responsiveness and personality issues. "InHouse Counsel Magazine ACC/Serengeti Managing Outside Counsel Survey," *InHouse Counsel Magazine,* 2010.
25. Richard Susskind, *The End of Lawyers* (Oxford: Oxford University Press, 2010).
26. Tupman, "The Leadership Imperative," *Law Management Group and Simon Tupman.*
27. Jordan Furlong, "You're Not Selling What We're Buying," *Law21 Blog,* November 30, 2016, https://www.law21.ca/2016/11/youre-not-selling-what-were-buying/.
28. "2015 Law Firms in Transition Survey," *Altman Weil, Inc.,* 2015, http://www.altmanweil.com/dir_docs/resource/1c789ef2-5cff-463a-863a-2248d23882a7_document.pdf.
29. Gluckman, "Too Many Lawyers?" *American Lawyer,* May 18, 2016.
30. The size of the 50 largest US law firms has increased more than ten times over the last 50 years, with offices throughout the world. "Law Firms in Transition: An Altman Weil Flash Survey," *Altman Weil,* 2015, 1–124, http://www.altmanweil.com/dir_docs/resource/1c789ef2-5cff-463a-863a-2248d23882a7_document.pdf. S.S Samuelson, "The Organizational Structure of Law Firms: Lessons from Management Theory," *Ohio State Law Journal* 51 (3): 645–74.

31. Most recently expanding in Canada, Latin America, and Southeast Asia. Yun Kriegler, "PwC Legal Pushes for Growth in Australia and SE Asia," *The Lawyer,* June 10, 2016, http://www.thelawyer.com/pwc-legal-pushes-for-growth-in-australia-and-se-asia/?cmpid=dnews_2355962; Kriegler, "PwC Legal Has Set Up a Foreign Law Practice in Singapore Under the Banner of PwC Legal International to Focus on Regional Transactions and Projects," *The Lawyer,* December 5, 2016, https://www.thelawyer.com/pwc-launches-singapore-foreign-law-practice/?cmpid=tlasia_2876703. For the Big Four's numerous advantages over law firms, see Susan Saltonstall Duncan,"Who Are Law Firms Really Competing With and Why?" *InFocus Blog,* January 18, 2017, http://www.rainmakingoasis.com/who-are-law-firms-really-competing-with-and-why/. See also "The Future of Legal Services," *Law Society,* January 28, 2016, http://www.lawsociety.org.uk/news/stories/future-of-legal-services/.
32. Chris Johnson, "For Many Chinese Law Firms, Revenue Doesn't Keep Pace With Size," *American Lawyer,* December 21, 2015; Staci Zaretsky, "Which U.S Firms Ranked Higher in the Asia 50, the Largest Law Firms in the Asia-Pacific Region?," *Above the Law,* January 2, 2013, http://abovethelaw.com/2013/01/which-american-firms-ranked-in-the-asia-50-the-largest-law-firms-in-the-asia-pacific-region/; David Lat, "The Global 100: The World's Largest Law Firms Ranked by Revenue and Profit," *Above the Law,* September 28, 2015, http://abovethelaw.com/2015/09/the-global-100-the-worlds-top-law-firms-ranked-by-revenue-profit-and-headcount/2/.
33. Kriegler "China's Top 30 Firms Post Combined Revenue up 55 Per cent," *The Lawyer,* November, 28, 2016, https://www.thelawyer.com/issues/online-november-2016/chinas-top-30-firms-post-combined-revenue-55-per-cent/?cmpid=tlasia_2854422.
34. Julie Triedman, "On U.S Tour, Chinese Lawyers Soak Up BigLaw Lessons," *American Lawyer,* June 14, 2016.
35. In 2016, 82 percent of law firm leaders believed that competition from non-traditional legal service providers will be a permanent trend. "Law Firms in Transition 2016: An Altman Weil Flash Survey," http://www.altmanweil.com/LFiT2016/. For a good overview of competitive forces at play, see Duncan, "Who Are Law Firms Really Competing With and Why?" *InFocus Blog.*
36. One estimate is that currently corporate legal departments comprise about 45 percent of total legal spending and rising. Mark A. Cohen, "Something's Gotta Give: Partner Profit Rises While Law Firm Market Share Declines," *Forbes,* December 11, 2016. Total legal spend grew to an all-time high of $102.3 billion in 2016, yet the portion of US spend on outside counsel remained relatively flat at $60.3 billion ($59.9 million in 2015), while in-house legal spend grew by $4 billion. "BTI's Market Outlook and Client Service Review 2017," *BTI Consulting Group,* December 5, 2016, http://www.bticonsulting.com/events/2016/12/5/btis-market-outlook-and-client-service-review-2017. Two-thirds of firms surveyed by Altman Weil in 2016 confirm the trend of decreasing budgets for outside legal counsel continuing and likely to accelerate, and also point to firms' increasing competition from other types of legal service providers. "Law Firms in Transition 2016: An Altman Weil Flash Survey," *Altman Weil,* 2016, http://www.altmanweil.com/LFiT2016/. Gluckman, "Too Many Lawyers?" *American Lawyer.*

Royal Dutch Shell is in the vanguard of a trend among clients of opening their own, often offshore, legal centers to service their entire operations. Kathryn McCann, "Offshoring Goes In-House: Shell to Launch External Legal Centre to Service Global Operations," *Legal Business,* May 31, 2016, http://www.legal-business.co.uk/index.php/lb-blog-view/6427-offshoring-goes-in-house-shell-to-launch-external-legal-centre-to-service-global-operations.

37. Rhode, "Developing Leadership," *Santa Clara Law Review,* 697.
38. Gabe Friedman, "Financial Check-In: Here's the State of the Legal Industry," *Bloomberg Law,* November 29, 2016, https://bol.bna.com/financial-check-in-heres-the-state-of-the-legal-industry/. This drop in demand follows a trend among chief legal officers for several years now. "2015 Chief Legal Officer Survey: An Altman Weil Flash Survey," *Altman Weil, Inc.,* 2015, 1–41, http://www.americanbar.org/content/dam/aba/administrative/litigation/materials/2016ccc/written_materials/1_2015_altman_weil_clo_survey.authcheckdam.pdf.
39. Thomas Markle, "A Call to Partner with Outside Capital: The Non-Lawyer Investment Approach Must Be Updated," *Arizona State Law Journal,* 2013, 1253.
40. SusanBeck,"AtABAMeeting,BarGroupSeesThreatfromNonlawyers," *TheAmLaw Daily,* February 4, 2016, http://www.americanlawyer.com/id=1202748892813/At-ABA-Meeting-Bar-Groups-See-Threat-from-Nonlawyers#ixzz48BC1ILsK.
41. Susan Beck, "Divided ABA Adopts Resolution on Nonlawyer Legal Services," *American Lawyer,* February 8, 2016.
42. Commission on the Future of Legal Services," *ABA.org,* 2016, *American Bar Association,* http://www.americanbar.org/groups/centers_commissions/commission-on-the-future-of-legal-services.html. The Commission was formed in August 2014 by incoming ABA President William Hubbard to improve access to justice.
43. Susan Beck, "Big Law Stays Silent as ABA Weighs Law Firm Ownership Rules," *American Lawyer,* May 9, 2016.
44. The merger agreed to in 2016 between Atlanta-based Sutherland, Asbill & Brennan and the UK's Eversheds keeps the US branch financially independent from the rest of the firm in a "limited by guarantee company." Under the British corporate system, LGC members act as guarantors of an umbrella business, but unlike traditional Swiss vereins in which members may share profits, LGC members cannot mix revenue. LGCs may also better insulate members from liabilities incurred by other members. Andrew Strickler, "Sutherland, Eversheds Partners to Vote on Merger," *Law360,* November 29, 2016. Jake Simpson, "Verein Tie-Ups Gain Allure as Firms Eye Global Expansion," *Law360.com,* August 3, 2014, http://www.law360.com/articles/563434/verein-tie-ups-gain-allure-as-firms-eye-global-expansion. In 2013 the UK's Norton Rose and Texas-based Fulbright & Jaworski created a five-branch verein now known as Norton Rose Fulbright.
45. Casey Sullivan, "The World's Largest Law Firm Will Have 7,300+ Lawyers," *Bloomberg Law,* November 17, 2015, https://bol.bna.com/the-worlds-largest-law-firm-will-have-7300-lawyers/.
46. "Future Trends for Legal Services," *Deloitte,* June, 2016, 1–10, https://www2.deloitte.com/global/en/pages/legal/articles/deloitte-future-trends-for-legal-services.html.

47. Friedrich Blase, "Sooner Than You Think! When Do Law Firms Need to Take Alternative Legal Providers Seriously?" *Thomson Reuters,* March 15, 2016, http://legalexecutiveinstitute.com/law-firms-need-take-alternative-legal-providers-seriously/.
48. "The 2017 Alternative Legal Service Study: Understanding the Growth and Benefits of These New Legal Providers," *Thomas Reuters,* http://legalsolutions.thomsonreuters.com/law-products/solutions/legal-outsourcing-services/outsourcing-insights/alternative-legal-service-provider-study-2017.
49. Michele Lange, "UK High Court Approves the Use of Predictive Coding in Litigation," *JDSupra.com,* April 8, 2016, http://www.jdsupra.com/legalnews/uk-high-court-approves-the-use-of-94748/. "The English High Court recently approved the use of predictive coding for disclosure in litigation . . . the possible disclosure of over two million documents done via traditional manual review would be disproportionate and 'unreasonable.'" See also Jill Switzer, "Old Lady Lawyer: How Much Should Lawyers Fear the Future?" *Above the Law,* March 16, 2016, http://abovethelaw.com/2016/03/old-lady-lawyer-how-much-should-lawyers-fear-the-future/.
50. Blase, "Sooner Than You Think! When Do Law Firms Need to Take Alternative Legal Providers Seriously?" *Thomson Reuters.* He projects that for every 1 percent growth in ALP revenue, traditional firms will lose 3 percent of theirs.
51. David J. Parnell, "Law Firm Leadership Survey: Top Strategic Initiatives of 2017," *Forbes,* February 27, 2017.
52. Roy Strom, "Forming Future Progressives," *Chicago Lawyer,* May, 2016. Dan Katz, law professor at the faculty at Chicago-Kent College of Law, created the Reinvent Law Laboratory at Michigan State University College of Law, which pitches to investor startups that "disrupt" the business of law by using technology and analytic-driven process improvements to lower costs and produce more predictable work. For example, algorithms alone can correctly predict the outcome of 70 percent of Supreme Court decisions.
53. Nick Hilborne, "Law Firms That Fail to Change 'No Longer Sustainable' After 2020, Report Predicts," *LegalFutures,* March 17, 2016, http://www.legalfutures.co.uk/latest-news/law-firms-that-fail-to-change-no-longer-sustainable-after-2020-report-predicts.
54. Regulatory authorities are increasingly using advanced software in compliance, filings, discovery, and litigation preparation. Ricci Disphan, "Ready or Not, Lawyers Are Increasingly Bound to AI by Ethical, Legal Standards," *Legaltechnews.com,* June 16, 2016, http://www.legaltechnews.com/id=1202760242618/Ready-or-Not-Lawyers-are-Increasingly-Bound-to-AI-by-Ethical-Legal-Standards#ixzz4BqbFkKTH. Richard Tromans, "Lawyers with Real Intelligence Will Defeat Artificial Intelligence," *Bloomberg,* March 26, 2015, https://bol.bna.com/lawyers-with-real-intelligence-will-defeat-artificial-intelligence/.
55. Ed Sohn, "alt.legal: Can Computers Beat Humans at Law?," *Above the Law,* March 23, 2016, http://abovethelaw.com/2016/03/alt-legal-can-computers-beat-humans-at-law/. Sharon D. Nelson and John W. Simek, "How Will Watson's Children Impact the Future of Law Practice?" *ABA Law Practice Magazine,* January/February 2016.

56. Susan Beck, "AI Pioneer ROSS Intelligence Lands Its First BigLaw Clients," *American Lawyer*, May 6, 2016; Jennifer Henderson, "Latham, Wisconsin Firm Reach ROSS Intelligence Partnerships," *American Lawyer*, May 20, 2016.
57. James Booth, "DLA Piper Strikes a Deal with Artificial Intelligence Firm," *Law.com*, June 14, 2016, http://www.law.com/sites/almstaff/2016/06/14/dla-piper-strikes-deal-with-artificial-intelligence-firm/#ixzz4BerLEj2Z; Ricci Dipshan, "21st Century Contract Review: Deloitte Announces Deployment of Kira A.I Software," *Legaltechnews.com*, March 8, 2016, http://www.legaltechnews.com/id=1202751683263/21st-Century-Contract-Review-Deloitte-Announces-Deployment-of-Kira-AI-Software-.
58. Booth, "Linklaters Signs Up to AI Service," *LegalWeek*, May 16, 2016, http://www.legalweek.com/legal-week/news/2458285/linklaters-signs-up-to-ai-service.
59. "Baker McKenzie forms new global innovation committee," February 10, 2017, *The Global Legal Post*, http://www.globallegalpost.com/global-view/baker-mckenzie-forms-new-global-innovation-committee-83694918/
60. Jonathan Manning, "Pinsent Masons Develops AI Software to Advise Clients on Brexit Issues," *The Lawyer*, November 8, 2016.
61. Dana Remus and Frank S. Levy. "Can Robots Be Lawyers? Computers, Lawyers, and the Practice of Law," November 27, 2016, https://papers.ssrn.com/sol3/papers.cfm?abstract_id=2701092.
62. James Manyika, Michael Chui, Mehdi Miremadi, Jacques Bughin, Katy George, Paul Willmott, and Martin Dewhurst, "Harnessing Automation for a Future That Works," *McKinsey*, http://www.mckinsey.com/global-themes/digital-disruption/harnessing-automation-for-a-future-that-works
63. "Lawyered Up: Deals to Legal Tech Up in 2016," *CB Insights Blog*, March 17, 2017, https://www.cbinsights.com/blog/legal-tech-startup-funding-deals-dollars/.
64. "Dentons launches NextLaw Labs and creates business accelerator," *Dentons.com*, May 19, 2015, http://www.dentons.com/en/whats-different-about-dentons/connecting-you-to-talented-lawyers-around-the-globe/news/2015/may/dentons-launches-nextlaw-labs-creates-legal-business-accelerator.
65. "Thomson Reuters and IBM Collaborate to Deliver Watson Cognitive Computing Technology," *Thomson Reuters.com*, October 8, 2015, http://thomsonreuters.com/en/press-releases/2015/october/thomson-reuters-ibm-collaborate-to-deliver-watson-cognitive-computing-technology.html
66. International Association for Artificial Intelligence and Law, http://www.iaail.org/.
67. "Ulster University launches new Legal Innovation Centre," Ulster University, https://www.ulster.ac.uk/news/2017/february/ulster-university-launches-new-legal-innovation-centre; Mark A. Cohen, "Allen & Overy: An Old Firm With A New Strategy," *Forbes*, April 10, 2017.
68. Mills, "What Are Humans Good for . . . in Legal Services?" *3 Geeks and a Law Blog*.
69. Choe Sang-Hun and John Markoff, "Master of Go Board Game is Walloped by Google Computer Program," *New York Times*, March 9, 2016.
70. Two-thirds of Americans believe that within the next fifty years, much of the work we humans presently do will be done by robots or computers, but more than one-third still believe their jobs will be safe. Switzer, "Old Lady Lawyer:

How Much Should Lawyers Fear the Future?" *Above the Law.* See also Mills, "What Are Humans Good For . . . in Legal Services?" *3 Geeks and a Law Blog,* for ways machines outperform lawyers, and don't.

71. Susskind, *The End of Lawyers? Rethinking the Nature of Legal Services.*
72. Susskind and Daniel Susskind, *The Future of the Professions: How Technology Will Transform the Work of Human Experts* (Oxford: Oxford University Press, 2016).
73. Jessica Stillman, "The World's First Robot Lawyer Has Arrived—And It's Great," *Inc.*, June 30, 2016, ? http://www.inc.com/jessica-stillman/meet-the-world-s-first-robot-lawyer.html.
74. Kevin J. Ryan, "It Turns Out Robots Make Surprisingly Good Trial Judges," *Inc.*, October 25, 2016; Nikolaos Aletras?, et al., "Predicting Judicial Decisions of the European Court of Human Rights: A Natural Language Processing Perspective," October 24, 2016, *PeerJ Computer Science,* https://peerj.com/articles/cs-93/.
75. "2015 Law Firms in Transition Survey," *Altman Weil, Inc.*, 2015. Gluckman, "Too Many Lawyers?" *American Lawyer.*
76. Kristin Rasmussen, "GCs Dissatisfied with Traditional Law Firms, Deloitte Report Finds," *Corporate Council,* June 21, 2016, http://www.corpcounsel.com/id=1202760553701/GCs-Dissatisfied-With-Traditional-Law-Firms-Deloitte-Report-Finds?slreturn=20170016155636.
77. D. Casey Flaherty, "When Will Lawyers Rise (Like Elevators) to the Occasion?" *ABA Journal,* March 17, 2016.
78. Geoff Colvin, "The Skills of Human Interaction Will Become Most Valuable in the Future," *New York Times,* March 9, 2016?. "We want to follow human leaders. We want to negotiate important agreements with people, hearing every lilt or lament in their voices, noting when they cross their arms, looking into their eyes." Geoff Colvin, *Humans Are Underrated: What High Achievers Know That Brilliant Machines Never Will* (New York: Portfolio/Penguin, 2015), 44. Susskind notes in the chapter entitled "Objections and Anxieties" that since empathy is not something many lawyers provide now, envisioning machines that lack that quality does not disqualify them from delivering expert legal services. Susskind and Susskind, *The Future of the Professions.*
79. Richard Tromans, "Lawyers with Real Intelligence Will Defeat Artificial Intelligence," *Bloomberg.*
80. Megan Beck and Barry Libert, "The Rise of AI Makes Emotional Intelligence More Important," *Harvard Business Review,* February 15, 2017.
81. Breslau and Daicoff, "The Illicit Relationship of Lawyers and Emotion," *Cutting Edge Law.*
82. Cremin, "Robots Are Learning to Fake Empathy," *Motherboard.*
83. "[M]arrying human intuition, creativity and empathy with a computer's brute-force ability to remember and calculate a staggering number of chess moves, countermoves and outcomes . . . produces a force that plays better chess than either humans or computers can manage on their own." Mike Cassidy, "Centaur Chess Shows Power of Teaming Human and Machine," *Huffington Post,* December 30, 2014, http://www.huffingtonpost.com/mike-cassidy/centaur-chess-shows-power_b_6383606.html.

84. Joe Hodnicki and Mark Giangrande, "Cognitive Computing at ROSS (now) and Thomson Reuters Legal (Forthcoming)," *Law Librarians*, March 24, 2016, https://llb2.com/2016/03/24/cognitive-computing-at-ross-now-and-thomson-reuters-legal-forthcoming/.
85. Flaherty, "The End of Lawyers, Period," *Legal Rebels.*
86. "2013 Client Advisory," *Hildebrandt Consulting Group, LLC,* 2013, 1–13, http://online.wsj.com/public/resources/documents/CitiHildebrandt2013 ClientAdvisory.pdf; Friedman, "Financial Check-In: Here's the State of the Legal Industry," *Bloomberg Law.*
87. Clayton M. Christensen, Dina Wang, and Derek van Bever, "Consulting on the Cusp of Disruption," *Harvard Business Review,* October, 2013, 107. "The legal market may be currently poised for what could be a dramatic reordering based on the same type of disruptive forces that have reordered many other businesses and industries." "2014: Report on the State of the Legal Market," *Center for the Study of the Legal Profession at Georgetown and Thomson Reuters,* January, 2014, 13.
88. Erin Fuchs, "The Eight Most Crushing Law Firm Implosions in the Nation's History," *Business Insider,* June 24, 2012, http://www.businessinsider.com/the-eight-most-spectacular-law-firm-collapses-in-history-2012-6?op=1.
89. "BigLaw's Banker: I've Got a 'Robust' List of Firms That May Fail," *Bloomberg,* produced by Lee Pacchia, October 26, 2012, YouTube Video [14:03], http://www.youtube.com/watch?v=JTlJCg5R0CY]; Mark A. Cohen, "Are Law Firms Becoming Obsolete?", *Forbes,* June 12, 2017.
90. "Developing Legal Talent: Stepping into the Future Law Firm," *Deloitte,* February, 2016, https://www2.deloitte.com/uk/en/pages/audit/articles/developing-legal-talent.html, 2.
91. Nick Hillborn, "Law Firms That Fail to Change 'No Longer Sustainable' after 2020, Report Predicts," *LegalFutures,* March 17, 2016, http://www.legalfutures.co.uk/latest-news/law-firms-that-fail-to-change-no-longer-sustainable-after-2020-report-predicts.
92. John Ryan, "Accelerating Performance: Five Leadership Skills You and Your Organization Can't Do Without," *Center for Creative Leadership,* August, 2010.
93. Petrie, *Future Trends in Leadership Development* (Greensboro, NC: Center for Creative Leadership, 2011), 7. See also André Martin, "What's Next? The 2007 Changing Nature of Leadership Study," *Center for Creative Leadership,* 2007, 9, http://www.ccl.org/wp-content/uploads/2015/04/WhatsNext.pdf. Competencies needed include "Participative Management, Putting People at Ease. Self-Awareness, Balance Between Personal Life and Work, Straightforwardness and Composure, Building and Mending Relationships, Doing Whatever It Takes, Decisiveness, Confronting Problem Employees and Change Management."
94. Roger Enrico, quoted in Stratford Sherman, "How Tomorrow's Leaders Are Learning Their Stuff," *Fortune Magazine,* November 27, 1995.
95. John Fleenor, "Creative Leadership, Tough Times: Soft Skills Make All the Difference," *Center for Creative Leadership,* 2003, http://www.prnewswire.com/news-releases/survey-by-center-for-creative-leadership-shows-soft-skills-make-a-difference-in-tough-times-75434152.html.

96. James M. Kouses and Barry Z. Posner, *The Leadership Challenge*, Elaine Beich, ed. (New York: Wiley, 2010), xv.
97. Leon C. Megginson, "Lessons from Europe for American Business," *Southwestern Social Science Quarterly* 44 (1): 1963.
98. Roland Smith, "The Struggles of Lawyer-Leaders and What They Need to Know," *NYSBA Journal*, March/April, 2009.
99. Jonah Lehrer, "The Power Trip," *The Wall Street Journal*, August 14, 2010. While Lehrer was disgraced for fabricating quotes, this comment is accurate.
100. Rhode, *Lawyers as Leaders*. At a time of "[i]ncreasing complexity, competition, scale, pace, conflict, amount of information, and divergence of experience and opinion . . . pressure to make complex decisions instantly . . . [i]ncreasing focus on financial bottom line . . . fewer equity partners are being made and conflict has exploded into open acrimony, defections and free agent mentality, and sometimes dissolution."
101. Tupman, "The Leadership Imperative," *Law Management Group and Simon Tupman*. Two-thirds of managing partners of 106 small and mid-sized law firms from New Zealand, Australia and the United Kingdom confirm their greatest challenges are "motivating their team" and "delivering on change."
102. Allison Spiegel, "Why So Many Young Lawyers Dislike Their Jobs," *The Globe and Mail*, June 8, 2016, http://www.theglobeandmail.com/report-on-business/small-business/sb-money/why-so-many-young-lawyers-dislike-their-jobs/article29807625/.
103. Ibid.
104. "2014: Report on the State of the Legal Market," *Thomson Reuters*.
105. Gluckman, "Too Many Lawyers?" *American Lawyer*.
106. The Creativity, Emotions, and the Arts project at Yale's Center for Emotional Intelligence studies the relationship of emotions to creativity and problem solving and develops museum-based workshops to teach visitors EI that promotes creative problem solving. "Emotions in Everyday Life," *Yale Center for Emotional Intelligence,*" 2013, http://ei.yale.edu/what-we-do/emotions-everyday-life/.
107. "Creativity and Emotional Intelligence," *SixSeconds.org*, February 10, 2011, http://www.6seconds.org/2011/02/10/creativity-and-emotional-intelligence/.
108. Some research indicates that those high in the personality trait Conscientiousness, as many lawyers are, are less likely to be creative. Gregory J. Feist, "A Meta-Analysis of Personality in Scientific and Artistic Creativity," November 1, 1998, *Personality and Social Psychology Review* 2 (4).
109. David and Congleton, "Emotional Agility," *Harvard Business Review*.
110. Jing Zhou and Jennifer M. George, "Awakening Employee Creativity: The Role of Leader Emotional Intelligence," *The Leadership Quarterly* 14 (5): 545–68. Positivity helps on this front as well: Alice M. Isen, Kimberley A. Daubman, and Gary P. Nowicki, "Positive Affect Facilitates Creative Problem Solving," *Journal of Personality and Social Psychology* 52 (1987): 1122–31.
111. "2013 Law Firms in Transition Survey," *Altman Weil*, 2013, http://www.altmanweil.com/dir_docs/resource/2d831a80-8156-4947-9f0f-1d97eec632a5_document.pdf, 34.
112. "2013 Chief Legal Officer Survey," *Altman Weil*.

113. Rhode, "Developing Leadership," *Santa Clara Law Review*, 690–91.
114. "Women Poised to Effectively Lead in Matrix Work Environments, Hay Group Research Finds," *Hay Group*, March 27, 2012, http://www.haygroup.com/ww/press/details.aspx?id=33283.
115. Aly R. Háji, "The Illusion Of Innovation At Canadian Law Firms," Independent MBA Study, McGill University, January 17, 2017, 10-11, https://jnper.com/lawfirms/. Asked about innovation leadership, 58 percent of associates felt there was "either no leadership for innovation or no awareness of any innovation leadership," compared to 84 percent of partners who believed there was such leadership; and 70 percent of associates lacked awareness of how to bring innovative ideas to firm leadership. The report concludes that despite partners' beliefs to the contrary, there was "a lack of incentives, leadership and structures in which to innovate." 15.
116. Amy J.C. Cuddy, Matthew Kohut, and John Neffinger, "Connect, Then Lead," *HBR Magazine Online*, July–August, 2013. Similarly, the leaders determined to be the most effective in the US Navy (not traditionally a feel-good group) were those who were warmer, more outgoing, emotionally expressive, and sociable. Wallace Bachman, "Nice Guys Finish First: A SYMLOG Analysis of U.S. Naval Commands," in *The SYMLOG Practitioner*, ed. Richard B. Polley, A. Paul Hare, and Philip J. Stone (New York: Praeger, 1988), 133–53. This concept may have been demonstrated during the 2016 presidential campaigns of Donald Trump and Hilary Clinton. While both were controversial and neither enjoyed high approval ratings, Trump appears to have struck an emotional chord in his supporters, while Clinton's (lawyerly) strength was in projecting her competence using position papers and the mastery of complex details. Commentators fretted over whether Trump would ever deliver on the substance and Clinton would ever warm up. Despite repeated attempts to convince her audiences of her bona fides, "untrustworthy" was one of the recurring characteristics Clinton was saddled with. "Warm and genuine" was how a cautious Paul Ryan described Trump after first conferring with him as the presumptive Republican nominee, which apparently started at least an initial thaw. Jennifer Steinhauer and Alexandra Burns, "Donald Trump and Paul Ryan Show Signs of Thaw," *New York Times*, May 12, 2016.
117. Cuddy, Kohut, and Neffinger, "Connect, Then Lead," *Harvard Business Review*.
118. See William Bridges, "Managing Transitions," June 2013. http://www.moravian.org/wp-content/uploads/2013/06/Bridges_Transition_Model.pdf.
119. Peter J. Jordan, Neal M. Ashkanasy, and Charmine E. J. Hartel, "Emotional Intelligence as a Moderator of Emotional and Behavioral Reactions to Job Insecurity," *The Academy of Management Review*, Vol. 27, No. 3 (July 2002), pp. 361–72.
120. "Press Release: insynergi Releases Whitepaper on How to Secure Successful Change Management," *insynergi.org*, November 25, 2013, http://www.realwire.com/releases/insynergi-releases-whitepaper-on-how-to-secure-successful-change-management. Of 10,640 projects from 200 companies across various industries in thirty countries studied by PwC, only 2.5 percent of the companies successfully completed 100 percent of their projects.

121. Tupman, "The Leadership Imperative," *Law Management Group and Simon Tupman.* "The best managing partners . . . have a high level of social awareness and the ability to sense and react appropriately to the emotions of others—if not to actually anticipate those emotions." John J. Michalik, "The Extraordinary Managing Partner: Reaching the Pinnacle of Law Firm Management," *Association of Legal Administrators,* 2011.
122. Ken Blanchard, "Mastering the Art of Change," *Training Journal,* January, 2010, 44–47.
123. Rhode, "Developing Leadership," *Santa Clara Law Review,* 690–91. In a survey of 75 managing partners of mid-size U.S. law firms, 40 percent said that "managing conflict" and 23 percent said managing "partner revolt or upheaval" had been what most put them to the test during the prior year. "Managing Partner Survey," *Managing Partner Forum,* 2013, 1–36.
124. "2013 Law Firms in Transition Survey," *Altman Weil,* 2013.
125. "Altman Weil Law Firms in Transition Survey," *Altman Weil,* 2016.
126. Tupman, "The Leadership Imperative," *Law Management Group and Simon Tupman.*
127. David Maister recalls the rainmaker at a major law firm saying: "I can't convince my partners that this is all about human beings. . . . My partners really don't want to express that level of intimacy with anyone at work," which, as Maister points out, "affects not only marketing and client relations, but also the way in which partners deal with each other and how firms are managed." Maister, "Are Law Firms Manageable?" *DavidMaister.com.*
128. Daicoff, "Expanding the Lawyer's Toolkit of Skills and Competencies," *Santa Clara Law Review,* 830.
129. Rajeev Peshawaria, formerly the Global Chief Learning Officer at Morgan Stanley and The Coca-Cola Company following senior stints at HSBC, American Express and Goldman Sachs, and currently the CEO of Iclif Leadership and Governance Center—Malaysia. Rajeev Peshawaria, "The Great Training Robbery: Why the $60 Billion Investment In Leadership Development Is Not Working," *Forbes,* November 1, 2011.
130. See William G. Johnson, "The Anatomy of Law Firm Failures," *Hildebrandt,* March, 2008, 1–5, and Rhode and Amanda K. Packel, "Ethics and Nonprofits," *Stanford Social Innovation Review,* 2009, 65–69.
131. Jordan Furlong, "The Four Cardinal Virtues of Law Firm Culture," *Edge International,* 2016, http://www.edge.ai/2016/04/the-4-cardinal-virtues-of-law-firm-culture/?key=eic.
132. Maister, "Are Law Firms Manageable?" *DavidMaister.com.*
133. "Firm Culture Matters Most," *FindLaw: For Legal Professionals,* 2013, http://www.infirmation.com/articles/one-article.tcl?article_id=2504.
134. "Of all the relationships we have at work, the one with our boss or supervisor has the greatest impact on our emotional and physical health." Mines, Meyer, and Mines, "Emotional Intelligence and Emotional Toxicity: Implications for Attorneys and Law Firms," *The Colorado Lawyer,* 93.
135. Steven J. Stein, Peter Papadogiannis, Jeremy A. Yip, and Gill Sitarenios, "Emotional Intelligence of Leaders: A Profile of Top Executives," *Leadership and Organization Development Journal* 30 (2009): 87. See Mihaly

Csikszentmihalyi, *Flow: The Psychology of Optimal Experience* (New York, NY: Harper and Row, 1990) for the many productivity advantages of achieving an emotionally balanced flow.

136. Triggers taken from Schwartz, *The Way We're Working Isn't Working*. Chip Scholz, "Emotional Hijacks at Work: Beware the Tiger," *Leader Snips Blog*, April 5, 2012, http://www.chipscholz.com/2012/04/05/emotional-hijacks-at-work-beware-the-tiger/.
137. Christine Porath, "The hidden toll of workplace incivility," *McKinsey Quarterly*, December, 2016. Porath is an associate professor at the McDonough School of Business at Georgetown University and author of the 2016 book *Mastering Civility*. She finds that incivility negatively charges work relationships, reducing productivity many times more than positive relationships can improve productivity.
138. Furlong, "The Four Cardinal Virtues of Law Firm Culture," *Edge International*.
139. "The B Word," *Lawyers Weekly*, June 3, 2013, https://www.lawyersweekly.com.au/features/14252-The-B-word.
140. R. Bacal, "Toxic Organizations—Welcome to the Fire of an Unhealthy Workplace," *The World of Work*, 2000, http://work911.com/articles/toxicorgs.htm.
141. Goleman, *Working with Emotional Intelligence*.
142. Mines, Meyer, and Mines, "Emotional Intelligence and Emotional Toxicity," *The Colorado Lawyer*, 92.
143. One article described an associate who was hospitalized for severe depression by the behavior of a partner dubbed the "smiling assassin" because of his tendency to make "friendly enquiries about a lawyer's weekend and the health of family members, while in the same breath criticizing their work." In a survey of Australian lawyers, 33 percent answered that partners were prone to bullying junior staff, and a further 29 percent said bullying was a problem at all levels of the firm, while only 10 percent said that bullying was dealt with decisively and quickly. "The B Word," *Lawyers Weekly*. A US partner claimed that he was suing his Michigan firm because he was forced out by managers who promoted "a culture of fear and intimidation." "This case is about . . . abuse of power by leaders of the largest law firm in Michigan," the partner alleged in his complaint. Paul Egan, "Fett & Fields, P.C Client Sues Principals of Michigan's Oldest and Largest Law Firm," *Detroit Free Press*, December 21, 2012.
144. Deena Shanker, "Why Are Lawyers Such Terrible Managers?" *Fortune*, January 11, 2013.
145. van der Elst, Razon, and Caponigro, "Do Bullies Feel Your Pain?" *Greater Good: The Science of a Meaningful Life*.
146. See DeFoe, "Bullying at Work [Legal Organizations], Coping Strategies, and Health Problems," *Psycholawlogy.com*, February 2, 2014, http://www.psycholawlogy.com/2014/02/06/bullying-work-legal-organizations-coping-strategies-health-problems/ for a discussion of how bullying can arise in and impact the legal workplace. See also the advice of Tom Grella, former Chair of the ABA Law Practice Section on handling bullying lawyers. Tom Grella, "Address Bullying Behavior Before Your Firm Gets a Black Eye,"

ABA Law Practice Magazine 38 (1), January/February 2012. "According to a report conducted by the Women Lawyers of Utah in 2010, 37% of women in firms said that they experienced verbal or physical behavior that created an unpleasant or offensive work environment, with 27% of those women feeling the situation was serious enough that they felt they were being harassed. And a whopping 86% felt that the basis for the harassment was their sex. The numbers for males were much lower, with only 22% reporting an unpleasant work environment and only 4% feeling it rose to levels of harassment." Sweeney, "The Female Lawyer Exodus," *The Daily Beast.*

147. Gaston Kroub, "Beyond Biglaw: 3 Reasons Law Firms Are Not Safe Spaces," *Above the Law,* March 22, 2016, http://abovethelaw.com/2016/03/beyond-biglaw-3-reasons-law-firms-are-not-safe-spaces/.
148. Stein, et al., "Emotional Intelligence of Leaders," *Leadership and Organization Development Journal.*
149. Brian Dalton, "Deviations from the Norm: The Lawyer 'Type' and Legal Hiring," *Above the Law,* May 20, 2014, http://abovethelaw.com/2014/05/deviations-from-the-norm-the-lawyer-type-and-legal-hiring/?rf=1.
150. Clutch, Clutch HR Employee Feedback Survey 2016, December 7, 2016, https://clutch.co/hr/resources/engage-millennial-employees-feedback-evaluation. Krieger and Sheldon, "What Makes Lawyers Happy?" *George Washington Law Review.*
151. Joseph Walker, "Meet the New Boss: Big Data," *The Wall Street Journal,* September 20, 2012. See also Lyle M. Spencer Jr. and Signe M. Spence, *Competence at Work: Models for Superior Performance* (New York: John Wiley and Sons, 1993).
152. "Q&A with Dr. TCP on Emotional Intelligence," *Hogan News,* March 4, 2014, http://info.hoganassessments.com/blog/bid/337710/Q-A-with-DrTCP-on-Emotional-Intelligence.
153. Suzanne Retzinger and Thomas Scheff, "Emotion, Alienation, and Narratives: Resolving Intractable Conflict," *Mediation Quarterly* 18 (1): 71.
154. Nelken, "If I'd Wanted to Learn about Feelings, I Wouldn't Have Gone to Law School," *Journal of Legal Education,* 422, 525.
155. Erica A. Fox, "Review Essay: Bringing Peace into the Room," *Negotiation Journal* 20 (3): 462.
156. Rhode, "Developing Leadership," *Santa Clara Law Review,* 690–91. Conflict can poison the culture and undermine morale, as well as make a substantial drain on management time and energy. In the 2013 MPF Survey of Managing Partners taken of seventy-five managing partners of midsize law firms, 40 percent answered that "managing conflict" was what "put [them] to the test most" in the prior year. "2012 Survey of Law Firm Economics," *MPF Managing Partner Survey,* August 6, 2012, http://www.managingpartnerforum.org/tasks/sites/mpf/assets/image/MPF%20-%202012%20Survey%20of%20LF%20Economics%20-%20Exec%20Summary%20-%209-20-12.pdf.
157. "2013 Managing Partner Survey," MPF *Managing Partner Forum,* 2013, 1–36. http://www.managingpartnerforum.org/tasks/sites/mpf/assets/image/MPF%20-%20Managing%20Partner%20Survey%20Results%20-%20Raw%20Data%20-%20FINAL%20-%205-9-131.pdf.

158. "The Emotional Intelligence Difference: Coaching for Behavior Change," *Empathia.com,* August 20, 2013, 4.
159. Tricia S. Jones, "Emotion in Mediation: Implications, Applications, Opportunities, and Challenges," in *The Blackwell Handbook of Mediation: Bridging Theory, Research, and Practice,* ed. Margaret S. Herrman (Oxford, UK: Blackwell Publishing, 2006), 278–79.
160. Bernard Mayer, *The Dynamics of Conflict Resolution: A Practitioner's Guide* (San Francisco, CA: Jossey-Bass 2000), 43.
161. Even when participating in difficult conversations, which inevitably raise the specter of conflict, experts advise making sure that "The Feelings Conversation" is acknowledged and included. Douglas Stone, Bruce Patton, and Sheila Heen, *Difficult Conversations: How to Discuss What Matters Most* (New York: Penguin Books, 1999).
162. Paul Ekman and Erika L. Rosenberg, eds., *Unmasking the Face, What the Face Reveals: Basic and Applied Studies of Spontaneous Expression Using the Facial Action Coding System (FACS)* (Oxford: Oxford University Press, 2003), 40.
163. Fallon et al., "Emotional Intelligence, Cognitive Ability and Information Search in Tactical Decision-Making," *Personality and Individual Differences,* 24–29. See, for example, Heather L. LaMarre, Kristin D. Landreville, and Michael A. Beam, "The Irony of Satire: Political Ideology and the Motivation to See What You Want to See in the Colbert Report," *The International Journal of Press/Politics* 14 (2): 212–31.
164. Kiser, for example, has documented examples of what looks like confirmation bias in a large portion of cases in which lawyers "turned down settlements only to find at trial that settlement would have been a better deal." Laura A. Kaster, "Review of *How Leading Lawyers Think: Expert Insights into Judgment and Advocacy* (Springer-Verlag 2011)," *NYSBA New York Dispute Resolution Lawyer,* 5 (1): 79. Kiser found that the less information lawyer decision-makers have in that situation, the more confident they feel, showing "considerable insensitivity to the extent of their knowledge." Kiser, *How Leading Lawyers Think,* 124.
165. "About Behavioral Economics: Why Hawks Always Win and Doves Always Lose," *Constable Research B.V,* May 29, 2009, http://hans.wyrdweb.eu/about-behavioral-economics/. Reviewing Kahneman and Jonathan Renshon, "Hawkish Biases," in Trevor Thrall and Jane Cramer, eds., *American Foreign Policy and the Politics of Fear: Threat Inflation Since 9/11* (New York: Routledge, 2009), 79–96.
166. Middleburg and Butterworth, "Emotional Intelligence," *The Barrister Magazine,* 2013.
167. Uwe Herwig et al., "Self-Related Awareness and Emotion Regulation," *Neuroimage* 50 (2010): 734–41.
168. One mediation model is "emotion analysis," a "way of clarifying the hurt and locating it within the relational matrix of conflict" for the parties to "'see' the conflict differently, resulting in a different emotional experience." One commentator proposes using "elicitive questioning" to identify emotions and reappraise the situation, while another has formulated eight "emotion-eliciting" strategies to use during conflict resolution. Another model proposes an emotional grid to chart the highs and lows of emotional interaction in a conflict in

terms of volume and intensity so as to identify triggers and complicating issues for each of the parties. Charlie Irvine, "Building Emotional Intelligence."

169. Herz, "Relationships Are King," *Touro Law Review,* 3.
170. Richard, "Herding Cats," *Altman Weil Report to Legal Management,* 1–12.
171. Fallon et al., "Emotional Intelligence, Cognitive Ability and Information Search in Tactical Decision-Making," *Personality and Individual Differences,* 24–29.
172. Richard, "The Lawyer Types," *ABA Journal*; Naomi L. Quenk, *In the Grip: Understanding Type, Stress, and the Inferior Function,* 2nd ed. (Mountain View, CA: CPP, Inc., 2000), 12–15. Four different ways of thinking, each on a two-sided scale, accounts for the 16 "types" in the MBTI. More than half of all practicing attorneys fall into one of four groups, and one type—INTJ—"occurs with five times greater frequency in lawyers than it does generally." Dalton, "Deviations from the Norm: The Lawyer 'Type' and Legal Hiring," Above the Law. The MBTI was developed because of a lawyer—Clarence Myers, the fiancé of Isabel Briggs—who was inscrutable to both his fiancé and her mother, Katharine Cook Briggs, prompting them to devise a system to identify their differences.
173. Quenk, *In the Grip.*
174. Jeff Foster, Larry Richard, Lisa Rohrer, and Mark Sirkin, "Understanding Lawyers: The Personality Traits of Successful Practitioners: Results from the Hogan Assessment Project on Lawyer Personality," *Hildebrandt Baker Robbins,* 2010, 5.
175. Peter J. Jordan and Ashlea Troth, "Emotional Intelligence and Conflict Resolution in Nursing," *Contemporary Nurse* 13 (1): 94–100.
176. Richard, "The Lawyer Types," *ABA Journal.*
177. Rhode, "Developing Leadership," *Santa Clara Law Review,* 709. One study, for example, found that "employees waste an average of $1,500 plus an additional eight hours of time for every difficult conversation they avoid." One of the advantages of dealing directly with conflict is that, "People who know how to discuss contentious issues are not as prone to complaining, feeling victimized, doing work-arounds and getting angry." "The Emotional Intelligence Difference: Coaching for Behavior Change," *Empathia.com,* 2013, http://www.empathia.com/objects/Emotional_intelligenceDesigned8-20-13.pdf.
178. Russ Edelman quoted in Meridith Levinson, "The Danger of Being Too Nice at Work," *CIO,* September 18, 2008, http://www.cio.com/article/450066/The_Danger_of_Being_Too_Nice_at_Work_?page=3&taxonomyId=3123.
179. Stone, Patton, and Heen, *Difficult Conversations: How to Discuss What Matters Most.*
180. Researchers who observed couples in conflict for only 15 minutes accurately predicted the health problems the men would develop over the next 20 years. Claudia M. Haase et al., "Interpersonal Emotional Behaviors and Physical Health: A 20-Year Longitudinal Study of Long-Term Married Couples," *Emotion* 16 (7): 965–77.
181. Herwig et al., "Self-Related Awareness and Emotion Regulation," 734–41.
182. Goleman, "The Brain and Emotional Intelligence," *Psychology Today.*
183. Nalini Ambady et al., "Surgeons' Tone of Voice: A Clue to Malpractice History," *Surgery* 132 (2002): 1, 8.

184. Larry Cebula, "A Man May Do an Immense Deal of Good, If He Does Not Care Who Gets the Credit," *Quote Investigator,* January 6, 2011, http://quote-investigator.com/2010/12/21/doing-good-selfless/.
185. Peters, formerly the Organization Effectiveness practice leader at McKinsey & Co., is author of *In Search of Excellence* and other bestsellers.
186. Mills, "What Are Humans Good For . . . in Legal Services?" *3 Geeks and a Law Blog*; Marc Andreeson, "Why Software Is Eating the World," *The Wall Street Journal,* August 20, 2011.
187. Salih Mujcic, "Leadership: Are You Ready for the Future?" *Revelian,* n.d., http://www.revelian.com/blog/leadership-are-you-ready-for-the-future/. "The ability of any single individual—as heroic or skilled or dedicated as he or she may be—is no longer enough to meet the complex challenges we face today." Petrie, *Future Trends in Leadership Development.*
188. Gardner, "The Collaboration Imperative for Today's Law Firms: Leading High-Performance Teamwork for Maximum Benefit," in R. Normand-Hochman ed., *Managing Talent for Success: Talent Development in Law Firms* (London, UK: Globe Business Publishing Ltd., 2013), 20. Heidi K. Gardner, Ph.D., is a Distinguished Fellow at ?Harvard Law School's Center on the Legal Profession, a Lecturer on Law, and Faculty Chair of the HLS's Accelerated Leadership Program and other executive education programs. Previously she served on the Organizational Behavior faculty of Harvard Business School. https://clp.law.harvard.edu/
189. Middleburg and Butterworth, "Emotional Intelligence," *The Barrister Magazine,* 2013.
190. Bithika Anand, "Collective Brilliance: Teamwork Defines Success," *EQ Edge,* February 2014, http://archive.constantcontact.com/fs148/1104176518924/archive/1116303782715.html.
191. Ben Heineman, former GE General Counsel and Distinguished Senior Fellow at the Harvard Law School Program on the Legal Profession, has described the lawyer-leaders of the future as "lawyers who are not just strong team members, but who can lead and build organizations: create the vision, the values, the priorities, the strategies, the people, the systems, the processes, the checks and balances, the resources and the motivation. Working on teams and leading them are interconnected: much of leadership today is not command and control of the troops but persuasion, motivation and empowerment of teams around a shared vision." Herb Rubenstein, *Leadership for Lawyers* (Chicago: American Bar Association, 2008), 19, quoting Ben Heineman.
192. Berman and Bock, "Developing Attorneys for the Future," *Santa Clara Law Review,* 888, 891.
193. "Legal Executive Briefing," *Thomson Reuters,* 2010, https://peermonitor.thomsonreuters.com/ThomsonPeer/docs/2011_Client_Advisory_FINAL.pdf.
194. Charles Duhigg, "What Google Learned from Its Quest to Build the Perfect Team," *The New York Times Magazine,* February 25, 2016.
195. Neal M. Ashkanasy, Claire E. Ashton-James, Peter J. Jordan "Performance Impacts of Appraisal and Coping with Stress in Workplace Settings: The Role of Affect and Emotional Intelligence," in Pamela L. Perrewe, Daniel

C. Ganster (eds.), *Emotional and Physiological Processes and Positive Intervention Strategies* (Research in Occupational Stress and Well-being, Volume 3) Emerald Group Publishing Limited 2003, 1–43. See Vanessa Urch Druskat and Steven B. Woolf, "Building the Emotional Intelligence of Groups," *Harvard Business Review* 79 (3) (2001): 81–90.

196. Elfenbein, "Learning in Emotion Judgments: Training and the Cross-Cultural Understanding of Facial Expression," *Journal of Nonverbal Behavior* 30 (2006): 21.

197. Luye Chang, Brian S. Connelly, and Alexis A. Geeza, "Separating Method Factors and Higher Order Traits of the Big Five: A Meta-Analytic Multitrait–Multimethod Approach," *Journal of Personality and Social Psychology* 102 (2): 408–426.

198. Gloria Barczak, Felicia Lassk, and Jay Mulki, "Antecedents of Team Creativity: An Examination of Team Emotional Intelligence, Team Trust and Collaborative Culture," *Creativity and Innovation Management* 19 (4): 333, 342. The authors defined creative teams as those able to "identify and exploit unique opportunities by using imaginative strategies to procure and orchestrate resources across functional groups."

199. See Druskat and Woolf, "Building the Emotional Intelligence of Groups," *Harvard Business Review.*

200. Mayer, Salovey, and Caruso, "Emotional Intelligence: Theory, Findings, and Implications," *Psychological Inquiry* 15 (3): 197–215 The study was of claims adjustment cases which require team collaboration and are rife with potential client dissatisfaction.

201. Etan Mark, "Expertise Articles: Emotional Intelligence Matters," *South Florida Legal Guide,* 2013, http://www.sflegalguide.com/index.php?plugin=News&id=110&title=emotional-intelligence—matters.

202. "When collaboration goes well, research demonstrates that oxytocin is released. This feel-good-because-you're-connecting neuro-hormone is released when our thoughts, feelings and actions blend with others. . . . On the other hand . . . when we perceive someone as a competitor or adversary, empathy and oxytocin plummet along with our willingness to explore the validity of other's ideas, or even hear their ideas." Colette Herrick and Joshua Freedman, "Emotional Intelligence and Collaboration in Health Care," *SixSeconds.org,* July 13, 2013, http://www.6seconds.org/2013/07/31/emotional-intelligence-collaboration-in-healthcare/.

203. Gardner, "The Collaboration Imperative for Today's Law Firms," in *Managing Talent for Success,* 7. She cites one firm that keeps a psychotherapist on retainer, who says that "trust issues" are the most prevalent, particularly for lateral hires and that "partners can learn to develop trust, but that it often takes many repeated, safe interactions." Gardner, "Harvard Study Part II: Collaboration Strategies for Rainmakers," *Bloomberg,* June 1, 2015, https://bol.bna.com/harvard-study-part-ii-collaboration-strategies-for-rainmakers/.

204. Jin Wook Chang, Thomas Sy, and Jin Nam Choi, "Team Emotional Intelligence and Performance Interactive Dynamics Between Leaders and Members," *Small Group Research* 43 (1): 84, 93. The research is "more relevant in small teams where members have frequent daily contact," and notes that

the same effectiveness doesn't exist among virtual teams not working face-to-face, although the essentials of open communication, fairness and emotional recognition that make teams effective generally are what make online teams effective as well. As an illustration of the importance of in-person interaction, Google engineered its cafeteria with a wait time and seating layout that encourages personal interaction, and Apple's new open headquarters are designed to bring people together physically. Mills, "What Are Humans Good For . . . in Legal Services?" *3 Geeks and a Law Blog.*

205. Freedman, "Case: EQ in the Navy and Marine Corps—Accelerating Change with Emotional Intelligence," *Six Seconds Emotional Intelligence Network,* June 23, 2010, http://www.6seconds.org/2011/06/23/case-navy-change/.
206. Druskat and Wolff, "Building the Emotional Intelligence of Groups," *Harvard Business Review,* 90.
207. Richard, "We Need a Chief Resilience Officer," *Lawyer Brain Blog,* August 21, 2013, http://www.lawyerbrainblog.com/2013/08/we-need-a-chief-resilience-officer/.
208. An Australian study in 2013 of 193 police officers found that as police officers increased their EI through training, their reported well-being rose, along with their job satisfaction, engagement and commitment. Mortimer, "Police 'Emotional Intelligence' Leads to Job Satisfaction," *My Daily News,* July 4, 2013, http://www.mydailynews.com.au/news/police-emotional-intelligence-leads-to-job-satisfa/1932767/.
209. Grewal and Davidson, "Emotional Intelligence and Graduate Medical Education," *Journal of the American Medical Association.*
210. Richard, "Accountability 101—Part Four," *Lawyer Brain Blog,* May 22, 2013, http://www.lawyerbrainblog.com/2013/05/accountability-101-part-four/.
211. See Deena Shanker, "Why Are Lawyers Such Terrible Managers?" *Fortune,* January 11, 2013. Kathy Caprino, "How Happiness Directly Impacts Your Success," *Forbes,* June 6, 2013.
212. Krieger and Sheldon, "What Makes Lawyers Happy?" *George Washington Law Review.*
213. Dan Bowling, formerly senior vice president of Human Resources for Coca-Cola worldwide and currently a professor at Duke Law School teaching positive psychology, proposes ten tips to make lawyers happier: (1) play to your strengths, (2) choose optimism, (3) keep perspective, (4) keep moving—literally, (5) be sociable, (6) practice gratitude, (7) be resilient, (8) pause/meditate, (9) keep a sense of humor, and (10) make law a calling—or get out. Vivia Chen, "10 Happy Tips for Lawyers," *The Careerist,* August 24, 2010, thecareerist.typepad.com/thecareerist/2010/08/happy-tips.html.
214. Gretchen Rubin, a Yale Law School graduate, was editor of the *Yale Law Journal* and clerked for Sandra Day O'Connor. Her bestseller *The Happiness Project (Or, Why I spent a Year Trying to Sing in the Morning, Clean My Closets, Fight Right, Read Aristotle, and Generally Have More Fun)* suggests cleaning your desk regularly, singing in the morning, and giving loved ones a long hug every day. According to Shawn Achor, author of *The Happiness Advantage,* "we need to train our brains for happiness and resilience. Here are two examples. If people regularly track what they are grateful for in their work/life, they

train themselves to be focused on what they like about their jobs. When people identify tasks they enjoy in their work and focus on doing more of these tasks they become more engaged over time." John Izzo, "Success Follows Happiness, Not the Other Way Around," *Huffington Post,* August 3, 2012, http://www.huffingtonpost.ca/john-izzo/happiness-in-business_b_1733860.html.

215. Happiness researcher Sonja Lyubomirsky's 2008 book *The How of Happiness: A New Approach to Getting the Life You Want* sets out twelve relatively simple happiness-enhancing strategies that can precipitate meaningful increases in happiness.
216. Lyubomirsky and Layous, "How Do Simple Positive Activities Increase Well-Being?" *Current Directions in Psychological Science,* 57–62.
217. Izzo, "Success Follows Happiness, Not the Other Way Around," *Huffington Post.*
218. Daniel Goleman, "Two Key Skills for High-Performance Leadership," December 5, 2016, *More Than Sound,* http://morethansound.net/tag/daniel-goleman/.
219. Richard, "We Need a Chief Resilience Officer," *LawyerBrain Blog.*
220. Rhode, *Lawyers as Leaders,* 107.
221. Charles Darwin, *The Autobiography of Charles Darwin,* ed. Nora Barlow (London, Collins: 1958), 139.
222. Mines, Meyer, and Mines, "Emotional Intelligence and Emotional Toxicity," *The Colorado Lawyer,* 93.
223. Kiser, *Beyond Right and Wrong,* 201.
224. Kiser, "The Emotionally Intelligent Lawyer: Balancing the Rule of Law with the Realities of Human Behavior," *Nevada Law Journal* 15 (2): 442–45. He notes that nearly one-half of all malpractice claims made from 2000 to 2007 reviewed by the ABA's Standing Committee on Lawyers Professional Liability, "allege errors relating to professional skills [that] necessarily entail an integration of substantive legal knowledge with a broader range of competencies embraced by *emotional intelligence* [emphasis added]—listening, understanding, communicating, conceptualizing, anticipating, simulating, and perspective-taking." A review of Kiser's book, *How Leading Lawyers Think,* describes how the successful litigators Kiser studied who are examples of low risk of liability are also high in EI: more empathic—"good at putting themselves in the juror's shoes and seeing the case from the perspective of the jury . . . they seek out third-party review from colleagues and outsiders and feedback on strengths and weaknesses . . . to counter overconfidence bias. . . . He sums up their habit of mind as 'responsibility, respect, resourcefulness and resiliency.'" Kaster, "Review of *How Leading Lawyers Think,*" 80.
225. In a poll of seven lawyers' professional liability insurers that on a combined basis insure more than 80 percent of the Am Law 250 firms, annual increases in claims of 10–40 percent were reported, as well as significantly larger amounts being sought. While the recession impacted claims, five of seven insurers surveyed attributed the rise to mergers and lateral hires. "Law Firms See Rise in Malpractice Claim Frequency, Severity," *Insurance Journal,* June 27, 2013.

226. Patrick Tandy, "AGC: Attorney Sanctions on the Rise," *Maryland State Bar Association Bulletin*, January 11, 2016, http://www.msba.org/Bar_Bulletin/2016/01_-_January/AGC__Attorney_Sanctions_on_the_Rise.aspx.
227. Warren E. Burger, "The Decline of Professionalism," *Tennessee Law Review* 61 (1): 5.
228. Eighteen percent rated lawyers high or very high. "Honesty/Ethics in Professions," *Gallup*, December 7–11, 2016, http://www.gallup.com/poll/1654/honesty-ethics-professions.aspx?version.
229. See Deborah Moss and Mark Hansen, "Lawyer's Perspective," *American Bar Association Journal* 77 (1989): 40.
230. Seth Rosner, "A Decade of Professionalism," *Prof. Law* 6 (2), 2, which deplores the shrinking demand for lawyers; growing numbers of legal malpractice suits; high incidences of fraud, theft, and fiduciary breaches by lawyers; and uncivil behavior by judges and lawyers. Among many instances are the litigator who admits to altering documents in a consumer class action, the tax lawyer who bribes IRS officials to accept tax positions, and the lawyer who bills a client for sex. Elie Mystal, "When I Get That Feeling, I Want Sexual Billing," *Above the Law*, January 15, 2013, http://abovethelaw.com/2013/01/when-i-get-that-feeling-i-want-sexual-billing/; see also plaintiff's attorney who assaulted opposing counsel: Andrew Strickler, "Atty Who Attacked Opponent Hasn't Withdrawn, Victim Says," *Law 360*, https://www.law360.com/articles/868288/atty-who-attacked-opponent-hasn-t-withdrawn-victim-says.
231. Michael E. McCabe, Jr., "Federal Judge Orders DOJ Prosecutors to Undergo Formal Ethics Training," *IP Ethics*, May 26, 2016, http://ipethicslaw.com/federal-judge-orders-doj-prosecutors-to-undergo-formal-ethics-training/#more-9092.
232. William M. Sullivan, Anne Colby, and Judith W. Wegner, *Educating Lawyers: Preparation for the Profession of Law* (San Francisco: Jossey-Bass, 2007), 133. The United Kingdom's Legal Education and Training Review also deplores the lack of law school training in ethics. Jonathan Ames, "Revealed at Last: Details of the Legal Education and Training Review," *The Lawyer*, June 25, 2013. Commissioned by the legal profession's three main watchdogs in the United Kingdom—the Solicitors Regulation Authority, the Bar Standards Board, and the Institute of Legal Executives' Professional Standards—the Review was issued in 2013 calling on regulators to consider major reforms.
233. Sandra Janoff, "The Influence of Legal Education on Moral Reasoning," *Minnesota Law Review* 76 (193): 219–34. There is some evidence that business school students similarly undergo a loss of caring.
234. For example, California Western School of Law expanded its professional responsibility course into a required six-credit set of courses called STEPPS ("Skills Training for Ethical and Preventive Practice and Career Satisfaction") focusing on "professional skills and identity development, problem solving, preventive law, and simulated cases with legal ethics." "STEPPS Program," *California Western School of Law*, https://www.cwsl.edu/academics/academic-initiatives/stepps-program.
235. Weiss, "Judge Holds Prosecutor in Contempt, Says His 'Emotional Intelligence Needs Strengthening,'" *ABA Journal*, January 6, 2017.

236. "Leadership and Behavior: Mastering the Mechanics of Reason and Emotion," *McKinsey Quarterly*, October 2016, http://www.mckinsey.com/business-functions/organization/our-insights/leadership-and-behavior-mastering-the-mechanics-of-reason-and-emotion.
237. Megan Zavieh, "Recovery After Bar Discipline," *Attorney at Work.com*, July 13, 2015, http://www.attorneyatwork.com/recovery-bar-discipline/.
238. Daicoff, *Lawyer, Know Yourself*, 106.
239. Kahneman, *Thinking Fast and Slow*.
240. Goleman, "The Brain and Emotional Intelligence," *Psychology Today*; Antoine Bechara, Hanna Damasio, and Damasio, "Emotion, Decision Making and the Orbitofrontal Cortex," *Cerebral Cortex* 10 (2000): 295–307; Larry Squire, "Memory Systems of the Brain: A Brief History and Current Perspective," *Neurobiology of Learning and Memory* 82 (2004): 171–77.
241. Defoe, "How Low Is Your GASP Score? Higher Guilt Proneness Is Better," *Psycholawlogy*, March 11, 2013, http://www.psycholawlogy.com/2013/03/11/how-low-do-you-gasp-lower-is-better/. There is mixed data on what feelings ethical or unethical acts produce. One study found that cheating on a test actually improved the cheater's mood, at least where there was no obvious victim, while noncheaters' moods declined slightly. Andrew O'Connell, "Cheating Makes People Feel Good (When There's No Victim)," *HBR Blog Network/The Daily Stat*, September 27, 2013, http://blogs.hbr.org/2013/09/cheating-makes-people-feel-good-when-theres-no-victim/.
242. Yip and Côté, "The Emotionally Intelligent Decision Maker," *Psychological Science*.
243. R. Abraham, "Emotional Intelligence in Organizations: A Conceptualization," *Genetic, Social, and General Psychology Monographs* 125 (2): 209–24.
244. Robin Wellford Slocum, "An Inconvenient Truth: The Need to Educate Emotionally Competent Lawyers," *Chapman University Law Research Paper*, July 19, 2011, 4. Vernellia R. Randall, "The Myers-Briggs Type Indicator, First Year Law Studies and Performance," *Cumberland Law Review*, 26 (199663): 92–93, 1996. Daicoff, "Lawyer, Know Thyself," *American University Law Review*, 46 (1997), 1427. Robert S. Rubin and Ronald E. Riggio, "The Role of Emotional Intelligence In Ethical Decision Making At Work," in Robert A. Giacalone, Carole L. Jurkiewicz, Craig Dunn ed. *Positive Psychology in Business Ethics and Corporate Responsibility*, 209–229, Information Age 2005. Publishinghttps://www.researchgate.net/profile/Robert_Rubin9/publication/305463783_The_role_of_emotional_intelligence_in_ethical_decision_making_at_work/links/578f95ac08aecbca4caddb0c.pdf?origin=publication_list.
245. Daniel C. Batson et al., "Is Empathic Emotion a Source of Altruistic Motivation?" *Journal of Personality and Social Psychology* 40 (1981): 290–302; People higher in empathy are more likely to help others in need, even when doing so goes against their self-interest. Jason Marsh, "The Limits of David Brooks' 'Limits of Empathy," *Greater Good: The Science of a Meaningful Life*, October 4, 2011, http://greatergood.berkeley.edu/article/item/the_limits_of_david_brooks_limits_of_empathy#c3751. A seminal study found that people who rescued Jews during the Holocaust had been encouraged at a young age to take the perspectives of others, which has also been demonstrated

more recently to reduce prejudice, racism, and bullying. Samuel P. Oliner and Pearl M. Oliner, *Altruistic Personality: Rescuers of Jews in Nazi Europe* (New York: The Free Press, 1988); Alex Dixon, "Can Empathy Reduce Racism?" *Greater Good: The Science of a Meaningful Life,* July 21, 2011, http://greatergood.berkeley.edu/article/item/empathy_reduces_racism/.

246. Freedman, "Case: EQ in the Navy and Marine Corps," *Six Seconds Emotional Intelligence Network,* 14.
247. Pham et al., "Feeling the Future: The Emotional Oracle Effect," *Journal of Consumer Research.*
248. Yip and Côté, "The Emotionally Intelligent Decision Maker," *Psychological Science.*
249. Stephané Côté quoted in Michael Roberto, "Emotional Intelligence and Risk-Taking," *Michael Roberto,* January 19, 2014, http://michael-roberto.blogspot.com/2014/01/emotional-intelligence-and-risk-taking.html.
250. Elam and Stratton, "Should Medical School Applicants Be Tested for Emotional Intelligence?" *American Medical Association Journal of Ethics,* 473–76. A breakdown of physician-patient communication is cited in over 40 percent of medical malpractice suits. Landro, "The Talking Cure for Health Care: Improving the Ways Doctors Communicate with Their Patients Can Lead to Better Care—And Lower Costs," *The Wall Street Journal.*
251. For example, the WellStar Health System, with five hospitals and more than 550 doctors, used training and coaches to improve doctors' communication and reduce malpractice claims. Patient reports of clear communication rose from 77.5 percent to 86.2 percent within a few months. Landro, "The Talking Cure for Healthcare," *The Wall Street Journal.*
252. "Ways to Avoid Legal Malpractice, as Claims Rise Industry-Wide," *YourABA,* December, 2016, http://www.americanbar.org/publications/youraba/2016/december-2016/legal-malpractice-claims-are-on-the-rise—but-you-can-take-steps.html.
253. Gary Steedly and Paula Raines, "Emotional Intelligence: The Secret Ingredient in Effective Leadership," February 18, 2007, (PowerPoint), slide 45. Poor communications is the most common of 30,000 complaints filed each year against Florida attorneys.
254. Kara MacKillop and Neil Vidmar, "Legal Malpractice: A Preliminary Inquiry," *First Annual Conference on Empirical Legal Studies Paper,* June 29, 2006. The Canadian agency is the Lawyers' Professional Indemnity Company (LAWPRO).
255. Ambady et al., "Surgeons' Tone of Voice: A Clue to Malpractice History," *Surgery,* 1, 8.
256. Landro, "The Talking Cure for Healthcare," *The Wall Street Journal.*
257. Coe, "GCs Say This Firm Is the Most Arrogant," *Law 360.* The list each year includes some of the most profitable BigLaw firms, and also those ranked high in client service.
258. Nancy S. Koven, "Specificity of Metaemotion Effects on Moral Decision-Making," *Emotion* 11 (5): 1255–61. Students asked to place the letter "E" on their forehead who had been pumped up with delusions of power invariably wrote the "E" backwards—how they would see it if they could see through their own forehead but without consideration for the viewpoint of others.

Adam Galinsky, "Research on Power Teaches Why Blagojevich Did What He Did (. . . and Why He Might Get Away with It)," *Huffington Post Blog,* August 3, 2010, http://www.huffingtonpost.com/adam-galinsky/research-on-power-teaches_b_691777.html.

259. Keith Darcy, Executive Director of the Ethics and Compliance Officer Association, quoted in Gael O'Brian, "The Ethics of Emotional Intelligence," *Business Ethics: The Magazine of Corporate Responsibility,* September 1, 2010.
260. Lehrer, "The Power Trip," *The Wall Street Journal.*
261. Kristy N. Bernard and Matthew L. Gibson, "Professional Misconduct by Mentally Impaired Attorneys: Is There a Better Way to Treat an Old Problem?" *Georgetown Journal of Legal Ethics* 17 (2004): 619–30.
262. Kiser, *Beyond Right and Wrong.*
263. See Daicoff, "Lawyer, Know Thyself," *American University Law Review.*
264. Kiser, *Beyond Right and Wrong.*
265. Beth Winegarner, "After Faruqi, More Female Attys to Sue for Sex Harassment," *Law360,* April 21, 2015, http://www.law360.com/articles/644709/after-faruqi-more-female-attys-to-sue-for-sex-harassment.
266. Gaston Kroub, "Beyond Biglaw: 3 Reasons Law Firms Are Not Safe Spaces," *Above the Law,* March 22, 2016, http://abovethelaw.com/2016/03/beyond-biglaw-3-reasons-law-firms-are-not-safe-spaces/.
267. Protected classes are "race, sex, religion, national origin, ethnicity, disability, age, sexual orientation, gender identity, marital status or socioeconomic status." "ABA Model Rules of Professional Conduct," *ABA,* 2017, http://www.americanbar.org/groups/professional_responsibility/committees_commissions/ethicsandprofessionalresponsibility/modruleprofconduct8_4.html.
268. The rule was proposed because such harassment and discrimination "undermines confidence in the legal profession and our legal system," according to comments to the proposed amendment. This is the whole amendment with comments: http://www.americanbar.org/content/dam/aba/administrative/professional_responsibility/final_revised_resolution_and_report_109.authcheckdam.pdf. See also Michael Downey, "Erin Andrews' Trial Shows Ethics Rule is Needed," *National Law Journal,* April 25, 2016.
269. While violation of the Rules does not necessarily produce liability, they are routinely cited in disciplinary actions and lawsuits, and their violation may be "evidence of breach of the applicable standard of conduct." Section 20 of the Preamble of the ABA Model Rules of Professional Conduct, as amended through August 2007, quoted in Dennis J. Quinn and Elizabeth A. Francis, "The Interaction between the Rules of Professional Conduct and Malpractice Actions in the District of Columbia, Maryland, and Virginia," *Carr Maloney P.C,* 1. "[F]or more than three decades, one-half of all law school graduates have been female. Yet female lawyers still make up less than 20% of the partners—and less than 10% of the equity partners—at most law firms." Downey, "Erin Andrews' Trial Shows Ethics Rule Is Needed," *National Law Journal.*
270. In an American College of Physician Executives survey, 55 percent of the respondents stated they were "very concerned" about the unethical business practices in healthcare, one-third reporting that "they knew of a physician within their own firm who was engaged in an unethical practice." David

Weber, "Unethical Business Practices in U.S. Health Care Alarm Physician Leaders," *Physician Executive* 31 (2005): 6–13.

271. Satish Deshpande, "A Study of Ethical Decision Making by Physicians and Nurses in Hospitals," *Journal of Business Ethics* 90 (2009): 393. See also Nele Libberecht et al., "Emotional Intelligence Predicts Success in Medical School," *Emotion* 14 (2014): 64–73. Similarly, a study assessing European medical students over three years concluded that, unlike cognitive ability or the personality trait Conscientiousness, only EI, and specifically the ability to regulate emotion, correlates positively with, among other things, dealing with ethical dilemmas. Todres et al., "The Emotional Intelligence of Medical Students: An Exploratory Cross-Sectional Study," *Medical Teacher* 32 (2010): e42–e48.
272. Christophe Bernard, "An Emotional Approach to Strategy Execution," October 17, 2014, *KPMG.com*, http://www.kpmg.com/global/en/issuesandinsights/articlespublications/family-business/pages/emotional-approach-strategy-execution.aspx.
273. Daicoff, "Lawyer, Know Thyself," *American University Law Review*, 1427.
274. Defoe, "Legal Talent Management Memo: Individual Differences and Moral Disengagement—Connections Which Can Predict Unethical Decisions," *Psycholawlogy*, September 23, 2012, http://www.psycholawlogy.com/2012/09/23/legal-talent-management-memo-individual-differences-and-moral-disengagementconnections-which-can-predict-unethical-decisions/.
275. They are (1) Moral Justification—making harm appear more morally justifiable, (2) Euphemistic Labeling—using morally neutral language to make bad conduct sound benign, (3) Advantageous Comparison—trivializing one's unethical behavior by comparing it with more harmful conduct, (4) Displacement of Responsibility—blaming someone else for bad behavior, (5) Diffusion of Responsibility—claiming no one individual but the whole group was responsible, (6) Distortion of Consequences—trivializing the harm by noting limited consequences, and (7) Dehumanization—not recognizing the target of the harm, and 8. Attribution of Blame—blaming the victim. Ibid.
276. "There is no group I can think of that practices the psychological act of compartmentalization with more dexterity and willingness than lawyers," according to a psychologist who specializes in treating lawyers. "Indeed, it may be the basic intellectual act of law practice." Chen, "Depressed People Make Better Lawyers," *The Careerist Blog*, July 22, 2010, http://thecareerist.typepad.com/thecareerist/2010/07/depressed-people-make-better-lawyers.html.
277. Defoe, "Legal Talent Management Memo," *Psycholawlogy*.
278. Daniel N. Jones and Delroy L. Paulhus, "Machiavellianism," in Mark R. Leary and Rick H. Hoyle eds., *Handbook of Individual Differences in Social Behavior* (New York: The Guilford Press, 2002), 257–73. While Goleman considers Machiavellianism to be a subclinical form of psychopathy, there seems to be no consensus other than that Machiavellianism and psychopathy overlap to some degree. Adam Grant, "The Dark Side of Emotional Intelligence," *The Atlantic*, January 2, 2014.

279. Kevin Dutton, *The Wisdom of Psychopaths: What Saints, Spies, and Serial Killers Can Teach Us about Success* (New York: Farrar, Straus and Giroux, 2012).
280. Rosalie Holihan, "Management Decision Making, Ethical Issues and "Emotional" Intelligence," *Management Decision* 44 (8): 1128.
281. Rhode, *Lawyers as Leaders*, 5. No doubt the narcissism is compounded by the implications of power.
282. Harvey Mansfield, "Niccolo Machiavelli," in *Encyclopedia Britannica Online*, last updated June 29, 2006, https://www.britannica.com/biography/Niccolo-Machiavelli.
283. Jones and Paulhus, "Machiavellianism," in *Handbook of Individual Differences in Social Behavior.*
284. University employees who tested higher in both emotion-regulation and Machiavellianism "exhibited a stronger positive association with interpersonal deviance in the workplace," deliberately engaging in the most harmful behaviors to their colleagues. Côté et al., "The Jekyll and Hyde of Emotional Intelligence: Emotion-Regulation Knowledge Facilitates Both Prosocial and Interpersonally Deviant Behavior," *Psychological Science* 22 (2011): 1073–80. Grant, "The Dark Side of Emotional Intelligence."
285. Chris Weller, "What's the Difference Between a Sociopath and a Psychopath," *Medical Daily*, March 6, 2014, http://www.medicaldaily.com/whats-difference-between-sociopath-and-psychopath-not-much-one-might-kill-you-270694.
286. According to criminal psychologist Robert Hare, who developed the Psychopathy Checklist-Revised (PCL-R), universally recognized for diagnosing psychopathy, "you're four times more likely to find a psychopath at the top of the corporate ladder than you are walking around the janitor's office," even though both share many of the same characteristics. Caitlin Dickson, "How to Spot a Sociopath (Hint: It Could Be You)," *The Daily Beast*, June 25, 2013, http://www.thedailybeast.com/articles/2013/06/25/how-to-spot-a-sociopath-hint-it-could-be-you.html. Hundreds of members of the American Psychological Association's Division 41 who specialize in psychology and law—criminal attorneys and psychology professors—agreed that the main difference between clients/patients who were psychopathic and successful and those who were unsuccessful (i.e., imprisoned) was conscientiousness: successful psychopaths have high levels of competence, order, and self-discipline, while unsuccessful ones are irresponsible, impulsive, and negligent. Otherwise, the two groups were virtually the same in all other respects. S. Mullins-Sweatt et al., "The Search for the Successful Psychopath," *Journal of Research in Personality* 44 (4): 554–58.
287. K.J. Mahaffey and D.K. Marcus, "Interpersonal Perception of Psychopathy: A Social Relations Analysis," *Journal of Social and Clinical Psychology* 25 (2006): 53–74.
288. A study of incarcerated men concluded that, "controlling for general intelligence, psychopathy was associated with lower EI. These findings suggest that individuals with psychopathy are impaired on a range of EI abilities and that EI is an important area for understanding deficits in psychopathy." Elsa Ermer et al., "Emotional Intelligence in Incarcerated Men with Psychopathic Traits," *Journal of Personality and Social Psychology* 103 (2012): 197. Brain

imaging reveals in sociopaths a thinning of the areas that connect the amygdala and other emotional centers to the prefrontal cortex, the location of emotional management, suggesting both a deficit in access to emotional data and a reduced ability to manage emotions. Damásio, "A Neural Basis for Sociopathy," *Archives of General Psychiatry* 57 (2000): 128–29.

289. People can employ "empathy to use other people, manipulating them through a savvy understanding of emotions." "[U]nderstanding someone's emotions (so-called 'cognitive empathy') and sharing those emotions (so-called 'emotional empathy') can split apart. Further, understanding without sharing is a dangerous pattern, which likely underlies intimidation, used car sales tactics, and all sorts of other manipulation. Of course, in many—and perhaps most—cases, we use our understanding of others to help them. . . . Empathic ability is value neutral, sometimes helping and other times hurting people." Jamil Zaki, "Using Empathy to Use People: Emotional Intelligence and Manipulation," *Scientific American: The Moral Universe Blog,* November 7, 2013, http://blogs.scientificamerican.com/moral-universe/2013/11/07/using-empathy-to-use-people-emotional-intelligence-and-manipulation/?goback=.gde_3708120_member_5804249847691231232#!.
290. Dickson, "How to Spot a Sociopath," *The Daily Beast.*
291. Paul Babiak and Robert D. Hare, *Snakes in Suits* (New York: Harper Business, 2006).
292. Douglas Richardson, "Don't Worry, Be Crazy," *Edge International Communiqué,* February, 2014, http://archive.constantcontact.com/fs148/1104176518924/archive/1116303782715.html.
293. "What makes leaders willing to accept the pressure, hours, scrutiny, and risks that come with the role?" Rhode asks. "For many individuals, it is not only commitment to a cause, an organization, or a constituency. It is also an attraction to power, status, admiration, and financial reward. Yet successful leadership requires subordinating these self-interests to a greater good. The result is what is variously labeled the 'leadership paradox' or the 'paradox of power.'" Rhode, "Developing Leadership," *Santa Clara Law Review,* 699, 700.
294. The economic recession that began in 2008 and damaged public trust, the general economy, and individual companies is viewed by many as attributable at least in part to unethical practices by lawyers, who were involved in all those mortgages and swaps and insurance products. Ryan McCarthy, "Wall Street Compensation Lawyer Steve Eckhaus: 'I Have Friends Who Blame Me for the Crisis,'" *Huffington Post,* February 26, 2011, http://www.huffingtonpost.com/2011/02/06/wall-street-compensation-_1_n_819221.html. While many bristle at these charges—"we were only doing our job"—others are not so sure of our innocence, as evidenced in a roundtable of lawyers' discussion entitled "Should Lawyers Shoulder Any Blame for the Financial Crisis?" Stephen J. Dodgett, "Not Guilty: *Legal Business*/Marsh Roundtable on Risk and the Financial Crisis," *Legal Business,* May, 2009, 32–37. Some professions have tightened their ethical standards in the wake of the recession. In 2012 economists, who were accused of failing to predict the 2007–2008 financial crisis and of helping create it—as highlighted in the film *Inside Job,* the 2011 Academy Award winner for best documentary—adopted more stringent

conflict-of-interest rules in their code of ethics. University of Illinois Professor Deirdre McCloskey said that economists too often had "acted like lawyers, standing up for a certain point of view regardless of the evidence." Ben Casselman, "Economists Set Rules on Ethics," *The Wall Street Journal*, January 9, 2012, quoting McCloskey. Our Model Rules of Professional Conduct stop short of an obligation to consider the common good, which some advocate for, simply encouraging the guidance of "personal conscience." "Model Rules of Professional Conduct," *ABA*, 2017. In 2013 a British tribunal "issued a 'severe reprimand' and a record fine of £14 million ($22 million) against Deloitte and a disbarment and fine against its corporate finance partner" for having "placed their own interests ahead of that of the public and compromised their own objectivity . . . a flagrant disregard of the professional standards expected and required," in connection with their work for the failed automaker MG Rover and four businessmen who took over the automaker and "ran it into the ground, taking out millions of pounds for themselves in highly dubious transactions." One of the businessmen "blamed Sue Lewis, a partner in Eversheds, a prominent law firm that was advising the company, for keeping them from realizing the full amount [of a suspect compensation package]," saying "'it wasn't her position to be raising questions about the directors' remuneration,' since the law firm "was not 'anybody's moral guardians.'" The tribunal wrote, "It has been put to us that in corporate finance work and tax work the only duty that a member owes is to his client . . . and that the public interest is not a matter that needs to concern him. We do not accept this." Floyd Norris, "When Accountants Act as Bankers," *New York Times*, September 12, 2013. Calls for greater emphasis on ethical leadership (Rhode, *Lawyers as Leaders*, 107) have not given rise to appreciably stricter standards for lawyers or to fewer cases of unethical conduct. Anecdotally, in 2013, in a complete sweep of the legal arena, within days of each other individual lawyers were convicted for "violating the trust placed in them as attorneys" (Andrew Keshner, "Convicted of Mortgage Fraud, Two Lawyers to Seek New Trial," *The New York Law Journal*, July 31, 2013), the ABA censured the University of Illinois College of Law and fined it $250,000 for fraudulently inflating credentials of incoming students, conduct which was "reprehensible and misleading to law school applicants, law students and law schools, and damaging to the reputation of the legal profession" (Sloan, "Hiring Partners: What's So Bad about Spring Recruitment?" *National Law Journal*, July 2, 2009, quoting the ABA), and the Ninth Circuit upheld a ruling that McGuireWoods "egregiously breached" its ethical duties in failing to disclose to class members that incentive awards would go to named plaintiffs (Amanda Bronstad, "Circuit Denies McGuireWoods Fees in BAR/BRI Case, Citing 'Egregious' Ethics Breach," *National Law Journal*, August 13, 2013).

295. Dutton, *The Wisdom of Psychopaths*. Dutton argues that the "wisdom of psychopaths" lies in seven core characteristics—Ruthlessness, Charm, Focus, Mental Toughness, Fearlessness, Mindfulness, and Action—that might help us get what we want, and if we engage in them judiciously, may not turn us into a complete villain.
296. Dickson, "How to Spot a Sociopath," *The Daily Beast*.

297. Ibid.
298. Mikolajczak et al. "Sensitive but Not Sentimental: Emotionally Intelligent People Can Put Their Emotions Aside When Necessary," *Personality and Individual Differences.*
299. Zaki, "Using Empathy to Use People," *Scientific American: The Moral Universe Blog.*
300. Côté et al., "The Jekyll and Hyde of Emotional Intelligence," *Psychological Science,* 1078.
301. Grant, "The Dark Side of Emotional Intelligence." EI can be used to manipulate or influence others in whatever direction is consistent with the person's goals, whether good or bad. Martin Kilduff, Dan S. Chiaburu, and Jochen I. Menges, "Strategic Use of Emotional Intelligence in Organizational Settings: Exploring the Dark Side," *Research in Organizational Behavior* 30 (2010): 129–52. Those high in EI who also had Machiavellian tendencies were found to be more likely to embarrass and demean their peers for their own benefit. Their behaviors in organizations included focusing on detecting the emotions of important others, disguising and expressing their own emotions, using misattribution to stir and shape emotions, and controlling the flow of emotion-laden communication to benefit themselves. In other words, they could "intentionally shape their emotions to fabricate favorable impressions of themselves," in effect deceiving more persuasively. In Côté et al., "The Jekyll and Hyde of Emotional Intelligence," *Psychological Science,* university employees who tested higher in both emotion-regulation knowledge and Machiavellianism "exhibited a stronger positive association with interpersonal deviance in the workplace," deliberately engaging in the most harmful behaviors to their colleagues. See also "The Dark Side of Emotional Intelligence," October 23, 2013, *Huffington Post,* http://www.huffingtonpost.com/2013/10/26/emotional-intelligence-manipulation-retaliation_n_4151648.html.
302. Discussing Dr. Robert Sutton, professor of management science and engineering at Stanford University, author of the classic "The No Asshole Rule: Building a Civilized Workplace and Surviving One That Isn't." Sylvia Lafair, "How the Dark Side of Emotional Intelligence Can Cost You," *The Business Journals,* December 16, 2016, http://www.bizjournals.com/bizjournals/how-to/human-resources/2016/12/how-the-dark-side-of-emotional-intelligence-costs.html.
303. Maister, *Practice What You Preach.* The most successful firms excelled by actually doing well on things to which most, if not all, firms pay only lip service, such as client service, teamwork, and employee development.
304. Middleburg and Butterworth, "Emotional Intelligence," *The Barrister Magazine,* 2013. Emotionally intelligent employees produce positive "organizational outcomes," including in "net profit, growth management, and employee management and retention." Stein et al. "Emotional Intelligence of Leaders," *Leadership and Organization Development Journal,* 30 (2009): 87.
305. "93% (i.e., 13/14ths) of the competencies predicting [financial] performance were from the emotional intelligence clusters." Boyatzis, "Using Tipping Points of Emotional Intelligence and Cognitive Competencies to Predict Financial Performance of Leaders," *Psicothema,* 130. The EI increases

of five times compared to an increase of only 50 percent in profitability for those with high cognitive competencies.

306. In a large beverage firm, 87 percent of the division presidents selected for EI competencies performed in the top third, outperforming their targets by 15–20 percent. McClelland, "Identifying Competencies with Behavioral-Event Interviews," *Psychological Science.* L'Oreal realized an average $91,370 increase in revenue per salesperson after selecting for EI skills. Lyle M. Spencer Jr. and Signe M. Spence, *Competence at Work: Models for Superior Performance.* By raising mid-management EI, an Italian chain achieved dramatic performance improvements—"massively" higher engagement and significantly higher retention—and ultimately higher profitability. Joshua Freedman, "The Amadori Case: Supplying McDonalds—Organizational Engagement, Emotional Intelligence and Performance," *SixSeconds.org,* April 3, 2013, http://www.6seconds.org/2013/04/03/amadori-case-engagement-emotional-intelligence/. Similarly, in 118 R&D teams, the project leaders' EI predicted the technical quality and also the profitability of both the products and the firm, in part due to teams working more efficiently. Nicholas Clarke, "Emotional Intelligence and Its Relationship to Transformational Leadership and Key Project Manager Competencies," *Project Management Journal* 41 (2010): 15–16. PepsiCo found that high EI executives generated 10 percent more in productivity, adding nearly $4 million in economic value. The hotel chain Sheraton attributes a 24 percent growth in market share in part to an EI initiative. "It's just emotion, taking HR over," *HC Online,* January 30, 2014, http://www.hcamag.com/hr-news/its-just-emotion-taking-hr-over-183565.aspx.
307. Groysberg and Sherman, "Baker and McKenzie (A)," *Harvard Business School Review.*
308. Cunningham, "Chief Legal Officers Tell Outside Counsel What They Want . . . and Don't," *C3,* June 20, 2013; see also the 16th Annual BTI Client Service All-Stars 2017, *BTI Consulting Group,* http://www.bticonsulting.com/client-service-all-stars-law.
309. Gerry Riskin, "Leadership Strategy from Gettysburg." *Amazing Firms Amazing Practices,* June 6, 2013, http://www.gerryriskin.com/leadership-strategy-from-gettysburg/.
310. Jim Collins, *Good to Great: Why Some Companies Make the Leap . . . and Others Don't* (New York: HarperBusiness, 2001).
311. Executives with EI skills—strong empathy, reality testing, problem-solving, and self-regard—have been demonstrated to be "more likely to yield high profit-earning companies." Stein et al., "Emotional Intelligence of Leaders," *Leadership and Organization Development Journal,* 87.
312. Peter Shankman (St. Martin's Press, 2013), https://www.shankman.com/about/.
313. Gardner, "The Collaboration Imperative for Today's Law Firms: Leading High-Performance Teamwork for Maximum Benefit," in R. Normand-Hochman ed., *Managing Talent for Success: Talent Development in Law Firms* (London, UK: Globe Business Publishing Ltd., 2013). Gardner conducted "quantitative analyses of a decade's worth of detailed financial and time-sheet

records at three global law firms and one accounting firm, case studies of professional services incumbents and new entrants, and surveys and interviews with hundreds of professionals in a range of sectors, including consulting, law, accounting, engineering, real estate brokerage, architecture, and executive search." She concludes that, "Multi-practice client service brings in significantly more revenue" due to "higher-value work and increased retention of clients and professionals." Gardner, "The Collaboration Imperative for Today's Law Firms," in *Managing Talent for Success,* 10, 11, 20.

314. Gardner, "When Senior Managers Won't Collaborate," *Harvard Business Review.*
315. A review of the compensation systems of 146 professional theater companies using one of three different valuation cultures—"a collaborative culture, a hierarchical one, or a so-called star culture"—concluded "that increasing a company's 'collaborative norms' rating by just one point could improve a firm's talent retention, revenues, and revenues coming from innovation, by as much as 10–15%." Patrick J. McKenna and Edwin B. Reeser, "Management Memo: Is Your Firm Creating a Star Culture?" *The Am Law Daily,* July 25, 2013.
316. Shanker, "Why Are Lawyers Such Terrible Managers?" *Fortune.*
317. Maister, "Are Law Firms Manageable?" *DavidMaister.com.*

Chapter Five

Four Steps to Achieving an Emotionally Intelligent Workplace

Corporate surveys find that more than two-thirds of major businesses apply some aspect of emotional intelligence in their recruiting, in promotions, and particularly in leadership development.[1]

—Daniel Goleman, author and emotional intelligence expert

[Even though] the ability to attract, develop, and retain talent has become one of the biggest competitive issues for law firms, they nevertheless often lack the experience, vision, and tools to do it.[2]

—Chris Frawley, customer experience consultant with Beyond Philosophy

[T]he model for personal emotional intelligence can be neatly applied to organizations that desire success in the larger world . . . With so many competing products and services that look alike in the mind of the customer, it will be the emotional intelligence embedded in the experience that will become the final differentiator.[3]

—Rebecca Normand-Hochman, editor of *Managing Talent for Success: Talent Development in Law Firms*

The vision of an emotionally intelligent organization is in stark contrast to what many believe is the current state of most legal workplaces. Just like being "smart" doesn't alone make us as good a lawyer as we could be, being smart is not enough to make the most productive organization.[4] Thankfully, a workplace can take steps toward realizing potentially geometric returns. Achieving that goal requires making emotional intelligence (EI) a priority and committing time and resources along the way.[5]

Google has been cited as a preeminently successful organization in part because of the founders Sergey Brin's and Larry Page's own emotional intelligence, and also because of their insistence on bringing that sensibility to their whole organization. When hiring a CEO, they placed an emphasis on finding someone who valued open emotional expression. Then together, the trio set out to create an emotionally supportive culture. Ranked number one in several national employee satisfaction surveys, the company has "shown empathy toward both its employees and society at large," offers its employees mindfulness and other nontraditional professional development programs that embrace EI, and founded a corporate charity, Google.org. "All in all, its founders' qualities in terms of both cognitive and emotional intelligence have helped Google develop a uniquely innovative, entrepreneurial, and stimulating atmosphere."[6]

Building an emotionally intelligent work environment is not easy. A checklist of what one hospital system did to achieve it demonstrates the extensive commitment that such an undertaking entails. A *Harvard Business Review* article recounts that the Cleveland Clinic: "(1) Publicized the problem internally. Seeing the hospital's dismal service scores shocked employees into recognizing that serious flaws existed. (2) Worked to understand patients' needs. Management commissioned studies to get at the root causes of dissatisfaction. (3) Made everyone a caregiver. An enterprise-wide program trained everyone, from physicians to janitors, to put the patient first. (4) Increased employee engagement. The Clinic instituted a 'caregiver celebration' program and redoubled other motivational efforts. (5) Established new processes. For example, any patient, for any reason, can now make a same-day appointment with a single call. (6) Set patients' expectations. Printed and online materials educate patients about their stays—before they're admitted." As the authors concluded, "Operating a truly patient-centered organization . . . isn't a program; it's a way of life."[7] The same can be said for client-centered organizations, as successful law practices must be.

The following sections discuss the four areas where lawyers can take both immediate and longer-term steps to achieve an emotionally intelligent workplace, the importance of finding that delicate but magical balance between demanding excellence and providing emotional support, and some of the frontrunners in our industry who are showing the way:

1. *Start at the Top: Emotionally Intelligent Leaders*
2. *Hire for Emotional Intelligence*
3. *Develop Emotional Intelligence*
4. *Emotionally Engage the Keepers*

   Find the Magical Balance

   Firms Daring to Lead

Step 1: Start at the Top: Emotionally Intelligent Leaders

> *[A]lthough technical excellence and intellect are critical factors for success as a lawyer, emotional intelligence is the differentiating factor for successful leadership.*[8]
>
> —Smith and Marrow, Center for Creative Leadership, "The Changing Nature of Leadership in Law Firms"

> *CEOs on average have the lowest EQ scores in the workplace . . . Yet, among executives, those with the highest EQ scores are the best performers.*[9]
>
> —Travis Bradberry, author and emotional intelligence expert, and Dr. Jean Greaves, author and CEO of TalentSmart

Institutionalizing EI starts with our leaders. Emotionally intelligent leaders are doubly effective. First, by overcoming their own lawyerly weaknesses, they can better grapple with the most common challenges legal workplaces face, and do so comfortably.[10] Second, the emotional intelligence of leaders reverberates throughout the culture, enhancing the EI of the whole firm.[11]

Recognizing the importance of using "a top-down" approach to raising workplace EI, the Yale Center and the Faas Foundation announced in early 2016 a joint initiative entitled "The Emotion Revolution in the Workplace" that focuses on the EI of leaders.[12] Similarly, in July 2015 the Wharton School established the Katz Fund for Research on Leadership and Emotional Intelligence with the goal of enhancing organizational EI starting from the top and supporting the Wharton Center for Leadership and Change Management.[13]

Yet in a puzzling paradox, while around the world high EI workers are consistently the best performers among their peers on all steps of the corporate ladder, top management is likely to have the lowest EI.[14] After surveying "half a million senior executives (including 1,000 CEOs), managers, and line employees across industries on six continents," TalentSmart concluded that "beyond middle management, there is a steep downward trend . . . CEOs, on average, have the lowest EQ scores in the workplace."[15]

Given lawyers' low EI tendencies, lawyer leaders may be even more likely than those in other industries to be bedeviled by low emotional intelligence.[16]

TEST YOURSELF: Try taking the short quiz designed by noted EI expert Dr. Annie McKee (also listed in the Appendix) to find out if you lead with emotional intelligence.[17]

Lawyer leaders can build more emotionally intelligent practices by doing the following:

Increase Feedback to Raise Self-Awareness
Invest in Leadership Development
Embrace Women Leaders
Use Emotional Contagion

Increase Feedback to Raise Self-Awareness

> *[G]reat leadership calls for a very high level of self-awareness. To develop self-awareness, we need to get feedback from people we trust, people who will tell us the truth.*[18]
>
> —John Ryan, President of Center for Creative Leadership and retired US Navy Vice Admiral

One of the primary reasons for the low level of EI at the top is leaders' low self-awareness.[19] Those most aware exhibit "congruence" between how they see themselves and how others see them, but those in the highest positions often rate themselves better on important aspects of their performance than others do.[20] In fact, the leaders rated the worst by others rate themselves substantially higher, and even higher than those leaders who rate themselves as average, signaling a profound deficit in self-awareness.[21]

Congruence is particularly lacking with respect to EI capabilities. In one review of almost 5,000 participants, the highest-level executives gave themselves significantly higher ratings than others gave them in nineteen of twenty EI competencies.[22] Senior executives also rate their organizations 49 percent higher on implementing measures to promote EI than do middle managers—another large gap.[23]

Why are so many of these top executives so clueless?[24] Simply rising to a position of power may itself lower EI by reducing empathy, which, in a vicious cycle, further reduces a leader's ability to recognize his or her impact on others.[25] Lawyers, known for arrogance, can be particularly at risk as they ascend to power, because arrogance itself "distorts a leader's capacity to read accurately situations."[26] The rise to power also carries with it other negative fallout like a narrowed focus in decision making, a phenomenon that can be seen even among Supreme Court Justices.[27]

Researchers suggest that "[t]oo many leaders are promoted because of what they know or how long they have worked, rather than for their skill in managing others. Once they reach the top, they spend less time interacting with staff."[28] There are few if any people above them, and those below them "are less inclined to give constructive feedback to higher status individuals" and less inclined to give "candid feedback that is less than flattering." So leaders are less likely to be called to task.[29]

Not only is feedback not volunteered to them, leaders affirmatively avoid seeking out feedback, even when they know they have considerable "blind spots."[30] In a survey of some 70,000 individuals, the behavior rated the least frequent of thirty leadership behaviors was "asks for feedback on how his/her actions affect others' performance." The authors put it bluntly: "Most leaders don't want honest feedback, don't ask for honest feedback, and don't get much of it unless it's forced on them."[31]

Many of the unwittingly overconfident senior partners that Randall Kiser surveyed likely do not routinely seek out review or feedback, unlike his highly successful litigators who attested to purposely "seek out third-party review from colleagues and outsiders and feedback . . . to counter overconfidence bias."[32]

Unfortunately, low EI leaders who do manage to receive feedback are unlikely to act on it. A study found that those with the lowest EI, who "vastly overestimated" their abilities, used what the authors termed "expedient escape" from doing anything about it by challenging the feedback's accuracy or dismissing its relevance.[33]

Lawyer leaders are in organizations that have few if any formal processes for giving them feedback. In the early 1970s British Airways developed one of the first upward feedback programs, which, while controversial, are now fairly ubiquitous among companies.[34] Still, less than half of law firms offer associates the opportunity to evaluate those above them, and few firms that do engage in the process make changes as a result.[35] Even fewer law firms and law departments provide peer or cross-performance appraisals.[36]

If, as Peter Drucker stresses in his book, *Management Challenges for the 21st Century*, self-awareness and the capacity to build mutually satisfying relationships are the backbone of strong management in the 21st century,[37] lawyer leaders must put in place processes to strengthen their leadership and develop and identify upcoming leaders in order to strengthen their organizations.

To institutionally increase feedback, top management should be regularly reviewed along with other lawyers in the firm, including receiving evaluations of their relationship-building, communication, collaboration, and other EI skills. Lawyer leaders should take EI-related assessments to make sure they recognize their specific strengths and weaknesses and to formulate steps for improvement, engage coaches informed by the assessment results in order to raise awareness and performance, and participate in EI training.[38]

Invest in Leadership Development

> *[In a pool of talented law firm partners,] it is the unusual individual who possesses the qualities of a successful business leader . . . [Are we lawyers] so naturally talented at leadership that we don't have to take any instruction? Unfortunately, the data shows otherwise.*[39]
>
> —Carl A. Leonard, former chair of Morrison & Foerster

Thankfully, emotionally intelligent leadership skills can be acquired.[40] Corporations around the world have long poured money into leadership development and are upping the ante in these more complex times. For each of the last few years US organizations have boosted leadership development spending by double-digit percentages to over $15 billion,[41] and in 2015 it remained the priority spending item for the third year in a row for 86 percent of companies globally.[42] Nearly all of these leadership development programs recognize the importance of EI skills and include instruction to improve them.[43]

Yet, despite the many leadership positions our profession holds in government and business, the legal industry has largely steered clear of leadership development. As of 2013 only 20 percent of large law firms and 38 percent of midsize firms report having any such programs, despite just 2 percent in a 2016 survey said they are doing an "excellent" job of grooming leaders.[44] Law departments that participate in corporate leadership training rarely have training that is customized for a legal setting.

The Center for Creative Leadership's white paper on "The Changing Nature of Leadership in Law Firms" maintains that a laissez-faire attitude toward leadership development is no longer an option: "A changing environment makes leadership development an imperative. Firms can no longer assume that leaders will simply emerge from the ranks of senior partners."[45]

Embrace Women Leaders

> *[W]omen may possess a unique and timely leadership quality.*[46]
>
> —Steven M. Savageau, Ed.D and Flight Administrator at Air Force Recruiting Service, in study of transformational leadership

The evidence points to our women lawyers as an untapped pool of emotionally intelligent leaders. What we see from performance evaluations of senior executives in industries around the world is that, regardless of whatever differences may exist between the genders in their experience or expression of emotions or in their levels of EI generally,[47] women perform well as leaders. In fact, as we advance through the 21st century, women may make better leaders than men.

In the 2013 book *The Athena Doctrine: How Women (and the Men Who Think Like Them) Will Rule the Future*, two male authors argue that "feminine" traits like connectedness, humility, candor, patience, and empathy are the new keys to corporate success,[48] a conclusion that fits with the more collaborative approach that others have concluded is necessary in 21st-century commerce, and specifically in law.[49]

An early meta-analysis found female leaders have better social skills, are more "interested in other people," and are "more friendly, pleasant, and socially sensitive" than male leaders.[50] In more recent studies, EI skills are significantly more present in executive-level women than their male peers: in some cases female managers average more than twice their male counterparts' self-awareness and empathy[51] and they are decidedly more effective in influencing others and resolving conflicts.[52] Simply including women on teams seems to raise team effectiveness because of the higher incidence of women having EI strengths.[53] Ruth Malloy, global managing director for leadership and talent at Hay Group, suggests that women have had to develop greater competence in these areas because of the barriers they have had to overcome to advance in their careers.[54]

Harvard Business Review's "Are Women Better Leaders Than Men?" reports that of over 7,000 leaders in an array of occupations and a broad swath of organizations, women at every level were perceived by colleagues to be at least marginally more effective leaders than men, and the higher they were on the totem pole, the better overall the women were rated: among top management, 67.7 percent of women were judged effective leaders versus 57.7 percent of men.[55] In a separate HBR study, female lawyers were also seen as edging out male lawyers as effective leaders—59.4 percent compared to 54.7 percent, respectively.[56] The conclusion must be that women lawyers are as likely, if not more so, than men to perform well in our legal leadership positions.

As Mary Robinson, a barrister who was the first female president of Ireland and then the United Nations high commissioner for human rights, observed, "women tend to be problem solvers and lead in a more participatory way. It's less hierarchical; there's more listening and nurturing. Everybody gets a chance to say their piece."[57]

These and other physiological and psychological differences outlined in *Leadership and the Sexes: Using Gender Science to Create Success in Business* are the basis for making a strong case that "More Than Ever the Time is Now for Female Led Leadership in Both Law Departments and Law Firms."[58]

But will we invest in women leaders? We certainly aren't doing so at the currently slow rate of making female partners and even slower rate of making female managing partners, members of executive committees, and chief legal officers.[59] Of course, few women stay in law.[60] They leave the profession, not just their jobs, in droves in part because of their discomfort with the low level of collegiality in their workplaces and the low regard for their attempts to make the culture more collaborative—what one referred to as "a toxic work culture."[61] Since managers who display EI have been demonstrated to be the ones who promote diversity and inclusiveness in their organizations,[62] low-EI lawyer leaders are more likely to perpetuate a "good ol' boys" culture that keeps cycling forward to the disadvantage of the organization.

When law firms and law departments start valuing and rewarding those among them who have the EI skills to be the best leaders, they are likely to find women well represented. Building a more emotionally intelligent workplace will help keep those valuable lawyers in their practices. Further, promoting women can bring a cultural change that encourages other women (and men) who have high emotional intelligence to stay.

Use Emotional Contagion

> *The creation of positive affect by people with higher EI may be especially important because it can spread among groups via emotional contagion.*[63]
>
> —John D. Mayer, Richard D. Roberts, and Sigal G. Barsade, psychologists and researchers

In the movie *Ghostbusters II*, our heroes discover that mounting negativity has created an evil slime that threatens humanity. In an attempt to disarm it, a large group of New Yorkers convenes in Central Park, holds hands, and sings "Kumbaya." And boom! The slime and its negativity start to dissolve.

That's sort of—ok, maybe only a little bit—how emotions spread through the workplace. Emotions are contagious. They can build up into a substantial store of negativity or positivity that permeates work environments and displaces other emotions and moods. The author of *Emotional Contagion* describes how we "catch other people's anxiety, depression or stress. Whatever they're feeling, we feel the same way." Physiologically, mirror neurons, which also produce empathy, are likely the mechanism through which this contagion spreads.[64]

Leaders can use emotional regulation to select the emotions they want to reverberate throughout the organization. By using emotional contagion, a high EI leader can raise a workplace's collective EI, and a low EI leader can radiate deep and broad dysfunction.

A leader's emotional contagion is hardly a new concept. In a 1920 letter, George C. Marshall noted that units led by those prone to negative emotions, or "calamity howlers," were "quickly infected with the same spirit and grew ineffective unless a more suitable commander was given charge."[65] More recently, Chip Conley, founder of the hotel chain Joie de Vivre and currently head of Global Hospitality and Strategy for Airbnb, calls CEOs "chief emotion officers" because they act as "emotional thermostats" for the organization and its clients.[66]

Emotions are so contagious, that, as one study demonstrated, when two people are sitting silently in a room, one person will transmit his or her emotion to the other person within two minutes. The person whose emotions are transmitted is either the one who is more expressive emotionally or, importantly for our purposes, the one who is more powerful.[67]

Here is the challenge for our general counsel, managing partners, and executive committee members—managing themselves well enough to express those emotions that will be most productive when amplified throughout their workplaces.[68]

What is the best mood for a leader to project? While positive feelings are not always appropriate, a leader who can project a positive mood enhances the mood and well-being of the group or organization, which, as has been pointed out, in turn produces a number of positives, like increases in performance, higher retention, and reduced conflict.[69] As Goleman posits, "The fundamental task of leaders is to prime good feeling in those they lead . . . a reservoir of positivity that frees the best in people."[70]

Dr. Kahneman has noted that each of our over 20,000 experiences a day is filed internally as either negative or positive, and we generally have a bias toward considering them negative, which lawyers are especially prone to.[71] Simply achieving a higher ratio of positive emotions in an organization can make "a quantum leap in well-being, with significantly greater job satisfaction, life satisfaction, relationships, work effectiveness, and other payoffs." For example, as mentioned before, doctors who are optimistic and in a good mood reach the right diagnosis 19 percent faster than doctors who are in an unhappy mood.[72]

The power of what we hear and see in influencing our own emotions was demonstrated when Facebook randomly altered the news feeds of 689,003 Facebook users by subtracting either happy or sad words. Those users were then found to reflect in their own posts fewer happy or sad words in accordance with how their news feeds had been altered.[73] Similarly, in an experiment at Yale University, a group of volunteers played the role of managers who worked together to allocate bonuses. A planted actor always spoke first, projecting one of four emotional states: active cheerfulness, calm warmth, passive sadness, and irritable hostility.[74] The actor infected the entire group with the emotion he or she projected, and the two positive emotions led both groups to improved cooperation, fairness, and overall better performance.[75]

One way for leaders to promote more positive feelings is by making more positive comments than negative ones, with some researchers proposing an ideal ratio in a business context of as many as six positive comments to each negative one.[76] Positive comments are typically far outweighed by the negative ones in our legal workplaces, and that same negativity impedes changing those engrained habits: "[I]ncreasing the Positivity Ratio in a law firm would produce hugely welcome and beneficial effects . . . greater collegiality, collaboration, and accountability, as well as better client service. But the very reason that such an approach is needed—i.e., the excessive skepticism, negativity and pessimism—may be the very reason that such an approach would never be accepted."[77]

One managing partner proved the advantage of using positive comments. He personally spoke to lawyers who elected to leave or who were terminated, and whatever the reason for their departure, he was known for his skill in making them feel good about the firm. When asked his secret, he said he always praised the person's contributions, encouraged his or her future endeavors, and offered to do whatever he could to make their transition easier, including giving references and contacting potential employers. He was rewarded by those he said good-bye to, regardless of their reasons for leaving, by their maintaining good relationships with the firm, giving testimonials to possible recruits, making client referrals or becoming clients, and sometimes even returning.[78]

What do you do if you, as a lawyer leader, really don't feel all that positive? Faking emotions produces tremendous stress on the part of the faker and reduces his or her career satisfaction.[79] Nonetheless, the favorable impact of a manager's positive emotions on colleagues, even those faked, appears to persist. One researcher attests to "how important it is that managers 'perform' or put on a public emotional show, even if they don't feel like it."[80]

Leaders who can regulate their emotional expressions so as to project a positive mood and include positive feedback, regardless of whether they are personally having a bad day and despite the ups and downs all organizations are subject to, can raise the moods and, ultimately, the performance of their charges.[81]

The managing partner of a mid-country, midsized regional law firm asked that I conduct a review to determine which departments were lagging in morale and productivity. It became apparent that he considered one department to be the prime candidate—"foregone conclusions" are what consultants are sometimes directed toward. Our corroborating opinion gives that conclusion the sheen of objectivity.

After interviewing representatives, junior and senior, of all departments, I called the managing partner and asked him to take me off the speakerphone and close his door. What I had found was that virtually everyone I interviewed had indeed reported the low morale that he had sensed, but they had also alluded to the affair the managing partner was having with a junior partner in his department. Lawyers high and low felt he unfairly gave her priority in case assignments and that he and the head of the department who he thought was causing low morale and productivity were rivals.

Of course, like most workplaces, law firms can be hotbeds of scandal. But this managing partner, blinded by something that looked to me to be mostly low EI, neither understood how his attitudes and actions were likely to be or were being received emotionally, nor was he able to detect that it was his actions that were the source of the low morale and productivity he saw.

START BY DEVELOPING EMOTIONAL INTELLIGENCE AT THE TOP

- Give leaders, who may exhibit the lowest emotional intelligence in the organization, feedback from assessments, upward and cross-reviews, and coaching to enhance their emotional intelligence, particularly their self-awareness, so as to better manage lawyers.
- Invest in emotional intelligence–denominated leadership training.
- Embrace women leaders.
- Use emotional contagion as a tool to spread positive, productive feelings throughout the organization.

Step 2: Hire Emotionally Intelligent Professionals

> *A firm is only as good as its people, and hiring the right people is both important and difficult. A bad hire drains a small firm financially and emotionally, and impedes its growth.*[82]
>
> —Tom Wallerstein, commercial litigator and partner in Venable's Litigation Group

> *Few organizations use less discipline, structure and intelligence in their hiring process than law firms.*[83]
>
> —Mark Levin, lawyer and management consultant, *The Right Profile*

Finding the best recruits, particularly those who can be the highest performers at the leadership level, is a dilemma faced by workplaces everywhere. *Harvard Business Review* reports that only 15 percent of companies in the United States and Asia and 30 percent of companies in Europe can fill leadership positions, so high is the demand compared with how few are up to the job.[84]

Considering the demonstrable link between emotional competencies and performance[85] and the finding that personal evaluations are more predictive as the job becomes more complex,[86] a majority of companies are screening recruits for these attributes.[87] AT&T was the first (in 1956) in the private sector to measure social and emotional competencies.[88] Daniel Goleman reports that "more than two-thirds of major businesses apply some aspect of emotional intelligence in their recruiting, in promotions and specifically in leadership development,"[89] including companies as diverse as Southwest Airlines, Apple, Google, FedEx, Ritz-Carlton, Xerox, and Goldman Sachs, which is developing its own software to measure EI and other factors.[90] Organizations using these assessments "have reduced turnover as much as 70 percent, while increasing productivity as much as 140 percent and bottom-line profitability as much as 130 percent."[91]

Legal workplaces can become more emotionally intelligent if they:

Recalibrate Hiring Practices
Screen for Emotional Intelligence and Other Competencies

Recalibrate Hiring Practices

In the legal recruiting environment, several circumstances have made the identification of applicant lawyers who are likely to succeed dramatically more difficult—and more compelling—than in the past, including the following:

The Pool of Traditionally Qualified Candidates Is Shrinking
Current Hiring Practices Are Expensive
Current Hiring Practices Result in Poor Hires
Applicants Are Dissatisfied

The Pool of Traditionally Qualified Candidates Is Shrinking. The number of applicants to law schools has been dropping dramatically, resulting in 2015 in "[f]ewer people . . . applying to law school than at any point in the past decade and a half."[92] This decline is remarkable since applications to law school traditionally rise during recessions. The applicants from Ivy League undergraduate schools have declined even faster than those from other schools, approaching 50 percent as of 2016.[93] The number of those entering law school, however, while the smallest class of students since the 1970s, is roughly the same as it was fifteen years ago.

Many of those with the highest LSAT scores are forgoing law school.[94] To meet their revenue goals, law schools are lowering their application standards, in some cases not even requiring LSAT scores, resulting in less impressive resumes, even at the best law schools, such as Harvard.[95] Applications to Harvard Law School, for example, dropped by 27 percent between 2009 and 2012, and the percentage of applicants admitted went up 42 percent.[96]

In addition, there is evidence that many of those going to law school now are no longer interested in a traditional law career after they graduate. A 2013 Kaplan Test Prep Survey found 50 percent of pre-law students plan to use their law degree in a nontraditional legal job.[97] Further, graduates from the best law schools are the lawyers least likely to stay in their legal jobs for the long term: "respondents with the most elite credentials—graduates of top law schools working in the most prestigious settings—are the least satisfied with their decision to become a lawyer."[98]

So the pool of new law graduates who are looking for and likely to stay in traditional legal jobs is significantly smaller and less accomplished by historical measures—undergraduate grade point averages and LSAT scores—than it has been in the past. Even though law firms are hiring fewer new lawyers than they did back in the heyday of growth, firms don't have much room for those lawyers they do hire to flame out, trade up, or simply decide the practice of law is not for them, all of which historically occur at high rates.[99] Further, more diverse applicants in the applicant pool challenge recruiters to both avoid discriminatory biases in selections and make valid choices among candidates with backgrounds they are less familiar with.[100]

Current Hiring Practices Are Expensive. Current hiring approaches are expensive in terms of recruiter time and lost potential earnings, the lost investment in hires who don't work out, and the lower profitability of poorer performers. The profit difference between a solid "A" associate and a "C–" one is projected to range from $100,000 to $250,000 per associate each year.[101] Laterals, about whom we know more and therefore should hire more successfully,[102] are even more expensive to hire and significantly more costly since they are less likely to stay in the long run,[103] and firms rarely break even financially on those who stay.[104] One estimate is that "it costs the legal industry roughly $9.1 billion annually for the turnover in just the 400 largest firms in the United States . . . more than double the annual salaries of all NFL players combined."[105]

Current Hiring Practices Result in Poor Hires. Not only is the current approach expensive, it is not effective in choosing the best candidates. An extensive review of the data concluded that "the current most popular hiring tool—the one-on-one interview—ranks only slightly above a coin-toss . . . Simply hiring someone because of a shared favorite sports team works just as well."[106] It also perpetuates cultural and personal biases, whether conscious or implicit. Fake resumes of high-standing second-tier law school students applying for BigLaw summer associate positions resulted overwhelmingly with offers for those who were male and higher-class socioeconomically—sailing and polo were the keys.[107]

Firms that look primarily to LSAT scores, grades, and class rank are destined to realize only mixed results. As tempting as those metrics are to rely on because of the ease of ascertaining them and the sheen of objectivity,[108] that data have been shown repeatedly not to correlate with success in law practice.[109] Even armed with information about currently practicing lateral candidates, firms persist in making poor hires and risking catastrophe, as illustrated by the series of firm collapses—Howrey, Dewey, and Bingham McCutchen—on the heels of stunning lateral growth.[110]

Applicants Are Dissatisfied. Recruits aren't singing the praises of the current recruitment process, either. In an article entitled, "Is This Any Way to Recruit Associates?" applicants to US law firms—specifically those from elite schools—complained about the superficial and repetitive nature of the traditional interviewing process: rounds of "short interviews, shallow questions and sheaves of boilerplate marketing materials."[111]

These circumstances amount to a mandate for change in how and whom we hire.[112] To change the odds in favor of hiring successful practitioners, we must overcome the statistical likelihood of hiring lawyers with low EI by, as Deloitte's 2016 legal industry report recommended, consciously "looking for lawyers who are not just technically competent, but who have a broader skill set."[113]

Screen for Emotional Intelligence and Other Competencies

Often legal workplaces have only a limited understanding of what the qualities for success in their practices are.[114] David Van Zandt, formerly Dean of Northwestern University School of Law, entreats law firms to develop a more nuanced model for selecting recruits. "I've long advocated that firms really need to look at their data . . . and identify the characteristics that they're looking for in their candidates," rather than "just go out and throw a wide net."[115]

Screening for EI and other competencies using assessments and other methods would be a formidable adjunct to achieving firms' retention and success objectives more cost effectively,[116] but few US firms have done so. The objections most frequently posed are not likely to offset the potential gains.

Use Emotional Intelligence and Other Competency Assessments. It has been estimated that 80 percent of the Fortune 500 and 89 percent of the Fortune 100 companies use EI assessments or other EI-sensitive processes in hiring.[117] Other professional services firms in the United States—like McKinsey & Co., Ernst & Young, and PwC—make use of various assessment data, which they report leads to higher acceptance rates and lower turnover.[118] The healthcare field is using evaluations of EI for selection into medical school and residencies, and to guide postselection development, and practitioners are urging their broader use.[119]

British law firms have incorporated assessments into hiring for years. Some require pre-interview online assessments.[120] Others invite twelve to twenty applicants at a time to attend "assessment days," typically involving "two 45-minute interviews (one with a case study component), an hour-long critical reasoning test, and a group negotiation exercise," with aptitude tests being the newest addition. Some firms also ask for a five-minute client pitch or written response to a client complaint.[121]

In the United States, there is only limited use of personal attribute evaluations for legal settings. Less than 5 percent of the largest 250 law firms in the country and 10 percent of midsize firms are estimated to use assessments of any sort in hiring, and "none uses instruments that are purpose-built for the legal profession."[122] Law schools often include style assessments in their repertoire of tools for assisting students in making career decisions (though not for purposes of admission), as do attorney out-placement firms.[123] Corporate law departments may use assessment data for hiring or development because their corporations successfully use them in other departments, but they are usually not customized for lawyers.[124]

Scholars and commentators have long advocated for the use of assessments in the selection and development of legal professionals.[125] As a white paper on lawyer hiring concluded, "personality assessments provide invaluable information to incorporate into the best possible recruitment and development decisions."[126] Consultant Bruce MacEwen notes, "Every other industry looks at tests. Are we saying that we lawyers are right and the rest of the world is wrong?"[127]

Bill Henderson, a law professor at Indiana Law School and the chief strategy officer for Lawyer Metrics, considers using interviews and assessments to evaluate candidates on the success attributes a firm is looking for several times more effective than what firms usually do. He finds the assessment piece critical: "There is simply no other effective way to screen."[128]

A Yale Law School professor suggests firms use traditional screening methods like grades to identify the initial pool of candidates, but then pay applicants who take a performance-based assessment, which will sort out those interested enough in the job to take the assessment and find undervalued students—"powerhouses who happen to interview poorly."[129] He believes competitive pressures would encourage most students to take the test, just as nearly all top college-football prospects voluntarily attend the diagnostic "Combine" where the NFL measures personal attributes that correlate with success as a football player.

Data from assessments, which are easily administered and take little time,[130] are valuable after hiring as well—to both the workplace and the individual lawyers.[131] From the perspective of the workplace, this information can bring an early understanding of what talents new hires are bringing to their job and how and where they are likely to work best. It can inform firm and department structure, committee and team composition, and succession and growth strategies, and produce a better understanding of the organizational dynamics at work and how to improve them.[132] These are all results that legal workplaces are no less in need of than the many businesses using assessment data for these purposes.

From the individual lawyer's perspective, we do them a disservice if we hire those who are unlikely to have the emotional stamina and skills not only to cope with a highly stressful environment with little room for error, but also to flourish. Insights into their strengths and challenges point lawyers to where their attention should go and can be a baseline for strategies for development and against which to clock improvements throughout their careers.[133]

Other Methods to Screen for Emotional Intelligence. Without an assessment, an applicant's emotional intelligence and other personal attributes can be much more difficult to determine, but several other approaches can provide information.

Behavioral or competence interviewing, or asking questions to ascertain certain competencies, is one of the tools corporations often use. Accenture, a consulting firm, has used behavioral interviews in hiring for more than a decade.[134] CareerBuilder's 2,600 hiring managers identify high EI applicants by asking questions that help the recruiters evaluate their ability to admit to and learn from mistakes, keep emotions in check, have thoughtful discussions on tough issues, listen as much or more than they talk, take criticism well, and show grace under pressure.[135]

Medical schools also use behavioral interviews, asking, for example, about specific quandaries or important events in the applicants' lives and what they learned from each situation to see "how the students articulated the way in which they reason, problem-solve and use self-awareness to interact effectively with others, to communicate empathy and to manage relationships."[136] A few law firms are employing a similar technique.[137] Emotion-related questions about applicants' greatest challenges, their experiences working in teams, through conflicts and complicated issues, the successes of which they are most proud, the undertakings that bring them the most satisfaction, and their values and aspirations would be useful in evaluating lawyer applicants.

Other possible evaluation vehicles include giving applicants critical reasoning tests and negotiation exercises, asking them to perform a case study on the spot, to respond to real-life scenarios, to present a short client pitch, and to draft a letter in response to a client's complaint.[138]

Objections. Lawyers usually first point to the same objections that early critics raised about EI generally and that have been summarily disposed of: EI is a fad,[139] the research produces conflicting results, and the assessments are ineffective[140] and can be gamed.[141] Even those who acknowledge the compelling conclusion of EI research sometimes question "pigeon-holing," fear assessments "will turn off associates," or object that "we'll be sued."

The point of assessment data is not to pigeonhole but to inform[142]: Jack Mayer, one of the original EI theorists, noted the impossibility of efficiently and accurately determining one's own or others' personal attributes without employing assessments.[143] The pigeonholing apprehension can be assuaged with reassurance: there are no "right" or "wrong" answers, no diagnosis or judgments are being made about anyone's mental health, data can change over time, and the assessments "are as much to ensure the applicant's success as to benefit the firm."[144]

Law firms may not be availing themselves of these tools, because as, prior to its merger with Dentons, McKenna Long & Aldridge's then head of recruitment and development said, "they are concerned with stigma—what will [candidates] think of us? They don't want to be different. We now have a market where firms could be more creative [about hiring], but lawyers don't thrive on change"[145]—textbook responses by the pessimistic and risk averse. Yet, as both consultant Dr. Larry Richard and I have found, "In actual practice, in those firms where we've used it, none of the dreaded consequences have come to pass."[146] As one firm said about their use: "The feedback from candidates has been overwhelmingly positive. They appreciate that we have put so much effort into the interview process to ensure a solid fit on both sides of the equation,"[147] a reaction that is likely to become more widespread among metric-loving Millennials.[148]

"'A lot of aspirational students quite like being tested,' says Lynn Johansen, head of trainee recruitment at Clifford Chance. 'I suggested a lighter process once for those who had done internships, but students said [they] would worry [that they] were not being taken seriously.'"[149] McKinsey & Co. reports that, rather than preferring a less extensive selection process, "Law students who go through [McKinsey's] interviews find them much more intellectually challenging," according to a partner there. "They see a value to that—to showing just what intellectually talented people they are."[150]

The more serious objection that often arises from lawyers, being lawyers, is the possibility of discrimination under Title VII of the Americans with Disabilities Act (ADA). Of course, no one is seriously advocating that personal assessments be the sole basis of hiring. Pre-hiring assessments of any sort must measure variables demonstrably linked to job performance without even unintentional discrimination against a protected class. The Equal Employment Opportunity Commission (EEOC) has approved a strategic enforcement plan for 2012–2016 that gives claims of systemic discrimination in recruitment and hiring, including pre-employment tests, high enforcement priority.[151] But so far legal challenges are relatively rare—only a reported 161 complaints out of 100,000 in 2011 related to testing—and the few that went to trial primarily sharpened the point of the importance of job relatedness, a standard that a well-prepared assessment should be able to meet.[152]

Finally, lawyers make the "we are unique" objection, claiming that these assessments don't provide relevant information because what we lawyers do is so special, so complex. The research, however, comes to the opposite conclusion. Emotional intelligence is even more relevant in a high managerial work demands (MWD) context—described as "challenging"; involving the "management of diverse individuals, functions, and lines of business"; "working with and through significant stakeholders"; and being accompanied by "stress and intense emotions"—because of "the cue rich environment of a high MWD job context."[153] Lawyers, as high MWD workers, are more dependent, not less, on EI skills to succeed. Also, in our high-pressure environments, lawyers with greater EI skills are better able to selectively distance themselves from unproductive emotions.[154] So measuring EI is highly relevant to assessing a lawyer's likely success.

As Daniel Goleman says, "once you're in a high-IQ position, intellect loses its power to determine who will emerge as a productive employee or an effective leader. For that, how you handle yourself and your relationships—in other words, the emotional intelligence skill set—matters more than your IQ."[155]

Yet for the most part, law firms persist in their sole reliance on their long-standing—many would say outdated—hiring processes. Whatever one thinks of using assessments and other techniques, the old system—hiring based on academic achievement and episodic interview impressions—produces wild variations in the quality of hires and is demonstrably less reliable than evaluations targeted to a success factor like emotional intelligence.

Aric Press, former publisher of the *American Lawyer,* is one of those making the plea for legal organizations to use assessments. In his article "Time for The Am Law 200 to Embrace Testing for Talent?" he summarizes the current situation: "[A]t most major firms testing and even coaching are tightly held, rarely used techniques . . . This all seems odd, given how important law firm talent is at the moment. Firms now hire fewer new associates than they once did; their margin for error has shrunk. At the same time, lateral partner acquisitions continue to grow, but no one thinks the success ratio has improved. Why don't more firms use these testing techniques as a way to improve their odds? . . . all of this pushes lawyers a bit out of their comfort zones. But a new era of developing human capital at law firms doesn't end with tiptoeing toward testing regimens."[156]

At a law firm cocktail party I attended, the piped-in music was interrupted by a young male voice who recounted how he had just been hired as an associate by this premier Texas law firm, even though he had never finished college or gone to law school. His father, whose boat he worked on, was a lawyer, and he could play a decent game of golf, he said, but his only work experience was bartending, as he was doing that night. Everyone's eyes turned to the bartender, who was holding a microphone. One of the senior lawyers had encouraged the young man to apply with a bogus resume to test the firm's hiring process. Needless to say, that lawyer soon started his own—ultimately quite successful—law practice.

HIRE EMOTIONALLY INTELLIGENT LAWYERS

More targeted recruiting is compelling because of a shrinking pool of highly qualified candidates who want to engage in a traditional law practice, the high cost of traditional recruiting methods, and the failure to identify the most successful candidates.

Lawyers should join the great majority of other businesses in using emotional intelligence assessments and emotional intelligence–sensitive evaluations like behavioral interviewing to hire for emotional intelligence and other success attributes appropriate to the demands of legal practice, an approach that:

- is more cost effective;
- produces better candidates;
- is better received by applicants;
- attracts Millennials, who appreciate metrics; and
- forges a better fit over the long run for both the individual and the organization.

Those firms that have used assessments have not felt stigmatized or had recruits resist taking them.

Assessments should not be the sole criteria for hiring, must measure variables demonstrably linked to job performance, and must not discriminate against protected classes.

Step 3: Develop Emotional Intelligence

> *There is a science of training that shows there is a right way and a wrong way to design, deliver, and implement a training program . . . Done well, training and development can have a significant impact on organizations' bottom line.*[157]
>
> —Eduardo Salas, psychology professor and researcher, Rice University

While lawyers identify "people issues" as the area of their organization they would most like to improve, many seem genuinely befuddled about what to do.[158] Well-designed professional development initiatives to improve emotional intelligence that use assessment data, training, coaching, performance and other reviews, and rewards and incentives can greatly improve law firm and law department functioning.[159]

In 2005, FedEx added a pilot EI piece to the curriculum at its state-of-the-art leadership university located in Memphis, Tennessee, to strengthen abilities critical to "a more careful, collaborative decision-making process to achieve sustainable success . . . in an extremely faced-paced, task-focused environment."[160] All new managers at FedEx Express—the urgent delivery arm of FedEx—participated in a five-day EI-based course with six-months of follow-up coaching.

When I recommend to lawyers professional development that focuses on emotions, I often get an immediate pushback, much like what came initially from FedEx: "The senior vice president scoffed . . . 'We don't want any emotional crying and stuff at work,'" and the human resources (HR) director, a "productivity guy," said he felt the same when he first heard about EI training: "I didn't want to hear the word emotion. I thought it was a lot of work and a lot of conversations that didn't need to be happening."[161]

But not long after the training took place, FedEx supervisors were emailing HR to find out what accounted for the positive changes they were seeing. Greater emotional intelligence correlated with "dramatic improvements in the particular outcomes FedEx was tracking . . . major improvements were made by 72% of participants in decision making, by 60% in quality of life, and by

58% in influence."[162] The results were so dramatic, FedEx instituted a $1.2 million EI training program around the globe, engaging over 100 facilitators to administer assessments and provide coaching.[163]

Providing a robust development program in universally useful EI skills will not only improve individual, team, and organizational performance but will also give firms access to a wider recruiting pool and produce a more loyal workforce.[164] Professional development is one of the most attractive benefits a legal workplace can offer to Gen Xers and Millennials, and its availability is a top reason they give for staying with an employer and for maintaining a relationship even after they leave.[165] Given that, in the *American Lawyer's* 2016 Midlevel Associate Survey, law firms got some of the lowest grades overall for training and development, firms that deliver on a robust program will have a recruiting and retention edge.[166]

Yet, as a Huron Legal Consulting Group report acknowledges, "Our experience is that few law firms or law departments invest the time and effort to develop higher levels of EI . . . Given the importance of these skills—and the critical impact on key relationships, morale and productivity—this greatly surprises us . . . We strongly recommend that senior lawyers invest as much time and effort into working on emotional intelligence skills and the so-called 'soft' skills as they do on other, technical, so-called 'hard' skills. In our experience, it is the soft skills that make the real difference leading to increased productivity, stronger leadership and higher levels of organizational impact and influence."[167]

All development efforts profit from EI assessment or other evaluation data, and require the willingness of participants to devote time and effort to the process.[168] To get buy-in, these programs must be perceived as a route to leadership, and not a punishment or remedial program for weakness, so there should be recognition for participation and rewards for progress. The conundrum is that those with higher EI are better equipped to make real improvements, while those with low EI, who are most in need of development and who have demonstrated to be the biggest gainers, are less likely to embrace it because of their sensitivity to criticism, insecurity, and worries about failure, the very attributes that these programs try to address.[169]

To develop emotional intelligence, legal workplaces can:

Institute EI Training Programs
Offer Coaching, Mentoring, and Other Feedback
Compensate, Reward, and Promote Emotional Intelligence

Institute Emotional Intelligence Training Programs

True education [lives in the] quickening of imagination, the widening of sympathy, the training of emotion.[170]

—Mary Parker Follett, 19th-century organizational theorist and author

Whereas IQ is very hard to change, EQ can increase with deliberate practice and training.[171]

—Dr. Tomas Chamorro-Premuzic, CEO of Hogan Assessment Systems, Professor of Business Psychology at University College London, and faculty member at Columbia University

To succeed on a sustained basis, today's lawyer needs to develop EI skills. Savvy law firm leaders recognize this, yet few law firms have made a commitment to teach these skills to their lawyers.[172]

—Dr. Larry Richard, consultant, "The Psychologically Savvy Leader"

Training is one of the best mechanisms to help identify and start on the path of realizing the benefits that emotional intelligence brings to lawyering.[173] Because of the brain's plasticity, the repetition of preferred responses that can be learned in a training environment can literally reshape the brain's pathways to make us emotionally smarter.[174]

EI training consists of instruction that raises awareness cognitively in the short run and also helps identify specific ways to exercise preferred responses over time. Even relatively short periods of in-class training—a single day,[175] 15 hours,[176] and 18 hours[177]—have been conclusively demonstrated to help raise EI and produce significant benefits professionally and personally. These results are especially encouraging because often those who begin the training with the lowest EI scores are the ones who make the most progress.[178]

The medical profession has registered notable success using EI training both in medical schools[179] and hospitals.[180] The Cleveland Clinic called training it provided in eight of its hospitals to help doctors create rapport, elicit views, and demonstrate empathy "transformative."[181] Training for EI has produced positive results in the educational setting also.[182] A meta-analysis found that among EI-trained grade-school students, positive behavior increased, negative behavior went down, and academic achievement scores jumped.[183] Further up the academic chain, at Case Western University's Weatherhead School of Management, in-depth EI assessments followed by seven weeks of training produced improvements in EI-related competencies in full-time students an average of 71 percent and 81 percent in part-time students, improvements retained even after five to seven years.[184]

In the corporate realm, a meta-analysis of many workplace EI training programs found an average improvement in relationship skills of 50 percent,[185] with even relatively short programs achieving increases in performance, revenues, stress management, and well-being.[186]

Although accounting firms years ago instituted formal EI trainings, few if any law firms have done so.[187] Business development, client management, and stress management courses offered in some legal workplaces may touch on aspects of EI, but these programs could benefit significantly from a more comprehensive approach, including the use of assessment data.[188]

Despite widespread evidence of the usefulness of EI trainings, both in person and online, there is no standard format and limited offerings.[189] Determining which program is best for your workplace requires consultation with a training expert and often a degree of customization based on the profile of your participants and your organizational goals.

The Appendix reviews a few training resources and training guidelines suggested by various authorities. Those interested in in-person or online emotional intelligence training, workshops, or coaching designed specifically for lawyers should contact Law People Management, LLC.

Because of our personal attributes, lawyers are particularly well-positioned to benefit from EI development. As psychology professor Seligman points out, "Given the degree of negative emotion and awful events that lawyers deal with daily, I can think of no other profession that would benefit more from resilience training," for example.[190]

Of course, those very attributes—including low resilience, high pessimism, and high skepticism—also make persuading lawyers to engage in "soft skills" training such a hard sell,[191] even when leaders recognize the necessity of doing so.[192] The goal can sound squishy and sentimental, without enough demonstrably immediate benefit. In addition, implementing a sustained training program indisputably takes attorneys' time and attention away from billable hours at a definite short-term cost.[193]

For those workplaces that step up to an investment in EI training, there are several factors that are important in making it successful. While the in-class portion of training may be relatively short, to change habits and behaviors that have formed over many years, an effective program still requires a relatively high commitment of time and effort by both the workplace and the individual during the training itself and afterward. Unlike learning legal principles, "you can't just sit in a lecture or read a book *about* emotional intelligence and then expect to be able to behave in a more emotionally intelligent way."[194]

The workplace needs to take the time to organize the program up front—identify participants, administer assessments, establish goals—and then deliver the training and provide support.[195] Before training starts, the organization should promote throughout the workplace its confidence in EI and the value of developing it, and leaders should lead by example by participating themselves. Throughout the training, participants should be lauded and encouraged to continue. Afterward, graduates should be publicly recognized and then supported by having opportunities to practice their new skills, such as serving on committees, which can be followed with evaluations and feedback on how they are performing and then encouragement to rededicate themselves to further improvement.[196] This cannot be a one-time event with little follow-up.[197]

Short of full-blown EI training, workplaces can put their toe in the EI training waters by offering stress management or mindfulness training.

Stress Management Training. In the CareerBuilder survey mentioned earlier, 71 percent of employers gave as their number one reason for preferring the emotionally intelligent that they are "more likely to stay calm under pressure"—that is, they are better able to manage stress.[198]

Stress management training sessions provided in the workplace, even as limited as they typically are, have repeatedly been found to be effective,[199] with one meta-analysis quantifying an average 35 percent reduction in stress.[200] They improve not only levels of stress, but also participants' awareness of stress,[201] and their ability to speed up and improve their recovery from the debilitating effects of stress.[202] And since most of these programs work by building emotional awareness and emotional regulation skills,[203] they can be an initial step toward raising overall EI.

Mindfulness Training. Legal workplaces should offer or encourage meditation to help cultivate mindfulness—one of the most well-documented mechanisms for attaining greater emotional intelligence, dealing with stress and producing more positive feelings.[204] Essentially, mindfulness allows us to step back and give our emotions and bodies a short vacation from the toll that stress and anxiety take, so we can return to our work refreshed and rejuvenated. It also sharpens our abilities to recognize emotions we had been inattentive to and to regulate our emotions by being able to interrupt our habitual responses and choose more productive ones.

A standard twenty minutes of meditation a day produces actual physical changes in the amygdala (the emotion center in the brain) that "correlate with less depression and more happiness."[205] Those who are more mindful during the day have more stable emotions, manage their mood and behavior better, and sleep more soundly (a critical ingredient for positive changes in brain plasticity).[206]

Mindfulness may also improve "moral discernment," and therefore ethical behavior, and it continues to confer these benefits even when we are not in a meditative state.[207]

Businesses are buying in to the "mindfulness revolution," as the February 2014 *Time* magazine cover article calls it. Aetna, McKinsey & Co., Apple, Twitter, General Mills, and Target all have instituted mindfulness programs at their workplaces.[208] A principal at McKinsey attributes to his meditation practice his ability to deal with "email addiction," cope with disappointment, and avoid becoming too insular.[209] Hospitals have also instituted mindfulness training to reduce physician stress and burnout.[210]

An engineer by background, Google's Chade-Meng Tan developed a seven-week mindfulness-based EI corporate training program outlined in his bestseller, *Search Inside Yourself: The Unexpected Path to Achieving Success, Happiness (and World Peace),* which quickly produced benefits like reductions in depression and anxiety, better stress management, more positive emotions, and even lower blood pressure.[211] Thousands participated in the program willingly every year because, Tan says, "Everybody already knows, emotional intelligence is good for my career, it's good for my team, it's good for my profits."[212] Johanna Sistek, a trademark lawyer at Google, says the emotional skills she refined in the class help her focus despite a "fire hose" of professional demands.[213]

Google's Tan also points to cultivating mindful compassion, a type of mindfulness, as "good for success and profits," citing LinkedIn CEO Jeff Weiner as a leading proponent of compassionate management.[214]

It's hardly necessary to point out that compassion is not one of the personal characteristics legal workplaces are usually gunning for, and, regardless of compelling research, few lawyers may aspire to that. But having compassion—the ability to care emotionally for ourselves and our own—while still being able to use our emotions in other contexts to compete and succeed is a valuable exercise of emotional intelligence.

Charles Halpern, former director of the Berkeley Initiative for Mindfulness in Law, lays out his vision: "more complete integration of mindfulness into law practice and legal education could have important consequences for the way in which law is practiced, legal institutions function and legal doctrines evolve. Such changes could help us collectively deal with the profound challenges of the 21st century. It is hard to see how we will meet those challenges successfully without moving legal institutions in the direction of mindfulness and empathy."[215]

Offer Coaching, Mentoring, and Other Feedback

> *To fulfil the expectations of millennials in particular, law firms need to become much more involved in coaching and mentoring than most are today.*[216]
>
> —Jane DiRenzo Pigott, Managing Director of R3 Group

> *[I]t is remarkable how many smart, highly motivated, and apparently responsible people rarely pause to contemplate their own behaviors . . . The most important aspect of effective EQ-coaching is giving people accurate feedback.*[217]
>
> —Dr. Tomas Chamorro-Premuzic, CEO of Hogan Assessment Systems, Professor of Business Psychology at University College London, and faculty member at Columbia University

Feedback from (1) coaches and mentors, (2) performance and other internal reviews, and (3) client reviews, whether in addition to or in lieu of assessments and training, can be instrumental in helping raise emotional intelligence.

Coaching/Mentoring. Coaching helps professionals better understand on an ongoing basis how they personally are perceived by others and what specific things they can do to improve or take advantage of that perception. A large-scale meta-analysis entitled "Effectiveness of Training in Organizations: Design and Evaluation Features" found that coaching was one of the most efficacious interventions and could "easily achieve improvements of 25%," with "average short-term improvements in interpersonal skills of 50%."[218] An organization-wide coaching program can significantly raise performance,[219] retention, and loyalty.[220]

Coaching has exploded as a profession, serving businesses globally. A study of companies with more than 1,000 employees found 52 percent had implemented coaching programs and another 37 percent had plans to do so.[221] Medical schools and hospitals use personal coaching both as an adjunct to EI training and a standalone tool to optimize the patient/doctor relationship and physician health.[222] Many businesses also incorporate coaching into their EI training programs,[223] and accounting firms provide different types of coaching, with some offering on-call telephonic or digital coaching.[224]

EI training programs are most effective, regardless of the industry, if they are followed up or paired with coaching. A sports organization that coupled three sessions of assessment-tailored EI workshops, totaling only eight hours, with six coaching sessions had what the manager described as "a massive impact upon how effective we are as an organization."[225]

A cost- and time-efficient approach to individual coaching is to set up coaching circles of small groups, ideally a team, that meet periodically as a group and possibly also individually.[226] The most important step, often neglected, is to make periodic evaluations of the program's effectiveness.[227]

In legal workplaces, the most common approach to one-on-one development is to encourage mentoring. Mentoring is usually by seasoned attorneys who provide advice and support to younger ones, either in a structured program involving some mentor training, periodic check-ins, and progress reports, or more informally simply in occasional conversations at lunch. Sometimes mentors are assigned; other times "chemistry" is left to couple the participants, with either the mentor or the mentee charged with making the approach.

Mentoring programs can produce positive results, but professional coaches have proven much more effective in developing EI skills. For starters, lawyers inside our workplaces are often not the best source of mentoring advice in the interpersonal arena, and most legal workplaces are not well equipped to identify those who are: mentoring in these areas cannot simply be delegated to the nonequity partner who doesn't have enough to do. Then, the core skill of mentoring—making the unwanted but constructive observation—may be a hard move for a lawyer mentor. Out of avoidance or acute awareness of how difficult this message is to hear, many lawyers avoid delivering it or, at the other extreme, appear to enjoy being brutally negative. Neither promotes successful mentoring.

Those who do mentor have a critical opportunity to use more positive feedback: "Only positive feedback can motivate people to continue doing what they're doing well, and do it with more vigor, determination, and creativity."[228] Or to quote one New York City BigLaw associate, "It's not even a question that when I like someone personally, I want to impress them more."[229] Research also shows that tone and body language are more memorable than the actual words spoken—a message with negative content delivered in a warm, positive way will be recalled as positive.[230] But lawyers often do not come naturally to a positive approach, making their mentoring less successful, or even counterproductive.

There are other disincentives to in-house mentoring. Firms that do not include mentoring toward minimum billable hours don't "pay" mentors, whether they do it well or not. Mentors may also see little incentive to invest in someone they consider likely to leave anyway. Unless mentoring programs are well structured, with periodic mentor training, consistency across the organization, and monitored follow-up, they can quickly devolve into "'call me if you need anything' approaches that create too much of a burden on junior lawyers."[231] And with increasing diversity, lawyers unschooled in coaching who mentor across age, gender, and racial and sexual orientation differences may well pose a risk for both the mentor and the firm. In short, "law firms cannot rely on their partners to invest appropriately and strategically in the associates they should seek to retain."[232]

Internal Reviews. Information from well-devised performance reviews that include a review of EI skills can be a valuable feedback supplement, but typical performance evaluations alone are not likely to be frequent, accurate, and insightful enough to move a lawyer's or, taken together, a firm's EI forward. Self-evaluations are also notoriously deficient.[233]

As discussed regarding leaders, few legal workplaces use upward or peer reviews to provide feedback. There are differing opinions about their value and the best way to design and use reviews,[234] but upward reviews offer useful information, especially to senior lawyers,[235] and give management important insight into those being considered for partnership or promotion,[236] including a method to gauge collaboration skills.[237] Peer reviews understandably scare some organizations, especially those that have problems handling aggressive, argumentative conflict, but these appraisals are useful toward many ends and can be at the crux of identifying peacemakers and resolving conflicts before they become cancerous. The point is to use workplace processes, both formal and informal, to increase the frequency and relevance of feedback.[238]

Client Feedback. Both individual lawyers and organizations can also benefit from client feedback in formulating their EI-based development. In a 2012 ALM Legal Intelligence Survey, only 56 percent of law firms say they have any plan to track client satisfaction to some extent. Despite priorities of growing revenue and improving profitability, "Client Performance Management and Client Satisfaction Measurement" came in as a fourth priority. Even of the firms that have a program in place, 47 percent said they formally ask for feedback from clients only "episodically."[239] Another survey found that 80 percent of the respondents either have "No Reliable Measures" or "Limited Measures" for determining client satisfaction.[240]

As one consultant counsels, "If law firms want to increase their revenue and profitability, having a formal and ongoing strategy for seeking and using client feedback will have to be part of the tool kit. Firms that have aggressively pursued a client feedback program together with a client account management (key client team) strategy report significantly higher profits."[241]

Clients should regularly be asked to evaluate our performance, preferably through anonymous surveys sent out automatically at points during the course of a matter or at least at its close. Those questions should include how individual lawyers and the team performed interpersonally, and we should listen to their responses.[242] Comments on various administrative and legal matters should, of course, be taken seriously, but comments regarding personal style and relationship interactions are a roadmap into how each attorney can provide better client service and the firm as a whole can profit.

Aggregating and carefully reviewing all the data from assessments, performance reviews, and client feedback, granular as it may seem, provides specific direction for and supports comprehensive professional development efforts. Together they help us improve our workplace emotional intelligence and drive our individuals and organizations to greater success.

The Emotional Intelligence Program at the University of Texas Center for Professional Education illustrates how various approaches can work together to raise emotional intelligence in a relatively short time. First, incoming students take EI assessments and are given written individual profiles. During one-day workshops, tutorials are conducted in how emotional intelligence allows individuals and teams to achieve exceptional results, workbook exercises focus on leadership and teamwork, and an interactive group format provides "hands-on, real-world practical instruction." Participants can develop a customized improvement plan that utilizes short-term one-on-one coaching. The process culminates in taking a 360-degree EI assessment to measure progress since the initial assessment. Taken together, the program helps students "cultivate a solid understanding of how to recognize and build emotional intelligence in themselves and others.[243]

Compensate, Reward, and Promote Emotional Intelligence

The old saw that "you get what you measure"[244] applies to professional development as well. Smart, competitive lawyers quickly learn what metrics, whether formally stated or not, are important to their success, and conform their behavior accordingly. Unfortunately, as Harvard Law professor Gardner recognizes, "the reward structure in legal practice undervalues interpersonal capabilities . . . necessary for successful leadership."[245]

Emotionally intelligent behavior needs to be one of the bases for compensation, recognition, and promotion in our legal workplaces. Gardner views the winner-take-all star culture that exists in most law firms as a barrier to collaboration, which she has concluded is the best way for firms to profit and which requires EI skills.[246] Yet she finds that "Too often, a firm espouses the desire for partners to collaborate, but then carries on remunerating people for individual results."[247]

Our up-or-out promotion systems encourage rivalry among associates, and the compensation structures champion competition among partners. After generations of institutionalized siloes and sharp elbows among the ranks, it is no surprise that those steeped in that value system don't instinctively bring in a colleague to help land a client or handle a matter.

Lawyers are quick to spot downsides of being more collaborative under prevailing systems.[248] Greater involvement by others can open the door to judgmental scrutiny of client interactions and threaten that fierce sense of autonomy. Cross-department work demands stronger interpersonal skills than simply delegating to junior staffers, can reduce one's personal leverage with the firm, and can also make a lawyer less attractive in the lateral sweepstakes. Rewarding collaboration and other behavior evidencing emotional intelligence can offset those disincentives.

Gardner believes that positive experience will overcome the initial suspicion of collaboration—that learning the value and expertise of other practices, finding how to share revenue fairly, and experiencing an enhanced reputation should eventually build trust and lower tension.[249] But in my experience few lawyers are going to undertake the risks—so that experience never comes—unless their workplace has made a full and clear commitment to reward their emotionally intelligent behavior in concrete ways.[250]

To show a firm's commitment, the objective of behaving in a more connected way should be made clear firm-wide. Emotional intelligence should be openly assessed and applauded as a workplace value, and its perks should be spelled out. Those who have high EI should be promoted to visible positions of power, and leaders should model the behaviors they are trying to develop—by including others on their matters, referring their matters to others, contributing to others' client work, and sharing credit. Putting in place internal and client reviews that include evaluations of interpersonal skills, such as responsiveness, communication, collegiality, and collaboration, help illustrate their value. As is done in most companies, supervising lawyers should be rated on their success in developing EI in their charges, and be rewarded for doing so.

Good marks should reap immediate benefits, whether in compensation credit, faster promotion, lower billable hours requirements, plum assignments, or even simple firm-wide recognition. Lawyers who bring others onto their team or refer matters to others should be rewarded financially, and those who coach, mentor, and resolve conflicts should have those contributions recognized in their compensation, just as pro bono or other nonbillable time is recognized. Those who have "single-handedly" scored or serviced a client or concluded a matter should be counseled that they could have benefited the client, the firm, and their own income/standing by taking a more multilawyer, interpersonally connected approach, and consequences for failing to improve should be spelled out and followed up on.

Groups as well as individuals should be encouraged to relate well. Department meetings should highlight collaborative efforts and successes. Each department should regularly meet with other departments to explore how their advice is interconnected, to identify possible common clients, and to build cross-department teams. Departments that are geographically or otherwise distant should be put in a position to better know each other, and to compare their firm and client experiences. Team effort that produces rising levels of client satisfaction and client retention, growth in revenue from existing accounts, and the acquisition of new clients in targeted areas are opportunities to publicly reinforce the benefits of emotionally intelligent behavior and the organization's dedication to achieving it.

DEVELOP EMOTIONAL INTELLIGENCE

- Practicing improved emotional responses learned in emotional intelligence training effectively raises emotional intelligence by rewiring neurological pathways.
- Short classes can raise emotional intelligence if followed by coaching/mentoring and opportunities to practice.
- Business development, stress management, and mindfulness training offer initial steps to start improving emotional intelligence.
- Effective emotional intelligence development programs require workplaces and individuals to dedicate their time and effort.
- Success depends on the individual's buy-in; those who could most benefit may be least interested.
- Feedback from assessments, performance reviews, and client reviews helps target development goals and gauge progress.
- Coaching is one of the most efficacious development interventions, and using professional coaches is preferable to most in-house mentoring programs.
- Positive feedback is more effective in molding behavior than negative feedback.
- Compensating, rewarding, and promoting those exhibiting emotionally intelligent behavior, such as collaboration, motivates and helps overcome lawyers' natural resistance and traditional workplace disincentives.

Step 4: Emotionally Engage the Keepers

If you want to build a ship . . . teach them to long for the endless immensity of the sea.[251]

—Antoine de Saint-Exupéry, *Citadelle*

The greatest competitive advantage in the modern economy is a positive and engaged workforce.[252]

—Shawn Achor, positive psychology expert and bestselling author of *The Happy Secret to Better Work* and *The Happiness Advantage*

> *The major challenge for CEOs over the next 20 years will be the effective deployment of human assets . . . getting one more individual to be more productive, more focused, more fulfilled than he was yesterday.*[253]
>
> —Marcus Buckingham, author and employee engagement expert

> *Engaged workers are much more productive at work, have fewer accidents and flat-out outperform disengaged workers.*[254]
>
> —Dan X. McGraw, business reporter and web producer

In the face of astronomically high attrition, keeping the professionals we want to keep is one of the more important consequences of achieving an emotionally intelligent workplace. However, the challenge is not just to retain those lawyers but to get and keep them engaged as well. There are good business reasons to do so, and emotional intelligence helps.

For starters, engagement matters.[255] "'Engaged workers . . . have bought into what the organization is about and are trying to make a difference,'" according to Gallup's Chief Scientist of Employee Engagement and Wellbeing.[256] From a database of more than one million surveys around the world, Gallup found the most "engaged" workplaces were 50 percent more likely to have lower turnover, 56 percent more likely to have higher-than-average customer loyalty, 38 percent more likely to have above-average productivity, and 27 percent more likely to report higher profitability.[257]

But a 2013 poll found only 30 percent of the American workforce "engaged" and "Gallup estimates that disengaged workers are costing businesses up to $550 billion a year."[258] While some evidence shows lawyers somewhat more engaged than other workers, the latest statistics also show that younger lawyers exhibit the least engagement, which could portend trouble.[259] Young lawyers' tendency to emotionally detach from their work evidently contributes to their being disengaged.[260]

The following twelve questions can illuminate whether workers are engaged, not engaged, or actively disengaged.[261] How would your workforce—lawyers and staff—answer them?

1. Do I know what is expected of me at work?
2. Do I have the materials and equipment that I need in order to do my work right?
3. At work, do I have the opportunity to do what I do best every day?
4. In the past seven days, have I received recognition or praise for doing good work?
5. Does my supervisor, or someone at work, seem to care about me as a person?
6. Is there someone at work who encourages my development?
7. At work, do my opinions seem to count?
8. Does the mission or purpose of my company make me feel that my job is important?
9. Are my coworkers committed to doing quality work?
10. Do I have a best friend at work?
11. In the past six months, has someone at work talked to me about my progress?
12. This past year, have I had opportunities at work to learn and grow?

Raising workers' EI is an antidote to disengagement.[262] Emotional intelligence increases a person's ability to be emotionally attached and engaged by equipping him or her with the skills to cope with the negative emotions that otherwise distance them from their work and others.[263] It also helps them to affirmatively connect with leaders, colleagues, and clients, building a personal stake in their work. Making a friend at the office, for example, dramatically increases a worker's engagement in his or her work and his or her satisfaction with his or her career.[264] And EI is the most powerful factor in quality and length of friendships.[265]

One study found that talent in every organization is a party to one of three types of psychological contracts: *affective*—"an emotional attachment," *normative*—"a sense of obligation and duty to stay," and *continuance*—"an assessment of the costs associated with leaving." The affective or emotional attachment produces the strongest commitment (and raises job satisfaction and mental and physical well-being), while the continuance contract, based on a cost/benefit analysis, produces the weakest commitment.[266]

What can legal workplaces do to encourage emotional engagement? Simply raising compensation is usually a red herring, but leaders have a significant role to play in raising emotional engagement both through their personal behavior and in their management of their workplace.

The Compensation Red Herring. Let's start out with what isn't effective. In an attempt to ensure performance and loyalty when hiring processes and culture haven't produced it, many law firms resort to paying higher salaries and bonuses—a remedy that in most cases doesn't work.[267]

Twenty years of research shows that "extrinsic rewards" are generally ineffective, if not counterproductive, to motivate the types of behavior that lawyers engage in: judgment, discrimination, and the use of intelligence, as Daniel Pink, a Yale Law School alum who was editor-in-chief of *The Yale Law & Policy Review*, reports in his book *Drive*.[268]

True to that research, an analysis by the *American Lawyer* of the 2011 Midlevel Associates Survey found that "there is no statistically significant relationship between associates' ranking of their compensation and benefits and their expectation that they will still be at their firm in two years," a finding echoed in an earlier analysis, which found the relationship "close to zero."[269] Money can't buy love.

Those findings do not undercut the value of using compensation in a highly competitive environment to reward and shape emotionally intelligent behaviors, they just make it apparent that compensation alone is not sufficient to get the best work or greatest commitment from people. Opportunities to control our work life, to master a subject or skill that we feel matters, to work with people we like and admire, and to participate in an undertaking greater than ourselves are all deeply felt motivators that do.[270] These can be optimized in an emotionally intelligent workplace.

The Role of Leaders. Feeling respected by their leaders is demonstrated to be the number one factor in garnering commitment and engagement from employees.[271] People prefer to work with leaders who can manage their own emotions well, and those working for high EI supervisors are more committed to their organizations than those working for lower EI supervisors.[272] In one instance, improving managers' emotional intelligence led to "massively" higher engagement, which fueled a 63 percent reduction in turnover and greater profit.[273] On the flip side, managers are reported to be the primary cause of employee disengagement,[274] especially managers with deficits in communication.[275]

Gary Kelly, CEO of Southwest, suggests that a leader model personal engagement by "spending time with employees, treating people with respect, having fun, being there for them personally and professionally, and putting people first—with empathy, kindness and compassion."[276]

Small steps can make a difference. Not long after FedEx introduced its pilot EI training program for managers, "simple, caring conversations about employees' lives were having a dramatic effect on results at work."[277] Or as legal consultant Gerry Riskin puts it, "You cannot help people perform better by buying a bigger whip and bigger boots."[278]

Despite what may be an elevated degree of discomfort, lawyers must purposefully approach and interact constructively with their colleagues and staff on a regular basis in part because of the hesitance of others to initiate those contacts themselves.

Here are some practices legal workplaces can adopt that make a difference in engagement:

Visualize the Greater Goal. Yes, we do litigation, regulatory compliance, transactions, tax, trusts and estates planning, and so on. We look at papers and argue and then bill our clients for it. But what is our greater contribution? We are in this business to help people and organizations make their way more comfortably, safely, and profitably. Whatever the practice, each organization has a greater good that it can articulate and rally engagement around.[279] Make that case.

Promote Civility. Maintaining civility is the responsibility of the organization. Make sure seniors are setting good examples, and ways to handle differences, difficult people, and common insensitivities are communicated and/or included in coaching and training. Develop a set of civility metrics to ensure that change is sustained.[280]

Give Support. Touro College Law Professor Marjorie Silver proposed years ago that firms provide ongoing support for lawyers similar to the supervision provided to young practitioners in helping professions.[281] Short of that, do less of "just buck up" and more of "how can we help?" to those who seem frustrated or overwhelmed. Consultant Dr. Larry Richard has suggested appointing a chief resilience officer, a dedicated internal champion whose official duties entail spotting and helping address those who are feeling down or falling behind.[282] Even without the official, make sure someone, internal or hired, is looking to identify and bolster those who are struggling.

Success Follows Happiness. Recognize and listen to what people are saying, particularly what they need, whether it is more training, different assignments, or better feedback, and do so with respect. Make time during performance evaluations or otherwise to elicit feelings, aspirations, suggestions, fears, and so on.[283] Success follows happiness.[284]

Encourage Collaboration and Teamwork. If you are recognizing and compensating these, workers will be more likely to participate on teams, which is an avenue to becoming more engaged.[285] Team members don't have to be best buddies; they just need to feel, as Google's research determined, that they are in a safe space that is sensitive and responsive to them.[286] Their performance and loyalty will follow.

Promote Person-to-Person Connection. Remember that online, technology-mediated collaboration is less effective in engaging people than personal interaction,[287] so make sure there are plenty of opportunities for the latter, and you will get more and better creative problem solving as well.[288]

Celebrate Often and Out in the Open. Any number of small and large accomplishments should be recognized or rewarded using whatever seems to appeal: lawyer-of-the-day, certificates, trophies, cupcakes, priority parking, gag awards, singing telegrams, in addition to more substantive benefits like participation on preferred matters or in coveted professional development programs.

Be Transparent. Transparency implies that no one is above the law when it comes to treating others unfairly or disrespectfully, and that abuses can be spotted. It is the best avenue for improving ethical conduct, especially by those in power.[289] Just the existence of mechanisms that promote transparency reduces unwanted behavior and gives that important sense of safety.

Improve Off-Boarding. Show that your organization values emotional ties, even after lawyers leave, by being supportive, generous, and interested in their future. Those ties can be very beneficial, making "happy quitters" "sources of valuable information, recommendations, and business opportunities."[290]

EMOTIONALLY ENGAGE THE KEEPERS

- Getting and keeping lawyers engaged is good for business: engagement raises productivity, performance, and retention and reduces absences.
- Emotional attachment to a workplace is a stronger bond than a sense of obligation or a financial attachment.
- Raising workers' emotional intelligence increases their emotional attachment and engagement.
- Raising compensation is not an effective way to increase engagement.
- Leaders' emotional intelligence has a major impact on workplace engagement.
- Workplaces can take steps to increase positive feelings and fuel engagement, such as giving people opportunities to control their work, to master a subject or skill they feel matters, to work with people they like and admire, and to participate in an undertaking greater than themselves.

Find the Magical Balance

Does this advice sound too indulgent? The question often arises whether being emotionally intelligent handicaps lawyers when it comes to being the biggest, baddest litigator or negotiator around. Leaders in particular ask: "Am I going to end up an ineffective softie?"

My experience is that the most difficult balance to achieve in all aspects of life, including managing a law practice, is that between giving support on one hand and requiring that standards are met on the other—the tension between nurturing and demanding. Jack Welch admits that managing talent with "just the right push-and-pull" is one of the hardest tasks for leaders to get right.[291] How do we set and enforce a standard that doesn't spoil or coddle weakness, but rather recognizes and fosters achievement without being harsh and uncompromising?

An important study undertook "to address some companies' fears that managers trained to be more emotionally intelligent would become sentimental and incapable of taking 'hard decisions.'" The results show that "emotional intelligence has nothing to do with sentimentality . . . Emotionally intelligent managers are not just nicer managers . . . [they] make better managers, as reflected by greater managerial competencies, higher team efficiency and less stressed subordinates . . . Actually, it is managers with low EI who have the greatest difficulties to put their emotions aside and not let them interfere when inappropriate."[292]

As one pundit put it, "There's a big difference between being a hard ass and just being an ass. You can have zero tolerance for failure and excuses, and connect with and care about someone at the same time."[293]

In short, for lawyers to flourish, we must recognize the significance and complexity of their emotions. That does not mean that we lower our standards or reduce the quality of our work. We can insist on excellence and still value the consideration of people's feelings so that we are all loyal, productive, and constructively engaged.[294]

The executive committee of a small but growing law firm in New York City asked me to review their associate compensation structure. They felt morale was sagging, particularly among associates, perhaps under the demands of growth, and they were considering revising compensation levels upward or giving bonuses. Most clients who come to me are looking to address a compensation issue. In this case, the firm allowed me to do a "red flag audit" to test their assessment of low morale and to see if I uncovered any issues other than workload or compensation that might be troubling the troops.

Cutting to the chase, I found that their associates at all levels recognized that they weren't being paid BigLaw salaries and bonuses, but they were content with their decision to exchange that compensation for a more intimate and collegial environment. They also recognized that the firm had been bursting at the seams recently with work, but almost to the lawyer, they welcomed the more frantic workload as a sign that the firm was prospering and their jobs were safe, and they seemed confident that the firm would over time make the appropriate adjustments in hiring and work management to regain the pace and closeness that they had enjoyed.

But there was a morale problem. The executive committee was right about that. In response to growth, the firm had to add offices on a separate elevator bank, which was reached by returning to the ground floor and changing elevators. The firm was pleased to maintain its current cost-advantaged lease and negotiated good terms on the additional space. Two departments had been moved to the new space a year before. The morale problem was that the intimate and collegial environment that the associates valued in this firm had been disrupted. Some lawyers went for days or weeks without seeing their colleagues on the other elevator bank. Spontaneous work discussions, drop-in mentoring, and casual socializing had changed. Teamwork was harder to arrange and execute. Further, speculation was rampant as to why the two departments had been chosen to be "exiled" to the floor that housed fewer executive committee members. The firm had been prepared to make across-the-board salary increases, when what the associates really wanted was a greater sense of connection.

The firm was not in a position to modify its physical footprint, so we devised a series of steps to help ease the associates' concerns. The executive committee's individual offices and their departments were divided between the two spaces, with a clear attempt to balance the power evenly. Space for support functions like accounting and file management was also provided on both floors, and staff rotated periodically between the two. Work space was made for lawyers from the other elevator bank who needed to work closely on joint projects. Coffee and bagels were served early Monday mornings in a conference room in one or the other space on a rotating basis. Late Friday afternoon snacks were also served rotating between the two spaces. Wednesday department lunches occasionally combined two departments that weren't on the same elevator bank. And so on.

These accommodations cost less than the additional compensation the firm was prepared to pay, and went far toward giving the firm a stronger sense of cohesion and better engagement among associates, despite its divided geography.

Dare to Lead

Few law firms or law departments use assessment tools during their hiring process. One of the oft-cited exceptions was Atlanta-based McKenna Long & Aldridge, which before it merged in 2015 with Dentons had for several years used a 30-minute online personality test, along with other methods, for assessing desired characteristics in recruits.[295]

McKenna Long was pleased with its untraditional recruiting formula: "Corporate America uses one-on-one interviews with psychologists; personality, leadership, and emotional intelligence assessments; simulations and case studies; written essays; and behavioral interviewing in making an informed hiring decision," the firm's then chief recruiting and development officer, Jennifer Queen, said. "Our hiring process has become more efficient and effective . . . Hundreds of candidates have taken the assessment, and only one student has declined. The feedback from candidates has been overwhelmingly positive. They appreciate that we have put so much effort into the interview process to ensure a solid fit on both sides of the equation. Now, how is that not a win-win for our clients, the firm, and the candidate?"[296]

Alan Fisch of intellectual property firm Fisch Sigler LLP, with offices in New York, Silicon Valley, and Washington DC, is proud of its use of unusual recruiting assessments: "Our recruiting is specifically designed to identify superstars with the right IQ and EQ fit for our organization. We acknowledge that our approach is uncommon, but so are the people we are seeking."[297]

Dentons is one of many US-headquartered firms with a UK presence or UK-headquartered firms, including Allen & Overy, Baker & McKenzie (now Baker McKenzie), Freshfields, Clifford Chance, DLA Piper, Eversheds, Freshfields, Herbert Smith, Freehills, Hill Dickinson, Hogan Lovells, Linklaters and Mayer Brown, that use online assessment centers in the United Kingdom to administer various aptitude and psychological assessments for lawyer applicants.[298]

Those workplaces experimenting with assessments in recruitment are not receiving applause from other quarters of the industry. John Sandberg of Sandberg, Phoenix, for one, "got a fair load of grief" from other firm leaders at a conference over his plans to use personality tests in recruiting, but he concluded that proceeding was worth the risk.[299]

Either short of assessments or in addition to them, some legal workplaces are employing behavioral interviewing techniques for both new recruits and laterals.[300] "Early adopters were Orrick, Herrington & Sutcliffe and DLA Piper; Baker Botts, Paul, Hastings, and Vinson & Elkins, among others, have joined them."[301]

Some firms use in-house personal style assessments administered after hiring for individual development purposes. Mayer Brown has tested associates for years for introversion to help them best use that characteristic in their work. Perkins Coie takes steps to accommodate introverts, including providing noise-cancelling headsets and smaller workspaces with doors, and provides programming on how introverts can advance in their careers and extroverts can work better with introverts.[302]

There is a notable increase in the number of lawyers who have taken the Myers-Briggs Type Indicator (MBTI) and a variety of other personal style assessments, often administered at firm and department retreats. "Lawyers have to get comfortable with the idea of personality and predictive tests before they'll embrace—or even use—them. And the relatively painless Myers-Briggs . . . may provide that comfort. But it's a hard slog. The combination of lawyer skepticism and low resilience gets in the way, the latter especially. [One consultant] says, 'If you don't believe in it or don't have enough self-awareness to reflect on what the test results are saying, then you won't use the test again.'"[303]

Some firms are taking steps toward raising emotional intelligence after hiring by offering leadership and client service programs with an EI component. Leadership training provided by Wharton Business School professors at Reed Smith University teaches lawyers to, among other things, "look at the world through other people's eyes while gaining an understanding of their own personality type." King & Spalding has put lawyers through Ritz-Carlton's Leadership Training emphasizing client service skills, and Alston Bird hired former Ritz-Carlton executive Leonardo Inghilleri to train lawyers in client service.[304]

With the rising recognition of lawyer distress, various stress management programs are increasingly being offered in legal settings. After LawCare, a health advice line for the legal profession in the United Kingdom, reported that the recession had led to record numbers of lawyers suffering from stress and depression, UK firm Herbert Smith launched a training program to help its staff to "recognize the symptoms of stress and deal with mental illness." A pilot program for partners and managers was later offered to all employees at the firm.[305] And in 2015, successor firm Herbert Smith Freehills launched a "Mental Health mentor programme . . . the first law firm to offer such a service to staff."[306]

Unfortunately, some attempts to improve emotional health come on the heels of tragedy. After the suicide of an intellectual property partner whose wife said her husband had felt "unsupported" at work, Hogan Lovells "pledged to examine its policies and procedures around workplace stress and mental health."[307] "[J]oining a growing number of U.K. law firms pushing for better mental health among its staff," the firm now offers a counselor on-site for confidential self-referrals two days a week, an in-house gym, onsite occupational health service, onsite physiotherapist, an employee assistance program, free health checks, healthcare advice, and "a number of seminars on topics such as emotional wellbeing."[308]

While most of the assessments being used in legal workplaces are long-standing ones used in other industries, attempts are being made to develop instruments specially for the legal profession, in some cases drawing on well-known assessments that touch on EI skills, such as the Hogan Assessments and the Caliper Profile, and even the Troutwine Athletic Profile, used by professional football teams.[309]

What should be encouraging is that these assessments have been found to be useful to legal workplaces in making the hiring process more data-based and efficient, and also in simply identifying the best hires. McKenna Long concluded before its merger with Dentons that "we are clear on the return on our investment [in an assessment]. Our hiring process has become more efficient and effective."[310] UK law firms have found that "as the recruiting process has grown more rigorous, firms have been able to make better hires," with some noting that those with high assessment scores were quickly outperforming those with middling scores—in one instance three times above average in legal ability and four times above in organizational skills.[311]

Using assessments is not the only EI-related talent management practice in which legal workplaces are finding success. Munger, Tolles & Olson, ranked by Vault as the number one firm in partner-associate relations and the number seven best law firm to work for in 2013, says it takes steps to be respectful and inclusive of its attorneys by putting associates on management committees, sharing the firms' financial statements with the rank-and-file, and incentivizing partners to treat people well by using a "free market system" where associates get their work by approaching partners they want to work with. "That is a motivating factor for our partners to be good people to work with . . . in order for them to attract the resources that they need for their cases or transactions, they need to be seen as good team leaders," Munger managing partner Sandra Seville-Jones is quoted as saying.[312]

Harvard Business School's case studies of Baker & McKenzie as it pioneered a global law practice—having grown at the time from a single Chicago office to sixty-nine offices in thirty-eight countries with more than 3,000 lawyers—is one of the most in-depth documentations of a law firm's experience with raising emotional intelligence. Given "an urgent focus on improving the soft skills and emotional intelligence that are so important to true 'counsel of choice' relationships," incoming Chairman of the Executive Committee John Conroy wanted a plan for guiding the firm's hiring, development, and retention of lawyers who could provide "the relationship development and 'value-added' service that clients are increasingly demanding." As one Baker & McKenzie insider said, "[T]he business we're in is really a relationship business. Technical expertise is a given. The real differentiator is the added value clients experience from counsel who inspire trust, who fully understand a client's needs and desires in the client's context, and who relate effectively with the client on a human level."[313]

The firm also wanted to address its high rate of attrition.[314] *"'Currently, we, collectively and individually, do not do a very good job of encouraging associates to aspire to be like us, partners at Baker & McKenzie, and, to a lesser extent, practicing attorneys. [These associates] suspect that many partners are unhappy, and they do not want to be.'"*[315]

So Baker & McKenzie "hired two industrial psychologists as consultants to help determine the qualities that were necessary for success . . . in terms of legal expertise and 'soft skills'" and to devise a "Development Framework" to instill higher levels of EI and "more opportunities for teamwork."[316] *Recognizing that "'These efforts will require expenditures of partner time, effort, and yes, probably money,'" they promised that "'Talent that has been carefully recruited and cultivated, and partners who have been successfully coached and mentored, whether for client service or practice management, are then far better placed to deliver value, either to clients or to the firm as managers. Talent management makes it far easier to create strong client teams through which the firm's lawyers can develop familiarity and intimacy with their clients such that those clients come to recognize that they can count on a Baker & McKenzie client team that is both personally and institutionally committed to that client's success.'"*[317]

Quality audits in which partners and staff visited each office, interviewing everyone from receptionists to partners, became standard throughout the firm. The firm conducted postmortems on cases and transactions, including surveying clients about work quality and service. It also invested in partner leadership training at the Center for Creative Leadership, an offering so popular there was a waiting list.

The firm's talent management strategy was named a "best practice" in both Harvard Business School case studies.[318] *In gauging the effectiveness of these efforts, according to Conroy, "When we look at what is successful internally—how you get along with people and who people support for advancement—some of the qualities that lead to success internally are the same qualities that lead to client satisfaction. So in terms of professional development, our strategy is to go beyond the technical legal training and to get into some of those other issues that are vitally important for effective client satisfaction."*[319]

The ultimate validation of the undertaking was the increase in Baker & McKenzie's revenue and profits: client retention promptly rose 39 percent,[320] *in the first two years, revenue grew 24 percent while profits grew 41 percent,*[321] *PPP climbed 85 percent in the first four years, the firm enjoyed unprecedented double-digit growth in profitability for years thereafter, and its performance continues to rise dramatically.*[322]

FOUR STEPS TO ACHIEVING AN EMOTIONALLY INTELLIGENT WORKPLACE

1. Start at the top: build more emotionally intelligent leaders by providing more feedback, investing in leadership development, embracing women leaders, and making use of emotional contagion.
2. Hire emotionally intelligent professionals using improved hiring practices that include screening for emotional intelligence and other competencies and/or using behavioral interviewing techniques.
3. Develop emotional intelligence by offering emotional intelligence training, coaching, mentoring, and other feedback sources, and compensating, rewarding, and promoting for emotional intelligence.
4. Emotionally engage the professionals you want to keep.

Find the magical balance that recognizes and fosters excellence without being emotionally harsh and uncompromising.

Be one of the legal workplaces that dare to lead in building emotional intelligence.

Chapter Endnotes

1. Goleman, "They've Taken Emotional Intelligence Too Far," *Time.*
2. Frawley, "The Emotionally Intelligent Organization and the Customer Experience," *Beyond Philosophy.*
3. Normand-Hochman, *Managing Talent for Success: Talent Development in Law Firms* (London: Globe Law and Business, 2013).
4. Stein et al., "Emotional Intelligence of Leaders," *Leadership and Organization Development Journal,* 87.
5. James I. Merlino and Anath Raman, "Healthcare's Service Fanatics," *Harvard Business Review,* May, 2013.
6. Walter, Humphrey, and Cole, "Unleashing Leadership Potential: Toward an Evidence-Based Management of Emotional Intelligence," *Organizational Dynamics,* 212–19.
7. Merlino and Raman, "Healthcare's Service Fanatics," *Harvard Business Review.*
8. Roland B. Smith and Paul Bennett Marrow, "The Changing Nature of Leadership in Law Firms," *New York State Bar Journal* 80 (2008): 33–38.
9. Bradberry and Greaves, *Emotional Intelligence 2.0,* 234–36.

10. Stein et al., "Emotional Intelligence of Leaders," *Leadership and Organization Development Journal,* 87.
11. "[I]n a study of 179 firms, associates with a high-ranking firm attributed that firm's success to the model behavior of the partners . . . the firm's leadership strove to 'nurture a culture of respect.' It is no coincidence that this firm had a high retention rate of associates, with only 3% reporting that they were looking for a new job." Mines, Meyer, and Mines, "Emotional Intelligence and Emotional Toxicity," *The Colorado Lawyer,* 94. The firm, Debevoise & Plimpton LLP, was rated as the ninth-ranking firm for quality of life.
12. "The Faas Foundation Announces Partnership with Yale Center for Emotional Intelligence to Study Role of Emotions in the Workplace," *SYS-Con Media,* February 22, 2016, http://news.sys-con.com/node/3688741.
13. "The Wharton School of the University of Pennsylvania Announces Gift to Establish the Katz Fund for Research on Leadership and Emotional Intelligence," *Wharton Magazine,* July 7, 2015, http://whartonmagazine.com/press-releases/launch-of-new-wharton-leadership-research/.
14. Giang, "Your Boss Probably Wouldn't Pass Yale's Emotional Intelligence Assessment," *Business Insider.*
15. Bradberry and Greaves, "Heartless Bosses?" *Harvard Business Review,* 24.
16. Richard, "Herding Cats," *Altman Weil Report to Legal Management,* 1–12.
17. https://hbr.org/2015/06/quiz-yourself-do-you-lead-with-emotional-intelligence
18. John Ryan, "Accelerating Performance: Five Leadership Skills You and Your Organization Can't Do Without," *Center for Creative Leadership,* August, 2010. Among 2,000 managers holding 41 different jobs from 12 different organizations, CCL identified self-awareness as both critical to modern leadership and one of the foundations of EI.
19. Kahneman, *Thinking Fast and Slow.*
20. A meta-analysis conducted in 2010 reported the large disparity between upper management's self-reports on how well they performed compared with reports from others in the organization, indicating the managers were not aware of what others thought of their performance. Harms and Credé, "Emotional Intelligence and Transformational and Transactional Leadership," *Journal of Leadership and Organizational Studies,* 5–17.
21. Boyatzis, *The Competent Manager: A Model for Effective Performance* (New York: John Wiley and Sons, 1982), Jack Zenger and Joseph Folkman, "Ten Fatal Flaws That Derail Leaders," *Harvard Business Review* 87 (2009): 18. Rhode, "Developing Leadership," *Santa Clara Law Review,* 719.
22. Steven B. Wolff, *Emotional Competence Inventory,* 37.
23. "While emotional intelligence . . . is rated a 4.5/5 on importance for solving the challenges, organizations earn a 2.6/5 on implementation—a 74% gap." "New Study of Leaders Reveals Emerging Global Talent Crisis, Emotional Intelligence Seen as Solution," *PR Newswire,* April 17, 2012, http://www.prnewswire.com/news-releases/new-study-of-leaders-reveals-emerging-global-talent-crisis-emotional-intelligence-seen-as-solution-147740315.html. In a telling survey of 4,000 senior managers, they believed improvements in their

competence in technology and finance should be their highest priority, while their employees overwhelmingly cited leadership and EI as top priorities for management improvement. Brett Steenbarger, "Becoming the Kind of Leader You Would Want to Follow," *Forbes*, April 9, 2016.

24. This failure of leaders to get feedback reaches up even to the presidency of the United States. Lyndon Johnson was characterized as increasingly isolated in the White House as he tried to avoid anyone who might tell him an unpleasant truth: "Self-deceptions multiplied in this hall of distorting mirrors," according to Pulitzer Prize–winning historian Doris Kearns Goodwin, who was Johnson's assistant during his presidency. Mark Lewis, "Doris Kearns Goodwin and the Credibility Gap," *Forbes*, February 27, 2002.
25. Kaster, "Review of *How Leading Lawyers Think*," *NYSBA New York Dispute Resolution Lawyer.*
26. Keith Darcy, Executive Director of the Ethics and Compliance Officer Association, quoted in O'Brian, "The Ethics of Emotional Intelligence," *Business Ethics: The Magazine of Corporate Responsibility.*
27. Deborah Gruenfeld, a psychologist at the Stanford Business School, in analyzing "more than 1,000 decisions handed down by the United States Supreme Court between 1953 and 1993 . . . found that, as justices gained power on the court, or became part of a majority coalition, their written opinions tended to become less complex and nuanced. They considered fewer perspectives and possible outcomes." Lehrer, "The Power Trip," *The Wall Street Journal.* See Annie McKee, "How the Most Emotionally Intelligent CEOs Handle Their Power," *Harvard Business Review*, December 8, 2016.
28. Bradberry and Greaves, *Emotional Intelligence 2.0*, 236.
29. Fabio Sala, "Do Programs Designed to Increase Emotional Intelligence at Work-Work?" *Consortium for Research on Emotional Intelligence in Organizations*, 2002.
30. Defoe, "Emotional Intelligence and 'Incompetent' [Lawyer and Law Firm] Leaders and the 'Double Curse': Low Performing, High Self-Evaluators and Resistance to Feedback via the 'Expedient Escape.'" *Psycholawlogy*, September 17, 2013, http://www.psycholawlogy.com/2013/09/17/emotional-intelligence-and-incompetent-managers-who-suffer-from-the-double-curse-low-performing-high-self-evaluators-resistance-to-feedback/.
31. Kouzes and Posner, *A Leader's Legacy*, 28. Leaders often appear to respect their own opinions more than the opinions of others, even many others. "It is as if their need to be 'right' overwhelms their ability to be right." Lester Levy and Mark Bently, "More 'Right' than 'Real': The Shape of Authentic Leadership in New Zealand," *Authentic Leadership Survey Results*, 2007, 4, http://nzli.co.nz/file/Research/more-right-than-real—authentic-leadership-report.pdf.
32. Kiser, *Beyond Right and Wrong*, 124.
33. Defoe, "Emotional Intelligence and 'Incompetent' [Lawyer and Law Firm] Leaders and the 'Double Curse': Low Performing, High Self-Evaluators and Resistance to Feedback via the 'Expedient Escape,'" *Psycholawlogy.*
34. Anita J. Zigman, "Upward Feedback Programs: A Primer for Law Firms." *Law Practice Today*, May, 2013, http://www.americanbar.org/content/newsletter/

publications/law_practice_today_home/lpt-archives/may13/upward-feedback-programs.html.
35. Cynthia L. Spanhel and Paula A. Patton, *How Associate Evaluations Measure Up: A National Study of Associate Performance Assessments* (Overland Park, KS: National Association for Law Placement [NALP] Foundation for Law Career Research and Education, 2006).
36. Susan Saab Fortney, "Are Law Firm Partners Islands unto Themselves? An Empirical Study of Law Firm Peer Review and Culture," *Georgetown Journal of Legal Ethics* 10 (1996): 271–316.
37. Peter Drucker, *Management Challenges for the 21st Century* (New York: HarperCollins, 1999).
38. Harms and Credé, "Emotional Intelligence and Transformational and Transactional Leadership," *Journal of Leadership and Organizational Studies,* 11.
39. Carl A. Leonard, "Does Your Firm Have a CEO? Managing Partners Coming of Age as Chief Executive Officers," *Legal Management,* March/April, 2000.
40. Riskin, "Leadership Strategy from Gettysburg," *Amazing Firms Amazing Practices.*
41. "Bersin by Deloitte Research Shows US Leadership Development Spending Up Again 14 Percent to More Than $15 Billion in 2013," *Bersin,* May 14, 2014, http://www.bersin.com/News/Content.aspx?id=17488.
42. "Global Human Capital Trends: Leading in the New World of Work," *Deloitte University Press,* 1–112. The average annual spending on development per person is $1,700 for first-level leaders; $2,700 for midlevels; $6,000 for seniors; and $7,100 for high potential leaders. Companies that excel at leadership development spend up to 60 percent more per participant on average than their less sophisticated peers, delivering, among other things, twenty times greater employee retention. Jack Zenger, "Does Leadership Development Really Work?" *Forbes,* May 2, 2012; "Leadership Development Factbook 2012: Benchmarks and Trends in U.S Leadership Development," *Bersin,* July 16, 2012, http://www.bersin.com/Store/details.aspx?docid=15587.
43. Goleman, "They've Taken Emotional Intelligence Too Far," *Time.*
44. Rhode, *Lawyers as Leaders;* "Building for the Future: The Courage to Invest in Your Clients, Your People, and Your Law Firm," *MPF Managing Partner Forum,* May 4–5, 2016, http://www.managingpartnerforum.org/tasks/sites/mpf/assets/image/MPF percent20- percent202016 percent20Leadership percent20Conference percent20- percent20Audience percent20Polling percent20Results percent20- percent205-5-16.pdf.
45. Roland B. Smith and Paul Bennett Marrow, "The Changing Nature of Leadership in Law Firms," *New York State Bar Journal 80,* September 2008, 33–38, http://www.ccl.org/leadership/pdf/news/releases/NYSBAJournal.pdf.
46. Steven M. Savageau, "The Correlation Between Transformational Leadership and Participation in Music Programs," PhD Diss, 2007, 58.
47. See, for example, Larry Richard and Lisa Roher, "A Breed Apart," *American Lawyer,* July 1, 2011, 44, noting that women score lower in ambition and sociability than men, but higher on interpersonal sensitivity.
48. For more, see John Gerzema and Michael D'Antonio, *The Athena Doctrine: How Women (and the Men Who Think Like Them) Will Rule the Future* (San Francisco, CA: Jossey-Bass, 2013).

49. Smith and Marrow, "The Changing Nature of Leadership in Law Firms," *New York State Bar Journal.* See also Gardner, "When Senior Managers Won't Collaborate," *Harvard Business Review.*
50. Cavallo and Brienza, *Emotional Competence and Leadership Excellence at Johnson & Johnson,* 5.
51. John Baldoni, "Few Executives Are Self-Aware, but Women Have the Edge," *Harvard Business Review,* May, 2013. This echoes a discovery by scientists who study primates. While female chimps console other chimps who are upset, alpha males, the troupe leaders, console even more often than do female chimps. According to Goleman, "In nature's design, leaders, it seems, need a large dose of empathic concern." Goleman, "Are Women More Emotionally Intelligent Than Men?" *Psychology Today.*
52. Among executives, "Empathy was found in 33% of women, compared to 15% of men; Effective conflict management was seen in 51% of women, vs. 29% of men; Effective influence was found in 32% of women, compared to 21% of men; and Self-awareness was strongly evident in 19% of women, but just 4% of men." "Women Poised to Effectively Lead in Matrix Work Environments," *Hay Group.* However, Malloy finds that among the stars—leaders in the top 10 percent of performance (which often indicates strong EI skills)—gender differences in EI abilities "wash out: The men are as good as the women, the women as good as the men, across the board." Goleman, "Are Women More Emotionally Intelligent Than Men?" *Psychology Today.*
53. Anita Woolley, Thomas W. Malone, and Christopher F. Chabris, "Why Some Teams Are Smarter Than Others," *New York Times,* January 16, 2015.
54. "Women Poised to Effectively Lead in Matrix Work Environments," *Hay Group.*
55. Jack Zenger and Joseph Folkman, "Are Women Better Leaders Than Men?" *Harvard Business Review,* March 15, 2012.
56. Jack Zenger and Joseph Folkman, "Gender Shouldn't Matter, But Apparently It Still Does," *Harvard Business Review,* April 4, 2012.
57. "Life's Work: Mary Robinson," *Harvard Business Review,* March, 2013.
58. Michael Gurian with Barbara Annis, *Leadership and the Sexes: Using Gender Science to Create Success in Business,* Jossey-Bass 2008. For a precis of the book's research, see https://www.leadershipnow.com/leadershop/9780787997038 excerpt.html. Stephen Maybe, "More Than Ever The Time Is Now for Female Led Leadership in Both Legal Departments and Law Firms," *Mondaq,* March 13, 2017, http://www.mondaq.com/canada/x/ 575102/Strategic+Planning/More+Than+Ever+The+Time+Is+Now+For+Female+Led+Leadership+In+Both+Legal+Departments+And+Law+Firms.
59. "2016 Report on Diversity in U.S. Law Firms," NALP, http://www.nalp.org/uploads/2016NALPReportonDiversityinUSLawFirms.pdf; "A Current Glance at Women in the Law," American Bar Association—Commission on Women in the Profession, January 2017, http://www.americanbar.org/content/dam/aba/marketing/women/current_glance_statistics_january2017.authcheckdam.pdf.
60. Sweeney, "The Female Lawyer Exodus," *The Daily Beast.*
61. In a survey one of the primary reasons given for women leaving was a "toxic work culture." "Survey Results: Why Are Women Really Leaving Firms?" *Montage Legal Group,* March 7, 2016, http://montagelegal.com/

survey-results-women-really-leaving-firms/. The significantly higher rate of MBTI "Feelers" among female lawyers than male lawyers may be a factor. "Feelers" value and promote harmony and rapport, an objective more attainable in a workplace that values EI skills, which may require, as Deborah Epstein Henry, a former lawyer and author of *Law & Reorder: Legal Industry Solutions for Restructure, Retention, Promotion & Work/Life Balance*, says, "30 percent representation of women on influential committees and boards—a critical mass." Sweeney, "The Female Lawyer Exodus," *The Daily Beast.*

62. David Thomas, "What Do Leaders Need to Understand about Diversity?" *Yale Insights*, January 1, 2011.
63. Mayer, Roberts, and Barsade, "Human Abilities: Emotional Intelligence," in *Annual Review of Psychology*, 524.
64. Elaine Hatfield, quoted in Amanda Enayati, "Don't Let Others Stress You Out," *CNN: The Chart*, September 7, 2011, http://thechart.blogs.cnn.com/2011/09/07/dont-let-others-stress-you-out/.
65. Thomas E. Ricks, "Whatever Happened to Accountability?" *Harvard Business Review*, October, 2012, 97.
66. Patrick Mayock, "Conley Talks Jobs, Careers, Callings," *Hotel News Now*, February 28, 2012, http://www.hotelnewsnow.com/Articles.aspx/7633/Conley-talks-jobs-careers-callings. In one Fortune 500 company where angry outbursts were common, raising emotional regulation skills, in not only the current leadership but also in those being groomed as upcoming leaders, significantly reduced the destructive anger throughout the company. "The Emotional Intelligence Difference," *Empathia.*
67. Goleman, "The Brain and Emotional Intelligence," *Psychology Today.*
68. Meyer, Roberts, and Barsade, "Human Abilities," *Annual Review of Psychology*, 524.
69. Thomas Sy, Stephane Cote, and Richard Saavedra, "The Contagious Leader: Impact of the Leader's Mood on the Mood of Group Members, Group Affective Tone, and Group Processes," *Journal of Applied Psychology* 90 (2005): 295–305. Jennifer George and Kenneth Bettenhausen, "Understanding Prosocial Behavior, Sales Performance, and Turnover: A Group Level Analysis in a Service Context," *Journal of Applied Psychology* 75 (1990): 698–709. Those who experience more positive affect are more academically successful, for example, than those who experience negative affect. Saklofske et al., "Relationships of Personality, Affect, Emotional Intelligence and Coping with Student Stress and Academic Success," *Learning and Individual Differences*, 256.
70. Goleman, Boyatzis, and McKee, *Primal Leadership*, ix. See Isen et al., "Positive Affect Facilitates Creative Problem Solving," *Journal of Personality and Social Psychology.*
71. Kahneman, *Thinking Fast and Slow.* Since earlier research had shown that human beings have a built-in negativity bias, "a larger quantity of positive emotion are needed to offset that bias and achieve the benefits of a positive mood . . . to achieve a quantum leap in well-being, with significantly greater job satisfaction, life satisfaction, relationships, work effectiveness, and other payoffs." Richard, "Accountability 101—Part Four," *Lawyer Brain Blog*, May 22, 2013, http://www.lawyerbrainblog.com/2013/05/accountability-101-part-four/. Thousands of

students across the country surveyed by the Yale Center for Emotional Intelligence reported that four out of the top five emotions they experience at school are predominantly negative. "The Emotion Revolution," *Yale Center for Emotional Intelligence*, 2015, http://ei.yale.edu/what-we-do/emotion-revolution/. The goal is not to generate exclusively positive feelings. Lawyers can sometimes make professional use of negative feelings. Forgas, "Don't Worry, Be Sad!" *Current Directions in Psychological Science*, 225–32.

72. Richard, "Accountability 101—Part Four," *Lawyer Brain Blog*. As reported in Shawn Achor's book *The Happiness Advantage*, doctors who are optimistic and in a good mood reach the right diagnosis 19 percent faster than doctors who are in an unhappy mood. Employees who are happy take fifteen less sick days every year than unhappy employees. Optimistic salespeople outsell pessimistic salespeople by 56 percent. A study that looked at the happiness of Catholic nuns who had produced journals when they were in their twenties found that happiness was a great predictor of how long they lived with about ten more years added to their lives!
73. While the impact of the manipulation appeared to be very small, a controversy arose because of the fear of potential mass emotional influence and because Facebook didn't notify users of the experiment or get their consent. Faye Flam, "Facebook Tried to Manipulate User Emotions for Study: Journalists Cite Improper Informed Consent," *UnDark*, June 30, 2014, http://undark.org/2014/06/30/facebook-tried-to-manipulate-user-emotions-for-study-journalists-cite-improper-informed-consent/.
74. Cherniss, "Emotional Intelligence."
75. Barsade, "The Ripple Effect: Emotional Contagion and Its Influence on Group Behavior," *Administrative Science Quarterly* 47 (2002): 644–75.
76. Jack Zenger and Joseph Folkman, "The Ideal Praise-to-Criticism Ratio," *Harvard Business Review*, March 15, 2013; Richard, "Accountability 101—Part Four," *Lawyer Brain Blog*. Early research recommended ratios of three to six positive comments to each negative one. Other studies established positivity ratios for successful married couples (5:1), and successful teams (5.5:1). The concept of a fixed positivity ratio was fairly thoroughly debunked in 2013: Dan Cossins, "'Positivity Ratio' Debunked," *The Scientist*, August 7, 2013, http://www.the-scientist.com/?articles.view/articleNo/36910/title/-Positivity-Ratio—Debunked/.
77. "My own informal, unscientific studies in several law firms show a dismal ratio of less than 1:1. In one firm I worked with, the ratio was 0.8:1 . . . [They say] it's important to be 'realistic,' to pay attention to threats, worst case scenarios, what could go wrong, etc. (This type of thinking generates negative emotions.) . . . research also shows how important it is to balance out this negative attention with a much larger attention to what's good, what works, and what positive developments might be just around the bend. (This type of thinking generates positive emotions.) Bottom line: Until the ratio gets beyond 3:1 (3 positive:1 negative), thriving is unlikely." Ibid.
78. Ravi S. Gajendran and Deepak Somaya, "Employees Leave Good Bosses Nearly as Often as Bad Ones," *Harvard Business Review*, March, 2016.
79. Joyce E. Bono et al., "Workplace Emotions: The Role of Supervision and Leadership," *Journal of Applied Psychology* 92 (2007): 1357–67.

80. "Good Managers Fake It," *Science Daily*, January 10, 2013, http://www.sciencedaily.com/releases/2013/01/130109215238.htm.
81. Bono et al., "Workplace Emotions," *Journal of Applied Psychology*.
82. Tom Wallerstein, "From Biglaw to Boutique: Bad Hires," *Above the Law*, December13,2012,http://abovethelaw.com/2012/12/from-biglaw-to-boutique-bad-hires/.
83. Mark Levin, "Law Firms Could Learn a Lot from the NFL Draft," *The Right Profile*, 2016, http://therightprofile.com/press-and-media/law-firms-could-learn-a-lot-from-the-nfl-draft/.
84. Claudio Fernández-Aráoz, Boris Groysberg, and Nitin Nohria, "How to Hang On to Your High Potentials," *Harvard Business Review*, October, 2011.
85. John E. Hunter, Frank L. Schmidt, and Michael K. Judiesch, "Individual Differences in Output Variability as a Function of Job Complexity," *Journal of Applied Psychology* 75 (1990): 28–42; Lex Borghans et al., "The Economics and Psychology of Personality Traits," *Journal of Human Resources* 43 (2008). Neal M. Ashkanasy and Ronald H. Humphrey, "Current Emotion Research in Organizational Behavior," *Emotion Review* 3 (2011): 214–24.
86. Huy Le et al., "Too Much of a Good Thing: Curvilinear Relationships between Personality Traits and Job Performance," *Journal of Applied Psychology* 96 (2011): 113–33.
87. In 2014, about 62 percent of companies used some sort of assessment tool as part of the hiring process, up from 48 percent in 2010. Camille Chatterjee, "Interview Test Prep: 6 Common Personality Assessments—And How Employers Use Them," *Forbes*, May 28, 2015. "More than 80% of midsize and large companies use personality and ability assessments for entry and midlevel positions as either pre-employment or new-employee orientation tools," according to Development Dimensions International, a global human-resources consultancy. Joseph Walker, "Do New Job Tests Foster Bias? As More Companies Adopt Personality Screening, Questions of Legality Emerge," *The Wall Street Journal*, September 20, 2012. Many corporate employers test for personality traits, even though they predict performance only to a small degree with respect to skilled and semi-skilled occupations. G.M. Hurtz and J.J. Donavan, "Personality and Job Performance: The Big Five Revisited," *Journal of Applied Psychology* 85 (2000): 869–79. Employers of large workforces with potentially large turnover rates use personal style data to better predict which potential employees are likely to stay longer and thereby reduce turnover by up to 50 percent. Even small companies have found reasons to use hiring assessments to address their specific concerns. For example, a small waste-disposal firm used an online test to gauge applicants' emotional stability, work ethic, and attitudes toward drugs and alcohol; its workers' comp claims fell 68 percent since using the test. Walker, "Meet the New Boss: Big Data," *The Wall Street Journal*.
88. Cherniss, "Emotional Intelligence." Introduced in 1956.
89. Goleman, "They've Taken Emotional Intelligence Too Far," *Time*. Other widely available assessment instruments that businesses use for hiring and advancement include the Birkman Method, the Caliper's Profile, the Myers-Briggs Type Indicator, the California Personality Inventory, Raymond Cattell's Institute for Personality and Ability Testing (IPAT), and the Minnesota Multiphasic

Personality Inventory (MMPI). The Gallup Organization and Professor Seligman have developed assessments to identify "signature strengths." "VIA Institute on Character," *VIA*, https://www.viacharacter.org/www/. Companies are even looking to handwriting and blood type experts to evaluate candidates. "Use Personality Assessment for Better Hiring," *FindLaw*, http://practice.findlaw.com/human-resources/use-personality-assessment-for-better-hiring.html#sthash.zlzA2o2i.dpuf.

90. Walker, "Meet the New Boss: Big Data," *The Wall Street Journal*. Xerox's analysis of its best employees found that work experience was of little relevance, while personal attributes were determinative, and six months after initiating a new hiring profile based on a pre-hiring personality assessment, attrition was cut by 20 percent. See also *Hiring for Attitude*, a 2012 book by Mark Murphy, which lists companies that hire people for their "attitudes" rather than for particular skills, despite the fact that the skills needed at each company are quite different. Since 2005, all the pilots Air Canada has hired have been tested for EI because "An airline captain is . . . a team leader . . . not only interacting with the other crew members but also with other departments within the airline." Marcia Hughes, Henry L. Thompson, and James Bradford Terrell, *Handbook for Developing Emotional and Social Intelligence: Best Practices, Case Studies, and Strategies* (New York: Wiley, 2010).
91. "Use Personality Assessment for Better Hiring," *FindLaw*. As global spending on talent-management software has risen, so has the value of companies producing that software, rising 15 percent to $3.8 billion in 2011. Large tech companies have been buying up these software companies. In August 2012, IBM bought Kenexa Corp, which uses data analysis for recruiting and retaining workers, for $1.3 billion. Oracle Corp. acquired job applicant tracking system company Taleo for $1.9 billion in February 2011, and in late 2011 SAP AG bought SuccessFactors, specializing in performance tracking, recruitment, and compensation, for $3.4 billion. Joseph Walker, "Do New Job Tests Foster Bias?" *The Wall Street Journal*, September 20, 2012.
92. Natalie Kitroeff, "Five Charts That Show You Should Apply to Law School This Year," *Bloomberg*, April 22, 2015, http://www.bloomberg.com/news/articles/2015-04-22/five-charts-that-show-you-should-apply-to-law-school-this-year. Complaints were being made by lawyer leaders already in 2007 that hiring the best people, while their highest priority, was stymied by, among other things, the limited pool of quality law graduates. Daniel J. DiLucchio, Jr., "Learnings for Managing Partners," *Altman Weil, Inc.*, November, 2007, http://www.altmanweil.com/index.cfm/fa/r.resource_detail/oid/1924bfae-530a-413b-8b09-5c15d41a7cb1/resource/Learnings_for_Managing_Partners.cfm. The situation has only gotten worse.
93. From 2008 to 2012, law school applications from Ivy Leaguers dropped 27 percent, surpassing the 20 percent decline for all applications for that same period. As of March 2016, applications since 2010 from these schools are down more than 48 percent. Jordan Weissmann, "Ivy League Students Are Still Avoiding Law School Like the Plague," *Slate*, March 14, 2016, http://www.slate.com/blogs/moneybox/2016/03/14/fewer_elite_college_students_are_applying_to_law_school.html.

94. Stephanie Francis Ward, "Those With Good LSAT Scores May be Choosing to Forgo Law School, Data Indicates," *ABA Journal,* June 13, 2017.
95. Delece Smith-Barrow, "As Law Schools Undergo Reform, Some Relax LSAT Requirements," *U.S News and World Report,* April 2, 2015, http://www.usnews.com/education/best-graduate-schools/top-law-schools/articles/2015/04/02/as-law-schools-undergo-reform-some-relax-lsat-requirements. Elizabeth Olson, "Harvard Law, Moving to Diversify Applicant Pool, Will Accept GRE Scores," *New York Times,* March 8, 2017.
96. Keith Lee, "Top University Students Are Increasingly Not Choosing Law School," *Associate's Mind,* August 12, 2013, http://associatesmind.com/2013/08/12/top-university-students-are-increasingly-not-choosing-law-school/.
97. Zach Warren, "Law School Class Size Decreasing, Says Survey," *InsideCounsel,* October, 2013.
98. Dinovitzer and Garth, "Lawyer Satisfaction in the Process of Structuring Legal Careers," *Law and Society Review,* 24.
99. The lure of law practice is fading. "Consider the statistics: Eighty-five percent of today's newest lawyers are carrying six-figure law school debt. Only about half of all those graduating from law school in 2012 found full-time long-term jobs requiring a J.D. A US Bureau of Labor Statistics employment report indicates that between December 2012 and December 2013, employment in the 'all legal services' category actually declined by 1,000 people. http://www.bls.gov/news.release/empsit.t17.htm As the profession was losing 1,000 jobs last year, law schools graduated a record number of new lawyers—46,000—and more large classes are in the pipeline. Sure, law school applications are down, but acceptance rates have gone way, way up to compensate, and recently revised BLS estimates suggest an ongoing lawyer glut for years to come." Steven J. Harper, "The Big Problem with the Ongoing Law School Bailout," *American Lawyer,* January 17, 2014.
100. Barry Schwartz's best-selling book, *The Paradox of Choice,* argues that having more possibilities can often produce paralysis instead of better choices, and may well impair not only decision-making ability but also the integrity of the decision-making process. Barry Schwartz, *The Paradox of Choice* (New York: Harper Collins, 2004).
101. Bill Henderson, Caren Ulrich Stacy, and Steve Gibson, "Everything You Think You Know about Lawyer Recruiting Is Wrong: The New Science of Evidence-Based Hiring Practices," *Bloomberg,* October 10, 2011, http://www.bna.com/new-science-of-evidence-based-hiring/.
102. Dalton, "Deviations from the Norm: The Lawyer 'Type' and Legal Hiring," *Above the Law.*
103. According to the NALP, "56% of entry-level associates will leave a firm within four years while 73% of laterals leave in the same period." Elizabeth Goldberg, "Is This Any Way to Recruit Associates?" *National Law Journal,* August 1, 2007.
104. "Managing partners responding to the Hildebrandt/Citi 2015 Client Advisory's confidential survey admitted that only about half of their lateral partners were break-even at best." Harper, "Big Law Leaders Perpetuating Mistakes," *The Belly of the Beast.*
105. Levin, "Law Firms Could Learn a Lot from the NFL Draft," *The Right Profile.*

106. Henderson, Stacy, and Gibson, "Everything You Think You Know about Lawyer Recruiting Is Wrong," *Bloomberg.* It takes an average of eight people who know each other well to get a reliable "intuitive" sense of another person. Elfenbein and Ambady, "Predicting Workplace Outcomes from the Ability to Eavesdrop on Feelings," *Journal of Applied Psychology,* 87 (2002): 963–71. "Culture fit is an absolutely critical determinant of longer-term fit, and not easy to discern in an interview," according to Jay Gaines, chief executive of Jay Gaines & Co., a New York executive search firm. Mantell, "Job Seekers, Get Ready for Personality Tests," *MarketWatch.* Evidently 81 percent of people lie about themselves during job interviews, which doesn't make it easier. "The Daily Stat," *Harvard Business Review.*
107. Weiss, "Like Polo and Sailing? Listing It on a Law Firm Resume Helped Men but Not Women, Study Finds," *ABA Journal,* October 24, 2016.
108. As one recruiter admitted: "Someone who was No. 2 in a class, we would talk ourselves into hiring. Oftentimes they wouldn't do well." And another one: "If a student got the thumbs-up from a Stanford Law School professor, then she must be smart and able to succeed." Goldberg, "Is This Any Way to Recruit Associates?" *National Law Journal.*
109. Shultz and Zedeck, "Predicting Lawyer Effectiveness," *Law and Social Inquiry,* 654.
110. David Lat, "More Info about the Morgan Lewis/Bingham McCutchen Deal," *Above the Law,* November 19, 2014; Julie Triedman, "Ex-Howrey Chair Discusses His New Shop, Old Firm's Demise," *American Lawyer,* January 28, 2016.
111. Goldberg, "Is This Any Way to Recruit Associates?" *National Law Journal.*
112. A mandate that hasn't been acted on in spite of near-unanimous agreement. In a survey of seventy-eight large law firms conducted by Thomson Reuters in 2010, 86 percent indicated that their firms were actively investing time and resources into innovatively changing their practices, which 82 percent rated either "important" or "extremely important" to the future of their firms. The two areas of innovation ranked most important were marketing and client development (82 percent) and talent acquisition, training, and management (76 percent). "2011 Client Advisory," *Hildebrandt Baker Robbins,* 2011, 16.
113. Hilborne, "Law Firms That Fail to Change 'No Longer Sustainable' After 2020, Report Predicts," *LegalFutures.*
114. In addition to the changing imperatives of personal style, technical expertise like information technology and artificial intelligence skills are becoming more critical abilities for zealously representing clients, particularly when governments and lawyers are on the other side, and "lawyers are required to use AI under ABA Model Rule 1.1 and Rule 1 of the Federal Rules of Civil Procedure (FRCP)." Dipshan, "Ready or Not, Lawyers Are Increasingly Bound to AI by Ethical, Legal Standards," *Legaltechnews,* June 16, 2016, http://www.legaltechnews.com/id=1202760242618/Ready-or-Not-Lawyers-are-Increasingly-Bound-to-AI-by-Ethical-Legal-Standards#ixzz4BqbHmBDD.
115. Sloan, "Hiring Partners: What's So Bad About Spring Recruitment?" *National Law Journal.*

116. In the United States, "Firms respond to cattle calls at top law schools. There, partners meet 20 students a day for 20 minutes at a time for several days in a row . . . [then] students are called back for a series of 30-minute office interviews. If a student is from a good school, has an acceptable resume, and decent social skills, he or she is practically guaranteed an offer. . . . And nine times out of 10, a summer job leads to an offer for a full-time associate position." It is an expensive process: by one calculation, after spending $250,000 to recruit each summer associate, only 28 percent of students offered a job will accept; and one hiring partner estimated that it took 6,000 hours of attorney time to recruit 57 summer associates, with expenses for travel, entertainment, and so on, additional. And it was not a very successful one in identifying loyal hires: "after associates do join a firm following their summer stints, 40 percent of them will leave by the end of their third year and 62 percent by the end of their fourth . . . according to NALP figures, firms report that 51 percent of associate departures every year are unwanted." Goldberg, "Is This Any Way to Recruit Associates?" *National Law Journal.*
117. Levin, "Law Firms Could Learn a Lot from the NFL Draft," *The Right Profile.* In 1999, when the American Management Association reported that 68 percent of Fortune 500 companies used psychometric testing for hiring, consultant Larry Richard estimated that less than 1 percent of law firms did. Richard, "Hiring Emotionally Intelligent Associates," *Bench and Bar of Minnesota.* John Remsen, Jr., "Building for the Future: Audience Polling Results from the MPF 2016 Leadership Conference," *LinkedIn.com,* June 17, 2016.
118. "McKinsey typically has candidates do five to seven hour-long interviews; each one includes a case study. Some applicants also take a multiple-choice test that presents real-life scenarios and requires some math to draw conclusions." Goldberg, "Is This Any Way to Recruit Associates?" *National Law Journal.*
119. Jain et al., "A Randomized Controlled Trial of Mindfulness Meditation versus Relaxation Training: Effects on Distress, Positive States of Mind, Rumination and Distraction," *Annals of Behavioral Medicine,* 11–21. A study of the competence of doctoral level clinical psychology trainees found that the best client-rated outcomes occurred with trainees who had the highest EI scores, while the worst client-rated outcomes occurred with trainees who had lower EI scores, and concluded by urging that doctoral candidates be screened for EI. Troy Rieck and Jennifer L. Callahan, "Emotional Intelligence and Psychotherapy Outcomes in the Training Clinic," *Training and Education in Professional Psychology,* Vol 7(1), February 2013, 42-52. http://psycnet.apa.org/?&fa=main.doiLanding&doi=10.1037/a0031659.
120. "Law Firm Verbal Reasoning and Situational Judgement Test Preparation," *Job Test Prep,* 2016, https://www.jobtestprep.co.uk/law-aptitude-test.
121. Goldberg, "Is This Any Way to Recruit Associates?" *National Law Journal.*
122. Levin, "Law Firms Could Learn a Lot from the NFL Draft," *The Right Profile.* Richard, "Hiring Emotionally Intelligent Associates," *Bench and Bar Minnesota.*
123. According to Keith S. Mullin, CEO of New York's Mullin & Associates/ Lincolnshire International, an out-placement firm, "Using testing to make hiring decisions is most effective when organizations have determined behavioral traits and competencies as success indicators and implemented them

into an effective performance appraisal system. . . . In my opinion, law firms could benefit from better understanding the kind of information collected, what the tests say about someone and how the results can be used." "Use Personality Assessment for Better Hiring," *FindLaw.*

124. Lauren Weber and Elizabeth Dwoskin, "Are Workplace Personality Tests Fair? Growing Use of Tests Sparks Scrutiny Amid Questions of Effectiveness and Workplace Discrimination," *Wall Street Journal,* September 29, 2014.
125. Sloan, "Hiring Partners: What's So Bad about Spring Recruitment?" *National Law Journal.*
126. Jeff Foster et al., "Understanding Lawyers: The Personality Traits of Successful Practitioners—Results from the Hogan Assessment Project on Lawyer Personality," *Hildebrandt Baker Robbins,* 6.
127. Press, "Time for the Am Law 200 to Embrace Testing for Talent?" *American Lawyer,* July 25, 2013.
128. Henderson, Stacy, and Gibson, "Everything You Think You Know about Lawyer Recruiting Is Wrong: The New Science of Evidence-Based Hiring Practices," *Bloomberg.*
129. Noah Messing, "Talent Assessments at Law Firms," *Above the Law,* June 28, 2013, http://abovethelaw.com/career-files/talent-assessment-at-law-firms/
130. "One advantage of the workplace personality assessments is the ability to quickly and cost-effectively administer these tests such that the results can be compiled and available even for a compressed on-campus interviewing timeline." Henderson, Stacy, and Gibson, "Everything You Think You Know about Lawyer Recruiting Is Wrong: The New Science of Evidence-Based Hiring Practices," *Bloomberg.*
131. Foster et al., "Understanding Lawyers," *Hildebrandt Baker Robbins,* 6.
132. In evaluating laterals, for example, using assessment data makes it more likely we can avoid "high-performing but selfish partners, who might be a toxic influence, and instead seek candidates who have a track record of working across boundaries." Gardner, "When Senior Managers Won't Collaborate," *Harvard Business Review.*
133. "A lot of the discussion tends to focus on using these tests in hiring decisions. But they arguably can be as helpful—and easier to accept—when making decisions about naming new practice group leaders or office chiefs. Understanding their tendencies toward teamwork or rigidity or pursuit of goals may help avoid mistakes as well as give otherwise promising candidates self-improvement agendas." Press, "Time for the Am Law 200 to Embrace Testing for Talent?" *American Lawyer.*
134. Goldberg, "Is This Any Way to Recruit Associates?" *National Law Journal.* "What it has done," says global recruiting director at Deloitte John Campagnino, "is allow us to move away from just-like-me recruiting—partners saying, 'You had a paper route, and I had a paper route, and I'm a partner, so you must do well.'"
135. "Seventy-One Percent of Employers Say They Value Emotional Intelligence Over IQ, According to CareerBuilder Survey," *PR Newswire,* August 18, 2011, http://newswire.com/news-releases/seventy-one-percent-of-employers-say-they-value-emotional-intelligence-over-iq-according-to-careerbuilder-survey-127995518.html.

136. "MD SELECT Program," *USF Health.*
137. Early adopters were Orrick, Herrington & Sutcliffe and DLA Piper, and Baker Botts, Paul, Hastings and Vinson & Elkins, among others, have joined them. Weiss, "Are You the Type That Likes to Run with Scissors? McKenna Long Has a Test to Exclude You," *ABA Journal,* April 22, 2011. A writing sample or case assessment is also a window into thought processes. Atlanta civil-rights boutique Barrett & Farahany requires applicants to interview a potential client and write a memo advising the firm whether to take the client's case—among other steps in the hiring process—which are compared to other candidates' memos. Messing, "Talent Assessment at Law Firms," *Above the Law,* June 28, 2013, http://abovethelaw.com/career-files/talent-assessment-at-law-firms/.
138. Goldberg, "Is This Any Way to Recruit Associates?" *National Law Journal.*
139. "[P]opular interest seems to have outstripped scientific interest." Frank J. Landy, "Some historical and scientific issues related to research on emotional intelligence," *Journal of Organizational Behavior,* April 14, 2005, 412. EI is hawked as the way to lose weight, to be a better poker player, and to improve your romantic and sex life. Susan Albers, *Eat Q: Unlock the Weight-Loss Power of Emotional Intelligence* (New York: HarperCollins, 2013); Stephen Bloomfield, "You Must Have Emotional Intelligence at the Poker Table," *Ante Up Magazine,* August 23, 2013, http://www.anteupmagazine.com/featured-column/you-must-have-emotional-intelligence-at-the-poker-table.htm; "Emotional Intelligence 'Aids Sex': Women Who Are More 'Emotionally Intelligent' Get Greater Pleasure from Sex, Research on Twins Suggests," *BBC News,* May 9, 2009, http://news.bbc.co.uk/2/hi/8044571.stm; Eric Ravenscroft, "Why You Make Bad Decisions When You're Attracted to Someone," *Lifehacker.com,* January 14, 2014, http://lifehacker.com/why-you-make-bad-decisions-when-youre-attracted-to-som-1501035149.
140. There are over 2,500 psychological and personal style assessments on the market, with more arriving every year. Not surprisingly then, some, even many, are ineffective. Fortunately, there is a scientific method for measuring the effectiveness of an assessment: it must have high levels of both validity (descriptive accuracy and effectiveness in prediction) and reliability (consistency over time). For a short primer on assessment statistics for lawyers, see H. Beau Baez III's article, "Personality Tests in Employment Selection: Use with Caution," *Cornell HR Review,* January 26, 2013.
141. Steve Tobak, "Why Emotional Intelligence Is Just a Fad," *CBS Money Watch,* February 13, 2012, http://www.cbsnews.com/8301-505125_162-57376240/why-emotional-intelligence-is-just-a-fad/. Some test takers evidently do fake at least a few answers, but these tests are constructed so that questions are "varied, complex, reinforcing and self-checking," making it hard to effectively fake any attribute in a significant way. The EQ-i, for example, has been singled out as being amenable to faking. W.L Grubb III and M.A McDaniel, "The Fakability of Bar-On's Emotional Quotient Inventory Short Form: Catch Me if You Can," *Human Performance* 20 (2007): 43–59.
142. As one EI researcher commiserated: "We are all unique human beings . . . It's bad enough for our banks, governments and supermarkets to treat us as just another number or category of customer without psychologists getting in on

the act!" Keith Beasley quoted in Mayer, "Measuring Emotional Intelligence," *Emotional Intelligence Information,* April 2013, http://www.unh.edu/emotional_intelligence/ei%20Measuring%20EI/eiMeasure%20why%20measure.htm.

143. "It is very difficult for people to understand themselves without some kind of independent feedback." Ibid.
144. "Use Personality Assessment for Better Hiring," *FindLaw.com.*
145. Vivia Chen, "McKenna Long's Recruiting Couch," *The Careerist,* January 25, 2011, http://thecareerist.typepad.com/thecareerist/2011/01/should-firms-use-psyche-test-in-hiring.html.
146. Richard, "Hiring Emotionally Intelligent Associates," *Minnesota Bar and Bench.*
147. Vivia Chen, "Our Secret Sauce," *The Careerist,* April 21, 2011, http://thecareerist.typepad.com/thecareerist/2011/04/our-secret-sauce.html.
148. Kristopher J. Brooks, "It's Time to Pay Attention to the Millennial Generation," *Democrat & Chronicle,* May 7, 2016, http://www.democratandchronicle.com/story/money/business/2016/05/06/s-time-pay-attention-millennial-generation/83918404/.
149. Goldberg, "Is This Any Way to Recruit Associates?" *National Law Journal.*
150. Quoted in Goldberg, "Is This Any Way to Recruit Associates?" *National Law Journal.*
151. "U.S. Equal Employment Opportunity Commission Strategic Enforcement Plan FY 2013–2016," *U.S Equal Employment Opportunity Commission,* 2013, https://www.eeoc.gov/eeoc/plan/sep.cfm. "The EEOC will target class-based intentional recruitment and hiring discrimination and facially neutral recruitment and hiring practices that adversely impact particular groups. Racial, ethnic, and religious groups, older workers, women, and people with disabilities continue to confront discriminatory policies and practices at the recruitment and hiring stages. These include exclusionary policies and practices, the channeling/steering of individuals into specific jobs due to their status in a particular group, restrictive application processes, and the use of screening tools (e.g., pre-employment tests, background checks, date-of-birth inquiries)." Walker, "Do New Job Tests Foster Bias?" *The Wall Street Journal.*
152. Those that don't meet the standard are likely touching on mental disabilities. Weber and Dwoskin, "Are Workplace Personality Tests Fair?" *The Wall Street Journal.* Talent Plus, one vendor of EI assessments, for example, claims that their assessments meet numerous rigorous guidelines set up by several professional societies and agencies, and only one court case has challenged its employment screening process, which was dismissed. "TalentPlus," *TalentPlus.com,* 2016, http://www.talentplus.com/.
153. C.I. Farh, M.G. Seo, and P.E. Tesluk, "Emotional Intelligence, Teamwork Effectiveness, and Job Performance: The Moderating Role of Job Context," *Journal of Applied Psychology* 97 (2012): 890–900. EI skills were found to be more relevant than personality, cognitive ability, emotional labor job demands, or job complexity.
154. J. Gooty et al., "The Wisdom of Letting Go and Performance: The Moderating Role of Emotional Intelligence and Discrete Emotions," *Journal of Occupational and Organizational Psychology* 87 (2014): 392–413. Another study found that

EI positively predicts performance for high emotional labor jobs, which lawyering undoubtedly is. Dana L. Joseph and Daniel A. Newman, "Emotional Intelligence: An Integrative Meta-Analysis and Cascading Model," *Journal of Applied Psychology* 95 (2010): 54–78. One study that found the association between EI and job performance and good "organizational citizenship behavior" grew stronger as cognitive intelligence decreased contrasts with a 2002 study finding that EI had a stronger relationship to job performance in emotionally demanding jobs. Côté and Miners, "Emotional Intelligence, Cognitive Intelligence, and Job Performance," *Administrative Science Quarterly*, 15–18.

155. Goleman, "They've Taken Emotional Intelligence Too Far," *Time*.
156. Press, "Time for the Am Law 200 to Embrace Testing for Talent?" *American Lawyer*.
157. Eduardo Salas et al., "The Science of Training and Development in Organizations: What Matters in Practice," *Psychological Science in the Public Interest* 13 (2012): 74–101.
158. A survey of the top 200 UK law partners identified people management as the area they would most like to improve, yet 45 percent reported their firm had made no improvement at all. Matt Byrne, "Lawyers Are Years Behind Accountants on Process and BD, *The Lawyer* Research Reveals," *The Lawyer*, June 24, 2013. In a 2010 Thomson Reuters annual survey of 78 large law firms, 86 percent of respondents indicated their firms were actively investing time and resources into changing aspects of their legal practice, with 82 percent rating these changes either "important" or "extremely important" to the future of their firms. The two areas ranked most important were marketing and client development (82 percent) and talent acquisition, training, and management (76 percent). "2011 Client Advisory," *Hildebrandt Baker Robbins*, 16.
159. Gardner, "When Senior Managers Won't Collaborate," *Harvard Business Review*.
160. Freedman, "Case Study: Emotional Intelligence for People-First Leadership at FedEx Express," *SixSeconds.org*, January 14, 2014, http://www.6seconds.org/2014/01/14/case-study-emotional-intelligence-people-first-leadership-fedex-express/.
161. Ibid.
162. Ibid.
163. "It's Just Emotion, Taking HR Over," *HC Online*.
164. Training at Shell Asia and GAMBRO DASCO, a medical dialysis company, for example, which included access to an EI coach, successfully boosted team cohesion and performance even three years after training ended. Granville D'Souza, "Case – EQ at Shell Asia: Enduring Boost for Teamwork from Blended EQ Program," *Six Seconds*, November 21, 2011; "EQ Blended Learning at GAMBRO DASCO," *Six Seconds*, July 7, 2010.
165. Gerry Riskin, "Retaining Associates with Potential: The Coaching Circle," *Amazing Firms, Amazing Practices*, 2017, http://www.gerryriskin.com/retaining-associates-with-potential-the-coaching-circle/.
166. MP McQueen, "Survey: Midlevel Associates Are Happier Than Ever," *American Lawyer*, September 1, 2016.

167. Middleburg and Butterworth, "Emotional Intelligence," *The Barrister Magazine,* 2013.
168. "[E]valuating clients' coachability levels at the start of the sessions can increase the effectiveness of coaching," illustrated by the "old joke about how many psychologists it takes to change a light bulb. Just one—so long as the light bulb wants to change." Chamorro-Premuzic, "Can You Really Improve Your Emotional Intelligence?" *Harvard Business Review.*
169. Rhode, "Developing Leadership," *Santa Clara Law Review,* 716.
170. From an address delivered at Boston University in late fall 1928. M.P Follett, "The Teacher–Student Relation," *Administrative Science Quarterly* 15 (1970): 146.
171. Chamorro-Premuzic, "Can You Really Improve Your Emotional Intelligence?" *Harvard Business Review.*
172. Richard, "The Psychologically Savvy Leader," *Lawyer Brain Blog,* November 14, 2013, http://www.lawyerbrainblog.com/2013/11/the-psychologically-savvy-leader/.
173. "The analysis of 34 information team leaders of an Italian company . . . showed a significant difference . . . between the Emotional Intelligence measured before and after the EQ training." Bradberry and Greaves, *Emotional Intelligence 2.0,* 21, 252. A Swedish training, replicated in the United States, Italy, and Australia, saw senior managers' total EI and most of their EI subscales rise, with emotional self-awareness and empathy increasing the most. The training involves first giving the participants an EI assessment, then having them participate in a 90-day training course "intended to teach emotional intelligence skills to managers." Lorenzo Fariselli, Joshua Freedman, and Massimiliano Ghini, "Increasing Emotional Intelligence," *SixSeconds.org,* January 8, 2008, http://prodimages.6seconds.org/media/WP_Increase_EQ.pdf.
174. There is ongoing research on the connection between training and the phenomenon of brain plasticity. The Max Planck Institute is one of the centers highly involved in "the plasticity of the social brain and the investigation of trainability of socio-affective functions . . . [including] empathy, compassion, affect regulation, cognitive perspective taking, mindfulness, attention, and memory. In the context of these studies, we are researching . . . the implementation of scientifically validated, effective training programs for schools and economic or political organizations." "Department of Social Neuroscience," *Max Planck Institute,* 2017, http://www.cbs.mpg.de/depts/singer/arb3. Neuropsychological studies suggest that, with adequate training, "people can become more pro-social, altruistic, and compassionate." Chamorro-Premuzic, "Can You Really Improve Your Emotional Intelligence?" *Harvard Business Review.* "Focused attention stimulates release of neurotransmitters that encourage plasticity and learning." Bridging Brain, Mind, and Behavior Research Award, James S. McDonnell Foundation quoted in Fariselli, Ghini, and Freedman, "Age and Emotional Intelligence," *SixSeconds.org,* http://prodimages.6seconds.org/media/WP_EQ_and_Age.pdf.
175. Dental employees successfully raised their EI scores after a single day-long training. B.B. Meyer, T.B. Fletcher, and S.J. Parker, "Enhancing Emotional Intelligence in the Health Care Environment," *Journal of Health Care Management* 23 (2004): 225–34.

176. The fifteen class hours of training over two-and-a-half days included information on understanding the relationship between "environmental triggers, beliefs, thoughts, emotions, and behaviors" in causing certain emotional reactions; recognizing the link between emotions and "habitual behaviors," thoughts, and reactions; how to use strategies to regulate emotion; how to express emotions and how to listen to others' expressions attentively. Participants were taught how to tackle "emotionally difficult and stressful situations in a more adaptive manner," and encouraged to deal with and manage emotions rather than ignore them. Those who received training experienced a decrease in cortisol levels (indicating lower levels of stress), and reported higher levels of well-being (emotional and physical) and better social and marital relationships, and the benefits remained a year later. Classes ranging in size from ten students conducting EI training over many years to more than 1,000 first discussed the "basic concepts of EI and emotion regulation in a class lecture"; then gave each student an EI self-assessment and application exercise asking them to rate themselves on different EI traits, including emotion regulation, and to consider specific approaches for applying EI and emotion regulation. Kotsou et al., "Emotional Plasticity: Conditions and Effects of Improving Emotional Competence in Adulthood," *Journal of Applied Psychology* 96 (2011): 3–5, 7–9.
177. An 18-hour training program with email follow-up produced sustainable improvements in "emotion regulation, emotion understanding, and overall emotional intelligence," as well as improvements in well-being, health, quality of social relationships, and work success. The training included "short lectures, role-playing games, group discussions, diary analysis and two-person interaction to teach participants basic principles about emotions." The emotional training group scored better on various emotional measures, became more extraverted, less neurotic, and more agreeable, and reported better physical and mental health, and happiness—even months later. The course also improved employability, as judged by human resources professionals who watched videotapes of interviews with participants before and after the course. Delphine Nelis et al., "Increasing Emotional Competence Improves Psychological and Physical Well-being, Social Relationships and Employability," *Emotion* 11 (2011): 361. See also Middleburg and Butterworth, "Emotional Intelligence," *The Barrister Magazine*, 2013.
178. Research conducted at the business school at the University of Queensland in Australia found that an EI skill development program helped low EI individuals "catch up to their colleagues' higher scores." Bar-On, "The Bar-On model of emotional-social intelligence," *Psicothema*.
179. Brown and Bylund, "Communication Skills Training: Describing a New Conceptual Model," *Academic Medicine* 83: 37–44.
180. F.J. Satterfield and E. Hughes, "Emotion Skills Training for Medical Students: A Systematic Review," *Medical Education* 41 (2007): 935–41. USF's medical school is planning on instituting EI training for all medical students. Grewal and Davidson, "Emotional Intelligence and Graduate Medical Education," *Journal of the American Medical Association*. Several Canadian medical schools are piloting EI skill training. "Physician Leadership Institute," *Canadian Medical*

Association. Some medical schools train for "relationship" skills like listening and building trust, which also help build EI. Filip Lievens, Deniz S. Ones, and Stephan Dilchert, "Personality Scale Validities Increase Throughout Medical School," *Journal of Applied Psychology* 94 (2009): 1514–35. The WellStar Health System used training and coaches for their more than 550 doctors in five hospitals. Patient reports of clear communication rose from 77.5 percent to 86.2 percent within only a few months. After over 1,000 doctors took online training, the Missouri School of Medicine Medical Center's patient-satisfaction scores went from some of the lowest in the country to over 90 percent in 2012. Landro, "The Talking Cure for Healthcare," *The Wall Street Journal*.

181. "[P]atient satisfaction jumped from about average to among the top 8% of the roughly 4,600 hospitals included. Hospital executives from all over the world now flock to Cleveland to study the Clinic's practices and to learn how it changed." Landro, "The Talking Cure," *The Wall Street Journal*. "The Clinic's journey also holds lessons for organizations outside healthcare—ones that until now have not had to compete by creating a superior experience for customers. Such enterprises often have workforces that were not hired with customer satisfaction in mind. Can they improve the customer experience without jeopardizing their traditional strengths? The Clinic's success suggests that they can." Merlino and Raman, "Health Care's Service Fanatics," *Harvard Business Review*.
182. Ilkay Ulutas and Esra Omeroglu, "The Effects of an Emotional Intelligence Education Program on the Emotional Intelligence of Children," *Social Behavior and Personality: An International Journal* 35 (2007): 1365–72. Rivers et al., "Improving the Social and Emotional Climate of Classrooms: A Clustered Randomized Controlled Trial Testing the RULER Approach," *Prevention Science*, 77–87.
183. Goleman, "Teach Emotional Intelligence in Schools," *LinkedIn*, May 19, 2013, http://www.linkedin.com/today/post/article/20130519223058-117825785-teach-emotional-intelligence-in-schools.
184. "Weatherhead MBA Program—Case Western Reserve University," *Consortium for Research on Emotional Intelligence in Organizations*, 2015, http://www.eiconsortium.org/model_programs/weatherhead_mba_program.html. Participants also continued to build new skills in the area.
185. Winfred Arthur Jr. et al., "Effectiveness of Training in Organizations: A Meta-Analysis of Design and Evaluation Features," *Journal of Applied Psychology* 88 (2003): 234–45.
186. A training program for the Hallmark Communities sales staff raised individual and team EI and performance significantly. Bradberry and Greaves, "Self Scores of Emotional Intelligence and Job Performance," *TalentSmart*. Managers at American Express Financial Services who completed a one-day EI workshop followed with colleague coaching achieved 25 percent higher rates of growth in funds under management, a 60–400 percent improvement in productivity over their peers, along with significant improvements in stress levels, positive emotional states, and quality of life. Frederic Luskin, Rick Aberman, and A. DeLorenzo, *The Training of Emotional Competence in Financial Services Advisors* (New Brunswick, NJ: Consortium for Research on Emotional

Intelligence in Organizations, 2002). A one-day seminar and three-day workshop given to the US Navy and Marines resulted in a 39 percent increase in awareness of the emotional dynamics of change, a 43 percent increase in tools for working through those dynamics and a 58 percent increase in tools for teaching others about EI. Freedman, "Case: EQ in the Navy and Marine Corps," *Six Seconds Emotional Intelligence Network.*

187. Richard, "Hiring Emotionally Intelligent Associates," *Bench & Bar of Minnesota.*
188. Press, "Time for the Am Law 200 to Embrace Testing for Talent?" *American Lawyer.*
189. Jeffrey D. Houghton et al., "Effective Stress Management: A Model of Emotional Intelligence, Self-Leadership, and Student Stress Coping," *Journal of Management Education* 36 (2012): 229.
190. Seligman quoted in Dan Bowling, "Stop Whining, You're in the Army Now," *The Careerist,* April 18, 2011, http://thecareerist.typepad.com/the-careerist/2011/04/stop-whining-youre-in-the-army-now.html. In Facebook COO Sheryl Sandberg's commencement speech to University of California Berkeley's Class of 2016, she said that after the sudden loss of her husband, she turned to Seligman to relearn resilience, which is the topic of her second book *Option B* (Knopf 2017), with Adam Grant. Wendy Lee, "Facebook's Sheryl Sandberg Urges Cal Graduates to Be Resilient," *San Francisco Chronicle,* May 14, 2016, http://www.sfgate.com/business/article/Facebook-s-Sheryl-Sandberg-urges-Cal-graduates-7468891.php.
191. Richard, "We Need a Chief Resilience Officer," *Lawyer Brain Blog.*
192. Richard, "The Psychologically Savvy Leader," *Lawyer Brain Blog.*
193. Marjorie A. Silver, "Supporting Attorneys' Personal Skills," *Revista Juridica de la Universidad de Puerto Rico* 78 (2009): 147–65.
194. Richard, "The Psychologically Savvy Leader," *Lawyer Brain Blog.*
195. Rachel Brushfield, "Feeling Decisions: Why Lawyers Need Emotional Intelligence," *ManagingPartner.com,* June 8, 2012, http://www.managing-partner.com/feature/hr/feeling-decisions-why-lawyers-need-emotional-intelligence.
196. Salas et al., "The Science of Training and Development in Organizations: What Matters in Practice," *Psychological Science in the Public Interest* 13 (2012): 74–101. For the benefits of team training in legal workplaces and methods for producing them, see the chapter entitled "Effective Teamwork and Collaboration," Heidi K. Gardner in ed. Rebecca Normand-Hochman, *Managing Talent for Success: Talent Development in Law Firms* (London: Globe Law and Business, 2013), 145–59.
197. "Trained and learned skills will not be demonstrated as job-related behaviors or performance if incumbents do not have the opportunity to perform them. . . . [T]he social context and the favorability of the post training environment play an important role in facilitating the transfer of trained skills to the job and may attenuate the effectiveness of training." Winifred Arthur Jr. et al., "Effectiveness of Training in Organizations: A Meta-Analysis of Design and Evaluation Features," *Journal of Applied Psychology* 88 (2003): 242.
198. "Seventy-One Percent of Employers Say They Value Emotional Intelligence Over IQ, According to CareerBuilder Survey," *PR Newswire,* August 18, 2011,

http://m.prnewswire.com/news-releases/seventy-one-percent-of-employers-say-they-value-emotional-intelligence-over-iq-according-to-careerbuilder-survey-127995518.html.

199. Katherine Richardson and Hannah R. Rothstein, "Effects of Occupational Stress Management Intervention Programs: A Meta-Analysis," *Journal of Occupational Health Psychology* 13 (2008): 69–93. Mark Slaski and Susan Cartwright, "Emotional Intelligence Training and Its Implications for Stress, Health and Performance," *Stress and Health* 19 (2003): 236.
200. A large-scale review of 36 studies representing 55 programs with an average length of 7.4 weeks and involving 2,847 participants reported "a significant medium to large effect." Cognitive-behavioral programs (which attempt to change behavior by changing how we think about our situation) produced larger effects than other types of interventions frequently used. Richardson and Rothstein, "Effects of Occupational Stress Management Intervention Programs," *Journal of Occupational Health Psychology*.
201. Slaski and Cartwright, "Emotional Intelligence Training and Its Implications for Stress, Health and Performance," *Stress and Health*.
202. Verena Hahn et al., "Learning How to Recover from Job Stress: Effects of a Recovery Training Program on Recovery, Recovery-Related Self-Efficacy, and Well-Being," *Journal of Occupational Health Psychology* 16 (2011): 202–16.
203. Houghton et al., "Effective Stress Management: A Model of Emotional Intelligence, Self-Leadership, and Student Stress Coping," *Journal of Management Education* 36 (2012): 220, 231.
204. Barbara L. Fredrickson et al., "Open Hearts Build Lives: Positive Emotions, Induced Through Loving-Kindness Meditation, Build Consequential Personal Resources," *Journal of Personality and Social Psychology* 95 (2008): 1045–62.
205. Emma Seppala, "Compassionate Mind, Healthy Body," *Greater Good*, July 24, 2013, http://greatergood.berkeley.edu/article/item/compassionate_mind_healthy_body.
206. Goleman, "Two Key Skills for High-Performance Leadership," *More Than Sound*.
207. Rhonda Magee, "Educating Lawyers to Meditate?" *UMKC Law Review*, 79 (2010): 1–60. See also "Meditation Appears to Produce Enduring Changes in Emotional Processing in the Brain," *Massachusetts General Hospital News Releases*, November 12, 2012, http://www.massgeneral.org/about/pressrelease.aspx?id=1520.
208. David Gelles, "At Aetna, a C.E.O.'s Management by Mantra," *New York Times*, February 27, 2015. Lawyer Janice Marturano, formerly general counsel and VP for public responsibility at General Mills, started a popular Mindful Leadership program at the company. Robin Rauzi, "Tapping into the Power of Mindfulness," *Los Angeles Times*, February 23, 2013.
209. Manish Chopra, "Want to Be a Better Leader? Observe More and React Less," *McKinsey Quarterly*, February 2016, http://www.mckinsey.com/global-themes/leadership/want-to-be-a-better-leader-observe-more-and-react-less?cid=other-eml-nsl-mip-mck-oth-1603I. Manish Chopra is a principal in McKinsey's New York office and author of The Equanimeous Mind, which chronicles his initial experiences with Vipassana meditation and the impact it had on his personal outlook and professional life.

210. Krasner et al. "Association of an Education Program in Mindful Communication with Burnout, Empathy, and Attitudes among Primary Care Physicians," *Journal of the American Medical Association* 302 (2009): 1284–93.
211. Lea Brovedani, "What's Love Got to Do with It?" *Six Seconds.org*, July 20, 2013, http://www.6seconds.org/2013/08/20/whats-love-got-to-do-with-it/.
212. Quoted in Carolyn Gregoire, "Google's 'Jolly Good Fellow' On the Power of Emotional Intelligence," *Huffington Post*, September 29, 2013, http://www.huffingtonpost.com/2013/09/29/googles-jolly-good-fellow_n_3975944.html. Drake Baer, "Here's What Google Teaches Employees in Its 'Search Inside Yourself' Course," *Business Insider*, August 5, 2014, http://www.businessinsider.com/search-inside-yourself-googles-life-changing-mindfulness-course-2014-8.
213. Caitlin Kelly, "Ok Google, Take a Deep Breath" *New York Times*, April 28, 2012.
214. Gregoire, "Google's 'Jolly Good Fellow' On the Power of Emotional Intelligence," *Huffington Post*.
215. Charles Halpern, "The Mindful Lawyer: Why Contemporary Lawyers Are Practicing Meditation," *Journal of Legal Education* 61 (2012): 641–46.
216. Jane DiRenzo Pigott, "Investing in Your High Potentials: Coaching Circles," *Legal Solutions*, March, 2016, http://info.legalsolutions.thomsonreuters.com/signup/newsletters/practice-innovations/2016-mar/article2.aspx.
217. Chamorro-Premuzic, "Can You Really Improve Your Emotional Intelligence?" *Harvard Business Review*.
218. Ibid.
219. Wolff, *Emotional Competence Inventory*, 37.
220. Pigott, "Investing in Your High Potentials: Coaching Circles," *Legal Solutions*.
221. "CFOs Value Interpersonal Skills," *Business Finance*, July 31, 2008, http://businessfinancemag.com/hr/cfos-value-interpersonal-skills.
222. Satterfield and Hughes, "Emotion Skills Training for Medical Students," *Medical Education*; Weng et al., "Doctors' Emotional Intelligence and the Patient–Doctor Relationship," *Medical Education* 42 (2008). The WellStar Health System produced significant improvements in communication in more than 550 doctors in five hospitals using coaches as an adjunct to training. Patient reports of clear communication rose from 77.5 percent to 86.2 percent within a few months. Landro, "The Talking Cure for Healthcare," *The Wall Street Journal*. USF intends to incorporate peer and faculty coaching in its EI training program for all medical students. Grewal and Davidson, "Emotional Intelligence and Graduate Medical Education," *Journal of the American Medical Association*.
223. Luskin, Aberman, and DeLorenzo, *The Training of Emotional Competence in Financial Services Advisors*.
224. Lisa Tierney, "CPAs Say Working with a Business Coach Gives Them 'Cutting Edge,'" *Accounting Web*, November 9, 2013, http://www.accountingweb.com/practice/growth/cpas-say-working-with-a-business-coach-gives-them-cutting-edge.
225. C.R Wagstaff, S. Hanton, and D. Fletcher, "Developing Emotion Abilities and Regulation Strategies in a Sport Organization: An Action Research Intervention," *Psychology of Sport and Exercise* 14 (2013): 476–87.
226. Riskin, "Retaining Associates with Potential," *Amazing Firms, Amazing Practices*.

227. Fewer than 15 percent of organizations evaluate their coaching initiatives. "Can EQ Be Measured and Developed?" *Kandidata Asia.*
228. Zenger and Folkman, "The Ideal Praise-to-Criticism Ratio," *Harvard Business Review.*
229. Shanker, "Why Are Lawyers Such Terrible Managers?" *Fortune.*
230. Goleman, "The Brain and Emotional Intelligence," *Psychology Today.*
231. Rhode, "Developing Leadership," *Santa Clara Law Review,* 716, citing the Minnesota State Bar Association's Best Practices Guide, which discusses "the lack of goals, evaluations, and requirements," and the reliance on junior attorneys. Rhode points out that these initiatives "often lack effective monitoring and reward structures, and a clear path to positions of power."
232. Riskin, "Retaining Associates with Potential," *Amazing Firms, Amazing Practices.*
233. Although "high intelligence, high achievement status, and internal locus of control were associated with more accurate self-evaluations." Using more objective data like assessment data, anonymous reporting, and comparisons to specific colleagues, along with more frequent self-evaluations, have been recommended to improve awareness of one's EI. Paul A. Mabe and Stephen G. West, "Validity of Self-Evaluation of Ability: A Review and Meta-Analysis," *Journal of Applied Psychology* 67 (1982): 280.
234. Companies such as Accenture and Adobe Systems have done away with annual reviews, while GE, for example, is expanding feedback from the annual review to more frequent feedback up and across via a mobile app. Rachel Emma Silverman, "GE Re-Engineers Performance Reviews, Pay Practices," *The Wall Street Journal,* June 8, 2016. Some law firms are following suit: Matthew Guarnaccia, "Allen & Overy Tries Out New Performance Review Program," *Law360,* May 4, 2017.
235. We've seen in Kiser's data, for example, the overconfidence senior litigators "who do not typically seek out review or feedback" are prone to. Martha Neil, "Lawyers—Especially Men—May Be Too Optimistic About Case Outcomes, Survey Says," *ABA Journal Online,* May 11, 2010, http://www.abajournal.com/news/article/lawyers—especially_men—may_be_too_optimistic_about_case_outcomes_survey_s.
236. Susan Saab Fortney, "Are Law Firm Partners Islands unto Themselves? An Empirical Study of Law Firm Peer Review and Culture," *Georgetown Journal of Legal Ethics* 10 (1996): 271–316.
237. "Only about forty percent of law firms offer associates opportunities to evaluate supervisors, and of those who engage in the process, only about five percent report changes for the better." Spanhel and Patton, *How Associate Evaluations Measure Up: A National Study of Associate Performance Assessments.*
238. Clutch, Clutch HR Employee Feedback Survey 2016, December 7, 2016, https://clutch.co/hr/resources/engage-millennial-employees-feedback-evaluation.
239. "Thinking Like Your Client: Strategic Planning in Law Firms," *ALM Legal Intelligence,* October, 2012, 1–36. Approximately 68 percent of law firms put "Growing the Firm's Revenue" as their top business strategy priority and 54 percent list "Improving Firm Profitability" as their number three priority.

240. "SURVEY RESULTS—Goals, Measures and Balanced Scorecards—December 2012 Strategy Topic of the Month," *Sterling Strategies,* December 26, 2012, http://sterlingstrat.com/survey-results-goals-measures-and-balanced-scorecards-december-2012-strategy-topic-of-the-month.html.
241. Duncan, "In 2013, Will More Firms Finally Understand That Client Feedback = Better Revenue and Profitability?" *InFocus Blog.*
242. Press, "Are Rainmakers a Breed Apart?" *American Lawyer,* February 24, 2014.
243. The center uses the EQ-i assessment. "PDC Offers Emotional Intelligence Certificate Program," *University of Texas at Austin,* February 13, 2014, https://extendedcampus.utexas.edu/?/stories/detail/emotional-intelligence-https://professionaled.utexas.edu/management-and-leadership
244. Dan Ariely, "You Are What You Measure," *Harvard Business Review,* June, 2010.
245. Rhode, *Lawyers as Leaders,* 1.
246. Gardner, "When Senior Managers Won't Collaborate," *Harvard Business Review.*
247. Gardner, "The Collaboration Imperative for Today's Law Firms," *Managing Talent for Success,* 8. Another sector confirms the bottom-line relevance of using compensation to promote collaboration. A review of three compensation systems of 146 professional theater companies found that the star compensation system fell behind more collaborative compensation systems in terms of both talent retention and revenue, and also scored the lowest of the three systems in producing revenue from innovation: "increasing a company's 'collaborative norms' rating by just one point could improve a firm's talent retention, revenues, and revenues coming from innovation by as much as 10–15 percent." Patrick McKenna and Edwin B. Reeser, "Management Memo: Is Your Firm Creating a Star Culture?" *The Am Law Daily,* July 25, 2013. http://www.americanlawyer.com/id=1202612505186/Management-Memo-Is-Your-Firm-Creating-A-Star-Culture.
248. Gardner, "When and Why Clients Want You to Collaborate," *American Lawyer,* June 28, 2016.
249. Gardner, "The Collaboration Imperative for Today's Law Firms," in *Managing Talent for Success,* 8.
250. See Gardner, "Is Your Firm Collaborative? What Your Client Sees," *American Lawyer,* May 23, 2016, for Gardner's list to check your firm's effectiveness in promoting collaboration.
251. Antoine de Saint-Exupery, *The Wisdom of the Sands,* 1948.
252. Shawn Achor, interviewed by Caprino, "How Happiness Directly Impacts Your Success," *Forbes Leadership Blog.* Author of bestselling *The Happy Secret to Better Work* and *The Happiness Advantage,* Shawn Achor is the winner of over a dozen distinguished teaching awards at Harvard University, where he delivered lectures on positive psychology in the most popular class at Harvard, and has become one of the world's leading experts on the connection between happiness and success. His TED talk is one of the most popular of all time with over 4 million views, and he has a lecture airing on PBS called "The Happiness Advantage."
253. Polly Labarre, "Marcus Buckingham Thinks Your Boss Has an Attitude Problem," *Fast Company,* August, 2001.

254. Dan X. McGraw, "Why Businesses Should Be Worried About Disengaged Workers," *Chron,* June 24, 2013, http://www.chron.com/jobs/article/Why-businesses-should-be-worried-about-disengaged-4618897.php?cmpid=classifiedshcat.
255. Richard," We Need a Chief Resilience Officer," *Lawyer Brain Blog.*
256. Susan Sorenson, "How Employee Engagement Drives Growth," June 20, 2013, *Gallup,* http://www.gallup.com/businessjournal/163130/employee-engagement-drives-growth.aspx.
257. Labarre, "Marcus Buckingham Thinks Your Boss Has an Attitude Problem," *Fast Company.*
258. Dan X. McGraw, "Why Businesses Should Be Worried About Disengaged Workers," *Chron,* June 24, 2013, http://www.chron.com/jobs/article/Why-businesses-should-be-worried-about-disengaged-4618897.php?cmpid=classifiedshcat. The impact of disengagement is dramatic: "Companies with 9.3 engaged workers for every disengaged worker saw 147 percent higher earnings," while those with only 2.6 engaged workers for every disengaged worker saw earnings shrink 2 percent.
259. "Life after law school," *Gallup,* 2016, http://www.gallup.com/opinion/gallup/190172/life-law-school.aspx
260. Mezrani, "Fear of Failure Holding Back Young Lawyers," *Lawyers Weekly.*
261. Labarre, "Marcus Buckingham Thinks Your Boss Has an Attitude Problem," *Fast Company.*
262. Mezrani, "Fear of Failure Holding Back Young Lawyers," *Lawyers Weekly.*
263. Gooty et al., "The Wisdom of Letting Go and Performance: The Moderating Role of Emotional Intelligence and Discrete Emotions," *Journal of Occupational and Organizational Psychology,* 392–413. A meta-analysis of EI and job performance confirmed that those high in EI by all three theoretical strands showed improved job satisfaction, organizational commitment, and turnover intentions; reduced negative feelings; and increased positive feelings. Researchers recommended that organizations "incorporate EI in employee recruitment, training, and development programs." Chao Miao, Ronald H. Humphrey, and Shanshan Qian, "A Meta-Analysis of Emotional Intelligence and Work Attitudes," *Journal of Occupational and Organizational Psychology* (2016): 1–26.
264. "We All Need Friends at Work," *Harvard Business Review,* July, 2013. "State of the American Workplace," *Gallup,* 2016, http://www.gallup.com/services/178514/state-american-workplace.aspx.
265. Anna Z. Czarna et al., "Do Narcissism and Emotional Intelligence Win Us Friends? Modeling Dynamics of Peer Popularity Using Inferential Network Analysis," *Personality and Social Psychology Bulletin* 42 (2016): 1588–99.
266. Rob Gray, "Employee Engagement Closely Tied to Health and Wellbeing," *HR Magazine,* April 16, 2014.
267. Silverman, "Big Data Upends the Way Workers Are Paid," *Wall Street Journal,* September 20, 2012.
268. *Drive: The Surprising Truth About What Motivates Us,* by Daniel H. Pink (New York: Riverhead Books, 2012). http://www.danpink.com/about/.

269. John Flood, "The Bonus Culture," *Random Academic Thoughts,* September 5, 2011, http://www.johnflood.com/blog/2011/09/the-bonus-culture/.
270. Pink, *Drive.* See a summary at http://marshallcf.com/wp-content/uploads/2017/02/Drive.pdf, *Marshall Commercial Funding,* 2009.
271. Porath, "The Hidden Toll of Workplace Incivility," *McKinsey Quarterly.*
272. S.J.S. Giles, "The Role of Supervisory Emotional Intelligence in Direct Report Organizational Commitment," master's thesis, 2001.
273. Freedman, "The Amadori Case: Supplying McDonalds—Organizational Engagement, Emotional Intelligence and Performance," *SixSeconds.org.*
274. Shanker, "Why Are Lawyers Such Terrible Managers?" *Fortune.*
275. Hannah Braime, "7 Practical Ways to Improve Your Emotional Intelligence," *Lifehack,* http://www.lifehack.org/articles/communication/7-practical-ways-improve-your-emotional-intelligence.html.
276. Quoted in Gill Garrett, *CBT at Work for Dummies* (New York: Wiley, 2015), 172.
277. "It's Just Emotion, Taking HR Over," *HC Online.*
278. Shanker, "Why Are Lawyers Such Terrible Managers?" *Fortune.*
279. Izzo, "Success Follows Happiness, Not the Other Way Around," *Huffington Post.* "[P]eople who see their work as a calling as opposed to a job are more productive, work longer hours and put more effort into their work. Having a purpose drives happiness, whereas having merely a job for survival drives unhappiness. And the interesting part is that this is true regardless of the nature of the work. It's just as true for housekeepers as it is for engineers! It's not 'what' you do, it's 'how' you do it and the attitude you bring." Microsoft found that to engage and retain Millennials, organizations should offer "a sense of purpose, with defined values and a strong mission." Cindy Bates, "Survey Reveals Four Secrets to Success for Attracting and Retaining Millennial Talent," *Microsoft US Small and Midsize Business Blog,* February 12, 2016, https://blogs.business.microsoft.com/en-us/2016/02/12/4761/.
280. Porath, "The Hidden Toll of Workplace Incivility," *McKinsey Quarterly.*
281. Silver, "Supporting Attorneys' Personal Skills," *Revista Juridica de la Universidad de Puerto Rico,* 1, 3.
282. Richard, "We Need a Chief Resilience Officer," *Laywer Brain Blog.*
283. "Do Something! Motivating Employees," *LegalEase,* July 21, 2010, http://legalease.blogs.com/legal_ease_blog/2010/07/do-something-motivating-employees.html#ixzz48HECpCc1.
284. "Happiness fuels success, not the other way around. When we are positive, our brains become more engaged, creative, motivated, energetic, resilient, and productive at work. This isn't just an empty mantra. This discovery has been borne out repeatedly by rigorous research in psychology and neuroscience, management studies, and the bottom lines of organizations around the world." Caprino, "How Happiness Directly Impacts Your Success," *Forbes Leadership Blog;* Izzo, "Success Follows Happiness, Not the Other Way Around," *Huffington Post.*
285. "Leadership and Behavior: Mastering the Mechanics of Reason and Emotion," *McKinsey Quarterly,* October, 2016, http://www.mckinsey.com/business-functions/organization/our-insights/leadership-and-behavior-mastering-the-mechanics-of-reason-and-emotion. Hebrew University economics professor

Eyal Winter, author *Feeling Smart: Why Our Emotions Are More Rational Than We Think* (PublicAffairs, 2014), and Harvard University economics professor and Nobel laureate Eric Maskin discuss how emotions are a key factor in designing compensation that makes workplaces supportive of diversity, motivation, collaboration, innovation, and connectedness.

286. Duhigg, "What Google Learned from Its Quest to Build the Perfect Team," *New York Times.* Microsoft's survey of Millennials found that "good team collaboration" was their first priority at work, and they preferred in-person interaction over remote. Bates, "Survey Reveals Four Secrets to Success for Attracting and Retaining Millennial Talent," *Microsoft US Small and Midsize Business Blog.*
287. Mills, "What Are Humans Good for . . . in Legal Services?" *3 Geeks and a Law Blog.*
288. Colvin, "The Skills of Human Interaction Will Become Most Valuable in the Future," *New York Times.*
289. Lehrer, "The Power Trip," *Wall Street Journal.*
290. Gajendran and Somaya, "Employees Leave Good Bosses Nearly as Often as Bad Ones," *Harvard Business Review.*
291. Jack Welch, "Four Sure-Fire Ways to Motivate Your People, and Dinner with You Isn't One of Them," *LinkedIn,* November 4, 2013, https://www.linkedin.com/pulse/20131104192204-86541065-four-sure-fire-ways-to-motivate-your-people-and-dinner-with-you-isn-t-one-of-them.
292. Mikolajczak et al., "Sensitive but Not Sentimental: Emotionally Intelligent People Can Put Their Emotions Aside When Necessary," *Personality and Individual Differences.*
293. Isaiah Hankel, "The Lost Art of Being a Hard Ass—5 Ways to Develop Others into Leaders, Not Followers," *IsaiahHankel.com,* 2015, http://www.isaiahhankel.com/the-lost-art-of-being-a-hard-ass-5-ways-to-develop-others-into-leaders-not-followers.
294. "Leadership and Behavior: Mastering the Mechanics of Reason and Emotion," *McKinsey Quarterly.* Hebrew University economics professor Eyal Winter's recent book, *Feeling Smart: Why Our Emotions Are More Rational Than We Think* (PublicAffairs, 2014), discusses how emotions are a key factor, not only in rational decision making but also in workplaces that support diversity, motivation, collaboration, innovation, and connectedness. "For partners looking to hold onto their best lawyers, the solutions may be surprisingly simple: Treat your associates like adults. Involve them in the business of the firm. Don't be a jerk. Stop yelling. And give positive feedback when it is deserved. . . . if you treat your associates better, they will do better work." Shanker, "Why Are Lawyers Such Terrible Managers?" *Fortune.*
295. The assessment was developed by TalentQuest. "Will You Be Ready When It's Time to Hire Again? Effective Assessment Solutions to Get the Best Talent First," *TalentQuest,* n.d, 1–11.
296. Chen, "Our Secret Sauce," *The Careerist.*
297. Teresa Lo, "IP Law Firm Gives Job Applicants Personality Quizzes," March 29, 2017, *JD Journal,* http://www.jdjournal.com/2017/03/29/ip-law-firm-gives-job-applicants-personality-quizzes/?utm_source=MENA&utm_medium=

Email&utm_campaign=t_17740—dt_20170331-cid_34870-Did_5100262-ad_JDJ~MENA-logid_[MCTS_CESLOGID]

298. "Law Firm Verbal Reasoning and Situational Judgement Test Preparation," *Job Test Prep*.
299. Goldberg, "Is This Any Way to Recruit Associates?" *National Law Journal*.
300. Laura Fries, "How to Screen Leadership Candidates for Emotional Intelligence," *Business Journals*, April 12, 2016, http://www.bizjournals.com/bizjournals/how-to/human-resources/2016/04/how-to-screen-leadership-candidates-for-eq.html.
301. Weiss, "Are You the Type That Likes to Run with Scissors? McKenna Long Has a Test to Exclude You," *ABA Journal*.
302. Gordon, "Most Lawyers Are Introverted and That's Not Necessarily a Bad Thing," *ABA Journal*, 37.
303. Press, "Time for the Am Law 200 to Embrace Testing for Talent?" *American Lawyer*.
304. Jeff Blumenthal, "Lawyers Take Lessons on Leadership," *Philadelphia Business Journal*, October, 2, 2006. See also John O. Cunningham, "The Ten Habits of Highly Successful Law Firms," *Legal Marketing Reader*, October, 2007, http://legalmarketingreader.com/effective_law_firms.html.
305. "Herbert Smith Trains Staff to Spot Stress," *The Lawyer*, September 27, 2009, http://www.thelawyer.com/1002095.article.
306. "Herbert Smith Freehills Expand Their Mental Health Mentor Programme," *City Mental Health Alliance*, August 16, 2016, http://citymha.org.uk/herbert-smith-freehills-expand-their-mental-health-mentor-programme/.
307. Catrin Griffiths, "Hogan Lovells to Review Stress Management in Wake of Partner's Suicide," *The Lawyer*, September 13, 2013, http://www.thelawyer.com/news/practice-areas/intellectual-property-news/hogan-lovells-to-review-stress-management-in-wake-of-partners-suicide/3009492.article.
308. Lucy Burton, "Hogan Lovells Brings Counselling In-House as City Pushes for Mental Well-Being," *The Lawyer*, February 20, 2014, http://www.thelawyer.com/news/regions/uk-news/hogan-lovells-brings-counselling-in-house-as-city-pushes-for-mental-well-being/3016573.article?cmpid=dnews_142625.
309. Mark Levin, a lawyer and chief marketing officer at Neal, Gerber & Eisenberg, working with a Chicago industrial psychologist, "developed an assessment test that would identify personality and work traits in lawyers. Along the way, he merged his efforts with Robert Troutwine, a psychologist famed for developing the Troutwine Athletic Profile (TAP), which is used by professional football teams—including the hugely successful New England Patriots and Indianapolis Colts—as they prepare for the annual draft of college players." Press, "Time for the Am Law 200 to Embrace Testing for Talent?" *American Lawyer*. They built some tests designed for those interested in becoming lawyers, for lawyers and for legal employers called The Right Profile: http://therightprofile.com/.
310. Chen, "Our Secret Sauce," *The Careerist*.
311. Goldberg "Is This Any Way to Recruit Associates?" *National Law Journal*.
312. Shanker, "Why Are Lawyers Such Terrible Managers?" *Fortune*.

313. Groysberg and Sherman, "Baker & McKenzie (A)" *Harvard Business School Review,* 3, 18.
314. Groysberg and Sherman, "Baker & McKenzie (A)," *Harvard Business Review,* 16. "We emphasize professional development across the board," said David Coleman, then director of Learning and Development. "[But] it was clear we needed to create special training opportunities for our top performers—[especially] those with the potential to provide the leadership we needed."
315. Groysberg and Sherman, "Baker & McKenzie (A)," *Harvard Business Review,* 16.
316. Groysberg and Sherman, "Baker & McKenzie (A)," *Harvard Business School Review,* 18, 16.
317. Ibid., 16, 20.
318. Chen, "Baker & McKenzie Aims for Global Elite," *American Lawyer,* October 7, 2008.
319. Groysberg and Sherman, "Baker & McKenzie (B): A New Framework for Talent Management," *Harvard Business School Review,* September 12, 2008, 1. Quoting John Conroy, member of the strategic planning task force at Baker & McKenzie at the time of the study.
320. "Client Feedback and Satisfaction," *BTI Consulting Group,* 2013, http://www.bticonsulting.com/client-feedback-evaluation/.
321. Groysberg and Sherman, "Baker & McKenzie (B)," *Harvard Business Review,* 1.
322. Matt Byrne, "Baker Unveils Record Results for 2012/13 with Revenue Topping $2.4bn," *The Lawyer,* August 28, 2013, http://www.thelawyer.com/news/regions/americas-news/bakers-unveils-record-results-for-2012/13-with-revenue-topping-24bn/3008820.article?cmpdate=The+Bakers+bread-making+machine+rolls+on&cmpid=dnews_1300503864&cmptype=newsletter&email=true. For the fiscal year ended June 30, 2016. Baker McKenzie reported global revenues of $2.62 billion, up 8% or 16% in constant currency, with net profit growing by 14% or 22% in constant currency, Profits per Equity Partner up 13% or 21% in constant currency, and 150 new partners. "Baker McKenzie Announces Global Revenues of US$2.62 billion," August 22, 2016, http://www.bakermckenzie.com/en/newsroom/2016/08/global-revenue-results-fy16/.

Chapter Six

What Is My Emotional Intelligence?

Did you ever take that test yourself?

—the replicant Rachael asks Rick Deckard, the Blade Runner (played by Harrison Ford) in Ridley Scott's 1982 film *Blade Runner,* who tries to identify replicants without advanced emotions by giving them the Voight-Kampff test

[EI is a product to some extent of genetics, but also of] deep-seated beliefs, experiences, emotional and other memories, culture, gender and habits that have developed over a person's entire lifetime.[1]

—Dr. Annie McKee, University of Pennsylvania's Chief Leadership Office Program Director and Senior Fellow, author and emotional intelligence expert

Our opinion of our own emotional intelligence (EI) may be flawed. Many of us suffer from overestimation of our abilities, called the "better-than-average effect."[2] For example, 80 percent of people think that their driving skills are better than average,[3] and we think we are smarter than others think we are.[4] The reasons for this phenomenon are that we are genuinely unaware of how we compare to others or of how others see us, and we also may unconsciously try to assuage any sense of inferiority we feel. So, as a meta-analysis comparing personal estimates with actual scores showed,[5] guessing our own emotional intelligence is likely to be incorrect.

Knowing our specific level of functioning currently in the various components of EI, no matter what that level is, is important because it allows us to understand ourselves best and to most efficiently improve.[6] There is no down side to getting this information—these assessments don't take long and do not indicate a disability or illness.

You can test your emotional intelligence by using the following:

Emotional Intelligence Assessments
Questions to Start You Thinking and Feeling
Worksheets to Illustrate Emotional Intelligence

Emotional Intelligence Assessments

The way to get the most accurate reading of your EI abilities is to take one of the widely recognized, confidential online EI assessments, which may require that you hire a professional administrator who can also explain your scores and possibly give you coaching on ways to improve them. These provide the most immediate and accurate information about not only your overall emotional intelligence compared to the general population but also those individual strengths and weaknesses where you would profit from improvement or from greater use.

Assessments to measure EI have proliferated in a short time, with the earliest dating from only the mid-1990s. By comparison, the most widely used scale of cognitive intelligence, the Wechsler Adult Intelligence Scale, has been in use for almost 100 years and the Five Factor Model (FFM) assessment of major personality traits, also referred to as the "Big Five"—Openness, Conscientiousness, Extraversion, Agreeableness, and Emotional Stability (or Neuroticism on the other side of that trait continuum)—was formulated in the early 1960s.

The various strands of EI research have resulted in several emotional intelligence models, often identified as "ability-based EI," "trait EI," "EI competencies," or "mixed models."[7] Each of the most widely used EI assessments has been developed based on one or more theoretical model(s), so different assessments ask different types of questions, often use different methods of administering the assessments, and have differing levels of validity and reliability, the typical gauges of an assessment's effectiveness.[8]

Divisions exist within the psychological community as to which of these instruments is best. The ability camp, which believes that EI is a distinct ability that can be developed, assesses EI based on performance in response to questions about scenarios, like an SAT. They trumpet the widely used Mayer-Salovey-Caruso Emotional Intelligence Test (MSCEIT), developed by the original EI researchers Jack Mayer and Peter Salovey.

One school of EI theorists call emotional intelligence a trait, which, like a personality trait, is unlikely to change. A long-standing trait or mixed-model assessment is the Emotional Quotient Inventory 2.0 (EQ-i 2.0) originally developed by Israeli psychologist Reuven Bar-On, which is available both as a "self-report" (in which you answer questions about yourself) and a "360-degree" assessment (in which others you work with answer those questions). The Emotional and Social Competence Inventory (ESCI) was originally developed by Daniel Goleman, who frames EI as a group of competencies. It uses a 360-degree assessment to measure those workplace competencies.[9]

Despite controversies,[10] all these assessments have proven effective in providing information about ourselves that other sources don't provide. EI theorists themselves acknowledge that, "the various models of EI tend to be complementary rather than contradictory."[11] A meta-analysis reviewing results of assessments using three different models of EI found all three to be more predictive of job performance than either personality traits or IQ scores: "The results support the overall validity of EI."[12]

These three long-standing and widely recognized EI assessments and their scoring methodology are summarized in the following box. See the Appendix for more information about these and other assessments.

THREE MAJOR THEORETICAL MODELS AND EMOTIONAL INTELLIGENCE ASSESSMENTS			
Model:	Abilities	Trait/Mixed	Competencies
Name:	MSCEIT	EQ-i 2.0	ECSI
Scoring:	SAT Style	Self and 360 Degree	360 Degree

See the Appendix for more information.

You can also take one of the less-recognized, low-cost, or free EI assessments or other assessments related to various aspects of EI that are listed in the Appendix.

Questions to Start You Thinking and Feeling

Daniel Goleman has posed these questions to "get you thinking about your own [EI] competencies," which, if answered in the affirmative, indicate emotional intelligence[13]:

1. Are you usually aware of your feelings and why you feel that way?
2. Are you aware of your limitations, as well as your personal strengths, as a leader?
3. Can you manage your distressing emotions well (e.g., recover quickly when you get upset or stressed)?
4. Can you adapt smoothly to changing realities?
5. Do you keep your focus on your main goals and know the steps it takes to get there?
6. Can you usually sense the feelings of the people you interact with and understand their way of seeing things?
7. Do you have a knack for persuasion and using your influence effectively?
8. Can you guide a negotiation to a satisfactory agreement and help settle conflicts?
9. Do you work well on a team, or prefer to work on your own?

Other yes/no questions that might help you tap into your emotional intelligence are the following:

1. Are you a good judge of character?
2. Do you find that your gut feelings are pretty accurate?
3. Are you able to anticipate others' reactions to your words or actions?
4. Are you able to predict what ensues after an interaction?
5. Are you able to calm yourself during stress?

For each of the questions above, a "yes" answer indicates an emotionally intelligent strength.

Here are some questions that require more extensive reflection than a simple yes/no:

1. Which emotions do you find most difficult to manage?
2. What strategies do you use to manage emotions?
3. What strategies are most effective in managing difficult emotions?
4. How often do you use denial, avoidance, or suppression to manage difficult emotions?
5. What have you found to be effective ways to manage others' difficult emotions?
6. What skills do your spouse/relatives/colleagues/clients compliment you on? Being a good listener? Being able to quickly read others' intentions? Recognizing when issues become emotional? Staying calm during emotional storms? Willing to talk out problems?
7. What do they complain about? You being unaware of problematic actions or situations? Being withdrawn or uncommunicative? Jumping to conclusions? Being too hard to understand? Being too critical?

WORKSHEETS TO ILLUSTRATE EMOTIONAL INTELLIGENCE

Here are a couple of worksheets to help you recognize illustrations of emotional intelligence in others and verbalize your competence in it:

1) What attributes have made your boss or client the worst or the best?
2) How have you resolved the worst jams you've gotten into at work?

Your Worst and Best Boss/Client

Drawing on your own experience working with managers, supervisors, colleagues, and clients is the best way to see the impact of differences in high-IQ and high-EI approaches at work. This simple exercise can help illuminate what your experience with others has taught you:

1. Recall the worst boss/senior partner/mentor/supervisor/ colleague/ client you've worked with.
2. List five characteristics that made that person difficult to work with.

   ____

   ____

   ____

   ____

   ____

3. Recall the best boss/senior partner/mentor/supervisor/colleague/ client you've worked with.
4. List five characteristics that made that person good to work with.

   ____

   ____

   ____

   ____

   ____

5. How many of these good or bad characteristics relate to IQ—the ability to analyze, calculate, read, or understand complex material, such as procedures, policies, or legal or financial documents?

   ____

6. How many of these characteristics relate to emotional intelligence—the ability to understand, relate to, and work well with others?

   ____

Your Worst and Best Performances at Work

List below what you think are the worst jams you've gotten into at work, what made the situation so problematic, and then characterize how you handled those situations as Great, OK, and Not So Great.

For example, maybe you had a problem with a fellow attorney because you mistakenly accused him or her of stealing away your young associate or paralegal, when it later turned out that the associate had asked the other attorney if he or she could work with him or her. Once you were in this spot, you figured out a greater-than-not solution by apologizing to the fellow attorney for your hasty accusation, clarifying with the associate/paralegal how work assignments are distributed, and asking why he or she was interested in working with the other attorney, in case there were those types of experiences you could offer said associate/paralegal. All parties seemed to be appeased.

1. Recall Your Five Worst Jams at Work, and Briefly Explain Why They Were So Problematic

    ______________________ Why? ____________________

    ______________________ Why? ____________________

    ______________________ Why? ____________________

    ______________________ Why? ____________________

    ______________________ Why? ____________________

2. Now Explain How You Resolved the Situation (Or Not) and Characterize That Outcome

    ______________________________ Great/OK/Not So Great

    ______________________________ Great/OK/Not So Great

    ______________________________ Great/OK/Not So Great

    ______________________________ Great/OK/Not So Great

    ______________________________ Great/OK/Not So Great

If you resolved two of your five worst jams with a great outcome, you are building some good EI skills. If you resolved three or more with a great outcome, you are well on your way to high emotional intelligence. If you resolved all of them with a great outcome or can't think of any jams, either you are not in need of most of what's in this book or you've done a real snow job on yourself.

DETERMINING YOUR EMOTIONAL INTELLIGENCE

The emotional intelligence and emotional intelligence–related assessments listed in the Appendix can help clarify your level of emotional intelligence:

- The best source of reliable information about your emotional intelligence is one of the widely recognized EI assessments, such as the MSCEIT, the EQ-i 2.0, or the ESCI, all described at greater length in the Appendix.
- Some consulting firms offer proprietary EI assessments that are also widely used, a few of whom are listed.
- Free EI assessments are plentiful but often not very informative or are of limited reliability. Use them with caution.
- Assessments of components of emotional intelligence and of attributes related to emotional intelligence can also give insight into your emotional intelligence, some of which are listed in the Appendix.

As a starting point, the questions and worksheets above can help you understand some of your personal attitudes toward and use of emotional intelligence.

Chapter Endnotes

1. Abhijit Bhaduri, "How to Develop Emotional Intelligence: An Interview with Annie McKee," *The Times of India,* April 12, 2013, http://blogs.timesofindia.indiatimes.com/just-like-that/entry/how-to-develop-emotional-intelligence.
2. Mark D. Alicke and Olesya Govorun, "The Better-Than-Average Effect," in Alicke, David A. Dunning, and Joachim Kreuger (eds.), *The Self in Social Judgement* (New York: Psychology Press, 2005), 85–106.
3. Kahneman, *Thinking Fast and Slow.*
4. Mabe and West, "Validity of Self-Evaluation of Ability," *Journal of Applied Psychology.*
5. Harms and Crede, "Emotional Intelligence and Transformational and Transactional Leadership," *Journal of Leadership and Organizational Studies.*
6. As one commentator noted, since "most people think they are better than they actually are . . . any intervention focused on increasing EQ must begin by helping people understand what their real strengths and weaknesses are." Chamorro-Premuzic, "Can You Really Improve Your Emotional Intelligence?" *Harvard Business Review.*
7. For an overview of the field, see EI Consortium, http://www.eiconsortium.org/.

8. Research that is published in academic journals and is peer reviewed is considered to be the most valid and reliable, the hallmarks of a good assessment. In this book, research results with respect to the major assessments as well as other EI assessments are included. While numerous "studies" relating to EI exist, many are simple surveys or promotional pieces for products, such as proprietary assessments or training, and have been included sparingly. For a short primer on assessment statistics for lawyers, see Baez, "Personality Tests in Employment Selection: Use with Caution," *Cornell HR Review.*
9. Cornelia A. Pauls and Nicolas W. Crost, "Effects of Faking on Self-Deception and Impression Management Scales," *Personality and Individual Differences* 37 (2004): 1137–51; Delroy L. Paulhus, "Measurement and Control of Response Bias," in John P. Robinson, Philip R. Shaver, and Lawrence S. Wrightsman, *Measures of Personality and Social Psychological Attitudes,* vol. 1 (San Diego: Academic Press, 1991), 17–59.
10. These differences in nomenclature may sound trifling but they signal important correlations, like whether or not EI is physiological or permanent. G. Matthews, M. Zeidner, and R.D. Roberts, *Emotional intelligence: Science and Myth* (Cambridge: MIT Press, 2004); Cherniss, "Emotional Intelligence and Why It Matters."
11. Juan Carlos Perez, K.V. Petrides, and Adrian Furnham, "Measuring Trait Emotional Intelligence," in Ralf Schulze and Richard D. Roberts (eds.), *Emotional Intelligence: An International Handbook* (Cambridge, MA: Hogrefe & Huber, 2005), 137.
12. O'Boyle, "The Relation between Emotional Intelligence and Job Performance: A Meta-Analysis," *Journal of Organizational Behavior,* 788; Another meta-analysis of EI and job performance confirmed that those high in EI by all three theoretical strands showed improved job satisfaction, organizational commitment, and turnover intentions. C. Miao, R.H. Humphrey, and S. Qian, "A Meta-Analysis of Emotional Intelligence and Work Attitudes," *Journal of Occupational and Organizational Psychology* (2016): 1–26.
13. Goleman, "How to Evaluate Your Own Emotional Intelligence," *LinkedIn.com,* June 27, 2013, http://www.linkedin.com/today/post/article/20130627123742-117825785-nine-ways-to-think-about-your-own-emotional-intelligence.

Chapter Seven

How Do I Raise My Emotional Intelligence?

All learning has an emotional base.

—Attributed to Plato

The good news is that emotional intelligence (EI) can be raised.[1] Data from around the world and from a diverse array of industries have documented instance after instance of overall emotional intelligence and specific EI skills being raised, regardless of an individual's age or stage in his or her career, thanks to our brain's "plasticity," or ability to change.[2] These improvements were often accomplished after relatively short instruction sessions, the results were sustained for a year or more, and improvements in some EI skills also helped advance other skills.[3]

Here are four routes to raising your overall emotional intelligence, followed by some specific behaviors that can raise each of the four components of EI discussed in this book.

Four Routes to Achieving an Emotional Intelligence Edge

What have researchers learned about how to raise our emotional intelligence? The following sections discuss four well-documented routes to higher EI:

1. *Expand Your Emotional Awareness*
2. *Participate in Training*

3. *Embrace Mindfulness*
4. *Persevere*

1. Expand Your Emotional Awareness

He who knows the universe and does not know himself knows nothing.[4]

—Jean de La Fontaine, 1679

Real knowledge is to know the extent of one's ignorance.[5]

—Confucius

Expanding emotional awareness is a sure-fire method for increasing your emotional intelligence. It informs all EI skills and is the foundation from which you can develop greater emotional empathy, understanding, and regulation. One way to expand emotional awareness is to increase the feedback you receive from all sources. Lawyers, who are smart and used to analyzing and applying data, are well-equipped to profit from that feedback.

Unfortunately, those low in EI often actively avoid feedback,[6] as did the "winningest" antitrust litigator mentioned earlier. Our low resilience makes us even more likely than other professionals to shy away from hearing, and to resist acting on, candid feedback that we fear might be criticism.[7]

In addition to taking one of the assessments discussed in the Appendix, you can take the following steps to expand your emotional awareness:

Sign Up a Coach, Mentor, or EI Buddy
Profit from Performance and Client Reviews
Listen Well

Sign Up a Coach or Mentor

Other avenues to gaining awareness include two reliable, institutional, and interactive methods that legal workplaces often employ, and which you can arrange even if your firm or department doesn't offer them: coaching and mentoring.

Executives, doctors, investment advisors, accountants, and teachers all take advantage of coaching to improve their professional performance.[8] Meta-analyses suggest that interpersonal skills are highly coachable, with average short-term improvements of 50 percent.[9] With the results of an EI assessment or EI-related assessment, a coach's work can be more targeted, with tailored goals against a baseline.

Some law firms and law departments offer colleague mentoring programs, either in a structured program or more informally, where mentors are assigned or the mentee approaches someone. For various reasons, coaching by a professional coach is nearly always a more reliable method for improving interpersonal skills than that offered by a colleague.[10]

Professional coaching is an increasingly popular benefit offered in law departments and law firms, most often on the West Coast, with some coaches specializing in improving emotional intelligence. The most common coaches—lawyers or not—brought in to law firms teach business development skills, which can help develop some EI skills as well. If your firm or department doesn't pay for outside coaching, they may consider splitting the cost with you or sponsoring coaching circles or workshops for a small group of lawyers.[11]

If your workplace offers neither mentoring nor coaching, use your bootstraps to find someone who you work with or who works in a similar environment and whose interpersonal skills you admire to play that role. People are invariably flattered that you think they have something valuable to offer. You should quantify the amount of time you are envisioning per visit (which doesn't always have to be in person) and for the whole process—an hour once or twice a month for six months is usually a minimum.

Don't get shut down by what may feel like criticism, no matter from whom it is coming. In most business arenas, as people progress up the ladder, the highest performers affirmatively seek and benefit from negative feedback—what isn't working well and should be addressed.[12] Yet many lawyers show little interest in knowing behaviors they could profit from changing. Truly hearing your coach/mentor's constructive observations may be your biggest challenge. Suppressing your emotions during what may be emotional interchanges risks both not clearly hearing or not clearly remembering the specifics of the conversation. Further, your lawyerly advocacy habit is likely to kick in and produce a barrage of protective defenses and distinctions that leave you with little useful enlightenment.

Here are some things you can do to maximize the effectiveness of your mentor/coach's feedback:

- *Prep your mentor/coach.* Approach this process with enthusiasm. Convey to your mentor/coach the reasons you think he or she and the process will be valuable to you. Ask to see any written evaluations and the proposed agenda or plan before you start so you can digest the process and look for positives you might gain. If there isn't an agenda or plan, take a stab at drafting one yourself.
- *Ask to take assessments.* Any feedback from assessments will help inform your agenda, make the advice more targeted, and make the milestones more apparent.
- *Know what you want to accomplish.* Carefully consider and then convey your objectives. Openly discuss your weaknesses—those you know of and any others that may be suggested. Also acknowledge your strengths, as they are helpful to your improvement.
- *Ask to hear the hard stuff.* Make it clear to your mentor/coach that you can handle any bad news, and then handle it. You can support yourself through "self-talk" that focuses on your many successes and your desire to move ahead in your career.
- *Go back for more.* After digesting the information you receive and licking your wounds, go back and summarize what you heard, then confirm that you got the correct message.
- *Try and try again.* Figure out how to practice new behaviors. Start at home and then bring them to the office? Start small at the office and then build more comprehensive changes? Make a change in supervisors or committees that allows you to focus on new skills?

- *Next steps.* Be sure to establish next steps. Would it be useful to check in with your mentor/coach periodically to assess your progress? Work more closely with someone in the office who exhibits skills you want to emulate? Have your mentor/coach get a periodic evaluation from your colleagues/supervisors? Do you need more specialized feedback that another assessment or advisor could provide? The goal is over time to align your perceptions of your EI and performance with the perceptions of the people you work with.

If neither coaching nor mentoring is available through your employment and you can't find a helpful volunteer, the Appendix lists a few organizations that provide EI coaching and Law People Management LLC provides services and references for coaching specifically designed for lawyers.

Even if you don't have access to or the time/money/patience for a mentoring or coaching relationship, steps you can take on your own to gain awareness include the following:

Find an EI Buddy. One of the most helpful things you can do is to identify someone who you believe has good EI instincts, and use that person as a sounding board. The person could be your spouse, your relative, a friend, or a colleague. Ideally, this is someone who often sees things differently than you and also seems to move in and out of difficult situations with aplomb. Describe a situation to him or her and ask for his or her assessment—what the body language and words and tones might mean, and how best to proceed. Get their take on your behavior as well.

Ask for Feedback in the Moment. Finally, this is a simple and immediate way to gain awareness. You are sitting across a conference table from a colleague and you suddenly feel like a cloud has passed over him or her, or that person says something in a way that surprises you. Ask whether the person is upset/angry/surprised, or whatever your instincts are telling you, or just ask what he or she is feeling. You might feel a little awkward, but if your tone is low and warm and nonthreatening, you are likely to get at least some response, and possibly an accurate one. You can then follow up with questions about what the problem is and what can be done to improve it. Or you can be relieved that you've misread the moment and are better informed the next time that look or comment shows up.

Profit from Performance and Client Reviews

Much of the advice given above about getting additional insights into your behavior and emotional intelligence through interactions with your coach, mentor, or EI buddy can be applied to gaining emotional awareness from your supervisors, peers, and clients via performance reviews and client reviews.

Performance reviews are not just about telling you what you're doing wrong. They should be calculated to improve your performance (a goal you likely share); done well, they can be instrumental in doing so, and can particularly succeed in elevating your awareness. You can still use performance reviews not done so well if your primary objective is to find out how you can improve and advance, and not just to defend yourself. The same questions you ask your coach/mentor or EI buddy can be posed to your performance reviewers. Going back to your reviewers in between formal evaluations with questions about your understanding of the input, your interim performance, and further goals is a powerful way to show your ability to "take" the comments that are made and turn those into higher performance. You will also gain even further awareness.

Similarly, client reviews provide extremely valuable feedback. You are in the client service business. Yes, you are smarter than the average bear, but the "smarts" that count for purposes of your continued employment, income, advancement, and ultimate success as a lawyer are those recognized and appreciated by your clients. Find out what kind of conduct your clients perceive as demonstrating smarts and cater shamelessly to them. The "best" lawyer in the world is not much good to anyone if no client wants his or her advice.

If your firm or department does not conduct either performance reviews or client reviews, or does so only annually, take it upon yourself to ask your supervisors, peers, and clients the same questions about your performance as those formal reviews should include: essentially, "How am I doing?" "What would you like to see more of?" and "What can I do differently?" Particularly with clients, don't forget to ask the "feeling" questions: "How do you feel about my work?" "What do you feel is most important?"

Listen Well

And then there is the all-around greatest of all tools for gaining emotional awareness: *listening*. Listening done well exercises an array of emotional intelligence muscles that can improve your emotional perception, empathy, understanding, and regulation. Here are some emotionally attuned ways to hear the emotional message:

Use Empathy. Listening is grounded in empathy—finding in ourselves the feelings we see in others in order to create a bond and open us to another's perspective. Rather than prioritizing your own agenda—what you will say or how you can best impress the client/witness/and so on—prioritize what the speaker is thinking/feeling/needing. "Listening to other people's points of view"[13] helped a PwC partner working in a developing country to find greater empathy.

Find a Shared Identity. Especially for those people who seem to be very different from you, think of what you might have in common—a shared leisure interest? a piece of geographical, religious, or ethnic background? These small bits of shared identity can help you build a bridge that makes you interested and/or sympathetic and thereby an even better listener.[14]

Practice Active Listening. Active listening engages us in interacting with the person speaking so that we are less likely to be internally distracted and therefore more likely to really hear what is being said. To do so,

- summarize what the speaker is saying—"As I understand it, you are interested in closing the factory at all costs";

- ask questions both to clarify—"What evidence do you have, again, of the fraud?"—and to confirm your understanding—"So you would like us to present all the possible approaches?"—and
- articulate and sympathize with both the spoken and unspoken feelings displayed—"It sounds like coming to this decision has been very hard for you" and "That experience must have been quite frightening."[15]

Behave "As If" You Are Listening. Even if you can't quite shut out the thoughts swirling around your mind, you can act as if you are listening, which encourages the speaker to reveal more of his or her thoughts. In *The Trusted Advisor*, professional services consultant David Maister emphasizes that to be a trusted advisor one must not only listen well but also be *perceived* to be listening.[16] Lawyers often fail to give the appropriate social cues—eye contact, the cognizant nod, the small sigh of acknowledgement, or a brief smile—that are little indications of having heard and wanting to hear more. Use attentive body language too: fidgeting or doodling will make the speaker feel ignored and clam up.[17]

Mirror the Speaker's Style. Personal style is a powerful reflection of someone's personality and worldview, and attentive listening gives us a shortcut to both.[18] Focus on *how* the speaker says certain things, not just *what* the speaker says: consider the rate of speech, tone of voice, and volume, and try to replicate those in your own speech. Mirroring his or her style makes the speaker more comfortable and makes you seem less alien, so he or she is more likely to open up.

Restrain from Talking Too Much. Limit your own talk. Be comfortable with conversational pauses, something that can be very difficult for high-urgency lawyers.[19] Give the speaker a chance to fill those spaces.

Use Emotion Words. Ask questions like "How did that make you feel?" "Why are you frowning?" "Is there something about this situation that especially annoys you?" to help reveal some of the perhaps unspoken feelings around the issues.

Manage Your Own Emotions. Limit and avoid not only your emotional distractions but also your own emotional "triggers"—such as concerns about your appearance, competence, or respect—so you can concentrate on what the speaker is saying. Take a break if that's useful to help clear your mind and emotions and return your attention to the speaker.

2. Participate in Training

Your firm or department, alum groups, bar associations, continuing legal education (CLE), and third-party providers may all offer trainings that could be useful in developing your emotional intelligence. Many professional development trainings can increase EI even if they are not denominated as EI trainings or use EI terms in instruction. Look for ones that burnish business development, client service, communication, and leadership skills. Emotional intelligence directly empowers success in all these areas.

A few organizations teach EI skills, both in person and online, with programs of varying lengths and cost. Online training in EI is well suited for sculpting your brain through repetition and has been found as effective as in-person trainings.[20] Even short trainings of only a few hours can set you off in the right direction, but following up by finding opportunities to practice new skills is critical to cement your progress and continue to improve.[21] The goal is to walk away from a training session with an understanding of the topic and of your strengths and deficits, and with exercises you can repeat to strengthen both.

The Appendix lists some training guidelines and offerings of different kinds that you or your firm/department can sign up for. If you are interested in in-person or online training, workshops, or coaching designed specifically for lawyers, contact Law People Management, LLC.

3. Embrace Mindfulness

> *Between stimulus and response there is a space. In that space is our power to choose our response. In our response lies our growth and our freedom.*[22]
>
> —Viktor E. Frankl, Austrian neurologist and psychiatrist, author of *Man's Search for Meaning*

> *With mindfulness you monitor whatever goes on within the mind.*[23]
>
> —Daniel Goleman, author and EI expert

A free and simple way to build emotional intelligence is through exercising mindfulness, a mental state achieved through the physical practice of meditation.[24] Initially, the benefits of mindfulness were thought to be primarily better pain and disease management,[25] but years of research have found many psychic benefits as well.[26]

Meditation is the locus for practicing mindfulness, which, rather than emptying our mind, as some assume, is a state in which we become aware of our internal flow of thoughts, emotions, and bodily sensations, recognize that those experiences are fleeting, and then detach ourselves from them for the moment. This detachment gives us an opportunity to step out of our automatic reactions, which for lawyers often include rumination, suppression, and negative self-talk. Focusing on your breath or a simple repeated mantra like "I am surrendering" can help you let all that you are experiencing go, as if it were floating away down a river.

As few as five minutes of meditation a day can start you on the path to becoming more mindful. You can meditate while walking, sitting at your desk, or even between reading cases. But as with other EI-building steps, repetition over time increases your abilities. As Daniel Goleman puts it, the "basic move" in mindfulness is to "notice when your mind has wandered and then detach from where it's wandered to, and bring your mind back to the point of focus . . . That is the essence of the practice, and it's the mental equivalent of going to the gym and going on a Cybex machine and doing repetitions to work a muscle. The more you do that, the stronger the circuitry for noticing the wandering, detaching, and moving it back gets."[27]

Mindfulness can produce improvements in several EI components. Enhanced brain functioning improves emotional perception [28] and builds greater empathy.[29] Mindfulness significantly improves our abilities to regulate our emotions, including stress and anxiety,[30] decreasing the activity and even the physical volume of the amygdala (which stimulates stress hormones).[31] Cognitive functioning improves,[32] and even physiological aging appears to slow, extending our lifespans.[33]

Mindfulness also promotes more positive feelings, a greater sense of well-being, and "less depression and more happiness."[34] The media labeled a monk who had spent most of his life meditating "The Happiest Man in the World" because of never-before-seen levels of activity in brain scans of his left prefrontal lobe (where positive emotions are experienced), giving him an abnormally large capacity for feeling positively.[35]

The benefits of mindfulness continue even when we are not in a meditative state,[36] giving us more stable emotions and better control over our mood and behavior during the day and a better night's sleep (critical for positive changes in brain plasticity).[37] Mindfulness may also help improve "moral discernment,"[38] and therefore raise ethical behavior.

One of the newer types of meditation may be difficult for hard-core lawyers to embrace. "Compassion meditation" is meditation in which you focus on generating compassionate feelings toward specific individuals and/or people in general. Extraneous thoughts and feelings are acknowledged and then let go, and a repeated mantra of goodwill may help concentrate your feelings. Compassion meditation can produce significant benefits quite quickly—after only minutes[39]—including reductions in depression, anxiety, self-criticism, and shame; increased production of oxytocin (the bonding hormone that promotes trust)[40]; better responses to stress[41]; lower blood pressure; and faster healing.[42]

The *ABA Journal* reports that at least a dozen bar associations have programs focused on some aspect of mindfulness.[43] The Canadian Bar Association offers workshops on developing mindfulness that have been very well received.[44] Some law schools, law firms, and law departments are promoting mindfulness training as well.[45] If your firm, company, or bar association does not offer such trainings, there are multiple offerings online and in apps, including some mentioned in the Appendix, that can be accessed at all times of the night and day to build your mindfulness—and the improvements in emotional intelligence that it brings—with as little as a few minutes a day of dedicated meditation.

4. Persevere

> *More than education, more than experience, more than training, a person's level of resilience will determine who succeeds and who fails.*[46]
>
> —Diane L. Couto, in "How Resilience Works"

While this may seem an obvious bit of advice in any quest to make improvements, lawyers are especially susceptible to failing to persevere in this undertaking.

The same characteristics that both reflect and exacerbate our low emotional intelligence also impede our improving it.[47] Taking the first difficult step of acknowledging the need for improvement in the emotional arena "is a bitter pill for many of us to swallow."[48] Then pervasive pessimism tells us the effort won't pay off or won't make enough difference, high skepticism makes us distrustful of both people and processes, and low resilience makes the possibility of failing frightening. So those with the most to gain, who are also most likely to "vastly overestimate" their EI, are the least likely to "get down to the hard work of changing."[49]

Yet this is an area where we must nevertheless persist in this uncomfortable position of feeling less confident and less competent, and be even more vigilant and persistent in our efforts than others, in order to reap substantial benefits.

While cognitive learning is easier for lawyers than emotional learning, learning cognitively what we should do does not necessarily enable us to do it. Since emotional capacities draw on different brain areas and require different neural pathways than cognitive capacities, emotional learning requires consciously rewiring entrenched neural connections that have become dominant over time and establishing new ones, a much more wrenching and time-intensive undertaking than cognitive learning.[50]

After learning cognitively about the concepts involved, after taking the EI classes and training, and after developing a list of behaviors you can personally commit to, achieving greater emotional intelligence is a slow and incremental process that requires diligently and repeatedly making an effort.[51]

For example, awareness of your anxiety and of strategies to keep that from hijacking the success of a negotiation have to become as conscious as the points you argue, and so too your preferred behavior in that situation has to be intentionally repeated again and again in order for it to become automatic.

Most habits require a minimum of three weeks of intensive repetition to establish.[52] For emotional learning, the arch may be even longer. Once you know the area you would like to work on and a few specific behaviors you want to adopt (which the following chapter may help you identify), allow yourself at least a six-week cycle to practice and reinforce the new approach. Once that period is over, you can gauge what further length of time might be required or change or add your choice of practice behaviors.

During this period of advancing, "self-talk" can either be your friend or your foe. What is going through your head as you make this conscious effort to improve? A large study of 75,000 (primarily) managers in over fifteen workplace sectors from 126 countries that found "an extremely strong, positive relationship between emotional intelligence test scores and success scores" also found that the greatest behavioral contributors to that success were a more affirmatively optimistic outlook and a conscious determination to motivate oneself.[53]

This does not come easily to lawyers. Consultant Dr. Larry Richard, a psychologist and lawyer who advises on, among other things, emotional intelligence, admits that he too has had to consciously change his self-talk from negative to positive as an antidote to the low resilience that undercuts persistence.[54]

If you are repeating the same pessimistic, negative thoughts—"I'm not good at this," "This will never work," "This takes too much time/effort"—you will either not make a concerted effort or simply fail in the endeavor. We are built to meet our expectations, whatever they are. During these weeks of practice, be your own cheerful champion, your own leader,[55] urging yourself onward with patience and understanding and an eye on the reward.

A literal "change of mind" can get us on a better path. Instead of doubling down on current strategies that sustain mediocre or deteriorating situations, imagine a better outcome—a less volatile, more energized, and productive relationship with an important person, for example—to provide the impetus to take a positive step in a new direction today, and then another one tomorrow.

We lawyers are intelligent, and that, together with our penchants toward analysis, hard work, and physical stamina, makes us well equipped to incrementally make improvements in our emotional intelligence despite challenging mindsets.

FOUR ROUTES TO RAISING MY EMOTIONAL INTELLIGENCE

1. Gain greater emotional awareness—through feedback from mentoring, coaching, an emotional intelligence buddy, performance and client reviews, and attentive listening.
2. Participate in training—in person and online from one of the many available resources.
3. Embrace mindfulness—meditate to become more mindful, which enhances emotional perception, empathy, and emotional regulation, and increases happiness.
4. Persevere—it takes time and repeated practice to forge the new neural connections that build higher emotional intelligence.

Raising the Four Components of Emotional Intelligence

In addition to and apart from using any or all of the four routes to raising overall emotional intelligence discussed above, you will find among the following suggestions behaviors you can practice on a regular basis in order to bolster any deficits, or deepen strengths, in any of the four components of EI.

Don't consider these suggestions to be laundry lists that you have to get through. Instead, start by picking one or two that appeal to you and that you can concentrate on practicing. Over time you can add other behaviors or change up the mix to achieve a balanced strength in all four components:

1. *Emotional Perception*
2. *Emotional Empathy*
3. *Emotional Understanding*
4. *Emotional Regulation*

1. Emotional Perception—Short-Circuiting Garbage In/Garbage Out

The greatest EI weakness that lawyers demonstrate is in accurately perceiving our own and others' emotions, a weakness that undermines any other EI strengths that we have. Any emotion management strategies we formulate will likely be flawed if the up-front perceptual data are incorrect: garbage in/garbage out! A colleague who is angry at us for something we have done presents a very different situation than one who is ashamed of his or her own conduct, and mistaking one for the other can lead us down a fruitless and even destructive path.

One of the simpler assessments of your ability to read emotional cues listed in the Appendix is the free online Reading the Mind in the Eyes Test.[56] For each set of eyes displayed, you choose one word out of four that is most descriptive of what you think the emotional clues in those eyes indicate about what the person is feeling. A report is given at the end of the session. Once you have an idea of your level of awareness, here are some suggestions for improvement.

Take Your Emotional Temperature. Start by taking your emotional temperature regularly. How do I feel? Is it good or bad? Energizing or enervating? Pleasant or unpleasant? Do I feel better or worse from the last time I checked in with myself?

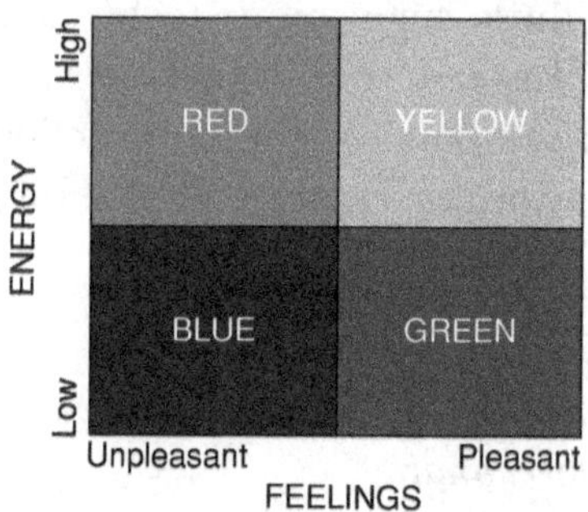

Figure 7-1: A mood meter.
Source: Deenie Melniker, "Mood Meter," *Tiny Tap*, http://www.tinytap.it/activities/g9kn/play/mood-meter.

Map Your Mood. The Yale Center for Emotional Intelligence recommends making a chart on a regular basis of how you feel, called a "mood meter," like that in Figure 7-1, which is made up of four colored quadrants that allow you to record your feelings on two axes: energy and pleasantness. The Mood Meter app can be downloaded.[57]

You can set your phone to alarm on whatever schedule you prefer—every hour, once or twice a day—and record where in the four quadrants your mood at that moment fits, creating a visual map of your moods for that day, week, and month. The point is not to change or like your moods, but to faithfully become aware of what you feel on those two dimensions. The quadrants represent the following:

- RED: feelings high in energy and low in pleasantness (e.g., angry, scared, anxious);
- BLUE: feelings low in energy and low in pleasantness (e.g., sad, disappointed, lonely);
- GREEN: feelings low in energy and high in pleasantness (e.g., calm, tranquil, relaxed); and
- YELLOW: feelings high in energy and high in pleasantness (e.g., happy, excited, curious).[58]

Figure 7-2 presents examples of words in various parts of this mood meter that you may find useful as a guide in placing your own emotions in the quadrants.

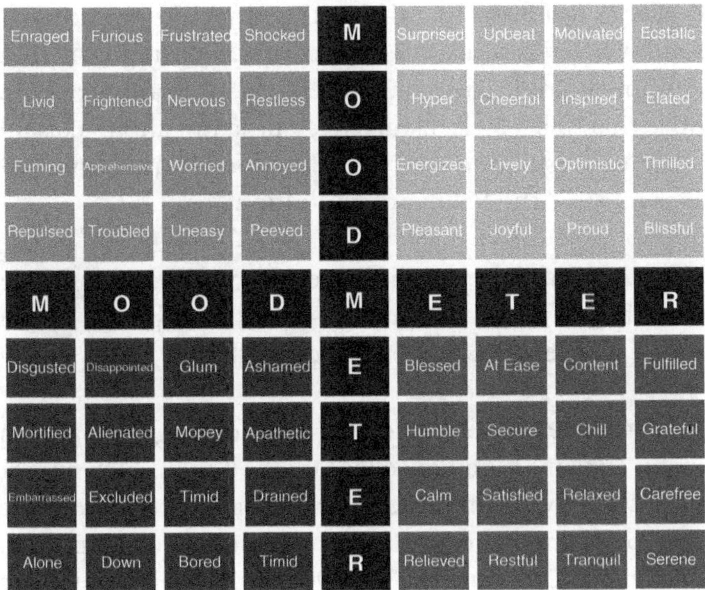

Figure 7-2: Mood meter emotional vocabulary.
Source: Eanes Elementary, http://eenhigby.weebly.com/mood-meter.html.

You can also record your emotions by regularly writing down your emotional experiences and what they feel like in an emotion journal, which allows you to review your observations later.

"Check Your Emotions at The Door."[59] If keeping a record sounds too burdensome, make a habit of checking in with your emotions using some trigger you are likely to experience several times a day: every time you walk through a doorway, for example, ask yourself what you are feeling.

Build Your Emotional Vocabulary. As you check in with your emotions, be more specific about what you're feeling so you can build a more extensive vocabulary. After placing the emotion within a large category, such as sadness or anger, then identify its degree of intensity—slight to severe, and give that a name, like melancholy or annoyance, sorrow or rage. The Mood Meter in Figure 7-2 includes various names of emotions that can help you build your vocabulary.

Pay Attention to Your Body. Identifying the physical sensations that go along with whatever you are feeling can help distinguish emotions. Are you hot or cold, tense or relaxed? As an example, you might recognize that "This feels disturbing, a little hot and makes me feel somewhat aggressive and energized but doesn't make me lose control. This must be the feeling of frustration."[60]

Try a Screen Vacation. Research indicates that putting away the devices for even a few days and interacting socially with others can significantly raise your emotional perception skills.[61]

Take the Silent Route. Watching movies on mute (a good way to spend time on an airplane) is an excellent method to build your emotion reading skills. Try to understand the action by the facial expressions and body language—you can turn on the sound periodically to verify or redirect your take. Are you surprised by the twists and turns of the plot even though you find you are correctly reading emotional cues? Then you might need to work on building your emotional understanding.

Involve Your EI Buddy. If you haven't already done so, engage a "high EI buddy" or even a "better EI buddy," preferably someone who knows your workplace and/or the players involved, to see if he or she agrees on your take on your own emotions or others' emotional cues.

Ask. Here's a low-tech suggestion: if you're not sure what emotion another person is experiencing, ask! You can say "it looks like you are [insert emotion here—angry, pleased, defiant, etc.]; is that correct?" or you can just ask what he or she is feeling.

Train. Paul Ekman found we can improve our ability to recognize other's emotions by systematically studying facial expressions. One or more of the seven programs in the Ekman Library, referenced in the Appendix, can help train you in reading facial cues in different settings.[62]

Play a Video Game. A video game called Crystals of Kaydor[63] could help your child or the child in you develop skill in reading nonverbal emotional cues. In it, an advanced robot that crash lands on an alien planet helps the natives solve problems by interpreting their body language and nonverbal cues.

TIPS FOR RAISING EMOTIONAL AWARENESS
• Test Your Emotional Temperature • Map Your Mood • Check Your Emotions at the Door • Build Your Emotional Vocabulary • Pay Attention to Your Body • Try a Screen Vacation • Take the Silent Route • Involve Your EI Buddy • Ask • Train • Play a Video Game

2. Emotional Empathy

After learning to associate the cues you see in another person with an identifiable emotion that you have experienced, are you able to conjure up in yourself the feelings that that emotion produces in them? Do you have emotional empathy?

Taking the Empathy Quotient (EQ),[64] a free sixty-item questionnaire, the Greater Good Empathy Quiz,[65] a free twenty-eight-question quiz, or one of the other empathy assessments listed in the Appendix can help you gauge your level of empathy.

Empathy can be raised in adults,[66] and the healthcare field has again led in experimenting with methods to increase empathy.[67] Research has confirmed that you can use your lawyerly analytic abilities to raise your empathy by purposely thinking about how you would feel if you were in another person's shoes, and analyzing his or her situation.[68]

Here are some specific strategies to help improve your empathy.[69]

Focus Your Attention Outward. As you build awareness of your own emotions, be sure to focus on the behaviors and expressions of other people in various circumstances so you can apply what you've learned about your own emotions to be more empathic toward others. Watch how babies and young children are instinctively attentive to and resonate with others' emotions.

Be Curious About Others. "Curiosity expands our empathy when we talk to people outside our usual social circle, encountering lives and worldviews very different from our own."[70] Exploring the pushes and pulls that impact others gives us information to better calculate what those others are feeling.

Use Your Imagination. Even when reading or watching the news, imagine what others are going through—what the details of their lives are like—and how they feel about their circumstances.

Find a Shared Identity. Especially for those people who seem to be very different from you, think of what it is you have in common. A shared leisure interest? A piece of geographical, religious, or ethnic background? These small bits of shared identity can help you build an empathic bridge.

Review Emotion-Reflective Writing. If you have kept a mood meter or an emotion journal, reviewing what you have felt can help you tap into how others might feel.[71]

Mimic Facial Expressions. While this may sound strange, it has been demonstrated to increase empathic feelings.[72] Our mirror neurons can convey to us the feelings of someone else by our replicating their outward expressions. If contorting your face in a meeting is a no-go, at least think consciously about those specific expressions.

Be Mindful. Being mindful can help us step back from automatic reactions to others and can also keep us from feeling overwhelmed in the face of others' negative feelings. Meditation—particularly meditation that focuses attention on concern or compassion for others—increases the capacity for empathy among both short-term and long-term meditators.[73]

Use Empathic Language. Empathic language reflects your sympathy with the other person regardless of whether you think their feeling is justified or you would feel that way in their situation. Verbally recognize their joy, their hopes, and their frustrations. Try to validate negative feelings rather than questioning or defending against them: "I can sense that you're feeling frustrated," or "I can understand how that situation could make you feel [angry, etc.]."

Act "As If." Even if you're not feeling it, research shows that acting as if you are empathic—using empathic language, giving little nonverbal nods of acknowledgement, keeping your body language directed to the other person—is often perceived by others as genuine empathy and these attempts to appear empathic can over time make you in fact more empathic.[74] So acting classes may be beneficial!

Join a Band. Playing music together with others boosts empathy in kids, and it may well help you as well.[75]

Reserve Judgment. Don't jump to conclusions about others: we feel less empathy when we assume that people are somehow getting what they deserve.[76]

Overcome Independence. Research suggests that attaining higher socioeconomic status may diminish empathy.[77] If you are financially successful, be more intentional about feeling empathy toward others, even though you may have less need to connect or cooperate with them.

Use Active Listening. As discussed before, active listening—particularly asking about and acknowledging spoken and unspoken emotions—encourages the speaker to share more and therefore expands your understanding of what they are feeling.[78]

Play a Video Game. There are several video games children or the child in you can play to increase empathy.[79] For example, the Learning Games Network, a spinoff of MIT and the University of Wisconsin–Madison, has developed a free, web-based science fiction game called Quandary that is designed to teach empathy and ethical decision making to ages eight and up.[80] Other games and apps are included in the Appendix.

TIPS FOR RAISING EMOTIONAL EMPATHY
• Focus Your Attention Outward • Be Curious About Others • Use Your Imagination • Find a Shared Identity • Review Emotion-Reflective Writing • Mimic Facial Expressions • Be Mindful • Use Empathic Language • Act "As If" • Join a Band • Reserve Judgment • Overcome Independence • Use Active Listening • Play a Video Game

3. Emotional Understanding

This is an area in which your IQ and analytic skills are valuable. Understanding emotions is gained by analyzing from an emotional perspective what we and others say and do. Ask yourself why the emotions you are sensing have arisen, what behaviors they provoke, how certain behaviors spark or change emotions, and vice versa, and how emotions blend with other emotions and change over time to create different emotions.

What are your own reactive patterns? Do you invariably bite back if you hear a negative tone? Do you immediately walk away from annoyance or irritation? Recognizing your patterns assists you in understanding both your emotional makeup and that of others. When your response is immediate, rigid, and repetitive, you are dealing with an engrained automatic reaction that will require conscious attention to fully understand and alter.

Studying the following graphs will expand your vocabulary and understanding of how emotions evolve and combine.

The pioneer of charting emotions is Robert Plutchik, who in 2001 plotted this "emotion circumplex" (Figure 7-3), which graphs how eight paired primary emotions—joy and sadness, anger and fear, trust and disgust, surprise and anticipation—can morph into stronger or weaker emotions, or combine with other emotions to produce different emotions.[81]

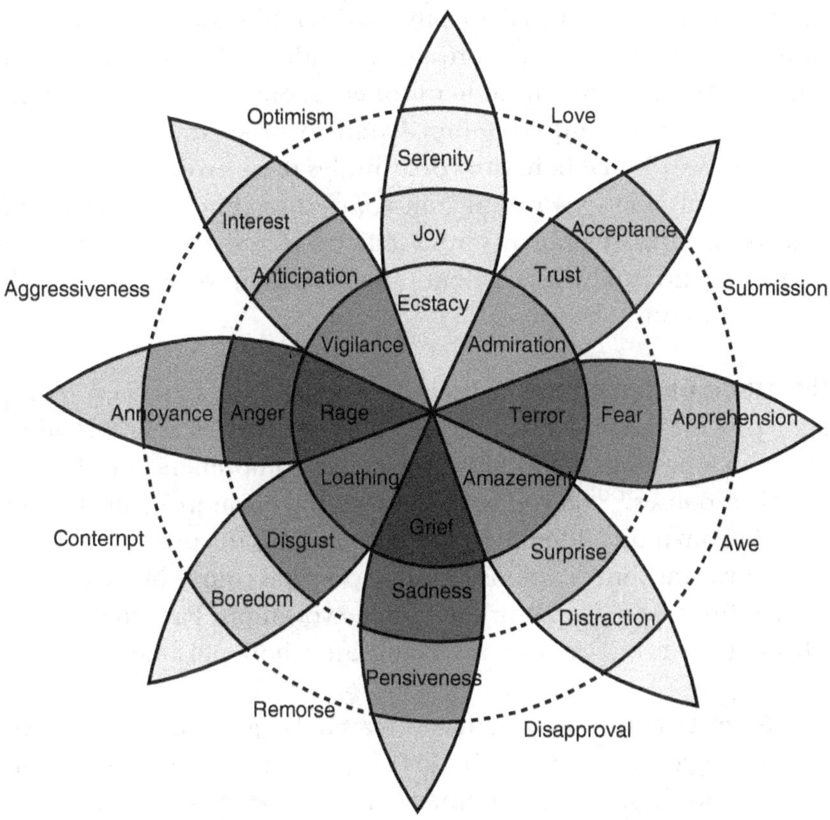

Figure 7-3: Emotion circumplex.
Source: Robert Plutchik, "The Nature of Emotions," *American Scientist* 89 (2001): 349.

The chart in Figure 7-4 recognizes "five core feelings: happiness, sadness, anger, fear and shame," and graphs variations those emotions change into with differing degrees of intensity.[82]

Here are some tips for improving your emotional understanding.

Read Literary Fiction. Research has found that people who read fiction are more attuned to others' emotions, how they arise, and their evolution.[83] Literature helps you gain a better understanding of literary characters from the inside out—people who, just as in real life, have complicated inner lives that are "rarely easily discerned but that warrant exploration."[84]

Expand Your Written Notes on Emotion. If you are keeping a mood meter, an emotion journal, or other written notes about your emotions, add notes on the circumstances under which they arise and change. Also note the ingredients of emotional blends—like when feelings of anger and contempt blend to make you feel disgust. You can record what behaviors or attitudes these evolutions or combinations of emotions produce in yourself or others. This written analytical work, which may sound tedious, is in the realm of typical lawyering and can bring tremendous advances in your understanding of emotions.

Listen to the Emotion in Music. Musical training, particularly at a young age, "provides an understanding of auditory nuances such as rhythm and semantics that could allow for better comprehension of emotional responses."[85] So you're not that young anymore? You can still benefit from music. Identifying which emotions the music you listen to is conveying and how those change over the course of a song can be helpful. Opera is rich in emotional evocations. Pay attention to what behaviors or circumstances motivate emotional changes.

Play Board Games. Neuroscience research suggests that when we compete against others, our brains project a "mental model" of the other person's thoughts and intentions and we get a first-hand seat to how those emotions evolve over time under changing circumstances.[86] Even if we are "trying to understand the other person so

Intensity of Feelings	HAPPY	SAD	ANGRY	AFRAID	ASHAMED
HIGH	Elated Excited Overjoyed Thrilled Exuberant Ecstatic Fired up Passionate	Depressed Agonized Alone Hurt Dejected Hopeless Sorrowful Miserable	Furious Enraged Outraged Boiling Irate Seething Loathsome Betrayed	Terrified Horrified Scared stiff Petrified Fearful Panicky Frantic Shocked	Sorrowful Remorseful Defamed Worthless Disagraced Dishonored Mortified Admonished
MEDIUM	Cheerful Gratified Good Relieved Satisfied Glowing	Heartbroken Somber Lost Distressed Let down Melancholy	Upset Mad Defended Frustrated Agitated Disgusted	Apprhensive Frightened Threatened Insecure Uneasy Intimidated	Apologetic Unworthy Sneaky Guilty Embarrassed Secretive
LOW	Glad Contented Pleasant Tender Pleased Mellow	Unhappy Moody Blue Upset Disappointed Dissatisfied	Perturbed Annoyed Uptight Resistant Irritated Touchy	Cautious Nervous Worried Timid Unsure Anxious	Bashful Ridiculous Regretful Uncomfortable Pitied Silly

The five core emotions run left to right across the top of the table. Manifestations of each emotion based upon the intensity felt are described down each of the columns in the table.

Figure 7-4: Variations of emotions and degrees of intensity.
Source: Bradberry and Greaves, ***Emotional Intelligence 2.0,*** 14–15. Chart adapted from Julia West. Reprinted with permission.

that we can *completely crush them*,"[87] looking into another person's strategies still helps us develop both empathy and an understanding of how their emotions influence them. We see in front of us the course of ambition, anger, resilience, determination, relief, and triumph.

Play Video Games. Video games like *The Sims 4* that have a greater emphasis on emotions may help develop emotional understanding.

TIPS FOR RAISING EMOTIONAL UNDERSTANDING
• Read Literary Fiction • Expend Your Written Notes on Emotion • Take up an Instrument or Listen to the Emotion in Music • Play Board Games • Play Video Games

4. Emotional Regulation

Having learned to recognize emotional signals, empathically experience what that emotion feels like and also understand how that nonrational data have arisen and could evolve or combine will give you a major leg up in the emotional regulation trenches, where most problem solving resides. What you don't want to do is automatically default to an emotional regulation strategy—like suppression or rumination—that is not constructive, or is even counterproductive.

Here are some suggestions to improve your emotional regulation.

Take a Deep Breath. Daniel Goleman heralds the importance of signaling a slowdown to your brain and your body by taking a deep oxygen-filled breath before taking any important actions.[88]

Count Yourself Down. It's true what your mother said—sometimes simply counting to ten works well to clear your mind for a better managed emotional response. It allows time for the rational brain to engage and survey the situation. Consciously asking questions or attempting to analyze the problem can also delay and help redirect a habitual emotional response to a more rationally engaged one.

Practice Mindfulness. Mindfulness allows us to make enough room mentally to detach from and examine our emotional responses and then gives us time to choose better ones.

Accept Your Thoughts and Emotions. Acceptance does not mean resigning yourself to negativity but responding to your ideas and emotions with an open attitude—letting yourself experience them without jumping to emotional conclusions, a danger for those of us high in a sense of urgency. This acceptance can bring relief, but it won't necessarily make you feel good. In fact, you may realize just how upset you really are. It is still a good place to start achieving better emotional regulation.

Walk It Off. Taking a walk outdoors has been demonstrated to improve mental functioning and positive well-being, and is a particularly good antidote to brooding, rumination, and depression. But it has to be outside in a natural setting, not in an urban one.[89]

Monitor Your Self-Talk. How we talk to ourselves can also help us manage our emotions. Telling ourselves repetitively our angry aggravations or negative predictions will not help us make good emotional regulation decisions.[90] Reframing our internal dialogue away from entrenched pessimism is a way to build a new response.[91] Get in the habit of marshalling credible counterarguments against the internal pessimistic voice that is predicting doom and gloom and blaming it all on you.[92]

Download an App. The GLS Studios develop video games and apps based on research by neuroscientists. Their app Tenacity focuses on learning self-regulation by maintaining attention and calm when serene scenes are bombarded with various distractions—a plane flying by, animals running past.[93] The Stanford University's Calming Technology Lab develops devices that help you respond to strong emotions, such as a belt it is working on that can detect breathing and connects to an app that helps calm you when you're feeling emotionally out of control.[94]

TIPS FOR RAISING EMOTIONAL REGULATION

- Take a Deep Breath
- Count Yourself Down
- Practice Mindfulness
- Accept Your Thoughts and Emotions
- Walk It Off
- Monitor Your Self-Talk
- Download an App

Chapter Endnotes

1. Goleman says that EI can be learned and improved at any age; Elkhonon Goldberg, clinical professor of neurology at New York University School of Medicine and director of the Institute of Neuropsychology and Cognitive Performance in New York, believes EI can be enhanced through training; and Howard Book, professor of psychiatry at the University of Toronto, suggests that EI increases with experience and age. Reilly, "Teaching a Law Student How to Feel" *Negotiation Journal*: 301–14.
2. Mines, Meyer, and Mines, "Emotional Intelligence and Emotional Toxicity," *The Colorado Lawyer*. Mayer, one of the original EI researchers, may be one of the most credentialed skeptics of our ability to raise that score. He argues that any true intelligence score, like IQ, tends to be static and not easily changed. Mayer, "Can Emotional Knowledge Be Changed?" *The Personality Laboratory at the University of New Hampshire*, 2013. Similarly, those who view EI as a "trait" expect it to remain fairly stable over time, unlike the skills associated with the trait, which can be improved. See Perez, Petrides, and Furnham, "Measuring Trait Emotional Intelligence," in *International Handbook of Emotional Intelligence*. Similarly, even Mayer acknowledges that if raw EI scores do not change, it is possible to increase emotional functioning. Mayer, Roberts and Barsade, "Human Abilities," *Annual Review of Psychology*, 513. Kotsou et al., "Emotional Plasticity," *Journal of Applied Psychology*, 827–39.
3. "Weatherhead MBA Program—Case Western Reserve University," *Consortium for Research on Emotional Intelligence in Organizations*, http://www.eiconsortium.org/model_programs/weatherhead_mba_program.html.

4. Quoted from Bradberry and Greaves, *Emotional Intelligence 2.0,* 53.
5. "Confucius Quotes," *Sources of Insight,* n.d., http://sourcesofinsight.com/confucius-quotes/.
6. O.J. Sheldon, D. Dunning, and D.R. Ames, "Emotionally Unskilled, Unaware, and Uninterested in Learning More: Reactions to Feedback About Deficits in Emotional Intelligence," *Journal of Applied Psychology,* 125–37.
7. Richard, "Herding Cats," *Altman Weil Report to Legal Management,* 1–12.
8. Satterfield and Hughes, "Emotion Skills Training for Medical Students: A Systematic Review," *Medical Education,* 935–41.
9. Arthur et al., "Effectiveness of Training in Organizations," *Journal of Applied Psychology,* 234–45.
10. Gerry Riskin, "Retaining Associates with Potential," *Amazing Firms, Amazing Practices.*
11. *Ibid.*
12. "[N]ovices sought and responded to positive feedback, and experts sought and responded to negative feedback . . . positive feedback increased novices' commitment and negative feedback increased experts' sense that they were making insufficient progress." Stacey R. Finkelstein and Ayelet Fishbach, "Tell Me What I Did Wrong: Experts Seek and Respond to Negative Feedback," *Journal of Consumer Research Inc.,* n.d., http://www.jstor.org/stable/10.1086/661934.
13. Robbins et al., *Management: The Essentials,* 260.
14. "Shared Identity," *Greater Good,* 2017, http://ggia.berkeley.edu/practice/shared_identity.
15. "Active Listening," *Greater Good,* 2017, http://ggia.berkeley.edu/practice/active_listening; Eric Fletcher, "Intentional Listening: How to Find Practice-Changing Opportunities," *Cordell Parvin Blog,* February 8, 2012, http://www.cordellblog.com/client-development/intentional-listening-how-to-find-practice-changing-opportunities/. These strategies are like those employed by a "listening system" medical and counseling schools sometimes teach called Basic Listening Sequence (BLS), which focuses on "microskills." It also encourages expressing "Positive Regard, Respect and Warmth, Concreteness, Immediacy, a Nonjudgmental Attitude, and Authenticity and Congruence." Defoe, "Emotional Intelligence, Lawyers, and Empathy—Using The Power of Listening with Care to Build Better Professional Relationships and Satisfy Clients," *Psycholawlogy Blog,* November 25, 2012, http://www.psycholawlogy.com/2012/11/25/emotional-intelligence-lawyers-and-empathyusing-the-power-of-listening-with-care-to-build-better-professional-relationships-and-satisfy-clients/.
16. Maister, Green, and Galford, *The Trusted Advisor.*
17. Cheryl Stephens, "Communications: Are You Listening?" *Plain Language Association InterNational,* 1998, http://www.heathersmithsmallbusiness.com/2008/11/27/to-hear-you-need-to-stop-talking-and-listen/.
18. See James W. Pennebaker, *The Secret Life of Pronouns: What Our Words Say About Us* (New York: Bloomsbury Press, 2011).
19. Stephens, "Communication: Are You Listening?" *Plain Language Association InterNational.*

20. Bradberry and Greaves, "Can You Develop Emotional Intelligence Online?" *TalentSmart.com,* 2003, https://www.talentsmart.com/media/uploads/pdfs/Can%20You%20Develop%20Emotional%20Intelligence%20Online.pdf.
21. For example, a fifteen-hour training session in five core emotional competencies with a four-week email follow-up was sufficient to yield significant increases in the competencies compared to no increase among a control group. The trained group reported enhanced physical and personal well-being and improved social and marital relationships, even a year later. Kotsou et al., "Emotional Plasticity," *Journal of Applied Psychology,* 827–39.
22. Frankl quoted in Leslie Becker-Phelps, "Don't Just React: Choose Your Response," *Psychology Today,* July 23, 2013.
23. Goleman, "What Mindfulness Is and Isn't," *LinkedIn,* February 16, 2014, http://www.linkedin.com/today/post/article/20140216161912-117825785-what-mindfulness-is-and-isn-t.
24. Jon Kabat-Zinn, *Full Catastrophe Living: Using the Wisdom of Your Body and Mind to Face Stress, Pain, and Illness* (New York: Random House, 1990).
25. Britta K. Hölzel et al., "Mindfulness Practice Leads to Increases in Regional Brain Gray Matter Density," *Psychiatry Research: Neuroimaging* 191 (2010): 36–43. It has proven effective against an increasing number of physical ailments. Richard J. Davidson et al., "Alterations in Brain and Immune Function Produced by Mindfulness Meditation," *Psychosomatic Medicine* 65 (2003): 564–70.
26. Jon Kabat-Zinn defined mindfulness as "moment-to-moment non-judgmental awareness," and in the late 1970s pioneered what became the Mindfulness Based Stress Reduction (MBSR) curriculum at the University of Massachusetts—eight weekly meditation classes and daily practice that had dramatic results: fifty-one patients who had been unsuccessfully treated by conventional methods reported significant decreases in pain, as well as significant reductions in mood disturbances and psychiatric symptoms. Kabat-Zinn, "An Outpatient Program in Behavioral Medicine for Chronic Pain Based on the Practice of Mindfulness Meditation," *General Hospital Psychiatry,* 4 (1982): 33–47. The formal MBSR program was initially available at more than 250 medical centers throughout the United States and continues to be the gold standard of mindfulness training.
27. Goleman quoted in "Back in Focus—Daniel Goleman and Joshua Freedman on Attention and Emotion, Part 2," *SixSeconds.org,* October 8, 2013, http://www.6seconds.org/2013/10/08/goleman-back-in-focus/.
28. T. Singer et al., "Empathy for Pain Involves the Affective but Not Sensory Components of Pain," *Science* 303 (2004): 1152–67. The insula and temporo-parietal junction in particular.
29. Jean Decety and Philip L. Jackson, "The Functional Architecture of Human Empathy," *Behavioral and Cognitive Neuroscience Reviews* 3 (2004): 71–100.
30. Fadel Zeidan et al., "Neural Correlates of Mindfulness Meditation-Related Anxiety Relief," *Social Cognitive Affective Neuroscience,* June 3, 2013, 1–9.
31. Catherine N.M. Ortner et al., "Mindfulness Meditation and Reduced Emotional Interference on a Cognitive Task," *Motivation and Emotion* 31 (2007): 271–83.

32. For instance, after only four days of mindfulness training for only twenty minutes each, participants show a significant improvement in critical cognitive skills, performing significantly higher in stressful cognitive tests than a control group. Zeidan et al., "Mindfulness Meditation Improves Cognition: Evidence of Brief Mental Training," *Consciousness and Cognition* 19 (2010): 597–605. Students who participate in mindfulness training for two weeks report a sixteen-point improvement in GRE test scores. Michael Mrazek et al., "Mindfulness Training Improves Working Memory Capacity and GRE Performance While Reducing Mind Wandering," *Psychological Science* 24 (2013): 776–81. Mindfulness training was found to protect cognitive functioning in members of the military in high-stress situations. Amishi Jha et al., "Examining the Protective Effects of Mindfulness Training on Working Memory Capacity and Affective Experience," *Emotion* 10 (2010): 54–64.
33. The lengths of telomeres found at the tips of chromosomes in every cell of our bodies are associated with rates of aging. Elissa Epel et al., "Can Meditation Slow Rate of Cellular Aging? Cognitive Stress, Mindfulness, and Telomeres," *Annals of the New York Academy of Sciences* 1172 (2009): 34–53. In 2010, Nobel Laureate Elizabeth Blackburn and colleagues found that the amount of telomerase, the enzyme that regulates and maintains the length of telomeres, increases through meditation, raising the likelihood of slower aging. Jacobs et al., "Intensive Meditation Training, Immune Cell Telomerase Activity, and Psychological Mediators," *Psychoneuroendocrinology* 36 (2010): 664–81. Similarly, in 2013 a professor at Harvard Medical School found that women who meditate with loving-kindness had longer telomeres, indicating less aging. Hoge et al., "Loving-Kindness Meditation Practice Associated with Longer Telomeres in Women," *Brain Behavior, and Immunity* 32 (2013): 159–63.
34. J. Carmody and R.A. Baer, "Relationships between Mindfulness Practice and Levels of Mindfulness, Medical and Psychological Symptoms and Well-Being in a Mindfulness-Based Stress Reduction Program," *Journal of Behavioral Medicine* 31 (2008): 23–33.
35. In a study reviewing the effects of participating in a nine-week loving-kindness meditation intervention program for twenty minutes a week for six weeks, researchers found that "the participants who went through the intervention experienced increased daily positive emotions, reduced depressive symptoms, and greater life satisfaction." Robert Chalmers, "Matthieu Ricard: Meet Mr. Happy," February 18, 2007, http://www.independent.co.uk/news/people/profiles/matthieu-ricard-meet-mr-happy-436652.html.
36. "Meditation Appears to Produce Enduring Changes in Emotional Processing in the Brain," *Massachusetts General Hospital News Releases,* November 12, 2012, http://www.massgeneral.org/about/pressrelease.aspx?id=1520.
37. Goleman, "Two Key Skills for High-Performance Leadership," *More Than Sound.*
38. Magee, "Educating Lawyers to Meditate?" *UMKC Law Review* 79 (2010).
39. Cendri A. Hutcherson et al., "Loving-Kindness Meditation Increases Social Connectedness," *Emotion* 8 (2008): 720–24.
40. Lea Brovedani, "What's Love Got to Do with It?" *Six Seconds.org,* July 20, 2013, http://www.6seconds.org/2013/08/20/whats-love-got-to-do-with-it/.

41. Paul Gilbert and Sue Procter, "Compassionate Mind Training for People with High Shame and Self-Criticism: Overview and Pilot Study of a Group Therapy Approach," *Clinical Psychology and Psychotherapy* 13 (2006): 353–79.
42. Linda E. Carlson et al., "Randomized Controlled Trial of Mindfulness-Based Cancer Recovery versus Supportive Expressive Group Therapy for Distressed Survivors of Breast Cancer," *Journal of Clinical Oncology* 31 (2013): 3119–26.
43. Gillespie, "Mindfulness in Legal Practice Is Going Mainstream," *ABA Journal*, February 1, 2013.
44. Lawrence Krieger, "The Mindful Lawyer Series," *Canadian Bar Association*, February 6, 2015, http://www.cbapd.org/details_en.aspx?id=ON_15OBA0206T.
45. Becy Beaupre Gillespie, "Mindful at Large: Contemplative Practice Is Emerging into the Mainstream," *ABA Journal*, 99 (2013): 24. Rogers' website on the subject—www.mindfulnessinlaw.org—has additional information on the numerous bar associations and law schools that offer mindfulness programs.
46. Diane L. Coutu, "How Resilience Works," *Harvard Business Review*, May 1, 2002.
47. Richard, "The Lawyer Types," *ABA Journal*.
48. Cherniss et al., *Bringing Emotional Intelligence to the Workplace* (New Brunswick, NJ: Consortium for Research on Emotional Intelligence in Organizations, 1998).
49. Sheldon, Dunning, and Ames, "Emotionally Unskilled, Unaware, and Uninterested in Learning More," *Journal of Applied Psychology* 99 (2014): 125–37.
50. Ibid.
51. R. Cabello and P. Fernández-Berrocal, "Implicit Theories and Ability Emotional Intelligence," *Frontiers in Psychology*, May 22, 2015.
52. Goleman, "3 Secrets to Habit Change," January 1, 2015, http://www.danielgoleman.info/daniel-goleman-3-secrets-to-habit-change/.
53. "Emotional Intelligence and Success," *Six Seconds.org*, March 25, 2016, http://www.6seconds.org/2016/03/25/research-emotional-intelligence-success/.
54. "How do you build Resilience in someone who is low to begin with? (My own Resilience score is 19 percent.) . . . [T]each the person to change their 'self-talk' from negative to positive . . . a positive mindset can fortify against a low-Resilience response. My lightbulb is that the converse is also true—a *negative* mindset can *cause* low Resilience in the first place." Richard, "Resilience and Lawyer Negativity," *Lawyer Brain Blog*, September 19, 2012, http://www.lawyerbrainblog.com/2012/09/resilience-and-lawyer-negativity/.
55. Daniel Bowling, formerly senior vice president of Human Resources for Coca Cola worldwide and currently a professor at Duke Law School teaching positive psychology, recommends the Army's training approach for building soft skills: test for and then align your abilities with work that requires those abilities; recognize and balance emotions in yourself and others; use prudent risk management and not just persistent negativity; and practice leading yourself through self-awareness, self-regulation and self-motivation. Bowling, "Stop Whining You're in the Army Now," *The Careerist*.
56. https://www.questionwritertracker.com/quiz/61/Z4MK3TKB.html
57. For more information, see "The Mood Meter App Is Here," *Yale Center for Emotional Intelligence*, 2014, http://ei.yale.edu/mood-meter-app/.
58. "Process," *Mood Meter*, http://moodmeterapp.com/process/.

59. Harry White, "A Check on Emotions," January 25, 2012, *Talent Management Magazine* http://www.talentmgt.com/2012/01/25/a-check-on-emotions/.
60. Ronald B. Adler and Russell F. Procter, *Looking Out Looking In* (Boston: Cengage Learning, 2011).
61. Yalda T. Uhlsa et al., "Five Days at Outdoor Education Camp without Screens Improves Preteen Skills with Nonverbal Emotion Cues," *Computers in Human Behavior,* 387–92.
62. Paul Ekman Group, n.d., "Paul Ekman Micro Expression Training," http://www.paulekman.com/micro-expression-training/.
63. GLS Studios, n.d., "Projects," http://glsstudios.com/games.html#sthash.Cl02tz0s.dpuf/. Empath is an emotion recognition program developed by Smartmedical Corp. that includes a number of applications businesses and video games can use. SmartMedicalCorp, n.d., "Vocal Emotion Recognition Test," https://webempath.net/lp-eng/.
64. "Empathy Quotient," *Psychology Tools,* n.d., https://psychology-tools.com/empathy-quotient/. The test was developed by Simon Baron-Cohen at ARC (the Autism Research Centre) at the University of Cambridge.
65. Greater Good, n.d., "Empathy Quiz," http://greatergood.berkeley.edu/quizzes/take_quiz/14. This assessment is drawn from three others: the Toronto Empathy Questionnaire, developed by Nathan Spreng and his colleagues; the Interpersonal Reactivity Index, developed by Mark Davis; and the Emotion Specific Empathy Questionnaire, developed by Sally Olderbak and her colleagues.
66. F.W. Platt and V.F. Keller, "Empathic Communication: A Teachable and Learnable Skill," *Journal of General Internal Medicine* 9 (1994): 222–26.
67. Sanyantani DasGupta and Rita Charon, "Personal Illness Narratives: Using Reflective Writing to Teach Empathy," *Academic Medicine: Journal of American Medical Colleges* 79 (2004): 351–56.
68. Christine Ma-Kellams and Jennifer Lerner, "Trust Your Gut or Think Carefully? Examining whether an Intuitive, versus a Systematic, Mode of Thought Produces Greater Empathic Accuracy," *Journal of Personality and Social Psychology,* 111 (2016): 674–85.
69. Taken in part from recommendations by the Greater Good Science Center at the University of California, Berkeley. "What Is Empathy?," *Greater Good.com,* n.d., http://greatergood.berkeley.edu/topic/empathy/definition#what; the nonprofit Playworks also offers eight strategies for developing empathy in children.
70. Roman Krznaric, author of the forthcoming: *Empathy: A Handbook for Revolution.*
71. DasGupta and Charon "Personal Illness Narratives: Using Reflective Writing to Teach Empathy," *Academic Medicine: Journal of American Medical Colleges.*
72. Ashley P. Taylor, n.d., "How Mimicking Facial Expressions Helps Us Read Emotions," *BrainDecoder.com,* https://www.braindecoder.com/how-mimicking-facial-expressions-helps-us-read-emotions-1597580336.html.
73. Antoine Lutz et al., "Regulation of the Neural Circuitry of Emotion by Compassion Meditation: Effects of Meditative Expertise," *Plos One,* March 26, 2008. Similarly, some research, including a study among male parolees enrolled in a substance abuse treatment program, has suggested that the

practice of Nonviolent Communication (NVC) (which includes meditation) can boost empathy.

74. Elliot M. Hirsch, "The Role of Empathy in Medicine: A Medical Student's Perspective," *Virtual Mentor.*
75. Stacey Kennelly, "Does Playing Music Boost Kids' Empathy?," *Greater Good.com,* June 8, 2012, http://greatergood.berkeley.edu/article/item/does_playing_music_boost_kids_empathy.
76. MIT Press Journals, n.d., http://www.mitpressjournals.org/action/showMultipleAbstracts#.VwPqmvkrIhc.
77. Jason Marsh, "You Can't Buy Empathy," *Greater Good.com,* December 14, 2010, http://greatergood.berkeley.edu/article/item/you_cant_buy_empathy.
78. "Active Listening," *Greater Good,* n.d., http://ggia.berkeley.edu/practice/active_listening.
79. "Top Games That Teach Empathy," *Common Sense Education,* 2017, https://www.graphite.org/top-picks/top-games-that-teach-empathy.
80. "FAQ," *Quandary,* 2017, https://www.quandarygame.org/faq.
81. Plutchik, "The Nature of Emotions," *American Scientist*: 349, Figure 6.
82. Bradberry and Greaves, *Emotional Intelligence 2.0,* 14–15. Chart adapted from a chart by Julia West.
83. Keith Oatley, "Changing Our Minds," *Greater Good.com,* December 1, 2008, http://greatergood.berkeley.edu/article/item/chaning_our_minds.
84. "Reading Literary Fiction Improves 'Mind-Reading' Skills Finds a Study from the New School of Social Research," *New School,* October 3, 2013, http://www.newschool.edu/pressroom/pressreleases/2013/CastanoKidd.htm.
85. "Music Training Leads to Better Emotional Comprehension," *GoodTheraphy.org,* November 9, 2012, http://www.goodtherapy.org/blog/music-training-emotional-comprehension-1109122. Musical education in children correlated with both higher IQs and also higher emotional comprehension scores.
86. Y. Zhu et al., "The Impact of Emotional Intelligence on Work Engagement of Registered Nurses: The Mediating Role of Organisational Justice," *Journal of Clinical Nursing* 24 (2015): 2115–24.
87. Annie Murphy Paul, "Beyond Strategy and Winning, How Games Teach Kids Empathy," *KQED News,* February 9, 2012, http://ww2.kqed.org/mindshift/2012/02/09/beyond-strategy-and-winning-how-games-teach-kids-empathy/.
88. Goleman, "Two Key Skills for High-Performance Leadership," *More Than Sound.*
89. Gregory N. Bratman et al., "Nature Experiences Reduces Rumination and Subgenual Prefrontal Cortex Activation," *Proceedings of the National Academy of Sciences* 112 (2015): 8567–72.
90. Michael P. Maslanka, "Seven Mindsets of Effective General Counsel," *Texas Lawyer,* June 10, 2013, http://www.law.com/jsp/tx/PubArticleTX.jsp?id=1202603032168&thepage=2.
91. "Pessimism narrows our focus, whereas positive thoughts widen our attention and receptiveness to the new and unexpected." Daniel Goleman, "The Focused Leader," *Harvard Business Review,* December 2013, 53.

92. See the exercises in Chapter 12 of Seligman's *Learned Optimism* (New York: Random House, 1990); "These techniques can teach lawyers to use optimism in their personal lives, yet maintain the adaptive pessimism in their professional lives. It is well documented that flexible optimism can be taught in a group setting, such as a law firm or class." Seligman, *Authentic Happiness*, 181.
93. Goleman, "The Focused Leader," *Harvard Business Review.*
94. Brittany Torez, "New Lab Aims to De-stress Technology Use," *The Stanford Daily*, May 28, 2013, http://www.stanforddaily.com/2013/05/28/new-lab-aims-to-de-stress-technology-use/.

Chapter Eight

The Role of Law Schools

[C]lients often bemoan the fact that lawyers often don't listen well, don't have a high emotional quotient and therefore have difficulty empathizing, and a number of other important qualities an effective adviser must have. If law schools don't screen for these success traits before admitting law students, and law schools don't develop coursework and training to enhance these skills, then it is no wonder practicing lawyers often do not have an abundance of these important skills.[1]

—Susan Saltonstall Duncan, legal consultant

[Law students are being trained] more for conflict than for the gentler arts of reconciliation and accommodation.[2]

—Derek Bok, former Harvard Law School Dean
and President of Harvard College

Today's law schools teach students how not to get emotionally involved in their cases. That's bullshit. If you are not emotionally involved, your client is not getting your best effort.[3]

—Joe Jamail, at his death the wealthiest practicing
attorney in the United States, referred to
as "the King of Torts"

If I'd wanted to learn about feelings, I wouldn't have gone to law school.[4]

—Law student

There is little controversy over whether law schools graduate emotionally intelligent lawyers. The consensus is that they do not. Commentators blame that failure on the confluence of several factors, including current law school admissions criteria and curricula.

Admissions Criteria. Some see the criteria for admitting law students as the primary culprit in our low emotional intelligence (EI) industry, and calls for using different criteria have been growing: "start administering emotional intelligence tests,"[5] one advisor begs. Factors such as LSAT scores and undergraduate grade point averages may be valid predictors of first-year law school grade point averages, but they don't predict overall law school grades or broader performance in law school. Rather, they lead to the admission of a disproportionate number of students who experience high levels of distress even during their first year of law school and then throughout their professional careers.[6]

Most importantly, existing admissions criteria don't correspond with success in practicing law.[7] As Shultz writes, "law schools, particularly elite law schools, assess applicants mainly on the basis of who will make a good law student rather than who will make a good lawyer,"[8] resulting in "successful" law students who "are unlikely to exhibit [the] strong emotional development" that successful practitioners require.[9]

Emotional intelligence and its components are what graduate schools for other professions are now screening for in admissions.[10] Medical schools recognize that, while "generally effective in identifying successful *matriculants,*" they had not been successful at identifying "students who will make good *doctors,*"[11] similar to the situation at law schools, so across the country many medical schools are adding EI testing or EI skill screening as part of entrance requirements.[12] Graduate business schools at Harvard, Yale, Columbia, Stanford, MIT, Pennsylvania, Dartmouth College and Notre Dame, who are adding EI-related data to admissions requirements, have early indications of positive results.[13]

Law School Curricula. Some blame the lack of emotional intelligence in our profession on the teaching model, called the Langdellian model[14]—"premised on the idea that law is a science, the study of which should be separate and distinct from the influence of emotions . . . a 19th century understanding of the human brain that is inherently flawed."[15]

At the 2012 symposium of the University of Connecticut Law School Law Review, a group of highly respected professors from law schools throughout the country agreed that the current curriculum is inadequate—touching on only one-quarter or less of the twenty-six success factors the Shultz/Zedeck study found employers and clients consider valuable.[16] Similarly, the 2016 Deloitte Report predicting major changes in the legal industry over the next decade recognizes that law firms and departments "have already identified a mismatch between the skills that are being developed through education and those currently required in the workplace."[17]

Perhaps law schools distance lawyers from their emotions in the mistaken belief that being "aggressively rational, linear, and goal oriented" will help them succeed.[18] The Georgetown study of Am Law 100 associates did cite one attribute of success as the ability to contain oneself emotionally.[19] However, developing the EI skills of emotional awareness and emotional management is a more sophisticated, targeted, and effective approach, both professionally and personally, to "containing" overwhelming emotions than the common lawyer habits of denial and suppression, for example.[20]

Apart from lowering distress and raising performance, teaching emotional intelligence in law school alongside other subjects could address the failure of law schools to develop various ethical skills,[21] a failure that the Carnegie Foundation report noted.[22] Similarly, research has established that feelings of relatedness, among others, that make ethical behavior more likely, are in fact eroded during the course of law school.[23]

Knowing that an ethical decision is being presented, which ethical standards are appropriate,[24] and how to address the emotional fallout from ethical decisions[25] are important practice skills that EI informs and that could raise ethical behavior in students and the profession generally.[26] But without affirmative guidance from our legal institutions, law students are left untutored in these and other important skills.[27]

Calls for the inclusion of emotional intelligence instruction in law schools have been building for decades,[28] and detailed recommendations have been made as to how to do so.[29] Empathy was identified early on as an ability that should be a priority for development: experts have outlined both intensive and lengthy empathy development programs, some taken from the healthcare field, that students could begin before starting law school, during their first year, and/or after graduation,[30] including an entire self-study curriculum.[31] Resilience is another EI-related skill that is well suited to instruction.[32]

Medical schools and graduate business schools are offering EI as a separate course of study, or are incorporating instruction in EI skills into classes for listening, building trust, and improving communication.[33] These measures, even when limited, have achieved good results.[34] One study found that medical students who took EI classes over the course of medical school scored higher in managing emotions in their third year than they did in each of the two years earlier,[35] and Weatherhead business students taking EI instruction for a few weeks showed substantial improvements in a number of EI subscores.[36]

First Steps. Some law schools have begun reworking their curricula to include more EI-related education: Harvard Law School overhauled its first-year curriculum in 2012, and Washington and Lee Law School revamped its third-year program with those considerations, among others, in mind.[37] Harvard and Georgetown both launched programs focused on building leadership, teamwork, and collaboration skills, all of which benefit from EI, to help "make the shift from lawyer to leader."[38] Courses attempting to bolster law students' interpersonal skills are starting to be offered at various law schools under a number of different titles—including professionalism, well-being, business skills, and ethics.[39]

Law schools are particularly interested in cultivating EI skills to help manage stress, a rising concern. Medical students, like law students, evidence mental health declines during their first year of graduate school, and studies have shown that mindfulness and other EI training affirmatively help improve medical students' overall well-being and ability to handle stress.[40]

Leonard Riskin launched the first Initiative for Mindfulness in Law and Dispute Resolution at the University of Missouri

School of Law in 2002,[41] and the University of Miami School of Law and University of California at Berkeley's Boalt Hall followed suit with initiatives.[42] The topic of Mindfulness in Legal Education brought together more than fifty professors and administrators from thirty-two law schools in 2013.[43] As of January 2016, twenty-five law schools offer or have offered mindfulness courses, both non-credit and for-credit, including Georgetown, Northwestern, Berkeley, the University of Missouri, and the University of San Francisco. Teaching mindfulness is also being integrated into law school classes on negotiation and professional responsibility.[44]

Student pressure is forcing more law schools to take other steps to help them deal with their emotions,[45] such as providing instruction on dealing with mental health challenges and substance abuse, hiring full-time counselors,[46] and setting up support networks. Law professors are starting to acknowledge their own mental health issues in solidarity with the students,[47] and private groups are offering support for law students in managing their most destructive emotions.[48]

Texas Tech Law School hired a dean of student affairs because he had a "different skill set" than lawyers. He has exhorted new students to "take care of each other" and introduced several initiatives to address student concerns.[49] The law school is also the first in the nation to offer a first-year class aimed solely at improving cognitive functioning, in no small part by drawing on and managing emotions.[50]

Worth the Effort? These efforts to produce greater well-being among law students might seem to some to be in service of a dubious goal. One article explored "a series of interrelated questions: Whether law schools can make law students happier. Whether making happier law students will translate into making happier lawyers, and the accompanying question of whether making law students happier would create better lawyers."[51]

The answers were a resounding yes to all three of those questions.[52] To make law students happier, they found that most importantly, law schools should promote social connectedness, which is correlated with overall happiness and promotes more effective lawyering by helping them more "'zealously represent' the interests of others."[53] Connectedness also helps support the emotional fallout from the isolation law students often experience. The ongoing value of promoting the personal connection in law school is demonstrated by a study finding that, "those [lawyers] who felt most supported on campus, who had professors who cared about them and made them excited about learning, and had mentors, tended to be more engaged and happy in their jobs and enjoyed greater overall well-being."[54]

That connectedness does not come any more naturally to law students, however, than to practicing lawyers. Law professor Silver acknowledges that her repeated attempts to conduct a pilot program providing support services to law students resulted in not a single volunteer student.[55] Since "[t]he vast majority of law students (88%) do not frequently work together with other students on projects,"[56] law schools could take the simple step of structuring projects so as to encourage and support group effort, and then reward emotional engagement and collaboration with recognition or as a consideration in the calculation of grades.

Some challenges to producing more emotionally intelligent law school students are systemic.[57] Law schools are for the most part still unfamiliar with non-rational-oriented goals and reluctant to push through changes to long-standing traditions. Legal educators are often averse—or at best ill equipped—to provide training in EI skills themselves,[58] since they are as likely as other lawyers to be low in EI.[59] One author reported that, in 2013, three law schools—the Charlotte School of Law, Florida Coastal School of Law, and Phoenix Schools of Law, all part of the Infilaw system of law schools—used a vendor's EI testing tools as part of their faculty hiring process, but most law schools did not use any personal style assessments to hire or promote faculty and that few professors take them on their own.[60]

Law schools should lead by publicly valuing emotional intelligence, screening for EI-related skills, offering classes in emotional intelligence, promoting student connectedness, and ensuring that law professors possess and are fluent in articulating EI skills.

HOW LAW SCHOOLS CAN HELP PRODUCE MORE EMOTIONALLY INTELLIGENT GRADS

- Articulate the value that law school places on emotional intelligence skills.
- Include personal style/emotional intelligence assessments and/or information in law school admissions criteria.
- Offer emotional intelligence and emotional intelligence–related classes, including mindfulness and stress management.
- Encourage connection, including by offering more group projects and rewarding emotionally intelligent behavior through recognition or as a component of grades.
- Address the risks that low emotional intelligence and other attributes pose through support groups, accessible counselling, and other initiatives.
- Include the consideration of emotional intelligence factors in the hiring and promotion of law professors.

Chapter Endnotes

1. Duncan, "Will Law Schools Finally Make Changes the Profession Needs?" *InFocus Blog,* December 30. 2012, http://www.rainmakingoasis.com/will-law-schools-finally-make-changes-the-profession-needs/.
2. Derek Bok, "A Flawed System," *Harvard Magazine* 85 (1983): 38–45.
3. Texas trial attorney famous for representing Pennzoil in its lawsuit against Texaco and winning a $10.53 billion verdict in 1985 (reduced on appeal to $8.53 billion). Mark Curriden, "Lions of the Trial Bar," *ABA Journal,* March, 2009, 34.
4. Nelken, "If I'd Wanted to Learn About Feelings, I Wouldn't Have Gone to Law School," *Journal of Legal Education,* 421.
5. Duncan, "Will Law Schools Finally Make Changes the Profession Needs?" *InFocus Blog.*
6. Shultz and Zedeck, "Predicting Lawyer Effectiveness," *Law & Social Inquiry,* 621, 639.
7. Ibid., 641.
8. Shultz, "Expanding the Definition of Merit," *Boalt Hall Transcript* 38 (2005): 22–24.
9. William D. Henderson, "The Bursting of the Pedigree Bubble," *NALP Bulletin,* 21 (2009): 14. Nelken, "If I'd Wanted to Learn About Feelings, I Wouldn't Have Gone to Law School," *Journal of Legal Education,* 421–22.

10. Linley Erin Hall notes that "Law schools are not the only entities interested in finding better ways to predict who will succeed in a profession," with changes being developed in the Medical College Admission Test (MCAT) to measure oral communication skills and in the Graduate Management Admission Test (GMAT) to gauge situational judgment. Linley Erin Hall, "What Makes for Good Lawyering?" *Boalt Hall Transcript* 38 (2005): 24.
11. "Tests like the medical college admission test (MCAT) have been developed to solely measure and emphasize scientific knowledge over emotional and social intelligence. Although students performing well on the MCAT are likely to do well during the first two didactic years of medical school, they may very well lack EI and social skills to do well during their clinical years and post-graduation residency." Ali Syed, "Medical Schools and Emotional Intelligence Screening," *The York Scholar* 8 (2011): 2. "Standardized tests such as the MCAT do not measure job competence, only an ability to do well on standardized tests. . . . [O]ne study demonstrated that in reviewing 12,000 correlations between aptitude test scores and various measures of later occupational success with 10,000 respondents, correlations did not exceed what would be expected by chance." Medical schools are often motivated to accept students primarily for their cognitive skills because of academic hospitals' interest in getting research grants. David C. McClelland, "Testing for Competence Rather Than 'Intelligence,'" *American Psychologist*: 3.
12. Nele Libberecht et al., "Emotional Intelligence Predicts Success in Medical School," *Emotion*, 64–73.
13. Korn, "Wanted: B-School Students With 'Soft Skills,'" *Wall Street Journal*.
14. Named after Christopher Columbus Langdell, the Dean at Harvard Law School who pioneered the early teaching model for law schools, including the Socratic method and the case method. See "Christopher Columbus Langdell," *Wikipedia*, https://en.wikipedia.org/wiki/Christopher_Columbus_Langdell.
15. Slocum, "An Inconvenient Truth," *Chapman University Law Research Paper*. Harold Anthony Lloyd, "Cognitive Emotion and the Law," *Law and Psychology Review*.
16. Duncan, "Will Law Schools Finally Make Changes the Profession Needs?" *InFocus Blog*.
17. "Changing client demands, employee expectations, technology and other external factors will alter the nature of jobs and skills required in the future." "Developing Legal Talent," *Deloitte*, 15. It goes on to predict that three "talent pools" will "form the structure of front-office employees within the law firm of the future": (1) partners and leaders, (2) traditional, permanent staff, and (3) nontraditional and transient employees, including "project managers, sales executives, deal makers, data and technology experts as well as lawyers." The report warns that with retirements over the next decade, a shortage of skilled workers and alternative career options could lead to an "employee-led" job market.
18. While most lawyers place a "premium on reaching sound decisions quickly," they were taught in law schools that "how they feel about the cases they read is irrelevant; what matters is the soundness of their logic." Nelken,"If I'd Wanted to Learn About Feelings, I Wouldn't Have Gone to Law School," *Journal of Legal Education*, 420.

19. Berman and Bock, "Developing Attorneys for the Future," *Santa Clara Law Review*, 895.
20. Daicoff, "Lawyer, Know Thyself," *American University Law Review*, 1426.
21. Sandra Janoff, "The Influence of Legal Education on Moral Reasoning," *Minnesota Law Review*, 76 (1991): 219–34. There is some evidence that business school students similarly undergo a loss of caring. Holihan, "Management Decision Making, Ethical Issues and 'Emotional' Intelligence,'" *Management Decision*.
22. The report noted that "law students' moral reasoning does not appear to develop to any significant degree during law school," nor later during practice. William Sullivan, Anne Colby, and Judith W. Wegner, *Educating Lawyers: Preparation for the Profession of Llaw* (San Francisco: Jossey-Bass, 2007), 133.
23. Krieger and Sheldon, "What Makes Lawyers Happy?" *George Washington Law Review*.
24. Abraham, "Emotional Intelligence in Organizations: A Conceptualization," *Genetic, Social, and General Psychology Monographs*: 209–24.
25. Slocum, "An Inconvenient Truth: The Need to Educate Emotionally Competent Lawyers," *Chapman University Law Research Paper*, 4. Randall, "The Myers-Briggs Type Indicator, First Year Law Studies and Performance," *Cumberland Law Review*, 92–93. Daicoff, "Lawyer, Know Thyself," *American University Law Review*, 1427.
26. "Predicting Academic Strength Emotionally," *InderScience Publishers*.
27. John Montgomery, "Incorporating Emotional Intelligence Concepts into Legal Education: Strengthening the Professionalism of Law Students," *University of Toledo Law Review*, 323 (2008).
28. Andrew S. Watson, "The Quest for Professional Competence: Psychological Aspects of Legal Education," *University of Cincinnati Law Review*, 91 (1968) emphasized the importance of lawyers being able to relate well with others, including clients. Because law students' predominately "Thinking" preference, which law school teaching reinforces, makes them "likely to undervalue factors, such as the importance of human relationships in legal problems, the human side of legal issues, the role of values in legal decision making, and the art of communication," law schools should "help them develop their less preferred [F]eeling" side to "appreciate the problems of people." Randall, "The Myers-Briggs Type Indicator, First Year Law Studies and Performance," *Cumberland Law Review*, 92–93. Daicoff comprehensively reviews the state of legal education, the extent of law student and lawyer distress, and proposes that law applicants' personal attributes, law school admissions practices, and law school curricula promote undesirable results, particularly cautioning against the potentially negative impact on professionalism and ethics that the emotional underdevelopment of lawyers has. Daicoff, "Lawyer, Know Thyself," *American University Law Review*. Daicoff identified forty-three intrapersonal and interpersonal skills enhanced by EI abilities that are taught in other disciplines. Daicoff, "Expanding the Lawyer's Toolkit of Skills and Competencies," *Santa Clara Law Review*, 52 (2012): 797–98. Silver's "Emotional Intelligence and Legal Education" was one of the earliest to focus on the necessity of teaching law students the critical new field of EI. Silver ascribed low EI in

law students to both the personalities of those drawn to law and the nature of legal education. Silver, "Love, Hate, and Other Emotional Interference in the Lawyer/Client Relationship," *Clinical Law Review* 259 (1999): 259–313. Ten years after her first plea, Silver renewed her appeal for EI training for law students, this time drawing on the model of how other helping professionals, such as clinical social workers, psychologists, and psychiatrists, are educated. Silver, "Supporting Attorneys' Personal Skills," *Revista Juridica de la Universidad de Puerto Rico,* 1.

29. Silver explained how the development of emotional skills could be incorporated into her own law school's curriculum. Silver, "Love, Hate, and Other Emotional Interference in the Lawyer/Client Relationship," *Clinical Law Review,* 259 (1999): 259–313. Slocum showed how instruction in four major emotional competency skills might be worked into legal curricula. Slocum, "An Inconvenient Truth," *Chapman University Law Research Paper,* 4–9, 15–27. Daicoff proposed how existing law school curricula could be used for teaching the "intrapersonal competencies and most of the interpersonal, conflict resolution, teamwork, problem solving, and planning skills" that Mayer and Salovey asserted could be taught. Daicoff, "Other, Expanding the Lawyer's Toolkit of Skills and Competencies," *Santa Clara Law Review,* 831.
30. Ian Gallacher, "Thinking Like Non-Lawyers: Why Empathy Is a Core Lawyering Skill and Why Legal Education Should Change to Reflect Its Importance," *Journal of the Association of Legal Writing Directors,* October 16, 2010. John Barkai and Virginia O. Fine, "Empathy Training for Lawyers and Law Students," *Southwestern University Law Review* 13 (1983): 505–29, describes a four-hour systematic training program for lawyers and law students that develops empathic or "active listening" communication skills, explains why empathetic responses are important for lawyers, and reviews the literature on empathy training in other disciplines.
31. Gerdy, "Clients, Empathy, and Compassion: Introducing First-Year Students to the 'Heart' of Lawyering," *Nebraska Law Review,* 41–42. She argues that law schools are perfectly suited to teach empathy—the "heart" of lawyering, a "vital" skill, a "must" have, the "cornerstone" of interpersonal relations and the "real mortar" of attorney-client relationships, and that the first year of law school is the ideal place to begin to fill this gap in legal education.
32. Law Professor Bowling, formerly senior vice president of Human Resources for Coca Cola worldwide and currently a professor at Duke Law School teaching positive psychology, advocates resilience training for law students, an intervention that benefited those in the US Army. Chen, "Depressed People Make Better Lawyers," *The Careerist.* The Army undertook an extensive $145 million assessment and training program that over 900,000 soldiers participated in with the goal of improving resilience and thereby combatting posttraumatic stress disorder using "positive emotion, engagement, relationships, meaning, and accomplishment." Seligman, "Building Resilience," *Harvard Business Review,* April, 2011.
33. Grewal and Davidson, "Emotional Intelligence and Graduate Medical Education," *Journal of the American Medical Association.* Eight out of the seventeen Canadian medical schools have piloted a Student Leadership Curriculum

that teaches components of EI. Bejjani, "Emotional Intelligence: Use in Medical Education and Practice," *McGill Journal of Medicine: MJM* 12 (2009): 5; "Physician Leadership Institute," *Canadian Medical Association.* The University of South Florida (USF) medical school intends to extend the SELECT EI training program to all medical students. "MD Select Program Overview," *USF Health.* Comrey, "Predicting Medical Students' Academic Performances by Their Cognitive Abilities and Personality Characteristics," *Academic Medicine,* 781–86; Lievens et al., "Personality Scale Validities Increase Throughout Medical School," *Journal of Applied Psychology,* 1514–35; Brown and Bylund, "Communication Skills Training," *Academic Medicine,* 37–44.

34. Satterfield and Hughes, "Emotion Skills Training for Medical Students: A Systematic Review," *Medical Education,* 935–41.
35. Todres et al., "The Emotional Intelligence of Medical Students," *Medical Teacher,* e42–e48. These trainings during medical school are particularly relevant in light of some findings that empathy decreases among doctors over time. See Ramzan Shahid, et al., "Assessment of Emotional Intelligence in Pediatric and Med-Peds Residents," *Journal of Contemporary Medical Education,* which showed higher than average EI scores for first year pediatric residents compared to the general population, but decreases in empathy and increases in assertiveness over the course of residency.
36. Boyatzis et al., "Competencies Can Be Developed, But Not the Way We Thought," *Capability* 2 (1996): 31. Participants also continued to build new skills in the area.
37. "J.D Program," *Harvard Law School,* 2017, http://law.harvard.edu/academics/degrees/jd/index.html; "J.D Application Overview: Washington and Lee," *Washington and Lee University,* 2017, http://law.wlu.edu/admissions/page.asp?pageid=311
38. Shanker, "Why Are Lawyers Such Terrible Managers?" *Fortune.*
39. See Daicoff, "Expanding the Lawyer's Toolkit of Skills and Competencies, *Santa Clara Law Review,* for examples of programs at various schools, including a class denominated as "emotional intelligence" offered at Indiana University Maurer School of Law and the University of San Francisco Law School's interpersonal dynamics class.
40. Craig Hassad et al., "Enhancing the Health of Medical Students: Outcomes of an Integrated Mindfulness and Lifestyle Program," *Advances in Health Science Education* 14 (2009): 387–98. Other studies show both measurable improvements in stress management and reduced burnout in students who participate in mindfulness programs. Tasha M. Felton, Lindsey Coates, and John Chambers Christopher, "Impact of Mindfulness Training on Counseling Students' Perceptions of Stress," *Mindfulness* 6 (2015): 159–69.
41. Since transferred to the University of Florida, Levin College of Law. Leonard L. Riskin, "The Contemplative Lawyer: On the Potential Contributions of Mindfulness Meditation to Law Students, Lawyers and Their Clients." *Harvard Negotiation Law Review* 7 (2002): 1–66.
42. Gillespie, "Mindful at Large: Contemplative Practice Is Emerging into the Mainstream," *ABA Journal,* 24. Scott Rogers is the founder of the Mindfulness in Law Program at the University of Miami Law School where he teaches

mindfulness, and is also the author of many books, including *The Six-Minute Solution: A Mindfulness Primer for Lawyers* and *Mindfulness for Law Students: Using the Power of Mindful Awareness to Achieve Balance and Success in Law School.* His website—www.mindfulnessinlawclass.org—lists many resources on mindfulness.

43. "Berkeley Initiative for Mindfulness in Law," *Berkeley Law,* http://www.law.berkeley.edu/mindfulness.htm.
44. Magee, "Justice Begins with a Breath," *ABA Journal,* January 1, 2016.
45. Sloan, "Yale Law Students Lobby for Better Services," *National Law Journal.* Mental Health Alliance, a Yale Law School student group, advocates for "raising awareness of mental health problems in law school and the legal profession, removing barriers for Yale law students seeking help . . . including limits on insurance coverage and lengthy wait times to see a mental health service provider," and for "expansion of the student health insurance and more therapists."
46. Sloan, "Law Schools Tackle Mental Health," *National Law Journal.*
47. Brian Clarke, "Professors' Candor About Problems Aids Students," *National Law Journal,* May 9, 2016.
48. The Dave Nee Foundation, for example, was founded to promote wellness among law students after Fordham University law graduate Dave Nee committed suicide while studying for the bar exam, and is active in promoting classes and interventions nationwide to help law students. "Dave Nee Foundation," http://www.daveneefoundation.org/.
49. Sloan, "Law School Helps Students Stay Emotionally Fit," *National Law Journal,* May 9, 2016. The law school offers, among other things, monthly lunch meetings to discuss mental health and substance abuse risks, has eliminated drinking at many campus events, and elicits annual student engagement surveys.
50. The SMART program developed at the Center for BrainHealth, a research division of the University of Texas at Dallas, focuses on strategic attention, "big-picture thinking," and "creative problem solving." Jenny B. Davis, "Texas Tech Adopts Smart Brain Training for Its 1Ls," *ABA Journal,* February, 2016, 10.
51. Levit and Linder, "Happy Law Students, Happy Lawyers," *Syracuse Law Review.*
52. This is consistent with other research. "Happiness fuels success, not the other way around. When we are positive, our brains become more engaged, creative, motivated, energetic, resilient, and productive at work. . . . This discovery has been borne out repeatedly by rigorous research in psychology and neuroscience, management studies, and the bottom lines of organizations around the world." Caprino, "How Happiness Directly Impacts Your Success," *Forbes Leadership Blog.*
53. Levit and Linder, "Happy Law Students, Happy Lawyers," *Syracuse Law Review.*
54. Sloan, "Would You Do Law School Again? 67% of Grads Said Yes," *National Law Journal,* March 23, 2016. Stephanie Marken, "Life After Law School," *Gallup,* March 24, 2016, http://www.gallup.com/opinion/gallup/190172/life-law-school.aspx.
55. Silver, "Supporting Attorneys' Personal Skills," *Revista Juridica de la Universidad de Puerto Rico,* 164.

56. "Law School Survey of Student Engagement, Engaging Legal Education: Moving Beyond the Status Quo," *Law School Survey of Student Engagement,* 2006, 8.
57. Brent W. Newton, "Preaching What They Don't Practice: Why Law Faculties' Preoccupation with Impractical Scholarship and Devaluation of Practical Competencies Obstruct Reform in the Legal Academy," *South Carolina Law Review* 105 (2010): 146–50.
58. Silver, "Love, Hate, and Other Emotional Interference in the Lawyer/Client Relationship," *Clinical Law Review,* 259 (1999): 259–313.
59. Daicoff, "Expanding the Lawyer's Toolkit of Skills and Competencies," *Santa Clara Law Review,* 797–98.
60. Baez, "Personality Tests in Employment Selection: Use with Caution," *Cornell HR Review.*

Chapter Nine

Now Is the Time to Lawyer with Emotional Intelligence

The greatest advantage lawyers have is that they compete only with other lawyers.[1]

—David Maister, author and professional services guru

The old saying that law firms are lucky that they only have to compete with other law firms no longer holds true. For law firms to continue to be profitable in a flattened field with more players, change is critical and urgent.[2]

—Karen MacKay, president of consulting firm Phoenix Legal, Inc., and Stephen Mabey, managing director of Applied Strategies, Inc.

In a 2013 online survey, consultant/commentator Jordan Furlong asked a wide range of lawyers to prioritize what "precise skills, talents and resources" among a possible fifteen should be in their "future legal survival kit." To Furlong's admitted surprise, the item that came out on top was "Emotional Intelligence," and three of the four next picks clearly benefit from emotional intelligence (EI).[3] The beauty of this survey is the simplicity of the list of factors and the clarity of those chosen—choices that are surprising to some and yet encouraging: lawyers recognize that employing emotional intelligence emotional intelligence is the rallying call for the 21st century.

That survey is consistent with others that have identified pressing, long-term trends in law that are already well upon us, such as the need for true responsiveness to clients, the rise of the importance of teams, the globalization of the legal marketplace, and the impact of technology.[4]

This book's comprehensive review of the research shows that equipping ourselves with high EI produces a plethora of advantages for lawyers, both professionally and personally, individually and in our organizations, that empower us to optimally deliver legal services into the stream of all those 21st-century trends.

Among those advantages are:

- Higher cognitive functioning
- More effective decision making and better decisions
- Enhanced performance in all fields of law
- Improved communication
- Greater leadership effectiveness
- More innovation
- Greater influence
- More effective change management
- Enhanced risk assessment
- Reduced conflict and improved conflict management
- Higher functioning teams
- More ethical conduct
- Lower risk of liability
- Improved interpersonal work relations
- Better social, family, and intimate relationships
- Greater mental and physical well-being—including improved career and life satisfaction and lower levels of depression and other signs of distress[5]

More specifically, by raising emotional intelligence, we get individual practitioners who are the best leaders, client service providers, supervisors, mentors, colleagues, and team players—lawyers who can hear and utilize uncomfortable feedback, make even the unpopular decisions, provide good counsel on the most difficult professional and personal issues and client imbroglios, spot and resolve conflict, encourage innovation, effectively forge change, and engender greater collaboration and collegiality.

We can start by putting our emotionally intelligent lawyers on the front line in external interactions—in client development and client service, talent recruitment, and community involvement—because they perform at the highest level professionally, producing loyal clients and valuable connections with the lowest risk of liability. Over time, those emotionally intelligent lawyers can model for others the most productive attitudes and behaviors within and without the workplace, building the organization's EI capacity and success over time.

Inside our organizations, we can build our individual and collective emotional intelligence by using EI screening, assessments, coaching, training, performance and client feedback, recognition and rewards to realize greater productivity, lower attrition, fewer expenses, and higher revenue.

Even if you're personally satisfied with your work and life, why wouldn't you want even more of whatever success you have already achieved? Particularly when enhanced EI promises to raise your legal game, income, and satisfaction at a time when the expanding complexities of practicing law we are confronting as we go forward into the 21st century threaten them all.

Raising emotional intelligence in our industry is not an easy undertaking, which I am the first to admit, but if both individual lawyers and organizations marshal the formidable talents that we are rightfully proud of—our intelligence, drive, hard work, and analytical abilities—toward that goal, I have no doubt that we can succeed.

What we cannot do is simply carry on in our stalwart way, turning a blind eye to mounting criticism, dissatisfied clients, distressed colleagues, a distrustful public, ill-equipped lawyers, rising misconduct, and failing workplaces impaired in their attempts to compete.

It is not, as law professor and author of *Lawyer, Know Yourself* Susan Daicoff recognizes, an either/or choice. "We must acknowledge the value of emotion; we need to learn to recognize our own feelings and those of others. We can integrate our thoughts and feelings, for greater personal and professional satisfaction and for the kind of connection with other people that acknowledges our mutual humanity."[6]

Chapter Endnotes

1. Maister, "Are Law Firms Manageable?" *DavidMaister.com.*
2. Karen MacKay and Stephen Mabey, "Profiting When the World Is Flat," *Law Practice,* July/August, 2012, http://www.phoenix-legal.com/documents/articles/profiting.pdf.
3. The next highest being Connections—Strong and Productive Relationships with Clients, Moral Fiber—Strength of Character and High Levels of Integrity, and Legal Knowledge—Old Fashioned Legal Know-How, followed by Innovation—Talent and Enthusiasm for Improving Current Practices. Furlong, "Ready for the Future? Your Survival Kit Survey Results," *Law 21 Blog,* August 15, 2013, https://www.law21.ca/2013/08/ready-for-the-future-your-survival-kit-survey-results/.
4. Smock et al., "Legal Marketplace: Outlook for 2013 and Beyond," *Managing Partner Forum: Advancing the Business of Law,* February, 2013.
5. Mayer, Roberts, and Barsade, "Human Abilities," *Annual Review of Psychology,* 507–36.
6. Breslau and Daicoff, "The Illicit Relationship of Lawyers and Emotion," *Cutting Edge Law.*

APPENDIX

Assessment and Development Resources

Emotional Intelligence and Emotional Intelligence–Related Assessments

Widely Used Emotional Intelligence Assessments

The following provides further information about the most widely used assessments coming out of the three main models of emotional intelligence (EI). To take an assessment, you may have to purchase it through a professional licensed to administer it or from assessment houses other than the product owner, in each case at a higher price. Assessments usually include a detailed report with your results, but feedback from a professional qualified in interpreting the results is highly recommended and can often be purchased in the form of a telephonic explanation or coaching session.

Ability Model: The MSCEIT

> *In regard to measuring emotional intelligence—I am a great believer that . . . ability testing . . . is the only adequate method to employ. Intelligence is an ability, and is directly measured only by having people answer questions and evaluating the correctness of those answers.*[1]
>
> —John D. Mayer

In 1990, John Mayer and Peter Salovey defined a new attribute called emotional intelligence as "the ability to monitor one's and others' feelings and emotions, to discriminate amongst them and to use this information to guide one's thinking and actions."[2] This theoretical framework employs arguably the narrowest definition of EI.

The Mayer/Salovey model considers emotional intelligence to be an ability, related to IQ and to personality traits, yet distinct from them, that can be assessed separately and also developed over time. The researchers concluded that, "[W]hat we have learned thus far is promising: emotional intelligence can be measured objectively, it predicts important life outcomes, and it appears that the skills that comprise the construct can be learned."[3]

In 1999, they and David Caruso developed the Meyer-Salovey-Caruso Emotional Intelligence Test (MSCEIT), the only widely recognized "ability-based" EI assessment, which is highly researched and academically vigorous with strong reliability and validity.[4] It replaced the earlier, lengthier Multifactor Emotional Intelligence Scale (MEIS) published in 1990, which was the first assessment expressly developed to measure EI.[5] The MSCEIT measures one's raw EI ability, whether or not that ability is used in full, just as people may under- or overperform their IQ.

The MSCEIT is a product of the assessment development and administration firm MHS, can be taken online, and consists of 141 items divided into four branches—(1) perceiving emotions, (2) using emotions (sometimes called emotional facilitation), (3) understanding emotions, and (4) managing emotions[6]—that take thirty to forty-five minutes to complete.[7] Each branch has two subscales:

- *Perceiving Emotions:* the Faces Task assesses the ability to identify how a person feels based on his or her facial expressions; the Pictures Task tests the ability to determine emotions expressed in music, art, and other external environments, including an audience or jury.
- *Using Emotions:* the Facilitating Task measures a person's knowledge of how moods interact and support thinking and reasoning; the Sensations Task compares different emotions

to different sensations, such as light, color, and temperature. Little research exists with respect to this branch.

- *Understanding Emotions:* the Blends Task rates the ability to connect situations with certain emotions and to assemble simple emotions into complex feelings—disgust, for example, is considered a blend of anger and disdain; the Changes Task assesses knowledge of emotional chains (i.e., how emotions transition from one to another in time or intensity, like from contentment to joy or annoyance to rage).
- *Regulating Emotions:* the Emotion Management Task measures the ability to manage and incorporate one's own emotions into decision making; the Emotional Relations Task measures the ability to manage and incorporate emotions into decision making that involves other people, in both cases in order to achieve certain results.

Rather than giving their opinion of their own or others' skills, subjects taking the MSCEIT perform tasks in real time, much like on an SAT, rating the best answer to questions or scenarios involving emotions. The results are scored based on the consensus of both experts and previous test-takers, a system that some see as a weakness.[8] Critics question whether the MSCEIT really assesses an ability or shows a cognitive understanding of emotions, without indicating whether the individual can do emotionally what he or she knows cognitively to do.[9]

The MSCEIT has demonstrated significantly less overlap with personality traits than the trait, competencies, or mixed-model assessments.[10] What the MSCEIT scores may correlate with is IQ.[11] Yet studies have concluded that the MSCEIT can predict more outcomes than other EI assessments, the Big Five personality traits, gender, or other factors.[12]

Mixed Model and Trait Models: The EQ-i 2.0 and the TEIQue

Another strand of research views emotional intelligence as a distinct trait, similar to a personality trait or a collection of personality characteristics, which tend to be unchangeable.

The original Emotional Quotient Inventory (EQ-i) was designed by US-born Israeli psychologist Reuven Bar-On and first presented to the American Psychological Association in Toronto, Canada, in 1996.[13] Rather than focusing on the internal processing of emotions, the Bar-On model of Emotional-Social Intelligence defines emotional intelligence as the ability to understand ourselves and others, to relate well to people, and to cope with environmental demands and pressures through such behaviors as awareness, stress tolerance, and problem solving. Hundreds of studies over the years have shown that EQ-i and successor scores are reliable and valid.[14]

The successor to the EQ-i, the EQ-i 2.0 is a 133-item "self-report" assessment developed by MHS.[15] It takes thirty minutes to complete and is available online and in many languages. One's total emotional quotient is determined based on five composite scales—self-perception, self-expression, interpersonal, decision making, and stress management—and fifteen subscales. The EQ 360 is the coordinating "multi-rater" assessment that has each of the same 133 assessment items as the EQ-i 2.0, resulting in a report that combines all others' reports with the self-report.

"Self-reports" gauge a person's EI from his or her answers to what that person considers his or her various strengths and weaknesses to be, whereas "360-degree" reports[16] reflect colleagues' evaluations of that person's skills. Those opinions are aggregated to form an EI profile—a "multi-rater" report—often noting any discrepancies between the self-report and the others' reports.

While offering a broad range of viewpoints, this methodology raises fundamental questions as to how well people know themselves and others, and whether either conscious or unconscious biases impact their reports. Also, self-reported EI has been found to overlap significantly with common personality traits, so much so that these assessments may be measuring the same or closely related traits,[17] which critics have noted.[18]

One of the more recently developed EI assessments is the Trait Emotional Intelligence Questionnaire (TEIQue), developed by Dr. K. V. Petrides at the London Psychometric Laboratory in University College London, which conceptualizes emotional intelligence as a separate and enduring personality trait. "Trait EI theory is unrelated to what lay people understand by 'emotional intelligence' or 'EQ' and incompatible with other models of the construct."[19]

The family of TEIQue instruments is used primarily for academic and clinical research.[20] The TEIQue Full Form is a self-report inventory with 153 items measuring fifteen facets, four factors, and global trait EI, and takes twenty-five minutes to complete. The TEIQue-Short Form is a thirty-item questionnaire taking five minutes to complete that measures "global trait EI" using two items from each of the fifteen facets. Assessments are also designed for young adults and children. All can be downloaded, with instructions for obtaining scoring, for a donation. Commercial use of the assessments is only granted upon application.

The Competencies Model: Goleman's ESCI

Another group of theorists views emotional intelligence as a set of skills called competencies. These are often also referred to as "mixed-model" theories, in that EI is considered to be neither a separate ability nor a personality trait but more a collection of behavioral skills that draw on emotional information, some of which have been found to be closely aligned with personality traits,[21] making this "mixed-model" the broadest theoretical formulation of EI.[22]

Daniel Goleman's widely used assessments of "a wide array of competencies and skills that drive managerial performance" are of this type.[23] Goleman reviewed data accumulated by the Hay Group from performance assessments of thousands of workers in American corporations and identified a large portion of those competencies correlated with optimal performance which he believed reflected emotional intelligence, a position that continues to stir controversy.[24]

The Emotional and Social Competence Inventory (ESCI)[25] was developed by Goleman in 2007 in collaboration with the Hay Group, and is the successor to the Emotional Competence Inventory (ECI) published in the late 1990s and a revised and expanded version, the ECI-2, published in 2005.[26]

The ESCI is a multi-rater product of the Hay Group, with twelve competencies divided into four quadrants: Self-Awareness,

Self-Management, Social Awareness, and Relationship Management. There is no self-assessment. The assessments' results are compared with the ratings in the Hay Group's extensive database.[27]

The Consortium for Research on Emotional Intelligence in Organizations gives further information on the above and other EI assessments.[28]

Six Seconds EQ Network recommends several EI assessments, which it says are all "statistically reliable" and measure "slightly (or significantly) different aspects of EQ."[29]

Vendor Emotional Intelligence Assessments

While many companies use vendor-developed assessments, these usually have not been as thoroughly tested by peer-reviewed research, so their validity and reliability are harder to gauge.[30]

TalentSmart's Emotional Intelligence Appraisal:[31] This ten-minute proprietary self-assessment with twenty-eight questions is available online at a relatively low cost. It "delivers scores for the key components of emotional intelligence: overall EQ, self-awareness, self-management, social awareness, and relationship management." A multi-rater 360-degree Appraisal is also available. The Emotional Intelligence Appraisal can be purchased together with a two-hour debriefing at a higher cost.

Six Seconds EQ Network's Six Seconds Emotional Intelligence Assessment:[32] Six Seconds developed a three-part EI model—Know Yourself, Choose Yourself, and Give Yourself—in 1997 drawing on the work of Peter Salovey (who serves on Six Seconds' advisory board), Jack Mayer, and Daniel Goleman. A self-assessment, the SEI "measures eight fundamentals of EQ, including emotional literacy, emotional management, and empathy," and is available online.

Free Emotional Intelligence Assessments

Free assessments of EI that have real value are hard to come by, even though an ever-growing number of websites promise to enlighten you. These free online assessments may give you a glimpse into aspects of your EI, but they have not been academically vetted.

1. Psychtests Emotional Intelligence Test:[33] Asks 341 questions, including some of the same types of questions as asked in the MSCEIT, and takes about sixty minutes to complete.
2. The Psychology Today Test:[34] Created by Psychtests and GoodTherapy.org (which has the same EI test) and promoted by *Psychology Today*. Asks test takers to rate 146 statements like "I adjust my behavior depending on who I am interacting with (e.g., calm and friendly with a child, serious and professional with my boss, etc.)" on scale of one to five (ranging from "completely true" to "completely false"). "After finishing the test, you will receive a Snapshot Report with an introduction, a graph and a personalized interpretation for one of your test scores." Takes about forty-five minutes to complete and a full report is available at a nominal fee.
3. Ghyst & Associates and Brent Darnell International's EI Test:[35] Asks forty-eight questions regarding six groupings (and subgroups) using the EQ-i (2.0) model of EI. Test-takers answer on a scale of one to five ("strongly disagree" to "strongly agree"), then tally total points for an explanation of what scores mean (e.g., if you score high on Independence, "Would rather work alone and be alone," if low, "Dependent on others for self-worth, would rather be told what to do").
4. Maetrix Emotional Intelligence Test also known as the Global Leadership Foundation's Global Emotional Intelligence Test:[36] "Uses 40 questions derived from the mætrîx *EI Capability Assessment* instrument, which contains 158 items . . . based on Goleman's four quadrant Emotional Intelligence Competency Model (2002)." Respondents choose one statement from a pair that they feel describes them best, for example: "My emotions have a strong impact on how I behave"; "My emotions have no impact on how I behave."
5. McGraw Hill Education's EI Quiz:[37] Asks test takers to choose from range of "strongly agree" to "strongly disagree" in response to twenty-five statements like: "I can think clearly and stay focused at a task at hand under pressure."

6. Institute for Health and Human Potential free IHHP EQ Quiz:[38] Includes seventeen questions, asking participant to rate how much he or she agrees with statements like "I can listen without jumping to judgment." They have a Facebook quiz available as well.
7. Mind Tools EI Quiz:[39] Quick, easy test of fifteen questions that gives a baseline EI.
8. The Other Kind of Smart EI Quiz:[40] Developed by Harvey Deutschendorf, author of *The Other Kind of Smart: Simple Ways to Boost Your Emotional Intelligence for Greater Personal Effectiveness and Success.* Simple quiz with fifteen questions on a scale from "Not true of me" to "Very often true of me."

Emotional Intelligence–Related Assessments

Listed below are some assessments, including some mentioned in this book, that purport to measure one or more aspects of EI, such as its components or its applications:

Leading with EI Quiz:[41] This short twenty-five-question quiz designed by noted EI researcher Dr. Annie McKee indicates your leadership EI. After getting your score, ask trusted friends or colleagues to answer the same questions about you to see if their responses match yours.

My Emotions:[42] This page of the University of Central Florida links to a wide variety of quizzes/tests looking at different aspects of EI, including the "Emotion Regulation Quiz," "Emotions and Job Preference Quiz," "Burnout Test," and "Emotional Labor Survey."

Awareness and Empathy:

1. Reading the Mind in the Eyes Test:[43] For each set of eyes displayed, you choose the one word out of four that is most descriptive of what the person is thinking or feeling, and a free report is given at the end of the session.

2. The Greater Good's free Facial Expression Quiz:[44] Test takers select from a range of emotions to describe the facial expression in twenty photo slides. Uses the Interpersonal Reactivity Index to measure empathy, though some question its accuracy as an empathy measurement tool.

Empathy:

1. The Empathy Quotient (EQ):[45] A free sixty-item questionnaire designed to measure empathy in adults developed by Simon Baron-Cohen at ARC (the Autism Research Centre) at the University of Cambridge.[46]
2. The Greater Good's free Empathy Quiz:[47] Contains twenty-eight questions drawn from three scientifically validated scales: the Toronto Empathy Questionnaire, the Interpersonal Reactivity Index, and the Emotion Specific Empathy Questionnaire. When you're done, you'll receive your empathy score, along with feedback interpreting this score and tips for strengthening your empathy skills.

The Ashoka Foundation's Start Empathy initiative[48] tracks educators' best practices for teaching empathy.[49] The nonprofit Playworks also offers eight strategies for developing empathy in children.[50] More suggestions for developing empathy are at this Greater Good site.[51]

Pessimism:

You can take Psychology Professor Martin Seligman's free online Optimism Test:[52] There is also a short, written version on page 84 of Seligman's *Authentic Happiness.*

Emotional Agility:

Susan David, on faculty at Harvard University, is a founder of the Harvard/McLean Institute of Coaching. She is the author of *Emotional Agility* (Avery, 2016),[53] based on the concept named by

Harvard Business Review as a Management Idea of the Year. Results from this short assessment are sent to your email address.[54]

Personality and Personal Style:

The Five Factor Model:[55] Long-standing, highly respected personality assessment evaluating the "Big Five" personality traits: Openness, Conscientiousness, Extraversion, Agreeableness, and Emotional Stability (or Neuroticism on the other side of that trait continuum).

Myers-Briggs Type Indicator (MBTI):[56] The Myers-Briggs Type Indicator® is a widely used self-report tool that indicates individual preferences in information collection and decision making. Originally developed because of a lawyer, the MBTI produces a four-letter code, among sixteen "types," suggesting the person's preferences in four different areas.[57] More than half of all practicing attorneys fall into one of four types, and one type—INTJ—"occurs with five times greater frequency in lawyers than it does generally."[58]

The Caliper Profile:[59] This widely used "in-depth personality assessment and job matching" assessment often used by businesses for career development purposes "has been validated by nearly a half-century of research and measures over twenty-five personality traits that relate to job performance."

The Hogan Personality Inventory (HPI):[60] The HPI measures how you relate to others when you are at your best, described as your "normal or bright-side personality," and is based on the Five-Factor Model (FFM) of personality traits. It was developed specifically for business applications to identify "the personality characteristics that distinguish individuals and predict career success."

Using the Hogan assessments, lawyers have been found to display low interpersonal sensitivity, and under stress become tense and overly critical, reluctant to take risks and make decisions, and inattentive to rules of conduct. Our tendencies to "become argumentative and critical of others" and "to physically or emotionally distance themselves from others and become uncommunicative" together mean we prefer "Moving Away" from conflict, in marked contrast to other professionals who favor the more successful "Moving Against" the conflict to solve or remove it.[61]

The Right Profile[62] was developed by a lawyer and the psychologist behind the Troutwine Athletic Profile used by professional football teams; it offers three assessments. "*The Should I Be a Lawyer Report* analyzes an individual's suitability for a career in law overall plus individual practice areas and work settings. The *Career Longevity Report* provides a deep analysis of the individual's legal career propensities plus a personalized fit analysis of practice areas and work settings. The *Attorney Assessment System* helps legal employers first identify candidates that are scientifically predicted to succeed and culturally fit with their organization and then provide the management and development tools to help them reach their full potential."

A Pre-Employment Attorney Test[63] is a relatively low cost online assessment that purports to identify individuals likely to have desirable and undesirable behaviors for lawyers—those who are "easy to get along with, not particularly self-centered or demanding, yet who have the aggressive personality with which to argue cases successfully." It consists of an untimed personality inventory with 133 questions, a forty-four item test of mental ability, and a set of open-ended questions to which the candidate must type in a short answer.

Conflict Style:

Thomas Kilmann Instrument:[64] "The Thomas-Kilmann Conflict Mode Instrument (TKI®) tool is the world's best-selling tool for helping people understand how different conflict-handling styles affect interpersonal and group dynamics—and for empowering them to choose the appropriate style for any situation. Using thirty multiple-choice questions, the TKI tool assesses an individual's typical behavior in conflict situations and describes it along two dimensions: assertiveness and cooperativeness."

Conflict Dynamics Profile:[65] "Unlike most conflict instruments, the CDP focuses on conflict behaviors rather than styles. That is, rather than identifying conflict 'styles'—which represent a combination of behavior, personality, and motivation that can be difficult to change—the CDP focuses exclusively on the behaviors people typically display when faced with conflict."

The US Institute of Peace's Conflict Styles Assessment:[66] "To find out your style, or tendency," you answer each of thirty prompts imagining a conflict scenario you have been in by choosing "the statement (either A or B) that best describes how you would respond. When you have finished, your scores will appear, along with an analysis of your results." It is based on the TKI.

This review of conflict analysis tools[67] represents a wide range of both micro- and macro-level approaches to conflict analysis primarily suited for governmental/political conflicts.

Emotional Intelligence Apps

These apps purport either to gauge EI or develop some aspect of it:

1. MEIT (Mobile Emotional Intelligence Test)[68] is a low-cost app that assesses EI using evaluations of emotions expressed by a series of human faces and decisions about how best to handle emotional situations.
2. The free Emotional Intelligence app by Movisol[69] helps individuals assess their EI.
3. The free Mood Meter app[70] developed by Yale provides an interactive tool for noting and managing emotions.
4. Six Seconds EQ Network offers several free apps using its EI model to improve EI—"Emotion Wheel," which evaluates and improves emotional literacy; "Intend," which helps focus attention; and "EQ Coach," which uses "cards" to ask

questions that help analyze and solve real-life situations (also available in a larger, low-cost version).[71]

5. There are several free or low-cost meditative apps to encourage and track meditation, including Insight Timer, Buddhify, and Calm.[72]

Stay on the lookout for new technological applications relating to EI. For example, Stanford University's Calming Technology Lab is developing relaxation devices to help respond to strong emotions, such as a belt (not yet commercially available) that can detect breathing and connects to an app that helps calm you when it determines that you're feeling emotionally uncontrolled.[73] Repeated could help build emotional regulation skills.

Emotional Intelligence Video Games

GLS (Games+Learning+Society) Studios develops video games and gaming that promote socioemotional development. In the game *Crystals of Kaydor,* developed using Paul Ekman's principles of facial recognition, the player is an advanced robot who crash-lands on an alien planet, where it helps locals solve problems through interpreting body language and nonverbal cues. In *Tenacity,* an app to help train emotional regulation, the player tries to maintain focus and calm in various settings despite distractions—planes flying by, animals running through.[74]

The online game *The Sims 4,* launched in 2015, has been redesigned so that the virtual characters have and are guided by their moods, including feeling body shame. One of the designers said that, "The key to *The Sims 4* emotions is that there isn't anything particularly better or worse. You have the ability of what to do with that emotion. If your Sim is furious, that may seem like a bad thing, but it actually means they can write a special book or paint a special painting or go for a really good run and have a really great workout."[75] Playing may improve emotional understanding.

The Learning Games Network, a spinoff of MIT and the University of Wisconsin–Madison, has developed a free, Web-based science fiction game called *Quandary* that teaches empathy, critical thinking, perspective taking, and ethical decision making. Players aged eight and up must make difficult decisions in which there are no clear right or wrong answers but important consequences—to themselves, to others in the colony, and to the planet Braxos.

If You Can is an empathy training iPad app using Yale's SEL curriculum to promote emotional learning designed for six- to twelve-year-olds and published by the founder of Electronic Arts, which also publishes Madden NFL.[76] Each episode is keyed to challenges in twenty areas that involve emotions, such as emotional awareness, resilience, gratitude, sensitivity, empathy, listening, humor, leadership, and collaboration.[77]

CommonSense.org lists video games children or the child in you can play to increase empathy, including their picks for the top thirteen games.[78]

Other Resources for Developing Emotional Intelligence

Workshops, classes, and seminars in EI are offered to the general public in many communities by local business groups, talent development professionals, libraries, colleges and universities, and other organizations. If you are interested in in-person or online training, workshops, or coaching designed specifically for lawyers, contact Law People Management, LLC.

Here are some additional resources offered to the general public for developing EI through training and coaching.

The American Management Association offers several two- to three-day seminars on EI, based on Daniel Goleman's work, both online and onsite currently at a cost of $2,000 to $2,600.[79] Some courses were developed in collaboration with Goleman, such as the "Emotional Intelligence Workshop," "Developing Your Emotional Intelligence," and "Leading with Emotional Intelligence."

The Institute for Social + Emotional Intelligence® uses their EI assessment—the Social + Emotional Intelligence Profile (SEIP)®—as the basis for online, self-paced EI programs with coaching support for six to twelve months currently ranging in cost from $3,995 to $10,250.[80]

The Center for Creative Leadership offers at several locations onsite leadership classes that include elements of emotional intelligence (currently at $4,200 per three-day session) and designs customized programs for organizations that can include online or telephonic assistance. It also provides coaching materials and services, that are fairly expensive, tailored to human resources or other leaders who can impact organizational culture.[81]

Among other offerings at various prices, Corporate Training Materials provides at an initial cost currently of $499 very basic customizable materials and instructions for training trainers in EI and other types of development workshops.[82]

Empathia provides both online and telephonic EI coaching for organizations, boasting 12 percent improvements in EI scores for online clients and 21 percent for those using telephone coaching.[83]

At a current cost of $49 to $299 each, one or more of the seven programs in the Ekman Library can help train you in reading facial cues in different settings.[84]

Six Seconds provides EI-related services to companies and individuals, including workshops and coaching.[85]

TalentSmart offers various programs to develop EI, including onsite and online coaching for individuals, teams and companies.[86]

For equestrians or simply the adventurous, Eponaquest[87] and others across the country have developed interactive equine programs for individuals and corporate groups that use EI concepts to boost awareness, communication, teamwork, and leadership.

Guidelines for Effective Emotional Intelligence Training

In 1998, twenty-two guidelines for effective organizational EI training were developed, consistent with principles for other types of training. They are organized into four phases—a preparation phase, a training phase, a transfer and maintenance phase, and an evaluation phase, as set forth in Figure A-1.[88]

"The initial phase, which is crucial for effective social and emotional learning, involves preparation for change at both the organizational and individual levels. The second phase, training, . . . includes the processes that help people change the way in which

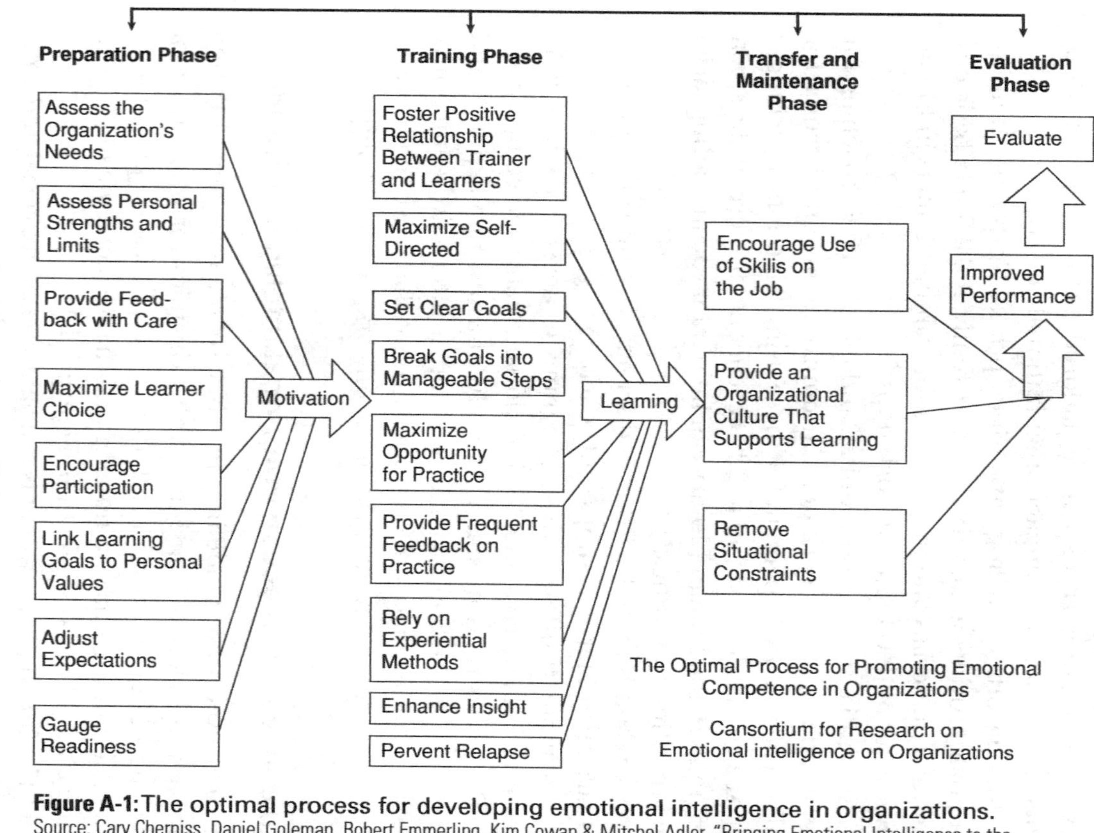

Figure A-1: The optimal process for developing emotional intelligence in organizations.
Source: Cary Cherniss, Daniel Goleman, Robert Emmerling, Kim Cowan & Mitchel Adler, "Bringing Emotional Intelligence to the Workplace: A Technical Report Issued by the Consortium for Research on Emotional Intelligence in Organizations," *Emotional Intelligence in Organizations,* 1998, http://www.eiconsortium.org/reports/technical_report.html.

they view the world and deal with its social and emotional demands. The third phase, transfer and maintenance, addresses what happens following the formal training experience. The final phase involves evaluation. Given . . . the complexity of programs designed to promote such learning and the great unevenness in the effectiveness of existing programs, evaluation always should be part of the process."

Consultant Larry Richard proposes that EI skills "can only be learned by employing an 'adult learning' methodology" following eight steps: "See the skill demonstrated. Try it yourself. Receive high quality operational feedback. Make course corrections and try it again. Repeat as needed. Tie it to a practical, meaningful goal. Build layers of skill complexity, one layer at a time. Practice and rehearse on a regular basis until the skill becomes second nature," the last being the most important and daunting step for lawyers.[89]

Kiser suggests that "we should shift our attention [from experience] to what psychologists call 'deliberate practice.' Deliberate practice requires systematic, objective measurement of professional performance, prompt and unfettered feedback, and increasingly difficult and complex challenges."[90]

Additional Resources

"Understanding Emotional Intelligence and Personality Type" discusses the use of the EQ-i, MBTI, and other assessments for managing and developing performance and leadership.[91]

"Can Apps Gauge Emotional Intelligence? Maybe" by Daniel Goleman cautions using apps that purport to gauge EI.[92]

TalentSmart's "Business Case for Emotional Intelligence"[93] presents arguments for using EI in business.

The Art of Speed Reading People: How to Size People Up and Speak Their Language by Paul D. Tieger and Barbara Barron-Tieger (Little Brown 1998) addresses how to read certain emotional cues.

The Other Kind of Smart: Simple Ways to Boost Your Emotional Intelligence for Greater Personal Effectiveness and Success by

Harvey Deutschendorf (American Management Association of New York).

Empathia's "The Emotional Intelligence Difference: Coaching for Behavior Change" extols the virtues of coaching.[94]

The Center for Creative Leadership's "The Coach's View: Best Practices for Successful Coaching Engagements" provides guidance on how to have successful coaching.[95]

Huron Legal's "Emotional Intelligence: What Can Learned Lawyers Learn from the Less Learned?" by Jonathan Middleburgh and Lucy Butterworth[96] reviews the EI literature and suggests what works best in teaching EI skills to lawyers.

Appendix Endnotes

1. Mayer, "Can Self-Report Measures Contribute to the Study of Emotional Intelligence? A Conversation between Joseph Ciarrochi and John D. Mayer," *Emotional Intelligence Information,* 2005, https://archive.org/stream/ERIC_ED499642/ERIC_ED499642_djvu.txt.
2. Mayer and Salovey, "Emotional Intelligence," *Imagination, Cognition, and Personality* 9 (1989): 185–211.
3. Brackett, Rivers, and Salovey, "Emotional Intelligence: Implications for Personal, Social, Academic, and Workplace Success." *Social and Personality Psychology Compass,* 5 (2011): 88-103.
4. Mayer, Salovey, and Caruso, "The Validity of the MSCEIT: Additional Analyses and Evidence," *Emotion Review* 4 (2012): 403–408.
5. Mayer, Salovey, and Caruso, *Mayer-Salovey-Caruso Emotional Intelligence Test User's Manual* (New York: Multi-Health Systems, 2002).
6. Mayer, Salovey, and Caruso, "The Validity of the MSCEIT: Additional Analyses and Evidence," *Emotion Review* 4 (2012): 403.
7. http://www.mhs.com/product.aspx?gr=io&id=overview&prod=msceit.
8. A. Ortony, W. Revelle, and R. Zinbarg, "Why Emotional Intelligence Needs a Fluid Component," in G. Matthews, M. Zeidner, and R.D. Roberts (eds.), *The Science of Emotional Intelligence* (Oxford: Oxford University Press, 2007).
9. Nathan Brody, "What Cognitive Intelligence Is and What Emotional Intelligence Is Not," *Psychological Inquiry* 15 (2004): 234–38.
10. Brackett and Mayer, "Convergent, Discriminant, and Incremental Validity of Competing Measures of Emotional Intelligence," *Personality and Social Psychology Bulletin* 29 (2003): 1147–58.
11. O'Boyle et al. "The Relation between Emotional Intelligence and Job Performance: A Meta-Analysis," *Journal of Organizational Behavior,* 793.

12. Côté et al., "Emotional Intelligence and Leadership Emergence in Small Groups," *Leadership Quarterly*, 21 (2010): 496–508.
13. Bar-On, "The Era of the 'EQ': Defining and Assessing Emotional Intelligence," paper presented at the 104th Annual Convention of the American Psychological Association, Toronto, Canada, August 13–14, 1996.
14. Bar-On, Kobus G. Maree, and Maurice Jesse Elias, eds., *Educating People to Be Emotionally Intelligent* (Westport, CT: Praeger Publishers, 2007).
15. https://tap.mhs.com/EQi20.aspx
16. Harms and Credé, "Emotional Intelligence and Transformational and Transactional Leadership," *Journal of Leadership and Organizational Studies*, 12.
17. Robert J. Emmerling and Daniel Goleman, "Emotional Intelligence: Issues and Common Misunderstandings," *Consortium for Research on Emotional Intelligence in Organizations*, October, 2003.
18. Petrides and Furnham, "Trait Emotional Intelligence," *European Journal of Personality* 15 (2001): 425–48; Robert P. Tett, Kevin E. Fox, and Alvin Wang, "Development and Validation of a Self-Report Measure of Emotional Intelligence as a Multidimensional Trait Domain," *Personality and Social Psychology Bulletin* 31 (2005): 859–88.
19. http://www.psychometriclab.com/Home/Default/6.
20. http://www.psychometriclab.com/Home/Default/14.
21. O'Boyle et al., "The Relation between Emotional Intelligence and Job Performance: A Meta-Analysis," *Journal of Organizational Behavior.* Boyatzis, *The Creation of the Emotional and Social Competency Inventory (ESCI)*. Mayer, Salovey, and Caruso, "The Validity of the MSCEIT," *Emotion Review*, 403–8.
22. Bar-On, *The Bar-On Emotional Quotient Inventory.*
23. Goleman, *Working with Emotional Intelligence.*
24. In the original edition of Goleman's book, he asserted that 80 percent of career success was attributable to EI. Goleman later changed that percentage to two-thirds of career success and over four-fifths of leadership success. Ibid. Mayer said "such claims are unrealistic in a number of ways," noting that the subtitle "Why It Can Matter More Than IQ" was not originally intended to be included on the cover of Goleman's book. See John D. Mayer, "Is EI the Best Predictor of Success in Life?" *Emotional Intelligence Information*, 2004, http://www.unh.edu/emotional_intelligence/ei%20Controversies/eicontroversy1%20best%20predictor.htm. A 2010 study, relying on more data, could not support Goleman's early claim. O'Boyle et al., "The Relation Between Emotional Intelligence and Job Performance: A Meta-Analysis," *Journal of Organizational Behavior*, 804. More recently, Goleman has warned others not to "jump to the conclusion that EQ alone makes up that 80% gap. . . . As the person who put the concept on the map, I can tell you that they are dead wrong." Goleman, "They've Taken Emotional Intelligence Too Far," *Time.*
25. http://www.haygroup.com/leadershipandtalentondemand/ourproducts/item_details.aspx?itemid=58&type=1&t=2&trk=profile_certification_title.
26. Cherniss, "Emotional Intelligence." About 40 percent of the items come from an older instrument, the Self-Assessment Questionnaire, which was developed by Dr. Richard Boyatzis and "validated against performance in hundreds of

competency studies of managers, executives, and leaders in North America," Italy, and Brazil. For more on these tests, see the Hay Group's website: "Emotional and Social Competency Inventory—University Edition (ESCI-U)—Online," *Hay Group*, 2017, http://www.haygroup.com/leadershipandtalentondemand/ourproducts/item_details.aspx?itemid=43&type=1&t=2.

27. http://www.eiconsortium.org/measures/eci_360.html.
28. http://www.eiconsortium.org/measures/measures.html.
29. http://www.6seconds.org/2011/07/18/comparison-of-eq-tests/
30. Harms and Credé, "Emotional Intelligence and Transformational and Transactional Leadership," *Journal of Leadership and Organizational Studies*, 13.
31. http://www.talentsmart.com/appraisal.
32. http://www.6seconds.org/newstore/products/sei/.
33. http://testyourself.psychtests.com/testid/3038.
34. http://psychologytoday.tests.psychtests.com/take_test.php?idRegTest=3203.
35. http://media.wix.com/ugd/c43b17_2721a60716b749d3b31923216e179572.pdf.
36. https://globalleadershipfoundation.com/geit/eitest.html.
37. http://www.mhhe.com/socscience/education/sadker/Sadker_EIQQ/sadker_eiqq.htm.
38. http://www.ihhp.com/free-eq-quiz/.
39. https://www.mindtools.com/pages/article/ei-quiz.htm.
40. http://theotherkindofsmart.com/ei-quiz.
41. https://hbr.org/2015/06/quiz-yourself-do-you-lead-with-emotional-intelligence.
42. http://psychology.cos.ucf.edu/myemotions-hxus/.
43. https://www.questionwritertracker.com/quiz/61/Z4MK3TKB.html.
44. http://greatergood.berkeley.edu/ei_quiz/.
45. https://psychology-tools.com/empathy-quotient/.
46. http://www.autismresearchcentre.com/arc_tests.
47. http://greatergood.berkeley.edu/quizzes/take_quiz/14.
48. http://startempathy.com/.
49. http://startempathy.com/how.
50. http://www.playworks.org/blog/teaching-empathy-your-child.
51. http://greatergood.berkeley.edu/topic/empathy/definition.
52. http://www.authentichappiness.sas.upenn.edu/register.aspx.
53. http://amzn.to/1RNPSlA.
54. http://quiz.susandavid.com/s3/eai.
55. http://www.personalitytest.org.uk/.
56. https://www.cpp.com/products/mbti/index.aspx.
57. http://www.myersbriggs.org/my-mbti-personality-type/mbti-basics/.
58. Dalton, "Deviations from the Norm," *Above the Law*. The MBTI was developed because lawyer Clarence Myers, the fiancé of Isabel Briggs, was inscrutable to both Briggs and her mother, Katharine Cook Briggs, prompting them to devise a system to identify their differences. MBTI has its share of critics. Lillian Cunningham, "Does It Pay to Know Your Type?" *The Washington Post*, December 14, 2012. See also Adam Grant, "Goodbye to MBTI, the Fad That Won't Die." *Psychology Today*, September 18, 2013. On the other hand,

according to CPP's director of research, "The validity and reliability of the Myers-Briggs Type Indicator® (MBTI®) instrument has been documented in thousands of peer-reviewed journals and case studies, and its publisher, CPP, Inc., freely makes its supporting data publicly available." Rich Thompson, "The Myers-Briggs Assessment is No Fad—It's a Research-Based Instrument That Delivers Results," *CPP Blog Central*, September 19, 2013.
59. https://www.calipercorp.com/products-and-solutions/pre-employment-assessments-3/caliper-profile/.
60. http://www.hoganassessments.com/content/hogan-personality-inventory-hpi.
61. Jeff Foster, Larry Richard, Lisa Rohrer, and Mark Sirkin, "Understanding Lawyers: The Personality Traits of Successful Practitioners: Results from the Hogan Assessment Project on Lawyer Personality." *Hildebrandt Baker Robbins.*
62. http://therightprofile.com/law/.
63. http://www.resourceassociates.com/tests/professional-tests/attorney-test.
64. https://www.cpp.com/products/tki/index.aspx.
65. http://www.conflictdynamics.org/products/conflictdynamics.php.
66. http://www.buildingpeace.org/act-build-peace/learn/conflict-styles.
67. http://local.conflictsensitivity.org/other_publication/conflict-analysis-tools/.
68. https://itunes.apple.com/us/app/meit-emotional-intelligence/id647313766?mt=8.
69. http://www.movisol.com/en/android/emotional-intelligence.aspx.
70. http://moodmeterapp.com/.
71. http://www.6seconds.org/tools/apps/.
72. http://www.healthline.com/health/mental-health/top-meditation-iphone-android-apps; https://insighttimer.com/; http://buddhify.com/; https://www.calm.com/.
73. Brittany Torrez, "New Lab Aims to De-stress Technology Use," *The Stanford Daily*, May 28, 2013, http://www.stanforddaily.com/2013/05/28/new-lab-aims-to-de-stress-technology-use/.
74. http://glsstudios.com/games.html; http://www.gameslearningsociety.org/games.php. Goleman, "The Focused Leader," *Harvard Business Review.*
75. https://www.thesims.com/the-sims-4. "New 'Sims 4' Lets Characters Have Body-Shame Issues, Too!" *NewNowNext*, August, 2013, http://www.newnownext.com/new-sims-4-lets-characters-have-body-shame-issues-too-watch/08/2013/.
76. https://www.ifyoucan.com/. Dean Takahashi, "Trip Hawkins Releases Second Chapter of His 'If' iPad Game for Teaching Kids Emotional Life Skills," *Venture Beat*, July 24, 2014, http://venturebeat.com/2014/07/24/trip-hawkins-releases-second-chapter-of-his-if-ipad-game-for-teaching-kids-emotional-life-skills/.
77. Wade Roush, 2014, "From Madden NFL to Emotional Intelligence: Trip Hawkins' Journey," *Xconomy*, January 27, http://www.xconomy.com/san-francisco/2014/01/27/from-madden-nfl-to-emotional-intelligence/?utm_source=rss&utm_medium=rss&utm_campaign=from-madden-nfl-to-emotional-intelligence.
78. https://www.commonsense.org/education/; https://www.commonsense.org/top-picks/top-games-that-teach-empathy; https://www.commonsense.org/blog/13-top-games-that-teach-empathy.

79. http://www.amanet.org/site-search-results.aspx?search_terms=emotional+intelligence.
80. http://the-isei.com/home.aspx, http://the-isei.com/business_leader_or_manager.aspx.
81. https://www.ccl.org/open-enrollment-programs/,http://www.ccl.org/leadership/solutions/index.aspx, http://www.ccl.org/Leadership/coaching/index.aspx.
82. http://corporatetrainingmaterials.com/Emotional_Intelligence/index.asp?gclid=CJ7u—WP-7gCFcxAMgodwlwAww
83. http://www.empathia.com/productive/professional-development/leader-coaching/, http://www.empathia.com/objects/Emotional_intelligenceDesigned8-20-13.pdf.
84. http://www.paulekman.com/micro-expression-training/
85. http://www.6seconds.org/tools/.
86. http://www.talentsmart.com/services/.
87. http://eponaquest.com/about/.
88. Cherniss et al., *Bringing Emotional Intelligence to the Workplace*, 8, 2. Figure 1 from Cherniss et al., 7.
89. Richard, "The Psychologically Savvy Leader," *Lawyer Brain Blog.*
90. "Hildebrandt Conversations: A Call for Data-Driven Law Practice," *Hildebrandt Baker Robbins*, April, 2010, 2–3, quoting Kiser.
91. http://www.qualifying.org/talent-management/clearer-perceptions.php.
92. http://www.huffingtonpost.com/dan-goleman/can-apps-gauge-emotional_b_5168699.html.
93. https://www.talentsmart.com/media/uploads/pdfs/The_Business_Case_For_EQ.pdf.
94. http://www.empathia.com/objects/Emotional_intelligenceDesigned8-20-13.pdf.
95. By Leigh Allen Whittier, Lisa Manning, Thomas E. Francis, and William A. Gentry (2011), http://www.ccl.org/leadership/pdf/research/TheCoachsView.pdf.
96. http://www.barristermagazine.com/barrister/index.php?id=480.

Bibliography

Adler, Herbert M. "The History of the Present Illness as Treatment: Who's Listening, and Why Does It Matter?" *Journal of the American Board of Family Practice* 10 (1997): 28–35.

Adler, Ronald B., and Russell F. Procter. *Looking Out, Looking In*, 13th Edition. Boston, MA: Cengage Higher Learning, 2011.

Adolphs, Ralph, Daniel Tranel, Antoine Bechara, Hanna Damasio, and Antonio R. Damasio. "Neuropsychological Approaches to Reasoning and Decision-Making." In *Neurobiology of Decision-Making*, edited by Antonio R. Damasio, Hanna Damasio, and Yves Christen, 157–179. New York, NY: Springer-Verlag, 1996.

Aletras, Nikolaos, Dimitrios Tsarapatsanis, Daniel Preotiuc-Pietro, and Vasileios Lampos. "Predicting Judicial Decisions of the European Court of Human Rights: A Natural Language Processing Perspective." *PeerJ Computer Science* (October 24, 2016), https://peerj.com/articles/cs-93/.

Alicke, Mark D., and Olesya Govorun. "The Better Than Average Effect." In *The Self in Social Judgment: Studies in Self and Identity*, edited by Mark D. Alicke, David A. Dunning, and Joachim I. Krueger, 85–106. New York, NY: Psychology Press, 2005.

Ambady, Nalini, Debi LaPlante, Thai Nguyen, Robert Rosenthal, Nigel Chaumeton, and Wendy Levinson. "Surgeons' Tone of Voice: A Clue to Malpractice History." *Surgery* 132 (2002): 5–9, http://www.stanford.edu/group/ipc/pubs/2002AmbadySurgery.pdf.

American Bar Association, Section of General Practice. *The Report of At the Breaking Point: A National Conference on the Emerging Crisis in the Quality of Lawyers' Health and Lives and Its Impact on Law Firms and Client Services.* Chicago, IL: American Bar Association, 1991.

Anestis, Michael D., Theodore W. Bender, Edward A. Selby, Jessica D. Riberio, and Thomas E. Joiner. "Sex and Emotion in the Acquired Capability for Suicide." *Archives of Suicide Research* 15 (2011): 172–182.

Anfossi, Maura, and Gianmauro Numico. "Empathy in the Doctor-Patient Relationship." *Journal of Clinical Oncology* 22 (2004): 2258–2259.

Anwar, Yasmin. "Emotional Intelligence Peaks as We Enter Our 60s, Research Suggests." *Berkeley Research,* December 16, 2010, http://vcresearch.berkeley.edu/news/emotional-intelligence-peaks-we-enter-our-60s-research-suggests.

Apple, Seth M. "What General Counsel Really Want in a Law Firm." *National Law Review,* January 14, 2013.

Ariely, Dan. "You Are What You Measure." *Harvard Business Review,* June, 2010.

Aronsson, Karin, Linda Jönsson, and Per Linell. "The Courtroom Hearing as a Middle Ground: Speech Accommodation by Lawyers and Defendants." *Journal of Language and Social Psychology* 6 (1987): 99–115.

Arthur, Winfred Jr., Winston Bennett, Jr., Pamela S. Edens, and Suzanne T. Bell. "Effectiveness of Training in Organizations: A Meta-Analysis of Design and Evaluation Features." *Journal of Applied Psychology* 88 (2003): 234–245.

Ashkanasy, Neal M. "The Case for Emotional Intelligence in Workgroups." Paper presented at The 16th Annual Conference of the Society for Industrial and Organizational Psychology, San Diego, CA, April 26–28, 2001.

Ashkanasy, Neal M., Ashton-James, Claire E., Jordan, Peter J. "Performance Impacts of Appraisal and Coping with Stress in Workplace Settings: The Role of Affect and Emotional Intelligence," in Pamela L. Perrewe, Daniel C. Ganster (eds.) *Emotional and Physiological Processes and Positive Intervention Strategies* (Research in Occupational Stress and Well-being, Volume 3), Emerald Group Publishing Limited, 2003, pp. 1–43.

Association of Corporate Counsel and Seregenti Law. "2010 ACC/Serengeti Managing Outside Counsel Survey: Assessing Key Elements of the In-House Counsel/Outside Counsel Relationship." *Association of Corporate Counsel and Seregenti Law,* 2010, http://www.acc.com/_cs_upload/vl/membersonly/Surveys/1249457_2.pdf.

Azimi, Shahram, Ali Asghar, Nejad Farid, M.J. Kharazi Fard, and N. Khoei. "Emotional Intelligence of Dental Students and Patient Satisfaction." *European Journal of Dental Education* 14 (2010): 129–132.

Bachman, John, Steven Stein, K. Campbell, and Gill Sitarenios. "Emotional Intelligence in the Collection of Debt." *International Journal of Selection and Assessment* 8 (2003): 176–182.

Bachman, Wallace. "Nice Guys Finish First: A SYMLOG Analysis of U.S. Naval Commands." In *The SYMLOG Practitioner*, edited by Richard B. Polley, A. Paul Hare, and Philip J. Stone, 133–153. New York, NY: Praeger, 1988.

Baez, Beau. "Personality Tests in Employment Selection: Use with Caution." *Cornell HR Review*, January 26, 2013.

Baez, Beau. *Tort Law in the USA*. Leiden: Kluwer Law International, 2010.

Baker, Alysha, Leanne ten Brinke, Stephen Porter. "Will Get Fooled Again: Emotionally Intelligent People Are Easily Duped by High-Stakes Deceivers." *Legal and Criminological Psychology* 18 (2013): 300–313.

Baltzly, Dirk. "Stoicism." In *The Stanford Encyclopedia of Philosophy*, edited by Edward N. Zalta, 2012.

Barbuto, John E. "A Critique of the Myers-Briggs Type Indicator and Its Operationalization of Carl Jung's Psychological Types." *Psychological Reports* 80 (1997): 611–625.

Barczak, Gloria, Felicia Lassk, and Jay Mulki. "Antecedents of Team Creativity: An Examination of Team Emotional Intelligence, Team Trust and Collaborative Culture." *Creativity and Innovation Management* 19 (2010): 332–345.

Bar-On, Reuven. *The Bar-On Emotional Quotient Inventory: A Test of Emotional Intelligence.* Toronto: Multi-Health Systems, 1997.

Bar-On, Reuven. "The Bar-On Model of Emotional Intelligence: A Valid, Robust and Applicable EI Model." *Organisations and People* 14 (2007): 27–34.

Bar-On, Reuven. "The Bar-On Model of Emotional-Social Intelligence (ESI)." *Psicothema* 17 (2006): 13–25, http://www.ressourcesetmanagement.com/Article%20prof%20%20Baron%20.pdf.

Bar-On, Reuven. "Emotional and Social Intelligence: Insights from the Emotional Quotient Inventory." In *The Handbook of Emotional Intelligence*, edited by Reuven Bar-On and James Donald Alexander Parker, 363–388. San Francisco, CA: Jossey-Bass, 2000.

Bar-On, Reuven. "The Era of the 'EQ': Defining and Assessing Emotional Intelligence." Paper presented at the 104th Annual Convention of the American Psychological Association, Toronto, CA, August 13–14, 1996.

Bar-On, Reuven, Richard Handley, and Suzanne Fund. "The Impact of Emotional Intelligence on Performance." In *Linking Emotional*

Intelligence and Performance at Work: Current Research Evidence, edited by Vanessa Druskat, Fabio Sala, and Gerald Mount, 3–19. Mahwah, NJ: Lawrence Erlbaum, 2005.

Bar-On, Reuven, Kobus G. Maree, and Maurice Jesse Elias, eds. *Educating People to Be Emotionally Intelligent.* Westport, CT: Praeger Publishers, 2007.

Bar-On, Reuven, Daneil Tranel, Natalie L. Denburg, and Antoine Bechara. "Exploring the Neurological Substrate of Emotional and Social Intelligence." *Brain* 126 (2003): 1790–1800.

Barrett, Lisa F., Batija Mesquita, and Maria Gendron. "Context in Emotion Perception." *Current Directions in Psychological Science* 20 (2011): 286–290.

Barsade, Sigal, and Donald Gibson. "Group Emotion: A View from Top and Bottom." In *Research on Managing Groups and Teams* Vol. 1, edited by Deborah Gruenfeld, Margaret Neale, and Elizabeth Mannix, 81–102. Greenwich, CT: JAI Press, 1999.

Bastian, Veneta A., Nicholas R. Burns, Ted Nettelbeck. "Emotional Intelligence Predicts Life Skills, But Not as Well as Personality and Cognitive Abilities." *Personal Individual Differences* 39 (2005): 1135–1145.

Batson, Daniel C., Bruce D. Duncan, Paula Ackerman, Terese Buckley, and Kimberly Birch. "Is Empathic Emotion a Source of Altruistic Motivation?" *Journal of Personality and Social Psychology,* 40 (1981): 290–302.

Bay, Darlene, and Kim McKeage. "Emotional Intelligence in Undergraduate Accounting Students: Preliminary Assessment." *Accounting Education: An International Journal* 15 (2006): 439–454.

BCG Attorney Search. "Firm culture matters most." *FindLaw: For Legal Professionals,* 2013, http://careers.findlaw.com/how-to-find-a-legal-job/firm-culture-matters-most.html.

Bechara, Antoine, Hanna Damasio, and Antonio Damasio. "Emotion, Decision-Making and the Orbitofrontal Cortex." *Cerebral Cortex* 10 (2000): 295–307.

Bechara, Antoine, with Antonio R. Damásio, Hanna Damásio, and Steven W. Anderson. "Insensitivity to Future Consequences following Damage to Human Prefrontal Cortex." *Cognition* 50 (1994): 7–15.

Bechtoldt, Myriam N. and Vanessa K. Schneider. "Predicting Stress from the Ability to Eavesdrop on Feelings: Emotional intelligence and Testosterone Jointly Predict Cortisol Reactivity." *Emotion* 16 (6) (2016): 815–825.

Beck, Connie, Bruce D. Sales, and G. Andrew H. Benjamin. "Lawyer Distress: Alcohol-Related Problems and Other Psychological Concerns among a Sample of Practicing Lawyers." *Journal of Law and Health* 10 (1996): 1–50.

Bejjani, Jimmy. "Emotional Intelligence: Use in Medical Education and Practice." *McGill Journal of Medicine: MJM* 12 (2009): 4–5.

Beldoch, M. "Sensitivity to Expression of Emotional Meaning in Three Modes of Communication." In *The Communication of Emotional Meaning,* by J. R. Davitz et al., 31–42. New York, NY: McGraw-Hill, 1964.

Benjamin, G. Andrew H. H, E.J. Darling, and Bruce D. Sales. "The Prevalence of Depression, Alcohol Abuse, and Cocaine Abuse among United States Lawyers." *Journal of Law and Psychiatry* 13 (1990): 223.

Berman, Lori, and Heather Bock. "Developing Attorneys for the Future: What Can We Learn from the Fast Trackers?" *Santa Clara Law Review* 52 (2012): 875–898.

Bernard, Kristy N., and Matthew L. Gibson. "Professional Misconduct by Mentally Impaired Attorneys: Is There a Better Way to Treat an Old Problem?" *Georgetown Journal of Legal Ethics* 17 (2004): 619–630.

Bhaduri, Abhijit. "How to Develop Emotional Intelligence: An Interview with Annie McKee." *Times of India,* April 12, 2013, http://blogs.timesofindia.indiatimes.com/just-like-that/how-to-develop-emotional-intelligence/.

Blanthorne, Cindy, Sak Bhamornsiri, and Robert E. Guinn. "Are Technical Skills Still Important?" *CPA Journal* 75 (2005): 64–65.

Bono, Joyce E., Hannah Jackson Foldes, Gregory Vinson, and John P. Muros. "Workplace Emotions: The Role of Supervision and Leadership." *Journal of Applied Psychology* 92 (2007): 1357–1367.

Borghans, Lex, Angela Lee Duckworth, James J. Heckman, and Bas ter Wee. "The Economics and Psychology of Personality Traits." *Journal of Human Resources* 43 (2008): 972–1059.

Boyatzis, Richard E. "Using Tipping Points of Emotional Intelligence and Cognitive Competencies to Predict Financial Performance of Leaders." *Psicothema* 18 (2006): 124–131, http://www.psicothema.com/pdf/3287.pdf.

Boyatzis, Richard E. *The Creation of the Emotional and Social Competency Inventory (ESCI).* Boston: Hay Group, 2007.

Boyatzis, Richard E. "Presentation at the Linkage Conference on Emotional Intelligence." Chicago, IL, September 27, 1999.

Boyatzis, Richard E. *The Competent Manager: A Model for Effective Performance.* New York, NY: John Wiley and Sons, 1982.

Boyatzis, Richard E., David Leonard, Kenneth Rhee, and Jane V. Wheeler. "Competencies Can Be Developed, But Not the Way We Thought." *Capability* 2 (1996): 25–41.

Boyatzis, Richard E., and Annie McKee. *Resonant Leadership.* Cambridge: Harvard Business Review Publications, 2005.

Brackett, Marc A., James L. Floman, Claire Ashton-James, Lillia Cherkasskiy, and Peter Salovey. "The Influence of Teacher Emotion on Grading Practices: A Preliminary Look at the Evaluation of Student Writing." *Teachers and Teaching: Theory and Practice* 19 (2013): 634–646.

Brackett, Marc A., and John D. Mayer. "Convergent, Discriminant, and Incremental Validity of Competing Measures of Emotional Intelligence." *Personality and Social Psychology Bulletin* 29 (2003): 1147–1158.

Brackett, Marc A., John D. Mayer, and Rebecca M. Warner. "Emotional Intelligence and Its Relation to Everyday Behavior." *Personality and Individual Differences* 36 (2004): 1387–1402.

Brackett, Marc A., Raquel Palomera, Justyna Mojsa-Kaja, Maria Regina Reyes, and Peter Salovey. "Emotion-Regulation, Burnout, and Job Satisfaction among British Secondary School Teachers." *Psychology in the Schools* 47 (2010): 406–417.

Brackett, Marc A., and Susan Rivers, "Transforming Students' Lives with Social and Emotional Learning." In *International Handbook of Emotions in Education,* edited by Reinhard Pekrun and Lisa Linnenbrink-Garcia, 366–386. New York, NY: Routledge, 2014.

Brackett, Marc A., Susan E. Rivers, and Peter Salovey. "Emotional Intelligence: Implications for Personal, Social, Academic, and Workplace Success." *Social and Personality Psychology Compass* 5 (2011): 88–103.

Bradberry, Travis. "Habits of Highly Emotionally Intelligent People." *PS News,* June 15, 2016, http://www.psnews.com.au/vic/508/personal_development/habits-of-highly-emotionally-intelligent-people.

Bradberry, Travis, and Jean Greaves. "Heartless Bosses?" *Harvard Business Review* 83 (2005): 24.

Bradberry, Travis, and Jean Greaves. *Emotional Intelligence 2.0.* San Diego, CA: TalentSmart, 2009.

Bradberry, Travis, and Jean Greaves. "Self Scores of Emotional Intelligence and Job Performance: An Analysis Across Industry and Position." Unpublished manuscript, 2003, http://www.talentsmart.com/media/uploads/pdfs/Technical_Manual.pdf.

Bradberry, Travis, and Lac D. Su. "China's Secret Weapon." *Forbes,* November 14, 2005.

Bradberry, Travis, Nick Tasler, and Lac D. Su. "Lawyers with Personality?" *TalentSmart* (2011): 1–3, http://www.talentsmart.com/media/uploads/articles/pdfs/Lawyers%20with%20Personality.pdf.

Bratman, Gregory N., J. Paul Hamilton, Kevin S. Hahn, Gretchen C. Daily, and James J. Gross. "Nature Experience Reduces Rumination and Subgenual Prefrontal Cortex Activation." *PNAS* 112 (2015): 8567–8572.

Beck, Megan, and Barry Libert. "The Rise of AI Makes Emotional Intelligence More Important." *Harvard Business Review.* February 15, 2017.

Breslau, Jill, and Susan Daicoff. "The Illicit Relationship of Lawyers and Emotion." *Cutting Edge Law,* September 1, 2008, http://cuttingedgelaw.com/content/illicit-relationship-lawyers-and-emotion.

Brody, Leslie R. "Gender and Emotion: Beyond Stereotypes." *Journal of Social Issues* 53 (1997): 369–393.

Brody, Nathan. "What Cognitive Intelligence Is and What Emotional Intelligence Is Not." *Psychological Inquiry* 15 (2004): 234–238.

Brushfield, Rachel. "Feeling Decisions: Why Lawyers Need Emotional Intelligence." *ManagingPartner.com,* June 8, 2012, http://www.managingpartner.com/feature/hr/feeling-decisions-why-lawyers-need-emotional-intelligence.

BTI Consulting Group. "Attorneys Pose Biggest Obstacle to Law Firm Growth." *BTI Consulting Group,* January 18, 2017, http://www.bticonsulting.com/themadclientist/2017/1/18/attorneys-pose-biggest-obstacle-to-law-firm-growth.

BTI Consulting Group. "Client Feedback and Satisfaction." *BTI Consulting Group,* 2013, http://www.bticonsulting.com/client-feedback-evaluation/.

BTI Consulting Group. "The 16th Annual BTI Client Service All-Stars 2017." *BTI Consulting Group,* 2017, http://www.bticonsulting.com/client-service-all-stars-law.

Bowling, Dan. "Stop Whining, You're in the Army Now." *The Careerist,* April 18, 2011, http://thecareerist.typepad.com/thecareerist/2011/04/stop-whining-youre-in-the-army-now.html

Burton, Lucy. "Hogan Lovells Brings Counselling In-House as City Pushes for Mental Well-Being." *The Lawyer,* February 20, 2014, http://www.thelawyer.com/news/regions/uk-news/hogan-lovells-brings-counselling-in-house-as-city-pushes-for-mental-well-being/3016573.article?cmpid=dnews_142625.

Byrne, Matt. "Lawyers Years Behind Accountants on Process and BD, The Lawyer Research Reveals." *The Lawyer,* June 24, 2013, http://m.thelawyer.com/3006303.article?mobilesite=enabled.

Cabello, Rosario, and Pablo Fernandez-Berrocal. "Implicit Theories and Ability Emotional Intelligence." *Frontiers in Psychology,* May 22, 2015.

Carlson, Linda E., Richard Doll, Joanne Stephen, Peter Faris, Rie Tamagawa, Elaine Drysdale, and Michael Speca. "Randomized Controlled Trial of Mindfulness-Based Cancer Recovery versus Supportive Expressive Group Therapy for Distressed Survivors of Breast Cancer." *Journal of Clinical Oncology* 31 (2013): 3119–3126.

Carrothers, Robert M., Stanford W. Gregory, Jr., and Timothy J. Gallagher. "Measuring Emotional Intelligence of Medical School Applicants." *Academic Medicine* 75 (2000): 456–463.

Carton, John S., Emily A. Kessler, and Christina L. Pape. "Nonverbal Decoding Skills and Relationship Well-Being in Adults." *Journal of Nonverbal Behavior* 23 (1999): 91–100.

Casselman, Ben. "Economists Set Rules on Ethics." *The Wall Street Journal,* January 9, 2012.

Cavallo, Kathleen, and Dottie Brienza. *Emotional Competence and Leadership Excellence at Johnson & Johnson: The Emotional Intelligence and Leadership Study.* New Brunswick, NJ: Consortium for Research on Emotional Intelligence in Organizations, Rutgers University, 2001. Also, *Europe's Journal of Psychology* 2 (2006).

Chamorro-Premuzic, Tomas. "Can You Really Improve Your Emotional Intelligence?" *Harvard Business Review Blog,* May 29, 2013.

Charan, Ram. "The Discipline of Listening." *Harvard Business Review,* June 21, 2012.

Chen, Vivia. "10 Happy Tips for Lawyers." *The Careerist,* August 24, 2010, http://thecareerist.typepad.com/thecareerist/2010/08/happy-tips.html.

Chen, Vivia. "Depressed People Make Better Lawyers." *The Careerist,* July 22, 2010, http://thecareerist.typepad.com/thecareerist/2010/07/depressed-people-make-better-lawyers.htmlhttp://thecareerist.typepad.

Chen, Vivia. "McKenna Long's Recruiting Couch." *The Careerist,* January 25, 2011, http://thecareerist.typepad.com/thecareerist/2011/01/should-firms-use-psyche-test-in-hiring.html.

Chen, Vivia. "Our Secret Sauce." *The Careerist,* April 21, 2011, http://thecareerist.typepad.com/thecareerist/2011/04/our-secret-sauce.html.

Cherniss, Cary. *The Business Case for Emotional Intelligence.* New Brunswick, NJ: Consortium for Research on Emotional Intelligence in Organizations, Rutgers University, 1999. http://www.eiconsortium.org/pdf/business_case_for_ei.pdf.

Cherniss, Cary. "Emotional Intelligence: What It Is and Why It Matters." Paper presented at the Annual Meeting of the Society for Industrial and Organizational Psychology, New Orleans, Louisiana, April 15, 2000. http://www.eiconsortium.org/reports/what_is_emotional_intelligence.html.

Cherniss, Cary, Daniel Goleman, Robert Emmerling, Kimberly Cowan, and Mitchel Adler. *Bringing Emotional Intelligence to the Workplace.* New Brunswick, NJ: Consortium for Research on Emotional Intelligence in Organizations, Rutgers University, 1998.

Cherry, M. Gemma, Ian Fletcher, Helen O'Sullivan, and Tim Dornan. "Emotional Intelligence in Medical Education: A Critical Review." *Medical Education* 48 (2014): 468–478.

ChildTrends. "Cambridge-Somerville Youth Study." *ChildTrends,* 2007, http://childtrends.org/?programs=cambridge-somerville-youth-study.

Christensen, Clayton M., Dina Wang, and Derek van Bever, "Consulting on the Cusp of Disruption." *Harvard Business Review,* October, 2013, 107.

Ciarrochi, Joseph, Frank P. Deane, and Stephen Anderson. "Emotional Intelligence Moderates the Relationship between Stress and Mental Health." *Personality and Individual Differences,* 32 (2) (January 2002): 197–209.

Clarke, Nicholas. "Emotional Intelligence and Its Relationship to Transformational Leadership and Key Project Manager Competencies." *Project Management Journal* 41 (2010): 5–20.

Clemson University. "Clemson Researcher Says High Blood Pressure May Lead to Missed Emotional Cues." *Clemson University,* November 3, 2011, http://www.clemson.edu/media-relations/3950/clemson-researcher-says-high-blood-pressure-may-lead-to-missed-emotional-cues/.

Codier, Estelle, Cindy Kamikawa, Barbara M. Kooker, and Jan Shoultz. "Emotional Intelligence, Performance, and Retention in Clinical Staff Nurse." *Nursing Administration Quarterly* 33 (2009): 310–316.

Coe, Aebra. "GCs Say This Firm Is the Most Arrogant." *Law360,* November 28, 2016, http://www.law360.com/articles/866039/gcs-say-this-firm-is-the-most-arrogant.

Cohen, Myer J. "The Impaired Lawyer." *American Bar Association Experience* 12 (2) (2002).

Colvin, Geoff. *Humans Are Underrated.* New York, NY: Penguin Random House, 2015.

Cook, Gail Lynn, Darlene Bay, Beth Visser, Jean E. Myburgh, and Joyce Njoroge. "Emotional Intelligence: The Role of Accounting Education and Work Experience." *Issues in Accounting Education* 26 (2011): 267–286.

Côté, Stephané, Katherine A. DeCelles, Julie M. McCarthy, Gerben A. Van Kleef, and Ivona Hideg. "The Jekyll and Hyde of Emotional Intelligence: Emotion-Regulation Knowledge Facilitates Both Prosocial and Interpersonally Deviant Behavior." *Psychological Science* 22 (2011): 1073–1080.

Côté, Stéphane, Anett Gyurak, and Robert W. Levenson. "The Ability to Regulate Emotion Is Associated with Greater Well-Being, Income, and Socioeconomic Status." *Emotion,* 10 (2010): 923–933.

Côté, Stéphane, P.N. Lopes, Peter Salovey, and CTH Miners. "Emotional Intelligence and Leadership Emergence in Small Groups." *Leadership Quarterly* 21 (2010): 496–508.

Côté, Stéphane, and Christopher T.H. Miners. "Emotional Intelligence, Cognitive Intelligence, and Job Performance." *Administrative Science Quarterly* 51 (2006): 1–28.

Côté, Stephané, Paul K. Piff, and Robb Willer. "For Whom Do the Ends Justify the Means? Social Class and Utilitarian Moral Judgment." *Journal of Personality and Social Psychology* 104 (2013): 490–503.

Coutu, Diane. "The Science of Thinking Smarter: A Conversation with Brain Expert John J. Medina." *Harvard Business Review* (May, 2008): 51–52.

Cowles, Kathryn Meagan. "Communication in the Courtroom," 2011, http://www.coastal.edu/media/administration/honorsprogram/pdf/Kathryn%20Cowles.pdf.

Csikszentmihalyi, Mihaly. *Flow: The Psychology of Optimal Experience.* New York, NY: Harper and Row, 1990.

Cuddy, Amy J.C., Matthew Kohut, and John Neffinger. "Connect, Then Lead." *HBR Magazine Online,* July–August, 2013, http://hbr.org/2013/07/connect-then-lead/ar/.

Cunningham, John O. "Chief Legal Officers Tell Outside Counsel What They Want . . . and Don't," *C3,* June 20, 2013, https://johnocunningham.wordpress.com/2013/06/20/chief-legal-officers-tell-outside-counsel-what-they-want-and-dont/.

Cunningham, Lillian. 2012. "Does It Pay to Know Your Type?" *The Washington Post,* December 14, 2012.

Cutuli, Debora. "Cognitive Reappraisal and Expressive Suppression Strategies Role in Emotion Regulation: An Overview on Their Modulatory Effects and Neural Correlates." *Frontiers in Systems Neuroscience* 175 (2014): 59–63.

Czarna, Anna Z., Philip Leifeld, Magdalena Śmieja, Michael Dufner, and Peter Salovey. "Do Narcissism and Emotional Intelligence Win Us Friends? Modeling Dynamics of Peer Popularity Using Inferential Network Analysis." *Personality and Social Psychology Bulletin,* September 27, 2016.

Daff, Lyn, Paul de Lange, and Beverley Jackling. "A Comparison of Generic Skills and Emotional Intelligence in Accounting Education." *Issues in Accounting Education* 27 (2012): 627–645.

Daicoff, Susan Swaim. "Asking Lawyers to Change Their Spots: Should Lawyers Change? A Critique of Solutions to Problems with Professionalism by Reference to Empirically-Derived Attorney Personality Attributes." *Georgetown Journal of Legal Ethics* 11 (1996): 547–597.

Daicoff, Susan Swaim. "Expanding the Lawyer's Toolkit of Skills and Competencies: Synthesizing Leadership, Professionalism, Emotional Intelligence, Conflict Resolution, and Comprehensive Law." *Santa Clara Law Review* 52 (2012): 795–894.

Daicoff, Susan Swaim. "Lawyer, Be Thyself: An Empirical Investigation of the Relationship Between the Ethic of Care, the Feeling Decision-Making Preference, and Lawyer Wellbeing." *Virginia Journal of Social Policy and Law* 16 (1997): 1337–1427.

Daicoff, Susan Swaim. *Lawyer, Know Yourself: A Psychological Analysis of Personality Strengths and Weaknesses.* Washington, DC: American Psychological Association, 2004.

Daicoff, Susan Swaim. "Lawyer, Know Thyself: A Review of Empirical Research on Attorney Attributes Bearing on Professionalism." *American University Law Review* 46 (1997): 1337, 1349, 1390–1391.

Daks, Martin C. "Compliance, Not Legal Fees, Named as GC's Chief Concern." *New Jersey Law Journal,* November 1, 2006.

Damásio, Antonio R. *Descartes' Error: Emotion, Reason, and the Human Brain,* New York, NY: Avon, 1994.

Damásio, Antonio R. "A Neural Basis for Sociopathy." *Archives of General Psychiatry* 57 (2000): 128–129.

Danescu-Niculescu-Mizil, Cristian, Lillian Lee, Bo Pan, and Jon Kleinberg. "Echoes of Power: Language Effects and Power Differences in Social Interaction." Paper presented at International World Wide Web Conference, Lyon, France, April 16–20, 2012. http://www.mpi-sws.org/~cristian/Echoes_of_power_files/echoes_of_power.pdf.

"Daniel Pink: Putting Your Best Pitch Forward in a Society of Salespeople." *Knowledge@Wharton*, January 30, 2013, http://knowledge.wharton.upenn.edu/article.cfm?articleid=3175.http://knowledge.wharton.upenn.edu/article.cfm?articleid=3175.

Danziger, Shai, Jonathan Levav, and Liora Avnaim-Pesso. "Extraneous Factors in Judicial Decisions." *Proceedings of the National Academy of Sciences*, 2011.

Dapretto, Mirella, Mari S. Davies, Jennifer H. Pfeifer, Ashley A. Scott, Marian Sigman, Susan Y. Bookheimer, and Marco Iacobini. "Understanding Emotions in Others: Mirror Neuron Dysfunction in Children with Autism Spectrum Disorders." *Nature Neuroscience* 9 (2006): 28–30.

Darwin, Charles. *The Autobiography of Charles Darwin*, ed. Nora Barlow. London: Collins, 1958, 139.

Darwin, Charles. *The Expression of the Emotions in Man and Animals*, 2nd ed. Chicago: University of Chicago Press, 1965 (1872).

Darwin, Charles. *The Origin of Species by Means of Natural Selection: Or, The Preservation of Favored Races in the Struggle for Life*, London: John Murray, Albemarle Street (1859). https://archive.org/details/onoriginofspec00darw.

DasGupta, Sayantani, and Rita Charon. "Personal Illness Narratives: Using Reflective Writing to Teach Empathy." *Academic Medicine* 79 (2004): 351–356, http://journals.lww.com/academicmedicine/Abstract/2004/04000/Personal_Illness_Narratives__Using_Reflective.13.aspx.

Daus, Catherine S., and Neal M. Ashkanasy. "The Case for the Ability-Based Model of Emotional Intelligence in Organizational Behavior." *Journal of Organizational Behavior* 26 (2005): 453–466.

David, Susan. "Recovering from an Emotional Outburst at Work." *Harvard Business Review*, May 8, 2015.

David, Susan, and Christina Congleton. "Emotional Agility." *Harvard Business Review Magazine*, November, 2012.

Davidson, Richard, and Sharon Begley. *The Emotional Life of Your Brain.* New York, NY: Penguin Group, 2013.

Davidson, R.J., and W. Irwin, "The Functional Neuroanatomy of Emotion and Affective Style." *Trends in Cognitive Style* 3 (1999): 11–21.

Davidson, Richard J., Jon Kabat-Zinn, Jessica Schumacher, Melissa Rosenkranz, Daniel Muller, Saki F. Santorelli, Ferris Urbanowski, Anne Harrington, Katherine Bonus, and John F. Sheridan. "Alterations in Brain and Immune Function Produced by Mindfulness Meditation." *Psychosomatic Medicine* 65 (2003): 564–570.

Defoe, Dan. "Bullying at Work [Legal Organizations], Coping Strategies, and Health Problems," *Psycholawlogy.com*, February 2, 2014, http://www.psycholawlogy.com/2014/02/06/bullying-work-legal-organizations-coping-strategies-health-problems/

Defoe, Dan. "Don't Grin When You [Lawyers] Win: The Social Benefits of Appearing 'Humble in Victory.'" *Psycholawlogy*, May 23, 2015, http://us9.campaign-archive1.com/?u=3d1a3948dc9d24fb867494685&id=45d515b7ac&e=c35e23051d.

Defoe, Dan. "Eavesdropping on Feelings, Emotional Intelligence, and Workplace Interventions." *Psycholawlogy Blog*, August 28, 2012, http://www.psycholawlogy.com/2012/08/28/eavesdropping-on-feelings-emotional-intelligence-and-workplace-interventions/.

Defoe, Dan. "Emotional Intelligence and 'Incompetent' [Lawyer and Law Firm] Leaders and the 'Double Curse': Low Performing, High Self-Evaluators & Resistance to Feedback via the 'Expedient Escape." *Psycholawlogy Blog*, September 17, 2013, http://www.psycholawlogy.com/2013/09/17/emotional-intelligence-and-incompetent-managers-who-suffer-from-the-double-curse-low-performing-high-self-evaluators-resistance-to-feedback/?utm_source=feedburner&utm_medium=email&utm_campaign=Feedpercent3A+Psycholawlogy+%28Psycholawlogy%29.

Defoe, Dan. "Emotional Intelligence, Lawyers, and Empathy—Using the Power of Listening with Care to Build Better Professional Relationships and Satisfy Clients." *Psycholawlogy Blog*, November 25, 2012, http://www.psycholawlogy.com/2012/11/25/emotional-intelligence-lawyers-and-empathyusing-the-power-of-listening-with-care-to-build-better-professional-relationships-and-satisfy-clients/.

Defoe, Dan. "Law Student Emotional Intelligence, Personality, Psychological Health: An Initial Understanding of Well-Being Indicators and Challenge to Educators," *Psycholawlogy Blog*, March 31, 2013, http://www.psycholawlogy.com/2013/03/31/emotional-intelligence-psychological-health-and-law-student-personalities-an-initial-understanding-of-well-being-indicators/.

Defoe, Dan. "The [Lawyer's] Smart Use of Unpleasant Emotions–Emotionally Intelligent Emotion Regulation." *Psycholawlogy*, June 7, 2013, http://

www.psycholawlogy.com/2013/06/07/the-lawyers-smart-use-of-unpleasant-emotionsemotionally-intelligent-emotion-regulation.

Defoe, Dan. "Legal Talent Management Memo: Individual Differences and Moral Disengagement—Connections which Can Predict Unethical Decisions." *Psycholawlogy Blog,* September 23, 2012, http://www.psycholawlogy.com/2012/09/23/legal-talent-management-memo-individual-differences-and-moral-disengagementconnections-which-can-predict-unethical-decisions/.

De Martino, Benedetto, Dharshan Kumaran, Ben Seymour, and Raymond J. Dolan. "Frames, Biases, and Rational Decision-Making in the Human Brain." *Science,* August 4, 313 (2006): 684–687.

Desbordes, Gaëlle, Lobsang T. Neg, Thaddeus W. W. Pace, B. Alan Wallace, Charles L. Raison, and Erick L. Schwartz. "Effects of Mindful-Attention and Compassion Meditation Training on Amygdala Response to Emotional Stimuli in an Ordinary, Non-meditative State." *Frontiers in Human Neuroscience* 6 (2012).

Descartes, René. *Discourse on the Method of Rightly Conducting the Reason and Seeking the Truth in the Sciences,* edited by Charles W. Eliot. New York, NY: P.F. Collier & Son, 2001.

Detert, James R., Linda Klebe Treviño, and Vicki L. Sweitzer. "Moral Disengagement in Ethical Decision Making: A Study of Antecedents and Outcomes." *Journal of Applied Psychology,* 93 (2008): 374–391.

Deutschendorf, Harvey. "5 Ways to Spot an Emotionally Intelligent Leader." *Business 2 Community,* November 6, 2013, http://www.business2community.com/leadership/5-ways-spot-emotionally-intelligent-leader-0673416#cPWBvzCAIDjYzzul.97.

Development Dimensions International. "What's the Number 1 Leadership Skill for Overall Success?" *Development Dimensions International,* February 23, 2016, http://www.ddiworld.com/global-offices/united-states/press-room/what-is-the-1-leadership-skill-for-overall-success.

Diamond, John L., Lawrence C. Levine, and Anita Bernstein. *Understanding Torts,* 4th ed. Danvers, MA: Matthew Bender & Company, 2010.

Dickson, Caitlin. "How to Spot a Sociopath (Hint: It Could Be You)." *The Daily Beast,* June 25, 2013, http://www.thedailybeast.com/articles/2013/06/25/how-to-spot-a-sociopath-hint-it-could-be-you.html?utm_medium=email&utm_source=newsletter&utm_campaign=cheatsheet_afternoon&cid=newsletter%3Bemail%3Bcheatsheet_afternoon&utm_term=Cheat%20Sheet.

Di Meglio, Francesca. "Want an MBA from Yale? You're Going to Need Emotional Intelligence." *Bloomberg Business Week,* May 15, 2013, http://www.businessweek.com/articles/2013-05-15/want-an-mba-from-yale-youre-going-to-need-emotional-intelligence.

Dinovitzer, Ronit, and Bryant G. Garth. "Lawyer Satisfaction in the Process of Structuring Legal Careers." *Law and Society Review,* 41 (2007): 1–52.

Dionne, E.J., Jr. "The Elusive Front-Runner; Gary Hart." *New York Times,* May 3, 1987.

Dixon, Alex. "Can Empathy Reduce Racism?" *Greater Good: The Science of a Meaningful Life,* University of California Berkeley, July 21, 2011, http://greatergood.berkeley.edu/article/item/empathy_reduces_racism/.

Dobbs, Richard, Jaana Remes, Sven Smit, James Manyika, Jonathan Woetzel, and Yaw Agyenim-Boateng. "Urban World: The Shifting Global Business Landscape." *McKinsey & Company,* October, 2013, http://www.mckinsey.com/insights/urbanization/urban_world_the_shifting_global_business_landscape?cid=other-eml-nsl-mip-mck-oth-1310

Dodgett, Stephen J. "Not Guilty: *Legal Business*/Marsh Roundtable on Risk and the Financial Crisis." *Legal Business,* May, 2009, 32–37.

Drucker, Peter. *Management Challenges for the 21st Century.* New York, NY: HarperCollins, 1999.

Druskat, Vanessa Urch, and Steven B. Wolff. "Building the Emotional Intelligence of Groups." *Harvard Business Review* 79 (2001): 81–90.

Duncan, Helen, and Peter H. Mason. "In-House Counsel Offer Their Advice to Law-Firm Litigators." *San Francisco Daily Journal,* September 27, 2004.

Duncan, Susan Saltonstall. "How to Sell: Stop Pitching and Start Listening and Relating," *InFocus Blog,* February 7, 2013, http://www.rainmakingoasis.com/wp-content/uploads/2016/08/How-to-Sell_Stop-Pitching-and-Start-Listening-and-Relating.pdf.

Duncan, Susan Saltonstall. "In 2013, Will More Firms Finally Understand That Client Feedback = Better Revenue and Profitability?" *InFocus Blog,* January 3, 2013, http://www.rainmakingoasis.com/in-2013-will-more-firms-finally-understand-that-client-feedback-better-revenue-and-profitability/

Duncan, Susan Saltonstall. "Who Are Law Firms Really Competing with and Why?" *InFocus Blog,* January 18, 2017, http://www.rainmakingoasis.com/who-are-law-firms-really-competing-with-and-why/.

Duncan, Susan Saltonstall. "Will Law Schools Finally Make Changes the Profession Needs?" *InFocus Blog,* December 30, 2012, http://www.rainmakingoasis.com/will-law-schools-finally-make-changes-the-profession-needs/.

Dutton, Kevin. *The Wisdom of Psychopaths: What Saints, Spies, and Serial Killers Can Teach Us About Success*. New York, NY: Farrar, Strauss & Giroux, 2012.

Eagly, Alice H., Mona G. Makhijani, and Bruce G. Klonsky. "Gender and the Evaluation of Leaders: A Meta-Analysis." *Psychological Bulletin* 111 (1992): 3–22.

Eisenberg, Nancy, and Paul A. Miller. "The Relation of Empathy to Prosocial and Related Behaviors." *Psychological Bulletin* 101 (1987): 91–119.

Ekman, Paul. ed. *Darwin and Facial Expression: A Century of Research in Review,* 2nd ed. Los Altos, CA: Malor Books, 2006.

Ekman, Paul. "Paul Ekman Micro Expression Training," *Paul Ekman Group,* n.d., http://www.paulekman.com/micro-expression-training/

Ekman, Paul, and Erika L. Rosenberg, eds. *Unmasking the Face, What the Face Reveals: Basic and Applied Studies of Spontaneous Expression Using the Facial Action Coding System (FACS).* Oxford: Oxford University Press, 2003.

Elam, Carol, and Terry D. Stratton. "Should Medical School Applicants Be Tested for Emotional Intelligence?" *American Medical Association Journal of Ethics* 8 (2006): 473–476.

Elbers, N.A., van Wees, K.A., Akkermans, A.J., Cuijpers, P., and Bruinvels, D.J. "Exploring Lawyer-Client Interaction: A Qualitative Study of Positive Lawyer Characteristics." *Psychological Injury and Law* 5 (2012): 89–94.

Elfenbein, Hillary Anger. "Learning in Emotion Judgments: Training and the Cross-Cultural Understanding of Facial Expression." *Journal of Nonverbal Behavior* 30 (2006).

Elfenbein, Hillary Anger, and N. Ambady. "Predicting Workplace Outcomes from the Ability to Eavesdrop on Feelings." *Journal of Applied Psychology* 87: 963–971.

Elfenbein, Hillary Anger, Maw Der Foo, Judith White, Hwee Hoon Tan, and Voon Chuan Aik. "Reading Your Counterpart: The Benefit of Emotion Recognition Accuracy for Effectiveness in Negotiation." *Journal of Nonverbal Behavior* 31 (2007): 205–223.

Emmerling, Robert J., and Daniel Goleman, "Emotional Intelligence: Issues and Common Misunderstandings." *Consortium for Research on Emotional Intelligence in Organizations,* October, 2003.

"The Emotional Oracle Effect." *Columbia Business School Newsroom,* February 24, 2012, http://www4.gsb.columbia.edu/news/item/7322632/The+Emotional+Oracle+Effect.

Epel, Elissa, Jennifer Daubenmier, Judith T. Moskowitz, Susan Folkman, and Elizabeth Blackburn. "Can Meditation Slow Rate of Cellular Aging? Cognitive Stress, Mindfulness, and Telomeres." *Annals of the New York Academy of Sciences* 1172 (2009): 34–53.

Erbas, Yasemin, Eva Ceulemans, Madeline Lee Pe, Peter Koval, and Peter Kuppens. "Negative Emotion Differentiation: Its Personality and Well-Being Correlates and a Comparison of Different Assessment Methods." *Cognition and Emotion* 28 (2014): 1196–1213.

Ermer, Elsa, Rachel E. Kahn, Peter Salovey, and Kent A. Peter. "Emotional Intelligence in Incarcerated Men with Psychopathic Traits." *Journal of Personality and Social Psychology* 103 (2012): 194–204.

Esmond-Kiger, Connie, Mary L. Tucker, and Christine A. Yost. "Emotional Intelligence: From the Classroom to the Workplace." *Management Accounting Quarterly* 7 (2006): 35–41.

Eva, Kevin W., Harold I. Reiter, Jack Rosenfeld, and Geoffrey R. Norman. "The Ability of the Multiple Mini-Interview to Predict Preclerkship Performance in Medical School." *Academic Medicine* 79 (2004): S40–S42.

Fahr, C.I., M.G. Seo, and P.E. Tesluk. "Emotional Intelligence, Teamwork Effectiveness, and Job Performance: The Moderating Role of Job Context." *Journal of Applied Psychology* 97 (2012): 890–900.

Fariselli, Lorenzo, Massimiliano Ghini, and Joshua Freedman. "Age and Emotional Intelligence." *SixSeconds: The Emotional Intelligence Network,* 2006, http://prodimages.6seconds.org/media/WP_EQ_and_Age.pdf.

Faucheux, Ron. "By the Numbers: Americans Lack Confidence in the Legal System." *The Atlantic,* July 6, 2012.

Feigenson, Neil, Jaihyun Park, and Peter Salovey. "Effect of Blameworthiness and Outcome Severity on Attributions of Responsibility and Damage Awards in Comparative Negligence Cases." *Law and Human Behavior* 21 (1997): 597–617.

Feist, Gregory J. "A Meta-Analysis of Personality in Scientific and Artistic Creativity." *Personality and Social Psychology Review* 2 (1998): 290–309.

Felton, Tasha M., Lindsey Coates, and John Chambers Christopher. "Impact of Mindfulness Training on Counseling Students' Perceptions of Stress." *Mindfulness,* 2013.

Feng-Jen, Tsai, Wei-Lun Huang, and Chang-Chuan Chan. "Occupational Stress and Burnout of Lawyers." *Journal of Occupational Health* 51 (2009): 443–450.

Fernández-Aráoz, Claudio, Boris Groysberg, and Nitin Nohria. "How to Hang on to Your High Potentials." *Harvard Business Review,* October, 2011.

Filipowicz, Allan, Sigal Barsade, and Shimul Melwani. "Understanding Emotional Transitions: The Interpersonal Consequences of Changing Emotions in Negotiations." *Journal of Personality and Social Psychology* 10 (2011): 541–556.

Filisko, G.M. "You're Out of Order! Dealing with the Costs of Incivility in the Legal Profession." *American Bar Association Journal,* January 1, 2013.

Fisher, Roger, and Daniel Shapiro. *Beyond Reason: Using Emotions as You Negotiate.* New York, NY: Viking, 2005.

Fisher, Roger, William L. Ury, and Bruce M. Patton. *Getting to YES: Negotiation Agreement Without Giving In.* New York, NY: Houghton Mifflin, 1991.

Greg Fleischmann, Kevin Iredell, and Kevin McMurdo, "Sales Professionals in Law Firms—Are We Finally Ready?" *LMA International,* September9,2015,http://blog.legalmarketing.org/sales-professionals-in-the-law-firm-are-we-finally-ready.

Fletcher, Eric. "Intentional Listening: How to Find Practice-Changing Opportunities." *Cordell Parvin Blog,* February 8, 2012, http://www.cordellblog.com/client-development/intentional-listening-how-to-find-practice-changing-opportunities/.

Flora, Carlin. "Gut Almighty." *Psychology Today,* May 1, 2007.

Flores, Rosa, and Rose Marie Arce. "Why Are Lawyers Killing Themselves?" *CNN,* January 19, 2014, http://www.cnn.com/2014/01/19/us/lawyer-suicides/.

Forgas, Joseph P. "Don't Worry, Be Sad! On the Cognitive, Motivational, and Interpersonal Benefits of Negative Mood." *Current Directions in Psychological Science* 22 (2013): 225–232.

Fortney, Susan Saab. "Are Law Firm Partners Islands unto Themselves? An Empirical Study of Law Firm Peer Review and Culture." *Georgetown Journal of Legal Ethics* 10 (1996): 271–316.

Forushani, Nasrin Zamani, and Mohammad Ali Besharat. "Relation Between Emotional Intelligence and Perceived Stress Among Female Students." *Procedia—Social and Behavioral Sciences* 30 (2011): 1109–1112.

Foster, Jeff, Larry Richard, Lisa Rohrer, and Mark Sirkin. "Understanding Lawyers: The Personality Traits of Successful Practitioners: Results from the Hogan Assessment Project on Lawyer Personality." *Hildebrandt Baker Robbins,* 2010. http://www.thresholdadvisors.com/

wp-content/uploads/2011/04/Understanding-Lawyers-White-Paper-Oct-2010-revised.pdf.

Fredrickson, Barbara L. "What Good Are Positive Emotions?" *Review of General Psychology* 2 (1998): 300–319.

Freedman, Joshua. "Case: EQ in the Navy and Marine Corps—Accelerating Change with Emotional Intelligence." *Six Seconds Emotional Intelligence Network,* June 23, 2011, http://www.6seconds.org/2011/06/23/case-navy-change/.

Freeman, David W. "High Blood Pressure May Blunt Emotional Intelligence." *CBS News Online,* November 4, 2011, http://www.cbsnews.com/8301-504763_162-57318462-10391704/high-blood-pressure-may-blunt-emotional-intelligence.

Freshman, Brenda, and Louis Rubino. "Emotional Intelligence: A Core Competency for Health Care Administrators." *Health Care Manager* 20 (2002): 1–9.

Freshman, Clark, Adele Hayes, and Greg Feldman. "The Lawyer-Negotiator as Mood Scientist: What We Know and Don't Know about How Mood Relates to Successful Negotiation." *Journal of Dispute Resolution* 1 (2002): 1–79.

Furlong, Jordan. "The Four Cardinal Virtues of Law Firm Culture," Edge International, 2016, http://www.edge.ai/2016/04/the-4-cardinal-virtues-of-law-firm-culture/?key=eic.

Furlong, Jordan. "Pricing to the Client Experience." *Law 21 Blog,* March 1, 2012, http://www.law21.ca/2012/03/pricing-to-the-client-experience/.

Furlong, Jordan. "Ready for the Future? Your Survival Kit Survey Results." *Law21 Blog,* August 15, 2013, https://www.law21.ca/2013/08/ready-for-the-future-your-survival-kit-survey-results/?utm_source=feedburner&utm_medium=email&utm_campaign=Feed%253A+law21+%2528Law21%2529.

Furlong, Jordan. "You're Not Selling What We're Buying," *Law21 Blog,* November 30, 2016, https://www.law21.ca/2016/11/youre-not-selling-what-were-buying/.

Gabbe, B. J., P. A. Cameron, O. D. Williamson, E. R. Edwards, S. E. Graves, and M. D. Richardson. "The Relationship Between Compensable Status and Long-Term Patient Outcomes Following Orthopaedic Trauma." *Medical Journal of Australia* 187 (2007): 14–17.

Gallacher, Ian. "Thinking Like Non-Lawyers: Why Empathy Is a Core Lawyering Skill and Why Legal Education Should Change to Reflect

Its Importance." *Journal of the Association of Legal Writing Directors,* October 16, 2010.

Gallup. "State of the American Workplace," *Gallup,* 2016, http://www.gallup.com/services/178514/state-american-workplace.aspx.

Gardner, Heidi. "The Collaboration Imperative for Today's Law Firms: Leading High-Performance Teamwork for Maximum Benefit." In R. Normand-Hochman ed., *Managing Talent for Success: Talent Development in Law Firms.* London, UK: Globe Business Publishing Ltd., 2013.

Gardner, Heidi. "Harvard Study Part II: Collaboration Strategies for Rainmakers." *Bloomberg,* June 1, 2015, https://bol.bna.com/harvard-study-part-ii-collaboration-strategies-for-rainmakers/.

Gardner, Heidi. "Is Your Firm Collaborative? What Your Client Sees." *American Lawyer,* May 23, 2016.

Gardner, Heidi. *Smart Collaboration: How Professionals and Their Firms Succeed by Breaking Down Silos.* Boston, MA: Harvard Business Review Press, 2016.

Gardner, Heidi. "When Senior Managers Won't Collaborate." *Harvard Business Review,* March 10, 2015.

Gardner, Heidi. "When and Why Clients Want You to Collaborate." *American Lawyer,* June 28, 2016.

Gardner, Howard. *Frames of Mind: The Theory of Multiple Intelligences.* New York: Basic Books, 1983.

Gasper, Karen, and Gerald L. Clore. "Do You Have to Pay Attention to Your Feelings to Be Influenced by Them?" *Peers Social Psychology Bulletin* 26: 698–711.

Gawande, Atul. "Letting Go." *The New Yorker,* August 2, 2010.

George, Jennifer, and Kenneth Bettenhausen. "Understanding Prosocial Behavior, Sales Performance, and Turnover: A Group Level Analysis in a Service Context." *Journal of Applied Psychology* 75 (1990): 698–709.

Gerdy, Kristin. "Clients, Empathy, and Compassion: Introducing First-Year Law Students to the 'Heart' of Lawyering." *Nebraska Law Review,* February, 2008.

Gigerenzer, G. *Gut Feelings: The Intelligence of the Unconscious.* New York: Viking, 2007.

Giles, S.J.S. *The Role of Supervisory Emotional Intelligence in Direct Report Organizational Commitment.* Unpublished master's thesis. University of New South Wales, Sydney, Australia, 2001.

Gilkey, Roderick, Ricardo Caceda, and Clinton Kilts. "When Emotional Reasoning Trumps IQ." *Harvard Business Review* 88 (2010): 20–21.

Gillespie, Becy Beaupre. "Mindful at Large: Contemplative Practice Is Emerging into the Mainstream." *ABA Journal* 99 (2013): 24.

Gilter, Jonathan D. "Study Finds Settling Is Better Than Going to Trial." *New York Times*, August 7, 2008.

Gohm, Carol L., Grant C. Corser, and David J. Dalsky. "Emotional Intelligence Under Stress: Useful, Unnecessary, or Irrelevant?" *Personal Individual Differences* 39 (2005): 1017–1028.

Goleman, Daniel. "Are Women More Emotionally Intelligent Than Men?" *Psychology Today*, April 29, 2011.

Goleman, Daniel. *The Brain and Emotional Intelligence: New Insights.* Florence, MA: More Than Sound, 2011.

Goleman, Daniel. *Emotional Intelligence: Why It Can Matter More Than IQ*, 10th Anniversary ed. New York, NY: Bantam Books, 2005.

Goleman, Daniel. "An EI-Based Theory of Performance." In *The Emotionally Intelligent Workplace: How to Select for, Measure, and Improve Emotional Intelligence in Individuals, Groups, and Organizations*, edited by Daniel Goleman and Cary Cherniss, 27–44. San Francisco: Jossey-Bass, 2000.

Goleman, Daniel. "The Focused Leader." *Harvard Business Review*, December 2013.

Goleman, Daniel. "How to Evaluate Your Own Emotional Intelligence," *LinkedIn*, June 27, 2013, http://www.linkedin.com/today/post/article/20130627123742-117825785-nine-ways-to-think-about-your-own-emotional-intelligence.

Goleman, Daniel. "Leadership That Gets Results." *Harvard Business Review*, March—April, 2000.

Goleman, Daniel. "Teach Emotional Intelligence in Schools." *LinkedIn*, May 19, 2013, http://www.linkedin.com/today/post/article/201305 19223058-117825785-teach-emotional-intelligence-in-schools.

Goleman, Daniel. "They've Taken Emotional Intelligence Too Far," *Time*, November 1, 2011, http://ideas.time.com/2011/11/01/theyve-taken-emotional-intelligence-too-far/.

Goleman, Daniel. "3 Secrets to Habit Change," January 1, 2015, http://www.danielgoleman.info/daniel-goleman-3-secrets-to-habit-change/

Goleman, Daniel. "Two Key Skills for High-Performance Leadership," *More Than Sound*, December 5, 2016, http://morethansound.net/tag/daniel-goleman/.

Goleman, Daniel. "What Mindfulness Is and Isn't," *LinkedIn*, February 16, 2014, http://www.linkedin.com/today/post/article/20140216161912-117825785-what-mindfulness-is-and-isn-t.

Goleman, Daniel. "The Decline of the Nice-Guy Quotient." *New York Times,* September 10, 1995.

Goleman, Daniel. "What Makes a Leader." *Harvard Business Review,* November–December 1998, 93–102.

Goleman, Daniel. *Working with Emotional Intelligence.* New York, NY: Bantam, 2000.

Goleman, Daniel, and Richard Boyatzis. "Social Intelligence and the Biology of Leadership." *Harvard Business Review* 86 (1998): 74–81.

Goleman, Daniel P., Richard E. Boyatzis, and Annie McKee. *Primal Leadership: Learning to Lead with Emotional Intelligence.* Cambridge, MA: Harvard Business Press, 2002.

Goleman, Daniel, Michael MacCoby, Thomas Davenport, John C. Beck, Dan Clampa, and Michael Watkins. *Harvard Business Review on What Makes a Leader.* Boston: Harvard Business School Publishing Corporation, 2001.

Goodman-Delahunty, Jane, Pär Anders Granhag, Maria Hartwig, and Elizabeth F. Loftus. "Insightful or Wishful: Lawyers' Ability to Predict Case Outcomes." *Psychology, Public Policy, and Law* 16 (2010): 133–157.

Gopnik, Adam. "Mindless: The New Neuro-skeptics." *The New Yorker,* September 9, 2013.

Gooty, J., M. B. Gavin, N. M. Ashkanasy, and J. S. Thomas. "The Wisdom of Letting Go and Performance: The Moderating Role of Emotional Intelligence and Discrete Emotions." *Journal of Occupational and Organizational Psychology* 87 (2014): 392–413.

Gordon, Leslie A. "Most Lawyers Are Introverted, and That's Not Necessarily a Bad Thing." *ABA Journal,* January 1, 2016.

Grant, Adam. "The Dark Side of Emotional Intelligence." *The Atlantic,* January 2, 2014.

Grant, Adam. "Goodbye to MBTI, the Fad That Won't Die." *Psychology Today,* September 18, 2013.

Grdinovac, J. A., and G. B. Yancey. "How Organizational Adaptations to Recession Relate to Organizational Commitment." *Psychologist-Manager Journal* 15 (2012): 6–24.

Greater Good. "What Is Empathy?" *Greater Good,* n.d. http://greatergood.berkeley.edu/topic/empathy/definition#what.

Greven, Corina, Tomas Chamorro-Premuzic, Adriane Arteche, and Adrian Furnham. "A Hierarchical Integration of Dispositional Determinants of General Health in Students: The Big Five, Trait Emotional

Intelligence and Humor Styles." *Personality and Individual Differences* 44 (2008): 1562–1573.

Grewal, Daisy, and Heather A. Davidson, "Emotional Intelligence and Graduate Medical Education." *Journal of the American Medical Association* 10 (2008): 1200–1202.

Griffith, Pat. "The Emotionally Intelligent Accountant: An Oxymoron?" *Pat Griffith Executive Development Blog,* March 15, 2011, http://www.patgriffith.com/2011/03/15/the-emotionally-intelligent-accountant-an-oxymoron/.

Griswold, Erwin N. "Law Schools and Human Relations." *Washington University Law Review* 3 (1955): 217–231.

Gross, Cynthia, Mary Jo Kreitzer, Maryanne Reilly-Spong, Melanie Wall, Nicole Y. Winbush, Robert Patterson, Mark Mahowald, and Michel Cramer-Bornemann. "Mindfulness-Based Stress Reduction versus Pharmacotherapy for Chronic Primary Insomnia: A Randomized Controlled Clinical Trial." *EXPLORE: Journal of Science and Healing* 7 (2011): 76–87.

Gross, James J. "Emotion Regulation: Affective, Cognitive, and Social Consequences." *Psychophysiology* 39 (2002): 281–291.

Grossman, Paul, Ulrike Tiefenthaler-Gilmer, Annette Raysk, and Ulrike Kesper. "Mindfulness Training as an Intervention for Fibromyalgia: Evidence of Postintervention and 3-Year Follow-up Benefits in Well-Being." *Psychotherapy and Psychosomatics* 76 (2007): 226–233.

Groysberg, Boris, and Eliot Sherman. "Baker & McKenzie (A): A New Framework for Talent Management." *Harvard Business School,* 2007.

Groysberg, Boris, and Eliot Sherman. "Baker & McKenzie (B): A New Framework for Talent Management." *Harvard Business School,* 2008.

Grubb III, W. L., and M. A. McDaniel. "The Fakability of Bar-on's Emotional Quotient Inventory Short Form; Catch Me If You Can." *Human Performance* 20 (2007): 43–59.

Guardian. "Emotional Intelligence: A Clincher in Lady Ashton's Diplomatic Triumph." *The Guardian ShortCuts Blog,* November 24, 2013, http://www.theguardian.com/science/shortcuts/2013/nov/25/emotional-intelligence-clincher-lady-ashton-eu-foreign-policy-iran#start-of-comments.

Gurian, Michael, with Barbara Annis. *Leadership and the Sexes: Using Gender Science to Create Success in Business.* San Francisco, CA: Jossey-Bass, 2008.

Hahn, Verena C., Carmen Binnewies, Sabine Sonnentag, and Eva J. Mojza. "Learning How to Recover from Job Stress: Effects of a Recovery

Training Program on Recovery-Related Self-Efficacy, and Well-Being." *Journal of Occupational Health Psychology* 16 (2011): 202–216.

Hall, Linley Erin. "What Makes for Good Lawyering?" *Boalt Hall Transcript*, Summer, 2005: 22–27, http://web.archive.org/web/20100508133459/http://www.law.berkeley.edu/beyondlsat/transcript.pdf.

Halpern, Charles. "The Mindful Lawyer: Why Contemporary Lawyers Are Practicing Meditation." *Journal of Legal Education* 61 (2012): 641–646.

Halpern, Jodi. "What Is Clinical Empathy?" *Journal of General Internal Medicine* 18 (2003): 670–674.

Hanson, Rick. *Buddha's Brain.* Oakland, CA: New Harbinger Publications, Inc., 2009.

Harms, Peter D., and Marcus Credé. "Emotional Intelligence and Transformational and Transactional Leadership: A Meta-Analysis." *Journal of Leadership and Organizational Studies* 17 (2010): 5–17.

Harper, Steven J. "Are Lawyers Becoming Happier?" *The Am Law Daily*, September 20, 2013, http://www.americanlawyer.com/PubArticleALD.jsp?id=1202619714994&Are_Lawyers_Becoming_Happier&slreturn=20130923171332#ixzz2fwFSmMrK.

Hartocollis, Anemona. "In Medical School Shift, Meeting Patients on Day 1." *New York Times*, September 2, 2010.

Haslett, Emma. "Author Q&A: Daniel Goleman, *Focus*." *Management Today*, November 6, 2013, http://www.managementtoday.co.uk/books/1219775/author-q-a-daniel-goleman-focus/.

Hassad, Craig, Steven De Lisle, Gavin Sullivan, and Ciaran Pier. "Enhancing the Health of Medical Students: Outcomes of an Integrated Mindfulness and Lifestyle Program." *Advances in Health Science Education* 14 (2009): 387–398.

Hatfield, Gary. "René Descartes." In *The Stanford Encyclopedia of Philosophy*, edited by Edward N. Zalta. http://plato.stanford.edu/archives/sum2011/entries/descartes/.

Hay Group. "Women Poised to Effectively Lead in Matrix Work Environments, Hay Group Research Finds: Overall, Competencies Required to Successfully Lead Matrix Teams Are in Short Supply." *Hay Group.com.* http://www.haygroup.com/ww/press/details.aspx?id=33283.

Hayward, Sonita. "Emotional Intelligence in Litigation." *Law Society Gazette*, July 31, 2015, http://www.lawgazette.co.uk/law/practice-points/emotional-intelligence-in-litigation/5050357.article.

Henderson, William D. "The Bursting of the Pedigree Bubble." *National Association for Law Placement Bulletin* 21 (2009): 1–14.

Hengstler, Gary A. "Vox Populi: The Public Perception of Lawyers: ABA Poll." *ABA Journal*, 1993.

Henry, John, and Peter MacLean. "Courting the Candidate-Customer: The Unlikely Art of Attraction." *Deloitte University Press*, July 24, 2014.

Herrick, Colette, and Joshua Freedman. 2013. "Emotional Intelligence and Collaboration in Health Care." *Six Seconds.org*, July 13, http://www.6seconds.org/2013/07/31/emotional-intelligence-collaboration-in-healthcare/.

Herwig, Uwe, Tina Kaffenberger, Lutz Janckec, and Annette B. Bruhl. "Self-Related Awareness and Emotion Regulation." *Nueroimage* 50 (2010): 734–741.

Herz, Arnie. "Relationships Are King." *Touro Law Review* 24 (2014): 1–15.

Herz, Arnie. "Client Empowerment 4: Great Expectations." November 20, 2012, http://arnieherz.com/client-empowerment-4-great-expectations/#more-.

Heskett, James L., Thomas O. Jones, Gary W. Loveman, W. Earl Sasser, Jr., and Leonard A. Schlesinger. "Putting the Service-Profit Chain to Work." *Harvard Business Review*, July, 2008. Originally published in 1994.

Hess, James D., and Arnold C. Bacigalupo. "Enhancing Decisions and Decision Making Processes Through the Application of Emotional Intelligence Skills." *Management Decision* 49 (2011): 710–721.

Hirsch, Elliot M. "The Role of Empathy in Medicine: A Medical Student's Perspective." *Virtual Mentor* 9 (2007): 423–427.

Hoerger, Michael, Benjamin P. Chapman, Ronald M. Epstein, .and Paul R. Duberstein. "Emotional Intelligence: A Theoretical Framework for Individual Differences in Affective Forecasting." *Emotion* 12 (2012): 716–725.

Hoge, Elizabeth A., Maxine M. Chen, Esther Orr, Christina A. Metcalf, Laura E. Fischer, Mark H. Pollack, Immaculata DeVivo, and Naomi M. Simon. "Loving-Kindness Meditation Practice Associated with Longer Telomeres in Women." *Brain, Behavior, and Immunity* 32 (2013): 159–163.

Hogenboom, Melissa. "Pyschopathic Criminals Have Empathy Switch." *BBC News*, July 24, 2013, http://www.bbc.co.uk/news/science-environment-23431793.

Hölzel, Britta K., James Carmody, Karleyton C. Evans, Elizabeth A. Hoge, Jeffery A. Dusek, Lucas Morgan, Roger K. Pitman, and Sara W.

Lazar. "Stress Reduction Correlates with Structural Changes in the Amygdala." *Social Cognitive and Affective Neuroscience* 5 (1): 11–17.

Hölzel, Britta K., James Carmody, Mark Vangel, Christina Congleton, Sita M. Yerramsetti, Tim Gard, and Sara W. Lazar. "Mindfulness Practice Leads to Increases in Regional Brain Gray Matter Density." *Psychiatry Research: Neuroimaging* 191 (2011): 36–43.

Howard, Philip K. *Life Without Lawyers: Restoring Responsibility in America.* New York, NY: W.W Norton & Company, 2009.

Hudson, Ruth. "The Importance of Emotional Intelligence for Lawyers." *Lawyers Weekly,* December 20, 2016, http://www.lawyersweekly.com.au/opinion/20258-the-importance-of-emotional-intelligence-for-lawyers.

Hunter, John E., Frank L. Schmidt, and Michael K. Judiesch. "Individual Differences in Output Variability as a Function of Job Complexity." *Journal of Applied Psychology* 75 (1990): 28–42.

Hutcherson, Cendri A., Emma M. Seppala, and James J. Gross. "Loving-Kindness Meditation Increases Social Connectedness." *Emotion* 8 (2008): 720–724.

Iacoboni, Marco, Roger P. Woods, Marcel Brass, Harold Bekkering, John C. Mzziotta, and Giacomo Rizzolatti. "Cortical Mechanisms of Human Imitation." *Science* 286 (1999): 2526–2528.

Imai, Lynn, and Michele J. Gelfand. "The Culturally Intelligent Negotiator: The Impact of Cultural Intelligence (CQ) on Negotiation Sequences and Outcomes." *Organizational Behavior and Human Decision Processes* 112 (2010): 83–98.

2010 InHouse Counsel magazine ACC/Serengeti Managing Outside Counsel Survey. http://www.acc.com/_cs_upload/vl/membersonly/Surveys/1249457_2.pdf.

Interscience. "Science News: Predicting Academic Strength Emotionally." *Science Daily,* June 28, 2011, http://www.sciencedaily.com/releases/2011/06/110628173051.htm.

Irvine, Charlie. "Building Emotional Intelligence." In *Choreography of Resolution,* edited by Michelle LeBaron, Carrie MacLeod, and Andrew Floyer Acland. Chicago, IL: American Bar Association, 2009, 107–121.

Isen, Alice M., Kimberley A. Daubman, and Gary P. Nowicki. "Positive Affect Facilitates Creative Problem Solving." *Journal of Personality and Social Psychology* 52 (1987): 1122–1131.

Jackson, Susan E., Jon A. Turner, and Arthur P. Brief. "Correlates of Burnout Among Public Service Lawyers." *Journal of Occupational Behaviour* 8 (1987): 339–349. http://onlinelibrary.wiley.com/doi/10.1002/job.4030080406/abstract.

Jacobs, Tonya L., Elissa S. Epel, Jue Line, Elizabeth H. Blackburn, Owen M. Wolkowitx, David A. Bridwell, Anthony P. Zanesco, Stephen R. Aichele, Baljinder K. Sahdra, Katherine A. MacLean, Brandon G. King, Phillip R. Shaver, Erika L. Rosenberg, Emilio Ferrer, B. Alan Wallace, and Clifford D. Saron. "Intensive Meditation Training, Immune Cell Telomerase Activity, and Psychological Mediators." *Psychoneuroendocrinology* 36 (2011): 664–681.

Jain, Shamini, Shauna L. Shapiro, Summer Swanick, Scott C. Roesch, Paul J. Mills, Iris Bell, and Gary E.R Schwartz. "A Randomized Controlled Trial of Mindfulness Meditation versus Relaxation Training: Effects on Distress, Positive States of Mind, Rumination and Distraction." *Annals of Behavioral Medicine* 33 (2007): 11–21.

James, Colin, Miles Bore, and Susanna Zito. "Emotional Intelligence and Personality as Predictors of Psychological Well-Being." *Journal of Psychoeducational Assessment* 30 (2012), 425–438.

Jameson, Jessica Katz, Andrea M. Bodtker, and Tim Linker, "Facilitating Conflict Transformation: Mediator Strategies for Eliciting Emotional Communication in a Workplace Conflict." *Negotiation Journal* 26 (2010): 25–48.

JD Journal. "McKenna Long & Aldridge to Include Psychological Test as Part of Its Hiring Process." *JD Journal*, January 28, 2011, http://www.jdjournal.com/2011/01/28/mckenna-long-aldridge-to-include-psychological-test-as-part-of-its-hiring-process/.

Jha, Amishi P., Elizabeth A. Stanley, Anastasia Kiyonaga, Ling Wong, and Lois Gelfand. "Examining the Protective Effects of Mindfulness Training on Working Memory Capacity and Affective Experience." *Emotion* 10 (2010): 54–64.

Johnson, Whitney. "Disrupt Yourself." *Harvard Business Review*, July–August, 2012, 149.

Jordan, Peter J., Neal M. Ashkanasy, and Charmine E. J. Hartel. "Emotional Intelligence as a Moderator of Emotional and Behavioral Reactions to Job Insecurity." *The Academy of Management Review* 27 (3) (July 2002): 361–372.

Jones, Tricia S. "Emotion in Mediation: Implications, Applications, Opportunities, and Challenges." In *The Blackwell Handbook of Mediation: Bridging Theory, Research, and Practice*, edited by Margaret S. Herrman. Oxford, UK: Blackwell Publishing, 2006, 277–306.

Joseph, Dana L., and Daniel A. Newman. "Emotional Intelligence: An Integrative Meta-Analysis and Cascading Model." *Journal of Applied Psychology* 95 (2010): 54–78.

Joyner, Fredricka F., and Derek T. Y. Mann. "Developing Emotional Intelligence in MBA Students: A Case Study of One Program's Success." *American Journal of Business Education (AJBE)* 4 (2011): 59–72.

Kabat-Zinn, Jon. *Full Catastrophe Living: Using the Wisdom of Your Body and Mind to Face Stress, Pain, and Illness.* New York, NY: Random House, 1990.

Kabat-Zinn, John. "An Outpatient Program in Behavioral Medicine for Chronic Pain Based on the Practice of Mindfulness Meditation." *General Hospital Psychiatry* 4 (1982): 33–47.

Kahneman, Daniel. *Thinking Fast and Slow.* New York, NY: Farrar, Strauss and Giroux, 2011.

Kasanoff, Bruce. "Intuition Is the Highest Form of Intelligence." *Forbes,* February 21, 2017.

Kasman, Deborah L., Kelly Fryer-Edwards, and Clarence H. Braddock III. "Educating for Professionalism: Trainees' Emotional Experiences on IM and Pediatrics Inpatient Wards." *Academic Medicine* 78 (2003): 730–741.

Kaster, Laura A. "Review of *How Leading Lawyers Think: Expert Insights into Judgment and Advocacy* (Springer-Verlag 2011)." *NYSBA New York Dispute Resolution Lawyer* 5 (2012): 79–80.

Kemper, Theodore D. "How Many Emotions Are There? Wedding the Social and the Autonomic Components." *American Journal of Sociology* 93 (1987): 263–289.

Keshner, Andrew. "Trial Founders on 'Personality Issues' Between Judge, Counsel." *New York Law Journal,* May 17, 2013, http://www.newyorklaw-journal.com/PubArticleNY.jsp?id=1202600442171&Trial_Founders_on_Personality_Issues_Between_Judge_Counsel#ixzz2Yg5ziBFr.

Kidwell, Blair, David M. Hardesty, Brian R. Murtha, and Shiben Sheng. "Emotional Intelligence in Marketing Exchanges." *Journal of Marketing* 75 (2011): 78–95.

Kim, See Joo, Jee In Kang, Kee Namkoong, and Dong-Ho Song. "The Effects of Serotonin Transporter Promoter and Monoamine Oxidase A Gene Polymorphisms on Trait Emotional Intelligence." *Neuropsychobiology* 64 (2011): 224–230.

Kimmel, Christopher M., Patrick A. Stewart, and William D. Schreckhise. "Of Closed Minds and Open Mouths: Indicators of Supreme Court Justice Votes during the 2009 and 2010 Sessions." *The Forum* 10 (2012).

Kiser, Randall. *Beyond Right and Wrong: The Power of Effective Decision Making for Attorneys and Clients.* Berlin: Springer-Verlag, 2010.

Kiser, Randall. "The Emotionally Intelligent Lawyer: Balancing the Rule of Law with the Realities of Human Behavior." *Nevada Law Journal* 15 (2015).

Kiser, Randall. *How Leading Lawyers Think: Expert Insights into Judgment and Advocacy.* New York, NY: Springer-Verlag, 2011.

Kiser, Randall L., Martin A. Asher, and Blakeley B. McShane. "Let's Not Make a Deal: An Empirical Study of Decision Making in Unsuccessful Settlement Negotiations." *Journal of Empirical Legal Studies* 5 (2008): 551–591.

Koch, Sarah-Neena. "Subcortical Brain Structures, Stress, Emotions, and Mental Illness." *MyBrainNotes™.com,* 2013, http://mybrainnotes.com/memory-brain-stress.html.

Kouzes, James M., and Barry Z. Posner. *A Leader's Legacy.* San Francisco, CA: John Wiley & Sons, 2006.

Krasner, Michael S., Ronald M. Epstein, Howard Beckman, Anthony L. Suchman, Benjamin Chapman, Christopher J. Mooney, and Timothy E. Quill. "Association of an Educational Program in Mindful Communication with Burnout, Empathy, and Attitudes Among Primary Care Physicians." *Journal of the American Medical Association* 302 (2009): 1284–1293, http://jama.jamanetwork.com/article.aspx?articleid=184621.

Kraus, Michael W., Stephane Cote, and Dacher Keltner. "Social Class Contextualism and Empathic Accuracy." *Psychological Science* 21 (2010): 1716–1723.

Kreamer, Anne. *It's Always Personal: Navigating Emotion in the New Workplace.* New York, NY: Random House, 2011.

Kreifelts, Benjamin, Thomas Ethofer, Elisabeth Huberle, Wolfgang Grodd, and Dirk Wildgruber. "Association of Trait Emotional Intelligence and Individual fMRI-Activation Patterns During the Perception of Social Signals from Voice and Face." *Human Brain Mapping* 31 (2010): 979–991.

Krieger, Lawrence S., and Kennon M. Sheldon, "What Makes Lawyers Happy?" *George Washington Law Review.*

Krill, Patrick R., Ryan Johnson, and Linda Albert. "The Prevalence of Substance Use and Other Mental Health Concerns Among American Attorneys." *Journal of Addiction Medicine* 10 (2016): 46–52.

Kronman, Anthony T. *The Lost Lawyer: Failing Ideals of the Legal Profession.* Cambridge, MA: Harvard University Press, 1993.

Labarre, Polly. "Marcus Buckingham Thinks Your Boss has an Attitude Problem." *Fast Company,* August, 2001, http://www.fastcompany.com/43419/marcus-buckingham-thinks-your-boss-has-attitude-problem.

Landa, Augusto, José María, Esther López-Zafra, Pilar Berrios Martos, and Maria del Carmen Aguilar-Luzón. "The Relationship Between Emotional Intelligence, Occupational Stress and Health in Nurses:

A Questionnaire Survey." *International Journal of Nursing Studies* 45 (2008): 888–901.

Landro, Laura. "The Talking Cure for Health Care: Improving the Ways Doctors Communicate with Their Patients Can Lead to Better Care—And Lower Costs." *Wall Street Journal*, April 8, 2013.

Law, David. "Did This Biglaw Partner Act Like a Big Tool? Let's Discuss." *Above the Law*, May 15, 2014.

"Law School Survey of Student Engagement, Engaging Legal Education: Moving Beyond the Status Quo." *Law School Survey of Student Engagement*, 2006.

Lazarus, R.S. "From Psychological Stress to the Emotions: A History of Changing Perspectives." *Annual Review of Psychology* 44 (1993): 1–21.

Lebanese American University. "News: Pharmacy Students Learn about Emotional Intelligence." *Lebanese American University*, July 3, 2013, http://www.lau.edu.lb/news-events/news/archive/pharmacy_students_learn_about/.

Lehrer, Jonah. "The Power Trip," *The Wall Street Journal*, August 14, 2010.

Levinson, Meridith. "The Danger of Being Too Nice at Work." *CIO*, September 18, 2008, http://www.cio.com/article/450066/The_Danger_of_Being_Too_Nice_at_Work_?page=3&taxonomyId=3123.

Levinson, Wendy, Debra L. Roter, John P. Mullooly, Valerie T. Dull, and Richard M. Frankel. "Physician-Patient Communication: The Relationship with Malpractice Claims Among Primary Care Physicians and Surgeons." *Journal of the American Medical Association* 277 (1997): 553–559.

Levit, Nancy, and Douglas Linder. "Happy Law Students, Happy Lawyers." *Syracuse Law Review* 58 (2008): 351–374.

Levy, Lester, and Mark Bentley. "More 'Right' Than 'Real': The Shape of Authentic Leadership in New Zealand." *Authentic Leadership Survey Results*, University of Auckland Business School, 2007.

Lewis, Natalie J., Charlotte E. Rees, J. Nicky Hudson, and Alan Bleakley. "Emotional Intelligence in Medical Education: Measuring the Unmeasurable?" *Advances in Health Sciences Education* 10 (2005): 339–355.

Libbrecht, Nele, Filip Lievens, Bernd Carette, and Stéphane Côté. "Emotional Intelligence Predicts Success in Medical School." *Emotion* 14 (2014): 64–73.

Lloyd, Harold Anthony. "Cognitive Emotion and the Law." *Law and Psychology Review*, August 1, 2016, https://poseidon01.ssrn.com/delivery.php

?ID=12300301706802912006900309700709300203500500007406608709012100700412309003002501811910002804301410306102101101202406900907609100005305708008602803006410910707300509106302803702508008409212606507510211912607208300311112706710109112712210811100200310612 4&EXT=pdf.

Lo, Teresa. "IP Law Firm Gives Job Applicants Personality Quizzes," *JD Journal*, March 29, 2017, http://www.jdjournal.com/2017/03/29/ip-law-firm-gives-job-applicants-personality-quizzes/?utm_source=MENA&utm_medium=Email&utm_campaign=t_17740—dt_20170331-cid_34870-Did_5100262-ad_JDJ~MENA-logid_[MCTS_CESLOGID].

Long, Gary, Greg Fowler, and Simon Castley. "DRI National Poll Uncovers Perceptions of Flaws in U.S. Civil Justice System." *Lexology*, September 27, 2012, http://www.lexology.com/library/detail.aspx?g=f64d5c01-d85b-4428-b65f-b996479144d3.

Lopes, Paulo N., Peter Salovey, and Rebecca Straus. "Emotional Intelligence, Personality, and the Perceived Quality of Social Relationships." *Personality and Individual Differences* 35 (2003): 641–658.

Lublin, Joann S. "Companies Try a New Strategy: Empathy Training," *Wall Street Journal*, June 21, 2016.

Lucas, Stephen E. *The Art of Public Speaking*, 11th ed. New York, NY: McGraw-Hill, 2012.

Lukasik, Daniel. "Judges and Depression." 2011, http://www.in.gov/judiciary/center/files/jedu-lib-social-dark-side-judging-depression-article.pdf.

Lukasik, Daniel. "Lawyers with Depression." http://www.lawyerswithdepression.com/.

Luskin, Frederic, Rick Aberman, and A. DeLorenzo. *The Training of Emotional Competence in Financial Services Advisors*. New Brunswick, NJ: Consortium for Research on Emotional Intelligence in Organizations, Rutgers University, 2002.

Lutz, Antoine, Julie Brefczynski-Lewis, Tom Johnston, snd Richard J. Davidson. "Regulation of the Neural Circuitry of Emotion by Compassion Meditation: Effects of Meditative Expertise." *Plos One* 3 (2008): e1897.

Lyubomirsky, Sonja, and Kristin Layous. "How Do Simple Positive Activities Increase Well-Being?" *Current Directions in Psychological Science* 22 (2013): 57–62.

Mabe, Paul A., and Stephen G. West. "Validity of Self-Evaluation of Ability: A Review and Meta-Analysis." *Journal of Applied Psychology* 67 (1982): 280–296.

MacKay, Karen, and Stephen Mabey. "Profiting When the World Is Flat." *Law Practice,* July/August, 2012, http://www.phoenix-legal.com/documents/articles/profiting.pdf.

MacKillop, Kara, and Neil Vidmar. "Legal Malpractice: A Preliminary Inquiry." *First Annual Conference on Empirical Legal Studies Paper,* 2006. http://papers.ssrn.com/sol3/papers.cfm?abstract_id=912963.

Maister, David. "Are Law Firms Manageable?" *David Maister.com,* 2006. http://davidmaister.com/articles/are-law-firms-manageable/.

Maister, David. "Do You Really Want Relationships?" *DavidMaister.com,* 2005, http://davidmaister.com/articles/2/80/.

Maister, David. *Practice What You Preach: What Managers Must Do to Create a High Achievement Culture.* New York, NY: Free Press, 2001.

Maister, David, Charles Green, and Robert Galford. *The Trusted Advisor.* New York, NY: Touchstone, 2000.

Ma-Kellams, Christine, and Jennifer Lerner. "Trust Your Gut or Think Carefully? Examining Whether an Intuitive, versus a Systematic, Mode of Thought Produces Greater Empathic Accuracy." *Journal of Personality and Social Psychology* 111 (2016): 674–685.

Managing Partner Forum. "The MPF 2013 Leadership Conference," May 9, 2013. http://www.managingpartnerforum.org/tasks/sites/mpf/assets/image/MPF%20-%20Managing%20Partner%20Survey%20Results%20-%20Raw%20Data%20-%20FINAL%20-%205-9-131.pdf.

Mann, Sandi. "Emotion at Work: To What Extent Are We Expressing, Suppressing, or Faking It?" *European Journal of Work and Organizational Psychology* 8 (1999): 347–369.

Manyika, James, Michael Chui, Mehdi Miremadi, Jacques Bughin, Katy George, Paul Willmott, and Martin Dewhurst. "Harnessing Automation for a Future That Works," *McKinsey,* http://www.mckinsey.com/global-themes/digital-disruption/harnessing-automation-for-a-future-that-works.

Marken, Stephanie. "Life After Law School." *Gallup,* March 24, 2016, http://www.gallup.com/opinion/gallup/190172/life-law-school.aspx.

Maroney, Terry A. "Angry Judges." *Vanderbilt Law Review* 65 (2012): 1207–1287.

Marsh, Jason. "The Limits of David Brooks' 'Limits of Empathy.'" *Greater Good: The Science of a Meaningful Life,* University of California

Berkeley, 2011, http://greatergood.berkeley.edu/article/item/the_limits_of_david_brooks_limits_of_empathy#c3751.

Marsh, Jason. "You Can't Buy Empathy." *Greater Good: The Science of a Meaningful Life,* December 14, 2010, http://greatergood.berkeley.edu/article/item/you_cant_buy_empathy.

Martin, Judy. "Workplace Stress Is Curveball Lobbed at Employee Emotional Intelligence." *Forbes Online,* November 19, 2012, http://www.forbes.com/sites/work-in-progress/2012/11/19/workplace-stress-is-curveball-lobbed-at-employee-emotional-intelligence/.

Martins, Alexandra, Nelson Ramalho, and Estelle Morin. "A Comprehensive Meta-Analysis of the Relationship between Emotional Intelligence and Health." *Personality and Individual Differences* 49 (2010): 554–564.

Mascaro, Jennifer S., James K. Rilling, Lobsang Tenzin Negi, and Charles L. Raison. "Compassion Meditation Enhances Empathic Accuracy and Related Neural Activity." *Social Cognitive and Affective Neuroscience* 8 (2013): 48–55.

Massachusetts General Hospital. "Meditation Appears to Produce Enduring Changes in Emotional Enduring Changes in Emotional Processing in the Brain: Imaging Study Finds Different Forms of Meditation May Have Varying Effects on Key Brain Structure." *Massachusetts General Hospital Website,* November 12, 2012, http://www.massgeneral.org/about/pressrelease.aspx?id=1520.

Massachusetts General Hospital. "News Release: Brief Training Program Improves Resident Physicians' Empathy with Patients." May 7, 2012, http://www.massgeneral.org/about/pressrelease.aspx?id=1461.

Matsumoto, David, Jeffery A. LeRoux, Roberta Bernhard, and Heather Gray. "Unraveling the Psychological Correlates of Intercultural Adjustment Potential." *International Journal of Intercultural Relations* 28 (2004): 281–309.

Matthews, Gerald, Amanda K. Emo, Gregory Funke, Moshe Zeidner, Richard D. Roberts, Paul T. Costa, Jr., and Ralf Schulze. "Emotional Intelligence, Personality, and Task-Induced Stress." *Journal of Experimental Psychology: Applied* 12 (2006): 96–107.

Matthews, G., M. Zeidner, and R. D. Roberts. *Emotional Intelligence: Science and Myth.* Cambridge, MA: MIT Press, 2004.

Mayer, Bernard. *The Dynamics of Conflict Resolution: A Practitioner's Guide.* San Francisco, CA: Jossey-Bass, 2000.

Mayer, Jane. "The Bush Six." *The New Yorker,* April 13, 2009.

Mayer, Jane. "Measuring Emotional Intelligence: Why Measure Emotional Intelligence." *Emotional Intelligence Information.* http://www.unh.edu/

emotional_intelligence/ei%20Measuring%20EI/eiMeasure%20why%20measure.htm.

Mayer, John D., Maria DiPaolo, and Peter Salovey. "Perceiving Affective Content in Ambiguous Visual Stimuli: A Component of Emotional Intelligence." *Journal of Personality Assessment* 544 (1990): 772–781.

Mayer, John D., and Peter Salovey. "Emotional Intelligence." *Imagination, Cognition, and Personality* 9 (1989): 185–211.

Mayer, John D., and Peter Salovey. "What Is Emotional Intelligence: Implications for Educators." In *Emotional Development and Emotional Intelligence: Educational Implications,* edited by Peter Salovey and D. Sluyter, 3–31. New York, NY: Basic Books, 1997.

Mayer, John D., Peter Salovey, and David Caruso. "Emotional Intelligence Meets Traditional Standards for an Intelligence." *Intelligence* 27 (1999): 267–298.

Mayer, John D., Peter Salovey, and David R. Caruso. "Emotional Intelligence: Theory, Findings, and Implications." *Psychological Inquiry* 15 (2004): 197–215.

Mayer, John D., Peter Salovey, and David Caruso. *Mayer-Salovey-Caruso Emotional Intelligence Test User's Manual.* New York, NY: Multi-Health Systems, 2002.

Mayer, John D., Peter Salovey, and David R. Caruso. "The Validity of the MSCEIT: Additional Analyses and Evidence." *Emotion Review* 4 (2012): 403–408.

Mayer, Richard D. Roberts, and Sigal G. Barsade. "Human Abilities: Emotional Intelligence." *Annual Review of Psychology* 59 (2008): 507–536.

Mayock, Patrick. "Conley Talks Jobs, Careers, Callings." *Hotel News Now,* February 28, 2012, http://www.hotelnewsnow.com/articles/14304/Conley-talks-jobs-careers-callings.

McCann, Greg K., David J. Tarbert, and Michael S. Lenetsky. "The Sound of No Students Clapping: What Zen Can Offer Legal Education." *University of San Francisco Law Review* 29 (1995): 313–314.

McClelland, David C. "Identifying Competencies with Behavioral-Event Interviews." *Psychological Science* 9 (1998): 331–339.

McClelland, David C. "Testing for Competence Rather Than 'Intelligence.'" *American Psychologist* 28 (1973): 1–14.

McCubbin, James A., Marcellus M. Merritt, John J. Sollers III, Michele K. Evans, Alan B. Zonderman, Richard D. Lane, and Julian F. Thayer. "Cardiovascular-Emotional Dampening: The Relationship Between

Blood Pressure and Recognition of Emotion." *Psychosomatic Medicine: Journal of Biobehavioral Medicine* 73 (2011): 743–750.

McEwan, Bruce S. "Protective and Damaging Effects of Stress Mediators: Central Role of the Brain." *Dialogues in Clinical Neuroscience* 8 (2006): 367–381.

McEwen, Bruce. *The End of Stress as We Know It.* Washington, DC: Joseph Henry Press, 2002.

McGrath, Charles. "A Lobotomy That He Says Didn't Touch His Soul." *New York Times,* November 16, 2005.

McKenna, Patrick J., and Edwin B. Reeser. "Management Memo: Is Your Firm Creating a Star Culture?" *Am Law Daily,* July 25, 2013, http://www.americanlawyer.com/PubArticleALD.jsp?id=1202612505186.

McKinsey & Company. "Leadership and Behavior: Mastering the Mechanics of Reason and Emotion." *McKinsey Quarterly,* October 2016, http://www.mckinsey.com/business-functions/organization/our-insights/leadership-and-behavior-mastering-the-mechanics-of-reason-and-emotion.

McLaughlin, Margaret, T. Richard-Cheatham, Keith V. Erickson, and Beth M. Waggenspack. "Juror Perceptions of Participants in Criminal Proceedings." *Journal of Applied Communication Research* 7 (1979): 91–102.

McPhail, Ken. "An Emotional Response to the State of Accounting Education: Developing Accounting Students' Emotional Intelligence." *Critical Perspectives on Accounting* 15: 629–648.

Merlino, James I., and Anath Raman. "Health Care's Service Fanatics." *Harvard Business Review,* May 1, 2013.

Mezrani, Leanne. "Fear of Failure Holding Back Young Lawyers." *Lawyers Weekly,* September 24, 2013, http://www.lawyersweekly.com.au/news/14721-fear-of-failure-holding-back-young-lawyers.

Miao, Chao, Ronald H. Humphrey, and Shanshan Qian. "A Meta-Analysis of Emotional Intelligence and Work Attitudes." *Journal of Occupational and Organizational Psychology* 90 (2016): 1–26.

Michalik, John J. "The Extraordinary Managing Partner: Reaching the Pinnacle of Law Firm Management." *Association of Legal Administrators,* 2011.

Middleburg, Jonathan, and Lucy Butterworth. "Emotional Intelligence: What Can Learned Lawyers Learn from the Less Learned?" *The Barrister Magazine,* 2013.

Mikolajczak, Moïra, Nathalie Balon, Martine Ruosi, and Ilios Kotsouet. "Sensitive But Not Sentimental: Emotionally Intelligent People Can

Put Their Emotions Aside When Necessary." *Personality and Individual Differences* 52(4) (2012): 537–540.

Mills, Michael. "What Are Humans Good For . . . in Legal Services," *3 Geeks and a Law Blog,* September 21, 2015, http://www.geeklawblog.com/2015/09/what-are-humans-good-for-in-legal.html?m=1.

Mines, Robert A., Rachel A. Meyer, and Michael R. Mines. "Emotional Intelligence and Emotional Toxicity: Implications for Attorneys and Law Firms." *The Colorado Lawyer* 33 (2004): 91–96.

Monahan, John, and Jeffrey Swanson. "Lawyers at Mid-Career: A 20-Year Longitudinal Study of Job and Life Satisfaction." *University of Virginia Law School Public Law and Legal Theory Working Paper Series,* 2008.

Mortimer, Luke. "Police 'Emotional Intelligence' Leads to Job Satisfaction." *My Daily News,* July 4, 2013, http://www.mydailynews.com.au/news/police-emotional-intelligence-leads-to-job-satisfa/1932767/.

Mueller, Jennifer S., and Jared R. Curhan. "Emotional Intelligence and Counterpart Mood Induction in a Negotiation." *International Journal of Conflict Management* 17 (2006): 110–128.

Mullins-Sweatt, S., N. Glover, K. Derefinko, J. Miller, and T. Widiger. "The Search for the Successful Psychopath." *Journal of Research in Personality* 44 (2010): 554–558.

Mrazek, Michael D., Michael S. Franklin, Dawa Tarchin Phillips, Benjamin Baird, and Jonathan W. Schooler. "Mindfulness Training Improves Working Memory Capacity and GRE Performance While Reducing Mind Wandering." *Psychological Science* 24 (2013): 776–781.

Neil, Martha. "Lawyers—Especially Men—May Be Too Optimistic About Case Outcomes, Survey Says." *ABA Journal Online,* May 11, 2010, http://www.abajournal.com/news/article/lawyers—especially_men—may_be_too_optimistic_about_case_outcomes_survey_s

Neisser, Ulric, ed. *The Rising Curve: Long-Term Gains in IQ and Related Measures.* Washington, DC: American Psychological Association, 1998.

Nelis, Delphine, Ilios Kotsou, Jordi Quoidbach, Michel Hansenne, Fanny Weytens, Pauline Dupuis, and Moïra Mikolajczak. "Increasing Emotional Competence Improves Psychological and Physical Well-Being, Social Relationships, and Employability." *Emotion* 11 (2011): 354–366.

Nelken, Melissa L. "Negotiation and Psychoanalysis: If I'd Wanted to Learn About Feelings, I Wouldn't Have Gone to Law School." *Journal of Legal Education* 46 (1996): 421–425.

Neuman, Ronald, and Fritz Strack. "'Mood Contagion': The Automatic Transfer of Mood Between Persons." *Journal of Personality and Social*

Psychology 79 (2000): 211–233, http://www.communicationcache.com/uploads/1/0/8/8/10887248/mood_contagion-_the_automatic_transfer_of_mood_between_persons.pdf.

Newberg, Andrew B., Nancy Wintering, Dharma S. Khalsa, Hannah Roggenkamp, and Mark R. Waldman. "Meditation Effects on Cognitive Function and Cerebral Blood Flow in Subjects with Memory Loss: A Preliminary Study." *Journal of Alzheimer's Disease* 20 (2010): 517–526.

Newton, Brent W. "Preaching What They Don't Practice: Why Law Faculties' Preoccupation with Impractical Scholarship and Devaluation of Practical Competencies Obstruct Reform in the Legal Academy." *South Carolina Law Review* 105 (2010): 146–150.

Norris, Floyd. "When Accountants Act as Bankers." *New York Times,* September 12, 2013, http://www.nytimes.com/2013/09/13/business/when-auditors-act-as-bankers.html?pagewanted=all&_r=1&.

O'Boyle, Ernest H., Ronald H. Humphrey, Jeffrey M. Pollack, Thomas H. Hawver, and Paul A. Story. "The Relation Between Emotional Intelligence and Job Performance: A Meta-Analysis." *Journal of Organizational Behavior* 32 (2011): 788–818.

Oliner, Samuel P., and Pearl M. Oliner. *The Altruistic Personality: Rescuers of Jews in Nazi Europe.* New York, NY: Macmillan, Inc., 1988.

Olson, Elizabeth. "Harvard Law, Moving to Diversify Applicant Pool, Will Accept GRE Scores," *New York Times,* March 8, 2017.

Oprah. "Oprah Interviews Sonia Sotomayor." *O Magazine,* February, 2013, 146.

Ortner, Catherine N. M., Sachne J. Kilner, and Philip David Zelazo. "Mindfulness Meditation and Reduced Emotional Interference on a Cognitive Task." *Motivation and Emotion* 31 (2007): 271–283.

Ortony, A., W. Revelle, and R. Zinbarg, "Why Emotional Intelligence Needs a Fluid Component." In *The Science of Emotional Intelligence,* edited by G. Matthews, M. Zeidner, and R.D. Roberts, 288–304. Oxford: Oxford University Press, 2007.

Palfai, Tibor P., and Peter Salovey. "The Influence of Depressed and Elated Mood on Deductive and Inductive Reasoning." *Imagination, Cognition and Personality* 13 (1993): 57–71.

Parrott, W. Gerrod. "The Nature of Emotion." In *The Blackwell Handbook of Social Psychology: Intraindvidual Processes,* edited by Abraham Tesser and Norbert Schwarz, 375–390. London: Blackwell Publishers, 2001.

Parmar, Belinda. "The Most (and Least) Empathetic Companies." *Harvard Business Review,* November 27, 2015.

Parvin, Cordell. "One Great Differentiator: Become Your Clients' Best Listener." *Cordell Parvin Blog*, July 10, 2012, http://www.cordellblog.com/client-development/one-great-differentiator-become-your-clients-best-listener/.

Paulhus, Delroy L. "Measurement and Control of Response Bias." In *Measures of Personality and Social Psychological Attitudes* vol. 1, edited by John P. Robinson, Phillip R. Shaver, and Lawrence S. Wrightsman, 17–59. San Diego, CA: Academic Press, 1991.

Pauls, Cornelia A., and Nicolas W. Crost. "Effects of Faking on Self-Deception and Impression Management Scales." *Personality and Individual Differences* 37 (2004): 1137–1151.

Pawlow, Jeffrey. "Emotional Intelligence Is Critical to Personal and Firm Success." *The Growth Partnership*, January 6, 2010, http://www.thegrowthpartnership.com/news/tgp_blog/emotional_intelligence_is_critical_to_personal_and_firm_success.

Payne, Wayne L. *A Study of Emotion: Developing Emotional Intelligence: Self-Integration; Relating to Fear, Pain and Desire.* Doctoral thesis, Union Institute, Cincinnati, OH, 1998.

Pérez, Juan Carlos, K. V. Petrides, and Adrian Furnham. "Measuring Trait Emotional Intelligence." In *International Handbook of Emotional Intelligence*, edited by Ralf Schulze and Richard D. Roberts, 124–143. Cambridge, MA: Hogrefe & Huber, 2005.

Perlini, Arthur H., and Trevor R. Halverson. "Emotional Intelligence in the National Hockey League." *Canadian Journal of Behavioural Science* 38 (2006): 109–119.

Petersen, Andrea. "Checking In? Hidden Ways Hotels Court Guests." *Wall Street Journal*, April 12, 2012.

Petrides, K. V., and Adrian Furnham. "Gender Differences in Measured and Self-Estimated Trait Emotional Intelligence." *Sex Roles* 42 (2000): 449–461.

Petrie, Nick. *Future Trends in Leadership Development*, unpublished manuscript. Greensboro, NC: Center for Creative Leadership, 2011, http://www.ccl.org/leadership/pdf/research/futureTrends.pdf.

Pham, Michel Tuan, Leonard Lee, and Andrew T. Stephen. "Feeling the Future: The Emotional Oracle Effect." *Journal of Consumer Research* 39 (2012): 461–477.

Phelps, Elizabeth A., Kevin J. O'Connor, William A. Cunningham, E. Sumie Funayama, J. Christopher Gatenby, John C. Gore, and Mahzarin R. Banaji. "Performance on Indirect Measures of Race Evaluation

Predicts Amygdala Activation." *Journal of Cognitive Neuroscience* 12 (2000): 729–738.

Piff, Paul K., Daniel M. Stancato, Stephane Cote, Rodolfo Mendoza-Denton, and Dacher Keltner. "Higher Social Class Predicts Increased Unethical Behavior." 2012. http://www-2.rotman.utoronto.ca/facbios/file/PredictionOfIncreasedUnethicalBehavior.pdf.

Pilling, Bruce K., and Sevo Eroglu. "An Empirical Examination of the Impact of Salesperson Empathy and Professionalism and Merchandise Salability on Retail Buyer's Evaluations." *Journal of Personal Selling and Sales Management* 14 (1994): 55–58.

Pink, Daniel. "Daniel H. Pink: 7 Questions in 10 Minutes—The New World of Sales and Selling." *Arts and Business Council of Greater Philadelphia Video,* 10:00, January 28, 2013. http://www.youtube.com/watch?v=O1bSwewzyjQ#t=145.

Pink, Daniel. *Drive: The Surprising Truth About What Motivates Us.* New York, NY: Riverhead Books, 2012.

Pink, Daniel. *To Sell Is Human: The Surprising Truth About Moving Others.* New York, NY: Riverhead Books, 2012.

Platsidou, Maria, and Layla Salman. "The Role of Emotional Intelligence in Predicting Burnout and Job Satisfaction of Greek Lawyers." *International Journal of Law, Psychology and Human Life* 1 (2012): 13–22.

Platt, F. W., and V. W. Keller. "Empathic Communication: A Teachable and Learnable Skill." *Journal of General Internal Medicine* 9 (1994): 222–226.

Plutchik, Robert. "The Nature of Emotions." *American Scientist* 89 (1980): 344–350.

Press, Aric. "Don't Look Down." *American Lawyer,* July 14, 2011, http://amlawdaily.typepad.com/amlawdaily/2011/07/julyaugust2011dicta.html.

Press, Aric. "Why Clients Hire and Fire Law Firms." *American Lawyer,* September 9, 2013, http://www.americanlawyer.com/PubArticleTAL.jsp?id=1202616219587&slreturn=20130928200943.

Reilly, Peter. "Teaching a Law Student How to Feel: Using Negotiations Training to Increase Emotional Intelligence." *Negotiation Journal* 21 (2005): 301–314.

Remus, Dana and Frank S. Levy. "Can Robots Be Lawyers? Computers, Lawyers, and the Practice of Law," November 27, 2016, Available at SSRN: https://papers.ssrn.com/sol3/papers.cfm?abstract_id=2701092.

Renaud, Michelle T., Carolyn Rutledge, and Laurel Shepherd. "Preparing Emotionally Intelligent Doctor of Nursing Practice Leaders." *Journal of Nursing Education* 51 (2012): 454–460.

Resnik, David B., and Gregg E. Dinse. "Do U.S Research Institutions Meet or Exceed Federal Mandates for Instruction in Responsible Conduct of Research? A National Survey." *Academic Medicine* 87 (2012): 1237–1242.

Retzinger, Suzanne, and Thomas Scheff. "Emotion, Alienation, and Narratives." *Mediation Quarterly* 18 (2000).

Reynolds, Michele. *An Investigation of the Emotional Intelligence Competencies of National Middle Schools to Watch Principals.* Ph.D, Dissertation, Eastern Kentucky University, 2011.

Rhode, Deborah L. "Developing Leadership." *Santa Clara Law Review* 52 (2012): 689–723.

Rhode, Deborah L. "Lawyers as Leaders." *Michigan State Law Review* 2 (2010): 413–422.

Rhode, Deborah L. *Lawyers as Leaders.* Oxford: Oxford University Press, 2013.

Rhode, Deborah L., and Amanda K. Packel. "Ethics and Nonprofits." *Stanford Social Innovation Review* 28 (2009): 65–69.

Richard, Larry. "Herding Cats: The Lawyer Personality Revealed." *Altman Weil Report to Legal Management* 29 (2002): 1–12.

Richard, Larry. "Hiring Emotionally Intelligent Associates." *Bench and Bar of Minnesota,* October 1999.

Richard, Larry. "Psychological Type and Job Satisfaction Among Practicing Lawyers in the United States." *Capital University Law Review* 29 (2002).

Richard, Larry. "The Psychologically Savvy Leader." *LawyerBrain Blog,* November 11, 2013, http://www.lawyerbrainblog.com/2013/11/the-psychologically-savvy-leader/.

Richard, Larry. "Resilience and Lawyer Negativity." *LawyerBrain™,* September 19, 2012, http://www.lawyerbrainblog.com/2012/09/resilience-and-lawyer-negativity/.

Richard, Larry. "We Need a Chief Resilience Officer." *Lawyer Brain Blog,* August 21, 2013, http://www.lawyerbrainblog.com/2013/08/we-need-a-chief-resilience-officer.

Richard, Larry. "Why Smart Lawyers Fail." Presentation to *American Bar Association,* 2007.

Richard, Larry, and Lisa Rohrer. "A Breed Apart?" *American Lawyer,* July 1, 2011.

Rieck, Troy, and Jennifer L. Callahan. "Emotional Intelligence and Psychotherapy Outcomes in the Training Clinic." *Training and Education in Professional Psychology* 7(1) (February 2013): 42–52.

Riskin, Leonard L. "Annual Saltman Lecture: Further Beyond Reason: Emotions, the Core Concerns, and Mindfulness in Negotiation." *Nevada Law Journal* 10 (2009): 294.

Riskin, Leonard L. "The Contemplative Lawyer: On the Potential Contributions of Mindfulness Meditation to Law Students, Lawyers and Their Clients." *Harvard Negotiation Law Review* 7 (2002): 1–66.

Riskin, Gerry. "Leadership Strategy from Gettysburg." *Amazing Firms Amazing Practices,* June 6, 2013, http://www.gerryriskin.com/leadership-strategy-from-gettysburg/.

Riskin, Gerry. "Retaining Associates with Potential: The Coaching Circle," *Amazing Firms, Amazing Practices,* 2017, http://www.gerryriskin.com/retaining-associates-with-potential-the-coaching-circle/.

Rivers, Susan E., Marc A. Brackett, Maria R. Reyes, Nicole A. Elbertson, and Peter Salovey. "Improving the Social and Emotional Climate of Classrooms: A Clustered Randomized Controlled Trial Testing the RULER Approach." *Prevention Science* 14 (2013): 77–87.

Robbins, Stephen A., and Timothy A. Judge. "Chapter 8: Moods and Emotions." In *Essentials of Organizational Behavior,* 10th edition, 258–297. Upper Saddle River, NJ: Prentice Hall, 2014.

Roberts, John G., Jr. "Oral Advocacy and the Re-emergence of a Supreme Court Bar." *Journal of Supreme Court History* 30 (2005): 68–81.

Rodriguez, Keri L., Nichole K. Bayliss, Stewart C. Alexander, Amy S. Jeffreys, Maren K. Olsen, Kathryn I. Pollak, Sarah K. Garrigues, James A. Tulsky, and Robert M. Arnold. "Effect of Patient and Patient–Oncologist Relationship Characteristics on Communication About Health-Related Quality of Life." *Psycho-Oncology* 20 (2011): 935–942.

Rosenzweig, Steven, Diane K. Reibel, Jeffrey M. Greeson, George C. Brainard, and Mohammadreza Hojat. "Mindfulness-Based Stress Reduction Lowers Psychological Distress in Medical Students." *Teaching and Learning in Medicine* 15 (2003): 88–92.

Rosete, David, and Joseph Ciarrochi. "Emotional Intelligence and Its Relationship to Workplace Performance Outcomes of Leadership Effectiveness." *Leadership and Organization Development Journal* 26 (2005): 388–399.

Rubin, Robert S., and Ronald E. Riggio. "The Role of Emotional Intelligence in Ethical Decision Making at Work." In *Positive Psychology in Business Ethics and Corporate Responsibility,* edited by Robert A. Giacalone, Carole L. Jurkiewicz, Craig Dunn, 209–229. Charlotte, NC: Information Age, 2005.

Saklofske, Donald H., Elizabeth J. Austin, Sarah M. Mastoras, Laura Beaton, and Shona E. Osborne. "Relationships of Personality, Affect, Emotional Intelligence and Coping with Student Stress and Academic Success: Different Patterns of Association for Stress and Success." *Learning and Individual Differences,* February 24, 2010, https://www.edu.uwo.ca/csmh/docs/publications/Saklofske%20Austin%20et%20al%202012.pdf.

Sala, Fabio. "Do Programs Designed to Increase Emotional Intelligence at Work-Work?" *Consortium for Research on Emotional Intelligence in Organizations,* 2002, http://www.eiconsortium.org/reports/do_ei_programs_work.html.

Salami, Samuel O. "Personality and Psychological Well-Being of Adolescents: The Moderating Role of Emotional Intelligence." *Social Behavior and Personality* 39 (2011): 785–794.

Salas, E., S. I. Tannenbaum, K. Kraiger, and K. A. Smith-Jentsch. "The Science of Training and Development in Organizations: What Matters in Practice." *Psychological Science in the Public Interest* 13 (2012): 74–101.

Salovey, Peter, David Caruso, and John D. Mayer. "Emotional Intelligence in Practice." In *Positive Psychology in Practice,* edited by Alex Linely and Stephen Joseph, 447–463. Hoboken, NJ: Wiley, 2004.

Salovey, Peter, John D. Mayer, Susan Lee Goldman, Carolyn Turvey, and Tibor P. Palfai. "Emotional Attention, Clarity, and Repair: Exploring Emotional Intelligence Using the Trait Meta-Mood Scale." In *Emotion, Disclosure, and Health,* edited by James W. Pennebaker, 125–154. Washington, DC: American Psychological Association, 1999.

Salovey, Peter, and Dennis C. Turk. "Some Effects of Mood on Clinicians' Memory." In *Reasoning, Inference, and Judgment in Clinical Psychology,* edited by Dennis C. Turk and Peter Salovey, 107–123. New York: Free Press, 1988.

Sandberg, Sheryl, and Adam Grant. *Option B.* New York: Knopf, 2017.

Schultz, Mike, and John Doerr. "How Clients Buy: 2009 Benchmark Report on Professional Services Marketing and Selling from the Client Perspective." *RainToday.com Research,* 2009, http://www.accountingweb.com/sites/default/files/How_Clients_Buy_09_-Excerpt-1.pdf.

Schutte, Nicola S., John M. Malouff, Einar B. Thorsteinsson, Navjot Bhullar, and Sally E. Rooke. "A Meta-Analytic Investigation of the Relationship between Emotional Intelligence and Health." *Personality and Individual Differences* 42 (2007): 921–933.

Schwartz, Tony. *The Way We're Working Isn't Working: The Four Forgotten Needs that Energize Great Performance.* New York: Simon and Schuster, 2010.

Scott, Sophie K., Andrew W. Young, Andrew J. Calder, Deborah J. Hellawell, John P. Aggleton, and Michael Johnsons. "Impaired Auditory Recognition of Fear and Anger Following Bilateral Amygdala Lessons." *Nature* 385 (1997): 254–257.

Scott-Halsell, Sheila A., Shane C. Blum, and Lynn Huffman. "A Study of Emotional Intelligence Levels in Hospitality Industry Professionals." *Journal of Human Resources in Hospitality and Tourism* 7 (2008): 135–152.

Seligman, Martin. *Authentic Happiness.* New York: Free Press, 2002.

Seligman, Martin. "Building Resilience." *Harvard Business Review,* April 2011.

Seppala, Emma. "Compassionate Mind, Healthy Body." *Greater Good: University of California, Berkeley,* July 24, 2013, http://greatergood.berkeley.edu/article/item/compassionate_mind_healthy_body.

Serani, Deborah. "The Emotional Blindness of Alexithymia." *Scientific American,* April 3, 2014.

Shahid, Ramzan, Jerold Stirling, and William Adams. "Assessment of Emotional Intelligence in Pediatric and Med-Peds Residents." *Journal of Contemporary Medical Education* 4(4), January 26, 2017.

Shankman, Peter. *Nice Companies Finish First: Why Cutthroat Management Is Over—And Collaboration Is In.* New York, NY: St. Martin's Press, 2013.

Shapiro, Johanna, and Desiree Lie. "A Comparison of Medical Students' Written Expressions of Emotion and Coping and Standardized Patients' Ratings of Student Professionalism and Communication Skills." *Medical Teacher* 26 (2004): 733–735.

Shellenbarger, Sure. "Even Lawyers Get the Blues; Opening Up about Depression." *Wall Street Journal,* December 13, 2007.

Shen, H., and Andrew L. Comrey. "Predicting Medical Students' Academic Performances by Their Cognitive Abilities and Personality Characteristics." *Academic Medicine* 72 (1997): 781–786.

Shultz, Marjorie. "Expanding the Definition of Merit." *Boalt Hall Transcript* 38 (2005): 22–24.

Shultz, Marjorie, and Sheldon Zedeck. "Phase I Final Report: Identification and Development of Predictors for Successful Lawyering," 2003. *Available from the authors.*

Shultz, Marjorie M., and Sheldon Zedeck. "Predicting Lawyer Effectiveness: Broadening the Basis for Law School Admission Decisions." *Law and Social Inquiry* 36 (2011): 620–661.

Silver, Marjorie A. "Love, Hate, and Other Emotional Interference in the Lawyer/Client Relationship." *Clinical Law Review* 259 (1999): 259–313.

Silver, Marjorie A. "Supporting Attorneys' Personal Skills." *Revista Juridica de la Universidad de Puerto Rico* 78 (2009): 147–165.

Simon, Robin W., and Leda E. Nath. "Gender and Emotion in the United States: Do Men and Women Differ in Self-Reports of Feelings and Expressive Behavior?" *American Journal of Sociology* 109 (2004): 1137–1176.

Singh, Angad. "'Emotional' Robot Sells Out in a Minute," *CNN,* June 23, 2015, http://www.cnn.com/2015/06/22/tech/pepper-robot-sold-out/.

Singh, Hardeep, Eric J. Thomas, Laura A. Petersen, and David M. Studdert. "Medical Errors Involving Trainees: A Study of Closed Malpractice Claims from 5 Insurers." *Archives of Internal Medicine* 167 (2007): 2030–2036.

Six Seconds. "New Study of Leaders Reveals Emerging Global Talent Crisis, Emotional Intelligence Seen as Solution." *PR Newswire,* April 17, 2012, http://www.globalbusinessnews.net/new-study-of-leaders-reveals-emerging-global-talent-crisis-emotional-intelligence-seen-as-solution/.

Slaski, Mark, and Susan Cartwright. "Emotional Intelligence Training and Its Implications for Stress, Health and Performance." *Stress and Health* 19 (2003): 233–239.

Sloan, Karen. "ABA Calls for Substance Abuse and Mental Health CLE." *National Law Journal.* February 6, 2017.

Sloan, Karen. "Hiring Partners: What's So Bad About Spring Recruitment?" *National Law Journal,* July 2, 2009.

Sloan, Karen. "Law School Helps Students Stay Emotionally Fit." *National Law Journal,* May 9, 2016.

Sloan, Karen. "Law Schools Tackle Mental Health." *National Law Journal,* May 9, 2016.

Sloan, Karen. "Would You Do Law School Again? 67% of Grads Said Yes." *National Law Journal,* March 23, 2016.

Sloan, Karen. "Yale Law Students Lobby for Better Services." *National Law Journal,* May 9, 2016.

Slocum, Robin Wellford. "An Inconvenient Truth: The Need to Educate Emotionally Competent Lawyers." *Chapman University Law Research Paper,* July 19, 2011.

Smee, Daniel E., James McGuire, Thomas Garrick, Shoba Sreenivasan, Daniel Dow, and Daniel Woehl. "Critical Concerns in Iraq/ Afghanistan War Veteran-Forensic Interface: Veterans Treatment

Court as Diversion in Rural Communities." *Journal of the American Academy of Psychiatry and Law* 41 (2013): 256–262.

Smith, Jacquelyn. "The Happiest and Unhappiest Jobs in America." *Forbes,* March 22, 2013.

Smith, Roland. "The Struggles of Lawyer-Leaders and What They Need to Know." *NYSBA Journal,* March/April 2009, http://www.ccl.org/leadership/pdf/landing/NYSBAJournalMarApr09.pdf.

Smith, Roland B., and Paul Bennett Marrow. "The Changing Nature of Leadership in Law Firms." *New York State Bar Journal* 80 (September 2008): 33–38, http://www.ccl.org/leadership/pdf/news/releases/NYSBAJournal.pdf.

Smock, John S., Peter A. Giuliani, Joseph V. Walker, and Gary B. Fiebert. "Legal Marketplace: Outlook for 2013 and Beyond." *Managing Partner Forum: Advancing the Business of Law,* February 2013, http://www.managingpartnerforum.org/tasks/sites/mpf/assets/image/MPF%20WHITE%20PAPER%20-%20Legal%20Marketplace%202013%20-%20SMOCK%20-%202-6-13.pdf.

Solon, Olivia. "Compassion Over Empathy Could Help Prevent Emotional Burnout." *Wired,* July 12, 2012.

Spanhel, Cynthia L., and Paula A. Patton. *How Associate Evaluations Measure Up: A National Study of Associate Performance Assessments.* Overland Park, KS: National Association for Law Placement (NALP) Foundation for Law Career Research and Education, 2006.

Spence, Gerry. *How to Argue and Win Every Time.* New York, NY: Macmillian, 1995.

Spencer, Jr., Lyle M., and Signe M. Spence. *Competence at Work: Models for Superior Performance.* New York, NY: John Wiley and Sons, 1993.

Squire, Larry. "Memory Systems of the Brain: A Brief History and Current Perspective." *Neurobiology of Learning and Memory* 82 (2004): 171–177.

Stanley, Colleen. *Emotional Intelligence for Sales Success: Connect with Customers and Get Results.* New York, NY: Amacom, 2012.

Stein, Steven J., and Howard E. Book. *The EQ Edge: Emotional Intelligence and Your Success,* 3rd ed. Toronto, Canada: Multi-Health Systems, Inc., 2011.

Stein, Steven J., Peter Papadogiannis, Jeremy A. Yip, and Gill Sitarenios. "Emotional Intelligence of Leaders: A Profile of Top Executives." *Leadership and Organization Development Journal* 30 (2009): 87–101.

Steinhauer, Jennifer, and Burns, Alexandra. "Donald Trump and Paul Ryan Show Signs of Thaw." *New York Times,* May 12, 2016.

Stephens, Cheryl. "Communications: Are You Listening?" *Plain Language Association InterNational,* 1988, http://www.plainlanguagenetwork.org/legal/listening.html.

Sternberg, Robert J., Elena Grigorenko, and Donald A. Bundy. "The Predictive Value of IQ." *Merrill-Palmer Quarterly* 47 (2001): 1–41.

Stone, Douglas, Bruce Patton, and Sheila Heen, *Difficult Conversations: How to Discuss What Matters Most.* New York, NY: Penguin Books, 1999.

Stratton, Terry D., and Carol L. Elam. "Should Medical Schools Applicants Be Tested for Emotional Intelligence?" *American Medical Association Journal of Ethics* 8 (2006): 473–476.

Stratton, Terry D., Carol L. Elam, Amy E. Murphy-Spencer, and Susan L. Quinlivan. "Emotional Intelligence and Clinical Skills: Preliminary Results from a Comprehensive Clinical Performance Examination." *Academic Medicine* 80 (2005): S34–S37.

Sullivan, William M., Anne Colby, and Judith W. Wegner. *Educating Lawyers: Preparation for the Profession of Law.* San Francisco, CA: Jossey-Bass, 2007.

Susskind, Richard. *The End of Lawyers.* Oxford: Oxford University Press, 2010.

Susskind, Richard and Daniel Susskind. *The Future of the Professions: How Technology Will Transform the Work of Human Experts.* Oxford: Oxford University Press, 2016.

Sweeney, Michael J. "The Devastation of Depression." *Bar Leader,* March–April, 1998, 11–13.

Sy, Thomas, Stéphane Côté, and Richard Saavedra. "The Contagious Leader: Impact of the Leader's Mood on the Mood of Group Members, Group Affective Tone, and Group Processes." *Journal of Applied Psychology* 90 (2005): 295–305.

Syed, Ali. "Medical Schools and Emotional Intelligence Screening." *York Scholar* 8 (2011): 2.

Tamblyn, Robyn, Michal Abrahamowicz, Dale Dauphinee, Elizabeth Wenghofer, André Jacques, Daniel Klass, Sydney Smee, David Blackmore, Nancy Winslade, Nadyne Girard, Roxane Du Berger, Ilona Bartman, David L. Buckeridge, and James A. Hanley. "Physician Scores on a National Clinical Skills Examination as Predictors of Complaints to Medical Regulatory Authorities." *Journal of the American Medical Association* 98 (2007): 993–1001.

Taylor, Ashley. "How Mimicking Facial Expressions Helps Us Read Emotions," *BrainDecoder.com,* n.d., https://www.braindecoder.com/how-mimicking-facial-expressions-helps-us-read-emotions-1597580336.html.

Taylor, Irene E. "Top 40: 40 and Under 40." *Lexpert*, November/December, 2004: 1–13. http://www.mccarthy.ca/pubs/top40under40.pdf.

Taylor, Scott N., and Jacqueline N. Hood. "It May Not Be What You Think: Gender Differences in Predicting Emotional and Social Competence." *Human Relations* 64 (2011): 627–652.

Tett, Robert P., Kevin E. Fox, and Alvin Wang. "Development and Validation of a Self-Report Measure of Emotional Intelligence as a Multidimensional Trait Domain." *Personality and Social Psychology Bulletin* 31 (2005): 859–888.

Thorndike, Edward L. "Intelligence and Its Uses." *Harper's Magazine* 140 (1920): 227–335.

Tillman, Zoe. "Ex-Judge Who Sued Dry Cleaners Over Lost Pants Faces Ethics Charges," *Law.com*, June 7, 2016, http://www.law.com/sites/almstaff/2016/06/07/ex-judge-who-sued-dry-cleaners-over-lost-pants-faces-ethics-charges/.

Tillman, Zoe. "Former White House Lawyer Disbarred in D.C," *The Blog of Legal Times*, July 1, 2015, http://www.nationallawjournal.com/legaltimes/id=1202731098423/Former-White-House-Lawyer-Disbarred-in-DC?slreturn=20170102125116.

Tolmage, Peskin, Harris, Falick Law Firm. "Non-verbal Communication: Non-verbal Communication in the Courtroom." *Tolmage, Peskin, Harris, Falick Law Firm*, 2013, http://www.stephanpeskin.com/NY-Injury-Resources/Resources-for-Attorneys/Non-Verbal-Communication.shtml.

Tupman, Simon. "The Leadership Imperative: A Study into Law Firm Leadership." *Law Management Group and Simon Tupman*, March, 2012, http://www.lawmanagementgroup.com/uploads/4/4/5/0/4450528/the_leadership_imperative_2012.pdf.

UC San Diego. "SEEC Research." *UC San Diego Empathy Center*, 2017, http://empathy.ucsd.edu/research/index.html.

Uhlsa, Yalda T., Minas Michikyan, Jordan Morris, Debra Garcia, Gary W. Small, Eleni Zgourou, and Patricia M. Greenfield. "Five Days at Outdoor Education Camp without Screens Improves Preteen Skills with Nonverbal Emotion Cues." *Computers in Human Behavior* 39 (2014): 387–392.

Ulutas, Ilkay, and Esra Omeroglu. "The Effects of an Emotional Intelligence Education Program on the Emotional Intelligence of Children." *Social Behavior and Personality: An International Journal* 35 (2007): 1365–1372.

University of Akron. "Identifying the Arrogant Boss." *Science Daily*, July 25, 2012, http://www.sciencedaily.com/releases/2012/07/120725105311.htm.

Vaillant, George E. *Triumphs of Experience: The Men of the Harvard Grant Study*. Cambridge, MA: Belknap Press, 2012.

Van der Elst, Kimberly, Na'amah Razon, and Janelle Caponigro. "Do Bullies Feel Your Pain?" *Greater Good: The Science of a Meaningful Life*, University of California–Berkeley, 2011, http://greatergood.berkeley.edu/article/research_digest/do_bullies_feel_your_pain.

Van Kleef, Gerben A., and Stéphane Côté. "Expressing Anger in Conflict: When It Helps and When It Hurts." *Journal of Applied Psychology* 92 (2007): 1557–1569.

Vega, Tanzina. "Trying to Burnish Its Image, J.&J. Turns to Emotions." *New York Times*, April 24, 2013.

Vernon, Philip A., K. V. Petrides, Denis Bratko, and Julie Aitken Schermer. "A Behavioral Genetic Study of Trait Emotional Intelligence." *Emotion* 8 (2008): 635–642.

Wagner, Ginger C. Moseley, Michael M. Grant, Johnathan R. Gore, and Christopher Owens. "Physicians' Emotional Intelligence and Patient Satisfaction." *Family Medicine* 34 (2002): 750–754.

Wagner, Peggy J. "Does High EI (Emotional Intelligence) Make Better Doctors?" *Virtual Mentor* 8 (2006): 477–479.

Walter, Frank, Ronald H. Humphrey, and Michael S. Cole. "Unleashing Leadership Potential: Toward an Evidence-Based Management of Emotional Intelligence." *Organizational Dynamics* 41 (2012): 212–219.

Ward, Stephanie Francis. "Pulse of the Legal Profession." *ABA Journal*, October 1, 2007.

Watson, Andrew S. "The Quest for Professional Competence: Psychological Aspects of Legal Education." *University of Cincinnati Law Review* 91 (1968).

Weare, Katherine, and Gay Gray. *What Works in Developing Children's Emotional and Social Competence and Wellbeing?* Nottingham: DfES Publications, 2003.

Wechsler, David. *The Measurement and Appraisal of Adult Intelligence*. Baltimore, MD: Williams and Wilkins, 1958.

Weed, Julie. "Checking In After Checkout." *New York Times*, May 27, 2013.

Weiss, Debra Cassens. "Are You the Type That Likes to Run with Scissors? McKenna Long Has a Test to Exclude You." *ABA Journal*, April 22, 2011.

Weiss, Debra Cassens. "Emphasis on Money Can Be Source of Depression in Law School." *ABA Journal*, March 13, 2008, http://www.abajournal.com/news/article/emphasis_on_money_can_be_source_of_depression_in_law_school.

Weiss, Debra Cassens. "Judge Holds Prosecutor in Contempt, Says His 'Emotional Intelligence Needs Strengthening.'" *ABA Journal*, January 6, 2017.

Weiss, Debra Cassens. "Like Polo and Sailing? Listing It on a Law Firm Resume Helped Men But Not Women, Study Finds." *ABA Journal*, October 24, 2016.

Weng, Hui-Ching, Hung-Chi Chen, Han-Jung Chen, Kang Lu, and Shin-Yuan Hung. "Doctors' Emotional Intelligence and the Patient–Doctor Relationship." *Medical Education* 42 (2008): 703–711.

Whalen, Paul J., Scott L. Rauch, Nancy L. Etcoff, Sean C. McInerney, Michael B. Lee, and Michael A. Jenike. "Masked Presentations of Emotional Facial Expressions Modulate Amygdala Activity Without Explicit Knowledge." *Journal of Neuroscience* 18 (1998): 411–418.

Wheeler, Michael. "Get in the Right State of Mind for Any Negotiation." *Harvard Business Review*, May 5, 2015.

Wolff, Steven B. *Emotional Competence Inventory (ECI) Technical Manual*, 2nd ed. St. Petersburg, FL: Hay Acquisition Company, Inc., 2005.

Wong, Bernie, and Neha John-Henderson. "Does Your Manager Feel Your Pain?" *Greater Good: The Science of a Meaningful Life*, May 13, 2011, University of California–Berkeley, http://greatergood.berkeley.edu/article/research_digest/does_your_manager_feel_your_pain.

Worldcrunch. "Argentina Schools Add 'Emotional Education' to Curriculum." *Gulf Times*, June 2, 2013, http://www.gulf-times.com/us-latin percent20america/182/details/354898/argentina-schools-add-percentE2percent80percent98emotional-educationpercentE2percent 80 percent99-to-curriculum.

Yip, Jeremy A., and Stéphane Côté. "The Emotionally Intelligent Decision Maker: Emotion-Understanding Ability Reduces the Effect of Incidental Anxiety on Risk Taking." *Psychological Science* 24 (2012): 48–55.

Young, Paul Thomas. *Emotion in Man and Animal: Its Nature and Relation to Attitude and Motive*. New York, NY: John Wiley and Sons, 1943.

Zaki, Jamil. "Using Empathy to Use People: Emotional Intelligence and Manipulation." *Scientific American, The Moral Universe Blog*, November 7, 2013, http://blogs.scientificamerican.com/moral-universe/2013/11/07/using-empathy-to-use-people-emotional-intelligence-and-manipulation/?goback=.gde_3708120_member_5804249847691231232#!.

Zeidan, Fadel, Susan K. Johnson, Bruce J. Diamond, Zhanna David, and Paula Goolkasian. "Mindfulness Meditation Improves Cognition: Evidence of Brief Mental Training." *Consciousness and Cognition* 19 (2010): 597–605.

Zeidan, Fadel, Katherine T. Martucci, Robert A. Kraft, John G. McHaffie, and Robert C. Coghill. "Neural Correlates of Mindfulness Meditation-Related Anxiety Relief." *Social Cognitive Affective Neuroscience,* June 3, 2013, 1–9.

Zenger, Jack. "Does Leadership Development Really Work?" *Forbes,* May 2, 2012.

Zenger, Jack, and Joseph Folkman. "Are Women Better Leaders Than Men?" *Harvard Business Review,* March 15, 2012.

Zenger, Jack, and Joseph Folkman. "Gender Shouldn't Matter, But Apparently It Still Does." *Harvard Business Review,* April 4, 2012.

Zenger, Jack, and Joseph Folkman. "The Ideal Praise to Criticism Ratio." *Harvard Business Review,* March 15, 2013.

Zenger, Jack, and Joseph Folkman. "Ten Fatal Flaws That Derail Leaders." *Harvard Business Review* 87 (2009): 18.

Zhu, Y., C. Liu, B. Guo, L. Zhao, and F. Lao. "The Impact of Emotional Intelligence on Work Engagement of Registered Nurses: The Mediating Role of Organisational Justice." *Journal of Clinical Nursing* 24 (2015): 2115–2124.

Zillman, Claire. "Survey: Generally Content, New Partners Fear Lack of Training Will Hamper Ability to Win Clients." *Am Law Daily,* October 22, 2012.

Zimmerman, Isiah M. "Isolation in the Judicial Career." *Court Review,* Winter, 2000.

Zinn, William. "The Empathic Physician." *Archives of Internal Medicine* 153 (1993): 306–312.

Index